Contents at a Glance

KU-536-563

Introduction   1

PART I: Packet-Filtering and Basic Security Measures

    CHAPTER 1: Preliminary Concepts Underlying Packet-Filtering Firewalls   7

    CHAPTER 2: Packet-Filtering Concepts   31

    CHAPTER 3: iptables: The Linux Firewall Administration Program   63

    CHAPTER 4: Building and Installing a Standalone Firewall   101

PART II: Advanced Issues, Multiple Firewalls, and Perimeter Networks

    CHAPTER 5: Firewall Optimization   181

    CHAPTER 6: Packet Forwarding   213

    CHAPTER 7: NAT—Network Address Translation   261

    CHAPTER 8: Debugging the Firewall Rules   281

PART III: Beyond iptables

    CHAPTER 9: Intrusion Detection and Response   315

    CHAPTER 10: Intrusion-Detection Tools   329

    CHAPTER 11: Network Monitoring and Attack Detection   345

    CHAPTER 12: Filesystem Integrity   381

    CHAPTER 13: Kernel Enhancements   399

PART IV: Appendices

    APPENDIX A: Security Resources   425

    APPENDIX B: Firewall Examples and Support Scripts   427

    APPENDIX C: VPNs   475

    APPENDIX D: Glossary   487

    INDEX   499

Table of Contents

Introduction   **1**

    The Purpose of This Book 2

    Who Should Read This Book 3

    Linux Distribution 3

    Errors in This Book 4

    Companion Website 4

PART I: **Packet-Filtering and Basic Security Measures**

    CHAPTER 1:   Preliminary Concepts Underlying Packet-Filtering Firewalls   **7**

    The OSI Networking Model 9

        Connectionless Versus Connection-Oriented Protocols 11

        Next Steps 12

    The IP 12

        IP Addressing and Subnetting 12

        IP Fragmentation 16

        Broadcasting and Multicasting 17

        ICMP 18

    Transport Mechanisms 20

        UDP 20

        TCP 20

    Don't Forget ARP 24

    Hostnames and IP Addresses 24

        IP Addresses and Ethernet Addresses 24

    Routing: Getting a Packet from Here to There 25

    Service Ports: The Door to the Programs on Your System 25

        A Typical TCP Connection: Visiting a Remote Website 27

    Summary 30

CHAPTER 2:   Packet-Filtering Concepts   **31**

A Packet-Filtering Firewall 33

Choosing a Default Packet-Filtering Policy 35

Rejecting Versus Denying a Packet 38

Filtering Incoming Packets 38

Remote Source Address Filtering 38

Local Destination Address Filtering 42

Remote Source Port Filtering 42

Local Destination Port Filtering 43

Incoming TCP Connection-State Filtering 43

Probes and Scans 43

Denial-of-Service Attacks 48

Source-Routed Packets 56

Filtering Outgoing Packets 56

Local Source Address Filtering 57

Remote Destination Address Filtering 57

Local Source Port Filtering 58

Remote Destination Port Filtering 58

Outgoing TCP Connection-State Filtering 59

Private Versus Public Network Services 59

Protecting Nonsecure Local Services 60

Selecting Services to Run 60

Summary 61

CHAPTER 3:   iptables: The Linux Firewall Administration Program   **63**

Differences Between IPFW and Netfilter Firewall Mechanisms 64

IPFW Packet Traversal 65

Netfilter Packet Traversal 66

Basic iptables Syntax 67

iptables Features 68

NAT Table Features 71

`mangle` Table Features 73

iptables Syntax 74

    `filter` Table Commands 75

    `filter` Table Target Extensions 80

    `filter` Table Match Extensions 82

    NAT Table Target Extensions 95

    `mangle` Table Commands 98

Summary 99

CHAPTER 4:   Building and Installing a Standalone Firewall   **101**

iptables: The Linux Firewall Administration Program 102

    Build Versus Buy: The Linux Kernel 104

    Source and Destination Addressing Options 104

Initializing the Firewall 106

    Symbolic Constants Used in the Firewall Examples 107

    Enabling Kernel-Monitoring Support 108

    Removing Any Preexisting Rules 109

    Resetting Default Policies and Stopping the Firewall 110

    Enabling the loopback Interface 111

    Defining the Default Policy 111

    Stealth Scans and TCP State Flags 112

    Using Connection State to Bypass Rule Checking 113

    Source Address Spoofing and Other Bad Addresses 114

Protecting Services on Assigned Unprivileged Ports 119

    Common Local TCP Services Assigned to Unprivileged Ports 120

    Common Local UDP Services Assigned to Unprivileged Ports . . . 122

Enabling Basic, Required Internet Services 124

    Allowing DNS (UDP/TCP Port **53**) 124

    Filtering the **AUTH** User Identification Service (TCP Port **113**) 130

Enabling Common TCP Services 132

    Email (TCP SMTP Port **25**, POP Port **110**, IMAP Port **143**) 133

    Accessing Usenet News Services (TCP NNTP Port **119**) 142

    Telnet (TCP Port **23**) 144

SSH (TCP Port 22) 146

FTP (TCP Ports 21, 20) 148

Web Services 153

Whois (TCP Port 43) 157

RealAudio, RealVideo, and QuickTime (TCP Ports 554
and 7070) 158

Enabling Common UDP Services 160

traceroute (UDP Port 33434) 160

Accessing Your ISP's DHCP Server (UDP Ports 67, 68) 162

Accessing Remote Network Time Servers (UDP Port 123) 165

Filtering ICMP Control and Status Messages 166

Error Status and Control Messages 167

ping Echo Request (Type 8) and Echo Reply (Type 0) Control
Messages 169

Logging Dropped Incoming Packets 170

Logging Dropped Outgoing Packets 172

Denying Access to Problem Sites Up Front 172

Installing the Firewall 173

Tips for Debugging the Firewall Script 174

Starting the Firewall on Boot with Red Hat and SUSE 175

Starting the Firewall on Boot with Debian 175

Installing a Firewall with a Dynamic IP Address 176

Summary 176

PART II: Advanced Issues, Multiple Firewalls, and Perimeter Networks

CHAPTER 5: Firewall Optimization   **181**

Rule Organization 181

Begin with Rules That Block Traffic on High Ports 182

Use the State Module for ESTABLISHED and
RELATED Matches 182

Consider the Transport Protocol 182

Place Firewall Rules for Heavily Used Services as
Early as Possible 184

Use the Multiport Module to Specify Port Lists 184

Use Traffic Flow to Determine Where to Place Rules for Multiple
Network Interfaces 184

User-Defined Chains 185

Optimized Example 188

User-Defined Chains in the Script 188

Firewall Initialization 190

Installing the Chains 192

Building the User-Defined `EXT-input` and `EXT-output` Chains . . 195

`tcp-state-flags` 204

`connection-tracking` 205

`local_dhcp_client_query` and `remote_dhcp_server_response` 206

`source-address-check` 207

`destination-address-check` 208

Logging Dropped Packets 208

What Did Optimization Buy? 210

Summary 212

CHAPTER 6: Packet Forwarding   **213**

The Limitations of a Standalone Firewall 213

Basic Gateway Firewall Setups 215

LAN Security Issues 217

Configuration Options for a Trusted Home LAN 218

LAN Access to the Gateway Firewall 220

LAN Access to Other LANs: Forwarding Local Traffic
Among Multiple LANs 221

Configuration Options for a Larger or Less Trusted LAN 222

Dividing Address Space to Create Multiple Networks 223

Selective Internal Access by Host, Address Range, or Port 225

A Formal Screened-Subnet Firewall Example 231

Symbolic Constants Used in the Firewall Examples 232

Setting the Stage on the Choke Firewall 234

Removing Any Preexisting Rules from the Choke Firewall 235

Defining the Choke Firewall's Default Policy 236

Enabling the Choke Machine's Loopback Interface 237

Stealth Scans and TCP State Flags 237

Using Connection State to Bypass Rule Checking 238

Source-Address Spoofing and Other Bad Addresses 238

Filtering ICMP Control and Status Messages 240

Enabling DNS (UDP/TCP Port 53) 241

Filtering the AUTH User Identification Service (TCP Port 113) 246

Email (TCP SMTP Port 25, POP3 Port 110, IMAP Port 143) 246

Accessing Usenet News Services (TCP NNTP Port 119) 248

Telnet (TCP Port 23) 249

SSH (TCP Port 22) 250

FTP (TCP Ports 21 and 20) 251

Web Services 253

Choke as a Local DHCP Server (UDP Ports 67 and 68) 256

Logging 258

Converting the Gateway from Local Services to Forwarding 258

Summary 258

CHAPTER 7: NAT—Network Address Translation   **261**

The Conceptual Background of NAT 261

iptables NAT Semantics 266

Source NAT 268

Destination NAT 270

Examples of SNAT and Private LANs 271

Masquerading LAN Traffic to the Internet 271

Applying Standard NAT to LAN Traffic to the Internet 273

Examples of DNAT, LANs, and Proxies 274

Host Forwarding 274

Host Forwarding and Port Redirection 275

Host Forwarding to a Server Farm 276

Host Forwarding to Servers in a Privately Addressed DMZ 277

Local Port Redirection—Transparent Proxying 279

Summary 280

CHAPTER 8: Debugging the Firewall Rules   **281**

General Firewall-Development Tips 281

Listing the Firewall Rules 284

    `filter` Table Listing Formats 285

    `nat` Table Listing Formats 291

    `mangle` Table Listing Formats 293

Checking the Input, Output, and Forwarding Rules 294

    Checking the Input Rules 295

    Checking the Output Rules 296

    Checking the Forwarding Rules 298

Interpreting the System Logs 300

    syslog Configuration 300

    Firewall Log Messages: What Do They Mean? 304

Checking for Open Ports 307

    `netstat -a [ -n -p -A inet ]` 308

    Checking a Process Bound to a Particular Port with `fuser` 311

    `strobe` 311

    `nmap` 312

Summary 312

PART III: **Beyond iptables**

CHAPTER 9: Intrusion Detection and Response   **315**

Detecting Intrusions 315

Symptoms Suggesting That the System Might Be Compromised 317

    System Log Indications 317

    System Configuration Indications 318

    Filesystem Indications 318

    User Account Indications 319

    Security Audit Tool Indications 320

    System Performance Indications 320

What to Do If Your System Is Compromised 320

Incident Reporting 322

   Why Report an Incident? 323

   What Kinds of Incidents Might You Report? 324

   To Whom Do You Report an Incident? 325

   What Information Do You Supply? 326

   Where Do You Find More Information? 327

Summary 327

CHAPTER 10: Intrusion Detection Tools   **329**

Intrusion Detection Toolkit: Network Tools 329

   Switches and Hubs and Why You Care 331

   Sniffer Placement 332

   ARPWatch 332

Rootkit Checkers 332

   Running Chkrootkit 333

   What If Chkrootkit Says the Computer Is Infected? 334

   Limitations of Chkrootkit and Similar Tools 335

   Using Chkrootkit Securely 336

   When Should Chkrootkit Be Run? 337

Filesystem Integrity 337

Log Monitoring 338

   Swatch 338

How to Not Become Compromised 340

   Secure Often 340

   Update Often 341

   Test Often 342

Summary 344

CHAPTER 11: Network Monitoring and Attack Detection   **345**

Listening to the Ether 345

   Three Valuable Tools 347

TCPDump: A Simple Overview 348

    Obtaining and Installing TCPDump 349

    TCPDump Options 350

    TCPDump Expressions 352

    Beyond the Basics with TCPDump 355

Using TCPDump to Capture Specific Protocols 355

    Using TCPDump in the Real World 356

    Attacks Through the Eyes of TCPDump 364

    Recording Traffic with TCPDump 369

Automated Intrusion Monitoring with Snort 371

    Obtaining and Installing Snort 372

    Configuring Snort 373

    Testing Snort 375

    Receiving Alerts 376

    Final Thoughts on Snort 377

Monitoring with ARPWatch 377

Summary 379

CHAPTER 12: Filesystem Integrity   **381**

Filesystem Integrity Defined 381

    Practical Filesystem Integrity 381

Installing AIDE 383

Configuring AIDE 383

    Creating an AIDE Configuration File 384

    A Sample AIDE Configuration File 386

    Initializing the AIDE DB 387

    Scheduling AIDE to Run Automatically 388

Monitoring AIDE for Bad Things 388

Cleaning Up the AIDE Database 390

Changing the Output of the AIDE Report 391

    Obtaining More Verbose Output 393

Defining Macros in AIDE 394

The Types of AIDE Checks 396

Summary 398

CHAPTER 13: Kernel Enhancements   **399**

Security Enhanced Linux 399

SELinux Architecture 400

Greater Security with GrSecurity 401

A Quick Look Around the Kernel 401

What'd You Call That? 402

What's Your Number? 402

The Kernel: From 20,000 Feet 403

To Patch or Not to Patch 404

Enhanced Security Without Grsec 405

Using a GrSecurity Kernel 405

Downloading Grsec and a Fresh Kernel 405

Compiling Your First Kernel 406

Improving the Kernel Build 415

GrSecurity 415

Applying the Grsec Patch 416

Choosing Grsec Features 417

Building the Grsec Kernel 419

Beyond the Basics with GrSecurity 421

Conclusion: Custom Kernels 421

PART IV: Appendices

APPENDIX A: Security Resources   **425**

Security Information Sources 425

Reference Papers and FAQs 426

Books 426

APPENDIX B: Firewall Examples and Support Scripts   **427**

   iptables Firewall for a Standalone System from Chapter 4 427

   Optimized iptables Firewall from Chapter 5 446

   iptables Firewall for a Choke Firewall from Chapter 6 463

APPENDIX C: VPNs   **475**

   Overview of Virtual Private Networks 475

   VPN Protocols 475

      PPTP 476

      IPSec 476

   Linux and VPN Products 480

      Openswan 480

      FreeS/WAN 481

      Virtual Private Network Daemon 481

      PPTP Linux Solutions 481

      Virtual Tunnel 482

   VPN Configurations 482

      Roaming User 482

   Connecting Networks 483

   VPN and Firewalls 483

   Summary 485

APPENDIX D: Glossary   **487**

Index   **499**

About the Authors

Steve Suehring is a technology architect with a diverse set of skills. He works with a wide array of technologies, from mainframe OS/390 through Microsoft Windows to several distributions of Linux. He has written a book on MySQL and numerous magazine articles. During his tenure as an editor for *LinuxWorld Magazine*, he focused on advocacy of Linux and open-source software, as well as computer security. He wrote a cover story for *LinuxWorld Magazine* featuring the WilliamsF1 team's use of Linux to design their Formula 1 car. Suehring is also a Cisco Certified Network Professional (CCNP), and he has contributed, according to him, "extremely small bits of code" to some open-source projects and lurks on a number of mailing lists, helping and answering questions when he can.

Robert Ziegler is a renowned firewall architect and consultant who has worked for a variety of organizations, including Nokia's router and access groups. He is well known as the author of the two previous editions of *Linux Firewalls*, and he operates a respected firewall resource site to share his design skills and evaluations of tools.

Dedication

To my wife, Rebecca

Acknowledgments

Thanks first to my family for being supportive while I write seemingly every day. I'd also like to thank my agent, Laura Lewin at Studio B, for all of her hard work and her constant help. Thanks also to A.J. Prowant for doing the technical edit on this project.

Chris and Nikie Tuescher deserve an acknowledgment for being great friends and understanding why we haven't come to Minneapolis lately—these books take time to write! Thanks to Aaron & Jodi Deering for having us over and for Aaron taking it easy on me at basketball. Thanks to Duff Damos for his continued friendship throughout the years. Pat Dunn, thanks for changing your password all the time and then forgetting it. Thanks to meek for his patience and constant help.

Here's the list, in no particular order. Though it maybe isn't readily apparent exactly how some of you helped, you have, in some way, contributed to this book (for better or worse). Andy Hale (let me know when you want to start fixing your floors), Dan Noah, Jim & Amy Leu, Kent & Amy Laabs, Michael Mittelstadt, Denise Sandell, The Pflugers, AWRC, Jake Buchholz, Richard Dean Anderson, Aaron Schrab, Beez, Rysch, HFB & The #JBS, The Guthries, The Heins, Tim McKeown, Pearl & Moff, Rob Konkol, Erin Thomas, Paul, Darrick, Jeff Sanner, Edward Van Halen, Peter DeLuise, The DBAs and the Data Architect team, Sarah Hagerman, Jay & Deb Schrank, Brian Page, Is Anyone Still Reading This, Mark Little, Nightmare Squad, Jim Oliva, John Eckendorf, 90fm, Scott & Karla Kluck, Amanda Tapping, The Steffens, Eliot Irons, Keith Imlach & the Data Security team, No, seriously, is anyone reading this, Sue Crawford, Erich Hartman, Commas are my best friend, Ron Mackay, The Chasteens, Darrin Davisson, If you haven't seen your name yet wait until my next book, Justin Hoerter, John Hein, Andy Berkvam, The Internets, Mike Wrzinski, , That was an extra comma because I love them so much, Chris Judge, Tony Falduto, Steve Hannan (I just thanked a Project Manager), Greg Rubey, Ryan Anderson, Suzi Limberg, Kevin Blake, Dave Dahlke, I get paid based on how many people I thank, Michael Shanks, Tom Lindley, This Space For Rent, Kevin Bedell, James Turner, Dee-Ann LeBlanc, Neil Peart, Norm & Crew @ Music Quest.

That was a long list and I'm sure that I forgot people, just like last time. I need to send this, the final deliverable, to the publisher as the deadline looms. If you weren't thanked explicitly here then know that I do thank you…even though I forgot about you when writing this.

We Want to Hear from You!

As the reader of this book, *you* are our most important critic and commentator. We value your opinion and want to know what we're doing right, what we could do better, what topics you'd like to see us cover, and any other words of wisdom you're willing to pass our way.

You can email or write me directly to let me know what you did or didn't like about this book—as well as what we can do to make our books better.

Please note that I cannot help you with technical problems related to the topic of this book and that due to the high volume of mail I receive I may not be able to reply to every message.

When you write, please be sure to include this book's title and author as well as your name and email address or phone number. I will carefully review your comments and share them with the author and editors who worked on the book.

Email: feedback@novellpress.com

Mail: Mark Taber
          Associate Publisher
          Novell Press/Pearson Education
          800 East 96th Street
          Indianapolis, IN 46240 USA

Reader Services

For more information about this book or others from Novell Press, visit our website at www.novellpress.com. Type the ISBN or the title of a book in the Search field to find the page you're looking for.

Introduction

This book is essentially about creating a software-based firewall using Netfilter and iptables in the Linux operating system. Beyond the basics of a firewall, this book also looks at the firewall in the context of a networked computing environment. To that end, topics such as intrusion detection and system security are also covered.

Computer security is an expansive subject area. Volumes have been written about it and volumes will continue to be written about it. Computer security is centered around protection of data assets using three principles: confidentiality, integrity, and availability. Confidentiality means that data is accessible only by those who are authorized to access the data and no one else. Integrity ensures that the data is verifiably good and is not tainted. Availability means that the data can be accessed when it needs to be accessed. These three principles guide the discussion of computer security and provide the framework for this book.

In addition to the three principles of confidentiality, integrity, and availability, I subscribe to an in-depth, risk-assessed approach to computer security. This means that I don't consider any single option to be an endpoint when it comes to securing data, rather that each item such as a firewall or antivirus software plays a role in securing data. However, there is a cost involved with each measure of security. Therefore, each additional measure or layer of security must be assessed to ensure that the cost of that layer doesn't exceed the benefit of being protected from that risk.

Consider this example: I use two firewalls, a choke and gateway (see Chapter 6, "Packet Forwarding"), for my home network. I consider the benefit of having a dual-firewall approach to outweigh the cost of operating and maintaining the firewalls. Other people use a single firewall or no firewall at all. They consider the risk of their data or systems being unavailable or attacked to be less costly than running a dual-firewall setup or even a single firewall for some. Many more examples of this cost/benefit assessment could be done. Unfortunately, this analysis is often overlooked for many areas of security, not just computer security. For more information on this type of analysis and a good read on top of it, see Bruce Schneier's works *Secrets and Lies* and *Beyond Fear*.

The Purpose of This Book

The goal of this book is to give the reader enough information that they may configure a firewall using iptables in Linux. A secondary goal is to educate the reader about system and network security. However, because this isn't a book on system and network security, those topics are indeed secondary even though they do consume a large portion of the book. There are also topics in this book that I haven't seen (yet) in other books to any great degree.

You are reading the third revision of this book and the first revision with a new author, Steve Suehring. Bob Ziegler wrote the original material and also revised the work into its second revision in 2001. Bob did an excellent job and I've built upon his solid foundation to bring you the third revision. In addition, the previous revision had some material contributed by Carl B. Constantine. You'll find Carl's contribution, though updated, in Appendix C of this revision, "VPNs."

I learned much of what I know about Linux security while working at an Internet service provider (ISP), beginning in 1995. Resisting the temptation to recite a "back when I was young" tale, I'll just say that most of what I learned was done with security in mind. It had to be. By definition at an ISP, you must run publicly available services and those services must be available 24x7. Having publicly available services means that there's a constant threat (and frequent execution) of attacks against the network and the systems therein. If we wouldn't have considered security to be central to our operation, we simply could not have ensured the reliability that our customers demanded, nor could we have guaranteed the integrity of the data that we housed. None of this takes into account the general lack of security tools, software, and books like this back in 1995, either.

That background also helps to answer the question "Why Linux?" The answer was and is quite simple: Linux and open-source tools were the only solution when I was tasked with solving these problems. There simply was no other way to provide Internet services with anywhere near the reliability that Linux and open-source software provided. No other operating system provided the same set of reliability and security while at the same time keeping down the Total Cost of Ownership (TCO). The same can largely be said today. With a pure technological decision, Linux wins. Factor in TCO and the picture only gets better for Linux and open-source software, regardless of the results from funded and paid studies. Why Linux? Because it works.

Who Should Read This Book

I've usually found these "Who Should Read This Book" sections to be somewhat useless simply because the goal is to get you to think that you should read the book. Therefore, to satisfy the publisher I'll tell you that everyone should read this book. In fact, everyone should read this book multiple times, buying a separate copy each time.

In all seriousness, I can't tell you whether you should be reading this book, but I can tell you about the book.

This book assumes that you have already chosen a Linux distribution and that you've already installed it. This book also assumes that you're not looking for an introductory "HOWTO" on Linux or *nix security such as the `chmod` command. There are many great resources about those topics already, many of them on the Internet, and I feel as though coverage of those issues gets away from the focus of this book. However, this book does deal rather extensively with introductory material on network security, packet filtering, and the layers in the OSI model (if you're unfamiliar with the OSI model, it's explained in the book).

This book tries to be helpful to those who know nothing about firewalls as well as to those who know a bit about Linux and Linux security but want to carry that to the next level. This book could be used successfully by home users and enterprise security administrators alike.

To get the most out of this book, you should be comfortable with, or at least not afraid of, the Linux command line, or shell. You should know how to move about in the file system and perform basic shell commands.

Linux Distribution

Linux and open-source books need to be more distribution neutral or cover more than one distribution. This book does both. A Linux firewall is built using the iptables firewall administration program on top of the Netfilter core software that resides in the Linux kernel. As such, the Linux distribution you choose is largely irrelevant. The book does, however, cover some commands and issues as seen through the eyes of SUSE, Red Hat/Fedora, and Debian. Yes, there are other distributions, many of them very good. Favoring those three distributions is certainly not meant to take away from any other distribution.

The second edition of this book covered only Red Hat. However, I undertook an effort early on in the revision process to remove the distribution-centric tone where it did show up. This was not done to intentionally favor any one distribution or to reject another. Rather, this was a pragmatic decision to provide material applicable to a larger audience and to prevent confusion as to file and command locations if you don't happen to be using the same distribution as the author.

Errors in This Book

Although every effort is made to check facts and figures, files and syntax, some errors will inevitably slip through the writing, technical editing, copyediting, and review process. Let me apologize in advance for any such errors as exist within these pages. I invite the reader to visit my web site at http://www.braingia.org/ for updates and other information about this book. I also invite you to send me feedback at steve.suehring@braingia.com. Although I can't guarantee that I'll have the answer, I will definitely try to respond and point you in the right direction.

Companion Website

Visit http://www.braingia.org/ for up-to-date information on this book and links to interesting security articles. Included on the website are the latest versions of some of the same scripts you'll see within the text.

## PART I

Packet-Filtering and Basic Security Measures

1   Preliminary Concepts Underlying Packet-Filtering Firewalls

2   Packet-Filtering Concepts

3   iptables: The Linux Firewall Administration Program

4   Building and Installing a Standalone Firewall

Preliminary Concepts Underlying Packet-Filtering Firewalls

A small site may have Internet access through a T1 line, a cable modem, DSL, ISDN, a PPP connection to a phone-line dial-up account, or wireless. The computer connected directly to the Internet is a point of focus for security issues. Whether you have one computer or a local area network (LAN) of linked computers, the initial focus for a small site will be on the machine with the direct Internet connection. This machine will be the firewall machine.

The term *firewall* has various meanings depending on its implementation and purpose. At this opening point in the book, *firewall* means the Internet-connected machine. This is where your primary security policies for Internet access will be implemented. The firewall machine's external network interface card is the connection point, or gateway, to the Internet. The purpose of a firewall is to protect what's on your side of this gateway from what's on the other side.

A simple firewall setup is sometimes called a *bastion firewall* because it's the main line of defense against attack from the outside. Many of your security measures are mounted from this one defender of your realm. Consequently, everything possible is done to protect this system.

Behind this line of defense is your single computer or your group of computers. The purpose of the firewall machine might simply be to serve as the connection point to the Internet for other machines on your LAN. You might be running local, private services behind this firewall, such as a shared printer or shared file systems. Or you might want all of your computers to have access to the Internet. One of your machines might host your private financial records. You might want to have Internet access from this machine, but you don't want anyone getting in. At some point, you might want to offer your own services to the Internet. One of the machines might be hosting your own website for the Internet. Another might function as your mail server or gateway. Your setup and goals will determine your security policies.

The firewall's purpose is to enforce the security policies you define. These policies reflect the decisions you've made about which Internet services you want to be accessible to your computers, which services you want to offer the world from your computers, which services you want to offer to specific remote users or sites, and which services and programs you want to run locally for your own private use. Security policies are all about access control and authenticated use of private or protected services, programs, and files on your computers.

Home and small-business systems don't face all the security issues of a larger corporate site, but the basic ideas and steps are the same. There just aren't as many factors to consider, and security policies often are less stringent than those of a corporate site. The emphasis is on protecting your site from unwelcome access from the Internet. A packet-filtering firewall is one common approach to, and one piece of, network security and controlling access to and from the outside.

Of course, having a firewall doesn't mean you are fully protected. Security is a process, not a piece of hardware. For example, even with a firewall in place it's possible to download spyware or adware or click on a maliciously crafted email, thereby opening up the computer and thus the network to the attack. It's just as important to have measures in place to mitigate successful attacks as it is to spend resources on a firewall. Using best practices inside of your network will help to lessen the chance of a successful exploit and give your network resiliency.

Something to keep in mind is that the Internet paradigm is based on the premise of end-to-end transparency. The networks between the two communicating machines are intended to be invisible. In fact, if a network device somewhere along the path fails, the idea is that traffic between the two endpoint machines will be silently rerouted.

Ideally, firewalls should be transparent. Nevertheless, they break the Internet paradigm by introducing a single point of failure within the networks between the two endpoint machines. Additionally, not all network applications use communication protocols that are easily passed through a simple packet-filtering firewall. It isn't possible to pass certain traffic through a firewall without additional application support or more sophisticated firewall technology.

Further complicating the issue has been the introduction of Network Address Translation (NAT, or "masquerading" in Linux parlance). NAT enables one computer to act on behalf of many other computers by translating their requests and forwarding them on to their destination. The use of NAT along with RFC 1918 private IP addresses has effectively prevented a looming shortage of IPv4 addresses. The combination of NAT and RFC 1918 address space makes the transmission of some types of network traffic difficult, impossible, complex, or expensive.

NOTE

Many router devices, especially those for DSL, cable modems, and wireless, are being sold as firewalls but are nothing more than NAT-enabled routers. They don't perform many of the functions of a true firewall, but they do separate internal from external. Be aware when purchasing a router that claims to be a firewall but only provides NAT. Although some of these products have some good features, the more advanced configurations are sometimes not possible.

A final complication has been the proliferation of multimedia and peer-to-peer (P2P) protocols used in both real-time communication software and popular networked games. These protocols are antithetical to today's firewall technology. Today, specific software solutions must be built and deployed for each application protocol. The firewall architectures for easily and economically handling these protocols are in process in the standards committees' working groups.

It's important to keep in mind that the combination of firewalling, DHCP, and NAT introduces complexities that cause sites to have to compromise system security to some extent in order to use the network services that the users want. Small businesses often have to deploy multiple LANs and more complex network configurations to meet the varying security needs of the individual local hosts.

Before going into the details of developing a firewall, this chapter introduces the basic underlying concepts and mechanisms on which a packet-filtering firewall is based. These concepts include a general frame of reference for what network communication is, how network-based services are identified, what a packet is, and the types of messages and information sent between computers on a network.

The OSI Networking Model

The OSI (Open System Interconnection) model represents a network framework based on layers. Each layer in the OSI model provides distinct functionality in relation to the other layers. The OSI model contains seven layers, as shown in Figure 1.1.

FIGURE 1.1
The seven layers of the OSI model.

The layers are sometimes referred to by number, with the lowest layer (Physical) being layer 1 and the highest layer (Application) being layer 7. If you hear someone refer to a "Layer 3 switch," he is referring to the third layer of the OSI model. As a person interested in security and intrusion detection, you must know the layers of the OSI model to fully understand the attack paths that could compromise your systems.

Each layer in the OSI model is important. The protocols you use every day, such as IP, TCP, ARP, NFS, and others, reside on the various layers of the model. Each layer has its own distinct function and role in the communication process.

The Physical layer of the OSI model is occupied by the media itself, such as the cabling and related signaling protocols, in other words, transferring the bits. For the most part, the Physical layer is of less concern to the network intrusion analyst beyond securing the devices and cabling themselves. Because this book doesn't really talk much about physical security (how interesting are door locks?), I won't be devoting more time to the Physical layer of the OSI model either. Naturally, the steps you take to secure physical wires are different from those you would take to attempt to secure wireless devices.

The next layer above Physical is the Datalink layer. The Datalink layer transfers the data over the given medium and is responsible for things such as detection and recovery from errors in transmission. The Datalink layer is also the layer where physical hardware addresses are defined, such as an Ethernet card's Media Access Control (MAC) address.

Above the Datalink layer, the Network layer is the all-important third layer in IP networks. This layer is responsible for the logical addressing and routing of data. IP is a Network layer protocol, which means that the Network layer is the layer on which IP addresses and subnet masks are used. Routers and some switches operate at layer three, moving data between both logically and physically divided networks.

The fourth layer, the Transport layer, is the primary layer on which reliability can be built. Protocols that exist at the Transport layer include TCP and UDP. The fifth layer is the Session layer, within which sessions are built between endpoints. The sixth layer, Presentation, is primarily responsible for communication with the Application layer above it, and it also defines such things as encryption to be used. Finally, the Application layer is responsible for displaying data to the user or application.

Aside from the OSI model, there exists another model, the DARPA model, sometimes called the TCP/IP reference model, which is only four layers. The OSI model has become the traditional or de facto model on which most network discussions take place.

As data moves from an application down the layers of the OSI model, the protocol at the next lower layer may add its own information onto the data. This data usually consists of a header that is prepended onto the data from the next highest level, though sometimes a trailer is added as well. This process, called encapsulation, continues until the data is transmitted across the physical medium. In the case of Ethernet, the data is known as a frame when it is transmitted. When the Ethernet frame arrives at its destination, the frame then begins the process of moving up the layers of the OSI model, with each layer reading the header (and possibly trailer) information from the corresponding layer of the sender. This process is called demultiplexing.

Connectionless Versus Connection-Oriented Protocols

At some layers of the OSI model, protocols can be defined in terms of one of their properties, connectionless or connection-oriented. This definition refers to the methods that the protocol contains for providing such things as error control, flow control, data segmentation, and data reassembly.

Think of connection-oriented protocols in terms of a telephone call. Generally there is an acceptable protocol for making a phone call and having a conversation. The person making the call, the initiator of the communication, opens the communication by dialing a telephone number. The person (or machine, as is the ever-increasing case) at the other end receives the request to begin a telephone conversation. The request to initiate a telephone conversation is frequently indicated by the ringing of the telephone on the receiver's end. The receiver picks up the telephone and says "Hello" or some other form of greeting. The initiator then acknowledges this greeting by responding in kind. At this point, it's safe to say that the conversation or call setup has been initiated. From this point forward, the conversation ensues. During the conversation if something goes wrong such as noise on the line, one of the parties may ask the other to repeat their last statement. Most of the time when a call is complete, both sides will indicate that they are done with the conversation by saying "Good-bye." The call ends shortly thereafter.

The example just given provides a semireasonable picture of a connection-oriented protocol such as TCP. There are exceptions to the rule, just as there can be exceptions or errors with the TCP protocol. For example, sometimes the initial call fails for technological reasons beyond the control of the caller or receiver.

On the other hand, a connectionless protocol is more akin to a postcard sent through the mail. After the sender writes a message on the postcard and drops it into the mailbox, the sender (presumably) loses control over that message. The sender receives no direct acknowl-edgment that the postcard was ever delivered successfully. Examples of connectionless proto-cols include UDP and IP itself.

Next Steps

From here, I'm going to jump into a more detailed look at the Internet Protocol (IP). However, I strongly recommend that you spend some additional time learning about the OSI model and the protocols themselves. Knowledge of the protocols and the OSI model is vital to a security professional. I highly recommend the book *TCP/IP Illustrated, Volume 1*, by W. Richard Stevens, as a book that is indispensable on any computer professional's desk.

The IP

The Internet Protocol is the basis on which the Internet operates. Together with protocols at other layers, the IP layer provides communications for countless applications. IP is a connec-tionless protocol providing layer 3 routing functions.

IP Addressing and Subnetting

As you already know, but I feel compelled to write, IP addresses for version 4 of IP consist of four 32-bit numbers separated by periods, known as the "dotted quad" or "dotted decimal" notation. Although seemingly everyone understands or at least has seen an IP address, it cer-tainly seems as though fewer and fewer understand subnetting and the subnet masks that are an important part of the IP addressing scheme. This section briefly looks at IP addressing and subnetting.

IP addresses are divided into different classes rather than being an entirely flat address space. The classes for IP addresses are shown in Table 1.1.

TABLE 1.1
Internet Addresses

CLASS	ADDRESS RANGE
A	0.0.0.0 to 127.255.255.255
B	128.0.0.0 to 191.255.255.255
C	192.0.0.0 to 223.255.255.255
D	224.0.0.0 to 239.255.255.255
E and unallocated	240.0.0.0 to 255.255.255.255

In practice, only addresses in Classes A through C are for general Internet use. However, some readers may have experience with Class D addresses, frequently used for multicast. Class E is the experimental and unallocated range.

SPECIAL IP ADDRESSES

There are three major special cases of IP addresses:

- *Network address* 0—As noted under Class A addresses, network address 0 is not used as part of a routable address. When used as a source address, its only legal use is during initialization when a host is attempting to have its IP address dynamically assigned by a server. When used as a destination, only address 0.0.0.0 has meaning, and then only to the local machine as referring to itself, or as a convention to refer to a default route.

- *Loopback network address* 127—As noted under Class A addresses, network address 127 is not used as part of a routable address. Loopback addresses refer to a private network interface supported by the operating system. The interface is used as the addressing mechanism for local network-based services. In other words, local network clients use it to address local servers. Loopback traffic remains entirely within the operating system. It is never passed to a physical network interface. Typically, 127.0.0.1 is the only loopback address used, referring to the local host.

- *Broadcast addresses*—Broadcast addresses are special addresses applying to all hosts on a network. There are two major categories of broadcast addresses. Limited broadcasts are not routed but are delivered to all hosts connected to the same physical network segment. All the bits in both the network and the host fields of the IP address are set to one, as 255.255.255.255. Network-directed broadcasts are routed, being delivered to all hosts on a specified network. The IP address's network field specifies a network. The host field is usually all ones, as in 192.168.10.255. Alternatively, you might sometimes see the address specified as the network address, as in 192.168.10.0.

13

The IP header consists of a number of fields and totals 20 bytes, not including optional option fields that can be included as part of the header. The IP header is shown in Figure 1.2.

FIGURE 1.2
The IP header.

Version	Hdr Len	TOS	Total Datagram Len	
Packet ID			FI	Fragment Offset
TTL		Protocol	Header Checksum	
Source Address				
Destination Address				
(IP Options)			(Padding)	

The IP header begins with 4 bits indicating the version, currently version 4, followed by the length of the header, which is normally 20 bytes plus optional options. The maximum length of the IP header is 60 bytes. The next field, type-of-service or TOS, contains 3 bits for precedence (not used), 4 bits for the TOS itself, and one bit that must be set to **0**. These are the four possible values for TOS:

- Minimize delay
- Maximize throughput
- Maximize reliability
- Minimize monetary cost

Under normal conditions these 4 bits are all zero, but certain applications might use various bits depending on their needs. For example, an SSH session might set the minimize delay bit because it is interactive by nature.

The first number of an IP address indicates the class of the address. Because each number within the dotted decimal notation is 8 bits, the possible values for each number are **0** through **255**. The class indicates the default number of bits devoted to the network portion of the address versus the number of bits devoted to the host identification with a given address. The division between the network portion of the address versus the host portion of the address is important because it is the basis of subnet addressing.

Aside from classes, there are three types of addresses available on the Internet: unicast, multicast, and broadcast. Unicast addresses correspond to a single host on the Internet. Multicast addresses correspond to a group of hosts that ask to be included within that group. Broadcast addresses are used by hosts that want to send data to every host on a given subnet.

Each class of address has a default subnet mask that indicates the division between the network and host portion of a given address. That's quite a mouthful, so I'll give examples and then there will be a quiz later. Kidding!

The default subnet masks for Classes A through C are given in Table 1.2.

TABLE 1.2
Default Subnet Masks

CLASS	DEFAULT SUBNET MASK
A	255.0.0.0
B	255.255.0.0
C	255.255.255.0

You've undoubtedly seen and typed these numbers when configuring network settings. As previously stated, the subnet mask indicates the division between the network and the host portions of an IP address. The unmasked portion, known as the host portion, of the address comprises the logical network on which a given host resides. In other words, with a Class C subnet mask of `255.255.255.0`, there can be a total of 254 hosts on the network. An astute reader might notice that there are really 256 addresses but only 254 hosts. Within a given logical IP network there are two special addresses, the network address and the broadcast address. This is true regardless of the size of the network. In the case of the Class C subnet example, the network address ends with `.0` and the broadcast address ends with `.255`.

As Table 1.2 illustrates, of the total 32 bits in an IPv4 address, a Class A subnet mask uses 8 bits, a Class B subnet mask uses 16 bits, and a Class C subnet mask uses 24 bits. When a network is divided along traditional address Class boundaries using the default subnet mask, it is said to be a classful network. As you might expect, there are times when it would be beneficial to use a much smaller network. For example, two IP routers that only need to transmit between each other would use an entire Class C network using traditional classful subnetting. Luckily, classless subnetting is also possible.

Using classless subnetting, officially called Classless Inter Domain Routing (CIDR), you can divide networks according to need by adding or subtracting bits from the subnet mask. This is useful for conservation of addresses because it enables the network administrator to customize the size of the network based more on need and convenience than on the classful boundaries.

Jumping back to the example with two routers that communicate solely with each other, using CIDR a network administrator can create a network of just two hosts with the resulting subnet mask being 255.255.255.252.

I'll carry that example a little further. The two routers only need to talk to each other within this network so that they can route traffic between two different IP networks. The network administrator assigns one router the address 192.168.0.1 and the other router 192.168.0.2 and gives both a subnet mask of 255.255.255.252. Given that subnet mask, there are two available IP addresses with which a host could be addressed. The network address for this logical network is 192.168.0.0 and the broadcast address is 192.168.0.3. Using CIDR, the network administrator can now use the remainder of the 192.168.0 network, following CIDR rules, for other hosts.

You'll frequently see subnet notation referred to with a /*NN* with *NN* being the number of bits to be masked. For example, a Class C has 24 bits for the network portion of the address, which means that it could be referred to as a /24. A Class B would be /16 and a Class A would be /8. Going back to the two-router example, the CIDR notation for this address is /30 because 30 bits of the address are consumed by the subnet.

Why is subnetting important? The simple answer is that a subnet defines the largest possible broadcast space for a given network. Within a given subnet a host can send a broadcast to all other hosts in that subnet. In practice, though, broadcasts are limited more by physical limitations than by the logical limitations presented by subnet masks. You can connect only so many devices to a switch before you may (I repeat, may) start to see performance degradation and would likely divide the network into smaller logical sections. Without subnetting we would have a very large, flat address space, which would be much slower than the hierarchical addressing currently used.

IP Fragmentation

There are times when an IP datagram is larger than the maximum allowed size for the physical medium on which it will be traveling. This maximum allowed size is known as the Maximum Transmission Unit, or MTU. If an IP datagram is larger than the MTU for the medium, the datagram will need to be split into smaller chunks before being transmitted. For Ethernet, the MTU is 1500 bytes. The process of splitting an IP datagram into smaller pieces is called fragmentation.

Fragmentation is handled at the IP layer of the OSI model and is thus transparent to higher layer protocols such as TCP and UDP. As an administrator, you should care about fragmentation insofar as it can affect application performance if one of the fragments of a large segment gets lost. In addition, as a security administrator, you should understand fragmentation because it has been a path for attack in the past. Realize, however, that any intermediary router or other devices within the communication path may cause fragmentation and you may not even know it.

Broadcasting and Multicasting

When a device wants to send data to other devices on the same network segment, it can send the data to a special address known as a broadcast address to accomplish this task. On the other hand, a multicast is sent to the devices that belong to the multicast group, sometimes called subscribers.

Imagine a large, flat network in which every computer and device is connected to the others. In such an environment every network device sees every other network device's traffic. In this type of network, each device sees the traffic and determines whether it cares about the traffic in question. In other words, it looks to see whether the data is addressed to it or to another device. If the data is addressed to the device, it passes the data up to the layers of the OSI model. At the interface level for Ethernet, the device looks for its MAC address or the hardware address associated with the network interface itself. Remember that IP addresses are relevant only to protocols at higher layers on the OSI model.

Aside from frames addressed to the device itself, two special cases exist that might cause an interface to accept data and pass it up to higher layers. These two special cases are multicast and broadcast. Multicast is a method for transmitting data to a subset of devices that are said to be subscribed to that multicast.

On the other hand, broadcasts are meant to be processed by every device that receives them. Primarily two types of broadcasts are available: directed broadcast and limited broadcast. By far, directed broadcasts are the most common. Limited broadcasts are used by devices attempting to configure themselves through DHCP, BOOTP, or another configuration protocol. A limited broadcast is sent to the address `255.255.255.255` and should never pass through a router. This is a key hint for anyone who controls a router or other routing device such as a routing firewall. If you receive a packet on your external, Internet-facing router interface addressed to `255.255.255.255`, chances are that there is a misconfigured device or, more likely, that a potential attacker is attempting to probe your network. You may see a limited broadcast on an internal interface for a router if you have devices that configure themselves on boot using DHCP.

Directed broadcasts are the most common form of broadcast you'll see on any given network. This is because broadcasts are used by the Address Resolution Protocol (ARP, discussed later) to determine the MAC address for an IP address on a given subnet. A directed broadcast is a broadcast that is limited by the network or subnet in which the sending device resides. By default, when a router interface encounters a directed broadcast, it does not pass it along to other subnets through the router. Most routers can be configured to allow this behavior; however, one should be careful so as not to create a broadcast storm by forwarding broadcasts through a router. A subnet broadcast is a data frame addressed to the broadcast address in a given subnet. This broadcast address varies depending on the subnet mask for the given subnet. In a Class C subnet (255.255.255.0 or /24), the default broadcast address is the highest available address, thus the one ending in .255. For example, in the 192.168.1.0/24 network, the broadcast address is 192.168.1.255.

ICMP

Holding a special place, some say, within the IP layer is ICMP. You're probably familiar with ICMP when you use the ping command because ping uses ICMP. ICMP, or Internet Control Message Protocol, has several uses, including being the underlying protocol for the ping command. There are 15 functions within ICMP each denoted by a type code. For instance, the type for an ICMP Echo Request (think: ping) is 8; the reply to that request, aptly titled an Echo Reply, is type 0. Within the different types there can also exist codes to specify the condition for the given type. The types and codes for ICMP messages are shown in Table 1.3.

TABLE 1.3
ICMP Message Types and Codes

TYPE	CODE	DESCRIPTION
0	0	Echo Reply
3		Destination Unreachable
	0	Network Unreachable
	1	Host Unreachable
	2	Protocol Unreachable
	3	Port Unreachable
	4	Fragmentation Needed and DF Set
	5	Source Route Failed
	6	Destination Network Unknown
	7	Destination Host Unknown
	8	Source Host Isolated
	9	Destination Network Administratively Prohibited
	10	Destination Host Administratively Prohibited
	11	Network Unreachable for Type of Service
	12	Host Unreachable for Type of Service

TABLE 1.3
ICMP Message Types and Codes (continued)

TYPE	CODE	DESCRIPTION
	13	Communication Administratively Prohibited
	14	Host Precedence Violation
	15	Precedence Cutoff in Effect
4		Source Quench
5		Redirect
	0	Network Redirect
	1	Host Redirect
	2	Type of Service and Network Redirect
	3	Type of Service and Host Redirect
8	0	Echo Request
9	0	Router Advertisement
10	0	Router Solicitation
11		Time Exceeded
	0	TTL (Time to Live) Exceeded in Transit
	1	Fragment Reassembly Time Exceeded
12	0	Parameter Problem
13	0	Timestamp Request
14	0	Timestamp Reply
15	0	Information Request
16	0	Information Reply
17	0	Address Mask Request
18	0	Address Mask Reply

The type and the code of an ICMP message are contained in the ICMP header, shown in Figure 1.3.

FIGURE 1.3
The ICMP header.

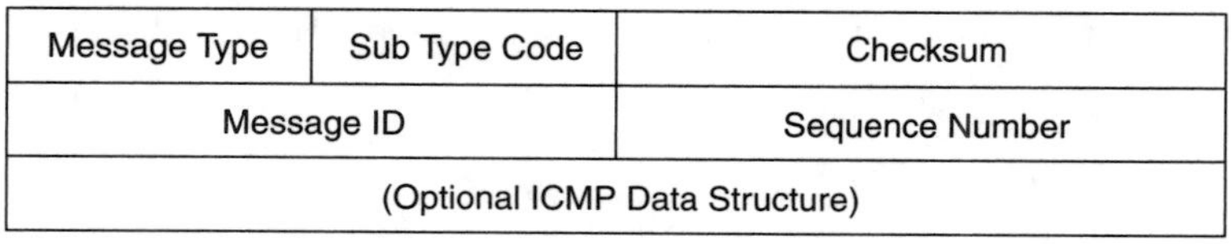

Message Type	Sub Type Code	Checksum	
Message ID		Sequence Number	
(Optional ICMP Data Structure)			

Transport Mechanisms

Internet Protocol defines a Network layer protocol of the OSI model. There are also other Network layer protocols, but I will be concentrating solely on IP because it is by far the most popular Network layer protocol in use today. Above the Network layer on the OSI model is the Transport layer. As you might expect, the Transport layer has its own set of protocols. Two of the Transport layer protocols are of interest: UDP and TCP. This section examines each of these protocols.

UDP

UDP, or User Datagram Protocol, is a connectionless protocol used for such services as DNS queries, SNMP, and RADIUS. Being connectionless, UDP is akin to a "fire and forget" type of protocol. The client sends a UDP packet, sometimes referred to as a datagram, and assumes that the server will receive the packet. It's up to a higher layer protocol to assemble the packets in order. The UDP header, shown in Figure 1.4, is 8 bytes in length.

FIGURE 1.4
The UDP header.

Source Port	Destination Port
UDP Packet Length	Checksum

The UDP header begins with the source port number and the destination port number. Next up is the length of the entire packet, including data. Obviously because the header itself is 8 bytes in length, the minimum value for this portion of the header is **8**. The final portion of the UDP header is the checksum, which includes both the header and the data.

TCP

TCP, an abbreviation for Transmission Control Protocol, is a connection-oriented protocol that is frequently used with IP. Referring to TCP as connection-oriented means that it provides reliable service to the layers above it. Recall the telephone conversation analogy given earlier in this chapter. As in that analogy, two applications wanting to communicate using TCP must also establish a connection (sometimes referred to as a session). The TCP header is shown in Figure 1.5.

FIGURE 1.5
The TCP header.

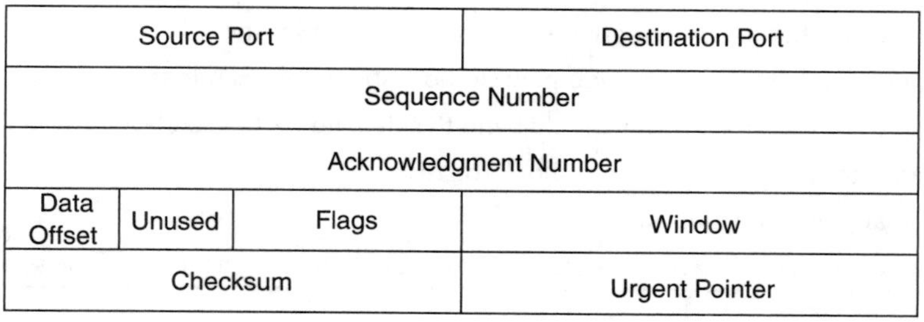

Source Port			Destination Port	
Sequence Number				
Acknowledgment Number				
Data Offset	Unused	Flags	Window	
Checksum			Urgent Pointer	

As you can see from Figure 1.5, the 20-byte TCP header is significantly more complicated than the other protocol headers shown in this chapter. Like the UDP header, the TCP header begins with both the source and the destination ports. The combination of the source and destination ports along with the IP addresses of the sender and receiver identifies the connection. The TCP header has a 32-bit sequence number and a 32-bit acknowledgment. Remember that TCP is a connection-oriented protocol and provides reliable service. The sequence and acknowledgment numbers are the primary (but not the only) mechanism used to provide that reliability. As data is passed down to the Transport layer, TCP divides the data into what it believes to be the most appropriate size. These pieces are known as TCP segments. As TCP sends data down the protocol stack, it creates a sequence number that indicates the first byte of data for the given segment. On the opposite end of the communication, the receiver sends an acknowledgment indicating that the segment has been received. The sender keeps a timer running, and if an acknowledgment isn't received in a timely fashion, the segment will be resent.

Another mechanism for reliability that TCP provides is a checksum on both the header and the data. If the checksum set within the header by the sender does not match the checksum as computed by the receiver, the receiver will not send an acknowledgment. If an acknowledgment gets lost in transit, the sender will likely send another segment with the same sequence number. In such an event, the receiver will simply discard the repeated segment.

A four-bit field is used for header length, including any options provided as part of the header. There are six individual bit flags within the TCP header: URG, ACK, PSH, RST, SYN, and FIN. A description of these flags is contained in Table 1.4.

TABLE 1.4
TCP Header Flags

FLAG	DESCRIPTION
URG	Indicates that the urgent pointer portion of the header should be examined.
ACK	Indicates that the acknowledgment number should be examined.
PSH	Indicates that the receiver should hand this data up to the next layer as soon as possible.
RST	Indicates that the connection should be reset.
SYN	Initiates a connection.
FIN	Indicates that the sender (could be either side of the connection) is done sending data.

The 16-bit Window field is used to provide a sliding window mechanism. The receiver sets the window number to indicate the size that the receiver is ready to receive, beginning with the acknowledgment number. This is a form of flow control for TCP.

The 16-bit urgent pointer indicates the offset from the sequence number where urgent data ends. This enables the sender to indicate that there is data that should be handled in an urgent manner and can be used in conjunction with the **PSH** flag as well.

Now that you have a feeling for the TCP header, it's time to examine how TCP connections are established and ended.

TCP CONNECTIONS

Whereas UDP is a connectionless protocol, TCP is a connection-oriented protocol. With UDP there is no concept of a connection, there is only a sender and a receiver of a UDP datagram. With TCP, on the other hand, either side of the connection can send or receive data, possibly doing both at the same time. This is what makes TCP a full-duplex protocol. The process of establishing a TCP connection is sometimes called the three-way handshake—you'll see why shortly.

With a connection-oriented protocol, there is a specific set of procedures that takes place in order to establish a TCP connection. During this process, various states exist for the TCP connection. The connection establishment procedures and their corresponding states are detailed next.

The side of the communication wanting to initiate the connection (client) sends a TCP segment with the **SYN** flag set, as well as an Initial Sequence Number (ISN) and the port number for the connection to the other side, normally referred to as the server side of the connection. This is frequently referred to as a SYN packet or SYN segment, and the connection is said to be in the **SYN_SENT** state.

The server side of the connection responds with a TCP segment with the SYN flag set as well as the ACK flag set. In addition, the server sets the ISN with a value one higher than the ISN sent by the client. This is frequently referred to as a SYN-ACK packet or SYN-ACK segment, and the connection is said to be in the SYN_RCVD state.

The client then acknowledges the SYN-ACK by sending another segment with the ACK flag set and by incrementing the ISN by one. This completes the three-way handshake and the connection is said to be in an ESTABLISHED state.

As with the protocol for connection initiation, there is also a protocol for connection termination. The protocol for terminating a TCP connection is four steps as opposed to the three for connection establishment. The additional step is due to the full duplex nature of a TCP connection insofar as either side may be sending data at any given time.

Closing a connection on one side is accomplished by that side sending a TCP segment with the FIN flag set. Either side of the connection can send a FIN to indicate that it is done sending data. The other side can still send data. However, in practice, after a FIN is received the connection termination sequence will normally begin. For this discussion I'll call the side wanting to terminate the connection the client side.

The termination process begins with the client sending a segment with the FIN flag set, known as the CLOSE_WAIT state on the server side and FIN_WAIT_1 on the client side. After the FIN is received by the server, the server sends an ACK back to the client, incrementing the sequence number by one. At this point the client goes into the FIN_WAIT_2 state. The server also indicates to its own higher layer protocols that the connection is terminated. Next the server closes the connection, which causes a segment with the FIN flag to be sent to the client, which in turn causes the server to go into a LAST_ACK state while the client goes into a TIME_WAIT state. Finally, the client acknowledges this FIN with an ACK and increments the sequence number by one, which causes the connection to go into a CLOSED state. Because TCP connections can be terminated by either side, a TCP connection can exist in a half-close mode in which one end has initiated the FIN sequence but the other side has not done so.

TCP connections can also be terminated by one end sending a segment with the reset (RST) flag set. This tells the other side to use an abortive release method. This is as opposed to the normal termination of a TCP connection sometimes referred to as an orderly release.

An optional part of the TCP connection sequence is the establishment of the Maximum Segment Size (MSS). The MSS is the maximum chunk of data that the respective end of communication is able to receive. Because the MSS is the maximum size that a given end of the connection can receive, it's perfectly fine to send a chunk of data smaller than the MSS. In general, you should consider a larger MSS to be good, keeping in mind that fragmentation should be avoided because it adds overhead (the additional bytes for each IP and TCP header required for fragmented packets).

Don't Forget ARP

Address Resolution Protocol, or ARP, is the protocol used to link a physical device such as a network card to an IP address. Network devices use a 48-bit address (known as a MAC address) that is unique across all devices in a given segment. Although sometimes devices have the same MAC address, this is quite rare within the same network segment.

When capturing traffic in a network, you will encounter ARP packets at varying frequencies as devices locate one another as they pass traffic. ARP requests are broadcast so that all devices will see them. However, most ARP replies are unicast so that only the requesting device will see the reply. ARP traffic is not normally passed between network segments. Therefore, a router can be configured to provide proxy ARP service so that it can answer for ARP requests in multiple network segments.

Hostnames and IP Addresses

People like to use words to name things, such as giving computers names like `mycomputer.mydomain.example.com`. Technically, it's not the computer that's being named, but the network interface in the computer. If the computer has multiple network cards, each card will typically have a different name and address, and will most likely be on a different network in a different subdomain.

Hostname elements are separated by dots. In the case of `mycomputer.mydomain.example.com`, the leftmost element, `mycomputer`, is the hostname. The `.mydomain`, `.example`, and `.com` are elements of the domains this network card is a member of. Network domains are hierarchical trees. What is a domain? It's a naming convention. The hierarchical domain tree represents the hierarchical nature of the global domain name service (DNS) database. DNS maps between the symbolic names people give to computers and networks and the numeric addresses the IP layer uses to uniquely identify network interfaces.

DNS maps in both directions: IP address to name and name to IP address. When you click on a URL in your web browser, the DNS database is consulted to find the unique IP address associated with that hostname. The IP address is passed to the IP layer to use as the destination address in the packet.

IP Addresses and Ethernet Addresses

Whereas the IP layer identifies network hosts by their 32-bit IP address, the subnet or link layer identifies the Ethernet card by its unique 48-bit Ethernet address, or MAC address, which the manufacturer burns into the card. IP addresses are passed between the endpoint hosts to identify themselves. Ethernet addresses are passed between adjacent hosts and routers.

Ordinarily, the Ethernet address could be ignored in a firewall discussion. The Layer 2 hardware Ethernet address is not visible to the Layer 3 IP level or Layer 4 Transport level. As you'll see in later chapters, iptables, the Linux firewall administration program, has the extended capability to access and filter on the MAC address. There are specialized uses for this firewall functionality, but it's important to remember that Ethernet addresses do not pass end-to-end across the network. Ethernet addresses are passed between adjacent network interfaces, or hosts and routers. They are not passed through a router unchanged.

Routing: Getting a Packet from Here to There

Neither a residential site nor most businesses are likely to run routing protocols such as RIP or OSPF. In these cases, routing tables are set up statically, by hand. There's a hint in there. If you're running a routing protocol such as RIP, chances are that you don't need to be; you could operate a more efficient network without that unnecessary overhead. Typically, most sites have a default gateway device, which is the network that interface packets are sent out on when the destination address's route is unknown. The service provider usually provides a single router address, which is the default Internet gateway for the site's local network.

Service Ports: The Door to the Programs on Your System

Network-based services are programs running on a machine that other computers on the network can access. The service ports identify the programs and individual sessions or connections taking place. Service ports are the numeric names for the different network-based services. They are also used as numeric identifiers for the endpoints of a particular connection between two programs. Service port numbers range from **0** to **65535**.

Server programs (that is, *daemons*) listen for incoming connections on a service port assigned to them. By historical convention, major network services are assigned well-known, or famous, port numbers in the lower range from **1** to **1023**. These port number–to–service mappings are coordinated by the Internet Assigned Numbers Authority (IANA) as a set of universally agreed-on conventions or standards.

An advertised service is simply a service available over the Internet from its assigned port. If your machine isn't offering a particular service, and someone tries to connect to the port associated with that service, nothing will happen. Someone is knocking on the door, but no one lives there to answer. For example, HTTP is assigned to port **80** (though, again, there's no reason why you couldn't run it on port **8080**, **20943**, or any available port). If your machine isn't running an HTTP-based web server and someone tries to connect to port **80**, the client program receives a connection shutdown message as an error message from your machine indicating that the service isn't offered.

The higher port numbers from **1024** to **65535** are called *unprivileged ports*. They serve a dual purpose. For the most part, these ports are dynamically assigned to the client end of a connection. The combination of client and server port number pairs, along with their respective IP host addresses, and the Transport protocol used, uniquely identifies the connection.

Additionally, ports in the **1024** through **49151** range are registered with the IANA. These ports can be used as part of the general unprivileged pool, but they are also associated with particular services such as SOCKS or X Window servers. Originally, the idea was that services offered on the higher ports were not running with root privilege. They were for use by user-level, nonprivileged programs. The convention may or may not hold in any individual case.

SERVICE NAME–TO–PORT NUMBER MAPPINGS

Linux distributions are supplied with a list of common service port numbers. The list is found in the /etc/services file.

Each entry consists of a symbolic name for a service, the port number assigned to it, the protocol (TCP or UDP) the service runs over, and any optional nicknames for the service. Table 1.5 lists some common service name–to–port number mappings, taken from Red Hat Linux.

TABLE 1.5
Common Service Name–to–Port Number Mappings

PORT NAME	PORT NUMBER/PROTOCOL	ALIAS
ftp	21/tcp	- -
telnet	23/tcp	- -
smtp	25/tcp	mail
nicname	43/tcp	whois
domain	53/tcp	nameserver
domain	53/udp	nameserver
finger	79/tcp	- -
http	80/tcp	www www-http
pop3	110/tcp	pop-3
auth	113/tcp	authentication tap ident

TABLE 1.5

Common Service Name–to–Port Number Mappings (continued)

PORT NAME	PORT NUMBER/PROTOCOL	ALIAS
nntp	119/tcp	readnews untp
ntp	123/udp	- -
https	443/tcp	- -

> Note that the symbolic names associated with the port numbers vary by Linux distribution and release. Names and aliases differ; port numbers do not.
>
> Also note that port numbers are associated with a protocol. The IANA has attempted to assign the same service port number to both the TCP and the UDP protocols, regardless of whether a particular service uses both transport modes. Most services use one protocol or the other. The domain name service uses both.

A Typical TCP Connection: Visiting a Remote Website

As an illustration, a common TCP connection is going to a website through your browser (connecting to a web server). This section illustrates the aspects of connection establishment and ongoing communication that will be relevant to IP packet filtering in later chapters.

What happens? As shown in Figure 1.6, a web server is running on a machine somewhere, waiting for a connection request on TCP service port **80**. You click on the link for a URL in Netscape. Part of the URL is parsed into a hostname; the hostname is translated into the web server's IP address; and your browser is assigned an unprivileged port (for example, TCP port **14000**) for the connection. An HTTP message for the web server is constructed. It's encapsulated in a TCP message, wrapped in an IP packet header, and sent out. For our purposes, the header contains the fields shown in Figure 1.6.

Additional information is included in the header that isn't visible at the packet-filtering level. Nevertheless, describing the sequence numbers associated with the **SYN** and **ACK** flags helps clarify what's happening during the three-way handshake. When the client program sends its first connection request message, the **SYN** flag is accompanied by a synchronization sequence number. The client is requesting a connection with the server and passes along a starting sequence number it will use as the starting point to number all the rest of the data bytes the client will send.

The packet is received at the server machine. It's sent to service port **80**. The server is listening to port **80**, so it's notified of an incoming connection request (the **SYN** connection synchronization request flag) from the source IP address and port socket pair (*your IP address*, 14000).

The server allocates a new socket on its end, (*web server IP address*, 80) and associates it with the client socket.

FIGURE 1.6
A TCP client connection request.

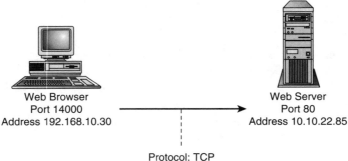

Protocol: TCP
Source Address: 192.168.10.30
Source Port: 14000
Destination Address: 10.10.22.85
Destination Port: 80 (www)
Flags: SYN (Connection Synchronization Request)

The web server responds with an acknowledgment (ACK) to the SYN message, along with its own synchronization request (SYN), as shown in Figure 1.7. The connection is now half open.

FIGURE 1.7
A TCP server connection request acknowledgment.

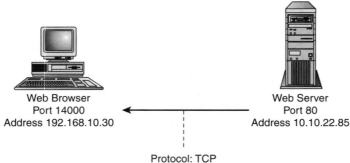

Protocol: TCP
Source Address: 10.10.22.85
Source Port: 80 (www)
Destination Address: 192.168.10.30
Destination Port: 14000
Flags: ACK (SYN Acknowledgment)
SYN (Connection Synchronization Request)

Two fields not visible to the packet-filtering level are included in the SYN–ACK header. Along with the ACK flag, the server includes the client's sequence number incremented by the number of contiguous data bytes received. The purpose of the acknowledgment is to acknowledge the data the client referred to by its sequence number. The server acknowledges this by incrementing the client's sequence number, effectively saying it received the data, and sequence number plus one is the next data byte the server expects to receive. The client is free to throw its copy of the original SYN message away now that the server has acknowledged receipt of it.

The server also sets the SYN flag in its first message. As with the client's first message, the SYN flag is accompanied by a synchronization sequence number. The server is passing along its own starting sequence number for its half of the connection.

This first message is the only message the server will send with the SYN flag set. This and all subsequent messages have the ACK flag set. The presence of the ACK flag in all server messages, as compared to the lack of an ACK flag in the client's first message, will be a critical difference when we get to the information available for constructing a firewall.

Your machine receives this message and replies with its own acknowledgment, after which the connection is established. Figure 1.8 shows a graphic representation of this. From here on, both the client and the server set the ACK flag. The SYN flag won't be set again by either program.

FIGURE 1.8
TCP connection establishment.

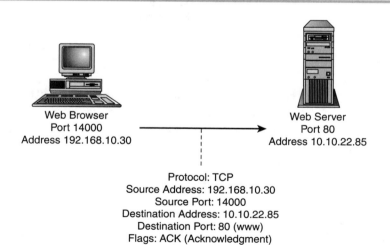

Web Browser
Port 14000
Address 192.168.10.30

Web Server
Port 80
Address 10.10.22.85

Protocol: TCP
Source Address: 192.168.10.30
Source Port: 14000
Destination Address: 10.10.22.85
Destination Port: 80 (www)
Flags: ACK (Acknowledgment)

With each acknowledgment, the client and server programs increment their partner process's sequence number by the number of contiguous data received, plus one, indicating receipt of that many bytes of data, and indicating the next data byte in the stream the program expects to receive.

As your browser receives the web page, your machine receives data messages from the web server with packet headers, as shown in Figure 1.9.

FIGURE 1.9
An ongoing TCP server-to-client connection.

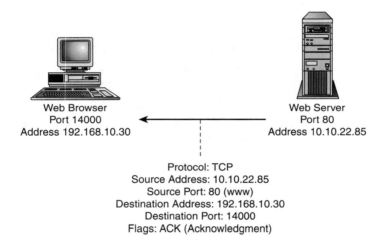

Web Browser
Port 14000
Address 192.168.10.30

Web Server
Port 80
Address 10.10.22.85

Protocol: TCP
Source Address: 10.10.22.85
Source Port: 80 (www)
Destination Address: 192.168.10.30
Destination Port: 14000
Flags: ACK (Acknowledgment)

Summary

The simple examples in this chapter illustrate the information that IP packet-filtering firewalls are based on. Chapter 2, "Packet-Filtering Concepts," builds on this introduction, describing how the ICMP, UDP, and TCP message types and service port numbers are used to define a packet-filtering firewall.

CHAPTER 2

Packet-Filtering Concepts

What is a firewall? Over the years, the term has changed in meaning. According to RFC 2647, "Benchmarking Terminology for Firewall Performance," a firewall is "a device or group of devices that enforces an access control policy between networks." This definition is very broad, purposefully so in fact. A firewall can encompass many layers of the OSI model and may refer to a device that does packet filtering, performs packet inspection and filtering, implements a policy on an application at a higher layer, or does any of these and more.

A nonstateful firewall usually performs some packet filtering based solely on the IP layer (layer 3) of the OSI model, though sometimes higher-layer protocols are involved in this type of firewall. An example of this type of device might include a border router that sits at the edge of a network and implements one or more access lists to prevent various types of malicious traffic from entering the network. Some might argue that this type of device isn't a firewall at all. However, it certainly appears to fit within the RFC definition.

A border router access list might implement many different policies depending on which interface the packet was received on. It's typical to filter certain packets at the edge of the network connecting to the Internet. These packets are discussed later in this chapter.

As opposed to a stateless firewall, a stateful firewall is one that keeps track of the packets previously seen within a given session and applies the access policy to packets based on what has already been seen for the given connection. A stateful firewall implies the basic packet filtering capabilities of a stateless firewall as well. A stateful firewall will, for example, keep track of the stages of the TCP three-way handshake and reject packets that appear out of sequence for that handshake. Being connectionless, UDP is somewhat trickier to a stateful firewall because there's no state to speak of. However, a stateful firewall tracks recent UDP exchanges to ensure that a packet that has been received relates to a recent outgoing packet.

An *Application-level gateway (ALG)*, sometimes referred to an as Application-layer gateway, is yet another form of firewall. Unlike the stateless firewall, which has knowledge of the Network and possibly Transport layers, an ALG primarily handles layer 7, the Application layer of the OSI model. ALGs typically have deep knowledge of the application data being passed and can thus look for any deviation from the normal traffic for the application in question.

An ALG will typically reside in between the client and the real server and will, for all intents and purposes, mimic the behavior of the real server to the client. In effect, local traffic never leaves the LAN, and remote traffic never enters the LAN.

ALG sometimes also refers to a module, or piece of software that assists another firewall. Many firewalls come with an FTP ALG to support FTP's port mode data channel, where the client tells the server what local port to connect to so that it can open the data channel. The server initiates the incoming data channel connection (whereas, usually, the client initiates all connections). ALGs are frequently required to pass multimedia protocols through a firewall because multimedia sessions often use multiple connections initiated from both ends and generally use a combination of TCP and UDP together.

ALG is a proxy. Another form of proxy is a circuit-level proxy. Circuit-level proxies don't usually have application-specific knowledge; but they can enforce access and authorization policies, and they serve as termination points in what would otherwise be an end-to-end connection. SOCKS is an example of a circuit-level proxy. The proxy server acts as a termination point for both sides of the connection, but the server doesn't have any application-specific knowledge.

In each of these cases, the firewall's purpose is to enforce the access-control or security policies that you define. Security policies are essentially about access control—who is and is not allowed to perform which actions on the servers and networks under your control.

Though not necessarily specific to a firewall, firewalls many times find themselves performing additional tasks, some of which might include Network Address Translation (NAT), antivirus checking, event notification, URL filtering, user authentication, and Network-layer encryption.

This book covers the ideas behind a packet-filtering firewall, both static and dynamic, or stateless and stateful. Each of the approaches mentioned controls which services can be accessed and by whom. Each approach has its strengths and advantages based on the differing information available at the various OSI reference model layers.

Chapter 1, "Preliminary Concepts Underlying Packet-Filtering Firewalls," introduced the concepts and information a firewall is based on. This chapter introduces how this information is used to implement firewall rules.

A Packet-Filtering Firewall

At its most basic level, a packet-filtering firewall consists of a list of acceptance and denial rules. These rules explicitly define which packets will and will not be allowed through the network interface. The firewall rules use the packet header fields described in Chapter 1 to decide whether to forward a packet to its destination, to silently throw away the packet, or to block the packet and return an error condition to the sending machine. These rules can be based on a wide array of factors, including the source or destination IP addresses, the source and (more commonly) destination ports, portions of individual packets such as the TCP header flags, the types of protocol, the MAC address, and more.

MAC address filtering is not common on Internet-connected firewalls. Using MAC filtering, the firewall blocks or allows only certain MAC addresses. However, in all likelihood you only see one MAC address, the one from the router just upstream from your firewall. This means that every host on the Internet will appear to have the same MAC address as far as your firewall can see. A common error among new firewall administrators is to attempt to use MAC filtering on an Internet firewall.

Using a hybrid of the TCP/IP reference model, a packet-filtering firewall functions at the Network and Transport layers, as shown in Figure 2.1.

The overall idea is that you need to very carefully control what passes between the Internet and the machine that you have connected directly to the Internet. On the external interface to the Internet, you individually filter what's coming in from the outside and what's going out from the machine as exactly and explicitly as possible.

For a single-machine setup, it might be helpful to think of the network interface as an I/O pair. The firewall independently filters what comes in and what goes out through the interface. The input filtering and the output filtering can, and likely do, have completely different rules. When speaking of a Linux firewall, the lists of rules defining what can come in and what can go out are called *chains*. The I/O pair is the list of rules on the input chain and the list of rules on the output chain. The lists are called *chains* because a packet is matched against each rule in the list, one by one, until a match is found or the list is exhausted, as depicted in Figure 2.2.

FIGURE 2.1
Firewall placement in the TCP/IP reference model.

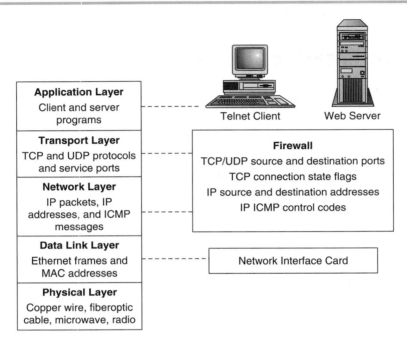

This sounds pretty powerful, and it is; but it isn't a surefire security mechanism. It's only part of the story, just one layer in the multilayered approach to data security. Not all application communication protocols lend themselves to packet filtering. This type of filtering is too low-level to allow fine-grained authentication and access control. These security services must be furnished at higher levels. IP doesn't have the capability to verify that the sender is who he or she claims to be. The only identifying information available at this level is the source address in the IP packet header. The source address can be modified with little difficulty. One level up, neither the network layer nor the transport layer can verify that the application data is correct. Nevertheless, the packet level allows greater, simpler control over direct port access, packet contents, and correct communication protocols than can easily or conveniently be done at higher levels.

Without packet-level filtering, higher-level filtering and proxy security measures are either crippled or potentially ineffective. To some extent, at least, they must rely on the correctness of the underlying communication protocol. Each layer in the security protocol stack adds another piece that other layers can't easily provide.

FIGURE 2.2
Input and output chains.

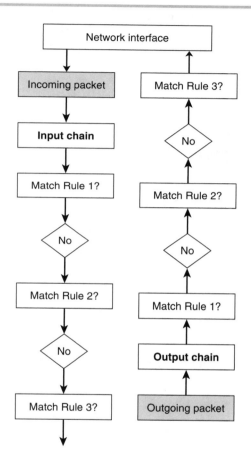

Choosing a Default Packet-Filtering Policy

As stated earlier in this chapter, a firewall is a device to implement an access control policy. A large part of this policy is the decision on a default firewall policy.

There are two basic approaches to a default firewall policy:

- Deny everything by default, and explicitly allow selected packets through.
- Accept everything by default, and explicitly deny selected packets from passing through.

Without question, the deny-everything policy is the recommended approach. This approach makes it easier to set up a secure firewall, but each service and related protocol transaction that you want must be enabled explicitly (see Figure 2.3). This means that you must understand the communication protocol for each service you enable. The deny-everything approach requires more work up front to enable Internet access. Some commercial firewall products support only the deny-everything policy.

FIGURE 2.3
The deny-everything-by-default policy.

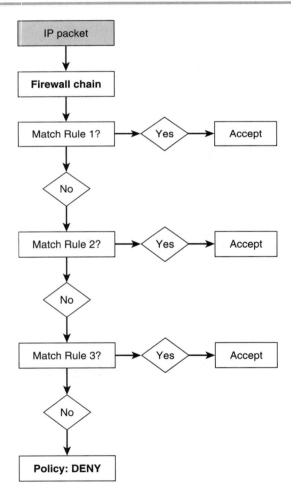

The accept-everything policy makes it much easier to get up and running right away, but it forces you to anticipate every conceivable access type that you might want to disable (see Figure 2.4). The danger is that you won't anticipate a dangerous access type until it's too late, or you'll later enable an insecure service without first blocking external access to it. In the end, developing a secure accept-everything firewall is much more work, much more difficult, almost always much less secure, and, therefore, much more error-prone.

FIGURE 2.4
The accept-everything-by-default policy.

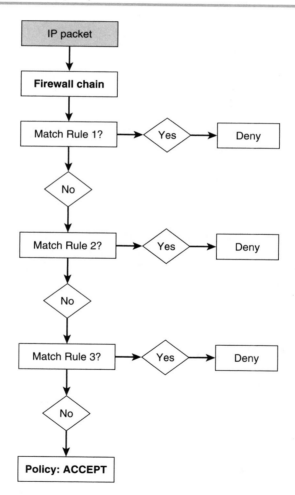

Rejecting Versus Denying a Packet

The Netfilter firewall mechanism in iptables gives you the option of either rejecting or dropping packets. What's the difference? As shown in Figure 2.5, when a packet is rejected, the packet is thrown away and an ICMP error message is returned to the sender. When a packet is dropped, the packet is simply thrown away without any notification to the sender.

FIGURE 2.5
Rejecting versus denying a packet.

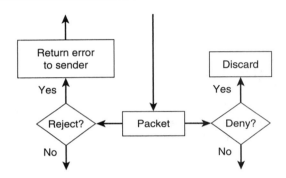

Silently dropping the packet is almost always the better choice, for three reasons. First, sending an error response doubles the network traffic. The majority of dropped packets are dropped because they are malevolent, not because they represent an innocent attempt to access a service you don't happen to offer. Second, a packet that you respond to can be used in a denial-of-service (DoS) attack. Third, any response, even an error message, gives the would-be attacker potentially useful information.

Filtering Incoming Packets

The input side of the external interface I/O pair, the input chain, is the more interesting in terms of securing your site. As mentioned earlier, you can filter based on source address, destination address, source port, destination port, and TCP status flags. You'll learn about all these pieces of information at one point or another in the following sections.

Remote Source Address Filtering

At the packet level, the only means of identifying the IP packet's sender is the source address in the packet header. This fact allows for the possibility of source address spoofing, in which the sender places an incorrect address rather than his or her own address in the source field. The address might be a nonexistent address, or it might be a legitimate address belonging to someone else. This can allow unsavory types to break into your system by appearing as local, trusted traffic; appearing to be you while attacking other sites; pretending to be someone else while attacking you; keeping your system bogged down responding to nonexistent addresses; or otherwise misleading you as to the source of incoming messages.

It's important to remember that you usually can't detect spoofed addresses. The address might be legitimate and routable but might not belong to the packet's sender. The next section describes the spoofed addresses you can detect.

SOURCE ADDRESS SPOOFING AND ILLEGAL ADDRESSES

There are 10 major classes of source addresses you should deny on your external interface in all cases. These are incoming packets claiming to be from the following:

- *Your IP address*—You will never see legal incoming packets claiming to be *from* your machine. Because the source address is the only information available and it can be modified, this is one of the forms of legitimate address spoofing you can detect at the packet-filtering level. Incoming packets claiming to be from your machine are spoofed. You can't be certain whether other incoming packets are coming from where they claim to be. (Note that some operating systems crash if they receive a packet in which both the source and the destination addresses belong to the host's network interface.)

- *Your LAN addresses*—You will rarely see legal incoming packets on the external, Internet interface claiming to be *from* your LAN. It's possible to see such packets if the LAN has multiple access points to the Internet, but it would probably be a sign of a misconfigured local network. In most cases, such a packet would be part of an attempt to gain access to your site by exploiting your local trust relationships.

- *Class A, B, and C private IP addresses*—These three sets of addresses in the historical Class A, B, and C ranges are reserved for use in private LANs. They aren't intended for use on the Internet. As such, these addresses can be used by any site internally without the need to purchase registered IP addresses. Your machine should never see incoming packets from these source addresses:

    - Class A private addresses are assigned the range from **10.0.0.0** to **10.255.255.255**.

    - Class B private addresses are assigned the range from **172.16.0.0** to **172.31.255.255**.

    - Class C private addresses are assigned the range from **192.168.0.0** to **192.168.255.255**.

- *Class D multicast IP addresses*—IP addresses in the Class D range are set aside for use as destination addresses when participating in a multicast network broadcast, such as an audiocast or a videocast. They range from `224.0.0.0` to `239.255.255.255`. Your machine should never see packets from these source addresses.

- *Class E reserved IP addresses*—IP addresses in the Class E range were set aside for future and experimental use and are not assigned publicly. They range from `240.0.0.0` to `247.255.255.255`. Your machine should never see packets from these source addresses—and mostly likely won't. (Because the entire address range is permanently reserved up through `255.255.255.255`, the Class E range can realistically be defined as `240.0.0.0` to `255.255.255.255`. In fact, some sources define the Class E address range to be exactly that.)

- *Loopback interface addresses*—The loopback interface is a private network interface used by the Linux system for local, network-based services. Rather than sending local traffic through the network interface driver, the operating system takes a shortcut through the loopback interface as a performance improvement. By definition, loopback traffic is targeted for the system generating it. It doesn't go out on the network. The loopback address range is `127.0.0.0` to `127.255.255.255`. You'll usually see it referred to as `127.0.0.1`, localhost, or the loopback interface, `lo`.

- *Malformed broadcast addresses*—Broadcast addresses are special addresses applying to all machines on a network. Address `0.0.0.0` is a special broadcast source address. A legitimate broadcast source address will be either `0.0.0.0` or a regular IP address. DHCP clients and servers will see incoming broadcast packets from source address `0.0.0.0`. This is the only legal use of this source address. It is not a legitimate point-to-point, unicast source address. When seen as the source address in a regular, point-to-point, nonbroadcast packet, the address is forged, or the sender isn't fully configured.

- *Class A network 0 addresses*—As suggested previously, any source address in the `0.0.0.0` through `0.255.255.255` range is illegal as a unicast address.

- *Link local network addresses*—DHCP clients sometimes assign themselves a link local address when they can't get an address from a server. These addresses range from `169.254.0.0` to `169.254.255.255`.

- *TEST-NET addresses*—The address space from `192.0.2.0` to `192.0.2.255` is reserved for test networks.

A number of other address blocks are reserved by IANA and are not in use. In my experience, it's good to filter out these additional blocks. There's a danger in doing so, however: As the IPv4 address space gets tighter and the number of Internet sites grows, IANA has been allocating these blocks more frequently since mid-2000. Unless you monitor the IANA block allocations on a regular basis, sooner or later you will be blocking legitimate addresses.

Unintentionally blocking newly allocated legitimate addresses is inconsequential for a residential site. Business sites must balance their need to maintain access against the cost of constantly monitoring the allocated address blocks. For Internet businesses that have been the subject of ongoing DoS attacks, it could very well be in their best interests to make the effort, simply to reduce the number of possible spoofed source addresses that their site will respond to.

BLOCKING PROBLEM SITES

Another common, but less frequently used, source address–filtering scheme is to block all access from a selected machine or, more typically, from an entire network's IP address block. This is how the Internet community tends to deal with problem sites and ISPs that don't police their users. If a site develops a reputation as a bad Internet neighbor, other sites tend to block it across the board.

On the individual level, blocking all access from selected networks is convenient when individuals in the remote network are habitually making a nuisance of themselves. This has historically been used as a means to fight unsolicited email, with some people going so far as to block an entire country's range of IP addresses.

LIMITING INCOMING PACKETS TO SELECTED REMOTE HOSTS

You might want to accept certain kinds of incoming packets from only specific external sites or individuals. In these cases, the firewall rules will define either specific IP addresses or a limited range of IP source addresses that these packets will be accepted from.

The first class of incoming packets is from remote servers responding to your requests. Although some services, such as web or FTP services, can be expected to be coming from anywhere, other services will legitimately be coming from only your ISP or specially chosen trusted hosts. Examples of servers that are probably offered only through your ISP are POP mail service, domain name service (DNS) name server responses, and possible DHCP or dynamic IP address assignments.

The second class of incoming packets is from remote clients accessing services offered from your site. Again, although some incoming service connections, such as connections to your web server, can be expected to be coming from anywhere, other local services will be offered to only a few trusted remote users or friends. Examples of restricted local services might be ssh and ping.

Local Destination Address Filtering

Filtering incoming packets based on the destination address is not much of an issue. Under normal operation, your network interface card ignores regular packets that aren't addressed to it. The exception is broadcast packets, which are broadcast to all hosts on the network.

Address 255.255.255.255 is the general broadcast destination address. It refers to all hosts on the immediate physical network segment, and it is called a limited broadcast. A broadcast address can be defined more explicitly as the highest address in a given subnet of IP addresses. For example, if your ISP's network address is 192.168.0.0 with a 24-bit subnet mask (255.255.255.0) and your IP address is 192.168.10.30, you would see broadcast packets addressed to 192.168.10.255 from your ISP. On the other hand, if you have a smaller range of IP addresses, say a /30 (255.255.255.252), then you have a total of four addresses, one network, two for hosts, and the broadcast. For example, consider the network 10.3.7.4/30. In this network, 10.3.7.4 is the network address, the two hosts would be 10.3.7.5 and 10.3.7.6, and the broadcast address would be 10.3.7.7. This /30 subnet configuration type is typically used between routers, though the actual addresses themselves may vary. The only way to know what the broadcast address will be for a given subnet is to know both an IP address within the subnet and the subnet mask. These types of broadcasts are called directed subnet broadcasts and are delivered to all hosts on that network.

Broadcast-to-destination address 0.0.0.0 is similar to the situation of point-to-point packets claiming to be from the broadcast source address mentioned earlier, in the section "Source Address Spoofing and Illegal Addresses." Here, broadcast packets are directed to source address 0.0.0.0 rather than to the destination address, 255.255.255.255. In this case, there is little question about the packet's intent. This is an attempt to identify your system as a Linux machine. For historical reasons, networking code derived from BSD UNIX returns an ICMP Type 3 error message in response to 0.0.0.0 being used as the broadcast destination address. Other operating systems silently discard the packet. As such, this is a good example of why dropping versus rejecting a packet makes a difference. In this case, the error message itself is what the probe is looking for.

Remote Source Port Filtering

Incoming requests and connections from remote clients to your local servers will have a source port in the unprivileged range. If you are hosting a web server, all incoming connections to your web server should have a source port between 1024 and 65,535. (That the server port identifies the service is the intention but not the guarantee. You cannot be certain that the server you expect is running at the port you expect.)

Incoming responses and connections from remote servers that you contacted will have the source port that is assigned to the particular service. If you connect to a remote website, all incoming messages from the remote server will have the source port set to **80** (or whatever port the local client specified), the `http` service port number.

Local Destination Port Filtering

The destination port in incoming packets identifies the program or service on your computer that the packet is intended for. As with the source port, all incoming requests from remote clients to your services generally follow the same pattern, and all incoming responses from remote services to your local clients follow a different pattern.

Incoming requests and connections from remote clients to your local servers will set the destination port to the service number that you assigned to the particular service. For example, an incoming packet destined for your local web server would normally have the destination port set to **80**, the `http` service port number.

Incoming responses from remote servers that you contacted will have a destination port in the unprivileged range. If you connect to a remote website, all incoming messages from the remote server will have a destination port between **1024** and **65,535**.

Incoming TCP Connection-State Filtering

Incoming TCP packet acceptance rules can make use of the connection state flags associated with TCP connections. All TCP connections adhere to the same set of connection states. These states differ between client and server because of the three-way handshake during connection establishment. As such, the firewall can distinguish between incoming traffic from remote clients and incoming traffic from remote servers.

Incoming TCP packets from remote clients will have the **SYN** flag set in the first packet received as part of the three-way connection establishment handshake. The first connection request will have the **SYN** flag set, but not the **ACK** flag.

Incoming packets from remote servers will always be responses to the initial connection request initiated from your local client program. Every TCP packet received from a remote server will have the **ACK** flag set. Your local client firewall rules will require all incoming packets from remote servers to have the **ACK** flag set. Servers do not normally attempt to initiate connections to client programs.

Probes and Scans

A probe is an attempt to connect to or get a response from an individual service port. A scan is a series of probes to a set of different service ports. Scans are often automated.

Unfortunately, probes and scans are rarely innocent anymore. They are most likely the initial information-gathering phase, looking for interesting vulnerabilities before launching an attack. In 1998, in particular, we saw an exponential rise in scans worldwide. Automated scan tools are widespread, and coordinated efforts by groups of hackers are common. The security, or lack thereof, of many hosts on the Internet, along with the proliferation of worms, viruses, and zombied machines, makes scans a constant issue on the Internet.

GENERAL PORT SCANS

General port scans are indiscriminate probes across a large block of service ports, possibly the entire range (see Figure 2.6). These scans are becoming less frequent—or, at least, less obvious—as more sophisticated, targeted stealth tools become available.

FIGURE 2.6
A general port scan.

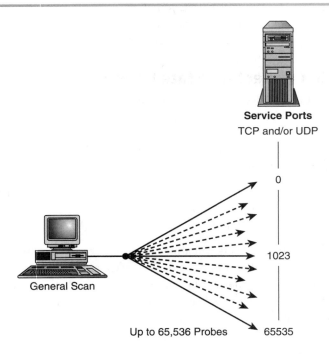

TARGETED PORT SCANS

Targeted port scans look for specific vulnerabilities (see Figure 2.7). The newer, more sophisticated tools attempt to identify the hardware, operating system, and software versions. These tools are designed to identify targets that might be prone to a specific vulnerability.

FIGURE 2.7
A targeted port scan.

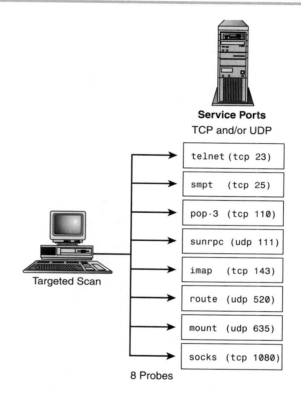

Service Ports
TCP and/or UDP

telnet (tcp 23)

smpt (tcp 25)

pop-3 (tcp 110)

sunrpc (udp 111)

imap (tcp 143)

route (udp 520)

mount (udp 635)

socks (tcp 1080)

Targeted Scan

8 Probes

COMMON SERVICE PORT TARGETS

Common targets often are individually probed as well as scanned. The attacker might be looking for a specific vulnerability, such as an insecure mail server, an unpatched web server, or an open RPC portmap daemon.

A more extensive list of ports can be found at http://www.iana.org/assignments/port-numbers. Only a few common ports are mentioned here, to give you the idea:

- Incoming packets from reserved port 0 are always bogus. This port isn't used legitimately.

- Probes of TCP ports 0 to 5 are a signature of the sscan program.

- telnet (23/tcp), smtp (25/tcp), dns (53/tcp/udp), pop-3 (110/tcp), sunrpc (111/udp/tcp), imap (143/tcp), snmp (161/udp), route (520/udp), and mount (635/udp) are favorite target ports. They represent some of the most potentially vulnerable openings to a system, whether intrinsically, due to common configuration errors, or due to known flaws in the software. Because these services are so common, they are good examples of why you want to either not offer them to the outside world, or very carefully offer them with controlled outside access to these services.

- NetBIOS (137-139/tcp/udp), SMB on Windows 2000/2003 (445/tcp), Netbus (12345/tcp), and older Back Orifice (31337/udp) probes are tediously common. They pose no threat to a Linux system. The target is a Windows system, in this case, but the scans are all too common due not to the popularity of Windows as a server on the Internet (Linux/Apache is the most popular web server), but rather to the relative insecurity of Microsoft Windows.

HISTORICALLY DANGEROUS PORTS

For further information on historically dangerous ports, see the "Packet Filtering for Firewall Systems" paper available at http://www.cert.org.

STEALTH SCANS

Stealth port scans, by definition, aren't meant to be detectable. They are based on how the TCP protocol stack responds to unexpected packets, or packets with illegal state flag combinations. For example, consider an incoming packet that has the ACK flag set but has no related connection. If the ACK were sent to a port with a listening server attached, the TCP stack wouldn't find a related connection and would return a TCP RST message to tell the sender to reset the connection. If the ACK were sent to an unused port, the system would simply return a TCP RST message as an error indication, just as the firewall might return an ICMP error message by default.

The issue is further complicated because some firewalls test only for the SYN flag or the ACK flag. If neither is set, or if the packet contains some other combination of flags, the firewall implementation might pass the packet up to the TCP code. Depending on the TCP state flag combination and the operating system receiving the packet, the system will respond with an RST or with silence. This mechanism can be used to help identify the operating system that the target system is running. In any of these cases, the receiving system isn't likely to log the event.

Inducing a target host to generate an RST packet in this manner also can be used to map a network, determining the IP addresses of systems listening on the network. This is especially helpful if the target system isn't a server and its firewall has been set to silently drop unwanted packets.

AVOIDING PARANOIA: RESPONDING TO PORT SCANS

Firewall logs normally show all kinds of failed connection attempts. Probes are the most common thing you'll see reported in your logs.

Are people probing your system this often? Yes, they are. Is your system compromised? No, it isn't. Well, not necessarily. The ports are blocked. The firewall is doing its job. These are failed connection attempts that the firewall denied.

At what point do you personally decide to report a probe? At what point is it important enough to take the time to report it? At what point do you say that enough is enough and get on with your life, or should you be writing `abuse@some.system` each time? There are no "right" answers. How you respond is a personal judgment call and depends in part on the resources available to you, how sensitive the information at your site is, and how critical the Internet connection is to your site. For obvious probes and scans, there is no clear-cut answer. It depends on your own personality and comfort level how you personally define a serious probe, and your social conscience.

With that in mind, these are some workable guidelines.

The most common attempts are a combination of automated probing, mistakes, legitimate attempts based on the history of the Internet, ignorance, curiosity, and misbehaving software.

You can almost always safely ignore individual, isolated, single connection attempts to `telnet`, `ssh`, `ftp`, `finger`, or any other port for a common service that you're not providing. Probes and scans are a fact of life on the Internet, all too frequent, and they usually don't pose a risk. They are kind of like door-to-door salespeople, commercial phone calls, wrong phone numbers, and junk postal mail. There isn't enough time in the day to respond to each one.

On the other hand, some probers are more persistent. You might decide to add firewall rules to block them completely, or possibly even their entire IP address space.

Scans of a subset of the ports known to be potential security holes are typically the precursor to an attack if an open port is found. More inclusive scans are usually part of a broader scan for openings throughout a domain or subnet. Current hacking tools probe a subset of these ports one after the other.

Occasionally, you'll see serious hacking attempts. This is unquestionably a time to take action. Write them. Report them. Double-check your security. Observe what they're doing. Block them. Block their IP address block.

Some system administrators take every occurrence seriously because, even if *their* machine is secure, other people's machines might not be. The next guy might not even have the capability of knowing that he is being probed. Reporting probes is the socially responsible thing to do, for everyone's sake.

How should you respond to port scans? If you write these people, their postmaster, their uplink service provider NOC, or the network address block coordinator, try to be polite. Give them the benefit of the doubt. Overreactions are misplaced more often than not. What might appear as a serious hacking attempt to you is often a curious kid playing with a new program. A polite word to the abuser, `root`, or postmaster will usually take care of the problem. More people need to be educated about Netiquette than need their network accounts rescinded. And they might be innocent of anything. Just as often, the person's system is compromised and that person has no idea what's going on. He'll be grateful for the information.

Probes aren't the only hostile traffic you'll see, however. Although probes are harmless in and of themselves, DoS attacks are not.

Denial-of-Service Attacks

DoS attacks are based on the idea of flooding your system with packets to disrupt or seriously degrade your Internet connection, tying up local servers to the extent that legitimate requests can't be honored, or, in the worst case, crashing your system altogether. The two most common results are keeping the system too busy to do anything useful and tying up critical system resources.

You can't protect against DoS attacks completely. They can take as many different forms as the attacker's imagination allows. Anything that results in a response from your system, anything that results in your system allocating resources (including logging of the attack), anything that induces a remote site to stop communicating with you—all can be used in a DoS attack.

DENIAL-OF-SERVICE ATTACKS

For further information on DoS attacks, see the "Denial of Service" paper available at http://www.cert.org.

These attacks usually involve one of several classic patterns, including TCP **SYN** flooding, `ping` flooding, UDP flooding, fragmentation bombs, buffer overflows, and ICMP routing redirect bombs.

TCP **SYN** **FLOODING**

A TCP **SYN** flood attack consumes your system resources until no more incoming TCP connections are possible (see Figure 2.8). The attack makes use of the basic TCP three-way handshaking protocol during connection establishment, in conjunction with IP source address spoofing.

FIGURE 2.8
A TCP SYN flood.

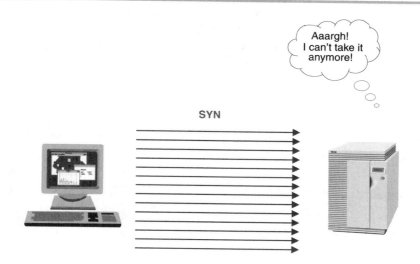

The attacker spoofs his source address as a private address and initiates a connection to one of your TCP-based services. Appearing to be a client attempting to open a TCP connection, the attacker sends you an artificially generated **SYN** message. Your machine responds by sending an acknowledgment, a **SYN ACK**. However, in this case, the address that you're replying to isn't the attacker's address. In fact, because the address is private, there is no one out there to respond. The spoofed host won't return an **RST** message to tear down the half-opened connection.

The final stage of TCP connection establishment, receiving an **ACK** in response, will never happen. Consequently, finite network connection resources are consumed. The connection remains in a half-opened state until the connection attempt times out. The attacker floods your port with connection request after connection request, faster than the TCP timeouts release the resources. If this continues, all resources will be in use and no more incoming connection requests can be accepted. This applies not only to the service being probed, but to all new connections as well.

Several aids are available to Linux users. The first is source address filtering, described previously. This filters out the most commonly used spoofed source addresses, but there is no guarantee that the spoofed address falls within the categories you can anticipate and filter against.

The second is to enable your kernel's **SYN** cookie module, a specific retardant to the resource starvation caused by **SYN** flooding. When the connection queue begins to get full, the system starts responding to **SYN** requests with **SYN** cookies rather than **SYN-ACKs**, and it frees the queue slot. Thus, the queue never fills completely. The cookie has a short timeout; the client must respond to it within a short period before the serving host will respond with the expected SYN-ACK. The cookie is a sequence number that is generated based on the original sequence number in the SYN, the source and destination addresses and ports, and a secret value. If the response to the cookie matches the result of the hashing algorithm, the server is reasonably well-assured that the SYN is valid.

Depending on the particular release, you may or may not need to enable the SYN cookie protection within the kernel by using the command echo 1 > /proc/sys/net/ipv4/ tcp_syncookies. Some distributions and kernel versions require you to explicitly configure the option into the kernel using make config, make menuconfig, or make xconfig, and then recompile and install the new kernel.

SYN **FLOODING AND IP SPOOFING**

For more information on SYN flooding and IP spoofing, see CERT_Advisory_CA-96.21, "TCP SYN Flooding and IP Spoofing Attacks," at http://www.cert.org.

ping **FLOODING**

Any message that elicits a response from your machine can be used to degrade your network connection by forcing the system to spend most of its time responding. The ICMP echo request message sent by ping is a common culprit. An attack called *smurf*, and its variants, forces a system to expend its resources processing echo replies. One method of accomplishing this is to spoof the victim's source address, and broadcast an echo request to an entire network of hosts. A single spoofed request message can result in hundreds or thousands of resulting replies being sent to the victim. Another way of accomplishing a similar result is to install trojans on compromised hosts across the Internet, and time them to each send echo requests to the same host simultaneously. Finally, a simple ping flood in which the attacker sends more echo requests and floods the data connection is another method for a DoS, though it's becoming less common. A typical ping flood is shown in Figure 2.9.

PING OF DEATH

An older exploit called the *Ping of Death* involved sending very large ping packets. Vulnerable systems could crash as a result. Linux is not vulnerable to this exploit, nor are many other current UNIX operating systems. If your firewall is protecting older systems or personal computers, those systems could be vulnerable.

FIGURE 2.9
A `ping` flood.

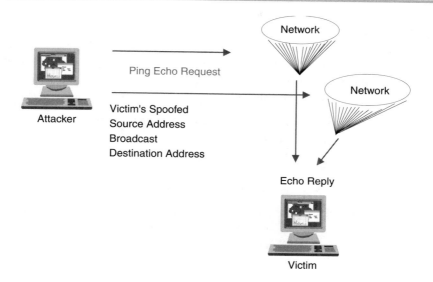

The Ping of Death exploit gives an idea of how the simplest protocols and message interactions can be used by the creative hacker. Not all attacks are attempts to break into your computer. Some are merely destructive. In this case, the goal is to crash the machine. (System crashes also might be an indicator that you need to check your system for installed trojan programs. You might have been duped into loading a trojan program, but the program itself might require a system reboot to activate.)

`ping` is a very useful basic networking tool. You might not want to disable `ping` altogether. In today's Internet environment, conservative folks recommend disabling incoming `ping` or at least severely limiting from whom you accept echo requests. Because of `ping`'s history of involvement in DoS attacks, many sites no longer respond to external `ping` requests from any but selected sources. This has always seemed to be an overreaction to the relatively small threat of a DoS based on ICMP when compared to the more ubiquitous and dangerous threats against applications and other protocols within the stack.

Dropping `ping` requests isn't a solution for the victim host, however. Regardless of how the recipient of the flood still reacts to the packets, the system (or network) can still be overwhelmed in the process of inspecting and dropping a flood of requests.

UDP FLOODING

The UDP protocol is especially useful as a DoS tool. Unlike TCP, UDP is stateless. Flow-control mechanisms aren't included. There are no connection state flags. Datagram sequence numbers aren't used. No information is maintained on which packet is expected next. There is not always a way to differentiate client traffic from server traffic based on port numbers. Without state, there is no way to distinguish an expected incoming response from an unsolicited packet arriving unexpectedly. It's relatively easy to keep a system so busy responding to incoming UDP probes that no bandwidth is left for legitimate network traffic.

Because UDP services are susceptible to these types of attacks (as opposed to connection-oriented TCP services), many sites disable all UDP ports that aren't absolutely necessary. As mentioned earlier, almost all common Internet services are TCP-based. The firewall we'll build in Chapter 4, "Building and Installing a Standalone Firewall," carefully limits UDP traffic to only those remote hosts providing necessary UDP services.

The classic UDP flood attack either involves two victim machines or works in the same way the smurf ping flood does (see Figure 2.10). A single spoofed packet from the attacker's UDP echo port, directed to a host's UDP chargen port, can result in an infinite loop of network traffic. The echo and chargen services are network test services. chargen generates an ASCII string. echo returns the data sent to the port.

FIGURE 2.10
A UDP flood.

Source Address: Intermediary
Destination Address: Victim
Source Port: UDP 7- chargen

Source Address: Victim
Destination Address: Intermediary
Source Port: UDP 7 - echo
Destination Port: UDP 19 - chargen

Source Address: Victim
Destination Address: Intermediary
Source Port: UDP 7 - echo
Destination Port: UDP 19 - chargen

FRAGMENTATION BOMBS

Different underlying network technologies (such as Ethernet, ATM, and token ring) define different limits on the size of the Layer 2 frame. As a packet is passed on from one router to the next along the path from the source machine to the destination machine, network gateway routers might need to cut the packet into smaller pieces, called fragments, before passing them on to the next network. In a legitimate fragmentation, the first fragment contains the usual source and destination port numbers contained in the UDP or TCP transport header. The following fragments do not.

For example, although the maximum theoretical packet length is 65,535 bytes, the maximum Ethernet frame size (Maximum Transmission Unit, or MTU) is 1,500 bytes.

When a packet is fragmented, intermediate routers do not reassemble the packet. The packets are reassembled either at the destination host or by its adjacent router.

Because intermediate fragmentation is ultimately more costly than sending smaller, nonfragmented packets, current systems often do MTU discovery with the target host at the beginning of a connection. This is done by sending a packet with the `Don't Fragment` option set in the IP header options field (the only generally legitimate current use of the IP options field). If an intermediate router must fragment the packet, it drops the packet and returns an ICMP 3 error, `fragmentation-required`.

One type of fragmentation attack involves artificially constructing very small packets. One-byte packets crash some operating systems. Current operating systems usually test for this condition.

Another use of small fragments is constructing the initial fragment so that the UDP or TCP source and destination ports are contained in the second fragment. (All networks' MTU sizes are large enough to carry a standard 40-byte IP and transport header.) Packet-filtering firewalls often allow these fragments through because the information that they filter on is not present. This form of attack is useful to get packets through the firewall that would not otherwise be allowed.

The Ping of Death exploit mentioned earlier is an example of using fragmentation to carry an illegally large ICMP message. When the `ping` request is reconstructed, the entire packet size is larger than 65,535 bytes, causing some systems to crash.

A classic example of a fragmentation exploit is the Teardrop attack. The method can be used to bypass a firewall or to crash a system. The first fragment is constructed to go to an allowed service. (Many firewalls don't inspect fragments after the first packet.) If it is allowed, the subsequent fragments will be passed through and reassembled by the target host. If the first packet is dropped, the subsequent packets will pass through the firewall, but the end host will have nothing to reconstruct and eventually will discard the partial packet.

The data offset fields in the subsequent fragments can be altered to overwrite the port information in the first fragment to access a disallowed service. The offset also can be altered so that offsets used in packet reassembly turn out to be negative numbers. Because kernel byte-copy routines usually use unsigned numbers, the negative value is treated as a very large positive number; the resulting copy trashes kernel memory and the system crashes.

Firewall machines and machines that do NAT for other local hosts should be configured to reassemble the packets before delivering them to the local target. Some of the iptables features require the system to reassemble packets before forwarding the packet to the destination host, and reassembly is done automatically.

BUFFER OVERFLOWS

Buffer overflow exploits can't be protected against by a filtering firewall. The exploits fall into two main categories. The first is simply to cause a system or server to crash by overwriting its data space or runtime stack. The second requires technical expertise and knowledge of the hardware and system software or server version being attacked. The purpose of the overflow is to overwrite the program's runtime stack so that the call return stack contains a program and a jump to it. This program usually starts up a shell with **root** privilege.

CGI scripts, used in many web applications, have historically been especially vulnerable unless you take precautions. Many of the current vulnerabilities in servers are a result of buffer overflows. It's important to install and keep up-to-date all the newest patches and software revisions.

CGI DENIAL-OF-SERVICE EXPLOITS

For a description of a DoS exploit using CGI scripts, see "How to Remove Meta-characters from User-Supplied Data in CGI Scripts," at http://www.cert.org, and "The World Wide Web Security FAQ," at http://www.w3.org.

ICMP REDIRECT BOMBS

ICMP redirect message Type 5 tells the target system to change its in-memory routing tables in favor of a shorter route. Redirects are sent by routers to their adjacent hosts. Their intention is to inform the host that a shorter path is available (that is, the host and new router are on the same network, and the new router is the router that the original would route the packet to as its next hop).

If you have a router running **routed** or **gated**, any redirect message is supposed to be ignored. Hosts are required to honor redirects and add the gateway to their route cache. An exception is indicated in RFC 1122, "Requirements for Internet Hosts—Communication Layers," Section 3.2.2.2: "A Redirect message SHOULD be silently discarded if the new gateway address it specifies is not on the same connected (sub-) net through which the Redirect arrived, or if the source of the Redirect is not the current first-hop gateway for the specified destination."

Redirects arrive on an almost-daily basis. They rarely originate from the adjacent router. For residential or business sites connected to an ISP, it's very unlikely that your adjacent router will generate a redirect message.

If your host uses static routing and honors redirect messages, it's possible for someone to fool your system into thinking that a remote machine is one of your local machines or one of your ISP's machines, or even to fool your system into forwarding all traffic to some other remote host.

DENIAL-OF-SERVICE ATTACKS AND OTHER SYSTEM RESOURCES

Network connectivity isn't the only concern in DoS attacks. Here are some examples of other areas to keep in mind while configuring your system:

- Your filesystem can overflow if your system is forced to write enormous numbers of messages to the error logs, or if your system is flooded with many copies of large email messages. You might want to configure resource limits and set up a separate partition for rapidly growing or changing filesystems.

EMAIL DENIAL-OF-SERVICE EXPLOITS

For a description of a DoS exploit using email, see "Email Bombing and Spamming," at http://www.cert.org.

- System memory, process table slots, CPU cycles, and other resources can be exhausted by repeated, rapid invocations of network services. You can do little about this other than set any configurable limits for each individual service, enabling **SYN** cookies, and denying rather than rejecting packets sent to unsupported service ports.

Source-Routed Packets

Source-routed packets employ a rarely used IP option that allows the originator to define the route taken between two machines, rather than letting the intermediate routers determine the path. As with ICMP redirects, this feature can allow someone to fool your system into thinking that it's talking to a local machine, an ISP machine, or some other trusted host, or to create the necessary packet flow for a man-in-the-middle attack.

Source routing has few legitimate uses in current networks. Some routers ignore the option. Some firewalls discard packets containing the option.

Filtering Outgoing Packets

If your environment represents a trusted environment, filtering outgoing packets might not appear to be as critical as filtering incoming packets. Your system won't respond to incoming messages that the firewall doesn't pass through. Residential sites often take this approach. Nevertheless, even for residential sites, symmetric filtering is important, particularly if the firewall protects Microsoft Windows machines. For commercial sites, outgoing filtering is inarguably important.

If your firewall protects a LAN of Microsoft Windows systems, controlling outgoing traffic becomes much more important. Recently, tens of thousands of compromised Windows machines have been used in coordinated DoS attacks. For this reason especially, it's important to filter what leaves your network.

Filtering outgoing messages also allows you to run LAN services without leaking into the Internet, where these packets don't belong. It's not only a question of disallowing external access to local LAN services. It's also a question of not broadcasting local system information into the Net. Examples of this would be if you were running a local `dhcpd`, `timed`, `routed`, or `rwhod` server for internal use. Other obnoxious services might be broadcasting `wall` or `syslogd` messages.

A related source is some of the personal computer software, which sometimes ignores the Internet service port protocols and reserved assignments. This is the personal computer equivalent of running a program designed for LAN use on an Internet-connected machine.

A final reason is simply to keep local traffic local that isn't intended to leave the LAN but that conceivably could. Keeping local traffic local is a good idea from a security standpoint but also as a means for bandwidth conservation.

Local Source Address Filtering

Filtering outgoing packets based on the source address is easy. For a small site or a single computer connected to the Internet, the source address is always your computer's IP address during normal operation. There is no reason to allow an outgoing packet to have any other source address, and the firewall should enforce this.

For people whose IP address is dynamically assigned by their ISP, a brief exception exists during address assignment. This exception is specific to DHCP and is the one case in which a host broadcasts messages using `0.0.0.0` as its source address.

For people with a LAN whose firewall machine has a dynamically assigned IP address, limiting outgoing packets to contain the source address of the firewall machine's IP address is mandatory. It protects you from several fairly common configuration mistakes that appear as cases of source address spoofing or illegal source addresses to remote hosts.

If your users or their software aren't 100% trustworthy, it's important to ensure that local traffic contains legitimate, local addresses only, to avoid participating in DoS attacks using source address spoofing.

This last point is especially important. RFC 2827, "Network Ingress Filtering: Defeating Denial of Service Attacks Which Employ IP Source Address Spoofing" (and updated by RFC 3704), is a current "best practices" document speaking to exactly this point. Ideally, every router should filter out the obvious illegal source addresses and ensure that traffic leaving the local network contains only routable source addresses belonging to that network.

Remote Destination Address Filtering

As with incoming packets, you might want to allow certain kinds of outgoing packets to be addressed only to specific remote networks or individual machines. In these cases, the firewall rules will define either specific IP addresses or a limited range of IP destination addresses to which these packets will be allowed.

The first class of outgoing packets to filter by destination address is packets destined to remote servers that you've contacted. Although some packets, such as those going to web or FTP servers, can be expected to be destined to anywhere on the Internet, other remote services will legitimately be offered from only your ISP or specially chosen trusted hosts. Examples of services that are probably offered only through your ISP are mail services such as SMTP or POP3, DNS services, DHCP dynamic IP address assignment, and the Usenet news service.

The second class of outgoing packets to filter by destination address is packets destined to remote clients who are accessing a service offered from your site. Again, although some outgoing service connections, such as responses from your local web server, can be expected to be going anywhere, other local services will be offered to only a few trusted remote sites or friends. Examples of restricted local services might be `telnet`, `ssh`, Samba-based services, and RPC services accessed via portmap. Not only will the firewall rules deny general incoming connections to these services, but the rules also won't allow outgoing responses from these services to just anyone.

Local Source Port Filtering

Explicitly defining which service ports on your network can be used for outgoing connections serves two purposes—one for your client programs and one for your server programs. Specifying the source ports allowed for your outgoing connections helps ensure that your programs are behaving correctly, and it protects other people from any local network traffic that doesn't belong on the Internet.

Outgoing connections from your local clients will almost always originate from an unprivileged source port. Limiting your clients to the unprivileged ports in the firewall rules helps protect other people from potential mistakes on your end by ensuring that your client programs are behaving as expected.

Outgoing packets from your local server programs will always originate from their assigned service port and will be in response to a request received. Limiting your servers to their assigned ports at the firewall level ensures that your server programs are functioning correctly at the protocol level. More important, it helps protect any private, local network services that you might be running from outside access. It also helps protect remote sites from being bothered by network traffic that should remain confined to your local systems.

Remote Destination Port Filtering

Your local client programs are designed to connect to network servers offering their services from their assigned service ports. From this perspective, limiting your local clients to connect only to their associated server's service port ensures protocol correctness. Limiting your client connections to specific destination ports serves a couple of other purposes as well. First, it helps guard against local, private network client programs inadvertently attempting to access servers on the Internet. Second, it does much to disallow outgoing mistakes, port scans, and other mischief potentially originating from your site.

Your local server programs will almost always participate in connections originating from unprivileged ports. The firewall rules limit your servers' outgoing traffic to only unprivileged destination ports.

Outgoing TCP Connection-State Filtering

Outgoing TCP packet-acceptance rules can make use of the connection-state flags associated with TCP connections, just as the incoming rules do. All TCP connections adhere to the same set of connection states, which differs between client and server.

Outgoing TCP packets from local clients will have the SYN flag set in the first packet sent as part of the three-way connection-establishment handshake. The initial connection request will have the SYN flag set, but not the ACK flag. Your local client firewall rules will allow outgoing packets with either the SYN or the ACK flags set.

Outgoing packets from local servers will always be responses to an initial connection request initiated from a remote client program. Every packet sent from your servers will have the ACK flag set. Your local server firewall rules will require all outgoing packets from your servers to have the ACK flag set.

Private Versus Public Network Services

One of the easiest ways to inadvertently allow uninvited intrusions is to allow outside access to local services that are designed only for LAN use. Some services, if offered locally, should never cross the boundary between your LAN and the Internet beyond. Some of these services annoy your neighbors, some provide information you'd be better off keeping to yourself, and some represent glaring security holes if they're available outside your LAN.

Some of the earliest network services, the r-* based commands in particular, were designed for local sharing and ease-of-access across multiple lab machines in a trusted environment. Some of the later services were intended for Internet access, but they were designed at a time when the Internet was basically an extended community of academicians and researchers. The Internet was a relatively open, safe place. As the Internet grew into a global network including general public access, it developed into a completely untrusted environment.

Lots of Linux network services are designed to provide local information about user accounts on the system, which programs are running and which resources are in use, system status, network status, and similar information from other machines connected over the network. Not all these informational services represent security holes in and of themselves. It's not that someone can use them directly to gain unauthorized access to your system. It's that they provide information about your system and user accounts that can be useful to someone who is looking for known vulnerabilities. They might also supply information such as usernames, addresses, phone numbers, and so forth, which you don't want to be readily available to everyone who asks.

Some of the more dangerous network services are designed to provide LAN access to shared filesystems and devices, such as a networked printer or fax machine.

Some services are difficult to configure correctly and some are difficult to configure securely. Entire books are devoted to configuring some of the more complicated Linux services. Specific service configuration is beyond the scope of this book.

Some services just don't make sense in a home or small-office setting. Some are intended to manage large networks, provide Internet routing service, provide large database informational services, support two-way encryption and authentication, and so forth.

Protecting Nonsecure Local Services

The easiest way to protect yourself is to not offer the service. But what if you need one of these services locally? Not all services can be protected adequately at the packet-filtering level. Multimedia services, such as RealAudio and instant messaging services, and UDP-based RPC services are notoriously difficult to secure at the packet-filtering level.

One way to safeguard your computer is to not host network services on the firewall machine that you don't intend for public use. If the service isn't available, there's nothing for a remote client to connect to. Let firewalls be firewalls.

A packet-filtering firewall doesn't offer complete security. Some programs require higher-level security measures than can be provided at the packet-filtering level. Some programs are too problematic to risk running on a firewall machine, even on a less secure residential host.

Small sites such as those in the home often won't have a supply of computers available to enforce access security policies by running private services on other machines. Compromises must be made, particularly for required services that are provided solely by Linux. Nevertheless, small sites with a LAN should not be running file sharing or other private LAN services on the firewall, such as Samba. The machine should not have unnecessary user accounts. Unneeded system software should be removed from the system. The machine should have no function other than that of a security gateway.

Selecting Services to Run

When all is said and done, only you can decide which services you need or want. The first step in securing your system is to decide which services and daemons you intend to run on the firewall machine, as well as behind the firewall in the private LAN. Each service has its own security considerations. When it comes to selecting services to run under Linux or any operating system, the general rule of thumb is to run only network services that you need and understand. It's important to understand a network service, what it does and who it's intended for, before you run it—especially on a machine connected directly to the Internet.

Summary

Between this and the preceding chapter, the basics of networking and firewalls have been laid out. The next chapter digs deeper into iptables itself before building an iptables firewall in Chapter 4.

iptables: The Linux Firewall Administration Program

Chapter 2, "Packet-Filtering Concepts," covers the background ideas and concepts behind a packet-filtering firewall. Each built-in rule chain has its own default policy. Each rule can apply not only to an individual chain, but also to a specific network interface, message protocol type (such as TCP, UDP, or ICMP), and service port or ICMP message type number. Individual acceptance, denial, and rejection rules are defined for the **INPUT** chain and the **OUTPUT** chain, as well as for the **FORWARD** chain, which you'll learn about at the end of this chapter and in Chapter 6, "Packet Forwarding." The next chapter pulls those ideas together to demonstrate how to build a simple, single-system, custom-designed firewall for your site.

This chapter covers the iptables firewall administration program used to build a Netfilter firewall. For those of you who are familiar with or accustomed to the older ipfwadm and ipchains programs used with the IPFW technology, iptables will look very similar to those programs. However, it is much more feature-rich and flexible, and it is very different on subtle levels.

There is indeed a difference between iptables and Netfilter, though you'll often hear the terms used interchangeably. Netfilter is the Linux kernel-space program code to implement a firewall within the Linux kernel, either compiled directly into the kernel or included as a set of modules. On the other hand, iptables is the userland program used for administration of the Netfilter firewall. Throughout this text, I will refer to iptables as being inclusive of both Netfilter and iptables, unless otherwise noted.

Differences Between IPFW and Netfilter Firewall Mechanisms

Because iptables is so different from the previous ipchains, this book won't attempt to cover the older implementation.

The next section is written for the reader who is familiar with or is currently using ipchains. If iptables is your first introduction to Linux firewalling, you can skip ahead to the section "Netfilter Packet Traversal."

If you are converting from ipchains, you'll notice several minor differences in the iptables syntax, most notably that the input and output network interfaces are identified separately. iptables is highly modularized, and the individual modules must occasionally be loaded explicitly. Logging is a rule target rather than a command option. Connection state tracking can be maintained. Address and Port Translation are now logically separate functions from packet filtering. Full Source and Destination Address Translation are implemented. Masquerading is now a term used to refer to a specialized form of source address NAT. Port forwarding and Destination Address Translation are supported directly without the need for third-party software support such as ipmasqadm.

> **MASQUERADING IN EARLIER VERSIONS OF LINUX**
>
> For those of you who are new to Linux, Network Address Translation (NAT) is fully implemented in iptables. Before this, NAT was called masquerading in Linux. A simple, partial implementation of Source Address Translation, masquerading was used by site owners who had a single public IP address and who wanted other hosts on their private network to be capable of accessing the Internet. Outgoing packets from these internal hosts had their source address masqueraded to that of the public, routable IP address.

The most important difference is in how packets are routed or forwarded through the operating system, making for subtle differences in how the firewall rule set is constructed.

For ipchains users, understanding the differences in packet traversal that are discussed in the next two sections is very important. iptables and ipchains look very much alike on the surface, but they are very different in practice. It's very easy to write syntactically correct iptables rules that have a different effect from what a similar rule would have done in ipchains. It can be confusing. If you already know ipchains, you must keep the differences in mind.

IPFW Packet Traversal

Under IPFW (ipfwadm and ipchains), three built-in filter chains were used. All packets arriving on an interface were filtered against the input chain. If the packet was accepted, it was passed to the routing module. The routing function determined whether the packet was to be delivered locally or forwarded to another outgoing interface. IPFW packet flow is pictured in Figure 3.1.

FIGURE 3.1
IPFW packet traversal. (Figure based on "Linux IPCHAINS-HOWTO," by Rusty Russel, v1.0.8.)

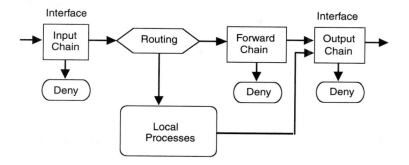

If forwarded, the packet was filtered a second time against the forward chain. If the packet was accepted, it was passed to the output chain.

Both locally generated outgoing packets and forwarded packets were passed to the output chain. If the packet was accepted, it was sent out the interface.

Received and sent local (loopback) packets passed through two filters. Forwarded packets passed through three filters.

The loopback path involved two chains. As shown in Figure 3.2, each loopback packet passed through the output filter before going "out" the loopback interface, where it was then delivered to the loopback's input interface. Then the input filter was applied.

Note that the loopback path demonstrates why people's X Window session hangs when starting a firewall script that either doesn't allow loopback traffic or fails before doing so when a deny by default policy is used.

In the case of response packets being demasqueraded before forwarding them on to the LAN, the input filters were applied. Rather than passing through the routing function, the packet was handed directly to the output filter chain. Thus, demasqueraded incoming packets were filtered twice. Outgoing masqueraded packets were filtered three times.

FIGURE 3.2
IPFW loopback and masqueraded packet traversal. (Figure based on "Linux IPCHAINS-HOWTO," by Rusty Russel, v1.0.8.)

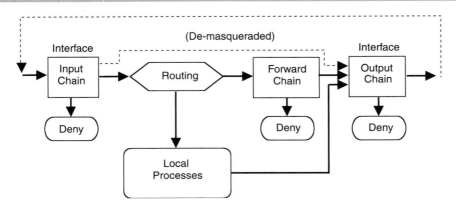

Netfilter Packet Traversal

Under Netfilter (iptables), built-in INPUT, OUTPUT, and FORWARD filter chains are used. Incoming packets pass through the routing function, which determines whether to deliver the packet to the local host's input chain or on to the forward chain. Netfilter packet flow is pictured in Figure 3.3.

FIGURE 3.3
Netfilter packet traversal. (Figure based on "Linux 2.4 Packet Filtering HOWTO," by Rusty Russel, v1.0.1.)

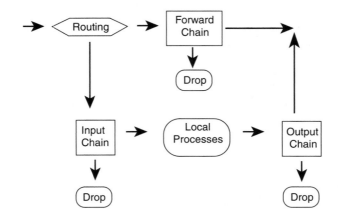

If a locally destined packet is accepted by the INPUT chain's rules, the packet is delivered locally. If a remotely destined packet is accepted by the FORWARD chain's rules, the packet is sent out the appropriate interface.

Outgoing packets from local processes are passed to the OUTPUT chain's rules. If the packet is accepted, it is sent out the appropriate interface. Thus, each packet is filtered once (except for loopback packets, which are filtered twice).

Basic iptables Syntax

Firewalls built with Netfilter are built through the iptables firewall administration command. The iptables command implements the firewall policies that you create and manages the behavior of the firewall. Netfilter firewalls have three individual tables: filter, NAT, and mangle. Within these tables, firewalls are built through chains, with each individual link in the chain being an individual iptables command.

Within the default filter table there is a chain for input or data coming into the firewall, a chain for output or data leaving the firewall, a chain for forwarding or data being sent through the firewall, and other chains including chains named and configured by the user, commonly (and appropriately) called user-defined chains. The NAT and mangle tables have specialty chains that will be discussed later. For now, it's sufficient to know that the filter table is the default table for implementing a basic firewall, the NAT table is used to provide NAT and related functions, and the mangle table is used when the packet will be altered by the firewall.

iptables commands are issued with very specific syntax. Many times, the ordering of the options given to iptables makes the difference between a successful command and a syntax error. The commands issued to iptables fall through, so a command that allows certain packets that follows a command that denies those same packets will cause the data to be dropped by the firewall.

The basic syntax for an iptables command begins with the iptables command itself, followed by one or more options, a chain, a set of match criteria, and a target or disposition. The layout of the command largely depends on the action to be performed. Consider this syntax:

```
iptables <option> <chain> <matching criteria> <target>
```

In building a firewall, the option is usually -A to append a rule onto the end of the ruleset. Naturally, there are several options depending on the target and the operation being performed. This chapter covers most of those options.

As previously stated, the chain can be an input chain, an output chain, a forwarding chain, or a user-defined chain. In addition, the chain might also be a specialty chain contained in the NAT or mangle tables.

The matching criteria in an iptables command sets the conditions for the rule to be applied. For example, the matching criteria would be used to tell iptables that all TCP traffic destined for port 80 is allowed into the firewall.

Finally, the target sets the action to perform on a matching packet. The target can be something as simple as DROP to silently discard the packet, or it can send the matching packet to a user-defined chain, or it can perform any other configured action in iptables.

The following sections of this chapter show hands-on examples using iptables to implement real-world rules for various tasks. Some of the examples include syntax and options that haven't yet been introduced. If you get lost, refer to this section or the iptables man page for more information on the syntax being used.

iptables Features

iptables uses the concept of separate rule tables for different kinds of packet processing functionality. These rule tables are implemented as functionally separate table modules. The three primary modules are the rule filter table, the NAT nat table, and the specialized packet-handling mangle table. Each of these three table modules has its own associated module extensions that are dynamically loaded when first referenced, unless you've built them directly into the kernel.

The filter table is the default table. The other tables are specified by a command-line option. The basic filter table features include these:

- Chain-related operations on the three built-in chains (INPUT, OUTPUT, and FORWARD) and on user-defined chains

- Help

- Target disposition (ACCEPT or DROP)

- IP header field match operations for protocol, source and destination address, input and output interfaces, and fragment handling

- Match operations on the TCP, UDP, and ICMP header fields

The filter table has two kinds of feature extensions: *target* extensions and *match* extensions. The target extensions include the REJECT packet disposition, the BALANCE and CLUSTERIP targets, the CLASSIFY target, CONNMARK, TRACE, and the LOG and ULOG functionalities. The match extensions support matching on the following:

- The current connection state

- Port lists (supported by the multiport module)

- The hardware Ethernet MAC source address or physical device
- The type of address, link-layer packet type, or range of IP addresses
- Various parts of IPSec packets or the IPSec policy
- The ICMP type
- The length of the packet
- The time the packet arrived
- Every *n*th packet or random packets
- The packet sender's user, group, process, or process group ID
- The IP header Type of Service (TOS) field (possibly set by the `mangle` table)
- The TTL section of the IP header
- The iptables mark field (set by the `mangle` table)
- Rate-limited packet matching

The `mangle` table has two target extensions. The **MARK** module supports assigning a value to the packet's `mark` field that iptables maintains. The **TOS** module supports setting the value of the **TOS** field in the IP header.

UPCOMING FEATURES IN IPTABLES

iptables is being actively developed and enhanced. Based on the source code and build environment, it is clear that additional modules will be available by the time this book is published. Some other modules are not intended for release in the public distributions.

For example, there is an experimental MIRROR target. This target retransmits a packet after reversing the source and destination sections of the IP header.

The **nat** table has target extension modules for Source and Destination Address Translation and for Port Translation. These modules support these forms of NAT:

- SNAT—Source NAT.
- DNAT—Destination NAT.
- MASQUERADE—A specialized form of source NAT for connections that are assigned a temporary, changeable, dynamically assigned IP address (such as a phone dial-up connection).
- REDIRECT—A specialized form of destination NAT that redirects the packet to the local host, regardless of the address in the IP header's destination field.

All TCP state flags can be inspected, and filtering decisions can be made based on the results. iptables can check for stealth scans, for example.

TCP can optionally specify the maximum segment size that the sender is willing to accept in return. Filtering on this one, single TCP option is a very specialized case. The TTL section of the IP header can also be matched and is a specialized case as well.

TCP connection state and ongoing UDP exchange information can be maintained, allowing packet recognition on an ongoing basis rather than on a stateless, packet-by-packet basis. Accepting packets recognized as being part of an established connection allows bypassing the overhead of checking the rule list for each packet. When the initial connection is accepted, subsequent packets can be recognized and allowed.

Generally, the TOS field is of historical interest only. The TOS field is either ignored or used with the newer Differentiated Services definitions by intermediate routers. IP TOS filtering has uses for local packet prioritizing—routing and forwarding among local hosts and the local router.

Incoming packets can be filtered by the MAC source address. This has limited, specialized uses for local authentication because MAC addresses are passed only between adjacent hosts and routers.

Individual filter log messages can be prefixed with user-defined strings. Messages can be assigned kernel logging levels as defined for `/etc/syslog.conf`. This allows logging to be turned on and off, and for the log output files to be defined, in `/etc/syslog.conf`. In addition, there is a `ULOG` option that sends logging to a userspace daemon, `ulogd`, to enable further detail to be logged about the packet.

Packet matches can be limited to an initial burst rate, after which a limit is imposed by the number of allowed matches per second. If match limiting is enabled, the default is that, after an initial burst of five matched packets, a rate limit of three matches per hour is imposed. In other words, if the system were flooded with `ping` packets, for example, the first five `ping`s would match. After that, a single `ping` packet could be matched 20 minutes later, and another one could be matched 20 minutes after that, regardless of how many `echo-request`s were received. The disposition of the packets, whether logged or not, would depend on any subsequent rules regarding the packets.

The `REJECT` target can optionally specify which ICMP (or `RST` for TCP) error message to return. The IPv4 standard requires TCP to accept either `RST` or `ICMP` as an error indication, although `RST` is the default TCP behavior. `iptable`'s default is to return nothing (`DROP`) or else to return an ICMP error (`REJECT`).

Along with REJECT, another special-purpose target is QUEUE. Its purpose is to hand off the packet via the netlink device to a user-space program for handling. If there is no waiting program, the packet is dropped.

RETURN is another special-purpose target. Its purpose is to return from a user-defined chain before rule matching on that chain has completed.

Locally generated outgoing packets can be filtered based on the user, group, process, or process group ID of the program generating the packet. Thus, access to remote services can be authorized at the packet-filtering level on a per-user basis. This is a specialized option for multiuser, multipurpose hosts because firewall routers shouldn't have normal user accounts.

Matching can be performed on various pieces of IPSec header, including the SPIs (security parameter indices) of the AH (authentication header) and ESP (encapsulating security payload).

The type of packet, be it broadcast, unicast, or multicast, is another form of match. This is done at the link layer.

A range of ports as well as a range of addresses are also valid matches with iptables. The type of address is another valid match as well. Related to type matching is the ICMP packet type. Recall that there are a number of valid types of ICMP packet types. Iptables can match against these types.

The length of the packet is a valid match, as is the time a packet arrived. This time matching is interesting. Using the time matches, you could configure the firewall to reject certain traffic after business hours or allow it only during certain times of day.

A good match for auditing, a random packet match is also available with iptables. Using this match, you can capture every *n*th packet and log it. This would be a method for auditing the firewall rules without logging too much information.

NAT Table Features

There are three general forms of NAT:

- *Traditional, unidirectional outbound NAT*—Used for networks using private addresses.
  - *Basic NAT*—Address Translation only. Usually used to map local private source addresses to one of a block of public addresses.
  - *NAPT (Network Address Port Translation)*—Usually used to map local private source addresses to a single public address (for example, Linux masquerading).
- *Bidirectional NAT*—Two-way address translation allows both outbound and inbound connections. A use of this is bidirectional address mapping between IPv4 and IPv6 address spaces.

- *Twice NAT*—Two-way Source and Destination Address Translation allows both outbound and inbound connections. Twice NAT can be used when the source and destination networks' address spaces collide. This could be the result of one site mistakenly using public addresses assigned to someone else. Twice NAT also can be used as a convenience when a site was renumbered or assigned to a new public address block and the site administrator didn't want to administer the new address assignments locally at that time.

iptables NAT supports source (SNAT) and destination NAT (DNAT). The NAT table allows for modifying a packet's source address or destination address and port. It has three built-in chains:

- The **PREROUTING** chain specifies destination changes to incoming packets before passing the packet to the routing function (DNAT). Changes to the destination address can be to the local host (transparent proxying, port redirection) or to a different host for host forwarding (**ipmasqadm** functionality, port forwarding in Linux parlance) or load sharing.

- The **OUTPUT** chain specifies destination changes to locally generated outgoing packets before the routing decision has been made (DNAT, REDIRECT). This is usually done to transparently redirect an outgoing packet to a local proxy, but it can also be used to port-forward to a different host.

- The **POSTROUTING** chain specifies source changes to outgoing packets being routed through the box (SNAT, MASQUERADE). The changes are applied after the routing decision has been made.

MASQUERADING IN IPTABLES

In iptables, masquerading is a specialized case of source NAT in the sense that the masqueraded connection state is forgotten immediately if the connection is lost. It's intended for use with connections (for example, dial-up) in which the IP address is assigned temporarily. If the user reconnected immediately, he would probably be assigned a different IP address than he had during the previous connection. (This is often not the case with many cable-modem and ADSL service providers. Often, after a connection loss, the same IP address is assigned upon reconnection.)

With regular SNAT, connection state is maintained for the duration of a timeout period. If a connection were reestablished quickly enough, any current network-related programs could continue undisturbed because the IP address hasn't changed, and interrupted TCP traffic would be retransmitted.

The distinction between MASQUERADE and SNAT is an attempt to avoid a situation that occurred in previous Linux NAT/MASQUERADE implementations. When a dial-up connection was lost and the user reconnected immediately, he was assigned a new IP address. The new address couldn't be used immediately because the old IP address and NAT information were still in memory until the timeout period expired.

Figure 3.4 shows the NAT chains in relation to the routing function and INPUT, OUTPUT, and FORWARD chains.

FIGURE 3.4
NAT packet traversal. (Figure based on "Linux 2.4 Packet Filtering HOWTO," v1.0.1, and "Linux 2.4 NAT HOWTO," v1.0.1.)

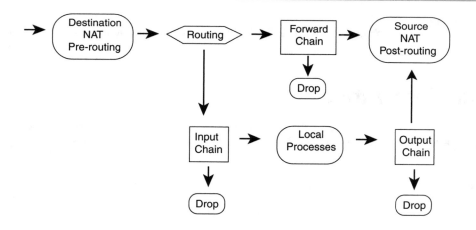

Note that, for outgoing packets, the routing function is implied between the local process and the OUTPUT chain. Static routing is used to determine which interface the packet will go out on, before the OUTPUT chain's filter rules are applied.

mangle **Table Features**

The mangle table allows *marking*, or associating a Netfilter-maintained value, with the packet, as well as making changes to the packet before sending the packet on to its destination. The mangle table has five built-in chains:

- The PREROUTING chain specifies changes to incoming packets as they arrive at an interface, before any routing or local delivery decision has been made.

- The INPUT chain specifies changes to packets as they are processed, but after the PREROUTING chain is traversed.

- The **POSTROUTING** chain specifies changes to packets as they are exiting the firewall, after the **OUTPUT** chain is traversed.

- The **FORWARD** chain specifies changes to packets that are forwarded through the firewall.

- The **OUTPUT** chain specifies changes to locally generated outgoing packets.

For the **TOS** field, the local Linux router can be configured to honor the **TOS** flags set by the **mangle** table or as set by the local hosts.

Little information is available about packet marking in the iptables documentation, beyond that it's used by the Linux Quality of Service implementation and that it's intended as a communication flag between iptables modules.

The preceding sections provided an overview of the features available in iptables and the general structure and functionality of the individual table modules. The following sections present the syntax used to invoke these features.

iptables Syntax

As presented earlier, iptables uses the concept of separate rule tables for different packet processing functionality. Nondefault tables are specified by a command-line option. Three tables are available:

- **filter**—The **filter** table is the default table. It contains the actual firewall filtering rules. The built-in chains include these:
    - INPUT
    - OUTPUT
    - FORWARD

- **nat**—The **nat** table contains the rules for Source and Destination Address and Port Translation. These rules are functionally distinct from the firewall filter rules. The built-in chains include these:
    - PREROUTING (DNAT/REDIRECT)
    - OUTPUT (DNAT/REDIRECT)
    - POSTROUTING (SNAT/MASQUERADE)

- **mangle**—The **mangle** table contains rules for setting specialized packet-routing flags. These flags are then inspected later by rules in the **filter** table. The built-in chains include these:

- PREROUTING (routed packets)

- INPUT (packets arriving at the firewall but after the PREROUTING chain)

- FORWARD (changes packets being routed through the firewall)

- POSTROUTING (changes packets just before they leave the firewall, after the OUTPUT chain)

- OUTPUT (locally generated packets)

SYNTAX FORMAT CONVENTIONS

The conventions used to present command-line syntax options are fairly standard in the computer world. For those of you who are new to Linux or to computer documentation in general, Table 3.1 shows the conventions used in the upcoming syntax descriptions.

TABLE 3.1
Conventions Representing Command-Line Syntax Options

ELEMENT	DESCRIPTION
|	A bar or pipe symbol separates alternate syntax options. For example, most of the iptables commands have both a short and a long form, such as -L and --list, and so they would be listed as alternate options because you would use one or the other of -L or --list.
<value>	Angle brackets indicate a user-supplied value, such as a string or numeric value.
[ ]	Square brackets indicate that the enclosed command, option, or value is optional. For example, most match operators can take a negation operator, !, which matches anything other than the value specified in the match. The negation operator is usually placed between the match operator and the value to be matched.
<value>:<value>	A colon indicates a range of values. The two values define the minimum and maximum values within the range. Because ranges themselves are optional, the convention is more often presented as <value>[:<value>].

filter **Table Commands**

The filter table commands are provided by the ip_tables module. The functionality is enabled by loading the module, which is done automatically with the first invocation of the iptables command, or it could be compiled into the kernel itself, which means you don't need to worry about modules being loaded at all.

`filter` **TABLE OPERATIONS ON ENTIRE CHAINS**

Table 3.2 shows the iptables operations on entire chains.

TABLE 3.2
iptables Operations on Entire Chains

OPTION	DESCRIPTION
`-N	--new-chain <chain>`	Creates a user-defined chain.
`-F	--flush [<chain>]`	Flushes the chain, or all chains if none is specified.
`-X	--delete-chain [<chain>]`	Deletes the user-defined chain, or all chains if none is specified.
`-P	--policy <chain> <policy>`	Defines the default policy for one of the built-in chains, INPUT, OUTPUT, or FORWARD. The policy is either ACCEPT or DROP.
`-L	--list [<chain>]`	Lists the rules in the chain, or all chains if none is specified.
`-Z	--zero`	Resets the packet and byte counters associated with each chain.
`-h	<some command> -h`	Lists the iptables commands and options, or if preceded by an iptables command, lists the syntax and options for that command.
`--modprobe=<command>`	Use <command> to load the necessary module(s) when adding or inserting a rule into a chain.
`-E	--rename-chain <old chain> <new chain>`	Renames the user-defined chain <old chain> to the user-defined chain <new chain>.

The `-h` help command is obviously not an operation on a chain nor is `--modprobe=<command>`, but I didn't know where else to list the command.

The list command takes additional options, as shown in Table 3.3.

TABLE 3.3
Options to the List Chain Command

OPTION	DESCRIPTION
-L -n | --numeric	Lists the IP addresses and port numbers numerically, rather than by name
-L -v | --verbose	Lists additional information about each rule, such as the byte and packet counters, rule options, and relevant network interface
-L -x | --exact	Lists the exact values of the counter, rather than the rounded-off values
-L -line-numbers	Lists the rule's position within its chain

filter TABLE OPERATIONS ON A RULE

The most frequently used commands to create or delete rules within a chain are shown in Table 3.4.

TABLE 3.4
Chain Commands on Individual Rules

COMMAND	DESCRIPTION
-A | --append <chain>	Appends a rule to the end of a chain
-I | --insert <chain>	Inserts a rule at the beginning of the chain
-R | --replace <chain> <rule number> <rule specification>	Replaces a rule in the chain
-D | --delete <chain> <rule number>	Deletes the rule at position rule number within a chain

BASIC filter TABLE MATCH OPERATIONS

The basic filter match operations supported in the default iptables filter table are listed in Table 3.5.

TABLE 3.5
`filter` Table Rule Operations

OPTION	DESCRIPTION
`-i` | `--in-interface` `[!]` `[<interface>]`	For incoming packets on either the INPUT or the FORWARD chains, or their user-defined subchains, specifies the interface name that the rule applies to. If no interface is specified, all interfaces are implied.
`-o` | `--out-interface` `[!]` `[<interface>]`	For outgoing packets on either the OUTPUT or the FORWARD chains, or their user-defined subchains, specifies the interface name that the rule applies to. If no interface is specified, all interfaces are implied.
`-p` | `--protocol` `[!]` `[<protocol>]`	Specifies the IP protocol that the rule applies to. The built-in protocols are `tcp`, `udp`, `icmp`, and all. The protocol value can be either the name or the numeric value, as listed in `/etc/protocols`.
`-s` | `--source` | `--src` `[!]` `<address>[</mask>]`	Specifies the host or network source address in the IP header.
`-d` | `--destination` | `--dst` `[!]` `<address>[</mask>]`	Specifies the host or network destination address in the IP header.
`-j` | `--jump` `<target>`	Specifies the target disposition for the packet if it matches the rule. The default targets include the built-in targets, an extension, or a user-defined chain.
`[!]` `-f` | `--fragment`	Specifies second and additional fragmented packets. The negated version of this specifies unfragmented packets.
`-c` | `--set-counters` `<packets>` `<bytes>`	Initializes the packet and byte counters.

RULE TARGETS ARE OPTIONAL

If the packet matches a rule that doesn't have a target disposition, the packet counters are updated, but list traversal continues.

tcp filter **TABLE MATCH OPERATIONS**

TCP header match options are listed in Table 3.6.

TABLE 3.6
tcp filter Table Match Operations

-p tcp **OPTION**	**DESCRIPTION**
--source-port | --sport [[!] <port>[:<port>]]	This command specifies the source ports.
--destination-port | --dport [!] <port>[:<port>]	This command specifies the destination ports.
--tcp-flags [!] <mask>[,<mask>] <set>[,<set>]	This command tests the bits in the mask list, out of which the following bits must be set in order to match.
[!] -syn	The SYN flag must be set as an initial connection request.
--tcp-option [!] <number>	The only legal tcp option is the maximum packet size that the sending host is willing to accept.

udp filter **TABLE MATCH OPERATIONS**

UDP header match options are listed in Table 3.7.

TABLE 3.7
udp filter Table Match Operations

-p udp **OPTION**	**DESCRIPTION**
--source-port | --sport [!] <port>[:<port>]	Specifies the source ports
--destination-port | --dport [!] <port>[:<port>]	Specifies the destination ports

icmp filter **TABLE MATCH OPERATIONS**

ICMP header match options are listed in Table 3.8.

TABLE 3.8
icmp filter Table Match Operations

MATCH	**DESCRIPTION**
--icmp-type [!] <type>	Specifies the ICMP type name or number. The ICMP type is used in place of a source port.

The major supported ICMP type names and numeric values are the following:

- echo-reply (0)
- destination-unreachable (3)
    - network-unreachable
    - host-unreachable
    - protocol-unreachable
    - port-unreachable
    - fragmentation-needed
    - network-unknown
    - host-unknown
    - network-prohibited
    - host-prohibited
- source-quench (4)
- redirect (5)
- echo-request (8)
- time-exceeded (10)
- parameter-problem (11)

ADDITIONAL ICMP SUPPORT

iptables supports a number of additional, less common or router-specific ICMP message types and subtypes. To see the entire list, use the following iptables help command:

iptables -p icmp -h

filter Table Target Extensions

The filter table target extensions include logging functionality and the capability to reject a packet rather than dropping it.

Table 3.9 lists the options available to the LOG target. Table 3.10 lists the single option available to the REJECT target.

TABLE 3.9
LOG Target Extension

-j LOG **OPTION**	**DESCRIPTION**
--log-level <syslog level>	Log level is either the numeric or the symbolic login priority, as listed in /usr/include/sys/syslog.h. These are the same log levels used in /etc/syslog.conf. The levels are emerg (0), alert (1), crit (2), err (3), warn (4), notice (5), info (6), memerg (0), alert (1), crit (2), err (3), warn (4), notice (5), info (6), and debut (7).
--log-prefix <"descriptive string">	The prefix is a quoted string that will be printed at the start of the log message for the rule.
--log-ip-options	This command includes any IP header options in the log output.
--log-tcp-sequence	This command includes the TCP packet's sequence number in the log output.
--log-tcp-option	This command includes any TCP header options in the log output.

TABLE 3.10
REJECT Target Extension

-j REJECT **OPTION**	**DESCRIPTION**
--reject-with <ICMP type 3>	By default, a rejected packet results in an ICMP type 3 icmp-port-unreachable message being returned to the sender. Other type 3 error messages can be returned instead, including icmp-net-unreachable, icmp-host-unreachable, icmp-proto-unreachable, icmp-net-prohibited, and icmp-host-prohibited.
--reject-with tcp-reset	Incoming TCP packets can be rejected with the more standard TCP RST message, rather than an ICMP error message.
--reject-with echo-reply	ping echo-request messages can be rejected with a faked echo-reply message. That is, the firewall generates the reply, but the request is not forwarded to the target host.

THE ULOG **TABLE TARGET EXTENSION**

Related to the LOG target is the ULOG target, which sends the log message to a userspace program for logging. Behind the scenes for ULOG, the packet gets multicast by the kernel through a netlink socket of your choosing (the default is socket 1). The userspace daemon would then read the message from the socket and do with it what it pleases. The ULOG target is typically used to provide more extensive logging than is possible with the standard LOG target.

As with the LOG target, processing continues after matches on a ULOG targeted rule. The ULOG target has four configuration options, as described in Table 3.11.

TABLE 3.11
ULOG Target Extension

OPTION	DESCRIPTION
--ulog-nlgroup <group>	Defines the netlink group that will receive the packet. The default group is 1.
--ulog-prefix <prefix>	Messages will be prefixed by this value, up to 32 characters in length.
--ulog-cprange <size>	The size in bytes to send to the netlink socket. The default is 0, which sends the entire packet.
--ulog-qthreshold <size>	The size in packets to queue within the kernel. The default is 1, which means that one packet is sent per message to the netlink socket.

filter **Table Match Extensions**

The filter table match extensions provide access to the fields in the TCP, UDP, and ICMP headers, as well as the match features available in iptables, such as maintaining connection state, port lists, access to the hardware MAC source address, and access to the IP TOS field.

MATCH SYNTAX

The match extensions require the -m or --match command to load the module, followed by any relevant match options.

multiport filter **TABLE MATCH EXTENSION**

multiport port lists can include up to 15 ports per list. Whitespace isn't allowed. There can be no blank spaces between the commas and the port values. Port ranges cannot be interspersed in the list. Also, the -m multiport command must exactly follow the -p <protocol> specifier.

Table 3.12 lists the options available to the multiport match extension.

TABLE 3.12

multiport Match Extension

m | --match multiport OPTION	DESCRIPTION
--source-port <port> [,<port>]	Specifies the source port(s).
--destination-port <port> [,<port>]	Specifies the destination port(s).
--port <port>[,<port>]	Source and destination ports are equal, and they match a port in the list.

The multiport syntax can be a bit tricky. Some examples and cautions are included here. The following rule blocks incoming packets arriving on interface eth0 destined for the UDP ports associated with NetBIOS and SMB, common ports that are exploited on Microsoft Windows computers and targets for worms:

```
iptables -A INPUT -i eth0 -p udp\
        -m multiport --destination-port 135,136,137,138,139 -j DROP
```

The next rule blocks outgoing connection requests sent through the eth0 interface to high ports associated with the TCP services NFS, socks, and squid:

```
iptables -A OUTPUT -o eth0 -p tcp\
        -m multiport --destination-port 2049,1080,3128 --syn -j REJECT
```

What is important to note in this example is that the multiport command must exactly follow the protocol specification. A syntax error would have resulted if the --syn were placed between the -p tcp and the -m multiport.

To show a similar example of --syn placement, the following is correct:

```
iptables -A INPUT -i <interface> -p tcp \
        -m multiport --source-port 80,443 ! --syn -j ACCEPT
```

However, this causes a syntax error:

```
iptables -A INPUT -i <interface> -p tcp ! --syn \
        -m multiport --source-port 80,443 -j ACCEPT
```

Furthermore, the placement of source and destination parameters is not obvious. The following two variations are correct:

```
iptables -A INPUT -i <interface> -p tcp -m multiport \
          --source-port 80,443 \
       ! --syn -d $IPADDR --dport 1024:65535 -j ACCEPT
```

and

```
iptables -A INPUT -i <interface> -p tcp -m multiport \
          --source-port 80,443 \
       -d $IPADDR ! --syn --dport 1024:65535 -j ACCEPT
```

However, this causes a syntax error:

```
iptables -A INPUT -i <interface> -p tcp -m multiport \
            --source-port 80,443 \
            -d $IPADDR --dport 1024:65535 ! --syn -j ACCEPT
```

This module has some surprising syntax side effects. Either of the two preceding correct rules produces a syntax error if the reference to the SYN flag is removed:

```
iptables -A INPUT -i <interface> -p tcp -m multiport \
            --source-port 80,443 \
        -d $IPADDR --dport 1024:65535 -j ACCEPT
```

The following pair of rules, however, does not:

```
iptables -A OUTPUT -o <interface> \
        -p tcp -m multiport --destination-port 80,443 \
        ! --syn -s $IPADDR --sport 1024:65535 -j ACCEPT

iptables -A OUTPUT -o <interface> \
        -p tcp -m multiport --destination-port 80,443 \
        --syn -s $IPADDR --sport 1024:65535 -j ACCEPT
```

Note that the --destination-port argument to the multiport module is not the same as the --destination-port or --dport argument to the module that performs matching for the -p tcp arguments.

limit filter **TABLE MATCH EXTENSION**

Rate-limited matching is useful for choking back the number of log messages that would be generated during a flood of logged packets.

Table 3.13 lists the options available to the limit match extension.

TABLE 3.13
limit Match Extension

-m | --match limit **OPTION**	**DESCRIPTION**
--limit <rate>	Maximum number of packets to match within the given time frame
--limit-burst <number>	Maximum number of initial packets to match before applying the limit

The burst rate defines the number of initial matches to be accepted. The default value is five matches. When the limit has been reached, further matches are limited to the rate limit. The default limit is three matches per hour. Optional time frame specifiers include /second, /minute, /hour, and /day.

In other words, by default, when the initial burst rate of five matches is reached within the time limit, at most three more packets will match over the next hour, one every 20 minutes, regardless of how many packets are received. If a match doesn't occur within the rate limit, the burst is recharged by one.

It's easier to demonstrate rate-limited matching than it is to describe it in words. The following rule will limit logging of incoming **ping** message matches to one per second when an initial five **echo-requests** are received within a given second:

```
iptables -A INPUT -i eth0 \
        -p icmp --icmp-type echo-request \
        -m limit --limit 1/second -j LOG
```

It's also possible to do rate-limited packet acceptance. The following two rules, in combination, will limit acceptance of incoming **ping** messages to one per second when an initial five **echo-requests** are received within a given second:

```
iptables -A INPUT -i eth0 \
        -p icmp --icmp-type echo-request \
        -m limit --limit 1/second -j ACCEPT

iptables -A INPUT -i eth0 \
        -p icmp --icmp-type echo-request -j DROP
```

The next rule limits the number of log messages generated in response to dropped ICMP **redirect** messages. When an initial five messages have been logged within a 20-minute time frame, at most three more log messages will be generated over the next hour, one every 20 minutes:

```
iptables -A INPUT -i eth0 \
        -p icmp --icmp-type redirect \
        -m limit -j LOG
```

The assumption in the final example is that the packet and any additional unmatched **redirect** packets are silently dropped by the default **DROP** policy for the **INPUT** chain.

dstlimit filter **TABLE MATCH EXTENSION**

The **dstlimit** match extension enables rate limiting on a per-destination basis, whether per IP address or per port. Note the difference between the **dstlimit** match extension and the **limit** match extension, which has one limit for packets of a certain type.

Table 3.14 lists the options for the **dstlimit** match extension.

TABLE 3.14
dstlimit Match Extension

OPTION	DEFINITION
--dstlimit <average>	Maximum average match rate in packets per second.
--dstlimit-mode <mode>	Defines the limit to be per IP (dstip), per IP and port tuple (dstip-dstport), per source IP and destination IP tuple (srcip-dstip), or per source IP and destination IP and destination port tuple (srcipdstip-dstport).
--dstlimit-name <name>	Specifies the name for the file to be placed in /proc/net/ipt_dstlimit/.
[--dstlimit-burst <burst>]	Specifies the number of packets that should be matched when received as a burst of packets. The default is 5.
[--dstlimit-htable-size <size>]	Defines the number of buckets in the hashtable.
[--dstlimit-htable-max <entries>]	Defines the limit for the number of entries in the hashtable.
[--dstlimit-htable-gcinterval <interval>]	Defines the length of time between cleanup of the hashtable. The value for <interval> is in milliseconds, with the default being 1000 ms.
[--dstlimit-htable-expire <time>]	Defines the amount of time before an idle entry is purged from the hashtable. The value is in milliseconds, with the default being 10000 ms.

state filter TABLE MATCH EXTENSION

Static filters look at traffic on a packet-by-packet basis alone. Each packet's particular combination of source and destination addresses and ports, the transport protocol, and the current TCP state flag combination is examined without reference to any ongoing context. ICMP messages are treated as unrelated, out-of-band IP Layer 3 events.

The state extension provides additional monitoring and recording technology to augment the stateless, static packet-filter technology. State information is recorded when a TCP connection or UDP exchange is initiated. Subsequent packets are examined not only based on the static tuple information, but also within the context of the ongoing exchange. In other words, some of the contextual knowledge usually associated with the upper TCP Transport layer, or the UDP Application layer, is brought down to the filter layer.

After the exchange is initiated and accepted, subsequent packets are identified as part of the established exchange. Associated ICMP messages are identified as being related to a particular exchange.

(In computer terminology, a collection of values or attributes that together uniquely identify an event or object is called a *tuple*. A UDP or TCP packet is uniquely identified by the tuple combination of its protocol, UDP or TCP, the source and destination addresses, and the source and destination ports.)

For session monitoring, the advantages of maintaining state information are less obvious for TCP because TCP maintains state information by definition. For UDP, the immediate advantage is the capability to distinguish responses from other datagrams. In the case of an outgoing DNS request, which represents a new UDP exchange, the concept of an established session allows an incoming UDP response datagram from the host and port the original message was sent to, within a certain time-limited window. Incoming UDP datagrams from other hosts or ports are not allowed. They are not part of the established state for this particular exchange. When applied to TCP and UDP, ICMP error messages are accepted if the error message is related to the particular session.

In considering packet flow performance and firewall complexity, the advantages are more obvious for TCP flows. Flows are primarily a firewall performance and optimization technology. The main goal of flows is to allow bypassing the firewall inspection path for a packet. Much faster TCP packet handling is obtained in some cases because the remaining firewall filters can be skipped if the TCP packet is immediately recognized as part of an allowed, ongoing connection. For TCP connections, flow state can be a major win in terms of filtering performance. Also, standard TCP application protocol rules can be collapsed into a single initial allow rule. The number of filter rules is reduced (theoretically, but not necessarily in practice, as you'll see later in the book).

The main disadvantage is that maintaining a state table requires more memory than standard firewall rules alone. Routers with 70,000 simultaneous connections, for example, would require tremendous amounts of memory to maintain state table entries for each connection. State maintenance is often done in hardware for performance reasons, where associative table lookups can be done simultaneously or in parallel. Whether implemented in hardware or software, state engines must be capable of reverting a packet to the traditional path if memory isn't available for the state table entry.

Also, table creation, lookup, and teardown take time in software. The additional processing overhead is a loss in many cases. State maintenance is a win for ongoing exchanges such as an FTP transfer or a UDP streaming multimedia session. Both types of data flow represent potentially large numbers of packets (and filter rule match tests). State maintenance is not a firewall performance win for a simple DNS or NTP client/server exchange, however. State buildup and teardown can easily require as much processing—and more memory—than simply traversing the filter rules for these packets.

The advantages are also questionable for firewalls that filter primarily web traffic. Web client/server exchanges tend to be brief and ephemeral.

Telnet and SSH sessions are in a gray area. On heavily trafficked routers with many such sessions, the state maintenance overhead may be a win by bypassing the firewall inspection. For fairly quiescent sessions, however, it's likely that the connection state entry will timeout and be thrown away. The state table entry will be re-created when the next packet comes along, after it has passed the traditional firewall rules.

Table 3.15 lists the options available to the `state` match extension.

TABLE 3.15
`state` Match Extension

`-m	--match state` **OPTION**	**DESCRIPTION**
`--state <state>[,<state>]`	Matches if the connection state is one in the list. Legal values are NEW, ESTABLISHED, RELATED, or INVALID.

TCP connection state and ongoing UDP exchange information can be maintained, allowing network exchanges to be filtered as NEW, ESTABLISHED, RELATED, or INVALID:

- NEW is equivalent to the initial TCP SYN request, or to the first UDP packet.

- ESTABLISHED refers to the ongoing TCP ACK messages after the connection is initiated, to subsequent UDP datagrams exchanged between the same hosts and ports, and to ICMP `echo-reply` messages sent in response to a previous `echo-request`.

- RELATED currently refers only to ICMP error messages. FTP secondary connections are managed by the additional FTP connection tracking support module. With the addition of that module, the meaning of RELATED is extended to include the secondary FTP connection.

- An example of an INVALID packet is an incoming ICMP error message that wasn't a response to a current session, or an `echo-reply` that wasn't a response to a previous `echo-request`.

Ideally, using the ESTABLISHED match allows the firewall rule pair for a service to be collapsed into a single rule that allows the first request packet. For example, using the ESTABLISHED match, a web client rule requires allowing only the initial outgoing SYN request. A DNS client request requires only the rule allowing the initial UDP outgoing request packet.

With a deny-by-default input policy, connection tracking can be used (theoretically) to replace all protocol-specific filters with two general rules that allow incoming and outgoing packets that are part of an established connection, or packets related to the connection. Application-specific rules are required for the initial packet alone.

Although such a firewall setup might very well work for a small or residential site in most cases, it is unlikely to perform adequately for a larger site or a firewall that handles many connections simultaneously. The reason goes back to the case of state table entry timeouts, in which a state entry for a quiescent connection is replaced because of table size and memory constraints. The next packet that would have been accepted by the deleted state entry requires a rule to allow the packet, and the state table entry must be rebuilt.

A simple example of this is a rule pair for a local DNS server operating as a cache-and-forward name server. A DNS forwarding name server uses server-to-server communication. DNS traffic is exchanged between source and destination ports **53** on both hosts. The UDP client/server relationship can be made explicit. The following rules explicitly allow outgoing (**NEW**) requests, incoming (**ESTABLISHED**) responses, and any (**RELATED**) ICMP error messages:

```
iptables -A INPUT -m state \
        --state ESTABLISHED,RELATED -j ACCEPT

iptables -A OUTPUT --out-interface <interface> -p udp \
        -s $IPADDR --source-port 53 -d $NAME_SERVER --destination-port 53 \
        -m state --state NEW,RELATED -j ACCEPT
```

DNS uses a simple query-and-response protocol. But what about an application that can maintain an ongoing connection for extended periods, such as an FTP control session or a telnet or SSH session? If the state table entry is cleared out prematurely for some reason, future packets won't have a state entry to be matched against to be identified as part of an **ESTABLISHED** exchange.

The following rules for an SSH connection allow for that possibility:

```
iptables -A INPUT -m state \
        --state ESTABLISHED,RELATED -j ACCEPT

iptables -A OUTPUT -m state \
        --state ESTABLISHED,RELATED -j ACCEPT

iptables -A OUTPUT --out-interface <interface> -p tcp \
        -s $IPADDR --source-port $UNPRIVPORTS \
        -d $REMOTE_SSH_SERVER --destination-port 22 \
        -m state --state NEW, -j ACCEPT
```

```
iptables -A OUTPUT --out-interface <interface> -p tcp ! --syn \
        -s $IPADDR --source-port $UNPRIVPORTS \
        -d $REMOTE_SSH_SERVER --destination-port 22 \
        -j ACCEPT

iptables -A INPUT --in-interface <interface> -p tcp ! --syn \
        -s $REMOTE_SSH_SERVER --source-port 22 \
        -d $IPADDR --destination-port $UNPRIVPORTS \
        -j ACCEPT
```

mac filter TABLE MATCH EXTENSION

Table 3.16 lists the options available to the mac match extension.

TABLE 3.16
mac Match Extension

-m | --match mac **OPTION**	**DESCRIPTION**
--mac-source [!] <address>	Matches the Layer 2 Ethernet hardware source address, specified as xx:xx:xx:xx:xx:xx:, in the incoming Ethernet frame

Remember that MAC addresses do not cross router borders (or network segments). Also remember that only source addresses can be specified. The mac extension can be used only on an in-interface, such as the INPUT, PREROUTING, and FORWARD chains.

The following rule allows incoming SSH connections from a single local host:

```
iptables -A INPUT -i <local interface> -p tcp \
        -m mac --mac-source xx:xx:xx:xx:xx:xx \
        --source-port 1024:65535 \
        -d <IPADDR> --dport 22 -j ACCEPT
```

owner filter TABLE MATCH EXTENSION

Table 3.17 lists the options available to the owner match extension.

TABLE 3.17
owner Match Extension

-m | --match owner **OPTION**	**DESCRIPTION**
--uid-owner <userid>	Matches on the creator's UID
--gid-owner <groupid>	Matches on the creator's GID
--pid-owner <processid>	Matches on the creator's PID
--sid-owner <sessionid>	Matches on the creator's SID or PPID
--cmd-owner <name>	Matches on a packet created by a process with command name name

The match refers to the packet's creator. The extension can be used on the OUTPUT chain only.

These match options don't make much sense on a firewall router; they make more sense on an end host.

So, let's say that you have a firewall gateway with a monitor, perhaps, but no keyboard. Administration is done from a local, multiuser host. A single user account is allowed to log in to the firewall from this host. On the multiuser host, administrative access to the firewall could be locally filtered as shown here:

```
iptables -A OUTPUT -o eth0 -p tcp \
        -s <IPADDR> --sport 1024:65535 \
        -d <fw IPADDR> --dport 22 \
        -m owner --uid-owner <admin userid> \
        --gid-owner <admin groupid> -j ACCEPT
```

mark filter TABLE MATCH EXTENSION

Table 3.18 lists the options available to the mark match extension.

TABLE 3.18
mark Match Extension

-m | -match mark **OPTION**	**DESCRIPTION**
--mark <value>[/<mask>]	Matches packets having the Netfilter-assigned mark value

The mark value and the mask are unsigned long values. If a mask is specified, the value and the mask are ANDed together.

In the example, assume that an incoming telnet client packet between a specific source and destination had been marked previously:

```
iptables -A FORWARD -i eth0 -o eth1 -p tcp \
        -s <some src address> --sport 1024:65535 \
        -d <some destination address> --dport 23 \
        -m mark --mark 0x00010070 \
        -j ACCEPT
```

The mark value being tested for here was set at some earlier point in the packet processing. The mark value is a flag indicating that this packet is to be handled differently from other packets.

tos filter TABLE MATCH EXTENSION

Table 3.19 lists the options available to the tos match extension.

TABLE 3.19
tos Match Extension

-m | --match tos **OPTION**	**DESCRIPTION**
--tos <value>	Matches on the IP TOS setting

The tos value can be one of either the string or numeric values:

- minimize-delay, 16, 0x10

- maximize-throughput, 8, 0x08

- maximize-reliability, 4, 0x04

- minimize-cost, 2, 0x02

- normal-service, 0, 0x00

THE VALUE OF TOS **BITS**

The TOS bits are of historical interest only. Linux does support their use locally, and various Linux firewall documents refer to the bits and their uses. Nevertheless, the fact remains that the TOS bits are not used or examined generally.

The TOS field has been redefined as the Differentiated Services (DS) field for use by the Differentiated Services Control Protocol (DSCP).

For more information on Differentiated Services, see these sources:

- RFC 2474, "Definition of the Differentiated Services Field (DS Field) in the IPv4 and IPv6 Headers"

- RFC 2475, "An Architecture for Differentiated Services"

- RFC 2990, "Next Steps for the IP QoS Architecture"

- RFC 3168, "The Addition of Explicit Congestion Notification (ECN) to IP"

- RFC 3260, "New Terminology and Clarifications for Diffserv"

unclean filter **TABLE MATCH EXTENSION**

The specific packet-validity checks performed by the unclean module are not documented. The module is considered to be experimental, and the iptables authors recommend against its use for now.

The following line shows the **unclean** module syntax. The module takes no arguments:

```
-m | --match unclean
```

The **unclean** extension might be "blessed" by the time this book is published. In the meantime, the module lends itself to an example of the **LOG** options:

```
iptables -A INPUT -p ! tcp -m unclean \
        -j LOG --log-prefix "UNCLEAN packet: " \
        --log-ip-options

iptables -A INPUT -p tcp -m unclean \
        -j LOG --log-prefix "UNCLEAN TCP: " \
        --log-ip-options \
        --log-tcp-sequence --log-tcp-options

iptables -A INPUT -m unclean -j DROP
```

addrtype filter TABLE MATCH EXTENSION

The **addrtype** match extension is used to match packets based on the type of address used, such as unicast, broadcast, and multicast. The types of addresses include those listed in Table 3.20.

TABLE 3.20
Address Types Used with the **addrtype** Match

NAME	DESCRIPTION
ANYCAST	An anycast packet
BLACKHOLE	A blackhole address
BROADCAST	A broadcast address
LOCAL	A local address
MULTICAST	A multicast address
PROHIBIT	A prohibited address
UNICAST	A unicast address
UNREACHABLE	An unreachable address
UNSPEC	An unspecified address

Two commands are used with the **addrtype** match, as listed in Table 3.21.

TABLE 3.21
addrtype Match Commands

OPTION	DESCRIPTION
--src-type <type>	Matches for addresses with a source of type <type>.
--dst-type <type>	Matches for addresses with a destination of type <type>.

iprange filter TABLE MATCH

Sometimes defining a range of IP addresses using CIDR notation is insufficient for your needs. For example, if you need to limit a certain range of IPs that don't fall on a subnet boundary or cross that boundary by only a couple addresses, the iprange match type will do the job.

Using the iprange match, you specify an arbitrary range of IP addresses for the match to take effect. The iprange match can also be negated. Table 3.22 lists the commands for the iprange match.

TABLE 3.22
iprange Match Commands

COMMAND	DESCRIPTION
[!] --src-range <ip address-ip address>	Specifies (or negates) the range of IP addresses to match. The range is given with a single hyphen and no spaces.
[!] --dst-range <ip address-ip address>	Specifies (or negates) the range of IP addresses to match. The range is given with a single hyphen and no spaces.

length filter TABLE MATCH

The length filter table match examines the length of the packet. If the packet's length matches the value given or optionally falls within the range given, the rule is invoked. Table 3.23 lists the one and only command related to the length match.

TABLE 3.23
length Match Command

COMMAND	DESCRIPTION
--length <length>[:<length>]	Matches a packet of <length> or within the range <length:length>

NAT Table Target Extensions

As mentioned earlier, iptables supports four general kinds of NAT: source NAT (SNAT); destination NAT (DNAT); masquerading (MASQUERADE), which is a specialized case of the SNAT implementation; and local port direction (REDIRECT) to the local host. As part of the NAT table, each of these targets is available when a rule specifies the nat table by using the -t nat table specifier.

SNAT NAT TABLE TARGET EXTENSION

Source Address and Port Translation (NAPT) is the kind of NAT people are most commonly familiar with. As shown in Figure 3.5, Source Address Translation is done after the routing decision is made. SNAT is a legal target only in the POSTROUTING chain. Because SNAT is applied immediately before the packet is sent out, only an outgoing interface can be specified.

FIGURE 3.5
NAT packet traversal.

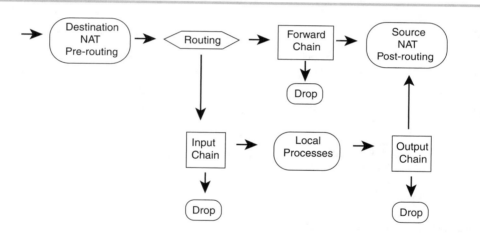

Some documents refer to this form of source NAT (the most common form) as NAPT, to acknowledge the port number modification. The other form of traditional, unidirectional NAT is basic NAT, which doesn't touch the source port. That form is used when you are translating between the private LAN and a pool of public addresses.

NAPT is used when you have a single public address. The source port is changed to a free port on the firewall/NAT machine because it's translating for any number of internal computers, and the port that the internal machine is using might already be in use by the NAT machine. When the responses come back, the port is all that the NAT machine has to determine that the packet is really meant for an internal computer rather than itself and then to determine which internal computer the packet is meant for.

The general syntax for **SNAT** is as follows:

```
iptables -t nat -A POSTROUTING --out-interface <interface>  ...  \
        -j SNAT --to-source <address>[-<address>][:<port>-<port>]
```

The source address can be mapped to a range of possible IP addresses, if more than one is available.

The source port can be mapped to a specific range of source ports on the router.

MASQUERADE NAT TABLE TARGET EXTENSION

Source Address Translation has been implemented in two different ways in iptables, as SNAT and as MASQUERADE. The difference is that the MASQUERADE target extension is intended for use with connections on interfaces with dynamically assigned IP addresses, particularly in the case in which the connection is temporary and the IP address assignment is likely to be different at each new connection. As discussed previously, in the section "NAT Table Features," MASQUERADE can be useful for phone dial-up connections in particular.

Because masquerading is a specialized case of SNAT, it is likewise a legal target only in the **POSTROUTING** chain, and the rule can refer to the outgoing interface only. Unlike the more generalized SNAT, MASQUERADE does not take an argument specifying the source address to apply to the packet. The IP address of the outgoing interface is used automatically.

The general syntax for **MASQUERADE** is as follows:

```
iptables -t nat -A POSTROUTING --out-interface <interface>  ...  \
        -j MASQUERADE [--to-ports <port>[-<port>]]
```

The source port can be mapped to a specific range of source ports on the router.

DNAT NAT TABLE TARGET EXTENSION

Destination Address and Port Translation is a highly specialized form of NAT. A residential or small business site is most likely to find this feature useful if its public IP address is dynamically assigned or if the site has a single IP address, and the site administrator wants to forward incoming connections to internal servers that aren't publicly visible. In other words, the DNAT features can be used to replace the previously required third-party port-forwarding software, such as `ipmasqadm`.

Referring back to Figure 3.5, Destination Address and Port Translation is done before the routing decision is made. DNAT is a legal target in the **PREROUTING** and **OUTPUT** chains. On the

PREROUTING chain, DNAT can be a target when the incoming interface is specified. On the OUTPUT chain, DNAT can be a target when the outgoing interface is specified.

The general syntax for DNAT is as follows:

```
iptables -t nat -A PREROUTING --in-interface <interface> ... \
        -j DNAT --to-destination <address>[-<address>][:<port>-<port>]
iptables -t nat -A OUTPUT --out-interface <interface> ... \
        -j DNAT --to-destination <address>[-<address>][:<port>-<port>]
```

The destination address can be mapped to a range of possible IP addresses, if more than one is available.

The destination port can be mapped to a specific range of alternate ports on the destination host.

REDIRECT NAT TABLE TARGET EXTENSION

Port redirection is a specialized case of DNAT. The packet is redirected to a port on the local host. Incoming packets that would otherwise be forwarded on are redirected to the incoming interface's INPUT chain. Outgoing packets generated by the local host are redirected to a port on the local host's loopback interface.

REDIRECT is simply an alias, a convenience, for the specialized case of redirecting a packet to *this* host. It offers no additional functional value. DNAT could just as easily be used to cause the same effect.

REDIRECT is likewise a legal target only in the PREROUTING and OUTPUT chains. On the PREROUTING chain, REDIRECT can be a target when the incoming interface is specified. On the OUTPUT chain, REDIRECT can be a target when the outgoing interface is specified.

The general syntax for REDIRECT is as follows:

```
iptables -t nat -A PREROUTING --in-interface <interface> ... \
        -j REDIRECT [--to-ports <port>[-<port>]]
iptables -t nat -A OUTPUT --out-interface <interface> ... \
        -j REDIRECT [--to-ports <port>[-<port>]]
```

The destination port can be mapped to a different port or to a specific range of alternate ports on the local host.

BALANCE NAT TABLE TARGET EXTENSION

The BALANCE target enables a round-robin method of sending connections to more than one target host. The BALANCE target uses a range of addresses for this purpose and thus provides a rudimentary load-balancing.

The general syntax for **BALANCE** is as follows:

```
iptables -t nat -A PREROUTING -p tcp -j BALANCE \
        --to-destination <ip address>-<ip address>
```

The **CLUSTERIP** target also provides some of these same options.

mangle **Table Commands**

The **mangle** table targets and extensions apply to the **OUTPUT** and **PREROUTING** chains. Remember, the **filter** table is implied by default. To use the **mangle** table features, you must specify the **mangle** table with the **-t mangle** directive.

mark mangle **TABLE TARGET EXTENSION**

Table 3.24 lists the target extensions available to the **mangle** table.

TABLE 3.24
mangle Target Extensions

-t mangle **OPTION**	**DESCRIPTION**
-j MARK --set-mark <value>	Sets the value of the Netfilter mark value for this packet
-j TOS --set-tos <value>	Sets the TOS value in the IP header

There are two **mangle** table target extensions: **MARK** and **TOS**. **MARK** contains the functionality to set the unsigned long **mark** value for the packet maintained by the iptables **mangle** table.

An example of usage follows:

```
iptables -t mangle -A PREROUTING --in-interface eth0 -p tcp \
        -s <some src address> --sport 1024:65535 \
        -d <some destination address> --dport 23 \
        -j MARK --set-mark 0x00010070
```

TOS contains the functionality to set the **TOS** bits in the IP header.

An example of usage follows:

```
iptables -t mangle -A OUTPUT ...  -j TOS --set-tos <tos>
```

The possible **tos** values are the same values available in the **filter** table's TOS match extension module.

Summary

This chapter covered the majority of features available in iptables—certainly, the features most commonly used. I've tried to give a general sense of the differences between Netfilter and IPFW, if for no other reason than to give you a "heads up" for the implementation differences that will appear in the following chapters. The modular implementation divisions of three separate major tables—`filter`, `mangle`, and `nat`—was presented. Within each of these major divisions, features were further broken down into modules that provide target extensions and modules that provide match extensions.

Chapter 4, "Building and Installing a Standalone Firewall," goes through a simple, standalone firewall example. Basic antispoofing, denial of service, and other fundamental rules are presented. The purpose of the chapter isn't to present a general firewall for people to cut and paste for practical use, as much as to demonstrate the syntax presented in this chapter in a functional way.

Subsequent chapters are more specific. User-defined chains, firewall optimization, LAN, NAT, and multihomed hosts are covered separately, as are larger local network architectures.

Building and Installing a Standalone Firewall

Chapter 2, "Packet-Filtering Concepts," covered the background ideas and concepts behind a packet-filtering firewall. Each firewall rule chain has its own default policy. Each rule not only applies to an individual INPUT or OUTPUT chain, but also can apply to a specific network interface, message protocol type (such as TCP, UDP, or ICMP), and service port number. Individual acceptance, denial, and rejection rules are defined for the INPUT chain and the OUTPUT chain, as well as for the FORWARD chain, which you'll learn about at the end of this chapter and in Chapter 6, "Packet Forwarding." This chapter pulls together those ideas to demonstrate how to build a simple, single-system firewall for your site.

The firewall that you'll build in this chapter is based on a deny-everything-by-default policy. All network traffic is blocked by default. Services are individually enabled as exceptions to the policy.

After the single-system firewall is built, Chapter 6 and Chapter 7, "NAT— Network Address Translation," move on to demonstrate how to extend the standalone firewall to a dual-homed firewall. A *multihomed firewall* has at least two network interfaces. It insulates an internal LAN from direct communication with the Internet. It protects your internal LAN by applying packet-filtering rules at the two forwarding interfaces and, with the addition of Network Address Translation (NAT), by acting as a proxying gateway between the LAN and the Internet. NAT is *not* a proxy service, in the sense that it does not provide an intermediate termination point for the connection. NAT *is* proxy-like in the sense that the local hosts are hidden from the public Internet.

The single-system and dual-homed firewalls are the least-secure forms of firewall architectures. If the firewall host were compromised, any local machines would be open to attack. As a standalone firewall, it's an all-or-nothing proposition. A single-homed host is found most often in a DMZ hosting a public Internet service or in a residential setting.

In the case of the single-system home or small-business setting, the assumption is that the majority of users have a single computer connected to the Internet or a single firewall machine protecting a small, private LAN. The assumption is that these sites simply don't have the resources to extend the model to an architecture with additional levels of firewalls.

The term "least secure" does not necessarily imply an insecure firewall, however. These firewalls are less secure than more complicated architectures involving multiple machines. Security is a compromise between available resources and diminishing returns on the next dollar spent. Chapter 6 introduces more secure configurations that allow for additional internal security protecting more complicated LAN and server configurations than a single-system firewall can.

iptables: The Linux Firewall Administration Program

This book is based on the 2.6 Linux kernel series, though much of it is applicable to the 2.4 kernel series as well. Most distributions of Linux come supplied with the Netfilter firewall mechanism introduced in Chapter 3, "iptables: The Linux Firewall Administration Program." This mechanism is usually referred to as iptables, its administration program's name. Older Linux distributions used the earlier IPFW mechanism. That firewall mechanism is usually referred to as **ipfwadm** or **ipchains**, the earlier version's administration program names.

iptables includes compatibility modules for both **ipchains** and **ipfwadm**. Some people might want to use one of these modules until their conversion to iptables is tested.

As a firewall administration program, iptables creates the individual packet-filter rules for the **INPUT** and **OUTPUT** chains composing the firewall. One of the most important aspects of defining firewall rules is the order in which the rules are defined.

Packet-filtering rules are stored in kernel tables, in an **INPUT**, **OUTPUT**, or **FORWARD** chain, in the order in which they are defined. Individual rules are inserted at the beginning of the chain or are appended to the end of the chain. All rules are appended in the examples in this chapter (with one exception at the end of the chapter). The order in which you define the rules is the order in which they'll be added to the kernel tables and, thereby, the order in which the rules will be compared against each packet.

As each externally originating packet arrives at the network interface, its header fields are compared against each rule in the interface's INPUT chain until a match is found. Conversely, as each locally generated packet is sent out, its header fields are compared against each rule in the interface's OUTPUT chain until a match is found. In either direction, when a match is found, the comparison stops and the rule's packet disposition is applied: ACCEPT, DROP, or, optionally, REJECT. If the packet doesn't match any rule on the chain, the default policy for that chain is applied. The bottom line is that *the first matching rule wins*.

The numeric service port numbers, rather than their symbolic names, as listed in /etc/ services, are used in all the filter examples in this chapter. iptables supports the symbolic service port names. The examples in this chapter use the numeric values because the symbolic names are not consistent across Linux distributions—or even from one release to the next. You could use the symbolic names for clarity in your own rules, but remember that your firewall could break with the next system upgrade. I've found it much more reliable to use the port numbers themselves. The last thing you want in a firewall is ambiguity, which is just what is introduced by using names instead of numbers for ports.

Most Linux distributions implement iptables as a set of loadable program modules. Most or all of the modules are dynamically and automatically loaded on first use. If you choose to build your own kernel, which I nearly always do, you'll need to compile in support for Netfilter, either as modules or directly into the kernel. The iptables command must be invoked once for each individual firewall rule you define. This is initially done from a shell script. This chapter will use a script called rc.firewall. The location of the script is dependent on the flavor of Linux where the script will be used. For example, on Red Hat and SUSE systems, the script should likely be within the /etc/rc.d/ directory whereas on Debian, /etc/init.d/ is the correct location. In cases in which shell semantics differ, the examples are written in Bourne (sh) or Bourne Again (bash) shell semantics.

The shell script sets a number of variables. Chief among these is the location of the iptables command itself. It's important to set this in a variable so that it is explicitly located. There's no excuse for ambiguity with a firewall script. The variable used to represent the iptables command in this chapter is $IPT. If you see $IPT, it is a substitute for the iptables command. You could just as easily execute the commands from the shell by typing iptables instead of $IPT. However, for use in a script (which is the intention in this chapter), setting this variable is a good idea.

The script should begin with the "shebang" line invoking the shell as the interpreter for the script. In other words, put this as the first line of the script:

```
#!/bin/sh
```

The examples are not optimized. They are spelled out for clarity. Firewall optimization and user-defined chains are discussed separately in Chapter 5, "Firewall Optimization."

Build Versus Buy: The Linux Kernel

There is great debate over whether it is advisable to compile a custom kernel or stick with the "stock" kernel that comes with a given Linux distribution. The debate also includes whether it is inherently better to compile a monolithic kernel (in which everything is compiled into the kernel) or use a modular kernel. As with any debate, there are pros and cons to each method. On the one hand there are those who always (or almost always) build their own kernel, sometimes called "rolling their own." On the other hand, there are those who rarely or never roll their own kernel. There are those who always build monolithic kernels and others who use modular kernels.

Building a custom kernel has a few advantages. First is the capability to compile in only the exact drivers and options necessary for the computer to run. This is great for a server such as a firewall because the hardware rarely, if ever, changes. Another advantage to compiling a custom kernel, if you choose a monolithic kernel, is the capability to completely prevent some types of attacks against the computer. Although attacks against monolithic kernels are possible, they are less common than attacks against modular kernels. Further, when you roll your own kernel you're not confined to the kernel version used by the distribution. This enables you to use the latest and greatest kernel, which may include bug fixes for your hardware. Finally, with a custom kernel you can apply additional security enhancements to the kernel itself. One such enhancement is covered in Chapter 13, "Kernel Enhancements."

Building a custom kernel is not without its own set of pitfalls. After you roll your own kernel, you can no longer use the distribution's kernel updates. Actually, you can revert to the distribution's kernel and use the updates, but it's likely that the distribution uses an earlier version of the kernel that may reintroduce bugs that were fixed in your custom version. Using a stock kernel also makes it easier to obtain support from the vendor for kernel issues.

As alluded to earlier, I nearly always roll my own kernel for production server machines. The situations in which direct support is an absolute requirement are the only exceptions. These are few and far between. I believe the capability to customize the kernel to the computer and add greater security through additional patches far outweighs the need to use official kernel updates from the distribution.

Source and Destination Addressing Options

A packet's source address and destination address can both be specified in a firewall rule. Only packets with that specific source or destination address match the rule. Addresses may be a specific IP address, a fully qualified hostname, a network (domain) name or address, a limited range of addresses, or all-inclusive.

IP ADDRESSES EXPRESSED AS SYMBOLIC NAMES

Remote hosts and networks may be specified as fully qualified hostnames or network names. Using a hostname is especially convenient for firewall rules that apply to an individual remote host. This is particularly true for hosts whose IP address can change or that invisibly represent multiple IP addresses, such as ISP mail servers sometimes do. In general, however, remote addresses are better expressed in dotted quad notation because of the possibility of DNS host hostname spoofing.

Symbolic hostnames can't be resolved until DNS traffic is enabled in the firewall rules. If hostnames are used in the firewall rules, those rules must follow the rules enabling DNS traffic, unless /etc/hosts contains entries for the hostnames.

Furthermore, some distributions such as Red Hat use a boot environment that installs the firewall rules before starting the network or any other services, including BIND. If symbolic host and network names are used in the firewall script, those names must have entries in /etc/hosts to be resolved.

iptables allows the address to be suffixed with a bit mask specifier. The mask's value can range from 0 through 32, indicating the number of bits to mask. As discussed in Chapter 1, "Preliminary Concepts Underlying Packet-Filtering Firewalls," bits are counted from the left, or most significant, bit. This mask specifier indicates how many of the leading bits in the address must exactly match the IP address specified.

A mask of 32, /32, means that all the bits must match. The address must exactly match what you've defined in the rule. Specifying an address as 192.168.10.30 is the same as specifying the address as 192.168.10.30/32. The /32 mask is implied by default; you don't need to specify it.

An example using masking is to allow connections to a particular service to be made only between your machine and your ISP's server machines. Let's say that your ISP uses addresses in the range of 192.168.24.0 through 192.168.27.255 for its server address space. In this case, the address/mask pair would be 192.168.24/22. As shown in Figure 4.1, the first 22 bits of all addresses in this range are identical, so any address matching on the first 22 bits will match. Effectively, you are saying that you will allow connections to the service only when offered from machines in the address range 192.168.24.0 through 192.168.27.255.

A mask of 0, /0, means that no bits in the address are required to match. In other words, because no bits need to match, using /0 is the same as not specifying an address. Any unicast address matches. iptables has a built-in alias for 0.0.0.0/0, any/0. Note that any/0, whether implied or stated, does not include broadcast addresses.

FIGURE 4.1
The matching first 22 bits in the masked IP address range 192.168.24.0/22.

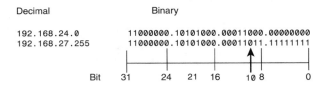

Initializing the Firewall

A firewall is implemented as a series of packet-filtering rules defined by options on the `iptables` command line. `iptables` is executed once for each individual rule. (Different firewalls can range from a dozen rules to hundreds.)

The `iptables` invocations should be made from an executable shell script, not directly from the command line. You should invoke the complete firewall shell script. Do not attempt to invoke specific `iptables` rules from the command line because this could cause your firewall to accept or drop packets inappropriately. When the chains are initialized and the default drop policy is enabled, all network services are blocked until acceptance filters are defined to allow the individual service.

Ideally, you should execute the shell script from the console. Only the brave execute the firewall shell script from either a remote machine or an X Window `xterm` session. Not only is remote network traffic blocked, but access to the local loopback interface used by X Windows is blocked until access to the interface is explicitly reenabled. Ideally, X Windows should not be running nor even installed on a firewall. It is a typical example of software that is not necessary and has been used as a means to exploit servers in the past.

As someone who manages Linux computers that are geographically hundreds to thousands of miles away, I can activate a firewall script only from a remote location. In these instances, it's advisable to do two things. First, change the default policy to **ACCEPT** for the first or first few executions of the firewall script. Do this to debug the syntax of the script itself, not the rules. After the script is syntactically correct, change that policy back to **DROP**.

A second and just as important tip for working with firewall scripts from remote locations is to create a cron job to stop the firewall at some point in the near future. Doing so will effectively allow you to enable the firewall and perform some testing but also enable you to get back into the computer if you lock yourself out through misplaced (or missing) rules. For example, when debugging a firewall script, I'll create a cron entry to disable the firewall every 2 minutes. I can then safely run the firewall script and find out whether I've locked out my

SSH session. If indeed I have locked myself out, I merely wait a few minutes for the firewall script to run and shut the firewall down, giving me the opportunity to fix the script and try again.

Furthermore, remember that firewall filters are applied in the order in which you've defined them on the **INPUT** or **OUTPUT** chain. The rules are appended to the end of their chain in the order in which you define them. The first matching rule wins. Because of this, firewall rules must be defined in a hierarchical order from most specific to more general rules.

Firewall initialization is used to cover a lot of ground, including defining global constants used in the shell script, enabling kernel support services (when necessary), clearing out any existing rules in the firewall chains, defining default policies for the **INPUT** and **OUTPUT** chains, reenabling the loopback interface for normal system operation, denying access from any specific hosts or networks you've decided to block, and defining some basic rules to protect against bad addresses and to protect certain services running on unprivileged ports.

Symbolic Constants Used in the Firewall Examples

A firewall shell script is easiest to read and maintain if symbolic constants are used for recurring names and addresses. The following constants either are used throughout the examples in this chapter or are universal constants defined in the networking standards. This example also includes the "shebang" interpreter line from above as a friendly reminder:

```
#!/bin/sh

IPT="/sbin/iptables"                    # Location of iptables on your system
INTERNET="eth0"                         # Internet-connected interface
LOOPBACK_INTERFACE="lo"                 # however your system names it
IPADDR="my.ip.address"                  # your IP address
MY_ISP="my.isp.address.range"           # ISP server & NOC address range
SUBNET_BASE="my.subnet.network"         # Your subnet's network address
SUBNET_BROADCAST="my.subnet.bcast"      # Your subnet's broadcast address
LOOPBACK="127.0.0.0/8"                  # reserved loopback address range
CLASS_A="10.0.0.0/8"                    # class A private networks
CLASS_B="172.16.0.0/12"                 # class B private networks
CLASS_C="192.168.0.0/16"                # class C private networks
CLASS_D_MULTICAST="224.0.0.0/4"         # class D multicast addresses
CLASS_E_RESERVED_NET="240.0.0.0/5"      # class E reserved addresses
BROADCAST_SRC="0.0.0.0"                 # broadcast source address
BROADCAST_DEST="255.255.255.255"        # broadcast destination address
PRIVPORTS="0:1023"                      # well-known, privileged port range
UNPRIVPORTS="1024:65535"                # unprivileged port range
```

Constants not listed here are defined in the context of the specific rules they are used with.

Enabling Kernel-Monitoring Support

Operating system support for various types of packet checking often overlaps with what the firewall can test for. When in doubt, aim for redundancy or defense in depth.

From the commands shown in the following lines, `icmp_echo_ignore_broadcasts` instructs the kernel to drop ICMP `echo-request` messages directed to broadcast or multicast addresses. (Another facility, `icmp_echo_ignore_all`, drops any incoming `echo-request` message. It should be noted that ISPs often rely on **ping** to help diagnose local network problems, and DHCP sometimes relies on `echo-request` to avoid address collision.)

```
# Enable broadcast echo Protection
echo 1 > /proc/sys/net/ipv4/icmp_echo_ignore_broadcasts
```

Source routing is rarely used legitimately today. Firewalls commonly drop all source-routed packets. These commands disable source routed packets:

```
# Disable Source Routed Packets
for f in /proc/sys/net/ipv4/conf/*/accept_source_route; do
    echo 0 > $f
done
```

TCP **SYN** cookies are a mechanism to attempt speedier detection of and recovery from **SYN** floods. This command enables **SYN** cookies:

```
# Enable TCP SYN Cookie Protection
echo 1 > /proc/sys/net/ipv4/tcp_syncookies
```

ICMP `redirect` messages are sent to hosts by their adjacent routers. Their purpose is to inform the host that a shorter path is available. That is, the host and both routers are on the same network, and the new router is the router to which the original would send the packet as its next hop.

Routers generate `redirect` messages for hosts; hosts do not. Hosts are required to honor `redirects` and add the new gateway to their route cache, except in the cases indicated in RFC 1122, "Requirements for Internet Hosts—Communication Layers," Section 3.2.2.2: "A Redirect message SHOULD be silently discarded if the new gateway address it specifies is not on the same connected (sub-) net through which the Redirect arrived [INTRO:2, Appendix A], or if the source of the Redirect is not the current first-hop gateway for the specified destination (see Section 3.3.1)." These commands enable redirects:

```
# Disable ICMP Redirect Acceptance
for f in /proc/sys/net/ipv4/conf/*/accept_redirects; do
    echo 0 > $f
done
```

```
# Don't send Redirect Messages
for f in /proc/sys/net/ipv4/conf/*/send_redirects; do
    echo 0 > $f
done
```

`rp_filter` attempts to implement source address validation as described in RFC 1812, "Requirements for IP Version 4 Routers," Section 5.3.8. In short, packets are silently dropped if their source address is such that the host's forwarding table would not route a packet with that destination address out the same interface on which the packet was received. According to RFC 1812, if implemented, routers should enable this feature by default. This form of address validation is often not enabled on routers, so these commands disable it:

```
# Drop Spoofed Packets coming in on an interface, which if replied to,
# would result in the reply going out a different interface.
for f in /proc/sys/net/ipv4/conf/*/rp_filter; do
    echo 1 > $f
done
```

`log_martians` logs packets received with impossible addresses, as defined in RFC 1812, Section 5.3.7. Impossible source addresses include multicast or broadcast addresses, addresses in the 0 and 127 networks, and the Class E reserved space. Impossible destination addresses include address 0.0.0.0, host 0 on any network, any host on the 127 network, and Class E addresses.

Currently, the Linux network code checks for the previously mentioned addresses. It does not check for private class addresses (nor could it do so without knowledge of the network a given interface was connected to). `log_martians` does not affect packet validity checking; it merely affects logging, which is set here:

```
# Log packets with impossible addresses.
for f in /proc/sys/net/ipv4/conf/*/log_martians; do
    echo 1 > $f
done
```

Removing Any Preexisting Rules

The first thing to do when defining a set of filtering rules is to remove any existing rules from their chains. Otherwise, any new rules that you define will be added to the end of existing rules. Packets could easily match a preexisting rule before reaching the point in the chain that you are defining from this point on.

Removal is called *flushing* the chain. Without an argument referring to a specific chain, the following command flushes all rules from all chains at once:

```
# Remove any existing rules from all chains
$IPT --flush
$IPT -t nat --flush
$IPT -t mangle --flush
```

The chains are empty, but any user-defined chains still exist. Flushing the chains does not affect the default policy state currently in effect.

The next step would be to delete any user-defined chains. They can be deleted with the following commands:

```
$IPT -X
$IPT -t nat -X
$IPT -t mangle -X
```

Resetting Default Policies and Stopping the Firewall

So far, the firewall has set some defaults that can be used regardless of the state of the Netfilter firewall. Before setting the default policies to DROP, I'll first reset the default policies to ACCEPT. This is useful for stopping the firewall completely, as you'll see shortly. These lines set the default policy:

```
# Reset the default policy
$IPT --policy INPUT    ACCEPT
$IPT --policy OUTPUT   ACCEPT
$IPT --policy FORWARD ACCEPT
$IPT -t nat --policy PREROUTING   ACCEPT
$IPT -t nat --policy OUTPUT ACCEPT
$IPT -t nat --policy POSTROUTING ACCEPT
$IPT -t mangle --policy PREROUTING ACCEPT
$IPT -t mangle --policy OUTPUT ACCEPT
```

Here's a final addition to what I term to be the beginning of the firewall script, namely the code to enable the firewall to be stopped easily. With this code placed below the previous code, when you call the script with an argument of "stop" the script will flush, clear, and reset the default policies and the firewall will effectively stop:

```
if [ "$1" = "stop" ]
then
echo "Firewall completely stopped!  WARNING: THIS HOST HAS NO FIREWALL RUNNING."
exit 0
fi
```

Enabling the `loopback` **Interface**

You need to enable unrestricted loopback traffic. This enables you to run any local network-based services that you choose—or that the system depends on—without having to worry about getting all the firewall rules specified.

Local services rely on the loopback network interface. After the system boots, the system's default policy is to accept all packets. Flushing any preexisting chains has no effect. However, if the firewall is being reinitialized and had previously used a deny-by-default policy, the drop policy would still be in effect. Without any acceptance firewall rules, the loopback interface would still be inaccessible.

Because the loopback interface is a local, internal interface, the firewall can allow loopback traffic immediately:

```
# Unlimited traffic on the loopback interface
$IPT -A INPUT  -i lo -j ACCEPT
$IPT -A OUTPUT -o lo -j ACCEPT
```

Defining the Default Policy

By default, you want the firewall to drop everything. The two available options for the built-in chains are **ACCEPT** and **DROP**. **REJECT** is not a legal policy in iptables. User-defined chains cannot be assigned default policies.

Using a default policy of **DROP**, unless a rule is defined to either explicitly allow or reject a matching packet, packets are silently dropped. What you more likely want is to silently drop unwanted incoming packets, but to reject outgoing packets and return an ICMP error message to the local sender. The difference for the end user is that, for example, if someone at a remote site attempts to connect to your web server, that person's browser hangs until his system returns a TCP timeout condition. There is no indication whether your site or your web server exists. On the other hand, if you attempt to connect to a remote web server, your browser receives an immediate error condition indicating that the operation isn't allowed:

```
# Set the default policy to drop
$IPT --policy INPUT   DROP
$IPT --policy OUTPUT  DROP
$IPT --policy FORWARD DROP
```

At this point, all network traffic other than local **loopback** traffic is blocked.

This firewall host has only one network interface. The **FORWARD** policy isn't necessary. Defining the **FORWARD** policy is a precaution for the future. For that reason, the following definitions should be added as well:

```
$IPT -t nat --policy PREROUTING  DROP
$IPT -t nat --policy OUTPUT DROP
$IPT -t nat --policy POSTROUTING DROP

$IPT -t mangle --policy PREROUTING DROP
$IPT -t mangle --policy OUTPUT DROP
```

DEFAULT POLICY RULES AND THE FIRST MATCHING RULE WINS

The default policies appear to be exceptions to the first-matching-rule-wins scenario. The default policy commands are not position dependent. They aren't rules, per se. A chain's default policy is applied after a packet has been compared to each rule on the chain without a match.

The default policies are defined first in the script to define the default packet disposition before any rules to the contrary are defined. If the policy commands were executed at the end of the script, and if the firewall script contained a syntax error causing it to exit prematurely, the default accept-everything policy could be in effect. If a packet didn't match a rule (and rules are usually accept rules in a deny-everything-by-default firewall), the packet would fall off the end of the chain and be accepted by default. The firewall rules would not be accomplishing anything useful.

Stealth Scans and TCP State Flags

Testing for common forms of TCP stealth scans is possible because iptables gives access to all the TCP state flags. The following rules block common stealth scan probes. None of the TCP state combinations tested for are legal combinations. In addition, the unclean match is used first in order to match packets with bad headers and other problems. This module has been experimental for a while, so use with caution. Should you see an error when attempting to load this module, it may not be available with your kernel version. In such an event, comment out the unclean match line by using a single pound sign "#" in front of the line loading the unclean module.

To reiterate statements made in Chapter 3, the first list of state flags lists the bits to be tested. Out of those bits, the second list of state flags lists the bits that must be set to match the test:

```
# Unclean
$IPT -A INPUT -m unclean -j DROP
# All of the bits are cleared
$IPT -A INPUT -p tcp --tcp-flags ALL NONE -j DROP
# SYN and FIN are both set
$IPT -A INPUT -p tcp --tcp-flags SYN,FIN SYN,FIN -j DROP
# SYN and RST are both set
$IPT -A INPUT -p tcp --tcp-flags SYN,RST SYN,RST -j DROP
# FIN and RST are both set
```

```
$IPT -A INPUT -p tcp --tcp-flags FIN,RST FIN,RST -j DROP
# FIN is the only bit set, without the expected accompanying ACK
$IPT -A INPUT -p tcp --tcp-flags ACK,FIN FIN -j DROP
# PSH is the only bit set, without the expected accompanying ACK
$IPT -A INPUT -p tcp --tcp-flags ACK,PSH PSH -j DROP
# URG is the only bit set, without the expected accompanying ACK
$IPT -A INPUT -p tcp --tcp-flags ACK,URG URG -j DROP
```

The `ACK,FIN FIN` test implicitly includes `xmastree` packets that contain `FIN-PSH`, `FIN-URG`, and `FIN-PSH-URG` as well.

Using Connection State to Bypass Rule Checking

Specifying the state match for previously initiated and accepted exchanges enables you to bypass the firewall tests for the ongoing exchange. The initial client request remains controlled by the service's specific filters, however.

Notice that both the `INPUT` and the `OUTPUT` filters are necessary to bypass the rules in both directions. A connection isn't treated as a two-way exchange by the state module, and a symmetric dynamic rule is not generated.

Because the state module can require more RAM than some Linux firewall machines have, the firewall example developed in this chapter provides the rules for both alternatives, with and without the state module.

Remember that use of the state module allows you to bypass the standard firewall rules for ongoing exchanges under normal operation. The standard rules must be included, however, if the state table entry for a connection is recycled or times out.

INCLUDING BOTH STATIC AND DYNAMIC FIREWALL RULES

Resource limits in terms of scalability and state table timeouts can require that both the static and the dynamic rules be used. The top limit is a selling point with large commercial firewalls.

The scalability issue comes up in large firewalls designed to handle 50,000–100,000 simultaneous connections—that's a lot of state. System resources run out at some point, and connection tracking can't be done. Either the new connection has to be dropped or the software has to fall back to stateless mode.

There's also the issue of timeouts. Connection state isn't kept forever. Slow and quiescent connections can have their state information easily cleaned out to make room for other more active connections. When a packet comes along later, the state information has to be rebuilt. In the meantime, the packet flow has to fall back to stateless mode while the transport stack looks up the connection information and informs the state module that the packet is indeed part of an established exchange:

```
if [ "$CONNECTION_TRACKING" = "1" ]; then
    $IPT -A INPUT  -m state --state ESTABLISHED,RELATED -j ACCEPT
    $IPT -A OUTPUT -m state --state ESTABLISHED,RELATED -j ACCEPT
    # Using the state module alone, INVALID will break protocols that use
    # bi-directional connections or multiple connections or exchanges,
    # unless an ALG is provided for the protocol. At this time, FTP and
    # IRC are the only protocols with ALG support.

    $IPT -A INPUT -m state --state INVALID -j LOG \
            --log-prefix "INVALID input: "
    $IPT -A INPUT -m state --state INVALID -j DROP

    $IPT -A OUTPUT -m state --state INVALID -j LOG \
            --log-prefix "INVALID output: "
    $IPT -A OUTPUT -m state --state INVALID -j DROP

fi
```

Source Address Spoofing and Other Bad Addresses

This section establishes some INPUT chain filters based on source and destination addresses. These addresses will never be seen in a legitimate incoming packet from the Internet.

At the packet-filtering level, one of the few cases of source address spoofing that you can identify with certainty as a forgery is your own IP address. This rule drops incoming packets claiming to be from you:

```
# Refuse spoofed packets pretending to be from
# the external interface's IP address
$IPT -A INPUT  -i $INTERNET -s $IPADDR -j DROP
```

There is no need to block outgoing packets destined to yourself. They won't return, claiming to be from you and appearing to be spoofed. Remember, if you send packets to your own external interface, those packets arrive on the loopback interface's input queue, not on the external interface's input queue. Packets containing your address as the source address never arrive on the external interface, even if you send packets to the external interface.

FIREWALL LOGGING

The -j LOG target enables logging for packets matching the rule. When a packet matches the rule, the event is logged in /var/log/messages, or wherever you've defined messages of the specified priority to be logged.

As explained in Chapter 1 and Chapter 2, private IP addresses are set aside in each of the Class A, B, and C address ranges for use in private LANs. They are not intended for use on the Internet. Routers are not supposed to route packets with private source addresses. Nevertheless, some routers do forward packets containing private source addresses.

Additionally, if someone on your ISP's subnet (that is, on your side of the router that you share) is leaking packets with private IP addresses, you'll see them even if the router doesn't forward them. Machines on your own LAN could also leak private addresses if your NAT or proxy configuration is set up incorrectly.

The next three sets of rules disallow incoming packets containing source addresses from any of the Class A, B, or C private network addresses. None of these packets should be seen on a public network:

```
# Refuse packets claiming to be from a Class A private network
$IPT -A INPUT  -i $INTERNET -s $CLASS_A -j DROP

# Refuse packets claiming to be from a Class B private network
$IPT -A INPUT  -i $INTERNET -s $CLASS_B -j DROP

# Refuse packets claiming to be from a Class C private network
$IPT -A INPUT  -i $INTERNET -s $CLASS_C -j DROP
```

The next rule disallows packets with a source address in the loopback network:

```
# Refuse packets claiming to be from the loopback interface
$IPT -A INPUT  -i $INTERNET -s $LOOPBACK -j DROP
```

Because loopback addresses are assigned to an internal, local software interface, any packet claiming to be from such an address is intentionally forged.

As with addresses set aside for use in private LANs, routers are not supposed to forward packets originating from the loopback address range. A router cannot forward a packet with a loopback destination address.

The next two rules primarily serve to log matching packets. The firewall's default policy is to deny everything. As such, broadcast addresses are dropped by default and must be explicitly enabled if they are wanted:

```
# Refuse malformed broadcast packets
$IPT -A INPUT  -i $INTERNET -s $BROADCAST_DEST -j LOG
$IPT -A INPUT  -i $INTERNET -s $BROADCAST_DEST -j DROP

$IPT -A INPUT  -i $INTERNET -d $BROADCAST_SRC  -j LOG
$IPT -A INPUT  -i $INTERNET -d $BROADCAST_SRC  -j DROP
```

The first pair of rules logs and denies any packet claiming to come from 255.255.255.255, the address reserved as the broadcast destination address. A packet will never legitimately originate from address 255.255.255.255.

The second pair of rules logs and denies any packet directed to destination address 0.0.0.0, the address reserved as a broadcast source address. Such a packet is not a mistake; it is a specific probe intended to identify a UNIX machine running network software derived from BSD. Because most UNIX operating system network code is derived from BSD, this probe is effectively intended to identify machines running UNIX.

CLARIFICATION ON THE MEANING OF IP ADDRESS 0.0.0.0

Address 0.0.0.0 is reserved for use as a broadcast source address. The Netfilter convention of specifying a match on any address, any/0, 0.0.0.0/0, or 0.0.0.0/0.0.0.0, doesn't match the broadcast source address. The reason is that a broadcast packet has a bit set in the Layer 2 frame header indicating that it's a broadcast packet destined for all interfaces on the network, rather than a point-to-point, unicast packet destined for a particular destination. Broadcast packets are handled differently than nonbroadcast packets. There is no legitimate nonbroadcast IP address 0.0.0.0.

The next two rules block two forms of directed broadcasts:

```
# Refuse directed broadcasts
# Used to map networks and in Denial of Service attacks
$IPT -A INPUT -i $INTERNET -d $SUBNET_BASE -j DROP
$IPT -A INPUT -i $INTERNET -d $SUBNET_BROADCAST -j DROP
```

With the deny-by-default policy and the firewall rules explicitly accepting packets based in part by matching on destination address, neither of these directed broadcast messages will be accepted by the firewall. These rules become more critical in larger setups in which the LAN uses real-world addresses.

With the use of variable-length network prefixes, a site's network and host fields may or may not fall on a byte boundary. For the sake of simplicity, the **SUBNET_BASE** is your network address, such as 192.168.1.0. The **SUBNET_BROADCAST** is your network's broadcast address, as in 192.168.1.255.

Just as with directed broadcast messages, limited broadcasts, confined to your local network segment, are likewise not accepted with the deny-by-default policy and the firewall rules explicitly accepting packets based in part by matching on destination address. Again, the following rule becomes more critical in larger setups in which the LAN uses real-world addresses:

```
# Refuse limited broadcasts
$IPT -A INPUT -i $INTERNET -d $BROADCAST_DEST -j DROP
```

It should be noted that an exception must be made in later chapters for DHCP clients. Broadcast source and destination addresses are used between the DHCP client and server ports initially.

Multicast addresses are legal only as destination addresses. The next rule drops spoofed multicast network packets:

```
# Refuse Class D multicast addresses
# illegal as a source address
$IPT -A INPUT -i $INTERNET -s $CLASS_D_MULTICAST -j DROP
```

Legitimate multicast packets are always UDP packets. As such, multicast messages are sent point-to-point, just as any other UDP message is. The difference between unicast and multicast packets is the class of destination address used (and the protocol flag carried in the Ethernet header). The next rule denies multicast packets carrying a non-UDP protocol:

```
$IPT -A INPUT -i $INTERNET -p ! udp -d $CLASS_D_MULTICAST -j DROP
```

Multicast functionality is a configurable option when you compile the kernel, and your network interface card can be initialized to recognize multicast addresses. The functionality is enabled by default in the default kernel from many newer distributions of Linux. You might want to enable these addresses if you subscribe to a network conferencing service that provides multicast audio and video broadcasts. (Multicast is also sometimes used on the local network for global resource discovery, such as with DHCP or routing.)

You won't generally see multicast destination addresses unless you've registered yourself as a recipient. Multicast packets are sent to multiple, but specific, targets by prior arrangement. I have seen multicast packets sent out from machines on my ISP's local subnet, however. The default policy drops multicast packets, even if you have registered as a recipient. You have to define a rule to accept the multicast address. The next rule allows incoming multicast packets for the sake of completeness:

```
$IPT -A INPUT  -i $INTERNET -p udp -d $CLASS_D_MULTICAST -j ACCEPT
```

Multicast registration and routing is a complicated process managed by its own IP layer-control protocol, the Internet Group Management Protocol (IGMP, protocol 2). For more information on multicast communication, refer to the "Multicast over TCP/IP HOWTO" at http://www.tldp.org/HOWTO/Multicast-HOWTO.html. Additional resources include RFC 1458, "Requirements for Multicast Protocols"; RFC 1112, "Host Extensions for IP Multicasting" (updated by RFC 2236, "Internet Group Management Protocol Version 2"); and RFC 2588, "IP Multicast and Firewalls."

Class D IP addresses range from 224.0.0.0 to 239.255.255.255. The CLASS_D_MULTICAST constant, 224.0.0.0/4, is defined to match on the first 4 bits of the address. As shown in Figure 4.2, in binary, the decimal values 224 (11100000B) to 239 (11101111B) are identical through the first 4 bits (1110B).

FIGURE 4.2
The matching first 4 bits in the masked Class D multicast address range 224.0.0.0/4.

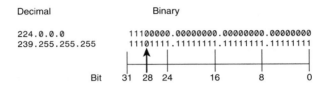

The next rule in this section drops packets claiming to be from a Class E reserved network:

```
# Refuse Class E reserved IP addresses
$IPT -A INPUT  -i $INTERNET -s $CLASS_E_RESERVED_NET -j DROP
```

Class E IP addresses range from 240.0.0.0 to 247.255.255.255. The CLASS_E_RESERVED_NET constant, 240.0.0.0/5, is defined to match on the first 5 bits of the address. As shown in Figure 4.3, in binary, the decimal values 240 (11110000B) to 247 (11110111B) are identical through the first 5 bits (11110B).

FIGURE 4.3
The matching first 5 bits in the masked Class E reserved address range 240.0.0.0/5.

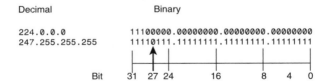

The IANA ultimately manages the allocation and registration of the world's IP address space. For more information on IP address assignments, see http://www.iana.org/_assignments/ipv4-address-space. Some blocks of addresses are defined as reserved by the IANA. These addresses should not appear on the public Internet.

Out of the entire set of the IANA's reserved address blocks, the 0.0.0.0/8, Link Local Network, and Test Net spaces are blocks that will not be assigned as public addresses. The remaining reserved blocks are not routable until assigned. In the meantime, they can be used as source addresses in denial-of-service attacks. The firewall could block the remaining reserved blocks as source addresses, but it turns out to be impractical for most sites because the IANA has been actively allocating these blocks since year 2000. The following lines drop packets from those sources:

```
# Refuse addresses defined as reserved by the IANA
# 0.*.*.*            - Can't be blocked unilaterally with DHCP
# 169.254.0.0/16     - Link Local Networks
# 192.0.2.0/24       - TEST-NET

$IPT -A INPUT -i $INTERNET -s 0.0.0.0/8 -j DROP
$IPT -A INPUT -i $INTERNET -s 169.254.0.0/16 -j DROP
$IPT -A INPUT -i $INTERNET -s 192.0.2.0/24 -j DROP
```

Protecting Services on Assigned Unprivileged Ports

Services intended for local or private use, in particular, often run on unprivileged ports. For TCP-based services, a connection attempt to one of these services can be distinguished from an ongoing connection with a client using one of these unprivileged ports through the state of the SYN and ACK bits. Blocking connection requests is sufficient. UDP-based services must simply be blocked unless the **state** module is used.

You should block incoming connection attempts to these ports for your own security protection. You want to block outgoing connection attempts to protect yourself and others from mistakes on your end and to log potential internal security problems. It's safer to block these ports across the board and route related traffic on an exceptional, case-by-case basis.

OFFICIAL SERVICE PORT NUMBER ASSIGNMENTS

Port numbers are assigned and registered by the IANA. The information was originally maintained as RFC 1700, "Assigned Numbers." That RFC is now obsolete. The official information is dynamically maintained by the IANA at http://www.iana.org/assignments/port-numbers.

What kinds of mistakes might you need protection from? The worst mistake is offering dangerous services to the world, whether inadvertently or intentionally. A common mistake is running local network services that leak out to the Internet and bother other people. Another is allowing questionable outgoing traffic, such as port scans, whether this traffic is generated by accident or intentionally is sent out by someone on your machine. A deny-everything-by-default firewall policy protects you from many mistakes of these types.

THE PROBLEM WITH PORT SCANS

Port scans are not harmful in themselves. They're generated by network-analysis tools. The problem with port scans today is that they are usually generated by people with less-than-honorable intentions. They are "analyzing" your network, not their own. Unfortunately, this leaves the merely curious looking guilty as well.

A deny-everything-by-default firewall policy enables you to run many private services behind the firewall without undue risk. These services must explicitly be allowed through the firewall to be accessible to remote hosts. This generalization is only an approximation of reality, however. Although TCP services on privileged ports are reasonably safe from all but a skilled and determined hacker, UDP services are inherently less secure, and some services are assigned to run on unprivileged ports. RPC services, usually run over UDP, are even more problematic. RPC-based services are bound to some port, often an unprivileged port. The `portmap` daemon maps between the RPC service number and the actual port number. A port scan can show where these RPC-based services are bound without going through the `portmap` daemon. Luckily, the use of `portmap` is becoming less and less common, so this isn't as much of a concern as it was a number of years ago.

Common Local TCP Services Assigned to Unprivileged Ports

Some services, usually LAN services, are offered through an officially registered, well-known unprivileged port. Additionally, some services, such as FTP and IRC, use more complex communication protocols that don't lend themselves well to packet filtering. The rules described in the following sections disallow local or remote client programs from initiating a connection to one of these ports.

FTP is a good example of how the deny-by-default policy isn't always enough to cover all the possible cases. The FTP protocol is covered later in this chapter. For now, the important idea is that FTP allows connections between two unprivileged ports. Because some services listen on registered unprivileged ports, and because the incoming connection request to these services is originating from an unprivileged client port, the rules allowing FTP can inadvertently allow incoming connections to these other local services as well. This situation is also an example of how firewall rules are logically hierarchical and order-dependent. The rules explicitly protecting a private, local service running on an unprivileged port must precede the FTP rules allowing access to the entire unprivileged port range.

As a result, some of these rules appear to be redundant and will be redundant for some people. For other people running other services, the following rules are necessary to protect private services running on local unprivileged ports.

DISALLOWING CONNECTIONS TO COMMON TCP UNPRIVILEGED SERVER PORTS

Connections to remote X Window servers should be made over SSH, which automatically supports X Window connections. By specifying the `--syn` flag, indicating the SYN bit, only connection establishment to the server port is blocked. Other connections initiated using the port as a client port are not affected.

X Window port assignment begins at port **6000** with the first running server. If additional servers are run, each is assigned to the next incremental port. As a small site, you'll probably run a single X server, so your server will listen only on port **6000**. Port **6063** is typically the highest assigned port, allowing 64 separate X Window managers running on a single machine, although ranges up to **6255** and **6999** are also seen sometimes:

```
XWINDOW_PORTS="6000:6063"              # (TCP) X Window
```

The first rule ensures that no outgoing connection attempts to remote X Window managers are made from your machine:

```
# X Window connection establishment
$IPT -A OUTPUT -o $INTERNET -p tcp --syn \
        --destination-port $XWINDOW_PORTS -j REJECT
```

The next rule blocks incoming connection attempts to your X Window manager. Local connections are not affected because local connections are made over the loopback interface:

```
# X Window: incoming connection attempt
$IPT -A INPUT -i $INTERNET -p tcp --syn \
        --destination-port $XWINDOW_PORTS -j DROP
```

The remaining TCP-based services can be blocked with a single rule by use of the `multiport` match extension. Blocking incoming connections isn't necessary if the machine isn't running the service, but it's safer in the long run, in case you later decide to run the service locally.

NFS usually binds to UDP port **2049** but can use TCP. You shouldn't be running NFS on a firewall machine, but if you are, external access is denied.

Connections to Open Window managers should not be allowed. Linux is not distributed with the Open Window manager. Incoming connections to port **2000** don't need to be blocked. (This will not be the case later, when the firewall's FORWARD rules are protecting other local hosts.)

Attempts to connect to remote SOCKS servers are fairly common and often involve intrusion exploits. SOCKS uses port **1080**.

`squid` is a web cache and proxy server. `squid` uses port **3128** by default but can be configured to use a different port.

The following rule blocks local clients from initiating a connection request to a remote NFS server, Open Window manager, SOCKS proxy server, or squid web cache server:

```
NFS_PORT="2049"                          # (TCP) NFS
SOCKS_PORT="1080"                        # (TCP) socks
OPENWINDOWS_PORT="2000"                  # (TCP) OpenWindows
SQUID_PORT="3128"                        # (TCP) squid

# Establishing a connection over TCP to NFS, OpenWindows, SOCKS or squid
$IPT -A OUTPUT -o $INTERNET -p tcp \
        -m multiport --destination-port \
        $NFS_PORT,$OPENWINDWS_PORT,$SOCKS_PORT,$SQUID_PORT \
        --syn -j REJECT

$IPT -A INPUT -i $INTERNET -p tcp \
        -m multiport --destination-port \
        $NFS_PORT,$OPENWINDWS_PORT,$SOCKS_PORT,$SQUID_PORT \
        --syn -j DROP
```

Common Local UDP Services Assigned to Unprivileged Ports

TCP protocol rules can be handled more precisely than UDP protocol rules because of TCP's connection establishment protocol. As a datagram service, UDP doesn't have a connection state associated with it. Unless the state module is used, access to UDP services should simply be blocked. Explicit exceptions are made to accommodate DNS and any of the few other UDP-based Internet services you might use. Fortunately, the common UDP Internet services are often the type used between a client and a specific server. The filtering rules can often allow exchanges with one specific remote host.

NFS is the main UNIX UDP service to be concerned with and also is one of the most frequently exploited. NFS runs on unprivileged port 2049. Unlike the previous TCP-based services, NFS is primarily a UDP-based service. It can be configured to run as a TCP-based service, but usually it isn't.

Associated with NFS is the RPC lock daemon, lockd, for NFS. lockd runs on UDP port 4045:

```
NFS_PORT="2049"                          # NFS
LOCKD_PORT="4045"                        # RPC lockd for NFS

# NFS and lockd
if [ "$CONNECTION_TRACKING" = "1" ]; then
    $IPT -A OUTPUT -o $INTERNET -p udp \
            -m multiport --destination-port $NFS_PORT,$LOCKD_PORT \
            -m state --state NEW -j REJECT
```

```
    $IPT -A INPUT -i $INTERNET -p udp \
        -m multiport --destination-port $NFS_PORT,$LOCKD_PORT \
        -m state --state NEW -j DROP
else
    $IPT -A OUTPUT -o $INTERNET -p udp \
        -m multiport --destination-port $NFS_PORT,$LOCKD_PORT \
        -j REJECT

    $IPT -A INPUT -i $INTERNET -p udp \
        -m multiport --destination-port $NFS_PORT,$LOCKD_PORT \
        -j DROP
fi
```

THE TCP AND UDP SERVICE PROTOCOL TABLES

The remainder of this chapter is devoted to defining rules to allow access to specific services. Client/server communication, for both TCP- and UDP-based services, involves some kind of two-way communication using a protocol specific to the service. As such, access rules are always represented as an I/O pair. The client program makes a query, and the server sends a response. Rules for a given service are categorized as client rules or server rules. The client category represents the communication required for your local clients to access remote servers. The server category represents the communication required for remote clients to access the services hosted from your machines.

The application messages are encapsulated in either TCP or UDP transport protocol messages. Because each service uses an application protocol specific to itself, the particular characteristics of the TCP or UDP exchange are, to some extent, unique to the given service.

The exchange between client and server is explicitly described by the firewall rules. Part of the purpose of firewall rules is to ensure protocol integrity at the packet level. Firewall rules, expressed in iptables syntax, are not especially human-readable, however. In each of the following sections, the service protocol at the packet-filtering level is presented as a table of state information, followed by the iptables rules expressing those states.

Each row in the table lists a packet type involved in the service exchange. A firewall rule is defined for each individual packet type. The table is divided into columns:

- *Description* contains a brief description of whether the packet is originating from the client or the server, and the packet's purpose.

- *Protocol* is the transport protocol in use, TCP or UDP, or the IP protocol's control messages, ICMP.

- *Remote Address* is the legal address, or range of addresses, that the packet can contain in the remote address field.

- *Remote Port* is the legal port, or range of ports, that the packet can contain in the remote port field.

- *In/Out* describes the packet's direction—that is, whether it is coming into the system from a remote location or whether it is going out from the system to a remote location.
- *Local Address* is the legal address, or range of addresses, that the packet can contain in the local address field.
- *Local Port* is the legal port, or range of ports, that the packet can contain in the local port field.
- TCP protocol packets contain a final column, *TCP Flag*, defining the legal SYN–ACK states that the packet may have.

The table describes packets as either incoming or outgoing. Addresses and ports are described as either remote or local, relative to your machine's network interface. Notice that, for incoming packets, Remote Address and Port refer to the source fields in the IP packet header; Local Address and Port refer to the destination fields in the IP packet header. For outgoing packets, Remote Address and Port refer to the destination fields in the IP packet header; Local Address and Port refer to the source fields in the IP packet header.

Finally, in the few instances when the service protocol involves ICMP messages, notice that the IP Network-layer ICMP packets are not associated with the concept of a source or destination port, as is the case for Transport-layer TCP or UDP packets. Instead, ICMP packets use the concept of a control or status message type. ICMP messages are not sent to programs bound to particular service ports. Instead, ICMP messages are sent from one computer to another. (The ICMP packet contains a copy of at least some of the original packet that resulted in the error message. The receiving host identifies the process that the error refers to by examining the packet carried in the ICMP packet's data area.) Consequently, the few ICMP packet entries presented in the tables use the source port column to contain the message type. For incoming ICMP packets, the source port column is the Remote Port column. For outgoing ICMP packets, the source port column is the Local Port column.

Enabling Basic, Required Internet Services

Only one service is truly required: the domain name service (DNS). DNS translates between hostnames and their associated IP addresses. You generally can't locate a remote host without DNS unless the host is defined locally.

Allowing DNS (UDP/TCP Port 53)

DNS uses a communication protocol that relies on both UDP and TCP. Connection modes include regular client-to-server connections, peer-to-peer traffic between forwarding servers and full servers, and primary and secondary name server connections.

Query lookup requests are normally done over UDP, both for client-to-server lookups and for peer-to-peer server lookups. The UDP communication can fail for a lookup if the information being returned is too large to fit in a single UDP DNS packet. The server sets a flag bit in the DNS message header indicating that the data is truncated. In this case, the protocol allows for a retry over TCP. Figure 4.4 shows the relationship between UDP and TCP during a DNS lookup. In practice, TCP isn't normally needed for queries. TCP is conventionally used for administrative zone transfers between primary and secondary name servers.

FIGURE 4.4
DNS client-to-server lookup.

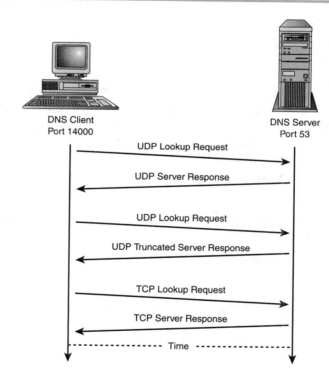

Zone transfers are the transfer of a name server's complete information about a network, or the piece (zone) of a network, that the server is authoritative for (that is, the official server). The authoritative name server is referred to as the primary name server. Secondary, or backup, name servers can periodically request zone transfers from their primary to keep their DNS caches up-to-date.

For example, one of your ISP's name servers is the primary, authoritative server for the ISP's address space. ISPs often have multiple DNS servers to balance the load, as well as for backup redundancy. The other name servers are secondary name servers, refreshing their information from the master copy on the primary server.

Zone transfers require careful access control between the primary and the secondary servers. A small system isn't likely to be an authoritative name server for a public domain's name space, nor is it likely to be a public backup server for that information. Larger sites could easily host both primary and secondary servers. Care must be taken that zone transfers are allowed only between these hosts. Numerous attacks have been successful because the attacker was able to grab a copy of an entire DNS zone and learn about the network topology in order to direct the attack at the most valuable assets.

Table 4.1 lists the complete DNS protocol the firewall rules account for.

TABLE 4.1
DNS Protocol

DESCRIPTION	PROTOCOL	REMOTE ADDRESS	REMOTE PORT	IN/OUT	LOCAL ADDRESS	LOCAL PORT	TCP FLAG
Local client query	UDP	NAMESERVER	53	Out	IPADDR	1024:65535	—
Remote server response	UDP	NAMESERVER	53	In	IPADDR	1024:65535	—
Local client query	TCP	NAMESERVER	53	Out	IPADDR	1024:65535	Any
Remote server response	TCP	NAMESERVER	53	In	IPADDR	1024:65535	ACK
Local server query	UDP	NAMESERVER	53	Out	IPADDR	53	—
Remote server response	UDP	NAMESERVER	53	In	IPADDR	53	—
Local zone transfer request	TCP	Primary	53	Out	IPADDR	1024:65535	Any
Remote zone transfer request	TCP	Primary	53	In	IPADDR	1024:65535	ACK

TABLE 4.1
DNS Protocol (continued)

DESCRIPTION	PROTOCOL	REMOTE ADDRESS	REMOTE PORT	IN/OUT	LOCAL ADDRESS	LOCAL PORT	TCP FLAG
Remote client query	UDP	DNS client	1024:65535	In	IPADDR	53	—
Local server response	UDP	DNS client	1024:65535	Out	IPADDR	53	—
Remote client query	TCP	DNS client	1024:65535	In	IPADDR	53	Any
Local server response	UDP	DNS client	53	Out	IPADDR	53	—
Remote zone transfer request	TCP	Secondary	1024:65535	In	IPADDR	53	Any
Local zone transfer response	TCP	Secondary	1024:65535	Out	IPADDR	53	ACK

ALLOWING DNS LOOKUPS AS A CLIENT

The DNS resolver client isn't a specific program. The client is incorporated into the network library code used by network programs. When a hostname requires a lookup, the resolver requests the lookup from a DNS server. Most computers are configured only as a DNS client. The server runs on a remote machine. For a home user, the name server is usually a machine owned by your ISP.

As a client, the assumption is that your machine is not running a local DNS server; if it is, you should ensure that you need to actually run the name server. There's no need to run extra services! Each client lookup goes through the resolver and is then sent to one of the remote name servers configured in /etc/resolv.conf. In general, it's better to install the client rules even if a local server is used. You'll avoid some confusing problems that could otherwise crop up at some point.

These rules must be installed in the firewall tables before any other rules could successfully specify a remote host by name, rather than by IP address, unless the remote host had an entry in the local /etc/hosts file.

DNS sends a lookup request as a UDP datagram:

```
NAMESERVER ="my.name.server"              # (TCP/UDP) DNS

if [ "$CONNECTION_TRACKING" = "1" ]; then
```

```
    $IPT -A OUTPUT -o $INTERNET -p udp \
            -s $IPADDR --sport $UNPRIVPORTS \
            -d $NAMESERVER --dport 53 \
            -m state --state NEW -j ACCEPT
fi

$IPT -A OUTPUT -o $INTERNET -p udp \
        -s $IPADDR --sport $UNPRIVPORTS \
        -d $NAMESERVER --dport 53 -j ACCEPT

$IPT -A INPUT  -i $INTERNET -p udp \
        -s $NAMESERVER --sport 53 \
        -d $IPADDR --dport $UNPRIVPORTS -j ACCEPT
```

If an error occurs because the returned data is too large to fit in a UDP datagram, the DNS client retries using a TCP connection.

The next two rules are included for the rare occasion when the lookup response won't fit in a DNS UDP datagram. They won't be used in normal, day-to-day operations. You could run your system without problems for months on end without the TCP rules. Unfortunately, every so often your DNS lookups hang without these rules. More typically, these rules are used by a secondary name server requesting a zone transfer from its primary name server:

```
if [ "$CONNECTION_TRACKING" = "1" ]; then
    $IPT -A OUTPUT -o $INTERNET -p tcp \
            -s $IPADDR --sport $UNPRIVPORTS \
            -d $NAMESERVER --dport 53 \
            -m state --state NEW -j ACCEPT
fi

$IPT -A OUTPUT -o $INTERNET -p tcp \
        -s $IPADDR --sport $UNPRIVPORTS \
        -d $NAMESERVER --dport 53 -j ACCEPT

$IPT -A INPUT -i $INTERNET -p tcp ! --syn \
        -s $NAMESERVER --sport 53 \
        -d $IPADDR --dport $UNPRIVPORTS -j ACCEPT
```

ALLOWING YOUR DNS LOOKUPS AS A FORWARDING SERVER

Configuring a local forwarding name server can be a big performance gain. As shown in Figure 4.5, when BIND is configured as a caching and forwarding name server, it functions both as a local server and as a client to a remote DNS server. The difference between a direct client-to-server exchange and a forwarded server-to-server exchange is in the source and destination ports used. Instead of initiating an exchange from an unprivileged port, BIND initiates the exchange from its own DNS port 53. (The query source port is now configurable. In newer versions of **BIND**, the local server makes its request from an unprivileged port, by default.) A second difference is that forwarding server lookups of this type are always done over UDP. (If the response is too large to fit in a UDP DNS packet, the local server must revert to standard client/server behavior to initiate the TCP request.)

FIGURE 4.5
A DNS forwarding server lookup.

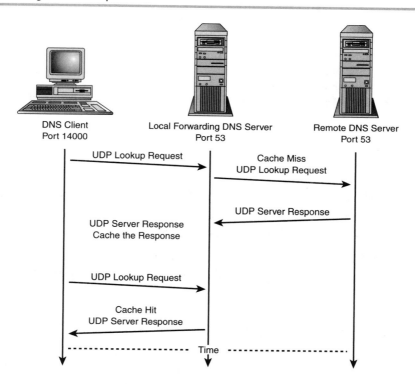

Local client requests are sent to the local DNS server. The first time, **BIND** won't have the lookup information, so it forwards the request to a remote name server. **BIND** caches the returned information and passes it on to the client. The next time the same information is requested, **BIND** finds it in its local cache (according to the record's time to live [TTL]) and doesn't do a remote request:

```
if [ "$CONNECTION_TRACKING" = "1" ]; then
    $IPT -A OUTPUT -o $INTERNET -p udp \
            -s $IPADDR --sport 53 \
            -d $NAMESERVER --dport 53 \
            -m state --state NEW -j ACCEPT
fi

$IPT -A OUTPUT -o $INTERNET -p udp \
        -s $IPADDR --sport 53 \
        -d $NAMESERVER --dport 53 -j ACCEPT

$IPT -A INPUT  -i $INTERNET -p udp \
        -s $NAMESERVER --sport 53 \
        -d $IPADDR --dport 53 -j ACCEPT
```

If the lookup fails because of UDP packet size, the server will fall back to a TCP client-mode lookup. If the lookup fails because the remote server doesn't have the information, the local server will query the root cache server. Because of this, the client rules would need to allow DNS traffic to any server, rather than to the specific servers listed in the local configuration.

The alternative **BIND** configuration is to configure it not only as a forwarding server, but also as a slave to the remote servers specified in the **BIND** configuration file, `named.conf`. As a slave, the general client UDP rules aren't required.

Filtering the AUTH User Identification Service (TCP Port 113)

The **AUTH**, or `identd`, user identification service is sometimes used when sending mail or posting a Usenet article. Some FTP sites are also configured to require a resolvable **AUTH** lookup. For logging purposes, the server initiates an **AUTH** request back to your machine to get the account name of the user who initiated the mail or news connection. Table 4.2 lists the complete client/server connection protocol for the **AUTH** service. It's becoming much less common for this service to be required though, and therefore I wouldn't recommend running it on your servers.

TABLE 4.2
identd Protocol

DESCRIPTION	PROTOCOL	REMOTE ADDRESS	REMOTE PORT	IN/OUT	LOCAL ADDRESS	LOCAL PORT	TCP FLAG
Local client query	TCP	ANYWHERE	113	Out	IPADDR	1024:65535	Any
Remote server response	TCP	ANYWHERE	113	In	IPADDR	1024:65535	ACK
Remote client query	TCP	ANYWHERE	1024:65535	In	IPADDR	113	Any
Local server response	TCP	ANYWHERE	1024:65535	Out	IPADDR	113	ACK

ALLOWING YOUR OUTGOING AUTH REQUESTS AS A CLIENT

Your machine would act as an AUTH client if you ran a mail or FTP server. Here are rules to allow your server to act as an AUTH client, should you choose to do so:

```
if [ "$CONNECTION_TRACKING" = "1" ]; then
    $IPT -A OUTPUT -o $INTERNET -p tcp \
            -s $IPADDR --sport $UNPRIVPORTS \
            --dport 113 -m state --state NEW -j ACCEPT
fi
$IPT -A OUTPUT -o $INTERNET -p tcp \
        -s $IPADDR --sport $UNPRIVPORTS \
        --dport 113 -j ACCEPT

$IPT -A INPUT -i $INTERNET -p tcp ! --syn \
        --sport 113 \
        -d $IPADDR --dport $UNPRIVPORTS -j ACCEPT
```

FILTERING INCOMING AUTH REQUESTS TO YOUR SERVER

Whether or not you decide to offer the service, you will likely receive incoming requests for the service when you send mail.

If you run the identd server, the following rules enable incoming identd connection requests:

```
if [ "$CONNECTION_TRACKING" = "1" ]; then
    $IPT -A INPUT  -i $INTERNET -p tcp \
            --sport $UNPRIVPORTS \
            -d $IPADDR --dport 113 \
            -m state --state NEW -j ACCEPT
fi
```

```
$IPT -A INPUT  -i $INTERNET -p tcp \
        --sport $UNPRIVPORTS \
        -d $IPADDR --dport 113 -j ACCEPT

$IPT -A OUTPUT -o $INTERNET -p tcp ! --syn \
        -s $IPADDR --sport 113 \
        --dport $UNPRIVPORTS -j ACCEPT
```

If you decide not to offer the service, it's a good practice to reject the connection request to avoid waiting for the TCP connection timeout. This is the case only when an incoming packet is rejected rather than dropped, in these examples:

```
$IPT -A INPUT -i $INTERNET -p tcp \
        --sport $UNPRIVPORTS \
        -d $IPADDR --dport 113 -j REJECT --reject-with tcp-reset
```

Alternatively, you could use the accept rules but not run the `identd` server. The result would be the same: The TCP layer would return a TCP **RST** message to the sender.

Enabling Common TCP Services

It's likely that no one will want to enable all the services listed in this section, but most everyone will want to enable some subset of them. These are the services most often used over the Internet today. As such, this section is more of a reference section than anything else. This section provides rules for the following:

- Email
- Usenet
- Telnet
- SSH
- FTP
- Web services
- Whois
- RealAudio, RealVideo, and QuickTime

Many other services are available that aren't covered here. Some of them are used on specialized servers, some are used by large businesses and organizations, and some are designed for use in local, private networks. Additional LAN and DMZ services are covered in Chapter 6.

Email (TCP SMTP Port 25, POP Port 110, IMAP Port 143)

Email is a service that almost everyone wants. How mail is set up depends on your ISP, your connection type, and your own choices. Email is sent across the network using the SMTP protocol assigned to TCP service port 25. Email is commonly received locally through one of three different protocols—SMTP, POP, or IMAP—depending on the services your ISP provides and on your local configuration.

SMTP is the general mail protocol. Mail is delivered to the destination host machine, as defined most commonly by the MX record in the DNS for the given domain. The endpoint mail server determines whether the mail is deliverable (addressed to a valid user account on the machine) and then delivers it to the user's local mailbox.

POP and IMAP are mail-retrieval services. POP runs on TCP port 110. IMAP runs on TCP port 143. ISPs commonly make incoming mail available to their customers using one or both of these two services. Both services are usually authenticated by username and password. As far as mail retrieval is concerned, the difference between SMTP and POP or IMAP is that SMTP receives incoming mail and queues it in the user's local mailbox. POP and IMAP retrieve mail into the user's local mail program from the user's ISP, where the mail had been queued remotely in the user's SMTP mailbox at the ISP. Table 4.3 lists the complete client/server connection protocols for SMTP, POP, and IMAP. SMTP also uses specialized delivery mechanisms that your local network might use, such as ETRN, that effectively transfer all mail for a given domain for local processing.

TABLE 4.3
SMTP, POP, and IMAP Mail Protocols

DESCRIPTION	PROTOCOL	REMOTE ADDRESS	REMOTE PORT	IN/OUT	LOCAL ADDRESS	LOCAL PORT	TCP FLAG
Send outgoing mail	TCP	ANYWHERE	25	Out	IPADDR	1024:65535	Any
Remote server response	TCP	ANYWHERE	25	In	IPADDR	1024:65535	ACK
Receive incoming mail	TCP	ANYWHERE	1024:65535	In	IPADDR	25	Any
Local server response	TCP	ANYWHERE	1024:65536	Out	IPADDR	25	ACK
Local client query	TCP	POP SERVER	110	Out	IPADDR	1024:65535	Any
Remote server response	TCP	POP SERVER	110	In	IPADDR	1024:65535	ACK

TABLE 4.3
SMTP, POP, and IMAP Mail Protocols (continued)

DESCRIPTION	PROTOCOL	REMOTE ADDRESS	REMOTE PORT	IN/OUT	LOCAL ADDRESS	LOCAL PORT	TCP FLAG
Remote client query	TCP	POP CLIENT	1024:65535	In	IPADDR	110	Any
Local server response	TCP	POP CLIENT	1024:65535	Out	IPADDR	110	ACK
Local client query	TCP	IMAP SERVER	143	Out	IPADDR	1024:65535	Any
Remote server response	TCP	IMAP SERVER	143	In	IPADDR	1024:65535	ACK
Remote client query	TCP	IMAP CLIENT	1024:65535	In	IPADDR	143	Any
Local server response	TCP	IMAP CLIENT	1024:65535	Out	IPADDR	143	ACK

SENDING MAIL OVER SMTP (TCP PORT 25)

Mail is sent over SMTP. But whose SMTP server do you use to collect your mail and send it onward? ISPs offer SMTP mail service to their customers. The ISP's mail server acts as the mail gateway. It knows how to collect your mail, find the recipient host, and relay the mail. With UNIX, you can host your own local mail server, if you want. Your server will be responsible for routing the mail to its destination.

RELAYING OUTGOING MAIL THROUGH AN EXTERNAL (ISP) GATEWAY SMTP SERVER

When you relay outgoing mail through an external mail gateway server, your client mail program sends all outgoing mail to your ISP's mail server. Your ISP acts as your mail gateway to the rest of the world. Your system doesn't need to know how to locate your mail destinations or the routes to them. The ISP mail gateway serves as your relay.

The following two rules enable you to relay mail through your ISP's SMTP gateway:

```
SMTP_GATEWAY="my.isp.server"          # external mail server or relay

if [ "$CONNECTION_TRACKING" = "1" ]; then
    $IPT -A OUTPUT -o $INTERNET -p tcp \
        -s $IPADDR --sport $UNPRIVPORTS \
        -d $SMTP_GATEWAY --dport 25 -m state --state NEW -j ACCEPT
fi

$IPT -A OUTPUT -o $INTERNET -p tcp \
        -s $IPADDR --sport $UNPRIVPORTS \
```

```
            -d $SMTP_GATEWAY --dport 25 -j ACCEPT

$IPT -A INPUT -i $INTERNET -p tcp ! --syn \
        -s $SMTP_GATEWAY --sport 25 \
        -d $IPADDR --dport $UNPRIVPORTS -j ACCEPT
```

SENDING MAIL TO ANY EXTERNAL MAIL SERVER

Alternatively, you can bypass your ISP's mail server and host your own. Your local server is responsible for collecting your outgoing mail, doing the DNS lookup on the destination host-name, and sending the mail to its destination. Your client mail program points to your local SMTP server rather than to the ISP's server.

The following two rules enable you to send mail directly to the remote destinations:

```
if [ "$CONNECTION_TRACKING" = "1" ]; then
    $IPT -A OUTPUT -o $INTERNET -p tcp \
            -s $IPADDR --sport $UNPRIVPORTS \
            --dport 25 -m state --state NEW -j ACCEPT
fi

$IPT -A OUTPUT -o $INTERNET -p tcp \
        -s $IPADDR --sport $UNPRIVPORTS \
        --dport 25 -j ACCEPT

$IPT -A INPUT -i $INTERNET -p tcp ! --syn \
        --sport 25 \
        -d $IPADDR --dport $UNPRIVPORTS -j ACCEPT
```

RECEIVING MAIL

How you receive mail depends on your situation. If you run your own local mail server, you can collect incoming mail directly on your Linux machine. If you retrieve your mail from your ISP account, you may or may not retrieve mail as a POP or IMAP client, depending on how you've configured your ISP email account, and depending on the mail delivery services the ISP offers.

RECEIVING MAIL AS A LOCAL SMTP SERVER (TCP PORT 25)

If you want to receive mail sent directly to your local machines from anywhere in the world, you need to run sendmail, qmail, or some other mail server program. These are the local server rules:

```
if [ "$CONNECTION_TRACKING" = "1" ]; then
    $IPT -A INPUT  -i $INTERNET -p tcp \
            --sport $UNPRIVPORTS \
            -d $IPADDR --dport 25 \
            -m state --state NEW -j ACCEPT
```

```
fi

$IPT -A INPUT  -i $INTERNET -p tcp \
       --sport $UNPRIVPORTS \
       -d $IPADDR --dport 25 -j ACCEPT

$IPT -A OUTPUT -o $INTERNET -p tcp ! --syn \
       -s $IPADDR --sport 25 \
       --dport $UNPRIVPORTS -j ACCEPT
```

Alternatively, if you'd rather keep your local email account relatively private and use your work or ISP email account as your public address, you can configure your work and ISP mail accounts to forward mail to your local server. In this case, you could replace the previous single rule pair, accepting connections from anywhere, with separate, specific rules for each mail forwarder.

RETRIEVING MAIL AS A POP CLIENT (TCP PORT 110)

Connecting to a POP server is a very common means of retrieving mail from a remote ISP or work account. If your ISP uses a POP server for customer mail retrieval, you need to allow outgoing client-to-server connections.

The server's address will be a specific hostname or address rather than the global, implied ANYWHERE specifier. POP accounts are user accounts associated with a specific user and password:

```
POP_SERVER="my.isp.pop.server"          # external pop server, if any

if [ "$CONNECTION_TRACKING" = "1" ]; then
    $IPT -A OUTPUT -o $INTERNET -p tcp \
           -s $IPADDR --sport $UNPRIVPORTS \
           -d $POP_SERVER --dport 110 -m state --state NEW -j ACCEPT
fi

$IPT -A OUTPUT -o $INTERNET -p tcp \
       -s $IPADDR --sport $UNPRIVPORTS \
       -d $POP_SERVER --dport 110 -j ACCEPT

$IPT -A INPUT -i $INTERNET -p tcp ! --syn \
       -s $POP_SERVER --sport 110 \
       -d $IPADDR --dport $UNPRIVPORTS -j ACCEPT
```

RECEIVING MAIL AS AN IMAP CLIENT (TCP PORT 143)

Connecting to an IMAP server is another common means of retrieving mail from a remote ISP or work account. If your ISP uses an IMAP server for customer mail retrieval, you need to allow outgoing client-to-server connections.

The server's address will be a specific hostname or address rather than the global, implied **$ANYWHERE** specifier. IMAP accounts are user accounts associated with a specific user and password:

```
IMAP_SERVER="my.isp.imap.server"        # external imap server, if any

if [ "$CONNECTION_TRACKING" = "1" ]; then
    $IPT -A OUTPUT -o $INTERNET -p tcp \
            -s $IPADDR --sport $UNPRIVPORTS \
            -d $IMAP_SERVER --dport 143 -m state --state NEW -j ACCEPT
fi

$IPT -A OUTPUT -o $INTERNET -p tcp \
        -s $IPADDR --sport $UNPRIVPORTS \
        -d $IMAP_SERVER --dport 143 -j ACCEPT

$IPT -A INPUT -i $INTERNET -p tcp ! --syn \
        -s $IMAP_SERVER --sport 143 \
        -d $IPADDR --dport $UNPRIVPORTS -j ACCEPT
```

EXAMPLES OF REAL-WORLD CLIENT AND SERVER EMAIL COMBINATIONS

Four common approaches to client and server email combinations are described in this section:

- Sending mail as an SMTP client and receiving mail as a POP client
- Sending mail as an SMTP client and receiving mail as an IMAP client
- Sending mail as an SMTP client and receiving mail as an SMTP server
- Sending mail as an SMTP server and receiving mail as an SMTP server

The first two are useful if you rely completely on your ISP's SMTP and POP or IMAP email services. The third example is a mixed approach, relaying outgoing mail through your ISP's SMTP mail server, but receiving mail directly through your local SMTP server. The fourth approach supports running your own complete, independent mail server for both outgoing and incoming mail.

SENDING MAIL AS AN SMTP CLIENT AND RECEIVING MAIL AS A POP CLIENT

If you are sending mail as an SMTP client and are receiving mail as a POP client, you are relying completely on a remote site for your mail services. The remote site hosts both an SMTP server for relaying your outgoing mail and a POP server for local mail retrieval:

```
SMTP_GATEWAY="my.isp.server"              # external mail server or relay

if [ "$CONNECTION_TRACKING" = "1" ]; then
    $IPT -A OUTPUT -o $INTERNET -p tcp \
            -s $IPADDR --sport $UNPRIVPORTS \
            -d $SMTP_GATEWAY --dport 25 -m state --state NEW -j ACCEPT
fi

$IPT -A OUTPUT -o $INTERNET -p tcp \
        -s $IPADDR --sport $UNPRIVPORTS \
        -d $SMTP_GATEWAY --dport 25 -j ACCEPT

$IPT -A INPUT -i $INTERNET -p tcp ! --syn \
        -s $SMTP_GATEWAY --sport 25 \
        -d $IPADDR --dport $UNPRIVPORTS -j ACCEPT

POP_SERVER="my.isp.pop.server"            # external pop server, if any

if [ "$CONNECTION_TRACKING" = "1" ]; then
    $IPT -A OUTPUT -o $INTERNET -p tcp \
            -s $IPADDR --sport $UNPRIVPORTS \
            -d $POP_SERVER --dport 110 -m state --state NEW -j ACCEPT
fi

$IPT -A OUTPUT -o $INTERNET -p tcp \
        -s $IPADDR --sport $UNPRIVPORTS \
        -d $POP_SERVER --dport 110 -j ACCEPT

$IPT -A INPUT -i $INTERNET -p tcp ! --syn \
        -s $POP_SERVER --sport 110 \
        -d $IPADDR --dport $UNPRIVPORTS -j ACCEPT
```

SENDING MAIL AS AN SMTP CLIENT AND RECEIVING MAIL AS AN IMAP CLIENT

If you are sending mail as an SMTP client and are receiving mail as an IMAP client, you are relying completely on a remote site for your mail services. The remote site hosts both an SMTP server for relaying outgoing mail and an IMAP server for local mail retrieval:

```
SMTP_GATEWAY="my.isp.server"              # external mail server or relay

if [ "$CONNECTION_TRACKING" = "1" ]; then
    $IPT -A OUTPUT -o $INTERNET -p tcp \
            -s $IPADDR --sport $UNPRIVPORTS \
            -d $SMTP_GATEWAY --dport 25 -m state --state NEW -j ACCEPT
fi
```

```
$IPT -A OUTPUT -o $INTERNET -p tcp \
        -s $IPADDR --sport $UNPRIVPORTS \
        -d $SMTP_GATEWAY --dport 25 -j ACCEPT

$IPT -A INPUT -i $INTERNET -p tcp ! --syn \
        -s $SMTP_GATEWAY --sport 25 \
        -d $IPADDR --dport $UNPRIVPORTS -j ACCEPT

IMAP_SERVER="my.isp.imap.server"        # external imap server, if any

if [ "$CONNECTION_TRACKING" = "1" ]; then
    $IPT -A OUTPUT -o $INTERNET -p tcp \
            -s $IPADDR --sport $UNPRIVPORTS \
            -d $IMAP_SERVER --dport 143 -m state --state NEW -j ACCEPT
fi

$IPT -A OUTPUT -o $INTERNET -p tcp \
        -s $IPADDR --sport $UNPRIVPORTS \
        -d $IMAP_SERVER --dport 143 -j ACCEPT

$IPT -A INPUT -i $INTERNET -p tcp ! --syn \
        -s $IMAP_SERVER --sport 143 \
        -d $IPADDR --dport $UNPRIVPORTS -j ACCEPT
```

SENDING MAIL AS AN SMTP CLIENT AND RECEIVING MAIL AS AN SMTP SERVER

If you are sending mail as an SMTP client and are receiving mail as an SMTP server, you are relying on a remote site to offer SMTP service to relay your outgoing mail to remote destinations. You run sendmail locally as a local SMTP server, allowing remote hosts to send mail to your machine directly. Outgoing mail is relayed through your ISP, but the local sendmail daemon knows how to deliver incoming mail to local user accounts:

```
SMTP_GATEWAY="my.isp.server"            # external mail server or relay

if [ "$CONNECTION_TRACKING" = "1" ]; then
    $IPT -A OUTPUT -o $INTERNET -p tcp \
            -s $IPADDR --sport $UNPRIVPORTS \
            -d $SMTP_GATEWAY --dport 25 -m state --state NEW -j ACCEPT
fi

$IPT -A OUTPUT -o $INTERNET -p tcp \
        -s $IPADDR --sport $UNPRIVPORTS \
        -d $SMTP_GATEWAY --dport 25 -j ACCEPT

$IPT -A INPUT -i $INTERNET -p tcp ! --syn \
        -s $SMTP_GATEWAY --sport 25 \
        -d $IPADDR --dport $UNPRIVPORTS -j ACCEPT
```

```
if [ "$CONNECTION_TRACKING" = "1" ]; then
    $IPT -A INPUT  -i $INTERNET -p tcp \
            --sport $UNPRIVPORTS \
            -d $IPADDR --dport 25 \
            -m state --state NEW -j ACCEPT
fi

$IPT -A INPUT  -i $INTERNET -p tcp \
        --sport $UNPRIVPORTS \
        -d $IPADDR --dport 25 -j ACCEPT

$IPT -A OUTPUT -o $INTERNET -p tcp ! --syn \
        -s $IPADDR --sport 25 \
        --dport $UNPRIVPORTS -j ACCEPT
```

SENDING MAIL AS AN SMTP SERVER AND RECEIVING MAIL AS AN SMTP SERVER

If you are sending mail as an SMTP server and are receiving mail as an SMTP server, you provide all your own mail services. Your local **sendmail** daemon is configured to relay outgoing mail to the destination hosts itself, as well as collect and deliver incoming mail:

```
if [ "$CONNECTION_TRACKING" = "1" ]; then
    $IPT -A OUTPUT -o $INTERNET -p tcp \
            -s $IPADDR --sport $UNPRIVPORTS \
            --dport 25 -m state --state NEW -j ACCEPT
fi

$IPT -A OUTPUT -o $INTERNET -p tcp \
        -s $IPADDR --sport $UNPRIVPORTS \
        --dport 25 -j ACCEPT

$IPT -A INPUT -i $INTERNET -p tcp ! --syn \
        --sport 25 \
        -d $IPADDR --dport $UNPRIVPORTS -j ACCEPT

if [ "$CONNECTION_TRACKING" = "1" ]; then
    $IPT -A INPUT  -i $INTERNET -p tcp \
            --sport $UNPRIVPORTS \
            -d $IPADDR --dport 25 \
            -m state --state NEW -j ACCEPT
fi

$IPT -A INPUT  -i $INTERNET -p tcp \
        --sport $UNPRIVPORTS \
        -d $IPADDR --dport 25 -j ACCEPT
```

```
$IPT -A OUTPUT -o $INTERNET -p tcp ! --syn \
        -s $IPADDR --sport 25 \
        --dport $UNPRIVPORTS -j ACCEPT
```

HOSTING A MAIL SERVER FOR REMOTE CLIENTS

Hosting public POP or IMAP services is unusual for a small system. You might do this if you offer remote mail services to a few friends, for example, or if their ISP mail service is temporarily unavailable. In any case, it's important to limit the clients your system will accept connections from, both on the packet-filtering level and on the server configuration level.

HOSTING A POP SERVER FOR REMOTE CLIENTS

POP servers are one of the most common and successful points of entry for hacking exploits. Firewall rules can offer some amount of protection, in many cases. Of course, you would limit access at the server configuration level as well. As always, and perhaps particularly so with mail server software, it is crucial to keep up-to-date with security updates for the software.

If you use a local system as a central mail server and run a local POP3 server to provide mail access to local machines on a LAN, you don't need the server rules in this example. Incoming connections from the Internet should be dropped. If you do need to host POP service for a limited number of remote individuals, the next two rules allow incoming connections to your POP server. Connections are limited to your specific clients' IP addresses:

```
if [ "$CONNECTION_TRACKING" = "1" ]; then
    $IPT -A INPUT   -i $INTERNET -p tcp \
            -s <my.pop.clients> --sport $UNPRIVPORTS \
            -d $IPADDR --dport 110 \
            -m state --state NEW -j ACCEPT
fi


$IPT -A INPUT   -i $INTERNET -p tcp \
        -s <my.pop.clients> --sport $UNPRIVPORTS \
        -d $IPADDR --dport 110 -j ACCEPT

$IPT -A OUTPUT -o $INTERNET -p tcp ! --syn \
        -s $IPADDR --sport 110 \
        -d <my.pop.clients> --dport $UNPRIVPORTS -j ACCEPT
```

If your site were an ISP, you could use network address masking to limit which source addresses you would accept POP connection requests from:

```
POP_CLIENTS="192.168.24.0/24"
```

If yours is a residential site with a handful of remote POP clients, the client addresses would need to be stated explicitly, with a separate rule pair for each client address.

HOSTING AN IMAP SERVER FOR REMOTE CLIENTS

IMAP servers are one of the most common and successful points of entry for hacking exploits. Firewall rules can offer some amount of protection, in many cases. Of course, you would limit access at the server configuration level as well. As always, and perhaps particularly so with mail server software, it is crucial to keep up-to-date with security updates for the software.

If you use a local system as a central mail server and run a local `imapd` server to provide mail access to local machines on a LAN, you don't need a server rule. Incoming connections from the Internet should be dropped. If you do need to host IMAP service for a limited number of remote individuals, the next two rules allow incoming connections to your IMAP server. Connections are limited to your specific clients' IP addresses:

```
if [ "$CONNECTION_TRACKING" = "1" ]; then
    $IPT -A INPUT  -i $INTERNET -p tcp \
            -s <my.imap.clients> --sport $UNPRIVPORTS \
            -d $IPADDR --dport 143 \
            -m state --state NEW -j ACCEPT
fi

$IPT -A INPUT  -i $INTERNET -p tcp \
        -s <my.imap.clients> --sport $UNPRIVPORTS \
        -d $IPADDR --dport 143 -j ACCEPT

$IPT -A OUTPUT -o $INTERNET -p tcp ! --syn \
        -s $IPADDR --sport 143 \
        -d <my.imap.clients> --dport $UNPRIVPORTS -j ACCEPT
```

If your site were an ISP, you could use network address masking to limit which source addresses you would accept IMAP connection requests from:

```
IMAP_CLIENTS="192.168.24.0/24"
```

If yours is a residential site with a handful of remote IMAP clients, the client addresses would need to be stated explicitly, with a separate rule pair for each client address.

Accessing Usenet News Services (TCP NNTP Port 119)

Usenet news is accessed over NNTP running on top of TCP through service port 119. Reading news and posting articles are handled by your local news client. Few systems require the server rules. Table 4.4 lists the complete client/server connection protocol for the NNTP Usenet news service.

TABLE 4.4
NNTP Protocol

DESCRIPTION	PROTOCOL	REMOTE ADDRESS	REMOTE PORT	IN/OUT	LOCAL ADDRESS	LOCAL PORT	TCP FLAG
Local client query	TCP	NEWS SERVER	119	Out	IPADDR	1024:65535	Any
Remote server response	TCP	NEWS SERVER	119	In	IPADDR	1024:65535	ACK
Remote client query	TCP	NNTP clients	1024:65535	In	IPADDR	119	Any
Local server response	TCP	NNTP clients	1024:65535	Out	IPADDR	119	ACK
Local server query	TCP	News feed	119	Out	IPADDR	1024:65535	Any
Remote server response	TCP	News feed	119	In	IPADDR	1024:65535	ACK

READING AND POSTING NEWS AS A USENET CLIENT

The client rules allow connections to your ISP's news server. Both reading news and posting articles are handled by these rules:

```
NEWS_SERVER="my.news.server"          # external news server, if any

if [ "$CONNECTION_TRACKING" = "1" ]; then
    $IPT -A OUTPUT -o $INTERNET -p tcp \
          -s $IPADDR --sport $UNPRIVPORTS \
          -d $NEWS_SERVER --dport 119 -m state --state NEW -j ACCEPT
fi

$IPT -A OUTPUT -o $INTERNET -p tcp \
        -s $IPADDR --sport $UNPRIVPORTS \
        -d $NEWS_SERVER --dport 119 -j ACCEPT

$IPT -A INPUT -i $INTERNET -p tcp ! --syn \
        -s $NEWS_SERVER --sport 119 \
        -d $IPADDR --dport $UNPRIVPORTS -j ACCEPT
```

HOSTING A USENET NEWS SERVER FOR REMOTE CLIENTS

A small site is very unlikely to host a news server for the outside world. Even hosting a local news server is unlikely. For the rare exception, the server rules should be configured to allow incoming connections from only a select set of clients:

```
if [ "$CONNECTION_TRACKING" = "1" ]; then
    $IPT -A INPUT  -i $INTERNET -p tcp \
            -s <my.news.clients> --sport $UNPRIVPORTS \
            -d $IPADDR --dport 119 \
            -m state --state NEW -j ACCEPT
fi

$IPT -A INPUT  -i $INTERNET -p tcp \
        -s <my.news.clients> --sport $UNPRIVPORTS \
        -d $IPADDR --dport 119 -j ACCEPT

$IPT -A OUTPUT -o $INTERNET -p tcp ! --syn \
        -s $IPADDR --sport 119 \
        -d <my.news.clients> --dport $UNPRIVPORTS -j ACCEPT
```

ALLOWING PEER NEWS FEEDS FOR A LOCAL USENET SERVER

A small, home-based site is unlikely to have a peer-to-peer news-feed server relationship with an ISP. Although news servers used to be fairly accessible to the general Internet, few open news servers are available anymore because of SPAM and server load issues.

If your site is large enough or rich enough to host a general Usenet server, you have to get your news feed from somewhere. The next two rules allow your local news server to receive its news feed from a remote server. The local server contacts the remote server as a client. The only difference between the peer-to-peer news-feed rules and the regular client rules is the name or address of the remote host:

```
if [ "$CONNECTION_TRACKING" = "1" ]; then
    $IPT -A OUTPUT -o $INTERNET -p tcp \
        -s $IPADDR --sport $UNPRIVPORTS \
        -d <my.news.feed> --dport 119 -m state --state NEW -j ACCEPT
fi

$IPT -A OUTPUT -o $INTERNET -p tcp \
        -s $IPADDR --sport $UNPRIVPORTS \
        -d <my.news.feed> --dport 119 -j ACCEPT

$IPT -A INPUT -i $INTERNET -p tcp ! --syn \
        -s <my.news.feed> --sport 119 \
        -d $IPADDR --dport $UNPRIVPORTS -j ACCEPT
```

Telnet (TCP Port 23)

Telnet had been the de facto standard means of remote login over the Internet for many years. As the nature of the Internet community has changed, telnet has come to be viewed more as an insecure service because it communicates in ASCII clear text. If you have the option, you should always use an encrypted service, such as SSH, rather than telnet. However, Microsoft Windows does not offer an SSH service and only offers telnet—so much for that security commitment!

The client and server rules here allow access to and from anywhere. If you use telnet, you can probably limit the external addresses to a *very* select subset at the packet-filtering level. Table 4.5 lists the complete client/server connection protocol for the telnet service.

TABLE 4.5
Telnet Protocol

DESCRIPTION	PROTOCOL	REMOTE ADDRESS	REMOTE PORT	IN/OUT	LOCAL ADDRESS	LOCAL PORT	TCP FLAG
Local client request	TCP	ANYWHERE	23	Out	IPADDR	1024:65535	Any
Remote server response	TCP	ANYWHERE	23	In	IPADDR	1024:65535	ACK
Remote client request	TCP	Telnet clients	1024:65535	In	IPADDR	23	Any
Local server response	TCP	Telnet clients	1024:65535	Out	IPADDR	23	ACK

ALLOWING OUTGOING CLIENT ACCESS TO REMOTE SITES

If you need to use telnet to access remote systems (SSH servers are very prevalent today), the next two rules allow outgoing connections to remote sites. If your site has multiple users, you should limit outgoing connections to the specific sites your users have accounts on, if at all possible, rather than allowing outgoing connections to anywhere:

```
if [ "$CONNECTION_TRACKING" = "1" ]; then
    $IPT -A OUTPUT -o $INTERNET -p tcp \
            -s $IPADDR --sport $UNPRIVPORTS \
            --dport 23 -m state --state NEW -j ACCEPT
fi

$IPT -A OUTPUT -o $INTERNET -p tcp \
        -s $IPADDR --sport $UNPRIVPORTS \
        --dport 23 -j ACCEPT

$IPT -A INPUT -i $INTERNET -p tcp ! --syn \
        --sport 23 \
        -d $IPADDR --dport $UNPRIVPORTS -j ACCEPT
```

ALLOWING INCOMING ACCESS TO YOUR LOCAL SERVER

Even if you need client access to remote servers, you may not need to allow incoming connections to your telnet server. If you do, the next two rules allow incoming connections to your server:

```
if [ "$CONNECTION_TRACKING" = "1" ]; then
    $IPT -A INPUT  -i $INTERNET -p tcp \
            --sport $UNPRIVPORTS \
            -d $IPADDR --dport 23 \
            -m state --state NEW -j ACCEPT
fi

$IPT -A INPUT  -i $INTERNET -p tcp \
        --sport $UNPRIVPORTS \
        -d $IPADDR --dport 23 -j ACCEPT

$IPT -A OUTPUT -o $INTERNET -p tcp ! --syn \
        -s $IPADDR --sport 23 \
        --dport $UNPRIVPORTS -j ACCEPT
```

Rather than allowing connections from anywhere, it is far preferable to define server rules for each specific host or network that an incoming connection can legitimately originate from. SSH clients are freely available for almost all systems in use today.

SSH (TCP Port 22)

With the expiration of the RSA patent in year 2000, OpenSSH, secure shell, is included in Linux distributions. It is also freely available from software sites on the Internet. SSH is considered far preferable to using telnet for remote login access because both ends of the connection use authentication keys for both hosts and users, and because data is encrypted. Additionally, SSH is more than a remote login service. It can automatically direct X Window connections between remote sites, and FTP and other TCP-based connections can be directed over the more secure SSH connection. Provided that the other end of the connection allows SSH connections, it's possible to route all TCP connections through the firewall using SSH. As such, SSH is something of a poor man's virtual private network (VPN).

The ports used by SSH are highly configurable. By default, connections are initiated between a client's unprivileged port and the server's assigned service port 22. The SSH client uses the unprivileged ports exclusively. The rules in this example apply to the default SSH port usage:

```
SSH_PORTS="1024:65535"          # RSA authentication
```

or

```
SSH_PORTS="1020:65535"          # Rhost authentication
```

The client and server rules here allow access to and from anywhere. In practice, you would limit the external addresses to a select subset, particularly because both ends of the connection must be configured to recognize each individual user account for authentication. Table 4.6 lists the complete client/server connection protocol for the SSH service.

TABLE 4.6
SSH Protocol

DESCRIPTION	PROTOCOL	REMOTE ADDRESS	REMOTE PORT	IN/OUT	LOCAL ADDRESS	LOCAL PORT	TCP FLAG
Local client request	TCP	ANYWHERE	22	Out	IPADDR	1024:65535	Any
Remote server response	TCP	ANYWHERE	22	In	IPADDR	1024:65535	ACK
Local client request	TCP	ANYWHERE	22	Out	IPADDR	513:1023	Any
Remote server response	TCP	ANYWHERE	22	In	IPADDR	513:1023	ACK
Remote client request	TCP	SSH clients	1024:65535	In	IPADDR	22	Any
Local server response	TCP	SSH clients	1024:65535	Out	IPADDR	22	ACK
Remote client request	TCP	SSH clients	513:1023	In	IPADDR	22	Any
Local server response	TCP	SSH clients	513:1023	Out	IPADDR	22	ACK

ALLOWING CLIENT ACCESS TO REMOTE SSH SERVERS

These rules allow you to connect to remote sites using SSH:

```
if [ "$CONNECTION_TRACKING" = "1" ]; then
    $IPT -A OUTPUT -o $INTERNET -p tcp \
            -s $IPADDR --sport $SSH_PORTS \
            --dport 22 -m state --state NEW -j ACCEPT
fi

$IPT -A OUTPUT -o $INTERNET -p tcp \
        -s $IPADDR --sport $SSH_PORTS \
        --dport 22 -j ACCEPT

$IPT -A INPUT -i $INTERNET -p tcp ! --syn \
        --sport 22 \
        -d $IPADDR --dport $SSH_PORTS -j ACCEPT
```

ALLOWING REMOTE CLIENT ACCESS TO YOUR LOCAL SSH SERVER

These rules allow incoming connections to your SSH server:

```
if [ "$CONNECTION_TRACKING" = "1" ]; then
    $IPT -A INPUT  -i $INTERNET -p tcp \
            --sport $SSH_PORTS \
            -d $IPADDR --dport 22 \
            -m state --state NEW -j ACCEPT
fi

$IPT -A INPUT  -i $INTERNET -p tcp \
        --sport $SSH_PORTS \
        -d $IPADDR --dport 22 -j ACCEPT

$IPT -A OUTPUT -o $INTERNET -p tcp ! --syn \
        -s $IPADDR --sport 22 \
        --dport $SSH_PORTS -j ACCEPT
```

FTP (TCP Ports 21, 20)

FTP remains one of the most common means of transferring files between two networked machines. Web-based browser interfaces to FTP have become common as well. Like telnet, FTP sends both authentication credentials and data communication in plain text over the network. Therefore, FTP is also considered to be an inherently insecure protocol. SFTP and SCP offer improvements to FTP in this regard.

FTP is used as the classic example of a protocol that isn't firewall- or NAT-friendly. Traditional client/server applications that communicate over TCP all work the same way. The client initiates the request to connect to the server.

Table 4.7 lists the complete client/server connection protocol for the FTP service.

TABLE 4.7
FTP Protocol

DESCRIPTION	PROTOCOL	REMOTE ADDRESS	REMOTE PORT	IN/OUT	LOCAL ADDRESS	LOCAL PORT	TCP FLAG
Local client query	TCP	ANYWHERE	21	Out	IPADDR	1024:65535	Any
Remote server response	TCP	ANYWHERE	21	In	IPADDR	1024:65535	ACK
Remote server port data channel request	TCP	ANYWHERE	20	In	IPADDR	1024:65535	Any

TABLE 4.7
FTP Protocol (continued)

DESCRIPTION	PROTOCOL	REMOTE ADDRESS	REMOTE PORT	IN/OUT	LOCAL ADDRESS	LOCAL PORT	TCP FLAG
Local client port data channel response	TCP	ANYWHERE	20	Out	IPADDR	1024:65535	ACK
Local client passive data channel request	TCP	ANYWHERE	1024:65535	Out	IPADDR	1024:65535	Any
Remote server passive data channel response	TCP	ANYWHERE	1024:65535	In	IPADDR	1024:65535	ACK
Remote client request	TCP	ANYWHERE	1024:65535	In	IPADDR	21	Any
Local server response	TCP	ANYWHERE	1024:65535	Out	IPADDR	21	ACK
Local server port data channel response	TCP	ANYWHERE	1024:65535	Out	IPADDR	20	Any
Remote client port data channel response	TCP	ANYWHERE	1024:65535	In	IPADDR	20	ACK
Remote client passive data channel request	TCP	ANYWHERE	1024:65535	In	IPADDR	1024:65535	Any
Local server passive data channel response	TCP	ANYWHERE	1024:65535	Out	IPADDR	1024:65535	ACK

FTP deviates from this standard TCP, client/server communication model. FTP relies on two separate connections, one for the control or command stream, and one for passing the data files and other information, such as directory listings. The control stream is carried over a traditional TCP connection. The client binds to a high, unprivileged port, and sends a connection request to the FTP server, which is bound to port **21**. This connection is used to pass commands.

In terms of the second data stream connection, FTP has two alternate modes for exchanging data between a client and server: port mode and passive mode. *Port mode* is the original, default mechanism. The client tells the server which secondary, unprivileged port it will listen on. The server initiates the data connection from port 20 to the unprivileged port the client specified.

This is the deviation from the standard client/server model. The server is initiating the secondary connection back to the client. This is why FTP is a protocol that requires ALG support for both the firewall and NAT. The firewall must account for an incoming connection from port 20 to a local unprivileged port. NAT must account for the destination address used for the secondary data stream connection. (The client has no knowledge that its network traffic is being NATed. The port and address it sent the server were its local, pre-NATed port and address.)

Passive mode is similar to the traditional client/server model in that the client initiates the secondary connection for the data stream. Again, the client initiates the connection from a high, unprivileged port. The server isn't bound to port 20 for the data connection, however. Instead, the server has told the client which high, unprivileged port the client should address the connection request to. The data stream is carried between unprivileged ports on both the client and the server.

In terms of traditional packet filtering, the firewall must allow TCP traffic between all unprivileged ports. Connection state tracking and ALG support allow the firewall to associate the secondary connection with a particular FTP control stream. NAT isn't an issue on the client side because the client is initiating both connections.

ALLOWING OUTGOING CLIENT ACCESS TO REMOTE FTP SERVERS

It's almost a given that most sites will want FTP client access to remote file repositories. Most people will want to enable outgoing client connections to a remote server.

OUTGOING FTP REQUESTS OVER THE CONTROL CHANNEL

The next two rules allow an outgoing control connection to a remote FTP server:

```
if [ "$CONNECTION_TRACKING" = "1" ]; then
    $IPT -A OUTPUT -o $INTERNET -p tcp \
            -s $IPADDR --sport $UNPRIVPORTS \
            --dport 21 -m state --state NEW -j ACCEPT
fi

$IPT -A OUTPUT -o $INTERNET -p tcp \
        -s $IPADDR --sport $UNPRIVPORTS \
        --dport 21 -j ACCEPT
```

```
$IPT -A INPUT -i $INTERNET -p tcp ! --syn \
        --sport 21 \
        -d $IPADDR --dport $UNPRIVPORTS -j ACCEPT
```

PORT-MODE FTP DATA CHANNELS

The next two rules allow the standard data channel connection, in which the remote server calls back to establish the data connection from server port **20** to a client-specified unprivileged port:

```
if [ "$CONNECTION_TRACKING" = "1" ]; then
    $IPT -A INPUT  -i $INTERNET -p tcp \
            --sport 20 \
            -d $IPADDR --dport $UNPRIVPORTS \
            -m state --state NEW -j ACCEPT
fi

$IPT -A INPUT  -i $INTERNET -p tcp \
        --sport 20 \
        -d $IPADDR --dport $UNPRIVPORTS -j ACCEPT

$IPT -A OUTPUT -o $INTERNET -p tcp ! --syn \
        -s $IPADDR --sport $UNPRIVPORTS \
        --dport 20 -j ACCEPT
```

This unusual callback behavior, with the remote server establishing the secondary connection with your client, is part of what makes FTP difficult to secure at the packet-filtering level.

PASSIVE-MODE FTP DATA CHANNELS

The next two rules allow the newer passive data channel mode used by most web browsers:

```
if [ "$CONNECTION_TRACKING" = "1" ]; then
    $IPT -A OUTPUT -o $INTERNET -p tcp \
            -s $IPADDR --sport $UNPRIVPORTS \
            --dport $UNPRIVPORTS -m state --state NEW -j ACCEPT
fi

    $IPT -A OUTPUT -o $INTERNET -p tcp \
            -s $IPADDR --sport $UNPRIVPORTS \
            --dport $UNPRIVPORTS -j ACCEPT

    $IPT -A INPUT -i $INTERNET -p tcp ! --syn \
            --sport $UNPRIVPORTS \
            -d $IPADDR --dport $UNPRIVPORTS -j ACCEPT
```

Passive mode is considered more secure than port mode because the FTP client initiates both the control and the data connections, even though the connection is made between two unprivileged ports. And, as stated earlier, passive mode doesn't have the problems with NAT that port mode does on the client side.

ALLOWING INCOMING ACCESS TO YOUR LOCAL FTP SERVER

Whether to offer FTP services to the world is a difficult decision. Although FTP sites abound on the Internet, FTP server configuration requires great care. Numerous FTP security exploits are possible.

If your goal is to offer general read-only access to some set of files on your machine, you might consider making these files available through a web server. If your goal is to allow file uploads to your machine from the outside, FTP server access should be severely limited on the firewall level, on the `xinetd` configuration level, on the `tcp_wrappers` level, and on the FTP configuration level.

In any case, if you decide to offer FTP services, and if you decide to allow incoming file transfers, write access should not be allowed via anonymous FTP. Remote write access to your file systems should be allowed only from specific, authenticated FTP user accounts, from specific remote sites, and to carefully controlled and limited FTP areas reserved in your file system. Hosting the FTP area from a `chroot` environment would be even better.

INCOMING FTP REQUESTS

The next two rules allow incoming control connections to your FTP server:

```
if [ "$CONNECTION_TRACKING" = "1" ]; then
    $IPT -A INPUT  -i $INTERNET -p tcp \
            --sport $UNPRIVPORTS \
            -d $IPADDR --dport 21 \
            -m state --state NEW -j ACCEPT
fi

$IPT -A INPUT  -i $INTERNET -p tcp \
        --sport $UNPRIVPORTS \
        -d $IPADDR --dport 21 -j ACCEPT

$IPT -A OUTPUT -o $INTERNET -p tcp ! --syn \
        -s $IPADDR --sport 21 \
        --dport $UNPRIVPORTS -j ACCEPT
```

PORT-MODE FTP DATA CHANNEL RESPONSES

The next two rules allow the FTP server to call back the remote client and establish the secondary data channel connection:

```
if [ "$CONNECTION_TRACKING" = "1" ]; then
    $IPT -A OUTPUT -o $INTERNET -p tcp \
```

```
                    -s $IPADDR --sport 20\
                    --dport $UNPRIVPORTS -m state --state NEW -j ACCEPT
fi


$IPT -A OUTPUT -o $INTERNET -p tcp \
            -s $IPADDR --sport 20 \
            --dport $UNPRIVPORTS -j ACCEPT


$IPT -A INPUT -i $INTERNET -p tcp ! --syn \
            --sport $UNPRIVPORTS \
            -d $IPADDR --dport 20 -j ACCEPT
```

PASSIVE-MODE FTP DATA CHANNEL RESPONSES

The next two rules allow the remote FTP client to establish the secondary data channel connection with the local server:

```
if [ "$CONNECTION_TRACKING" = "1" ]; then
    $IPT -A INPUT   -i $INTERNET -p tcp \
            --sport $UNPRIVPORTS \
            -d $IPADDR --dport $UNPRIVPORTS \
            -m state --state NEW -j ACCEPT
fi


$IPT -A INPUT   -i $INTERNET -p tcp \
            --sport $UNPRIVPORTS \
            -d $IPADDR --dport $UNPRIVPORTS -j ACCEPT


$IPT -A OUTPUT -o $INTERNET -p tcp ! --syn \
            -s $IPADDR --sport $UNPRIVPORTS \
            --dport $UNPRIVPORTS -j ACCEPT
```

CAUTION

Don't use TFTP on the Internet! TFTP offers a simplified, unauthenticated, UDP version of the FTP service. It is intended for loading boot software into routers and diskless workstations over a local network from trusted hosts. Some people confuse TFTP as an alternative to FTP. Don't use it over the Internet, period. Preferably, don't install TFTP on your system at all.

Web Services

Web services are based on the Hypertext Transfer Protocol (HTTP). Client and server connections use the standard TCP conventions. Several higher-level, special-purpose communication protocols are available in addition to the standard general HTTP access, including secure access over SSL or TLS, and access via an ISP-provided web server proxy. These different access protocols use different service ports.

STANDARD HTTP ACCESS (TCP PORT 80)

In normal use, web services are available over `http` service port 80. Table 4.8 lists the complete client/server connection protocol for the HTTP web service.

TABLE 4.8
HTTP Protocol

DESCRIPTION	PROTOCOL	REMOTE ADDRESS	REMOTE PORT	IN/OUT	LOCAL ADDRESS	LOCAL PORT	TCP FLAG
Local client request	TCP	ANYWHERE	80	Out	IPADDR	1024:65535	Any
Remote server response	TCP	ANYWHERE	80	In	IPADDR	1024:65535	ACK
Remote client request	TCP	ANYWHERE	1024:65535	In	IPADDR	80	Any
Local server response	TCP	ANYWHERE	1024:65535	Out	IPADDR	80	ACK

ACCESSING REMOTE WEBSITES AS A CLIENT

It's almost inconceivable in today's world that a home-based site would not want to access the World Wide Web from a web browser. The next two rules allow access to remote web servers:

```
if [ "$CONNECTION_TRACKING" = "1" ]; then
    $IPT -A OUTPUT -o $INTERNET -p tcp \
            -s $IPADDR --sport $UNPRIVPORTS \
            --dport 80 -m state --state NEW -j ACCEPT
fi

$IPT -A OUTPUT -o $INTERNET -p tcp \
        -s $IPADDR --sport $UNPRIVPORTS \
        --dport 80 -j ACCEPT

$IPT -A INPUT -i $INTERNET -p tcp ! --syn \
        --sport 80 \
        -d $IPADDR --dport $UNPRIVPORTS -j ACCEPT
```

ALLOWING REMOTE ACCESS TO A LOCAL WEB SERVER

If you decide to run a web server of your own and host a public website, the following general server rules allow all typical incoming access to your site. This is all that most people need in order to host a website:

```
if [ "$CONNECTION_TRACKING" = "1" ]; then
    $IPT -A INPUT  -i $INTERNET -p tcp \
            --sport $UNPRIVPORTS \
            -d $IPADDR --dport 80 \
            -m state --state NEW -j ACCEPT
fi

$IPT -A INPUT  -i $INTERNET -p tcp \
        --sport $UNPRIVPORTS \
        -d $IPADDR --dport 80 -j ACCEPT

$IPT -A OUTPUT -o $INTERNET -p tcp ! --syn \
        -s $IPADDR --sport 80 \
        --dport $UNPRIVPORTS -j ACCEPT
```

SECURE WEB ACCESS (SSL AND TLS) (TCP PORT 443)

Secure Sockets Layer (SSL) and Transport Layer Security (TLS) are used for secure, encrypted web access. The protocols use TCP port 443. You will most often encounter this if you go to a commercial website to purchase something, use online banking services, or enter a protected web area where you'll be prompted for personal information. The Apache web server shipped with Red Hat Linux 7.1 includes OpenSSL support. Table 4.9 lists the complete client/server connection protocol for the service.

TABLE 4.9
SSL and TLS Protocol

DESCRIPTION	PROTOCOL	REMOTE ADDRESS	REMOTE PORT	IN/OUT	LOCAL ADDRESS	LOCAL PORT	TCP FLAG
Local client request	TCP	ANYWHERE	443	Out	IPADDR	1024:65535	Any
Remote server response	TCP	ANYWHERE	443	In	IPADDR	1024:65535	ACK
Remote client request	TCP	ANYWHERE	1024:65535	In	IPADDR	443	Any
Local server response	TCP	ANYWHERE	1024:65535	Out	IPADDR	443	ACK

ACCESSING REMOTE WEBSITES OVER SSL OR TLS AS A CLIENT

Most people will want client access to secure websites at some point:

```
if [ "$CONNECTION_TRACKING" = "1" ]; then
    $IPT -A OUTPUT -o $INTERNET -p tcp \
            -s $IPADDR --sport $UNPRIVPORTS \
```

```
                    --dport 443 -m state --state NEW -j ACCEPT
fi

$IPT -A OUTPUT -o $INTERNET -p tcp \
        -s $IPADDR --sport $UNPRIVPORTS \
        --dport 443 -j ACCEPT

$IPT -A INPUT -i $INTERNET -p tcp ! --syn \
        --sport 443 \
        -d $IPADDR --dport $UNPRIVPORTS -j ACCEPT
```

ALLOWING REMOTE ACCESS TO A LOCAL SSL OR TLS WEB SERVER

If you conduct some form of e-commerce or have a user-authenticated web area, you'll most likely want to allow incoming connections to encryption-protected areas of your website. Otherwise, you won't need local server rules.

Both the OpenSSL included with Linux and commercial SSL support packages are available for the Apache web server. See http://www.apache.org for more information.

The next two rules allow incoming access to your web server using the SSL or TLS protocols:

```
if [ "$CONNECTION_TRACKING" = "1" ]; then
    $IPT -A INPUT  -i $INTERNET -p tcp \
            --sport $UNPRIVPORTS \
            -d $IPADDR --dport 443 \
            -m state --state NEW -j ACCEPT
fi

$IPT -A INPUT  -i $INTERNET -p tcp \
        --sport $UNPRIVPORTS \
        -d $IPADDR --dport 443 -j ACCEPT

$IPT -A OUTPUT -o $INTERNET -p tcp ! --syn \
        -s $IPADDR --sport 443 \
        --dport $UNPRIVPORTS -j ACCEPT
```

WEB PROXY ACCESS (TCP PORTS 8008, 8080)

Publicly accessible web server proxies are most common at ISPs. As a customer, you configure your browser to use a remote proxy service. Web proxies are often accessed through one of two unprivileged ports assigned for this purpose, ports **8008** or **8080**, as defined by the ISP. In return, you get faster web page access when the pages are already cached locally at your ISP's server and the relative anonymity of proxied access to remote sites. Your connections are not direct, but instead they are done on your behalf by your ISP's proxy. Table 4.10 lists the complete client/server connection protocol for the web proxy service.

TABLE 4.10
Web Proxy Protocol

DESCRIPTION	PROTOCOL	REMOTE ADDRESS	REMOTE PORT	IN/OUT	LOCAL ADDRESS	LOCAL PORT	TCP FLAG
Local client request	TCP	WEB PROXY SERVER	WEB PROXY PORT	Out	IPADDR	1024:65535	Any
Remote server response	TCP	WEB PROXY SERVER	WEB PROXY PORT	In	IPADDR	1024:65535	ACK

If you use a web proxy service offered by your ISP, the specific server address and port number will be defined by your ISP. The client rules are as shown here:

```
WEB_PROXY_SERVER="my.www.proxy"       # ISP Web proxy server, if any
WEB_PROXY_PORT="www.proxy.port"       # ISP Web proxy port, if any
                                      # typically 8008 or 8080
if [ "$CONNECTION_TRACKING" = "1" ]; then
    $IPT -A OUTPUT -o $INTERNET -p tcp \
            -s $IPADDR --sport $UNPRIVPORTS \
            -d $WEB_PROXY_SERVER --dport $WEB_PROXY_PORT \
            -m state --state NEW -j ACCEPT
fi

$IPT -A OUTPUT -o $INTERNET -p tcp \
        -s $IPADDR --sport $UNPRIVPORTS \
        -d $WEB_PROXY_SERVER --dport $WEB_PROXY_PORT -j ACCEPT

$IPT -A INPUT -i $INTERNET -p tcp ! --syn \
        -s $WEB_PROXY_SERVER --sport $WEB_PROXY_PORT \
        -d $IPADDR --dport $UNPRIVPORTS -j ACCEPT
```

Whois (TCP Port 43)

The whois program accesses the InterNIC Registration Services database. Table 4.11 lists the complete client/server connection protocol for the whois service.

TABLE 4.11
Whois Protocol

DESCRIPTION	PROTOCOL	REMOTE ADDRESS	REMOTE PORT	IN/OUT	LOCAL ADDRESS	LOCAL PORT	TCP FLAG
Local client request	TCP	ANYWHERE	43	Out	IPADDR	1024:65535	Any
Remote server response	TCP	ANYWHERE	43	In	IPADDR	1024:65535	ACK

The next two rules enable you to query an official remote server:

```
if [ "$CONNECTION_TRACKING" = "1" ]; then
    $IPT -A OUTPUT -o $INTERNET -p tcp \
            -s $IPADDR --sport $UNPRIVPORTS \
            --dport 43 -m state --state NEW -j ACCEPT
fi

$IPT -A OUTPUT -o $INTERNET -p tcp \
        -s $IPADDR --sport $UNPRIVPORTS \
        --dport 43 -j ACCEPT

$IPT -A INPUT -i $INTERNET -p tcp ! --syn \
        --sport 43 \
        -d $IPADDR --dport $UNPRIVPORTS -j ACCEPT
```

RealAudio, RealVideo, and QuickTime (TCP Ports 554 and 7070)

RealAudio, RealVideo, and QuickTime use the same ports. The control connection to the server is built on top of the Real-Time Streaming Protocol (RTSP). See RFC 2326, "Real Time Streaming Protocol (RTSP)," for more information on the protocol. The incoming data stream is built on top of the Real-Time Transport Protocol (RTP). See RFC 3550, "RTP: A Transport Protocol for Real-Time Applications," for more information on the RTP protocol. See http://www.realnetworks.com for more information on RealAudio and RealVideo firewall requirements.

The client programs can be configured to use TCP solely, to use TCP for the control connection and UDP for the data stream (the UDP port can be configured to be a single port or one from a range of ports), or to use the HTTP application protocol solely. The TCP server ports, 554 or 7070 and 7071, depend on the client and server versions. The UDP client ports range between 6970 and 7170 for newer clients. If your site uses the older RealAudio version 3.0 player, the UDP client port range is 6770 to 7170. The actual port range supported can vary by application and platform.

Typically, the client program uses the most efficient transport combination available. The client determines this by attempting the different methods. Because bidirectional protocols usually have problems getting through a firewall without ALG support, the data stream will usually arrive over the TCP or HTTP protocols.

In other words, without a firewall support module for RealAudio, your options are to use HTTP for the incoming stream, to open the specific TCP or UDP ports and not use the `state` module (or, at least, not use the `INVALID` match), or to open the required ports and place the rules for the data stream before the `state` match rules.

Table 4.12 lists the control and data streams for a local client.

TABLE 4.12
RealAudio Protocol

DESCRIPTION	PROTOCOL	REMOTE ADDRESS	REMOTE PORT	IN/OUT	LOCAL ADDRESS	LOCAL PORT	TCP FLAG
Local client control request	TCP	ANYWHERE	554,7070	Out	IPADDR	1024:65535	Any
Remote server control response	TCP	ANYWHERE	554,7070	In	IPADDR	1024:65535	ACK
Local client TCP data request	TCP	ANYWHERE	7071	Out	IPADDR	1024:65535	Any
Remote server TCP data response	TCP	ANYWHERE	7071	In	IPADDR	1024:65535	ACK
Remote server UDP data stream	UDP	ANYWHERE	1024:65535	In	IPADDR	6970:71709	—

The next rule pair establishes the control connection with the server:

```
if [ "$CONNECTION_TRACKING" = "1" ]; then
    $IPT -A OUTPUT -o $INTERNET -p tcp \
            -m multiport --source-port 554,7070 \
            --syn -s $IPADDR --sport $UNPRIVPORTS \
            -m state--state NEW -j ACCEPT
fi

$IPT -A OUTPUT -o $INTERNET -p tcp \
        -m multiport --destination-port 554,7070 \
        --syn -s $IPADDR --dport $UNPRIVPORTS -j ACCEPT

$IPT -A INPUT -i $INTERNET -p tcp \
        -m multiport --destination-port 554,7070 \
        ! --syn -d $IPADDR --dport $UNPRIVPORTS -j ACCEPT
```

The next rule allows the preferred incoming UDP data stream from the server:

```
$IPT -A INPUT -i $INTERNET -p udp \
        --sport $UNPRIVPORTS \
        -d $IPADDR --dport 6970:7170 -j ACCEPT
```

The next rule pair establishes the TCP data stream connection with the server:

```
if [ "$CONNECTION_TRACKING" = "1" ]; then
    $IPT -A OUTPUT -o $INTERNET -p tcp \
            -s $IPADDR --sport $UNPRIVPORTS \
            --dport 7071 -m state --state NEW -j ACCEPT
fi

$IPT -A OUTPUT -o $INTERNET -p tcp \
        -s $IPADDR --sport $UNPRIVPORTS \
        --dport 7071 -j ACCEPT

$IPT -A INPUT -i $INTERNET -p tcp ! --syn \
        --sport 7071 \
        -d $IPADDR --dport $UNPRIVPORTS -j ACCEPT
```

Enabling Common UDP Services

The stateless UDP protocol is inherently less secure than the connection-based TCP protocol. Because of this, many security-conscious sites completely disable, or else limit as much as possible, all access to UDP services. Obviously, UDP-based DNS exchanges are necessary, but the remote name servers can be explicitly specified in the firewall rules. As such, this section provides rules for only three services:

- traceroute
- Dynamic Host Configuration Protocol (DHCP)
- Network Time Protocol (NTP)

traceroute (UDP Port 33434)

On Unix and Linux systems, traceroute is a UDP service that causes intermediate systems to generate ICMP Time Exceeded messages to gather hop count information, and that causes the target system to return a Destination Unreachable message, indicating the endpoint of the route to the host. By the default deny policy, the firewall being developed in this chapter blocks incoming UDP traceroute packets because traceroute default ports are not explicitly enabled. As a result, outgoing ICMP responses to incoming traceroute requests won't be sent. Table 4.13 lists the complete client/server connection protocol for the traceroute service.

TABLE 4.13
traceroute Protocol

DESCRIPTION	PROTOCOL	REMOTE ADDRESS	REMOTE PORT / ICMP TYPE	IN/OUT	LOCAL ADDRESS	LOCAL PORT / ICMP TYPE
Outgoing traceroute probe	UDP	ANYWHERE	33434:33523	Out	IPADDR	32769:66535
Time exceeded (intermediate hop)	ICMP	ANYWHERE	11	In	IPADDR	—
Port not found (termination)	UDP	ANYWHERE	3	In	IPADDR	—
Incoming traceroute probe	UDP	ISP	32769:65535	In	IPADDR	33434:33523
Time exceeded (intermediate hop)	ICMP	ISP	—	Out	IPADDR	11
Port not found (termination)	ICMP	ISP	—	Out	IPADDR	3

traceroute can be configured to use any port or port range. As such, it's difficult to block all incoming traceroute packets by listing specific ports. However, it often uses source ports in the range from 32,769 to 65,535 and destination ports in the range from 33,434 to 33,523. Because traceroute can be configured to use any source and destination port, the most effective way to block incoming traceroute is to block the outgoing ICMP messages generated in response. Symbolic constants are defined for traceroute's default source and destination ports:

```
TRACEROUTE_SRC_PORTS="32769:65535"
TRACEROUTE_DEST_PORTS="33434:33523"
```

ENABLING OUTGOING traceroute REQUESTS

If you intend to use traceroute yourself, you must enable the UDP client ports. Note that you must allow incoming ICMP Time Exceeded and Destination Unreachable messages from anywhere for outgoing traceroute to work:

```
$IPT -A OUTPUT -o $INTERNET -p udp \
        -s $IPADDR --sport $TRACEROUTE_SRC_PORTS \
        --dport $TRACEROUTE_DEST_PORTS -j ACCEPT
```

Because traceroute is a less secure UDP service and can be used to identify your edge router, map your LAN, or attack other UDP services, allowing incoming traceroute isn't recommended.

Accessing Your ISP's DHCP Server (UDP Ports 67, 68)

DHCP exchanges, if any, between your site and your ISP's server will necessarily be local client-to-remote server exchanges. Most often, DHCP clients receive temporary, or semipermanent, dynamically allocated IP addresses from a central server that manages the ISP's customer IP address space. The server also typically provides your local host with other configuration information, such as the network subnet mask; the network MTU; the default, first-hop router addresses; the domain name; and the default TTL.

If you have a dynamically allocated IP address from your ISP, you need to run a DHCP client daemon on your machine. It's not uncommon for bogus DHCP server messages to fly around your ISP's local subnet if someone runs the server by accident. For this reason, it's especially important to filter DHCP messages to limit traffic between your client and your specific ISP DHCP server as much as possible.

Table 4.14 lists the DHCP message type descriptions, as quoted from RFC 2131, "Dynamic Host Configuration Protocol."

TABLE 4.14
DHCP Message Types

DHCP MESSAGE	DESCRIPTION
DHCPDISCOVER	Client broadcast to locate available servers
DHCPOFFER	Server to client in response to DHCPDISCOVER with offer of configuration parameters
DHCPREQUEST	Client message to servers either (a) requesting offered parameters from one server and implicitly declining offers from all others; (b) confirming correctness of previously allocated address after, for example, system reboot; or (c) extending the lease on a particular network address
DHCPACK	Server to client with configuration parameters, including committed network address
DHCPNAK	Server to client indicating that client's notion of network address is incorrect (for example, client has moved to new subnet) or client's lease has expired

TABLE 4.14
DHCP Message Types (continued)

DHCP MESSAGE	DESCRIPTION
DHCPDECLINE	Client to server indicating that network address is already in use
DHCPRELEASE	Client to server relinquishing network address and canceling remaining lease
DHCPINFORM	Client to server, asking only for local configuration parameters; client already has externally configured address

In essence, when the DHCP client initializes, it broadcasts a **DHCPDISCOVER** query to discover whether any DHCP servers are available. Any servers receiving the query may respond with a **DHCPOFFER** message indicating their willingness to function as server to this client; they include the configuration parameters that they have to offer. The client broadcasts a **DHCPREQUEST** message to accept one of the servers and to inform any remaining servers that it has chosen to decline their offers. The chosen server responds with a broadcast **DHCPACK** message, indicating confirmation of the parameters that it originally offered. Address assignment is complete at this point. Periodically, the client sends the server a **DHCPREQUEST** message requesting a renewal on the IP address lease. If the lease is renewed, the server responds with a unicast **DHCPACK** message. Otherwise, the client falls back to the initialization process. Table 4.15 lists the complete client/server exchange protocol for the DHCP service.

TABLE 4.15
DHCP Protocol

DESCRIPTION	PROTOCOL	REMOTE ADDRESS	REMOTE PORT	IN/OUT	LOCAL ADDRESS	LOCAL PORT
DHCPDISCOVER; DHCPREQUEST	UDP	255.255.255.255	67	Out	0.0.0.0	68
DHCPOFFER	UDP	0.0.0.0	67	In	255.255.255.255	68
DHCPOFFER	UDP	DHCP SERVER	67	In	255.255.255.255	68
DHCPREQUEST; DHCPDECLINE	UDP	DHCP SERVER	67	Out	0.0.0.0	68
DHCPACK; DHCPNACK	UDP	DHCP SERVER	67	In	ISP/NETMASK	68
DHCPACK	UDP	DHCP SERVER	67	In	IPADDR	68
DHCPREQUEST; DHCPRELEASE	UDP	DHCP SERVER	67	Out	IPADDR	68

The DHCP protocol is far more complicated than this brief summary, but the summary describes the essentials of the typical client and server exchange. For more information, refer to the section "Choke as a Local DHCP Server (UDP Ports **67** and **68**)," in Chapter 6.

The following firewall rules allow communication between your DHCP client and a remote server:

```
DHCP_SERVER="my.dhcp.server"              # if you use one

# Initialization or rebinding: No lease or Lease time expired.

$IPT -A OUTPUT -o $INTERNET -p udp \
        -s $BROADCAST_SRC --sport 68 \
        -d $BROADCAST_DEST --dport 67 -j ACCEPT

# Incoming DHCPOFFER from available DHCP servers

$IPT -A INPUT  -i $INTERNET -p udp \
        -s $BROADCAST_SRC --sport 67 \
        -d $BROADCAST_DEST --dport 68 -j ACCEPT

# Fall back to initialization
# The client knows its server, but has either lost its lease,
# or else needs to reconfirm the IP address after rebooting.

$IPT -A OUTPUT -o $INTERNET -p udp \
        -s $BROADCAST_SRC --sport 68 \
        -d $DHCP_SERVER --dport 67 -j ACCEPT

$IPT -A INPUT  -i $INTERNET -p udp \
        -s $DHCP_SERVER --sport 67 \
        -d $BROADCAST_DEST --dport 68 -j ACCEPT

# As a result of the above, we're supposed to change our IP
# address with this message, which is addressed to our new
# address before the dhcp client has received the update.
# Depending on the server implementation, the destination address
# can be the new IP address, the subnet address, or the limited
# broadcast address.

# If the network subnet address is used as the destination,
# the next rule must allow incoming packets destined to the
# subnet address, and the rule must precede any general rules
# that block such incoming broadcast packets.

$IPT -A INPUT  -i $INTERNET -p udp \
```

```
            -s $DHCP_SERVER --sport 67 \
            --dport 68 -j ACCEPT

# Lease renewal

$IPT -A OUTPUT -o $INTERNET -p udp \
            -s $IPADDR --sport 68 \
            -d $DHCP_SERVER --dport 67 -j ACCEPT
$IPT -A INPUT  -i $INTERNET -p udp \
            -s $DHCP_SERVER --sport 67 \
            -d $IPADDR --dport 68 -j ACCEPT
```

Notice that DHCP traffic cannot be completely limited to your DHCP server. During initialization sequences, when your client doesn't yet have an assigned IP address or even the server's IP address, packets are broadcast rather than sent point-to-point. At the Layer 2 level, the packets may be addressed to your network card's hardware address.

Accessing Remote Network Time Servers (UDP Port 123)

Network time services such as NTP allow access to one or more public Internet time providers. This is useful to maintain an accurate system clock, particularly if your internal clock tends to drift, and to establish the correct time and date at bootup or after a power loss. A small-system user should use the service only as an Internet client. Few small sites have a satellite link to Greenwich, England; a radio link to an atomic clock; or an atomic clock of their own lying around.

ntpd is the server daemon. In addition to providing time service to clients, ntpd uses a peer-to-peer relationship among servers. Few small sites require the extra precision ntpd provides. ntpdate is the client program and uses a client-to-server relationship. The client program is all that a small site will need. Table 4.16 lists only the client/server exchange protocol for the NTP service. There is rarely, if ever, a reason to run ntpd itself because that's the server component. If you must run the NTP server (as opposed to the client), do so in a chroot environment.

TABLE 4.16
NTP Protocol

DESCRIPTION	PROTOCOL	REMOTE ADDRESS	REMOTE PORT	IN/OUT	LOCAL ADDRESS	LOCAL PORT
Local client query	UDP	TIMESERVER	123	Out	IPADDR	1024:65535
Remote server response	UDP	TIMESERVER	123	In	IPADDR	1024:65535

The ntpd startup script that is run at boot time uses ntpdate to query a series of public time service providers. The ntpd daemon is started after the server's reply. These hosts would be individually specified in a series of firewall rules:

```
TIME_SERVER="my.time.server"          # external time server, if any

if [ "$CONNECTION_TRACKING" = "1" ]; then
    $IPT -A OUTPUT -o $INTERNET -p udp \
            -s $IPADDR --sport $UNPRIVPORTS \
            -d $TIME_SERVER --dport 123 \
            -m state --state NEW -j ACCEPT
fi

$IPT -A OUTPUT -o $INTERNET -p udp \
        -s $IPADDR --sport $UNPRIVPORTS \
        -d $TIME_SERVER --dport 123 -j ACCEPT

$IPT -A INPUT  -i $INTERNET -p udp \
        -s $TIME_SERVER --sport 123 \
        -d $IPADDR --dport $UNPRIVPORTS -j ACCEPT
```

Note that the previous rules are written for a standard client/server UDP communication. Depending on your particular client and server software, it's possible that one or both of them will use the NTP server-to-server communication model, with both the client and the server using UDP port 123.

Filtering ICMP Control and Status Messages

ICMP control messages are generated in response to a number of error conditions, and they are produced by network analysis programs such as ping and traceroute.

ICMP MESSAGE TYPES AND IPTABLES

iptables supports the use of either the ICMP numeric message type or the alphabetic symbolic name.

iptables also supports use of the message subtypes, or codes. This is especially useful for finer filtering control over type 3 Destination Unreachable messages. For example, you could specifically disallow outgoing Port Unreachable messages to disable an incoming traceroute, or you could specifically allow only outgoing Fragmentation Needed messages.

To see a list of all supported ICMP symbolic names in iptables, run iptables -p icmp -h. To see the official RFC assignments, go to http://www.iana.org/assignments/icmp-parameters.

Error Status and Control Messages

Four ICMP control and status messages need to pass through the firewall: Source Quench, Parameter Problem, incoming Destination Unreachable, and outgoing Destination Unreachable of subtype Fragmentation Needed. Four other ICMP message types are optional: Echo Request, Echo Reply, other outgoing Destination Unreachable subtypes, and Time Exceeded. Other message types can be ignored, to be filtered out by the default policy.

Of the message types that can—or should—be ignored, only redirect is considered dangerous because of its role in denial-of-service attacks as a redirect bomb. (See Chapter 2 for more information on redirect bombs.) As with redirect, the remaining ICMP message types are specialized control and status messages intended for use between routers.

The following sections describe the message types important to an endpoint host machine, as opposed to an intermediate router, in more detail.

FRAGMENTED ICMP MESSAGES

An ICMP message will never be fragmented under normal circumstances. An ICMP message should fit entirely within a Layer 2 frame. It's safe to drop fragmented ICMP messages. Such packets are usually used in denial-of-service attacks:

```
$IPT -A INPUT  -i $INTERNET --fragment -p icmp -j LOG \
        --log-prefix "Fragmented ICMP: "

$IPT -A INPUT  -i $INTERNET --fragment -p icmp -j DROP
```

SOURCE QUENCH CONTROL (TYPE 4) MESSAGES

ICMP message type 4, Source Quench, can be sent when a connection source, usually a router, is sending data faster than the next destination router can handle it. Source Quench is used as a primitive form of flow control at the IP Network layer, usually between two adjacent, point-to-point machines:

```
$IPT -A INPUT  -i $INTERNET -p icmp \
        --icmp-type source-quench -d $IPADDR -j ACCEPT

$IPT -A OUTPUT -o $INTERNET -p icmp \
        -s $IPADDR --icmp-type source-quench -j ACCEPT
```

The router's next hop or destination machine sends a **Source Quench** command. The originating router responds by sending packets at a slower rate, gradually increasing the rate until it receives another Source Quench message.

In practice, Source Quench is not much used within the Internet anymore. Flow control is left to the higher-level protocols. The message type is seen on LANs, however.

PARAMETER PROBLEM STATUS (TYPE 12) MESSAGES

ICMP message type 12, Parameter Problem, is sent when a packet is received containing illegal or unexpected data in the header, or when the header checksum doesn't match the checksum generated by the receiving machine:

```
$IPT -A INPUT  -i $INTERNET -p icmp \
       --icmp-type parameter-problem -d $IPADDR -j ACCEPT

$IPT -A OUTPUT -o $INTERNET -p icmp \
       -s $IPADDR --icmp-type parameter-problem -j ACCEPT
```

DESTINATION UNREACHABLE ERROR (TYPE 3) MESSAGES

ICMP message type 3, Destination Unreachable, is a general error status message:

```
$IPT -A INPUT  -i $INTERNET -p icmp \
       --icmp-type destination-unreachable -d $IPADDR -j ACCEPT

$IPT -A OUTPUT -o $INTERNET -p icmp \
       -s $IPADDR --icmp-type fragmentation-needed -j ACCEPT

# Don't log dropped outgoing ICMP error messages
$IPT -A OUTPUT -o $INTERNET -p icmp \
       -s $IPADDR --icmp-type destination-unreachable -j DROP
```

The ICMP packet header for type 3 messages, Destination Unreachable, contains an error code field identifying the particular kind of error. Ideally, you'd want to drop outgoing type 3 messages. This message type is what is sent in response to a port scan used to map your service ports or address space. An attacker can create a denial-of-service condition by forcing your system to generate large numbers of these messages by bombarding your unused ports. Worse, an attacker can spoof the source address, forcing your system to send them to the spoofed hosts. Unfortunately, the Destination Unreachable message creates a Catch-22 situation. One of the message subtypes, Fragmentation Needed, is used to negotiate packet fragment size. Your network performance can be seriously degraded without this negotiation.

TIME EXCEEDED STATUS (TYPE 11) MESSAGES

ICMP message type 11, Time Exceeded, indicates a timeout condition—or, more accurately, that a packet's maximum hop count has been exceeded. On networks today, incoming Time Exceeded is mostly seen as the ICMP response to an outgoing UDP **traceroute** request:

```
$IPT -A INPUT  -i $INTERNET -p icmp \
       --icmp-type time-exceeded -d $IPADDR -j ACCEPT
```

If you want to use `traceroute`, you must allow incoming ICMP Time Exceeded messages. Because your machine is not an intermediate router, you have no other use for Time Exceeded messages.

`ping` Echo Request (Type 8) and Echo Reply (Type 0) Control Messages

`ping` uses two ICMP message types. The request message, Echo Request, is message type 8. The reply message, Echo Reply, is message type 0. `ping` is a simple network-analysis tool dating back to the original DARPANet. The name `ping` was taken from the idea of the audible ping played back by sonar systems. (DARPA is the Defense Advanced Research Projects Agency, after all.) Similar to sonar, an Echo Request message broadcast to all machines in a network address space generates Echo Reply messages, in return, from all hosts responding on the network.

> ### `smurf` ATTACKS
>
> Don't broadcast anything out unto the Internet. The `ping` broadcast mentioned previously is the basis of the `smurf` IP denial-of-service attack. See CERT Advisory CA-98.01.smurf at http://www.cert.org for more information on `smurf` attacks.

OUTGOING `ping` TO REMOTE HOSTS

The following rule pair enables you to `ping` any host on the Internet:

```
if [ "$CONNECTION_TRACKING" = "1" ]; then
    # allow outgoing pings to anywhere
    $IPT -A OUTPUT -o $INTERNET -p icmp \
            -s $IPADDR --icmp-type echo-request \
            -m state --state NEW -j ACCEPT
fi

# allow outgoing pings to anywhere
$IPT -A OUTPUT -o $INTERNET -p icmp \
        -s $IPADDR --icmp-type echo-request -j ACCEPT

$IPT -A INPUT  -i $INTERNET -p icmp \
        --icmp-type echo-reply -d $IPADDR -j ACCEPT
```

INCOMING `ping` FROM REMOTE HOSTS

The approach shown here allows only selected external hosts to `ping` you:

```
if [ "$CONNECTION_TRACKING" = "1" ]; then
    # allow incoming pings from trusted hosts
    $IPT -A INPUT  -i $INTERNET -p icmp \
            -s $MY_ISP --icmp-type echo-request -d $IPADDR \
            -m state --state NEW -j ACCEPT
fi

# allow incoming pings from trusted hosts
$IPT -A INPUT  -i $INTERNET -p icmp \
        -s $MY_ISP --icmp-type echo-request -d $IPADDR -j ACCEPT

$IPT -A OUTPUT -o $INTERNET -p icmp \
        -s $IPADDR --icmp-type echo-reply -d $MY_ISP -j ACCEPT
```

For the purposes of the example you've been building in this chapter, external hosts allowed to **ping** your machine are machines belonging to your ISP. Chances are good that your network operations center or customer support will want to **ping** your external interface. If your machine is a DHCP client, it's possible that the DHCP implementation depends on **ping** as well. Except for those from your local network neighbors, other incoming Echo Requests are denied. **ping** has been used in several types of denial-of-service attacks.

Logging Dropped Incoming Packets

Any packet matching a rule can be logged by using the **-j LOG** target. Logging a packet has no effect on the packet's disposition, however. The packet must match an accept or drop rule. Some of the rules presented previously had logging enabled, before matching the packet a second time to drop it. Some of the IP address spoofing rules are examples.

Rules can be defined for the explicit purpose of logging certain kinds of packets. Most typically, packets of interest are suspicious packets indicating some sort of probe or scan. Because all packets are denied by default, if logging is desired for certain packet types, explicit rules must be defined before the packet falls off the end of the chain and the default policy takes effect. Essentially, out of all the denied packets, you might be interested in logging some of them, using rate-limited logging for some, and silently dropping others.

Which packets are logged is an individual matter. Some people want to log all dropped packets. For other people, logging all dropped packets could soon overflow their system logs. Some people, secure in the knowledge that the packets are dropped, don't care about them and don't want to know about them. Other people are interested in the obvious port scans or in some particular packet type.

Because of the first-matching-rule-wins behavior, you could log all dropped incoming packets with a single rule. The assumption here is that all packet-matching acceptance rules have been tested, and the packet is about to drop off the end of the chain and be thrown away:

```
$IPT -A INPUT -i $INTERNET -j LOG
```

For some people, this will produce too many log entries—or too many uninteresting log entries. For example, you might want to log all dropped incoming ICMP traffic with the exception of `ping` because it is a common service, regardless of whether your site responds to `ping` requests:

```
$IPT -A INPUT -i $INTERNET -p icmp \
        --icmp-type ! 8 -d $IPADDR -j LOG
```

You might want to log dropped incoming TCP traffic to all ports and log dropped incoming UDP traffic to your privileged ports:

```
$IPT -A INPUT -i $INTERNET -p tcp \
        -d $IPADDR -j LOG

$IPT -A INPUT -i $INTERNET -p udp \
        -d $IPADDR --dport $PRIVPORTS -j LOG
```

Then again, you might want to log all dropped privileged port access, with the exception of commonly probed ports that you don't offer service on anyway:

```
$IPT -A INPUT -i $INTERNET -p tcp \
        -d $IPADDR --dport 0:19 -j LOG

# skip ftp, telnet, ssh
$IPT -A INPUT -i $INTERNET -p tcp \
        -d $IPADDR --dport 24 -j LOG
# skip smtp
$IPT -A INPUT -i $INTERNET -p tcp \
        -d $IPADDR --dport 26:78 -j LOG
# skip finger, www
$IPT -A INPUT -i $INTERNET -p tcp \
        -d $IPADDR --dport 81:109 -j LOG
# skip pop-3, sunrpc
$IPT -A INPUT -i $INTERNET -p tcp \
        -d $IPADDR --dport 112:136 -j LOG
# skip NetBIOS
$IPT -A INPUT -i $INTERNET -p tcp \
        -d $IPADDR --dport 140:142 -j LOG
# skip imap
$IPT -A INPUT -i $INTERNET -p tcp \
        -d $IPADDR --dport 144:442 -j LOG
```

```
# skip secure_web/SSL
$IPT -A INPUT -i $INTERNET -p tcp \
        -d $IPADDR --dport 444:65535 -j LOG


#UDP rules
$IPT -A INPUT -i $INTERNET -p udp \
        -d $IPADDR --dport 0:110 -j LOG
# skip sunrpc
$IPT -A INPUT -i $INTERNET -p udp \
        -d $IPADDR --dport 112:160 -j LOG
# skip snmp
$IPT -A INPUT -i $INTERNET -p udp \
        -d $IPADDR --dport 163:634 -j LOG
# skip NFS mountd
$IPT -A INPUT -i $INTERNET -p udp \
        -d $IPADDR --dport 636:5631 -j LOG
# skip pcAnywhere
$IPT -A INPUT -i $INTERNET -p udp \
        -d $IPADDR --dport 5633:31336 -j LOG
# skip traceroute's default ports
$IPT -A INPUT -i $INTERNET -p udp \
        --sport $TRACEROUTE_SRC \
        -d $IPADDR --dport $TRACEROUTE_DEST -j LOG


# skip the rest
$IPT -A INPUT -i $INTERNET -p udp \
        -d $IPADDR --dport 33434:65535 -j LOG
```

Logging Dropped Outgoing Packets

Logging outgoing traffic blocked by the firewall rules is necessary for debugging the firewall rules and to be alerted to local software problems.

With the exception of outgoing ICMP type 3 errors, which were dropped previously, possibly all traffic about to be dropped by the default policy could be logged:

```
$IPT -A OUTPUT -o $INTERNET -j LOG
```

Denying Access to Problem Sites Up Front

If some site is making a habit of scanning your machine or otherwise being a nuisance, you might decide to deny it access to everything, at least until the problem behavior is corrected.

One way to do this without editing the `rc.firewall` script each time is to include a separate file of specific drop rules. By inserting the rules into the **INPUT** chain rather than appending them, the site will be blocked even if subsequent rules would otherwise allow them access to some service. The file is named **/etc/rc.d/rc.firewall.blocked**. To avoid a possible runtime error, check for the file's existence before trying to include it:

```
# Refuse packets claiming to be from the banned list
if [ -f /etc/rc.d/rc.firewall.blocked ]; then
    . /etc/rc.d/rc.firewall.blocked
fi
```

An example of a global drop rule in the `rc.firewall.blocked` file is this:

```
$IPT -I INPUT -i $INTERNET -s <address/mask> -j DROP
```

As an alternative to inserting the rules at the very beginning of the chains, which would precede state checking, the rules could be append rules, and the file could be included in the spoofed source address section of the ruleset.

Any packet from this source address range is dropped, regardless of message protocol type or source or destination port.

Installing the Firewall

This section assumes that the firewall script is called `rc.firewall`. There's no reason that the script couldn't be called simply **fwscript** or something else either. In fact, on Debian systems the standard is closer to the single name, **fwscript**, rather than a name prefixed with an **rc.** as is the case on Red Hat. This section covers the commands as if the script was installed in either **/etc/rc.d/** for a Red Hat or SUSE system and **/etc/init.d/** for a Debian system.

As a shell script, initial installation is simple. The script should be owned by **root**. On Red Hat and SUSE:

```
chown root.root /etc/rc.d/rc.firewall
```

On Debian:

```
chown root.root /etc/init.d/rc.firewall
```

The script should be writable and executable by **root** alone. Ideally, the general user should not have read access. On Red Hat and SUSE:

```
chmod u=rwx /etc/rc.d/rc.firewall
```

On Debian:

```
chmod u=rwx /etc/init.d/rc.firewall
```

To initialize the firewall at any time, execute the script from the command line. There is no need to reboot:

```
/etc/rc.d/rc.firewall start
```

Technically, the **start** argument isn't required there, but it's a good habit anyway—again, I'd rather err on the side of completeness than have ambiguity with a firewall. The script includes a **stop** action that flushes the firewall entirely. Therefore, if you want to stop the firewall, call the same command with the **stop** argument:

```
/etc/rc.d/rc.firewall stop
```

Be forewarned: If you stop the firewall in this way, you are running with no protection. The attorneys tell me that I should tell you, "Always leave the firewall enabled!"

On Debian, change the path for the command to **/etc/init.d**. Start the firewall:

```
/etc/init.d/rc.firewall start
```

Stop the firewall on Debian:

```
/etc/init.d/rc.firewall stop
```

Tips for Debugging the Firewall Script

When you're debugging a new firewall script through an SSH or another remote connection, it's quite possible that you might lock yourself out of the system. Granted, this isn't a concern when you're installing the firewall from the console, but as someone who manages remote Linux servers, I find that access to the console is rarely possible. Therefore, a method is necessary for stopping the firewall automatically after it gets started, just in case the firewall locks out my connection. Cron to the rescue.

Using a cron entry, you can stop the firewall by running the script with a **stop** argument at some predefined interval. I find that every 2 minutes works well during initial debugging. If you'd like to use this method, set a cron entry with the following command as **root** (on Debian):

```
crontab -e
*/2 * * * * /etc/init.d/rc.firewall stop
```

On Red Hat and SUSE:

```
crontab -e
*/2 * * * * /etc/rc.d/rc.firewall stop
```

With this cron entry in place, you can start the firewall and have it stop every 2 minutes. Using such a mechanism is somewhat of a trade-off though, because you have to do your initial debugging before the clock hits a minute divisible by two! Additionally, it's up to you to remember to remove this cron entry when you've debugged the firewall. If you forget to remove this entry the firewall will stop and you'll be running with no firewall again!

Starting the Firewall on Boot with Red Hat and SUSE

On Red Hat and SUSE, the simplest way to initialize the firewall is to edit `/etc/rc.d/rc.local` and add the following line to the end of the file:

```
/etc/rc.d/rc.firewall start
```

After the firewall rules are debugged and stable, Red Hat Linux provides a more standard way to start and stop the firewall. If you chose `iptables` while using one of the runlevel managers, the default runlevel directory contains a link to `/etc/rc.d/init.d/_iptables`. As with the other startup scripts in this directory, the system will start and stop the firewall automatically when booting or changing runlevels.

One additional step is required to use the standard runlevel system, however. You must first manually install the firewall rules:

```
/etc/rc.d/rc.firewall
```

Then execute the command:

```
/etc/init.d/iptables save
```

The rules will be saved in a file, `/etc/sysconfig/iptables`. After this, the startup script will find this file and load the saved rules automatically.

A word of caution is in order about saving and loading the firewall rules using this method. The `iptables save` and `load` features are not fully debugged at this point. If your particular firewall configuration results in a syntax error when saving or loading the rules, you must continue using some other startup mechanism, such as executing the firewall script from `/etc/rc.d/rc.local`.

Starting the Firewall on Boot with Debian

As with many other things, configuring the firewall script to start on boot is simpler on Debian than on other distributions. You can make the firewall start and stop on boot with the `update-rc.d` command. Run `update-rc.d` with the firewall script in `/etc/init.d`, and set your current directory to `/etc/init.d/` as well:

```
cd /etc/init.d
update-rc.d rc.firewall defaults
```

See the man page for `update-rc.d` for more information on its usage beyond that shown here.

Other aspects of the firewall script depend on whether you have a registered, static IP address or a dynamic, DHCP-assigned IP address. The firewall script as presented in this chapter is set up for a site with a statically assigned, permanent IP address.

Installing a Firewall with a Dynamic IP Address

If you have a dynamically assigned IP address, the standard firewall installation method won't work without modification. The firewall rules would be installed before the network interfaces are brought up, before the system is assigned an IP address, and possibly before being assigned a default gateway router or name servers.

The firewall script itself needs the **IPADDR** and **NAMESERVER** values defined. Both the DHCP server and the local /etc/resolv.conf file can define up to three name servers. Also, any given site may or may not know the addresses of their name servers, default gateway router, or DHCP server ahead of time. Furthermore, it's not uncommon for your network mask, subnet, and broadcast addresses to change over time as the ISP renumbers its network. Some ISPs assign a different IP address on a frequent basis, with the result that your IP address can change numerous times during the course of an ongoing connection.

Your site must provide some means of dynamically updating the installed firewall rules as these changes occur. Appendix B, "Firewall Examples and Support Scripts," provides sample scripts designed to handle these changes automatically.

In addition, if you're using a DSL connection, there's a chance that the MTU might cause problems. If this is the case, here's a firewall rule to fix the problem:

```
$IPT -A OUTPUT -o $INTERNET -p tcp --tcp-flags SYN,RST \
    SYN -j TCPMSS --clamp-mss-to-pmtu
```

The firewall script could read these shell variables directly from the environment or could read them from a file. In any case, the variables would not be hard-coded into the firewall script, as they are in the example in this chapter.

Summary

This chapter led you through the processes involved in developing a standalone firewall using iptables. The deny-by-default policy was established. Some commonly used attack vectors were fixed at the beginning of the script, including source address spoofing, protecting services running on unprivileged ports, and DNS. Examples of rules for popular network services were shown. ICMP messages, the control and status messages used by the underlying IP Network layer, were handled as well. Examples of controlling the level of logging produced were demonstrated. Finally, the issues involved in firewall installation were described, both for sites with a static IP address and for sites with a dynamically assigned IP address.

Chapter 5 uses the standalone firewall as the basis for building an optimized firewall. Chapter 6 uses it as the basis for a more complicated firewall architecture. A screened subnet architecture using two firewalls separating a DMZ perimeter network is described in Chapter 6. A small business could easily have the need and the resources for this more elaborate configuration. Chapter 7 uses the standalone firewall as the basis for its examples but does not build on this example directly.

PART II

Advanced Issues, Multiple Firewalls, and Perimeter Networks

5 Firewall Optimization

6 Packet Forwarding

7 NAT—Network Address Translation

8 Debugging the Firewall Rules

## CHAPTER 5

Firewall Optimization

Chapter 4, "Building and Installing a Standalone Firewall," used the iptables firewall administration program to build a simple, single-system, custom-designed firewall. This chapter introduces firewall optimization. Optimization can be divided into three major categories: rule organization, use of the state module, and user-defined chains. The example in the preceding chapter was shown both with and without the use of the state module. This chapter focuses on rule organization and user-defined chains.

Rule Organization

Little optimization can be done using only the INPUT, OUTPUT, and FORWARD chains. Chain traversal is top to bottom, one rule at a time, until the packet matches a rule. The rules on a chain must be ordered hierarchically, from most general to most specific.

There is no hard-and-fast formula for rule organization. The two main underlying factors are which services are hosted on the machine and the machine's primary purpose, noting especially the heaviest traffic services on the machine. The requirements of a dedicated firewall and packet forwarder are very different from those of a bastion firewall protecting a dedicated web or mail server. Likewise, a site administrator is likely to place different performance priorities on a firewalled machine that serves primarily as a workstation than a firewall that serves as both a residential gateway and a Linux server for a home.

The third underlying factor to consider when preparing to organize rules for firewall optimization is the available network bandwidth, the speed of the Internet connection. Optimization isn't likely to buy much, if anything, for a site with a residential-speed Internet connection. Even for a heavily accessed website, the machine's CPU isn't likely to break a sweat. The bottleneck is the Internet connection itself.

Begin with Rules That Block Traffic on High Ports

As the example in Chapter 4 demonstrated, the bulk of the rules are antispoofing rules, or rules blocking traffic on specific high ports (such as NFS or X Windows). These types of rules must come before the rules allowing traffic to specific services. Obviously, the FTP data channel rules must come near the end of the rule list, even though you'd want the rules to be near the top of the list because FTP transfers tend to be large.

Use the State Module for ESTABLISHED and RELATED Matches

Using the state module's ESTABLISHED and RELATED matches essentially allows for moving all rules for ongoing exchanges to the head of the chains, as well as eliminating the need for specific rules for the server half of a connection. In fact, bypassing filter matching for ongoing, recognized, previously accepted exchanges is one of the two primary purposes of the state module.

The state module's second primary purpose is to serve a firewall-filtering function. Connection-state tracking allows the firewall to associate packets with ongoing exchanges. This is particularly useful for connectionless, stateless UDP exchanges.

Consider the Transport Protocol

The transport protocol that the service runs over is another factor. In a static firewall, the overhead of testing every single incoming packet against all the spoofing rules is a big loss.

TCP SERVICES: BYPASS THE SPOOFING RULES

Even without the state module, for TCP-based services, the rule for the remote server half of a connection can bypass the spoofing rules. The TCP layer will drop incoming spoofed packets with the ACK bit set because the packet won't match any of the TCP layer's established connection states.

The remote client half of a rule pair must follow the spoofing rules, however, because the typical client rule covers both the initial connection request and the ongoing traffic from the client. If the SYN and ACK flags are tested for individually, the rules testing for the ACK flag in packets arriving from remote clients can bypass the spoofing tests. The spoofing tests must apply to only the initial SYN request.

Use of the state module also allows the rule for the remote client's incoming connection request, the initial SYN packet, to be logically separate from the rule for the client's subsequent ACK packets. Only the initial connection request, the initial NEW packet, needs to be tested against the spoofing rules.

UDP SERVICES: PLACE INCOMING PACKET RULES AFTER SPOOFING RULES

Without the state module, for UDP-based services the rule for incoming packets must always follow the spoofing rules. The concept of client and server is maintained at the application level, assuming that it's maintained at all. At the firewall and UDP levels, without connection state, there is no indication of initiator and responder, other than the service port or unprivileged port used. As you saw in Chapter 4, some UDP services use the associated well-known service port for both the client and the server, whereas other services use unprivileged ports for both.

DNS is an example of a connectionless UDP service. Without connection state, there isn't a mapping between the destination address where the client sent a query and the source address in an incoming response packet. One of the reasons DNS cache poisoning is possible is that DNS server implementations do not check whether an incoming packet was a legitimate response from the server previously queried or whether the packet was sent from some other address. Furthermore, some implementations do not even ensure that a client made a request. An incoming, unrequested rogue packet could be used to update the local DNS cache even without an initial query having been made.

TCP VERSUS UDP SERVICES: PLACE UDP RULES AFTER TCP RULES

Overall, UDP rules should be placed later in the firewall chains, after any TCP rules. This is because most Internet services run over TCP, and connectionless UDP services are typically simple, single-packet query-and-response services. Testing the single or UDP packet or a handful of them against the preceding rules for ongoing TCP connections doesn't add noticeable drag to a UDP query and response. A notable exception is streaming media, such as the RealAudio data stream. However, as stated in Chapter 4, multimedia and other bidirectional, multiconnection session protocols are not firewall-friendly to begin with. Such services cannot pass through a firewall or NAT without specific ALG support.

ICMP SERVICES: PLACE THEIR RULES LATE IN THE RULE CHAIN

ICMP is another protocol whose firewall rules can be placed late in the rule chain. ICMP packets are small control and status messages. As such, they are sent relatively infrequently. Legitimate ICMP packets usually consist of a single, nonfragmented packet. With the exception of echo-request, ICMP packets are almost always sent as a control or status message in response to an exceptional outgoing packet of some kind.

Place Firewall Rules for Heavily Used Services as Early as Possible

Generally, there are no hard-and-fast rules for firewall rule placement in a list. Rules for heavily used services, such as the HTTP-related rules for a dedicated web server, should be placed as early as possible. Rules for applications that involve high, ongoing packet counts also should be placed as early as possible. However, as mentioned earlier, the data stream protocols for applications such as FTP and RealAudio require the rules to be placed near the end of the chain, after any other application rules.

Use the Multiport Module to Specify Port Lists

Some small gains can be had by using the multiport module to specify port lists, thereby collapsing several rules into one. Both the number of rules in the list and the number of specific match tests performed are reduced. Effectively, the packets matching one of the ports in the list share a single instance of the tests for the interface, protocol, TCP flags, and source and destination address. The actual amount of gain seen is dependent on the specific services the firewall accepts. Obviously, the services represented by the ports must share identical transport header characteristics to share the specific set of tests the rule represents.

Use Traffic Flow to Determine Where to Place Rules for Multiple Network Interfaces

If the host has multiple network interfaces, rules specific to a given interface should be placed with regard to which interfaces will have the heaviest traffic flow. Rules for those interfaces should precede rules for other interfaces. Interface considerations are probably of little interest to a residential site, but they can have a major impact on throughput for a commercial site.

As a case in point, this issue came up several years ago with a small ISP that had built a firewall based on the ipfwadm and ipchains examples on Bob Ziegler's website. As shown in Figure 5.1 and Figure 5.2, the path that packets take through the operating system is very different between IPFW and Netfilter. Unlike Netfilter and iptables, with ipchains, packets passing between network interfaces are passed from the input chain to the forward chain to the output chain. The examples on the website were intended as examples for people at home. The input and output rules for the LAN were the last rules in the scripts. The rules specific to the local Linux host came first. The ISP's firewall was primarily functioning as a router or gateway. Through experimentation, the ISP found that moving the I/O rules for the LAN interface to the beginning of the input and output chains resulted in more than a megabit-per-second increase in throughput.

FIGURE 5.1
IPFW loopback and masqueraded packet traversal.

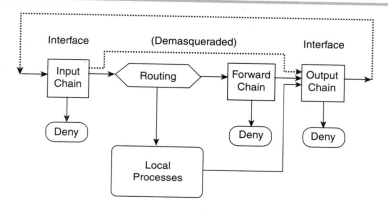

FIGURE 5.2
Netfilter packet traversal.

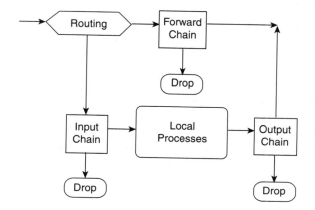

User-Defined Chains

The `filter` table has three permanent, built-in chains: `INPUT`, `OUTPUT`, and `FORWARD`. iptables enables you to define chains of your own, called user-defined chains. These user-defined chains are treated as rule targets—that is, based on the set of matches specified in a rule, the target can branch off or jump to a user-defined chain. Rather than the packet being accepted or dropped, control is passed to the user-defined chain to perform more specific match tests relative to packets matching the branch rule. After the user-defined chain is traversed, control returns to the calling chain, and matching continues from the next rule in the calling chain unless the user-defined chain matched and took action on the packet.

Figure 5.3 shows the standard, top-down rule traversal using the built-in chains.

FIGURE 5.3
Standard chain traversal.

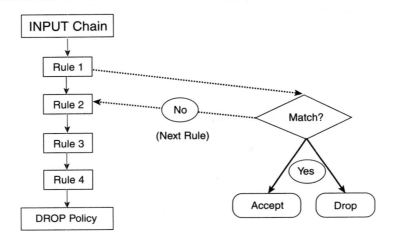

User-defined chains are useful in optimizing the ruleset and therefore are often used. They allow the rules to be organized into categorical trees. Rather than relying on the straight-through, top-down check-off list type of matching inherent in the standard chain traversal, packet match tests can be selectively narrowed down based on the characteristics of the packet. Figure 5.4 shows initial packet flow. After initial tests common to all incoming packets are performed, packet matching branches off based on the destination address in the packet.

Branching is based on destination address in this example. Source address matching is done later in relation to specific applications, such as remote DNS or mail servers. In most cases, the remote address will be "anywhere." Matching on destination address at this point distinguishes between unicast packets targeted to this machine, broadcast packets, multicast packets, and (depending on whether it's the **INPUT** or **FORWARD** chain) packets targeted to internal hosts.

Figure 5.5 details the user-defined chain for the protocol rules for packets specifically addressed to this host. As shown, user-defined chains can jump to other user-defined chains containing even more specific tests.

FIGURE 5.4
User-defined chains based on destination address.

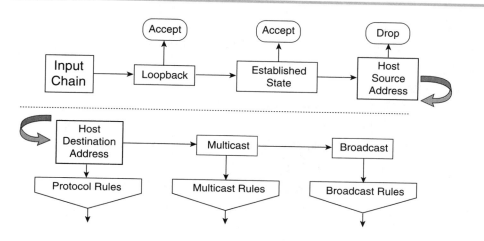

FIGURE 5.5
User-defined chains based on protocol.

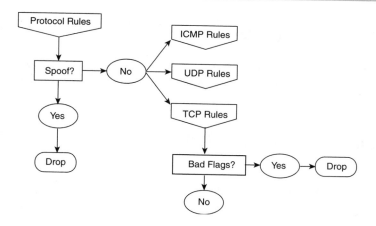

This list summarizes the characteristics of user-defined chains from Chapter 3, "iptables: The Linux Firewall Administration Program":

- User-defined chains are created with the **-N** or **--new-chain** operations.
- User-defined chain names can be up to 30 characters in length.

- User-defined chain names can contain hyphens (-) but not underscores (_).
- User-defined chains are accessed as rule targets.
- User-defined chains do not have default policies.
- User-defined chains can call other user-defined chains.
- If the packet doesn't match a rule on the user-defined chain, control returns to the next rule in the calling chain.
- The user-defined chain can be exited early, with control returning to the next rule in the calling chain, via use of the RETURN target.
- User-defined chains are deleted with the -X or --delete-chain operations.
- A chain must be empty before it can be deleted.
- A chain cannot have any references to it from other chains to be deleted.
- A chain is emptied specifically by name, or all existing chains are emptied if no chain is specified, with the -F or --flush operations.

The next section takes advantage of user-defined chains and the concepts presented in the section on rule organization to optimize the single-system firewall presented in Chapter 4.

Optimized Example

In the example that follows, the shell variables and kernel-level protection services are the same as those listed in the example in Chapter 4. One new variable is declared, USER_CHAINS, which contains the names of all the user-defined chains used in the script.

User-Defined Chains in the Script

The chains are listed here:

- tcp-state-flags—Contains the rules to check for invalid TCP state flag combinations.
- connection-tracking—Contains the rules to check for state-related matches, INVALID, ESTABLISHED, and RELATED.
- source-address-check—Contains the rules to check for illegal source addresses.
- destination-address-check—Contains the rules to check for illegal destination addresses.
- EXT-input—Contains the interface-specific user-defined chains for the INPUT chain. In this example, the host has one interface connected to the Internet.

- **EXT-output**—Contains the interface-specific user-defined chains for the **OUTPUT** chain. In this example, the host has one interface connected to the Internet.

- **local_dns_server_query**—Contains the rules for outgoing queries from either the local DNS server or local clients.

- **remote_dns_server_response**—Contains the rules for incoming responses from a remote DNS server.

- **local_tcp_client_request**—Contains the rules for outgoing TCP connection requests and locally generated client traffic to remote servers.

- **remote_tcp_server_response**—Contains the rules for incoming responses from remote TCP servers.

- **remote_tcp_client_request**—Contains the rules for incoming TCP connection requests and remotely generated client traffic to local servers.

- **local_tcp_server_response**—Contains the rules for outgoing responses to remote clients.

- **local_udp_client_request**—Contains the rules for outgoing UDP client traffic to remote servers.

- **remote_udp_server_response**—Contains the rules for incoming responses from remote UDP servers.

- **EXT-icmp-out**—Contains the rules for outgoing ICMP packets.

- **EXT-icmp-in**—Contains the rules for incoming ICMP packets.

- **EXT-log-in**—Contains the logging rules for incoming packets before dropping them by the default **INPUT** policy.

- **EXT-log-out**—Contains the logging rules for outgoing packets before dropping them by the default **OUTPUT** policy.

- **log-tcp-state**—Contains the logging rules for TCP packets with illegal state flag combinations, before dropping them.

- **remote_dhcp_server_response**—Contains the rules for incoming packets from this host's DHCP server.

- **local_dhcp_client_query**—Contains the rules for outgoing DHCP client packets.

Some interface-specific chains are prefaced with **EXT** to differentiate them from any user-defined chains containing rules for any LAN interfaces. This firewall example assumes that there is only one interface, the external interface. The point is to suggest that different rules and security policies could be defined on a per-interface basis.

The actual declaration in the firewall shell script would be as shown here:

```
USER_CHAINS="EXT-input          EXT-output \
            tcp-state-flags      connection-tracking  \
            source-address-check destination-address-check  \
            local-dns-server-query   remote-dns-server-response  \
            local-tcp-client-request remote-tcp-server-response \
            remote-tcp-client-request local-tcp-server-response \
            local-udp-client-request remote-udp-server-response \
            local-dhcp-client-query  remote-dhcp-server-response \
            EXT-icmp-out         EXT-icmp-in \
            EXT-log-in           EXT-log-out \
            log-tcp-state"
```

Firewall Initialization

The firewall script starts out identically to the example in Chapter 4. Recall that a number of shell variables were set, including one called $IPT to define the location of the iptables firewall administration command:

```
#!/bin/sh
```

```
IPT="/sbin/iptables"                   # Location of iptables on your system
INTERNET="eth0"                        # Internet-connected interface
LOOPBACK_INTERFACE="lo"                # however your system names it
IPADDR="my.ip.address"                 # your IP address
MY_ISP="my.isp.address.range"          # ISP server & NOC address range
SUBNET_BASE="my.subnet.network"        # Your subnet's network address
SUBNET_BROADCAST="my.subnet.bcast"     # Your subnet's broadcast address
LOOPBACK="127.0.0.0/8"                 # reserved loopback address range
CLASS_A="10.0.0.0/8"                   # class A private networks
CLASS_B="172.16.0.0/12"                # class B private networks
CLASS_C="192.168.0.0/16"               # class C private networks
CLASS_D_MULTICAST="224.0.0.0/4"        # class D multicast addresses
CLASS_E_RESERVED_NET="240.0.0.0/5"     # class E reserved addresses
BROADCAST_SRC="0.0.0.0"                # broadcast source address
BROADCAST_DEST="255.255.255.255"       # broadcast destination address
PRIVPORTS="0:1023"                     # well-known, privileged port range
UNPRIVPORTS="1024:65535"               # unprivileged port range
```

A number of kernel parameters were also set; refer to Chapter 4 for an explanation of these parameters:

```
# Enable broadcast echo Protection
echo 1 > /proc/sys/net/ipv4/icmp_echo_ignore_broadcasts
# Disable Source Routed Packets
for f in /proc/sys/net/ipv4/conf/*/accept_source_route; do
```

```
    echo 0 > $f
done
# Enable TCP SYN Cookie Protection
echo 1 > /proc/sys/net/ipv4/tcp_syncookies
# Disable ICMP Redirect Acceptance
for f in /proc/sys/net/ipv4/conf/*/accept_redirects; do
    echo 0 > $f
done

# Don't send Redirect Messages
for f in /proc/sys/net/ipv4/conf/*/send_redirects; do
    echo 0 > $f
done
# Drop Spoofed Packets coming in on an interface, which, if replied to,
# would result in the reply going out a different interface.
for f in /proc/sys/net/ipv4/conf/*/rp_filter; do
    echo 1 > $f
done
# Log packets with impossible addresses.
for f in /proc/sys/net/ipv4/conf/*/log_martians; do
    echo 1 > $f
done
```

The built-in chains and any preexisting user-defined chains are emptied:

```
# Remove any existing rules from all chains
$IPT --flush
$IPT -t nat --flush
$IPT -t mangle --flush
```

The next step would be to delete the user-defined chains. They can be deleted with the following commands:

```
$IPT -X
$IPT -t nat -X
$IPT -t mangle -X
```

The default policy is first set to **ACCEPT** for all built-in chains:

```
# Reset the default policy
$IPT --policy INPUT   ACCEPT
$IPT --policy OUTPUT  ACCEPT
$IPT --policy FORWARD ACCEPT
$IPT -t nat --policy PREROUTING  ACCEPT
$IPT -t nat --policy OUTPUT ACCEPT
$IPT -t nat --policy POSTROUTING ACCEPT
$IPT -t mangle --policy PREROUTING ACCEPT
$IPT -t mangle --policy OUTPUT ACCEPT
```

Here is the final code for the beginning of the firewall script, namely the code to enable the firewall to be stopped easily. With this code placed below the preceding code, when you call the script with an argument of **stop** the script will flush, clear, and reset the default policies, and the firewall will effectively stop.

```
if [ "$1" = "stop" ]
then
echo "Firewall completely stopped!  WARNING: THIS HOST HAS NO FIREWALL RUNNING."
exit 0
fi
```

Now reset the real default policy to **DROP**:

```
$IPT --policy INPUT    DROP
$IPT --policy OUTPUT   DROP
$IPT --policy FORWARD DROP
$IPT -t nat --policy PREROUTING DROP
$IPT -t nat --policy OUTPUT DROP
$IPT -t nat --policy POSTROUTING DROP
$IPT -t mangle --policy PREROUTING DROP
$IPT -t mangle --policy OUTPUT DROP
```

Traffic through the loopback interface is enabled:

```
# Unlimited traffic on the loopback interface
$IPT -A INPUT   -i lo -j ACCEPT
$IPT -A OUTPUT -o lo -j ACCEPT
```

Now the script starts differing from the example in Chapter 4.

The user-defined chains can now be created. Their names were included in the single shell variable, USER_CHAINS, for just this purpose:

```
# Create the user-defined chains
for i in $USER_CHAINS; do
    $IPT -N $i
done
```

Installing the Chains

Unfortunately, the function call–like nature of building and installing the chains doesn't lend itself to a serial, step-by-step explanation without the capability to show different places in the script simultaneously, side by side.

The idea is to place the rules on the user-defined chains and then to install those chains on the built-in **INPUT**, **OUTPUT**, and **FORWARD** chains. If the script contains an error and exits while building the user-defined chains, the built-in chains will contain no rules, the default DROP policy will be in effect, and, presumably, the loopback traffic will be enabled.

So, this first installation section is actually placed at the end of the firewall script. The first step is to check for illegal TCP state flag combinations:

```
# If TCP: Check for common stealth scan TCP state patterns
$IPT -A INPUT  -p tcp -j tcp-state-flags
$IPT -A OUTPUT -p tcp -j tcp-state-flags
```

Notice that the same chain can be referenced from more than one calling chain. The rules on the user-defined chains needn't be duplicated for the INPUT and OUTPUT chains. Now when the packet processing reaches this point, the processing will "jump" to the user-defined tcp-state-flags chain. When the processing is complete within that chain, the processing will be passed back here and continue on, unless a final disposition for the packet was found in the user-defined chain.

If the state module is being used, the next step is to bypass the firewall altogether if the packet is part of an ongoing, previously accepted exchange:

```
if [ "$CONNECTION_TRACKING" = "1" ]; then
    # Bypass the firewall filters for established exchanges
    $IPT -A INPUT  -j connection-tracking
    $IPT -A OUTPUT -j connection-tracking
fi
```

If the machine is a DHCP client, a provision must be made for the broadcast messages sent between the client and the server during initialization. A provision must also be made to accept the broadcast source address, 0.0.0.0. The source and destination address-checking tests would drop the initial DHCP traffic:

```
if [ "$DHCP_CLIENT" = "1" ]; then
    $IPT -A INPUT  -i $INTERNET -p udp \
            --sport 67 --dport 68 -j remote-dhcp-server-response
    $IPT -A OUTPUT -o $INTERNET -p udp \
            --sport 68 --dport 67 -j local-dhcp-client-query
fi
```

Now jump to the user-defined chain to drop incoming packets that are using this host's IP address as their source address. Then test for other illegal source and destination addresses:

```
# Test for illegal source and destination addresses in incoming packets
$IPT -A INPUT  -p ! tcp -j source-address-check
$IPT -A INPUT  -p tcp --syn -j source-address-check
$IPT -A INPUT  -j destination-address-check
```

```
# Test for illegal destination addresses in outgoing packets
$IPT -A OUTPUT -j destination-address-check
```

Locally generated outgoing packets don't need their source address checked because the firewall rules explicitly require this host's IP address in the source field. Destination address checking is performed on outgoing packets, however.

At this point, regular incoming packets addressed to this host's IP address can be handed off to the main section of the firewall. Any incoming packet that doesn't match a rule on the EXT-input chain will return here to be logged and dropped:

```
# Begin standard firewall tests for packets addressed to this host
$IPT -A INPUT -i $INTERNET -d $IPADDR -j EXT-input
```

A final set of tests on destination address is necessary. Broadcast and multicast packets are not addressed to this host's unicast IP address. They are addressed to a broadcast or multicast address.

As mentioned in Chapter 4, multicast packets won't be received unless you register to receive packets addressed to a particular multicast address. If you want to receive multicast packets, you must either accept all of them or add a rule specific to the particular address and port used for any given session. The following code enables you to choose whether to drop or accept the traffic:

```
# Multicast traffic
$IPT -A INPUT  -i $INTERNET -p udp -d $CLASS_D_MULTICAST -j [ DROP | ACCEPT ]
$IPT -A OUTPUT -o $INTERNET -p udp -s $IPADDR -d $CLASS_D_MULTICAST \
    -j [ DROP | ACCEPT ]
```

At this point, regular outgoing packets from this host can be handed off to the main section of the firewall. Any outgoing packet that doesn't match a rule on the EXT-_output chain will return here to be logged and dropped:

```
# Begin standard firewall tests for packets sent from this host
# Source address spoofing by this host is not allowed due to the
# test on source address in this rule.
$IPT -A OUTPUT -o $INTERNET -s $IPADDR -j EXT-output
```

Any broadcast messages are implicitly ignored by the last input and output rules. Depending on the nature of the public or external network that the machine is directly connected to, broadcasts could be very common on the local subnet. You probably don't want to log such messages, even with rate-limited logging.

Finally, any remaining packets are dropped by the default policy. Any logging would be done at this point:

```
# Log anything of interest that fell through,
# before the default policy drops the packet.
$IPT -A INPUT  -j EXT-log-in
$IPT -A OUTPUT -j EXT-log-out
```

This marks the end of the firewall and is the last reference to the INPUT and OUTPUT chains.

Building the User-Defined EXT-input and EXT-output Chains

This section describes the construction of the user-defined chains that were jumped to in the preceding section. At the top level, rules are built on the general EXT-input and EXT-output chains. These rules are jumps to more specific sets of matches contained in the dedicated user-defined chains you've created.

Note that the EXT-input and EXT-output layer is not necessary. The following rules and jumps could just as easily have been associated with the built-in INPUT and OUTPUT chains.

Using these chains has one advantage, however. Because the jumps to these chains were dependent on the source or destination address, you know at this point that the incoming packet is addressed to this host and has a source address believed to be legitimate. The outgoing packet is addressed from this host and has a destination address believed to be legitimate. Also, if the state module is in use, the packet is either the first packet in an exchange or a new, unrelated ICMP packet.

In summary, the EXT-input and EXT-output chains will be used to select traffic by protocol and by direction, in terms of client or server. Each rule will provide the branch point to the firewall rules specific to that protocol and packet characteristics. The matches performed by the EXT-input and EXT-output rules are the heart of the optimization available with user-defined chains.

DNS TRAFFIC

The rules to identify DNS traffic come first. Until the DNS rules are installed, your network software won't be capable of locating services and hosts out on the Internet unless you use the IP address.

The first pair of rules match on queries from the local cache and forward name server, if you have one, and responses from the remote DNS server. The local server is configured as a slave to the remote, primary server, so the local server will fail if the lookup doesn't succeed. This configuration is less common for a small office/home office:

```
$IPT -A EXT-output -p udp --sport 53 --dport 53 \
      -j local-dns-server-query
```

```
$IPT -A EXT-input -p udp --sport 53 --dport 53 \
        -j remote-dns-server-response
```

The next pair of rules match on standard DNS client lookup requests over TCP, when the server's response is too large to fit in a UDP DNS packet. These rules would be used by both a forwarding name server and a standard client:

```
$IPT -A EXT-output -p tcp \
        --sport $UNPRIVPORTS --dport 53 \
        -j local-dns-server-query

$IPT A EXT-input -p tcp ! --syn \
        --sport 53 --dport $UNPRIVPORTS \
        -j remote-dns-server-response
```

What follows are the user-defined chains containing the actual **ACCEPT** and **DROP** rules.

local_dns_server_query **AND** remote_dns_server_response

These two user-defined chains, `local_dns_server_query` and `remote_dns_server_response`, perform the final determination on the packet.

The `local_dns_server_query` chain selects the outgoing request packets based on the remote server's destination address. For this chain, you must define the nameservers you'd like to use:

```
NAMESERVER_1="your.name.server"
NAMESERVER_2="your.secondary.nameserver"
NAMESERVER_3="your.tertiary.nameserver"

# DNS Forwarding Name Server or client requests
if [ "$CONNECTION_TRACKING" = "1" ]; then
    $IPT -A local-dns-server-query \
            -d $NAMESERVER_1 \
            -m state --state NEW -j ACCEPT

    $IPT -A local-dns-server-query \
            -d $NAMESERVER_2 \
            -m state --state NEW -j ACCEPT

    $IPT -A local-dns-server-query \
            -d $NAMESERVER_3 \
            -m state --state NEW -j ACCEPT
fi

$IPT -A local-dns-server-query \
        -d $NAMESERVER_1 -j ACCEPT
```

```
$IPT -A local-dns-server-query \
        -d $NAMESERVER_2 -j ACCEPT

$IPT -A local-dns-server-query \
        -d $NAMESERVER_3 -j ACCEPT
```

The `remote_dns_server_response` chain selects the incoming response packets based on the remote server's source address:

```
# DNS server responses to local requests
$IPT -A remote-dns-server-response \
        -s $NAMESERVER_1 -j ACCEPT

$IPT -A remote-dns-server-response \
        -s $NAMESERVER_2 -j ACCEPT

$IPT -A remote-dns-server-response \
        -s $NAMESERVER_3 -j ACCEPT
```

Notice that the final rules select on only the remote server's IP address. The calling rules on the `EXT-input` and `EXT-output` chains already have matched on the UDP or TCP header fields. Those match tests don't need to be performed again.

`local_dns_client_request` **AND** `remote_dns_server_response`

These two user-defined chains, `local_dns_client_request` and `remote_dns_server_response`, perform the final determination on packets exchanged between local TCP clients and remote servers.

The `local_dns_client_request` chain selects the outgoing request packets based on the remote server's destination address and port. The `remote_dns_server_response` chain selects the incoming response packets based on the remote server's source address and port.

LOCAL CLIENT TRAFFIC OVER TCP

The next pair of rules match on standard, local client traffic to remote servers over TCP:

```
$IPT -A EXT-output -p tcp \
        --sport $UNPRIVPORTS \
        -j local-tcp-client-request

$IPT -A EXT-input -p tcp ! --syn \
        --dport $UNPRIVPORTS \
        -j remote-tcp-server-response
```

Remember that these rules normally are not tested when the state module is used, with the exception of the first outgoing **SYN** request.

The specific reference to the TCP protocol is required in the following rules, even though the protocol field was matched on by the calling rule, because the source or destination port is specified. This is a syntactic requirement of iptables. Also note that you need to define the source and destination hosts within these rules, as indicated by the `<selected host>` and other such calls. In addition, if you use these rules, be sure to define variables for the ones you choose, such as `POP_SERVER`, `MAIL_SERVER`, `NEWS_SERVER`, and so on. The following code enables TCP traffic from local clients:

```
# Local TCP client output and remote server input chains

# SSH client
if [ "$CONNECTION_TRACKING" = "1" ]; then
    $IPT -A local-tcp-client-request -p tcp \
            -d <selected host> --dport 22 \
            -m state --state NEW \
            -j ACCEPT
fi

$IPT -A local-tcp-client-request -p tcp \
        -d <selected host> --dport 22 \
        -j ACCEPT

$IPT -A remote-tcp-server-response -p tcp ! --syn \
        -s <selected host> --sport 22  \
        -j ACCEPT

# Client rules for HTTP, HTTPS and FTP control requests
if [ "$CONNECTION_TRACKING" = "1" ]; then
    $IPT -A local-tcp-client-request -p tcp \
            -m multiport --destination-port 80,443,21 \
            --syn -m state --state NEW \
            -j ACCEPT
fi
$IPT -A local-tcp-client-request -p tcp \
        -m multiport --destination-port 80,443,21 \
        -j ACCEPT

$IPT -A remote-tcp-server-response -p tcp \
        -m multiport --source-port 80,443,21  ! --syn \
        -j ACCEPT

# POP client
if [ "$CONNECTION_TRACKING" = "1" ]; then
    $IPT -A local-tcp-client-request -p tcp \
            -d $POP_SERVER --dport 110 \
            -m state --state NEW \
```

```
                    -j ACCEPT
      fi

$IPT -A local-tcp-client-request -p tcp \
          -d $POP_SERVER --dport 110 \
          -j ACCEPT

$IPT -A remote-tcp-server-response -p tcp ! --syn \
          -s $POP_SERVER --sport 110 \
          -j ACCEPT

# SMTP mail client
if [ "$CONNECTION_TRACKING" = "1" ]; then
    $IPT -A local-tcp-client-request -p tcp \
              -d $MAIL_SERVER --dport 25 \
              -m state --state NEW \
              -j ACCEPT
fi

$IPT -A local-tcp-client-request -p tcp \
          -d $MAIL_SERVER --dport 25 \
          -j ACCEPT

$IPT -A remote-tcp-server-response -p tcp ! --syn \
          -s $MAIL_SERVER --sport 25 \
          -j ACCEPT

# Usenet news client
if [ "$CONNECTION_TRACKING" = "1" ]; then
    $IPT -A local-tcp-client-request -p tcp \
              -d $NEWS_SERVER --dport 119 \
              -m state --state NEW \
              -j ACCEPT
fi
$IPT -A local-tcp-client-request -p tcp \
          -d $NEWS_SERVER --dport 119 \
          -j ACCEPT

$IPT -A remote-tcp-server-response -p tcp ! --syn \
          -s $NEWS_SERVER --sport 119 \
          -j ACCEPT

# FTP client - passive mode data channel connection
if [ "$CONNECTION_TRACKING" = "1" ]; then
    $IPT -A local-tcp-client-request -p tcp \
              --dport $UNPRIVPORTS \
```

```
            -m state --state NEW \
            -j ACCEPT
fi

$IPT -A local-tcp-client-request -p tcp \
        --dport $UNPRIVPORTS -j ACCEPT

$IPT -A remote-tcp-server-response -p tcp  ! --syn \
        --sport $UNPRIVPORTS -j ACCEPT
```

LOCAL SERVER TRAFFIC OVER TCP

The next pair of rules match on standard, local server traffic to remote clients over TCP. These would be applicable only if you're actually offering services to remote hosts:

```
$IPT -A EXT-input -p tcp \
        --sport $UNPRIVPORTS \
        -j remote-tcp-client-request

$IPT -A EXT-output -p tcp ! --syn \
        --dport $UNPRIVPORTS \
        -j local-tcp-server-response
```

The next pair of rules handle incoming data channel connections from remote FTP servers when using port mode:

```
# Kludge for incoming FTP data channel connections
# from remote servers using port mode.
# The state modules treat this connection as RELATED
# if the ip_conntrack_ftp module is loaded.

$IPT -A EXT-input -p tcp \
        --sport 20 --dport $UNPRIVPORTS \
        -j ACCEPT

$IPT -A EXT-output -p tcp ! --syn \
        --sport $UNPRIVPORTS --dport 20 \
        -j ACCEPT
```

`remote_tcp_client_request` **AND** `local_tcp_server_response`

These two user-defined chains, **remote_tcp_client_request** and **local_tcp_server_response**, perform the final determination on packets exchanged between remote TCP clients and local servers.

The **remote_tcp_client_request** chain selects the incoming request packets based on the remote client's source address and port. The **local_tcp_server_response** chain selects the outgoing response packets based on the remote client's destination address and port:

```
# Remote TCP client input and local server output chains

# SSH server
if [ "$CONNECTION_TRACKING" = "1" ]; then
    $IPT -A remote-tcp-client-request -p tcp \
            -s <selected host> --destination-port 22 \
            -m state --state NEW \
            -j ACCEPT
fi

$IPT -A remote-tcp-client-request -p tcp \
        -s <selected host> --destination-port 22 \
        -j ACCEPT

$IPT -A local-tcp-server-response -p tcp  ! --syn \
        --source-port 22 -d <selected host> \
        -j ACCEPT

# AUTH identd server
$IPT -A remote-tcp-client-request -p tcp \
        --destination-port 113 \
        -j REJECT --reject-with tcp-reset
```

LOCAL CLIENT TRAFFIC OVER UDP

The next pair of rules match on standard, local client traffic to remote servers over UDP:

```
# Local UDP client, remote server
$IPT -A EXT-output -p udp \
        --sport $UNPRIVPORTS \
        -j local-udp-client-request

$IPT -A EXT-input -p udp \
        --dport $UNPRIVPORTS \
        -j remote-udp-server-response
```

BYPASSING SOURCE ADDRESS CHECKING WITHOUT USING THE STATE MODULE

If you aren't using the state module, most TCP rules could still be placed before the source address spoofing rules. TCP maintains connection state information itself. Only the first incoming connection request, the first SYN packet, requires source address checking. You can do this by reorganizing the rules and splitting the rule for incoming client traffic into two tests, one for the initial SYN flag and one for all subsequent ACK flags.

Using the rules for a local web server as an example, the first rule would follow the spoofing rules:

```
        if [ "$CONNECTION_TRACKING" = "1" ]; then
            $IPT -A remote-tcp-client-request -p tcp \
                    --destination-port 80 \
                    -m state --state NEW \
                    -j ACCEPT
        else
            $IPT -A remote-tcp-client-request -p tcp --syn \
                    --destination-port 80 \
                    -j ACCEPT
        fi

The next two rules would precede the spoofing rules:

        $IPT -A INPUT -p tcp ! --syn \
                --source-port $UNPRIVPORTS \
                -d $IPADDR --destination-port 80 \
                -j ACCEPT

        $IPT -A OUTPUT -p tcp  ! --syn \
                -s $IPADDR --source-port 80  \
                --destination-port $UNPRIVPORTS \
                -j ACCEPT
```

local_udp_client_request **AND** remote_udp_server_response

These two user-defined chains, `local_udp_client_request` and
`remote_udp_server_response`, perform the final determination on packets exchanged
between local UDP clients and remote servers.

The `local_udp_client_request` chain selects the outgoing request packets based on the
remote server's destination address and port. The `remote_udp_server_response` chain selects
the incoming response packets based on the remote server's source address and port. Be sure
to define the `TIME_SERVER` variable before implementing this rule:

```
# NTP time client
if [ "$CONNECTION_TRACKING" = "1" ]; then
    $IPT -A local-udp-client-request -p udp \
            -d $TIME_SERVER --dport 123 \
            -m state --state NEW \
            -j ACCEPT
fi
$IPT -A local-udp-client-request -p udp \
        -d $TIME_SERVER --dport 123 \
        -j ACCEPT

$IPT -A remote-udp-server-response -p udp \
        -s $TIME_SERVER --sport 123 \
        -j ACCEPT
```

ICMP TRAFFIC

Finally, the last pair of rules match on incoming and outgoing ICMP traffic:

```
# ICMP traffic
$IPT -A EXT-input -p icmp -j EXT-icmp-in

$IPT -A EXT-output -p icmp -j EXT-icmp-out
```

EXT-icmp-in **AND** EXT-icmp-out

These two user-defined chains, **EXT-icmp-in** and **EXT-icmp-out**, perform the final determination on ICMP packets exchanged between the local host and remote machines.

The **EXT-icmp-in** chain selects the incoming ICMP packets based on the message type. The **EXT-icmp-out** chain selects the outgoing ICMP packets based on the message type:

```
# Log and drop initial ICMP fragments
$IPT -A EXT-icmp-in --fragment -j LOG \
        --log-prefix "Fragmented incoming ICMP: "

$IPT -A EXT-icmp-in --fragment -j DROP

$IPT -A EXT-icmp-out --fragment -j LOG \
        --log-prefix "Fragmented outgoing ICMP: "

$IPT -A EXT-icmp-out --fragment -j DROP

# Outgoing ping
if [ "$CONNECTION_TRACKING" = "1" ]; then
    $IPT -A EXT-icmp-out -p icmp \
            --icmp-type echo-request \
            -m state --state NEW \
            -j ACCEPT
fi

$IPT -A EXT-icmp-out -p icmp \
        --icmp-type echo-request -j ACCEPT

$IPT -A EXT-icmp-in -p icmp \
        --icmp-type echo-reply -j ACCEPT

# Incoming ping

if [ "$CONNECTION_TRACKING" = "1" ]; then
    $IPT -A EXT-icmp-in -p icmp \
            -s $MY_ISP \
            --icmp-type echo-request \
```

```
                -m state --state NEW \
                -j ACCEPT
fi

$IPT -A EXT-icmp-in -p icmp \
        --icmp-type echo-request \
        -s $MY_ISP -j ACCEPT

$IPT -A EXT-icmp-out -p icmp \
        --icmp-type echo-reply \
        -d $MY_ISP -j ACCEPT

# Destination Unreachable Type 3
$IPT -A EXT-icmp-out -p icmp \
        --icmp-type fragmentation-needed -j ACCEPT

$IPT -A EXT-icmp-in -p icmp \
        --icmp-type destination-unreachable -j ACCEPT

# Parameter Problem
$IPT -A EXT-icmp-out -p icmp \
        --icmp-type parameter-problem -j ACCEPT

$IPT -A EXT-icmp-in -p icmp \
        --icmp-type parameter-problem -j ACCEPT

# Time Exceeded
$IPT -A EXT-icmp-in -p icmp \
        --icmp-type time-exceeded -j ACCEPT

# Source Quench
$IPT -A EXT-icmp-out -p icmp \
        --icmp-type source-quench -j ACCEPT

$IPT -A EXT-icmp-in -p icmp \
        --icmp-type source-quench -j ACCEPT
```

tcp-state-flags

The **tcp-state-flags** chain is the very first user-defined chain you will attach to both the built-in **INPUT** and **OUTPUT** chains. The tests match on TCP state flag combinations that are artificially crafted and often are used in stealth scans:

```
# All of the bits are cleared
$IPT -A tcp-state-flags -p tcp --tcp-flags ALL NONE -j log-tcp-state
```

```
# SYN and FIN are both set
$IPT -A tcp-state-flags -p tcp --tcp-flags SYN,FIN SYN,FIN -j log-tcp-state

# SYN and RST are both set
$IPT -A tcp-state-flags -p tcp --tcp-flags SYN,RST SYN,RST -j log-tcp-state

# FIN and RST are both set
$IPT -A tcp-state-flags -p tcp --tcp-flags FIN,RST FIN,RST -j log-tcp-state

# FIN is the only bit set, without the expected accompanying ACK
$IPT -A tcp-state-flags -p tcp --tcp-flags ACK,FIN FIN -j log-tcp-state

# PSH is the only bit set, without the expected accompanying ACK
$IPT -A tcp-state-flags -p tcp --tcp-flags ACK,PSH PSH -j log-tcp-state

# URG is the only bit set, without the expected accompanying ACK
$IPT -A tcp-state-flags -p tcp --tcp-flags ACK,URG URG -j log-tcp-state
```

log-tcp-state

The log-tcp-state chain is used for two reasons. First, the log message is prefixed with a specific explanatory message, and because this is a crafted packet, any IP or TCP options are reported. Second, the matching packet is dropped immediately. The two generalized logging chains that come up later are written under the assumption that the logged packets will be dropped by the default policy immediately upon return from the chains:

```
$IPT -A log-tcp-state -p tcp -j LOG \
        --log-prefix "Illegal TCP state: " \
        --log-ip-options --log-tcp-options

$IPT -A log-tcp-state -j DROP
```

connection-tracking

The connection-tracking chain is the second user-defined chain you will attach to both the built-in INPUT and OUTPUT chains. Matching packets bypass the firewall rules and are accepted immediately:

```
if [ "$CONNECTION_TRACKING" = "1" ]; then
    # Bypass the firewall filters for established exchanges
    $IPT -A connection-tracking -m state \
            --state ESTABLISHED,RELATED \
            -j ACCEPT
```

```
$IPT -A connection-tracking -m state --state INVALID \
        -j LOG --log-prefix "INVALID packet: "
$IPT -A connection-tracking -m state --state INVALID -j DROP
fi
```

local_dhcp_client_query and remote_dhcp_server_response

The local_dhcp_client_query and remote_dhcp_server_response chains contain the rules required of a DHCP client. Placement of these rules in the chain hierarchy is important in relation to any spoofing or generalized broadcast rules. Furthermore, the host will not configure its IP address until after receiving the **DHCPACK** commitment message from the server. The destination address that the server uses in the **DHCPACK** message depends on the particular server implementation. If you want to use this rule, you'll need to set **DHCP_CLIENT** to **1** and also define the **DHCP_SERVER** variable:

```
# Some broadcast packets are explicitly ignored by the firewall.
# Others are dropped by the default policy.
# DHCP tests must precede broadcast-related rules, as DHCP relies
# on broadcast traffic initially.

if [ "$DHCP_CLIENT" = "1" ]; then
    DHCP_SERVER="my.dhcp.server"

    # Initialization or rebinding: No lease or Lease time expired.

    $IPT -A local-dhcp-client-query \
            -s $BROADCAST_SRC \
            -d $BROADCAST_DEST -j ACCEPT


    # Incoming DHCPOFFER from available DHCP servers

    $IPT -A remote-dhcp-server-response \
            -s $BROADCAST_SRC \
            -d $BROADCAST_DEST -j ACCEPT


    # Fall back to initialization
    # The client knows its server, but has either lost its lease,
    # or else needs to reconfirm the IP address after rebooting.

    $IPT -A local-dhcp-client-query \
            -s $BROADCAST_SRC \
            -d $DHCP_SERVER -j ACCEPT
```

```
$IPT -A remote-dhcp-server-response \
       -s $DHCP_SERVER \
       -d $BROADCAST_DEST -j ACCEPT

# As a result of the above, we're supposed to change our IP
# address with this message, which is addressed to our new
# address before the dhcp client has received the update.
# Depending on the server implementation, the destination address
# can be the new IP address, the subnet address, or the limited
# broadcast address.

# If the network subnet address is used as the destination,
# the next rule must allow incoming packets destined to the
# subnet address, and the rule must precede any general rules
# that block such incoming broadcast packets.

$IPT -A remote-dhcp-server-response \
       -s $DHCP_SERVER -j ACCEPT

# Lease renewal

$IPT -A local-dhcp-client-query \
       -s $IPADDR \
       -d $DHCP_SERVER -j ACCEPT

fi
```

source-address-check

The **source-address-check** chain tests for identifiably illegal source addresses. The chain is attached to the **INPUT** chain alone. The firewall rules guarantee that packets generated by this host contain your IP address as their source address. Notice that these rules would need some adjustment if the host had more than one network interface or if a private LAN was using private class IP addresses.

A DHCP client needs to handle DHCP-related broadcast traffic before performing these tests:

```
# Drop packets pretending to be originating from the receiving interface
$IPT -A source-address-check -s $IPADDR -j DROP

# Refuse packets claiming to be from private networks

$IPT -A source-address-check -s $CLASS_A -j DROP
$IPT -A source-address-check -s $CLASS_B -j DROP
$IPT -A source-address-check -s $CLASS_C -j DROP
$IPT -A source-address-check -s $CLASS_D_MULTICAST -j DROP
```

```
$IPT -A source-address-check -s $CLASS_E_RESERVED_NET -j DROP
$IPT -A source-address-check -s $LOOPBACK  -j DROP

$IPT -A source-address-check -s 0.0.0.0/8 -j DROP
$IPT -A source-address-check -s 169.254.0.0/16 -j DROP
$IPT -A source-address-check -s 192.0.2.0/24 -j DROP
```

destination-address-check

The `destination-address-check` chain tests for broadcast packets, misused multicast addresses, and well-known unprivileged service ports. The chain is attached to both the **INPUT** and **OUTPUT** chains. A DHCP client needs to handle DHCP-related broadcast traffic before performing these tests:

```
# Block directed broadcasts from the Internet

$IPT -A destination-address-check $BROADCAST_DEST -j DROP
$IPT -A destination-address-check -d $SUBNET_BASE -j DROP
$IPT -A destination-address-check -d $SUBNET_BROADCAST -j DROP
$IPT -A destination-address-check -p ! udp \
        -d $CLASS_D_MULTICAST -j DROP

# Avoid ports subject to protocol and system administration problems

# TCP unprivileged ports
# Deny connection requests to NFS, SOCKS and X Window ports
$IPT -A destination-address-check -p tcp -m multiport \
        --destination-port $NFS_PORT,$OPENWINDOWS_PORT,$SOCKS_PORT,$SQUID_PORT \
        --syn -j DROP

$IPT -A destination-address-check -p tcp --syn \
        --destination-port $XWINDOW_PORTS -j DROP

# UDP unprivileged ports
# Deny connection requests to NFS and lockd ports
$IPT -A destination-address-check -p udp -m multiport \
        --destination-port $NFS_PORT,$LOCKD_PORT -j DROP
```

Logging Dropped Packets

The **EXT-log-in** and **EXT-log-out** chains contain the rules that log packets immediately before the packets fall off the end of their respective chains and are dropped by the default policy. Almost all outgoing packets to be dropped are logged because they indicate either a problem in the firewall rules or an unknown (or unauthorized service) attempting to contact the outside world:

```
# ICMP rules

$IPT -A EXT-log-in -p icmp \
        --icmp-type ! echo-request -m limit -j LOG

# TCP rules

$IPT -A EXT-log-in -p tcp \
        --dport 0:19 -j LOG

# skip ftp, telnet, ssh
$IPT -A EXT-log-in -p tcp \
        --dport 24 -j LOG

# skip smtp
$IPT -A EXT-log-in -p tcp \
        --dport 26:78 -j LOG

# skip finger, www
$IPT -A EXT-log-in -p tcp \
        --dport 81:109 -j LOG

# skip pop-3, sunrpc
$IPT -A EXT-log-in -p tcp \
        --dport 112:136 -j LOG

# skip NetBIOS
$IPT -A EXT-log-in -p tcp \
        --dport 140:142 -j LOG

# skip imap
$IPT -A EXT-log-in -p tcp \
        --dport 144:442 -j LOG

# skip secure_web/SSL
$IPT -A EXT-log-in -p tcp \
        --dport 444:65535 -j LOG

#UDP rules

$IPT -A EXT-log-in -p udp \
        --dport 0:110 -j LOG

# skip sunrpc
$IPT -A EXT-log-in -p udp \
        --dport 112:160 -j LOG
```

```
# skip snmp
$IPT -A EXT-log-in -p udp \
        --dport 163:634 -j LOG

# skip NFS mountd
$IPT -A EXT-log-in -p udp \
        --dport 636:5631 -j LOG

# skip pcAnywhere
$IPT -A EXT-log-in -p udp \
        --dport 5633:31336 -j LOG

# skip traceroute's default ports
$IPT -A EXT-log-in -p udp \
        --sport $TRACEROUTE_SRC \
        --dport $TRACEROUTE_DEST -j LOG

# skip the rest
$IPT -A EXT-log-in -p udp \
        --dport 33434:65535 -j LOG

# Outgoing Packets

# Don't log rejected outgoing ICMP destination-unreachable packets
$IPT -A EXT-log-out -p icmp \
        --icmp-type destination-unreachable -j DROP

$IPT -A EXT-log-out -j LOG
```

What Did Optimization Buy?

The goal of optimization is to get the packet through the filter processing as quickly as possible, with as few unnecessary tests as possible. Ideally, you want the packets flowing through at line speed.

In terms of the firewall itself, three factors affect performance: the number of rules installed in the kernel; the chain traversal length, or the number of rules that any given packet is tested against before it matches; and the total number of match tests performed on the packet. Also, when it comes to using the state module, remember that the trade-off is speed versus memory.

By way of example, consider the FTP client-out and server-in rules, and compare the straight-through firewall presented in Chapter 4 with the optimized ruleset presented in this chapter. We'll also examine the differences that the state module makes.

Note that some of the variations in the tables are artifacts of how the sample scripts in Chapter 4 and this chapter are organized, as well as some differences in the TCP state flag and source address checks between the two examples.

The optimized versions have more rules than their straight-through counterparts! Even more surprising, the connection-tracking versions have more rules than the classic, stateless versions! Didn't we already conclude that use of the state match module reduces the number of rules by eliminating individual **ACCEPT** rules for server responses to client requests? Yes and no.... The absolute number of rules increases, because the static rules must remain present to account for any cases in which a state table entry has timed out or been replaced due to a resource shortage. The number of input rules *traversed* can drop dramatically.

Using user-defined chains results in a few more rules as well. The additional rules perform the intermediate packet selection and branching. There's a small amount of overhead in the top-level branching decisions. The overhead isn't significant and even the small amount of apparent overhead is deceiving. The number of rules traversed isn't as critical of a perform-ance metric as the number of individual header field match tests performed.

Optimization with user-defined chains can significantly reduce the number of rules that a response packet must be tested against before reaching its final matching rule. What isn't obvious here is that the straight-through ruleset includes a set amount of overhead because of the antispoofing rules. Because the example firewalls were client-centered, the straight-through server traversal lengths are much longer than the client lengths as a result of the address checking done on the incoming packets.

Using the state module and thereby bypassing the firewall for established traffic dramatically reduces list traversal length for established connections. The increase in number of rules tra-versed for new connections is the result of the duplicate rules, the connection-tracking rules, and their static counterparts.

Even with the state module, the initial packet always takes the static path. So the gain that the classic optimized version shows over the straight-through version still applies to the first packet.

Finally, the benefits of both optimization and connection state tracking are obvious! The categorization being performed by the user-defined chains dramatically reduces the actual number of tests that a packet is tested against in a classic packet-filtering firewall. Use of the state modules reduces the number of tests even further by skipping the rules altogether. Furthermore, the data channel connection is matched immediately as a **RELATED** connection.

What is perhaps least obvious, unless you've read the kernel firewall code, is that the real per-formance issue isn't the number of rules traversed, per se, but the number of comparison tests performed. Each unmatched, traversed rule represents at least one comparison (for example, is the incoming packet an ICMP packet or a TCP packet, or is it arriving on the loopback interface or some other specific interface?). User-defined chains allow the comparisons to be partitioned by branching off into dedicated chains at critical comparison decision points.

Summary

Chapter 4 introduced iptables by walking through the steps of building a simple firewall for a standalone system. This chapter discussed the ideas behind firewall optimization and then built user-defined chains to optimize the firewall example from Chapter 4. Finally, the effects of optimization were examined, as were the effects of using the state module.

## CHAPTER 6

Packet Forwarding

This chapter covers some of the basic issues underlying LAN security, the forwarding of gateway firewalls, and perimeter networks. Security policies are defined relative to the site's level of security needs, the importance or value of the data being protected, and the cost of lost data or privacy. This chapter opens by reviewing the firewalls presented in earlier chapters and then discusses issues that the site's policy maker must address when choosing server placement and determining security policies.

You may need Network Address Translation (NAT) to access the Internet from internal machines. NAT is not discussed until Chapter 7, "NAT—Network Address Translation." This chapter focuses on forwarding alone.

For readers familiar with `ipchains` or `ipfwadm`, forwarding and NAT were combined syntactically. Both functions were specified by a single forward rule. These logically distinct functions are clearly distinct in iptables. In fact, the two functions are handled by separate tables with separate chains. All forwarded packets, NATed or not, require forwarding rules. NAT is applied separately at a different point in the packet's traversal path through the system. This chapter focuses on the iptables services available in the `filter` table and in its extensions. Chapter 7 looks at the services available in the `nat` table and in its extensions.

The Limitations of a Standalone Firewall

The single-system firewall presented in Chapter 4, "Building and Installing a Standalone Firewall," is a basic bastion firewall, using only the `INPUT` and `OUTPUT` chains. When the firewall is a packet-filtering router that has a network interface connected to the Internet and another connected to your LAN (referred to as a *dual-homed* system), the firewall applies rules to decide whether to forward or block packets crossing between the two interfaces. In this case, the packet-filtering firewall is a static router with traffic-screening rules enforcing local policies concerning which packets are allowed through the network interfaces.

As pointed out in Chapter 3, "iptables: The Linux Firewall Administration Program," Netfilter handles forwarded packets quite differently from the previous IPFW mechanism. Forwarded packets are inspected by the **FORWARD** chain alone. The **INPUT** and **OUTPUT** rules don't apply. Network traffic related to the local firewall host and network traffic related to the LAN have completely different sets of rules and rule chains.

Rules on the **FORWARD** chain can specify both the incoming and the outgoing interface. For a dual-homed host setup with a LAN, the firewall rules applied to the incoming and outgoing network interfaces represent an I/O pair—one rule for arriving packets and a reverse rule for departing packets. The rules are directional. The two interfaces are handled as a unit.

Traffic is not routed directly between the Internet and the LAN automatically. Packets to be forwarded won't flow without a rule pair to accept the traffic. The filtering rules applied to the two interfaces act as a firewall and static router between the two networks.

The firewall configuration presented in Chapter 4 is perfectly adequate for an individual home system with a single network interface.

As a standalone gateway firewall protecting a LAN, if the firewall machine is ever compromised, it's all over. Even if the firewall's local interfaces have completely different policies from those for forwarded traffic, if the system has been compromised, it won't be long before the interloper has gained **root** access. At that point, if not before, the internal systems are wide open as well. Chances are, a home LAN will never have to face this situation if the services offered to the Internet are chosen carefully and a stringent firewall policy is enforced. Still, a standalone gateway firewall represents a single point of failure. It's an all-or-nothing situation.

Many larger organizations and corporations rely on a single firewall setup, and many others use one of two other architectures: a screened-host architecture with no direct routing, or a screened-subnet architecture with proxy services, along with a perimeter DMZ network created either between or alongside the external firewall, separated from the private LAN. Public servers in the DMZ network have their own specialized, bastion firewalls as well. This means that these sites have a lot more computers at their disposal—and a staff to manage them.

DMZ: A PERIMETER NETWORK BY ANY OTHER NAME

A perimeter network between two firewalls is called a demilitarized zone (DMZ). The purpose of a DMZ is to establish a protected space from which to run public servers (or services) and to isolate that space from the rest of the private LAN. If a server in the DMZ is compromised, that server remains isolated from the LAN; the gateway firewalls and bastion firewalls running on the other DMZ servers offer protection against the compromised server.

In addition to the single-system, standalone firewall, the firewall presented in Chapter 4 can be expanded to form the basis for a dual-homed gateway firewall protecting the host, which offers one or a few public services. A home LAN is often protected by a single gateway firewall that both filters forwarded traffic and offers public services.

What options are available for a dual-homed system that can't afford the risk of a single gateway firewall or the cost of many computers and a staff to manage them? Fortunately, a dual-homed firewall and LAN offer stronger security when the system is configured carefully. The question is this: Is the extra effort worth the increased security in a trusted environment?

Basic Gateway Firewall Setups

Two basic gateway firewall setups are used here. As shown in Figure 6.1, the gateway has two network interfaces: one connected to the Internet and one connected to the DMZ. Public Internet services are offered from machines in the DMZ network. The gateway firewall offers no services. A second firewall, a choke firewall, is also connected to the DMZ network, separating the internal, private networks from the quasi-public server machines in the perimeter network. Private machines are protected behind the choke firewall on the internal LAN. Additionally, each of the server machines in the DMZ runs a specialized firewall of its own. If the gateway firewall or one of the servers fails, the public server machines in the DMZ continue to run their individual firewalls. The choke firewall protects the internal LAN from a compromised gateway or from any other compromised machine in the perimeter network. Traffic between the LAN and the Internet passes through both firewalls and crosses the perimeter network.

In the second setup, the gateway has three network interfaces: one connected to the Internet, one connected to the DMZ, and one connected to the private LAN. As shown in Figure 6.2, traffic between the LAN and the Internet, and traffic between the DMZ and the Internet, share nothing except the gateway's external network interface.

FIGURE 6.1
A DMZ between a dual-homed gateway and a choke firewall.

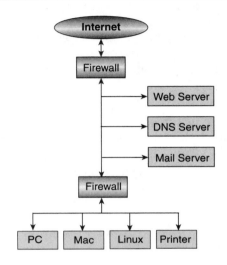

FIGURE 6.2
A tri-homed firewall separating a LAN and a DMZ.

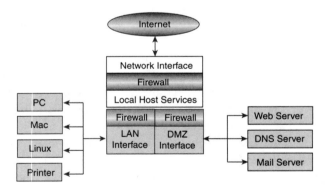

An advantage of this configuration over the first is that neither the LAN nor the DMZ shares the traffic load of both networks. Another advantage is that it's easier to define rules that refer to all LAN or DMZ traffic specifically, as opposed to traffic related to the other network. Another advantage is that a single-gateway host is less expensive than two separate firewall devices.

The disadvantage of this configuration over the first is that the gateway becomes a single point of failure for both networks. Also, the firewall rules in the single host include all the complexity related to both the DMZ and the LAN. This complexity can become a confusing issue when you're developing firewall rules by hand.

A common third alternative is to add a filtering router that separates LAN and DMZ traffic. DMZ servers run their own bastion firewalls. There may or may not be a generalized firewall between the router and the DMZ. As shown in Figure 6.3, the gateway firewall is separate from the router and protects the LAN. The filtering router performs some of the basic filtering for both the LAN and the DMZ. The gateway firewall doesn't need to provide this basic filtering, and it effectively functions similarly to the choke firewall in the first setup.

FIGURE 6.3
A filtering router in front of LAN and DMZ firewalls.

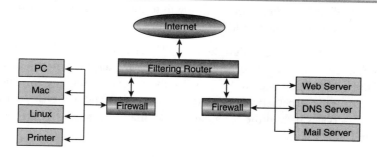

LAN Security Issues

Security issues are largely dependent on the size of the LAN, its architecture, and what it's used for. The services and architecture are also influenced by the public IP addressing available to the site. Perhaps even more basic than that is the type of Internet connection the site has: dial-up, DSL, wireless, cable, satellite, ISDN, leased line, or any of the other types of Internet connections. Following are some questions you should consider when creating a security policy for your site.

Is a public IP address dynamically and temporarily assigned via DHCP or IPCP? Does the site have a single permanently assigned public IP address or a block of them?

Are services offered to the Internet? Are these services hosted on the firewall machine, or are they hosted on internal machines? For example, you might offer email service from the gateway firewall machine but serve a website from an internal machine in the DMZ. When services are hosted from internal machines, you want to place those machines on a perimeter network and apply completely different packet filtering and access policies to those machines. If services are offered from internal machines, is this fact visible to the outside, or are the services proxied or transparently forwarded via NAT so that they appear to be available from the firewall machine?

How much information do you want to make publicly available about the machines on your LAN? Do you intend to host local DNS services? Are local DNS database contents available to the Internet?

Can people log in to your machines from the Internet? How many and which local machines are accessible to them? Do all user accounts have the same access rights? Will incoming connections be proxied for additional access control?

Are all internal machines equally accessible to local users and from all local machines? Are external services equally accessible from all internal machines? For example, if you use a screened-host firewall architecture, users must log in to the firewall machine directly to have access to the Internet. No routing would be done at all.

Are private LAN services running behind the firewall? For example, is NFS used internally, or do you use NIS, or Samba, or a networked printer, or the Berkeley remote commands, such as rsh, rlogin, and rcp? Do you need to keep any of these services from leaking information or broadcast traffic to the Internet, such as SNMP, DHCP, timed, ntpd, ruptime, or rwho? Maintaining such services behind the secondary choke firewall ensures complete isolation of these services from the Internet.

Related to services designed for LAN use are questions about local versus external access to services designed for Internet use. Will you offer FTP internally but not externally, or will you possibly offer different kinds of FTP services to both? Will you run a private web server or configure different parts of the same site to be available to local users as opposed to remote users? Will you run a local mail server to send mail but use a different mechanism to retrieve incoming mail from the Internet (that is, will your mail be delivered directly to your machine's user accounts, or will you explicitly retrieve mail from an ISP)?

Configuration Options for a Trusted Home LAN

You must consider two kinds of internal network traffic. The first kind is local access to the gateway firewall, through the internal interface, as shown in Figure 6.4. The second is local access to the Internet, through the gateway machine's external interface.

FIGURE 6.4
LAN traffic to the firewall machine and to the Internet.

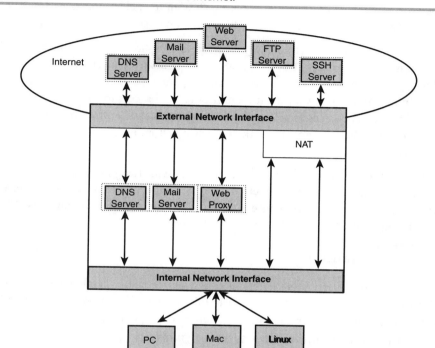

Presumably, most small systems have no reason to filter packets between the firewall and the local network in general. However, because most home-based sites are assigned a single IP address, one exception arises: NAT. Presumably, the only internal filtering-related action you must take will be to enable your own form of source address spoofing by applying NAT packets moving between your internal machines and the Internet. Most of the emphasis is on filtering packets between the firewall and the Internet.

HOW TRUSTWORTHY ARE "TRUSTED HOME LANS"?

Although small-business and residential sites often like to view their networks as "trusted," this is often not the case. The problem isn't the local users, but rather the high incidence rate of compromise among these systems. For more information, see CERT Advisory CA-2001-20, "Continuing Threats to Home Users," at http://www.cert.org/advisories/CA-2001-20.html. For additional information on networking in general, and security in particular, see CERT's informational paper, "Home Network Security," at http://www.cert.org/tech_tips/home_networks.html.

LAN Access to the Gateway Firewall

In a home environment, chances are good that you'll want to enable unrestricted access between the LAN machines and the gateway firewall. (Some parents have reason to disagree.)

The assumption in this section is that any public services are hosted on the firewall. LAN hosts are purely client machines. The LAN is allowed to initiate connections to the firewall, but the firewall is not allowed to initiate connections to the LAN. There will be exceptions to this rule of thumb. You might want the firewall host to have access to a local, networked printer, for example. (A business site would never make this choice. The firewall would be as protected against problems originating in the LAN as it is from problems originating on the public Internet.)

Starting with the firewall developed in Chapter 4 as the basis, two more constants are needed in the firewall example to refer to the internal interface connecting to the LAN. This example defines the internal network interface as eth1; the LAN is defined as including Class C addresses ranging from 192.168.1.0 to 192.168.1.255:

```
LAN_INTERFACE="eth1"
LAN_ADDRESSES="192.168.1.0/24"
```

Allowing unrestricted access across the interfaces is a simple matter of allowing all protocols and all ports by default. Notice that the LAN can initiate new connections to remote servers, but new incoming connections from remote sites are not accepted:

```
$IPT -A FORWARD  -i $LAN_INTERFACE -o $EXTERNAL_INTERFACE \
        -p tcp -s $LAN_ADDRESSES --sport $UNPRIVPORTS \
        -m state --state NEW,ESTABLISHED,RELATED -j ACCEPT

$IPT -A FORWARD -i $EXTERNAL_INTERFACE_1 -o $LAN_INTERFACE \
        -m state --state ESTABLISHED,RELATED -j ACCEPT
```

Notice also that these two rules forward traffic. They do not affect local traffic between the LAN and the firewall itself. To access services on the firewall host, local INPUT and OUTPUT rules are needed as well:

```
$IPT -A INPUT  -i $LAN_INTERFACE \
        -p tcp -s $LAN_ADDRESSES --sport $UNPRIVPORTS -d $GATEWAY \
        -m state --state NEW,ESTABLISHED,RELATED -j ACCEPT

$IPT -A OUTPUT -o $LAN_INTERFACE \
        -m state --state ESTABLISHED,RELATED -j ACCEPT
```

Both the forwarding and the internal interface rules could be as service-specific as the external interface rules in Chapter 4. In today's world, the internal interface and forwarding rules should be that specific. The rules in this section merely lay the groundwork, introducing the forwarding rules themselves.

LAN Access to Other LANs: Forwarding Local Traffic Among Multiple LANs

If the machines on your LAN, or on multiple LANs, require routing among themselves, you need to allow access among the machines for the service ports that they require, unless they have alternate internal connection paths. In the former case, any local routing done between LANs would be done by the firewall.

The assumption in this section is that there is a gateway firewall with two network interfaces, a DMZ server network, an internal choke firewall with two network interfaces, and the LAN private network. This is the setup shown earlier in Figure 6.1. Traffic between the LAN and the Internet crosses through the DMZ network between the choke and gateway firewalls. This setup is common in smaller sites.

This example renames the internal network interface on the gateway as `DMZ_INTERFACE`. Another constant is needed for the firewall. The DMZ is defined as including Class C private addresses ranging from `192.168.3.0` to `192.168.3.255`:

```
DMZ_INTERFACE="eth1"
DMZ_ADDRESSES="192.168.3.0/24"
```

The following first two rules allow local access to the gateway firewall host from the LAN. In practice, the LAN would not be allowed access to all ports on the firewall. The second two rules allow the firewall itself to access specific services offered in the DMZ on a server-by-server basis. Again, a firewall in a larger setting would have little or no reason to access services hosted in the DMZ. In most cases, the firewall host wouldn't offer any services to the DMZ at all. In larger sites, it's probable that the firewall wouldn't offer any services to the LAN either:

```
$IPT -A INPUT  -i $DMZ_INTERFACE -s $LAN_ADDRESSES -d $GATEWAY \
        -m state --state NEW,ESTABLISHED,RELATED -j ACCEPT

$IPT -A OUTPUT -o $DMZ_INTERFACE -s $GATEWAY -d $LAN_ADDRESSES \
        -m state --state ESTABLISHED,RELATED -j ACCEPT

$IPT -A OUTPUT -o $DMZ_INTERFACE -s $GATEWAY -d $DMZ_ADDRESSES \
        -m state --state NEW,ESTABLISHED,RELATED -j ACCEPT
$IPT -A INPUT  -i $DMZ_INTERFACE -s $DMZ_ADDRESSES -d $GATEWAY \
        -m state --state ESTABLISHED,RELATED -j ACCEPT
```

The next rules forward traffic between the internal networks and the Internet. The DMZ and LAN traffic are handled separately. The DMZ traffic represents incoming connection requests from the Internet. The LAN traffic represents outgoing connection requests to the Internet. Again, in practice the DMZ rules would be very specific by server address and service:

```
$IPT -A FORWARD  -i $EXTERNAL_INTERFACE -o $DMZ_INTERFACE \
        -d $DMZ_ADDRESSES \
        -m state --state NEW,ESTABLISHED,RELATED -j ACCEPT

$IPT -A FORWARD -i $DMZ_INTERFACE -o $EXTERNAL_INTERFACE \
        -s $DMZ_ADDRESSES \
        -m state --state ESTABLISHED,RELATED -j ACCEPT

$IPT -A FORWARD -i $DMZ_INTERFACE -o $EXTERNAL_INTERFACE \
        -s $LAN_ADDRESSES \
        -m state --state NEW,ESTABLISHED,RELATED -j ACCEPT

$IPT -A FORWARD  -i $EXTERNAL_INTERFACE -o $DMZ_INTERFACE \
        -d $LAN_ADDRESSES \
        -m state --state ESTABLISHED,RELATED -j ACCEPT
```

Note that the preceding forwarding rules for the DMZ are not complete. Servers in the DMZ sometimes initiate outgoing connections as well, such as connection requests from a web proxy server or a mail gateway server.

On the choke firewall, the following rules forward traffic between the LAN and DMZ networks. Notice that the LAN can initiate new connections, but new incoming connections from either the DMZ or the Internet to the LAN are not accepted. Again, in practice, the LAN would be given more controlled access to the DMZ as well as to the gateway firewall, assuming that the gateway provided any services:

```
$IPT -A FORWARD  -i $LAN_INTERFACE -o $DMZ_INTERFACE \
        -s $LAN_ADDRESSES \
        -m state --state NEW,ESTABLISHED,RELATED -j ACCEPT

$IPT -A FORWARD -i $DMZ_INTERFACE -o $LAN_INTERFACE \
        -m state --state ESTABLISHED,RELATED -j ACCEPT
```

Configuration Options for a Larger or Less Trusted LAN

A business or an organization, and many home sites, would use more elaborate, specific mechanisms than the simple, generic forwarding firewall rules presented in the preceding two sections for a trusted home LAN. In less trusted environments, firewall machines are protected from internal users as strongly as from external users.

Port-specific firewall rules are defined for the internal interfaces as well as for the external interfaces. Internal rules might be a mirror image of the rules for the external interfaces, or the rules might be more inclusive. What is allowed through the choke firewall machine's internal network interface depends on the types of systems running on the LAN and the types of local services running in the DMZ, as well as which Internet services are accessible to the LAN according to local security policies.

For example, you might want to block local broadcast messages from reaching the gateway firewall. If not all your users are completely trusted, you might want to restrict what passes into the choke firewall from internal machines as strongly as what comes in from the Internet. Additionally, you should keep the number of user accounts to a bare minimum on the firewall machine. Ideally, a firewall has no user accounts, with the exception of a single unprivileged administrative account.

A home-based business might have a single IP address, requiring LAN Network Address Translation. However, businesses often lease several publicly registered IP addresses or an entire network address block. Public addresses are usually assigned to a business's public servers. With public IP addresses, outgoing connections are forwarded and incoming connections are routed normally. A local subnet can be defined to create a local, public DMZ.

Dividing Address Space to Create Multiple Networks

IP addresses are divided into two pieces: a network address and a host address within that network. As stated in Chapter 1, "Preliminary Concepts Underlying Packet-Filtering Firewalls," Class A, B, and C addresses are something of an artifact, but they remain the easiest addresses to use as examples because their network and host fields fall on byte boundaries. Class A, B, and C network addresses are defined by their first 8, 16, and 24 bits, respectively. Within each address class, the remaining bits define the host part of the IP address. This is shown visually in Table 6.1.

TABLE 6.1
Network and Host Fields in an IP Address

	CLASS A	CLASS B	CLASS C
Leading Network Bits	0	10	110
Network Field	1 byte	2 bytes	3 bytes
Host Field	3 bytes	2 bytes	1 byte
Network Prefix	/8	/16	/24
Address Range	1–126	128–191	192–223
Network Mask	255.0.0.0	255.255.0.0	255.255.255.0

Subnetting is a local extension to the network address part of the local IP addresses. A local network mask is defined as one that treats some of the most significant host address bits as if they were part of the network address. These additional network address bits serve to define multiple networks locally. Remote sites are not aware of local subnets. They see the address range as normal Class A, B, or C addresses.

For example, let's take the Class C private address block, `192.168.1.0`. The base address, known as the network address, is `192.168.1.0` for this example. The network mask for this example is `255.255.255.0`, exactly matching the first 24 bits, the network address, of the `192.168.1.0/24` network.

This network can be divided into two local networks by defining the first 25 bits, rather than the first 24 bits, as the network portion of the address. In current parlance, we say that the local network has a prefix length of 25 rather than 24. The most significant bit of the host address field is now treated as part of the network address field. The host field now contains 7 bits rather than 8. The network mask becomes `255.255.255.128`, or /25 in CIDR notation. Two subnetworks are defined: `192.168.1.0`, addressing hosts from `1` to `126`, and `192.168.1.128`, addressing hosts from `129` to `254`. Each subnet loses two host addresses because each subnet uses the lowest host address, `0` or `128`, as the network address, and uses the highest host address, `127` or `255`, as the broadcast address. Table 6.2 shows this in tabular form.

TABLE 6.2
Class C Network `192.168.1.0` Subnetted into Two Subnets

SUBNET NUMBER	NONE	0	1
Network Address	192.168.1.0	192.168.1.0	192.168.1.128
Network Mask	255.255.255.0	255.255.255.128	255.255.255.128
First Host Address	192.168.1.1	192.168.1.1	192.168.1.129
Last Host Address	192.168.1.254	192.168.1.126	192.168.1.254
Broadcast Address	192.168.1.255	192.168.1.127	192.168.1.255
Total Hosts	254	126	126

Subnetworks `192.168.1.0` and `192.168.1.128` can be assigned to two separate internal network interface cards. Each subnet consists of two independent networks, each containing up to 126 hosts.

Subnetting allows for the creation of multiple internal networks, each containing different classes of client or server machines and each with its own independent routing. Different firewall policies can then be applied to the networks.

Of course, this example showed the network being divided into two portions. The network can in fact be divided into many parts in order to create a number of smaller networks. It's quite common to see a network with a subnet mask of 255.255.255.252 or /30 used between routers at two locations. Table 6.3 takes the process one step further and shows the same network divided into four subnets.

TABLE 6.3
Class C Network 192.168.1.0 Subnetted into Four Subnets

SUBNET NUMBER	0	1	2	3
Network Address	192.168.1.0	192.168.1.64	192.168.1.128	192.18.1.192
Network Mask	255.255.255.192	255.255.255.192	255.255.255.192	255.255.255.192
First Host Address	192.168.1.1	192.168.1.65	192.168.1.129	192.168.1.193
Last Host Address	192.168.1.62	192.168.1.126	192.168.1.190	192.168.1.254
Broadcast Address	192.168.1.63	192.168.1.127	192.168.1.191	192.168.1.255
Total Hosts	62	62	62	62

Selective Internal Access by Host, Address Range, or Port

Traffic through a firewall machine's internal interface can be selectively limited, just as traffic through the external interface is. For example, on a firewall for a small, residential site, rather than letting everything through on the internal interface, traffic could be limited to DNS, SMTP, POP, and HTTP. In this case, let's say that a firewall machine provides these services for the LAN. Local machines are not allowed any other access to outside services. In this case, forwarding isn't done.

POINT OF INTEREST

In this example, local hosts are limited to the specific services: DNS, SMTP, POP, and HTTP. Because POP is a local mail-retrieval service in this case, and because DNS, SMTP, and HTTP are proxied services, no direct Internet access is being made by LAN clients. In each case, the local clients are connecting to local servers. POP is a local LAN service. The three other servers establish remote connections on the client's behalf.

This example would be used only by a small, likely residential, site. Placing the mail gateway and POP services on the firewall host can require the host to have user accounts. It is not necessary that these accounts be login accounts, however.

CONFIGURATION OPTIONS FOR AN INTERNAL LAN

The following example considers a firewall machine with an internal interface connected to a LAN. Constants for the internal interface are as shown here:

```
LAN_INTERFACE="eth1"            # internal interface to the LAN
LAN_GATEWAY="192.168.1.1"       # firewall machine's internal
                                # interface address
LAN_ADDRESSES="192.168.1.0/24"  # range of addresses used on the LAN
```

LAN machines point to the firewall machine's internal interface as their name server:

```
# Generic gateway response rule
$IPT -A OUTPUT  -o $LAN_INTERFACE \
        -s $LAN_GATEWAY \
        -d $LAN_ADDRESSES --dport $UNPRIVPORTS \
        -m state --state ESTABLISHED,RELATED -j ACCEPT


# Service-specific LAN request rules

$IPT -A INPUT -i $LAN_INTERFACE -p udp \
        -s $LAN_ADDRESSES --sport $UNPRIVPORTS \
        -d $LAN_GATEWAY --dport 53 \
        -m state --state NEW,ESTABLISHED,RELATED -j ACCEPT

$IPT -A INPUT -i $LAN_INTERFACE -p tcp \
        -s $LAN_ADDRESSES --sport $UNPRIVPORTS \
        -d $LAN_GATEWAY --dport 53 \
        -state --state NEW,ESTABLISHED,RELATED -j ACCEPT
```

LAN machines also point to the firewall as their SMTP and POP server:

```
# Sending mail - SMTP

$IPT -A INPUT  -i $LAN_INTERFACE -p tcp \
        -s $LAN_ADDRESSES --sport $UNPRIVPORTS \
        -d $GATEWAY --dport 25 \
        -state --state NEW,ESTABLISHED,RELATED -j ACCEPT


# Receiving Mail - POP
```

```
$IPT -A INPUT  -i $LAN_INTERFACE -p tcp \
       -s $LAN_ADDRESSES --sport $UNPRIVPORTS \
       -d $GATEWAY --dport 110 \
       -state --state NEW,ESTABLISHED,RELATED -j ACCEPT
```

The sendmail server will initiate an AUTH lookup request to the mail client. You won't likely be running the AUTH daemon, but you can send a REJECT for AUTH requests which can, on certain mail configurations, prevent a delay:

```
$IPT -A OUTPUT -o $LAN_INTERFACE -p tcp \
       -s $GATEWAY --sport $UNPRIVPORTS  \
       -d $LAN_ADDRESSES --dport 113 -j REJECT

$IPT -A INPUT  -i $LAN_INTERFACE ! --syn -p tcp \
       -s $LAN_ADDRESSES --sport 113 \
       -d $GATEWAY --dport $UNPRIVPORTS -j REJECT
```

Finally, a local web caching proxy server is running on the firewall machine on port 8080. Internal machines point to the web server on the firewall as their proxy, and the web server forwards any outgoing requests on their behalf, along with caching any pages retrieved from the Internet. All connections to the proxy are via port 8080. Secure web and FTP access to remote sites is initiated by the proxy server:

```
$IPT -A INPUT  -i $LAN_INTERFACE -p tcp \
       -s $LAN_ADDRESSES --sport $UNPRIVPORTS \
       -d $GATEWAY --dport 8080 \
       -state --state NEW,ESTABLISHED,RELATED -j ACCEPT
```

Remember that the web server will use the FTP passive mode protocol to retrieve data from remote FTP sites. The firewall's external interface will need input and output rules to access remote FTP, HTTP, and HTTPS service ports. The gateway host must also have rules for the external interface to account for email and local DNS queries to remote hosts.

CONFIGURATION OPTIONS FOR MULTIPLE LANS

Adding a second internal LAN allows this example to be developed further. The next example can be better secured than the preceding example. As shown in Figure 6.5, the DNS, SMTP, POP, and HTTP services are offered from server machines in a second LAN rather than from the firewall machine. The second LAN may or may not serve as a public DMZ. It's equally possible that the second LAN represents an internal service LAN, and its services are not offered to the Internet (although, in that case, the firewall could be required to at least be a mail gateway, depending on the local firewall configuration). In either case, firewall hosts do not typically host services. In this example, traffic is routed between the two LANs by the internal interfaces on the firewall machine.

FIGURE 6.5
Separating clients and servers in multiple LANs.

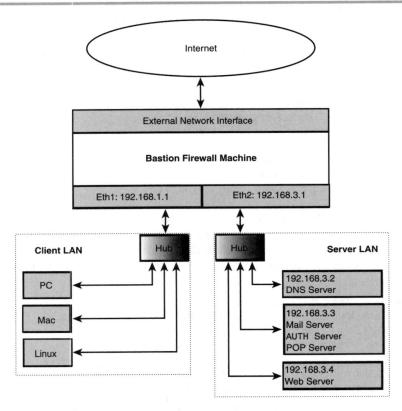

The following variables are used to define the LAN, network interfaces, and server machines in this example:

```
CLIENT_LAN_INTERFACE="eth1"          # internal interface to the LAN
SERVER_LAN_INTERFACE="eth2"          # internal interface to the LAN
CLIENT_ADDRESSES="192.168.1.0/24"    # range of addresses used on the client LAN
SERVER_ADDRESSES="192.168.3.0/24"    # range of addresses used on the server LAN
DNS_SERVER="192.168.3.2"             # LAN DNS server
MAIL_SERVER="192.168.3.3"            # LAN Mail and POP server
POP_SERVER="192.168.3.3"             # LAN Mail and POP server
WEB_SERVER="192.168.3.4"             # LAN Web server
```

The first rule covers all server responses back to clients in the client LAN:

```
$IPT -A FORWARD  -i $SERVER_LAN_INTERFACE -o $CLIENT_LAN_INTERFACE \
        -s $SERVER_ADDRESSES -d $CLIENT_ADDRESSES \
        -m state --state ESTABLISHED,RELATED -j ACCEPT
```

The second rule covers all ongoing connection traffic from the LAN clients to the local servers in the server LAN:

```
$IPT -A FORWARD  -i $CLIENT_LAN_INTERFACE -o $SERVER_LAN_INTERFACE \
        -s $CLIENT_ADDRESSES -d $SERVER_ADDRESSES \
        -m state --state ESTABLISHED,RELATED -j ACCEPT
```

The third rule covers all remote server responses back to client requests from the local servers in the server LAN:

```
$IPT -A FORWARD  -i $EXTERNAL_INTERFACE -o $SERVER_LAN_INTERFACE \
        -d $SERVER_ADDRESSES \
        -m state --state ESTABLISHED,RELATED -j ACCEPT
```

The fourth rule covers all local server responses back to client requests from the remote hosts on the Internet:

```
$IPT -A FORWARD  -i $SERVER_LAN_INTERFACE -o $EXTERNAL_INTERFACE \
        -s $SERVER_ADDRESSES \
        -m state --state ESTABLISHED,RELATED -j ACCEPT
```

Local machines use the DNS server in the **SERVER_LAN** as their name server. Just as with the rules between the firewall's internal interface and external interface, *server* access rules are defined for the client LAN's interface. *Client* access rules are defined for the server LAN's interface:

```
$IPT -A FORWARD -i $CLIENT_LAN_INTERFACE -o $SERVER_LAN_INTERFACE -p udp \
        -s $CLIENT_ADDRESSES --sport $UNPRIVPORTS \
        -d $DNS_SERVER --dport 53 \
        -m state --state NEW -j ACCEPT
```

```
$IPT -A FORWARD -i $CLIENT_LAN_INTERFACE -o $SERVER_LAN_INTERFACE -p tcp \
        -s $CLIENT_ADDRESSES --sport $UNPRIVPORTS \
        -d $DNS_SERVER --dport 53 \
        -m state --state NEW -j ACCEPT
```

The DNS server on the second LAN needs to get its information from an external source. If the local server were a cache-and-forward server to an external server, forwarding unresolved lookups to the external server, the firewall's forwarding rules for its internal server LAN interface and external Internet interface would be this:

```
$IPT -A FORWARD -i $SERVER_LAN_INTERFACE -o $EXTERNAL_INTERFACE -p udp \
        -s $DNS_SERVER --sport 53 \
        -d $NAME_SERVER_1 --dport 53 \
        -m state --state NEW -j ACCEPT

$IPT -A FORWARD -i $SERVER_LAN_INTERFACE -o $EXTERNAL_INTERFACE -p udp \
        -s $DNS_SERVER --sport $UNPRIVPORTS \
        -d $NAME_SERVER_1 --dport 53 \
        -m state --state NEW -j ACCEPT

$IPT -A FORWARD -i $SERVER_LAN_INTERFACE -o $EXTERNAL_INTERFACE -p tcp \
        -s $DNS_SERVER --sport $UNPRIVPORTS \
        -d $NAME_SERVER_1 --dport 53 \
        -m state --state NEW -j ACCEPT
```

The hosts in the **CLIENT_LAN** point to the **MAIL_SERVER** as their mail gateway for sending mail:

```
# Sending Mail - SMTP
# -------------------

$IPT -A FORWARD -i $CLIENT_LAN_INTERFACE -o $SERVER_LAN_INTERFACE -p tcp \
        -s $CLIENT_ADDRESSES --sport $UNPRIVPORTS \
        -d $MAIL_SERVER --dport 25 \
        -m state --state NEW -j ACCEPT
```

The SMTP server on the **SERVER_LAN** needs to send the mail to remote destinations. The server requires access through the firewall to the Internet:

```
$IPT -A FORWARD -i $SERVER_LAN_INTERFACE -o $EXTERNAL_INTERFACE -p tcp \
        -s $MAIL_SERVER --sport $UNPRIVPORTS --dport 25 \
        -m state --state NEW -j ACCEPT
```

The local mail server also needs to receive incoming mail from remote sites:

```
$IPT -A FORWARD  -i $EXTERNAL_INTERFACE -o $SERVER_LAN_INTERFACE -p tcp \
        --sport $UNPRIVPORTS -d $MAIL_SERVER --dport 25 \
        -m state --state NEW -j ACCEPT
```

Note that, for incoming mail to be addressed to the mail server, the name server must have a publicly accessible MX record advertising the host as the site's mail server. In this particular set of examples, the DNS rules do not allow for incoming DNS queries from the Internet. Thus, the remote name server would need to provide this service. (Alternative solutions using NAT and host forwarding are described in Chapter 7.) Be aware that some *spam conscious* Internet providers prevent incoming and outgoing connections on port 25, the common SMTP port. This of course breaks the end-to-end nature of the Internet.

The clients on the CLIENT_LAN point to the POP_SERVER machine to retrieve mail:

```
# Receiving Mail - POP
# --------------------

$IPT -A FORWARD -i $CLIENT_LAN_INTERFACE -o $SERVER_LAN_INTERFACE -p tcp \
        -s $CLIENT_ADDRESSES --sport $UNPRIVPORTS \
        -d $POP_SERVER --dport 110 \
        -m state --state NEW -j ACCEPT
```

Finally, a local web proxy server is running on a server machine in the server LAN, bound to port 8080. Internal machines point to the web server as their caching proxy, and the web server forwards any outgoing requests on their behalf:

```
# WWW PROXY
# ---------

$IPT -A FORWARD -i $CLIENT_LAN_INTERFACE -o $SERVER_LAN_INTERFACE -p tcp \
        -s $LAN_ADDRESSES --sport $UNPRIVPORTS \
        -d $WEB_SERVER --dport 8080 \
        -state --state NEW -j ACCEPT
```

The web server on the server LAN needs Internet access to remote servers listening on TCP ports 80 and 443, as well as FTP's TCP port 21:

```
$IPT -A FORWARD  -i $SERVER_LAN_INTERFACE -o $EXTERNAL_INTERFACE -p tcp \
        -m multiport --destination-port 80,443,21 \
        --syn -s $WEB_SERVER --sport $UNPRIVPORTS \
        -m state --state NEW -j ACCEPT
```

A Formal Screened-Subnet Firewall Example

A small or medium-size business might have reason to invest in a more elaborate firewall architecture. The remainder of the chapter focuses on a single example using the configuration from Figure 6.1, in which the DMZ sits between a dual-homed gateway firewall and an internal choke firewall.

The gateway firewall separates both the DMZ and the LAN from the Internet. Its internal interface connects directly to the DMZ rather than to the private LAN. Public services are hosted from machines on the perimeter DMZ network, each with a separate bastion firewall and security policy of its own. The public servers may or may not have publicly visible interfaces, depending on how your public IP addresses are assigned. The choke firewall separates the DMZ from the LAN. Depending on the network hardware used in the DMZ, the traffic between the LAN and Internet may or may not "share a wire" with the DMZ.

Unlike the firewall example in Chapter 4, this setup does not have a potential single point of failure. Services with different security policies can be hosted from different security zones within the internal networks.

The main idea is to physically isolate the private LAN from the external gateway firewall machine through the use of an internal choke firewall. The perimeter network does not have to be a full network with its own servers; it's a conceptualization. The perimeter network could be implemented as simply as a crossover cable between the gateway's internal interface and the choke's external interface.

Implementing a DMZ as a simple crossover cable might sound silly. It buys a small site two firewalls, just as a full perimeter network does. Two firewalls don't represent a single point of failure. Local LAN services are hosted on the choke machine or within the LAN itself rather than on the gateway host, and they are completely isolated from the gateway or the Internet.

The setup in the remainder of the chapter uses a minimum of six sets of firewall rules—one each for the external and internal interfaces of both firewall machines, plus the forwarding rules on the two machines, which is where the bulk of the work is done.

The conceptual difference between this example and the example in Chapter 4 is the addition of the DMZ perimeter network—the new rules applied to the gateway's internal interface and to the choke firewall's external interface. On the detail level, the difference is also in the input and output rules because the gateway firewall offers no services itself—or a mere handful, at most. The forwarding rules for the two interfaces are mirror images of each other. Public servers on the DMZ network have their own individualized firewall rules as well. Public servers in the DMZ are usually specialized, dedicated, single-service machines. Their firewall rules are simple and highly restrictive to the particular services that they host. Additionally, the overhead of the antispoofing and high service port protection rules aren't needed because the gateway is providing this service.

The choke firewall's symbolic constants and initial rules are largely identical to the gateway's. Because the gateway hosts no services, the input and output rules largely move to the FORWARD chain. The major emphasis of this chapter's example is on the choke's firewall rules and on the symmetry between the forwarding rules on the gateway and the choke. The example's rules will be very familiar by this point. For the most part, the rules from Chapter 4 are moving to the FORWARD chains on both firewalls.

Symbolic Constants Used in the Firewall Examples

As with the firewall example in Chapter 4, the gateway's external interface is assigned to eth0, leading to the Internet. Just for the sake of confusion, I'm going to divide the address space. As shown in Table 6.4, the gateway's public interface remains with IP address 192.168.1.1.

The internal interface address will be 192.168.1.65 on eth1, leading to the perimeter DMZ network. The choke firewall machine's external interface address will be 192.168.1.126 on its eth0, leading to the perimeter DMZ network. The choke firewall machine's internal interface address will be 192.168.1.129 on eth1, leading to the private LAN.

The address space available to the DMZ hosts is 192.168.1.66 to 192.168.1.125 because the DMZ will be in the 192.168.1.64/26 network. The broadcast address is 192.168.1.127.

The address space available to the LAN hosts in the 192.168.1.128 network range is from 192.168.1.130 to 192.168.1.190. The broadcast address is 192.168.1.191.

TABLE 6.4
Class C Network 192.168.1.0 Subnetted into Four Subnets

SUBNET	0	1		2	3
Firewall	Gateway External Interface	Gateway DMZ Interface	Choke DMZ Interface	Choke LAN Interface	Unused Subnet
Network Address	192.168.1.0	192.168.1.64		192.1.128	192.168.1.192
Network Mask	255.255.255.192	255.255.255.192		255.255.255.192	255.255.255.192
IP Address	192.168.1.1	192.168.1.65	192.168.1.126	192.168.1.129	unused
First Free Host Address	unused	192.168.1.66		192.168.1.130	192.168.1.193
Last Free Host Address	unused	192.168.1.125		192.168.1.190	192.168.1.254
Broadcast Address	192.168.1.63	192.168.1.123		192.168.1.191	192.168.1.255
Total Hosts	62	62		62	62

ADDITIONAL CONSTANTS FOR THE PUBLIC GATEWAY FIREWALL

The following constants are added to the gateway's firewall script to refer to the gateway's internal interface, the choke's IP address, and the network address block for the DMZ:

```
DMZ_INTERFACE="eth1"             # network interface to the DMZ
DMZ_IPADDR="192.168.1.65"        # DMZ IP address
CHOKE_IPADDR="192.168.1.126"     # choke firewall DMZ address
DMZ_ADDRESSES="192.168.1.64/26"  # DMZ IP address range
```

```
DMZ_BROADCAST="192.168.1.127"      # DMZ broadcast address
LAN_ADDRESSES="192.169.1.128/26"   # LAN IP address range
LOCAL_ADDRESSES="192.168.1.0/24"   # any local IP address
```

CONSTANTS FOR THE PRIVATE CHOKE FIREWALL

A firewall shell script is easier to read and maintain if symbolic constants are used for recurring names and addresses. The following constants either are used throughout the examples in this chapter or are universal constants defined in the networking standards:

```
DMZ_INTERFACE="eth0"               # network interface to the DMZ
LAN_INTERFACE="eth1"               # network interface to the LAN
LOOPBACK_INTERFACE="lo"            # however your system names it

DMZ_IPADDR="192.168.1.126"         # DMZ IP address
GATEWAY_IPADDR="192.168.1.65"      # gateway firewall - the router
DMZ_ADDRESSES="192.168.1.64/26"    # DMZ IP address range
DMZ_NETWORK="192.168.1.64"         # DMZ subnet base address
DMZ_BROADCAST="192.168.1.127"      # DMZ broadcast address
LAN_IPADDR="192.168.1.129"         # LAN IP address
LAN_ADDRESSES="192.168.1.128/26"   # LAN IP address range
LAN_NETWORK="192.168.1.128"        # DMZ subnet base address
LAN_BROADCAST="192.168.1.191"      # DMZ broadcast address

LOOPBACK="127.0.0.0/8"             # reserved loopback address range
CLASS_A="10.0.0.0/8"               # Class A private networks
CLASS_B="172.16.0.0/12"            # Class B private networks
CLASS_C="192.168.0.0/16"           # Class C private networks
CLASS_D_MULTICAST="224.0.0.0/4"    # Class D multicast addresses
CLASS_E_RESERVED_NET="240.0.0.0/5" # Class E reserved addresses
BROADCAST_SRC="0.0.0.0"            # broadcast source address
BROADCAST_DEST="255.255.255.255"   # broadcast destination address
PRIVPORTS="0:1023"                 # well-known, privileged
                                   # port range
UNPRIVPORTS="1024:65535"           # unprivileged port range
```

Constants not listed here are defined within the context of the specific rules that they are used with.

Setting the Stage on the Choke Firewall

The following steps are identical to those in Chapter 4. The choke firewall's preamble is identical to the gateway's:

```
# Enable broadcast echo Protection
echo 1 > /proc/sys/net/ipv4/icmp_echo_ignore_broadcasts
```

```
# Disable Source Routed Packets
for f in /proc/sys/net/ipv4/conf/*/accept_source_route; do
    echo 0 > $f
done

# Enable TCP SYN Cookie Protection
echo 1 > /proc/sys/net/ipv4/tcp_syncookies

# Disable ICMP Redirect Acceptance
for f in /proc/sys/net/ipv4/conf/*/accept_redirects; do
    echo 0 > $f
done

# Don't send Redirect Messages
for f in /proc/sys/net/ipv4/conf/*/send_redirects; do
    echo 0 > $f
done

# Drop Spoofed Packets coming in on an interface, which, if replied to,
# would result in the reply going out a different interface.
for f in /proc/sys/net/ipv4/conf/*/rp_filter; do
    echo 1 > $f
done

# Log packets with impossible addresses.
for f in /proc/sys/net/ipv4/conf/*/log_martians; do
    echo 1 > $f
done
```

Removing Any Preexisting Rules from the Choke Firewall

The first thing to do when defining a set of filtering rules is to remove any existing rules from the rule chains. Otherwise, any new rules that you define will be added to the end of existing rules. Packets could easily match a preexisting rule before ever reaching the point in the chain you are defining from this point on. The following command flushes the rules of all three built-in filter table chains—INPUT, OUTPUT, and FORWARD—at once. (User-defined chains are flushed, too, but none is used in this chapter.) This is the same as found on the gateway firewall built in previous chapters:

```
# Flush any existing rules from all chains
$IPT --flush
$IPT -t nat --flush
$IPT -t mangle --flush
$IPT -X
$IPT -t nat -X
$IPT -t mangle -X
```

The chains are empty. You're starting from scratch. The system is in its default accept-everything policy state if the system has just booted. If the firewall is being reinitialized, the default policies are whatever they had been previously set to. Flushing the rules does not affect the default policies.

Defining the Choke Firewall's Default Policy

The choke policy is to reject all traffic in either direction. To return an ICMP 3 error message, the REJECT target must be used. The easiest method is to end the chains with a general REJECT rule to catch anything that hasn't matched an ACCEPT rule. This results in meaningful error messages being delivered immediately, rather than forcing the local hosts to wait for a timeout. Note that this is different from the gateway's firewall where the default policy is to silently drop traffic using DROP.

To create a known-good environment where the firewall script can be used to stop the firewall, the first default policy is to ACCEPT. This is the same policy setup as seen in previous chapters:

```
$IPT --policy INPUT    ACCEPT
$IPT --policy OUTPUT   ACCEPT
$IPT --policy FORWARD ACCEPT
$IPT -t nat --policy PREROUTING  ACCEPT
$IPT -t nat --policy OUTPUT ACCEPT
$IPT -t nat --policy POSTROUTING ACCEPT
$IPT -t mangle --policy PREROUTING ACCEPT
$IPT -t mangle --policy OUTPUT ACCEPT
```

Next, the bits to create the stop action are added. Again, these are the same as in previous chapters:

```
if [ "$1" = "stop" ]
then
echo "Firewall completely stopped!  WARNING: THIS HOST HAS NO FIREWALL RUNNING."
exit 0
fi
```

Both firewalls drop or reject everything by default rather than accepting everything by default:

```
# Set the default policy to reject on the choke firewall
$IPT --policy INPUT REJECT
$IPT --policy OUTPUT REJECT
$IPT --policy FORWARD REJECT
```

At this point, all network traffic is blocked.

Enabling the Choke Machine's Loopback Interface

You need to enable unrestricted loopback traffic. This enables you to run any local network services that you choose, or that the system depends on, without having to worry about getting all the firewall rules specified:

```
# Unlimited traffic on the loopback interface
$IPT -A INPUT  -i $LOOPBACK_INTERFACE -j ACCEPT
$IPT -A OUTPUT -o $LOOPBACK_INTERFACE -j ACCEPT
```

Stealth Scans and TCP State Flags

Testing for common forms of TCP stealth scans is possible because iptables gives access to all the TCP state flags. The following rules block common stealth scan probes. None of the TCP state combinations tested for is a legal combination.

Because specific interfaces aren't matched in the following input and forward rules, the rules apply to all interfaces. Again, the code is the same as for the gateway firewall:

```
# All of the bits are cleared
$IPT -A INPUT   -p tcp --tcp-flags ALL NONE -j DROP
$IPT -A FORWARD -p tcp --tcp-flags ALL NONE -j DROP

# SYN and FIN are both set
$IPT -A INPUT   -p tcp --tcp-flags SYN,FIN SYN,FIN -j DROP
$IPT -A FORWARD -p tcp --tcp-flags SYN,FIN SYN,FIN -j DROP

# SYN and RST are both set
$IPT -A INPUT   -p tcp --tcp-flags SYN,RST SYN,RST -j DROP
$IPT -A FORWARD -p tcp --tcp-flags SYN,RST SYN,RST -j DROP

# FIN and RST are both set
$IPT -A INPUT   -p tcp --tcp-flags FIN,RST FIN,RST -j DROP
$IPT -A FORWARD -p tcp --tcp-flags FIN,RST FIN,RST -j DROP

# FIN is the only bit set, without the expected accompanying ACK
$IPT -A INPUT   -p tcp --tcp-flags ACK,FIN FIN -j DROP
$IPT -A FORWARD -p tcp --tcp-flags ACK,FIN FIN -j DROP

# PSH is the only bit set, without the expected accompanying ACK
$IPT -A INPUT   -p tcp --tcp-flags ACK,PSH PSH -j DROP
$IPT -A FORWARD -p tcp --tcp-flags ACK,PSH PSH -j DROP

# URG is the only bit set, without the expected accompanying ACK
$IPT -A INPUT   -p tcp --tcp-flags ACK,URG URG -j DROP
$IPT -A FORWARD -p tcp --tcp-flags ACK,URG URG -j DROP
```

Using Connection State to Bypass Rule Checking

Specifying the state match for previously initiated and accepted exchanges enables you to bypass the firewall tests for the ongoing exchange. The initial client request remains controlled by the service's specific filters, however. The following code checks for established connections:

```
$IPT -A INPUT  -m state --state ESTABLISHED,RELATED -j ACCEPT
$IPT -A OUTPUT -m state --state ESTABLISHED,RELATED -j ACCEPT

$IPT -A FORWARD -m state --state ESTABLISHED,RELATED -j ACCEPT
# Using the state module alone, INVALID will break protocols that use
# bidirectional connections or multiple connections or exchanges,
# unless an ALG is provided for the protocol. At this time, FTP is the
# only protocol with ALG support.

$IPT -A INPUT -m state --state INVALID -j LOG \
        --log-prefix "INVALID input: "
$IPT -A INPUT -m state --state INVALID -j DROP

$IPT -A OUTPUT -m state --state INVALID -j LOG \
        --log-prefix "INVALID output: "
$IPT -A OUTPUT -m state --state INVALID -j DROP

$IPT -A FORWARD -m state --state INVALID -j LOG \
        --log-prefix "INVALID forward: "
$IPT -A FORWARD -m state --state INVALID -j DROP
```

Source-Address Spoofing and Other Bad Addresses

This section establishes some filters based on source and destination addresses. These addresses will never be seen in a legitimate packet.

At the packet-filtering level, one of the few cases of source-address spoofing that you can identify as a forgery with certainty is your own IP address. These rules deny incoming packets claiming to be from you:

```
# Refuse spoofed packets pretending to be from you
$IPT -A INPUT -s $DMZ_IPADDR -j DROP
$IPT -A INPUT -s $LAN_IPADDR -j DROP

$IPT -A FORWARD -s $DMZ_IPADDR -j DROP
$IPT -A FORWARD -s $LAN_IPADDR -j DROP

$IPT -A INPUT -i $DMZ_INTERFACE \
        -s $LAN_ADDRESSES -j DROP
```

The preceding rules are redundant if you have activated the `rp_filter` kernel facility. It's good practice to define the rules explicitly.

Likewise, the firewall rules drop packets that don't contain a local source address. Regardless, it's good practice to explicitly define a rule to implement RFC 2827, "Network Ingress Filtering: Defeating Denial of Service Attacks Which Employ IP Source Address Spoofing":

```
$IPT -A FORWARD -i $DMZ_INTERFACE \
        -s $LAN_ADDRESSES -j DROP

$IPT -A FORWARD  -i $LAN_INTERFACE \
        -s ! $LAN_ADDRESSES -j DROP

$IPT -A OUTPUT -o $DMZ_INTERFACE -s ! $DMZ_IPADDR -j DROP
$IPT -A OUTPUT -o $LAN_INTERFACE -s ! $LAN_IPADDR -j DROP
```

We'll skip the rules from Chapter 4 that checked for private network source addresses. The gateway firewall is performing that function.

The next sets of rules are primarily for completeness. Both of the firewall's default policies are to drop everything. As such, broadcast addresses are dropped by default and must be explicitly enabled when they are wanted:

```
# Refuse malformed broadcast packets
$IPT -A FORWARD -i $LAN_INTERFACE -o $DMZ_INTERFACE \
        -d $BROADCAST_SRC  -j DROP

$IPT -A FORWARD -i $LAN_INTERFACE -o $DMZ_INTERFACE \
        -d $BROADCAST_SRC  -j DROP

# Don't forward directed broadcasts
$IPT -A FORWARD -i $LAN_INTERFACE -o $DMZ_INTERFACE \
        -d $DMZ_NETWORK -j DROP
$IPT -A FORWARD -i $LAN_INTERFACE -o $DMZ_INTERFACE \
        -d $DMZ_BROADCAST -j DROP

# Don't forward limited broadcasts in either direction
$IPT -A FORWARD -d $BROADCAST_DEST -j DROP
```

Multicast is always sent over UDP. Whether or not you add rules to accept incoming multicast, the following rules block illegal multicast packets:

```
$IPT -A INPUT    -p ! udp -d $CLASS_D_MULTICAST -j DROP
$IPT -A FORWARD -p ! udp -d $CLASS_D_MULTICAST -j DROP
```

Filtering ICMP Control and Status Messages

When the connection state tracking is used, ICMP error messages are forwarded for existing connections, and incoming and outgoing messages are accepted. The error messages are RELATED messages. Otherwise, ICMP traffic would require explicit acceptance rules.

ping's echo-request message type must be allowed explicitly, in any case. echo-request and echo-reply are diagnostic messages rather than error messages related to an ongoing exchange. Also of note regarding echo-request is that DHCP sometimes relies on echo-request to discover whether an address that is about to be assigned is already in use by a host on the local network.

Rather than duplicating the ICMP rules from Chapter 4, I'll assume that you are using the state module. echo-request and time-exceeded do need special consideration, however.

ECHO REQUEST (TYPE 8) AND ECHO REPLY (TYPE 0) MESSAGES

ping uses two ICMP message types. The request message, echo-request, is message Type 8. The reply message, echo-reply, is message Type 0. echo-request messages are not forwarded into the LAN from anywhere. External echo-request to the choke are allowed from only the gateway firewall:

```
$IPT -A INPUT   -i $DMZ_INTERFACE -p icmp --icmp-type echo-request \
       -s $GATEWAY_IPADDR -j ACCEPT
```

Some sites might choose to block outgoing echo-reply messages even if incoming echo-request messages are dropped. Some trojans, such as loki, use unsolicited echo-reply messages to carry covert login sessions in the packets' data area from your local hosts to remote servers:

```
$IPT -A OUTPUT  -o $DMZ_INTERFACE -p icmp --icmp-type echo-reply \
       -d $GATEWAY_IPADDR -j ACCEPT
$IPT -A FORWARD -o $DMZ_INTERFACE -p icmp --icmp-type echo-reply -j DROP
```

TIME EXCEEDED STATUS (TYPE 11) MESSAGES

ICMP message Type 11, time-exceeded, indicates a timeout condition—or, more accurately, that a packet's maximum hop count has been exceeded. On networks today, time-exceeded is mostly seen as the ICMP response to a traceroute request.

Many people use traceroute to pinpoint a problem in the network. Additionally, traceroute is useful in network mapping and locating critical gateways. Whether or not you choose to use traceroute, it's a good idea to block outgoing time-exceeded messages. There are few legitimate reasons for someone to map your internal network, and plenty of hostile reasons to do so. It should be noted that some versions of traceroute, notably those on *nix platforms, use UDP as the transport mechanism rather than ICMP.

If you need to allow any kind of incoming UDP traffic on the unprivileged ports, it's easier and more effective to block your outgoing response than it is to try to block the incoming requests. `traceroute` starts at UDP port `33434`, by default, but the base port is settable by command-line option and optionally can use ICMP `echo-request` rather than UDP as well:

```
$IPT -A OUTPUT  -o $DMZ_INTERFACE -p icmp --icmp-type time-exceeded -j DROP
$IPT -A FORWARD -o $DMZ_INTERFACE -p icmp --icmp-type time-exceeded -j DROP
```

If new incoming UDP packets are dropped by default, your system won't return the ICMP Type 3 `port-unreachable` message that endpoint hosts return.

Enabling DNS (UDP/TCP Port 53)

DNS relies on both UDP and TCP. Connection modes include regular client-to-server connections, server-to-server lookup traffic, and DNS zone transfers.

It's unlikely that a residential site will host public DNS service or pay the fee to have a top-level public pointer to its name server, though Dynamic DNS services are changing this paradigm. Smaller businesses may or may not do so. It's common to hire a DNS service or to have the service provided by the ISP or ASP. Larger organizations usually do host publicly accessible name servers, as well as run local, private name servers internally.

CLASSIC DNS SETUP FOR A LAN

Some sites need the additional sense of security that comes with a classic DNS setup that hides local hosts—security through obscurity, if you will. The attraction of this setup is that sensitive, local, personal, and account information can be centrally stored in the internal DNS database.

The idea is that a publicly visible host runs its own DNS server for the public. The server is configured as the authoritative source for the site, but the information is incomplete. The public name server knows nothing about internal machines. DNS clients on the public name server machine, if any, possibly don't use the local name server. Instead, `/etc/resolv.conf` on the public server points to an internal, private machine as the name server for the local clients. Incoming queries from the Internet are handled by the public DNS server. Local queries are handled by the internal DNS server.

The internal server is also configured as the authoritative source for the site. In this case, the information is correct. Local queries, possibly queries from the public server's local clients, and queries from the private LAN are all handled by this internal, private DNS server. As shown in Figure 6.6, when the local server doesn't have the requested lookup information, it queries the public server, which, in turn, forwards the query to an external name server.

FIGURE 6.6
Public dummy and private authoritative DNS name servers.

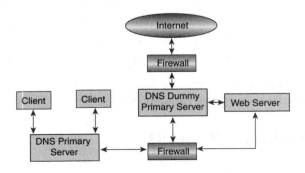

A similar configuration is the case shown in Figure 6.7. The public server claims to be authoritative for the entire site. It knows only about the DMZ servers and answers queries about them. The forwarding server knows about local hosts and answers local queries. Local machines are probably not publicly addressable from the Internet. Both servers are primary authorities for their local domain. The forwarding server may or may not have hard-coded DNS information about hosts in the DMZ.

FIGURE 6.7
Authoritative public and private DNS name servers.

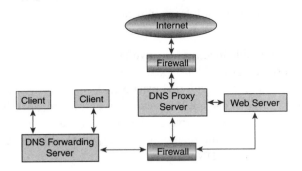

In the case in Figure 6.8, both servers hold the same DNS LAN database. Local hosts are visible to the Internet. The secondary, public server gets its information about the LAN from the primary server.

FIGURE 6.8
Secondary public and primary internal DNS name servers.

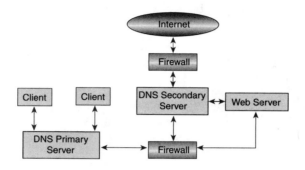

The primary could be the primary for both the LAN and the DMZ. On the other hand, it could be the primary for the LAN, and the DMZ server could be the primary for the DMZ. It's possible for DNS servers to be both primary and secondary servers for different domains at the same time.

In practice, larger sites may have multiple domain spaces and public and private name servers for load sharing and service reliability. One server is the primary server for each domain. The rest are secondary servers that refresh and update their databases, as needed, by requesting zone transfers from the primary.

In the following examples, the public DNS servers are running in the DMZ, and a private server is running on the choke firewall machine. There is no requirement that the site be configured this way. A public server could be hosted on the gateway. The private server could be on some other host in the LAN. This would in fact be the recommended approach because it's never a good idea to run extra services on the firewall machine.

As the site's network architecture becomes larger and more formal, it becomes more likely that the DMZ servers will be dedicated to hosting a single service. The gateway functions only as a filter and a router. All services are moved to the DMZ or the LAN.

GATEWAY CONFIGURATION FOR A PUBLIC DMZ NAME SERVER

The DMZ contains the public name servers. One possible configuration is to have all local DNS clients use the private name server running on the choke machine. If the choke server can't service a query, it forwards the request to one of the public servers, which, in turn, queries designated remote servers or the root name servers, in the most general case.

The gateway firewall forwards DNS traffic between the public servers in the DMZ and remote servers, as well as incoming lookup requests from the Internet. For this example, you must define a **DNS_SERVER** constant, and the DMZ servers use the standard DNS client/server protocols:

```
# DNS name server (53) - requests to remote servers
# --------------------------------------------------

$IPT -A FORWARD  -i $DMZ_INTERFACE -o $EXTERNAL_INTERFACE -p udp \
        -s $DNS_SERVER --sport $UNPRIVPORTS --dport 53 \
        -m state --state NEW -j ACCEPT

$IPT -A FORWARD  -i $DMZ_INTERFACE -o $EXTERNAL_INTERFACE -p tcp \
        -s $DNS_SERVER --sport $UNPRIVPORTS --dport 53 \
        -m state --state NEW -j ACCEPT

# DNS name server (53) - requests from remote clients
# ---------------------------------------------------

$IPT -A FORWARD -i $EXTERNAL_INTERFACE -o $DMZ_INTERFACE -p udp \
        --sport $UNPRIVPORTS -d $DNS_SERVER --dport 53 \
        -m state --state NEW -j ACCEPT

$IPT -A FORWARD -i $EXTERNAL_INTERFACE -o $DMZ_INTERFACE -p tcp \
        --sport $UNPRIVPORTS -d $DNS_SERVER --dport 53 \
        -m state --state NEW -j ACCEPT
```

Naturally, the single pair of generic rules is required to forward **ESTABLISHED** and **RELATED** traffic.

CHOKE DMZ CONFIGURATION AS A PRIVATE NAME SERVER

The choke hosts the private name server in this example. (The server, or servers, could just as easily run in the LAN itself or in a separate local server network.) LAN clients use the private name server. If the choke server can't service a query from its DNS cache, it forwards the request to the public server running in the DMZ.

The private DNS server receives client queries from the client programs running on machines in the LAN. In this example, requests from DMZ clients go to the private server so that they have access to DNS information about LAN clients:

```
# DNS LAN clients to private server (53)
# --------------------------------------

$IPT -A INPUT  -i $LAN_INTERFACE -p udp \
        -s $LAN_ADDRESSES --sport $UNPRIVPORTS \
        -d $LAN_IPADDR --dport 53 \
        -m state --state NEW -j ACCEPT
```

```
$IPT -A INPUT  -i $LAN_INTERFACE -p tcp \
        -s $LAN_ADDRESSES --sport $UNPRIVPORTS \
        -d $LAN_IPADDR --dport 53 \
        -m state --state NEW -j ACCEPT

$IPT -A INPUT  -i $DMZ_INTERFACE -p udp \
        -s $DMZ_ADDRESSES --sport $UNPRIVPORTS \
        -d $DMZ_IPADDR --dport 53 \
        -m state --state NEW -j ACCEPT

$IPT -A INPUT  -i $DMZ_INTERFACE -p tcp \
        -s $DMZ_ADDRESSES --sport $UNPRIVPORTS \
        -d $DMZ_IPADDR --dport 53 \
        -m state --state NEW -j ACCEPT
```

The TCP rule handles both large DNS responses and zone-transfer requests from local secondary name servers.

The private DNS server sends recursive server requests to the public DNS server for queries that the choke server can't resolve. When using this code, don't forget to define a **DNS_SERVER** constant as well:

```
# DNS caching & forwarding name server (53)
# ---------------------------------------

$IPT -A OUTPUT -o $DMZ_INTERFACE -p udp \
        -s $DMZ_IPADDR --sport 53 \
        -d $DNS_SERVER --dport 53 \
        -m state --state NEW -j ACCEPT

$IPT -A OUTPUT -o $DMZ_INTERFACE -p udp \
        -s $DMZ_IPADDR --sport $UNPRIVPORTS \
        -d $DNS_SERVER --dport 53 \
        -m state --state NEW -j ACCEPT

$IPT -A OUTPUT -o $DMZ_INTERFACE -p tcp \
        -s $DMZ_IPADDR --sport $UNPRIVPORTS \
        -d $DNS_SERVER --dport 53 \
        -m state --state NEW -j ACCEPT
```

In this example, the forwarding name server is assumed to be configured as a slave to the public server. I always include the standard UDP client rules as a precaution.

Filtering the AUTH User Identification Service (TCP Port 113)

The ident or AUTH user identification service provides the username associated with the connection. This is a historic protocol not used widely on the Internet anymore. You don't need
to run the AUTH service but it's common to send a REJECT or TCP RST for AUTH requests.

REJECTING AUTH REQUESTS

The following rule blocks AUTH requests at the gateway by using REJECT rather than DROP so
that the requests get a TCP RST right away rather than being blocked silently:

```
$IPT -A INPUT -i $EXTERNAL_INTERFACE -p tcp \
        --dport 113 -j REJECT
```

Email (TCP SMTP Port 25, POP3 Port 110, IMAP Port 143)

Mail is typically handled by a central SMTP server. As a workable example, this section is
based on the assumption that a machine in the DMZ is the local mail gateway and mail host.
Local clients will retrieve incoming mail from the mail host using its local POP3 or IMAP server. It's equally likely that the mail server in the DMZ is no more than a relay agent and SPAM
filter, and incoming mail would be forwarded from the mail relay in the DMZ to a mail server
in the private LAN for access by local users.

Two common approaches to client and server email combinations are described in this
section:

- Sending mail through a DMZ SMTP mail relay and receiving mail as a DMZ POP3 client
- Sending mail through a DMZ SMTP mail relay and receiving mail as a DMZ IMAP client

FORWARDING MAIL THROUGH THE GATEWAY (TCP PORT 25)

When you relay outgoing mail through a remote gateway server, your client mail program
sends all outgoing mail to your ISP's mail server. Your ISP acts as your mail gateway to the rest
of the world. Your system doesn't need to know how to locate the mail destinations. The ISP
mail gateway serves as your relay.

In this example, your site is hosting its own mail server. Your local server is responsible for
collecting your outgoing mail, doing the DNS lookup on the destination hostname, and relaying the mail to its destination. Your client mail program points to your local SMTP server
rather than to a remote server.

If you are relaying outgoing mail as an SMTP server and are receiving mail as an SMTP client,
you provide all your own mail services. Your local sendmail daemon is configured to relay

outgoing mail to the remote destination hosts itself, as well as collect and possibly deliver incoming mail.

For these examples, don't forget to define a constant for the MAIL_SERVER, such as this:
MAIL_SERVER="192.168.1.10"

The first rule enables you to relay outgoing mail and is applied to the gateway firewall:

```
$IPT -A FORWARD  -i $DMZ_INTERFACE -o $EXTERNAL_INTERFACE -p tcp \
       -s $MAIL_SERVER --sport $UNPRIVPORTS --dport 25 \
       -m state --state NEW -j ACCEPT
```

The next rule enables you to receive incoming mail and is also applied to the gateway firewall:

```
$IPT -A FORWARD -i $EXTERNAL_INTERFACE -o $DMZ_INTERFACE -p tcp \
       --sport $UNPRIVPORTS -d $MAIL_SERVER --dport 25 \
       -m state --state NEW -j ACCEPT
```

Finally, the gateway might generate mail to local hosts or to some central administrative server:

```
$IPT -A OUTPUT -o $DMZ_INTERFACE -p tcp \
       -s $DMZ_IPADDR --sport $UNPRIVPORTS -d $MAIL_SERVER --dport 25 \
       -m state --state NEW -j ACCEPT
```

CHOKE SMTP CLIENT CONFIGURATION

This rule set enables you to forward mail from LAN machines and send mail from the choke firewall itself. When using this code, don't forget to define a MAIL_SERVER constant:

```
$IPT -A FORWARD -i $LAN_INTERFACE -o $DMZ_INTERFACE -p tcp \
       -s $LAN_ADDRESSES --sport $UNPRIVPORTS \
       -d $MAIL_SERVER --dport 25 \
       -m state --state NEW -j ACCEPT

$IPT -A OUTPUT -o $DMZ_INTERFACE -p tcp \
       -s $DMZ_IPADDR --sport $UNPRIVPORTS \
       -d $MAIL_SERVER --dport 25 \
       -m state --state NEW -j ACCEPT
```

RETRIEVING MAIL AS A POP CLIENT THROUGH THE CHOKE FIREWALL (TCP PORT 110)

How you receive mail depends on your situation. If you run your own local mail server, you can collect incoming mail directly on your Linux machine. If you retrieve your mail from your ISP account, you may or may not retrieve mail as a POP or IMAP client, depending on how you've configured your ISP email account, and depending on the mail-delivery services that the ISP offers.

In this example, incoming mail is delivered to the local mail server. LAN clients retrieve their mail from the local mail host using POP. The mail host also functions as a POP server. This rule is applied to the choke firewall, and you would need to define the constant for the POP3 server as POP_SERVER if you use this code:

```
$IPT -A FORWARD -i $LAN_INTERFACE -o $DMZ_INTERFACE -p tcp \
        -s $LAN_ADDRESSES --sport $UNPRIVPORTS \
        -d $POP_SERVER --dport 110 \
        -m state --state NEW -j ACCEPT
```

RETRIEVING MAIL AS AN IMAP CLIENT THROUGH THE CHOKE FIREWALL (TCP PORT 143)

Connecting to an IMAP server is another common means of retrieving mail from a mail host. The following example demonstrates the firewall rules necessary to retrieve mail from an IMAP server running in the DMZ.

The next rule forwards client connections from the LAN to the IMAP server running on the mail host in the DMZ and is applied to the choke firewall with the IMAP_SERVER constant predefined:

```
$IPT -A FORWARD -i $LAN_INTERFACE -o $DMZ_INTERFACE -p tcp \
        -s $LAN_ADDRESSES --sport $UNPRIVPORTS \
        -d $IMAP_SERVER --dport 143 \
        -m state --state NEW -j ACCEPT
```

Accessing Usenet News Services (TCP NNTP Port 119)

Usenet news is accessed over the NNTP protocol running on top of TCP through service port 119. Reading news and posting articles are handled by your local news client.

A non-ISP site isn't likely to host a news server for the outside world. Even hosting a local news server is unlikely for a small site. For the site that represents the rare exception, the server rule should be configured to allow incoming connections from only a select set of external clients or external networks. A local public server would run on a machine in the DMZ, and the gateway would forward incoming NNTP connections to the local NNTP server machine.

GATEWAY NNTP CONDUIT AND SERVER DMZ CONFIGURATIONS

The server rule allows local client connections to your ISP's news server. Both reading news and posting articles are handled by this rule set:

```
$IPT -A FORWARD  -i $DMZ_INTERFACE -o $EXTERNAL_INTERFACE -p tcp \
        -s $LAN_ADDRESSES --sport $UNPRIVPORTS \
        -d $NEWS_SERVER --dport 119 \
        -m state --state NEW -j ACCEPT
```

If a local news server is running on a machine in the DMZ, offering public service to select remote clients, a set of server rules allowing remote clients to connect to this machine's NNTP port is defined:

```
DMZ_NEWS_SERVER="192.168.1.70"

$IPT -A FORWARD -i $EXTERNAL_INTERFACE -o $DMZ_INTERFACE -p tcp \
        -s <my.news.clients> --sport $UNPRIVPORTS \
        -d $DMZ_NEWS_SERVER --dport 119 \
        -m state --state NEW -j ACCEPT
```

If the local news server provides public Usenet newsgroups as well as local newsgroups, the local server requires a news feed from a remote server. The local server retrieves articles as a client to the remote server. The following rule allows access to a remote news server acting as a news feed:

```
NEWS_FEED="<my.remote.news.feed>"

$IPT -A FORWARD -i $DMZ_INTERFACE -o $EXTERNAL_INTERFACE -p tcp \
        -s $DMZ_NEWS_SERVER --sport $UNPRIVPORTS \
        -d $NEWS_FEED --dport 119 \
        -m state --state NEW -j ACCEPT
```

CHOKE NNTP CLIENT DMZ CONFIGURATIONS

The next rule allows local clients to access remote news servers in either the DMZ or on the Internet and would require a NEWS_SERVER constant to be defined:

```
$IPT -A FORWARD -i $LAN_INTERFACE -o $DMZ_INTERFACE -p tcp \
        -s $LAN_ADDRESSES --sport $UNPRIVPORTS \
        -d $NEWS_SERVER --dport 119 \
        -m state --state NEW -j ACCEPT
```

Telnet (TCP Port 23)

Some types of equipment, such as lower-end routers and other networking gear, allow only telnet connections for configuration. Therefore, you may find yourself forced to use it when you'd rather use a more secure protocol such as SSH.

The rules here allow LAN access to the DMZ machines using telnet. The DMZ hosts aren't allowed to connect to hosts in the LAN. The choke firewall is allowed telnet access to the LAN, however. You should not allow incoming telnet connections from remote sites; rather, you should use SSH to connect into the DMZ and then use telnet from the DMZ if you are absolutely forced to use telnet. These rules are applied to the choke firewall for telnet:

```
$IPT -A FORWARD -i $LAN_INTERFACE -o $DMZ_INTERFACE -p tcp \
        -s $LAN_ADDRESSES --sport $UNPRIVPORTS \
        -d $DMZ_ADDRESSES --dport 23 \
        -m state --state NEW -j ACCEPT

$IPT -A OUTPUT -o $DMZ_INTERFACE -p tcp  \
        -s $DMZ_IPADDR --sport $UNPRIVPORTS  \
        -d $DMZ_ADDRESSES --dport 23 \
        -m state --state NEW -j ACCEPT

$IPT -A OUTPUT -o $LAN_INTERFACE -p tcp  \
        -s $LAN_IPADDR --sport $UNPRIVPORTS  \
        -d $LAN_ADDRESSES --dport 23 \
        -m state --state NEW -j ACCEPT
```

SSH (TCP Port 22)

The client and server rules here demonstrate three separate approaches to SSH. In practice, non-ISP sites would probably limit the external addresses to a select subset, particularly because both ends of the connection should be configured to recognize each individual user account. sshd can use TCPWrappers with access lists in **/etc/hosts.allow** and **/etc/hosts.deny**.

GATEWAY SSH CONFIGURATION

The first rule allows local connections from the choke machine to an **sshd** server running on the gateway. All of these rules are applied on the gateway firewall:

```
$IPT -A INPUT  -i $DMZ_INTERFACE -p tcp \
        -s $CHOKE_IPADDR --sport $UNPRIVPORTS \
        -d $DMZ_IPADDR --dport 22 \
        -m state --state NEW -j ACCEPT
```

The next rule forwards connections from LAN clients to any remote server:

```
$IPT -A FORWARD  -i $DMZ_INTERFACE -o $EXTERNAL_INTERFACE -p tcp \
        -s $LAN_ADDRESSES --sport $UNPRIVPORTS --dport 22 \
        -m state --state NEW -j ACCEPT
```

The last rule forwards connections from a selected remote client address to a specific local server:

```
$IPT -A FORWARD  -i $EXTERNAL_INTERFACE -o $DMZ_INTERFACE -p tcp \
        -s <selected remote host> --sport $UNPRIVPORTS \
        -d <selected local host> --dport 22 \
        -m state --state NEW -j ACCEPT
```

CHOKE SSH CONFIGURATION

The first rule allows local connections from the choke machine to `sshd` servers running in the DMZ, including the gateway firewall host:

```
$IPT -A OUTPUT  -o $DMZ_INTERFACE -p tcp \
       -s $DMZ_IPADDR --sport $UNPRIVPORTS \
       -d $DMZ_ADDRESSES --dport  22 \
       -m state --state NEW -j ACCEPT
```

The next rule forwards connections from LAN clients to any remote server:

```
$IPT -A FORWARD  -i $LAN_INTERFACE -o $DMZ_INTERFACE -p tcp \
       -s $LAN_ADDRESSES --sport $UNPRIVPORTS --dport 22 \
       -m state --state NEW -j ACCEPT
```

The last rule forwards connections from a selected remote client address to a specific local host, which, in this case, resides in the LAN:

```
$IPT -A FORWARD  -i $DMZ_INTERFACE -o $LAN_INTERFACE -p tcp \
       -s <selected remote host> --sport $UNPRIVPORTS \
       -d <selected LAN host> --dport 22 \
       -m state --state NEW -j ACCEPT
```

FTP (TCP Ports 21 and 20)

FTP has two modes for exchanging data between a client and a server: normal data channel port mode and passive data channel mode. Port mode is the default mechanism when using the FTP client program and connecting to a remote FTP site. Passive mode is the mechanism used when connecting to an FTP site through a web browser. Occasionally, you might encounter an FTP site that supports only one mode.

Two approaches to client and server FTP combinations are described in this section:

- The gateway is simply a gateway to remote FTP servers; the choke machine and the LAN hosts are clients.

- An FTP server runs in the DMZ; the choke, LAN hosts, and remote hosts are clients.

GATEWAY AS CONDUIT TO REMOTE FTP SERVERS

It's almost a given that most sites will want FTP client access to remote file repositories. The first section allows internal hosts to connect to remote FTP servers.

The following rules allow outgoing FTP client connections from the choke host and the LAN machines. The constants are those used on the gateway:

```
# Outgoing FTP Client Request
# -------------------------

$IPT -A FORWARD -i $DMZ_INTERFACE -o $EXTERNAL_INTERFACE -p tcp \
-s $LAN_ADDRESSES --sport $UNPRIVPORTS --dport 21 \
        -m state --state NEW -j ACCEPT

$IPT -A FORWARD -i $DMZ_INTERFACE -o $EXTERNAL_INTERFACE -p tcp \
        -s $CHOKE_IPADDR --sport $UNPRIVPORTS --dport 21 \
        -m state --state NEW -j ACCEPT
```

The `ip_conntrack_ftp` module takes care of the port or passive mode data connection as part of the **RELATED** state. Specific rules for the data connection aren't required.

The two pairs of data channel connection request rules are included here for the sake of completeness:

```
# Port Mode Data Channel Responses
# -------------------------------------

$IPT -A FORWARD -i $EXTERNAL_INTERFACE -o $DMZ_INTERFACE -p tcp \
        --sport 20 -d $LAN_ADDRESSES --dport $UNPRIVPORTS \
        -m state --state NEW -j ACCEPT

$IPT -A FORWARD -i $EXTERNAL_INTERFACE -o $DMZ_INTERFACE -p tcp \
        --sport 20 -d $CHOKE_IPADDR --dport $UNPRIVPORTS \
        -m state --state NEW -j ACCEPT

# Passive Mode Data Channel Responses
# --------------------------------

$IPT -A FORWARD -i $DMZ_INTERFACE -o $EXTERNAL_INTERFACE -p tcp \
        -s $LAN_ADDRESSES --sport $UNPRIVPORTS --dport $UNPRIVPORTS \
        -m state --state NEW -j ACCEPT

$IPT -A FORWARD -i $DMZ_INTERFACE -o $EXTERNAL_INTERFACE -p tcp \
        -s $CHOKE_IPADDR --sport $UNPRIVPORTS --dport $UNPRIVPORTS \
        -m state --state NEW -j ACCEPT
```

The choke's client rule is included in the upcoming section "Choke as Conduit and Client to an FTP Server."

FTP SERVER IN DMZ, CHOKE, LOCAL HOSTS, AND REMOTE HOSTS AS CLIENTS

This section defines rules to allow incoming client requests using FTP.

GATEWAY AS CONDUIT TO AN FTP DMZ SERVER

On the gateway, the next rule forwards incoming FTP client connections from any remote machine to the server in the DMZ. When using this code, note that it requires a constant of DMZ_FTP_SERVER to be defined:

```
$IPT -A FORWARD -i $EXTERNAL_INTERFACE -o $DMZ_INTERFACE -p tcp \
      --sport $UNPRIVPORTS -d $DMZ_FTP_SERVER --dport 21 \
      -m state --state NEW -j ACCEPT
```

CHOKE AS CONDUIT AND CLIENT TO AN FTP SERVER

The following rules allow outgoing FTP client connections from the LAN and the choke machine to an FTP server anywhere. The choke's rules don't refer to the DMZ specifically.

The first rule forwards outgoing FTP client connections from any LAN machine to any server:

```
$IPT -A FORWARD -i $LAN_INTERFACE -o $DMZ_INTERFACE -p tcp \
      -s $LAN_ADDRESSES --sport $UNPRIVPORTS --dport 21 \
      -m state --state NEW -j ACCEPT
```

The second rule allows FTP client access from the choke host itself:

```
$IPT -A OUTPUT -o $DMZ_INTERFACE -p tcp  \
      -s $DMZ_IPADDR --sport $UNPRIVPORTS --dport 21 \
      -m state --state NEW -j ACCEPT
```

Web Services

Web services generally are based on the HTTP protocol. Several higher-level communication protocols are used for special purposes, including a special protocol for web proxy and cache access (**webcache** on TCP port **8080** in **/etc/services**), and SSL and TLS for secure access (**https** on TCP port **443** in **/etc/services**). The **squid** web proxy uses TCP port **3128** by default (**squid** on TCP port **3128** in **/etc/services**).

Four approaches to client and server web combinations are described in this section:

- The gateway is simply a conduit for local web clients connecting to remote web servers; the choke machine and the LAN are clients.

- The choke acts as both a forwarder and a client.

- A web server runs in the DMZ; the choke, LAN, and remote hosts are clients.

- A web proxy runs in the DMZ; the choke and the LAN are clients.

THE GATEWAY AS A CONDUIT FOR LOCAL WEB CLIENTS

The first section of the following code allows local hosts to connect to web servers running on remote hosts.

On the gateway, the following rules forward local client connections from the choke machine, as well as from machines on the private LAN behind the choke firewall:

```
$IPT -A FORWARD  -i $DMZ_INTERFACE -o $EXTERNAL_INTERFACE -p tcp \
        -s $LAN_ADDRESSES --sport  $UNPRIVPORTS --dport 80 \
        -m state --state NEW -j ACCEPT

$IPT -A FORWARD  -i $DMZ_INTERFACE -o $EXTERNAL_INTERFACE -p tcp \
        -s $LAN_ADDRESSES --sport  $UNPRIVPORTS --dport 443 \
        -m state --state NEW -j ACCEPT

$IPT -A FORWARD  -i $DMZ_INTERFACE -o $EXTERNAL_INTERFACE -p tcp \
        -s $CHOKE_IPADDR --sport  $UNPRIVPORTS --dport 80 \
        -m state --state NEW -j ACCEPT

$IPT -A FORWARD  -i $DMZ_INTERFACE -o $EXTERNAL_INTERFACE -p tcp \
        -s $CHOKE_IPADDR --sport  $UNPRIVPORTS --dport 443 \
        -m state --state NEW -j ACCEPT
```

THE CHOKE AS A FORWARDER AND WEB CLIENT

The choke acts as both a forwarder and a client in this example. The following rules forward local client connections from the LAN and also allow client connections from the choke itself:

```
$IPT -A FORWARD  -i $LAN_INTERFACE -o $DMZ_INTERFACE -p tcp \
        -s $LAN_ADDRESSES --sport  $UNPRIVPORTS --dport 80 \
        -m state --state NEW -j ACCEPT

$IPT -A OUTPUT  -o $DMZ_INTERFACE -p tcp \
        -s $DMZ_IPADDR --sport  $UNPRIVPORTS --dport 80 \
        -m state --state NEW -j ACCEPT

$IPT -A FORWARD  -i $LAN_INTERFACE -o $DMZ_INTERFACE -p tcp \
        -s $LAN_ADDRESSES --sport  $UNPRIVPORTS --dport 443 \
        -m state --state NEW -j ACCEPT

$IPT -A OUTPUT  -o $DMZ_INTERFACE -p tcp \
        -s $DMZ_IPADDR --sport  $UNPRIVPORTS --dport 443 \
        -m state --state NEW -j ACCEPT
```

A PUBLIC WEB SERVER IN THE DMZ; THE CHOKE, LAN, AND REMOTE HOSTS AS CLIENTS

In this example, the site hosts a public web server in the DMZ.

The gateway is a bidirectional conduit, allowing public access to the local server, as well as continuing to allow local access to remote sites using the rules presented in the preceding section. These rules apply to the gateway and would require a predefined constant of DMZ_WEB_SERVER:

```
$IPT -A FORWARD  -i $EXTERNAL_INTERFACE -o $DMZ_INTERFACE -p tcp \
        --sport $UNPRIVPORTS -d $DMZ_WEB_SERVER --dport 80 \
        -m state --state NEW -j ACCEPT

$IPT -A FORWARD  -i $EXTERNAL_INTERFACE -o $DMZ_INTERFACE -p tcp \
        --sport $UNPRIVPORTS -d $DMZ_WEB_SERVER --dport 443 \
        -m state --state NEW -j ACCEPT

$IPT -A FORWARD  -i $DMZ_INTERFACE -o $EXTERNAL_INTERFACE -p tcp \
        -s $LAN_ADDRESSES --sport $UNPRIVPORTS --dport 80 \
        -m state --state NEW -j ACCEPT

$IPT -A FORWARD  -i $DMZ_INTERFACE -o $EXTERNAL_INTERFACE -p tcp \
        -s $LAN_ADDRESSES --sport $UNPRIVPORTS --dport 443 \
        -m state --state NEW -j ACCEPT

$IPT -A FORWARD  -i $DMZ_INTERFACE -o $EXTERNAL_INTERFACE -p tcp \
        -s $CHOKE_IPADDR --sport $UNPRIVPORTS --dport 80 \
        -m state --state NEW -j ACCEPT

$IPT -A FORWARD  -i $DMZ_INTERFACE -o $EXTERNAL_INTERFACE -p tcp \
        -s $CHOKE_IPADDR --sport $UNPRIVPORTS --dport 443 \
        -m state --state NEW -j ACCEPT
```

The choke's rules remain the same as they were in the preceding section.

A WEB PROXY IN THE DMZ; THE GATEWAY AS A CONDUIT; CHOKE AND LAN AS CLIENTS

Although it's possible to offer public web service from an internal LAN server, it isn't usually done because of the greater potential for security breaches with misconfigured servers and CGI scripts, and the tendency to isolate private information from public information. That is, sites that host both a private, internal website and a public website usually run multiple web servers on different machines in different LANs. A more common scenario would be to host the public website from a host on the perimeter network.

In the case of a *very* small personal or business home site, one possibility is to run a public server on the gateway machine. (Hosting a public web server on the firewall host would otherwise be considered a dangerous idea.) Possibly, a second, private proxy web server runs on an internal machine. In this situation, the public server may or may not offer SSL service. The internal web server offers proxy service. The private server isn't accessible from the gateway machine.

The proxy server in this example could run in the LAN, but there wouldn't be an "example" because the firewall rules on both the gateway and the choke would remain the same as in the first web section. Placing the proxy web server in the DMZ or on the choke host demonstrates the difference between the client-side rules and the server-side rules.

From the gateway's perspective, the internal web proxy appears to be a web client initiating connections to remote servers. This example requires a constant of DMZ_WWW_PROXY:

```
$IPT -A FORWARD  -i $DMZ_INTERFACE -o $EXTERNAL_INTERFACE -p tcp \
       -s $DMZ_WWW_PROXY --sport  $UNPRIVPORTS --dport 80 \
       -m state --state NEW -j ACCEPT

$IPT -A FORWARD  -i $DMZ_INTERFACE -o $EXTERNAL_INTERFACE -p tcp \
       -s $DMZ_WWW_PROXY --sport  $UNPRIVPORTS --dport 443 \
       -m state --state NEW -j ACCEPT
```

The choke's rules must account for the port that the web proxy is bound to, thus the WEB_PROXY_PORT constant in this example. From the choke's perspective, the local web proxy appears to be a server running on a port other than TCP port **80**, as these rules show:

```
$IPT -A FORWARD  -i $LAN_INTERFACE -o $DMZ_INTERFACE -p tcp \
       -s $LAN_ADDRESSES --sport  $UNPRIVPORTS \
       -d $DMZ_WWW_PROXY --dport $WEB_PROXY_PORT \
       -m state --state NEW -j ACCEPT

$IPT -A OUTPUT  -o $DMZ_INTERFACE -p tcp \
       -s $DMZ_IPADDR --sport  $UNPRIVPORTS \
       -d $DMZ_WWW_PROXY --dport $WEB_PROXY_PORT \
       -m state --state NEW -j ACCEPT
```

Choke as a Local DHCP Server (UDP Ports 67 and 68)

DHCP provides network configuration information to hosts. We often think of DHCP mostly in terms of assigning IP addresses, but it also can provide information such as your network mask and MTU, the address of the first-hop router, name server addresses, and the domain name.

Although you should never send DHCP server messages to the Internet (with the notable exception of your gateway that might need to contact your ISP's DHCP server), some people run a private DHCP server to assign IP addresses to local machines. DHCP can be useful not only for assigning IP addresses on a larger LAN with many machines, but also for very small personal home LANs. In fact, some people with a single standalone system sometimes run the DHCPD server locally if they carry a laptop computer between home and work. If the work environment assigns IP addresses dynamically, using DHCP at home makes transporting the laptop between networks easier. Additionally, some networked printers and wireless devices can or do use DHCP to discover their IP address when they come online.

For this example, the **dhcpd** server is running on the choke machine, providing dynamic IP address assignment for machines on the private LAN:

```
$IPT -A INPUT  -i $LAN_INTERFACE -p udp \
        -s $BROADCAST_SRC --sport 68 \
        -d $BROADCAST_DEST --dport 67 -j ACCEPT

$IPT -A OUTPUT -o $LAN_INTERFACE -p udp \
        -s $BROADCAST_SRC --sport 67 \
        -d $BROADCAST_DEST --dport 68 -j ACCEPT

$IPT -A OUTPUT -o $LAN_INTERFACE -p udp \
        -s $LAN_IPADDR --sport 67 \
        -d $BROADCAST_DEST --dport 68 -j ACCEPT

$IPT -A INPUT  -i $LAN_INTERFACE -p udp \
        -s $BROADCAST_SRC --sport 68 \
        -d $LAN_IPADDR --dport 67 -j ACCEPT

$IPT -A OUTPUT -o $LAN_INTERFACE -p udp \
        -s $LAN_IPADDR --sport 67 \
        -d $LAN_ADDRESSES --dport 68 -j ACCEPT

$IPT -A OUTPUT -o $LAN_INTERFACE -p udp \
        -s $LAN_IPADDR --sport 67 \
        -d $LAN_ADDRESSES --dport 68 -j ACCEPT

$IPT -A INPUT  -i $LAN_INTERFACE -p udp \
        -s $LAN_ADDRESSES --sport 68 \
        -d $LAN_IPADDR --dport 67 -j ACCEPT
```

Logging

Logging dropped packets on the internal interfaces is a good idea, even if the LAN is a relatively trusted environment. Logging is a major tool when debugging firewall problems and understanding communication protocols, both in cases in which different vendors have not strictly adhered to the protocol standards and in cases in which you don't know just what the protocol is. Application protocol information is often difficult to find or is incomplete because network-application writers usually are thinking in terms of an unfiltered, open network. If all traffic were allowed between the private LAN and the choke machine, logging still might be enabled on a port-specific basis or for broadcast traffic. However, although allowing all local traffic is easier in the short term for trusted environments, it can make debugging more difficult when packets are then dropped by the forwarding rules or by the gateway's firewall rules.

Converting the Gateway from Local Services to Forwarding

The gateway firewall from Chapter 4 needs some further adjustments to its rules. The services that had been hosted on the gateway have moved to the DMZ. This chapter has shown the forwarding rules on at least one of the two firewalls when the rules were the same, and on both firewalls when the respective rules were a bit different. I don't want to be unnecessarily repetitive and belabor the rules on the gateway.

In the interests of space and patience, yours and mine, the modified prelude to the example from Chapter 4 is not presented here. The modifications are simply to convert the error-checking rules from the local **INPUT** and **OUTPUT** chains to the **FORWARD** chain because the local services are moving into the DMZ. Both examples, from Chapter 4 and from this chapter, are presented in their entirety, without interspersed text, in Appendix B, "Firewall Examples and Support Scripts."

Summary

This chapter covered some of the firewall options available when you're protecting a LAN. Security policies are defined relative to the site's level of security needs, the importance of the data being protected, and the cost of lost data or privacy. Starting with the bastion firewall developed in Chapter 4 as the basis, LAN and firewall setup options were discussed in increasingly complex configurations.

The major emphasis in this chapter was to use the firewall example from Chapter 4 as the basis to develop a formal, elaborate, textbook type of firewall. The bastion became a forwarding gateway firewall with two network interfaces: one connected to the Internet and one connected to a perimeter network, or DMZ. Public Internet services were offered from machines in the DMZ network. A second firewall, a choke firewall, was also connected to the DMZ network, separating the internal, private LAN from the quasi-public server machines in the perimeter network. Private machines were protected behind the choke firewall on the internal LAN. The choke firewall protected any other machine in the perimeter network.

Some services, such as IRC or RealAudio, do not lend themselves to packet filtering because of their application communication protocols, such as requiring incoming connections from the server or multiple client/server exchanges over both TCP and UDP. These types of services require additional help from application-level proxies.

## CHAPTER 7

NAT—Network Address Translation

Network Address Translation is a technology to substitute one source or destination address in the IP header with another address. Traditionally, it's an IP address translation technology to map packets between two different addressing realms. NAT's most common use is to map outgoing connections between a privately addressed local network and the publicly addressable Internet. In fact, that was what it was originally proposed to do, primarily in conjunction with the then newly defined private class address spaces; both were attempts to alleviate the IPv4 address space shortage.

This chapter introduces the concept of NAT and tells what the various types of NAT are typically used for.

The Conceptual Background of NAT

NAT was first presented in 1994 in RFC 1631, which was later replaced by RFC 3022. NAT was proposed as a possible short-term, temporary solution (to be used until IPv6 was deployed) to the growing shortage of public IP addresses. NAT also was seen as a possible solution to the growing demands on routers that handled noncontiguous address blocks. It was thought that NAT might possibly reduce or eliminate the need for CIDR, which, in turn, was prompting address reallocations and changes to router software and network configurations. NAT was also seen as a means to avoid the cost and overhead of local network renumbering when the address spaces were reallocated, or when a site changed service providers and was assigned a new public address block.

NAT was seen not only as a short-term solution, but also as a solution that conceivably would cause more problems than it solved. With the exception of FTP, most problematic application protocols were thought to be legacy protocols that would gradually fall into disuse. It was assumed that, in the face of NAT, network application developers would naturally become more mindful of end-to-end considerations, would be careful not to embed address information in new applications' data, and would avoid diverging from the standard client/server model.

Just the opposite turned out to be the case. IPv6 has yet to be deployed, giving NAT permanent, long-term status. Use of NAT became almost universal as Internet access became more available to the general public and available IPv4 addresses became ever more scarce. The standard application protocols of the time and the common standard protocols still in use today—including DNS, HTTP, SMTP, POP, and NNTP—work just fine with NAT, and all NAT implementations provide special support for FTP.

NAT's success at transparent translation is a result of the standard client/server connection characteristics of these common protocols. The exceptions didn't turn out to be a few legacy and oddball applications, however. Internet applications have become increasingly interactive. Newer applications sometimes don't have a clear client/server relationship. Sometimes a single server coordinates communication among multiple users, who may also initiate communication among themselves, independent of the server. Multiple servers can operate in conjunction with distributed services running across multiple NAT address domains, or with services that are provided by different kinds of servers operating cooperatively. Multimedia and other multistreaming and two-way, multiconnection sessions can initiate connections in both directions, may have many simultaneous connections per session, and may rely on both TCP and UDP simultaneously. The client isn't always a stationary, permanently addressable entity, as with dynamic client location in terms of mobile devices and telecommuting employees. Some services rely on end-to-end packet and data integrity, as do the IPSec encryption and authentication protocols.

These newer network applications do not work with NAT transparently. Specific application-layer gateway (ALG) support for each application must be provided for NAT to be capable of translating these packets correctly. In the case of encryption, end-to-end Transport-layer security protocols using encryption and authentication methods don't work, period.

Regardless of the difficulties associated with NAT, its usefulness ensures that it's here to stay for the duration of IPv4. In the meantime, firewall folks are looking at alternative ways of firewalling to solve the problems that the newer protocols introduce, both in terms of NAT and in terms of packet filtering itself.

We need alternative firewalling methods because firewalling itself has problems when implemented with current technology. NAT isn't the only problem. Multimedia, and the cost and overhead of application-level gateways, are gradually forcing the issue. Some of these protocols simply cannot be filtered with current firewall (and NAT) approaches.

Three general categories of NAT exist, as described in RFC 2663, "IP Network Address Translator (NAT) Terminology and Considerations":

- Traditional, outbound, unidirectional NAT is used for networks with private address space. Outgoing sessions can be initiated from the private LAN to remote Internet hosts. Incoming sessions cannot be initiated from remote hosts to local hosts in the privately addressed LAN.

  Traditional NAT is divided into two general subtypes, although the two subtypes can overlap in practice:

  - Basic NAT performs address translation only. It is usually used to map local private source addresses to one from a pool of public addresses. For the duration of all sessions initiated by a particular local host, there is a one-to-one mapping between a particular public and private address pair.

  - Network Address and Port Translation (NAPT) performs address translation but also replaces the local LAN host's source port with a source port on the NAT device. It is usually used to map local private source addresses to a single public address (as in Linux masquerading). Because the NAT device has a single IP address to map all outgoing private LAN connections to, the private and public source port pair is used to associate a particular connection with a particular private host address and a particular connection from that host.

- Bidirectional NAT performs two-way address translation, allowing both outbound and inbound connections. There is a one-to-one mapping between a public address and a private address. Effectively, the public address is a public alias for the local host's private address. This allows remote hosts to address the private host by the public address associated with it. The NAT device translates the public destination address in the incoming packet to the private address that the local host is actually assigned.

  One use of this is bidirectional address mapping between IPv4 and IPv6 address spaces. Although both addresses are routable within their own address spaces, IPv6 addresses are not routable within the IPv4 address space. A host in the IPv4 address space cannot directly reference a host in the IPv6 address space. Likewise, a host in the IPv6 space can directly reference a host in the IPv4 space. It is the IPv6 host's address that is being translated back and forth between the two addressing realms.

  Another use for bidirectional NAT that is more relevant to Linux users is to forward connections between the Internet and privately addressed local servers when the site offers public services from a LAN but has a single public IP address.

- Twice NAT performs two-way source and destination address translation, but both the source and destination addresses are translated in both directions. Twice NAT is used when the source and destination networks' address spaces collide. This could be because one site mistakenly used public addresses assigned to someone else. Twice NAT can be used as a convenience when a site is renumbered or assigned to a new public address block but the owner doesn't want to administer the new address assignments immediately.

The advantages of NAT include these:

- Packets containing standard application protocol data are transparently translated between networks.
- Standard client/server services "just work" with NAT.
- NAT alleviates the problems caused by the growing shortage of available IP addresses by sharing one public address or a small block of public addresses among an entire local network.
- NAT reduces the need for both local and public IP address renumbering.
- NAT reduces the need to deploy and administer more complicated routing schemes within larger local networks.
- In NAT's most common form in conjunction with private IP addresses, unwanted incoming traffic isn't passed along because the local machines aren't addressable.
- In one of NAT's other forms, it's used to allow virtual servers, in which a server farm appears to be a single, addressable server for load balancing.

The disadvantages of NAT include these:

- NAT introduces single points of failure within the network by maintaining critical state within the network itself.
- Maintaining critical state on the NAT device breaks the Internet paradigm in that packets can no longer be automatically rerouted around failed NAT routers.
- NAT breaks the Internet paradigm of end-to-end transparency by modifying packet contents en route.
- As a result of modifying addressing information, application-specific NAT support is required for any application that embeds local addresses or ports in the application payload.

- As a result of modifying addressing information for applications that embed local addresses or ports in the application payload, incoming packets destined to a NAT host must be defragmented before forwarding.

- NAT increases resource and performance requirements for NAT devices, which otherwise would be dedicated to fast datagram forwarding. NAT represents not only the overhead of defragmentation, packet inspection, and packet modification, but also the overhead of state maintenance, state timeouts, and state garbage collection.

- Because of state maintenance within the network and the associated resource requirements, NAT devices are not infinitely scalable. Additionally, without complicated sharing techniques, hosts cannot use multiple peer NAT devices, an aspect of the single point of failure.

- Bidirectional, multistream protocols require application-specific NAT support to forward incoming secondary streams to the proper local host. (Note that these protocols generally require ALG support for firewalling as well.)

- NAT can break the capability to run multiple instances of the same local network client application in connection with the same remote server. This problem tends to occur with network games and IRC, where the session has associated incoming streams.

- NAT cannot be used with transport mode IPSec for end-to-end security for a few reasons:

  - End-to-end Transport-layer security techniques are not possible because the techniques rely on end-to-end integrity of the packet header contents for authentication.

  - End-to-end Transport-layer security techniques are not possible because the techniques rely on end-to-end integrity of the packet's data payload, which also relies on packet header integrity.

  - End-to-end Transport-layer security techniques are not possible because data encryption renders the packet's contents unavailable for inspection. NAT modifications are not possible to change embedded address and port information.

  - Security trust relationships must be extended into the network from the endpoint hosts, possibly to a point outside the local site altogether. IPSec and most VPN technologies must be extended to the NAT device (in other words, IPSec tunnel mode). Again, the NAT device becomes a single point of failure because the NAT device must terminate the VPN and establish a new link as a proxy to the destination.

iptables NAT Semantics

iptables provides full NAT functionality, including both source (SNAT) and destination (DNAT) address mapping. The term *full NAT* isn't a formal term; I'm referring to the capability to perform both source and destination NAT, to specify one or a range of translation addresses, to perform port translation, and to perform port remapping. iptables supports the three general types of NAT (traditional NAT, bidirectional NAT, and twice NAT), as defined in RFC 2663.

A partial implementation of NAPT, known as masquerading among Linux users, was provided in earlier Linux releases. It was used to map all local, private addresses to the single public IP address of the site's single public network interface.

NAT and forwarding were often spoken of as two components of the same thing because masquerading was specified as part of the forward rule's semantics. Blurring the concepts was irrelevant functionally. Now it's very important to keep the distinction in mind. Forwarding and NAT are two distinct functions and technologies.

Forwarding is routing traffic between networks. Forwarding routes traffic between network interfaces *as is*. Connections can be forwarded in either direction.

Masquerading sits on top of forwarding as a separate kernel service. Traffic is masqueraded in both directions, but not symmetrically. Masquerading is unidirectional. Only outgoing connections can be initiated. As traffic from local machines passes through the firewall to a remote location, the internal machine's IP address and source port are replaced with the address of the firewall machine's external network interface and a free source port on the interface. The process is reversed for incoming responses. Before the packet is forwarded to the internal machine, the firewall's destination IP address and port are replaced with the real IP address and port of the internal machine participating in the connection. The firewall machine's port determines whether incoming traffic, all of which is addressed to the firewall machine, is destined to the firewall machine itself or to a particular local host.

The semantics of forwarding and NAT are separated in iptables. The function of forwarding the packet is done in the **filter** table using the **FORWARD** chain. The function of applying NAT to the packet is done in the **nat** table, using one of the **nat** table's **POSTROUTING**, **PREROUTING**, or **OUTPUT** chains:

- Forwarding is a routing function. The **FORWARD** chain is part of the **filter** table.

- NAT is a translation function that is specified in the **nat** table. NAT takes place either before or after the routing function. The **nat** table's **POSTROUTING**, **PREROUTING**, and **OUTPUT** chains are part of the **nat** table. Source NAT is applied on the **POSTROUTING** chain after a packet has passed through the routing function. Source NAT is also applied on the OUTPUT chain for locally generated, outgoing packets. (The `filter` table OUTPUT chain and the `nat` table OUTPUT chain are two separate, unrelated chains.) Destination NAT is applied on the PREROUTING chain before passing the packet to the routing function.

A word of caution is in order for readers who are used to the combined `forward` and MASQ semantics of ipfwadm and ipchains. In iptables, maintaining the clear demarcation between prerouting, forwarding, and post-routing has serious repercussions in terms of the forwarding and NAT rules, as compared to those in ipfwadm and ipchains. In iptables forwarding, the rules are usually specified as a pair, one for each direction between the two interfaces. Use of the state module can hide this fact by allowing all ESTABLISHED rules to be collapsed into a single pair.

In iptables NAT, a single rule is specified. The NAT table entry is created when the first packet in the exchange is received or sent. NAT recognizes returning responses by their destination address and port pair, and it automatically reverses the original process. Because forwarding and NAT are applied on different chains at different points in the packet's path, all three rules are needed: the two rules in the forwarding rule pair and the single NAT rule.

Perhaps a more insidious issue is just what the address in the packet is on any given chain. Associated rules on the PREROUTING, POSTROUTING, FORWARD, INPUT, and OUTPUT chains will see different addresses in the same packet. The various rules applying to the same packet will have to match on different addresses.

WHICH DESTINATION ADDRESS IS SEEN WHERE?

Destination NAT is applied on the `nat` table's PREROUTING chain, before the routing decision is made. Rules on the PREROUTING chain must match on the original destination address in the packet's IP header. Rules on the `filter` table's INPUT or FORWARD chain must match on the modified, NATed address in the same packet header. Likewise, if that same packet were to also have source NAT applied after the routing decision is made, and if the destination address were important to match on, the rule on the `nat` table's POSTROUTING chain would match on the modified destination address.

Source NAT is applied on the `nat` table's POSTROUTING chain, after the routing decision is made. Rules on any chain match on the original source address. The source address is modified immediately before sending the packet on to the next hop or destination host. The modified source address isn't seen on the host applying the source NAT.

None of these distinctions between forwarding and NAT was an apparent issue with ipfwadm and ipchains. The forwarding rule pair wasn't necessary when masquerading. Two-way forwarding and NAT were implied by a single rule. The incoming local interface was implied by the source address. The translated source address was taken from the outgoing public interface specification. Reverse translation for response packets was implied without an explicit rule.

DON'T GO OVERBOARD USING NAT SYNTAX

The rest of this chapter presents the nat table syntax. Another word of caution is called for when looking at the complete NAT syntax. The following sections describe the simpler, more general syntax used with NAT, which is what will be used most commonly. The average site won't have a use for the specialized features available in the nat table.

Both SNAT and DNAT rules can specify the protocol, source and destination addresses, source and destination ports, and state flags, in addition to the translated address and ports. When this is done, the nat table rules look very much like `filter` table rules. It's very easy to confuse NAT rules with firewall rules, especially for people who are used to ipchains syntax. Actual filtering is done in the FORWARD chain.

You could mirror the match fields between the FORWARD rules and the NAT rules; the two sets of rules could look nearly identical. For large rule sets, it would quickly become an error-prone, administrative nightmare and would accomplish very little.

Remember that iptables forwarding and NAT are two completely separate functions. The actual firewall filtering is done by the rules in the `filter` table. For most people, it's best to keep the nat table rules simple.

Source NAT

Two forms of source NAT exist in the iptables **nat** table, specified as two distinct targets, SNAT and MASQUERADE. SNAT is standard source address translation. MASQUERADE is a specialized form of source NAT for use in environments in which an arbitrary, dynamically assigned IP address is assigned on a temporary, connection-by-connection basis.

Both targets are used on the **nat** table's **POSTROUTING** chain. Source address modifications are applied after the routing decision has been made to choose the proper outgoing interface. Thus, SNAT rules are associated with an outgoing interface, not with an incoming interface.

STANDARD SNAT

This is the general syntax for SNAT:

```
iptables -t nat -A POSTROUTING -o <outgoing interface> ... \
        -j SNAT --to-source <address>[-<address>][:port-port]
```

The address is the source address to substitute for the original source address in the packet, presumably the address of the outgoing interface. Source NAT is what NAT is traditionally used for, to allow outgoing connections. Specifying a single translation address performs NAPT, allowing all local, privately addressed hosts to share your site's single, public IP address.

Optionally, a range of source addresses can be specified. Sites that have a block of public addresses would use this range. Outgoing connections from local hosts would be assigned one of the available addresses, with the public address being associated with a particular local host's IP address. Specifying a range of addresses represents what traditional, basic NAT is usually used for, although iptables SNAT is internally implemented as NAPT in both cases.

The final port specification is another option. The range of ports defines the pool of source ports to choose from on the NAT device's outgoing interface.

The ellipsis represents any other packet selectors that are specified. For example, SNAT could be applied only to a select local host or only for TCP connections. Another use might be for VPN, where connections between two sites might be made between two specific source and destination addresses. An alternative with VPN is that connections might be made between specific source and destination ports.

Why might a site add these match selectors to a NAT rule? These selections are—or should be—made on the `filter` table's INPUT, OUTPUT, and FORWARD chains. In the case of applying NAT to select hosts, the site might be excluding hosts containing sensitive information. The site might contain networked devices such as printers or local wireless devices, and it might not be clear just what kinds of traffic these devices generate. Matching on TCP might be done as an added assurance that UDP traffic is not being exchanged with the Internet or that UDP traffic is passed only through specific application proxies.

MASQUERADE SOURCE NAT

The general syntax for MASQUERADE is as follows:

```
iptables -t nat -A POSTROUTING -o <outgoing interface> ... \
        -j MASQUERADE [--to-ports <port>[-port]]
```

MASQUERADE doesn't have an option to specify a particular source address to use on the NAT device. The source address used is the address of the outgoing interface.

The optional port specification is one source port or a range of source ports to choose from on the NAT device's outgoing interface.

As with SNAT, the ellipsis represents any other packet selectors that are specified. For example, MASQUERADE could be applied to only a select local host.

Destination NAT

Two forms of destination NAT exist in the iptables **nat** table, specified as two distinct targets: DNAT and REDIRECT. DNAT is standard destination address translation. REDIRECT is a specialized form of destination NAT that redirects packets to the NAT device's input or loopback interface.

The two targets can be used on either of the **nat** table's **PREROUTING** or **OUTPUT** chains. Destination address modifications are applied before the routing decision is made to choose the proper interface. Thus, on the **PREROUTING** chain, DNAT and REDIRECT rules are associated with an incoming interface for packets that are to be forwarded through the device or that are addressed to this host's incoming interface. On the **OUTPUT** chain, DNAT and REDIRECT rules refer to locally generated, outgoing packets from the NAT host itself.

STANDARD DNAT

The general syntax for **DNAT** is as shown here:

```
iptables -t nat -A PREROUTING -i <incoming interface> ... \
        -j DNAT --to-destination <address>[-<address>][:port-port]
```

and

```
iptables -t nat -A OUTPUT -o <outgoing interface> ... \
        -j DNAT --to-destination <address>[-<address>][:port-port]
```

The address is the destination address to substitute for the original destination address in the packet, presumably the address of a local server.

Optionally, a range of destination addresses can be specified. Sites that have a pool of public, peer servers would use this range. Incoming connections from remote sites would be assigned to one of the servers. These addresses could be public addresses assigned to the internal machines. For example, a pool of peer servers appears to be a single server to remote hosts. Alternatively, the addresses could be private addresses, and the servers wouldn't be directly visible or addressable from the Internet. In the latter case, the site probably doesn't have public addresses to assign to the servers. Remote hosts attempt to connect to the service on the NAT host. The NAT host forwards the connections transparently to the privately addressed internal server.

The final port specification is another option. The port specifies the destination port, or port range, on the target host's incoming interface that the packet should be sent to.

The ellipsis represents any other packet selectors that are specified. For example, **DNAT** could be applied to redirect incoming connections from a specific remote host to an internal host. Another use might be to redirect incoming connections to a particular service port to the actual server running in the local network.

REDIRECT DESTINATION NAT

The general syntax for REDIRECT is shown here:

```
iptables -t nat -A PREROUTING -i <incoming interface> ... \
        -j REDIRECT [--to-ports <port[-port]>
```

and

```
iptables -t nat -A OUTPUT -o <outgoing interface> ... \
        -j REDIRECT [--to-ports <port[-port]>
```

Remember, REDIRECT redirects the packet to this host, which is the host performing the REDIRECT.

Packets arriving on the incoming interface are presumably addressed to some other local host. Another alternative could be that the packet is targeted to a particular local service port, and the packet is redirected to a different port on the host transparently.

Locally generated packets, destined for somewhere else, are redirected back to the loopback interface on this host. Again, a packet targeted to a specific remote service might be redirected back to the local machine, perhaps to a caching proxy, for example.

Optionally, a different destination port or port range can be specified. If no port is specified, the packet is delivered to the destination port that the sender defined in the packet.

The ellipsis represents any other packet selectors that are specified. For example, REDIRECT could be applied to redirect incoming connections to a specific service to a server, logger, authenticator, or some kind of inspection software on the local host. The packet could be sent on from this host after some kind of inspection function was performed. Another use might be to redirect outgoing connections to a particular service back to a server or an intermediate service on this host.

Examples of SNAT and Private LANs

Source NAT is by far the most common form of NAT. Using NAT to give outgoing Internet access to local, privately addressed hosts was the original purpose of NAT. The following sections provide some simple, real-world examples of using the **nat** table's MASQUERADE and SNAT targets.

Masquerading LAN Traffic to the Internet

The MASQUERADE version of source NAT is intended for people with dial-up accounts who get a different IP address assigned at each connection. It also is used by people with *always on* connections, but whose ISP assigns them a different IP address on a regular basis.

The simplest example is a PPP connection. These sites often use a single rule to masquerade all outgoing connections from the LAN:

```
iptables -t nat -A POSTROUTING -o ppp0 -j MASQUERADE
```

Masquerading—and NAT in general—is set up with the first packet. With masquerading, a single **nat** rule can be sufficient. The NAT and connection state tracking take care of the incoming packets. The FORWARD rule pair is necessary, though, as in this example:

```
iptables -A FORWARD -o ppp0 \
        -m state --state NEW,ESTABLISHED,RELATED -j ACCEPT

iptables -A FORWARD -o <LAN interface> \
        -m state --state ESTABLISHED,RELATED -j ACCEPT
```

In this simple type of setup, the incoming interface doesn't need to be specified. FORWARD rules refer to traffic crossing between interfaces. If the host has a single network interface and a single **ppp** interface, anything forwarded out one interface must necessarily originate from the other interface. Anything accepted by the FORWARD rules in the `filter` table during routing will be masqueraded by the POSTROUTING rule in the **nat** table.

Even with short-term phone connections, the single FORWARD rule allowing outgoing NEW connections should be broken out into rules for specific services. Depending on the networked devices in the LAN and how they operate, you most likely want to limit what LAN traffic gets forwarded.

Here's an example of a single FORWARD rule pair:

```
iptables -A FORWARD -i <LAN interface> -o ppp0 \
        -m state --state NEW,ESTABLISHED,RELATED -j ACCEPT

iptables -A FORWARD -i -ppp0 -o <LAN interface> \
        -m state --state ESTABLISHED,RELATED -j ACCEPT
```

In this example, the single FORWARD rule pair is broken out into several more specific rules allowing only DNS queries and standard web access. Other LAN traffic isn't forwarded, as shown by these commands:

```
iptables -A FORWARD -i -ppp0 -o <LAN interface> \
        -m state --state ESTABLISHED,RELATED -j ACCEPT
iptables -A FORWARD -o ppp0  \
        -m state --state RELATED,ESTABLISHED -j ACCEPT

iptables -A FORWARD -o ppp0 -p udp \
        --sport 1024:65535 -d <name server> --dport 53 \
        -m state --state NEW -j ACCEPT
```

```
iptables -A FORWARD -o ppp0 -p tcp \
         --sport 1024:65535 -d <name server> --dport 53 \
         -m state --state NEW -j ACCEPT

iptables -A FORWARD -o ppp0 -p tcp \
         -s <local host> --sport 1024:65535 --dport 80 \
         -m state --state NEW -j ACCEPT
```

The single MASQUERADE rule on the **nat** table's POSTROUTING chain remains unchanged. All forwarded traffic is masqueraded. (Locally generated traffic going out the **ppp0** interface is not masqueraded because the traffic is identified with the interface's IP address, by definition.) The FORWARD rules in the **filter** table are limiting what traffic is forwarded and, therefore, what traffic is seen at the POSTROUTING chain.

Applying Standard NAT to LAN Traffic to the Internet

Assuming that that same site had a dynamically assigned but semipermanent IP address or that it has a permanently assigned IP address, the more general SNAT version of source NAT would be used. Just as in the masquerading example, small residential sites often forward and NAT all outgoing LAN traffic:

```
iptables -t nat -A POSTROUTING -o <external interface> \_-j SNAT \
             --to-source <external address>
```

As with masquerading, a single SNAT rule can be sufficient. The NAT and connection state tracking take care of the incoming packets. The FORWARD rule pair is necessary, however, as in the following example:

```
iptables -A FORWARD -o <external interface>\
          -m state --state NEW,ESTABLISHED,RELATED -j ACCEPT

iptables -A FORWARD -o <LAN interface> \
          -m state --state ESTABLISHED,RELATED -j ACCEPT
```

In the case of small sites with 24x7 connections, it's especially important to be selective about what traffic gets forwarded. The single FORWARD rule allowing outgoing *new* connections isn't sufficient. Trojans and viruses are common. The newer networked devices can tend to be somewhat promiscuous about what they do over the network. There's a good chance that Microsoft Windows machines and devices such as networked printers are generating far more traffic than you realize. Also, much of that local traffic is broadcast. It's a good idea to avoid the risk of forwarding broadcast traffic. Routers are no longer supposed to forward directed broadcast traffic by default, but many still do. (Limited broadcasts don't cross network boundaries without a relay agent to duplicate the packet and pass it on. Most devices use limited broadcasts.) A final reason is the case of attaching work laptops to the home network. Many employers don't want offsite laptops to have Internet access without VPN or the protection of their corporate firewalls and antivirus software.

Examples of DNAT, LANs, and Proxies

For the residential and small-business site, destination NAT is probably the most welcome addition to Linux NAT.

Host Forwarding

DNAT provides the host-forwarding capability that, until now, was available only through third-party solutions. For small sites with a single public IP address, DNAT allows incoming connections to local services to be transparently forwarded to a server running in a DMZ. Public services aren't required to run on the firewall machine.

With a single IP address, remote sites send client requests to the firewall machine. The firewall is the only local host that's visible to the Internet. The service (for example, a web or mail server) itself is hosted internally in a private network. For packets arriving on that service's port, the firewall changes the destination address to that of the local server's network interface and forwards the packet to the private machine. The reverse is done for server responses. For packets from the server, the firewall changes the source address to that of its own external interface and forwards the packet on to the remote client.

The most common example is forwarding incoming HTTP connections to a local web server:

```
iptables -t nat -A PREROUTING -i <public interface> -p tcp \
        --sport 1024:65535 -d <public address> --dport 80 \
        -j DNAT --to-destination <local web server>
```

The tricky part is the question of what address is seen on each chain. Destination NAT was applied before the packet reached the FORWARD chain. So the rule on the FORWARD chain must refer to the internal server's private IP address rather than to the firewall's public address:

```
iptables -A FORWARD -i <public interface> -o <DMZ interface> -p tcp \
        --sport 1024:65535 -d <local web server> --dport 80 \
        -m state --state NEW -j ACCEPT
```

Connection tracking and NAT automatically reverse the translation for packets returning from the server. Because the initial connection request was accepted, a generic FORWARD rule suffices to forward the return traffic from the local server to the Internet:

```
iptables -A FORWARD -i <DMZ interface> -o <public interface> \
        -m state --state ESTABLISHED,RELATED -j ACCEPT
```

Of course, don't forget that ongoing traffic from the client must be forwarded as well because the convention used in this book has been to separate individual service rules specifying the NEW state from a single rule for all ESTABLISHED or RELATED traffic:

```
iptables -A FORWARD -i <public interface> -o <DMZ interface> \
    -m state --state ESTABLISHED,RELATED -j ACCEPT
```

Host Forwarding and Port Redirection

DNAT can modify the destination port as well as the destination address. By way of example, I'll set up a rather contrived situation and build on the previous example. Let's say that this site has a second semiprivate web server. The server is bound to port 81 on the same internal host. The internal host is running two separate web servers, hosting two different websites. Clients direct their requests to port 80 on the firewall. Port 81 is closed on the firewall. Incoming connections to the semiprivate server are accepted from only specific remote addresses.

In other words, all incoming web connection requests are targeted to the firewall host's TCP port 80. Requests from general client addresses are NATed and forwarded to port 80 on the server in the DMZ. Requests from specific remote clients are NATed and forwarded to a second web server on port 81 on the same server in the DMZ.

The NAT rule translates both the destination address and the destination port. The order of the two NAT rules is important here. The client traffic is originally targeted to port 80 in both cases. Firewall rules are ordered from most specific to most general. The selected clients must be selected out and redirected to port 81 before their packets match the more general rule that matches all clients and redirects packets to port 80 on the internal host:

```
iptables -t nat -A PREROUTING -i <public interface> -p tcp \
    -s <allowed remote host> --sport 1024:65535 \_
    -d <public address> --dport 80 \
    -j DNAT --to-destination <local web server>:81
iptables -t nat -A PREROUTING -i <public interface> -p tcp \
    --sport 1024:65535 -d <public address> --dport 80 \
    -j DNAT --to-destination <local web server>
```

The rule on the FORWARD chain must refer to the internal server's private IP address and port 81 rather than to the firewall's public address and port 80. Rule order is not important here. The NAT modification was done previously on the PREROUTING chain. The forwarding rules see the modified packets:

```
iptables -A FORWARD -i <public interface> -o <DMZ interface> -p tcp \
    --sport 1024:65535 -d <local web server> --dport 81 \
    -m state --state NEW -j ACCEPT
```

```
iptables -A FORWARD -i <public interface> -o <DMZ interface> -p tcp \
        --sport 1024:65535 -d <local web server> --dport 80 \
        -m state --state NEW -j ACCEPT
```

As in the previous example, the single generic **FORWARD** rule pair for ongoing connections is repeated here:

```
iptables -A FORWARD -i <DMZ interface> -o <public interface> \
        -m state --state ESTABLISHED,RELATED -j ACCEPT
```

```
iptables -A FORWARD -i <public interface> -o <DMZ interface> \
        -m state --state ESTABLISHED,RELATED -j ACCEPT
```

Host Forwarding to a Server Farm

DNAT can accept a range of destination addresses to translate to, and it selects one of the addresses when the exchange is initiated. As an example of multiple destination addresses, let's say that this site has a handful of public addresses. A web server is advertised as running on one of these addresses. Five duplicate web servers are running in the DMZ, each assigned a different private IP address ranging from **192.168.1.1** to **192.168.1.5**. Remote clients address the web server at the single public address.

The NAT rule translates the original destination address to one of the addresses in the NAT list:

```
iptables -t nat -A PREROUTING -i <public interface> -p tcp \
        --sport 1024:65535 -d <public Web address> --dport 80 \
        -j DNAT --to-destination 192.168.1.1-192.168.1.5
```

The private server address range was chosen to allow the **FORWARD** rule to use an address mask to match any of the servers' addresses:

```
iptables -A FORWARD -i <public interface> -o <DMZ interface> -p tcp \
        --sport 1024:65535 -d 192.168.1.0/29 --dport 80 \
        -m state --state NEW -j ACCEPT
```

As in the previous examples, the single generic **FORWARD** rule pair for ongoing connections is repeated here:

```
iptables -A FORWARD -i <DMZ interface> -o <public interface> \
        -m state --state ESTABLISHED,RELATED -j ACCEPT
```

```
iptables -A FORWARD -i <public interface> -o <DMZ interface> \
        -m state --state ESTABLISHED,RELATED -j ACCEPT
```

There are, of course, multiple ways to accomplish this same task with Linux including the Linux Virtual Server, which enables more robust configuration of load balancing and redundancy.

Host Forwarding to Servers in a Privately Addressed DMZ

It's fairly common for a small SOHO site to have a handful of public IP addresses. The site offers multiple services from a DMZ. Although the site has enough public addresses to assign to each server, there won't be enough if the address block is divided into multiple subnets. The public addresses can't be assigned to the servers in the DMZ without dividing the subnets or bridging because routing requires that the firewall's public and DMZ interface addresses belong to different address domains. Some sites use a network mask to allow the public interface to accept any address in the public block. The servers in the DMZ are advertised as running at one of these public addresses, but the servers themselves are assigned private addresses. NAT is used to transparently translate between the public address that's associated with the server and the server's actual private address.

As a final example of DNAT, let's say that the site is assigned eight public IP addresses. The site's network information is listed in Table 7.1.

TABLE 7.1
Sample SOHO Public Address Block with Eight IP Addresses

ADDRESS BLOCK	IP ADDRESS
Network Address	169.254.25.80/29
Network Mask	255.255.255.248
Router Address	169.254.25.81
Firewall/DNS Address	169.254.25.82
First Host Address	169.254.25.83
Last Host Address	169.254.25.86
Broadcast Address	169.254.25.87
Total Local Hosts	5

The site's server's address mapping information is listed in Table 7.2.

TABLE 7.2
Sample Logical Mapping Between Public and Private Server Addresses

SERVER	PUBLIC ADDRESS	PRIVATE DMZ ADDRESS
Public Web Server	169.254.25.83	192.168.1.3
Customer Web Server	169.254.25.84	192.168.1.4
FTP Server	169.3254.25.85	192.168.1.5
Mail Server	169.254.25.86	192.168.1.6

The NAT rules follow. The addresses in Table 7.2 are replaced with shell variables or constant names for clarification:

```
iptables -t nat -A PREROUTING -i <public interface> -p tcp \
        --sport 1024:65535 -d $PUBLIC_WEB_SERVER --dport 80 \
        -j DNAT --to-destination $DMZ_PUBLIC_WEB_SERVER
iptables -t nat -A PREROUTING -i <public interface> -p tcp \
        --sport 1024:65535 -d $CUSTOMER_WEB_SERVER --dport 443 \
        -j DNAT --to-destination $DMZ_CUSTOMER_WEB_SERVER
iptables -t nat -A PREROUTING -i <public interface> -p tcp \
        --sport 1024:65535 -d $FTP_SERVER --dport 21 \
        -j DNAT --to-destination $DMZ_FTP_SERVER
iptables -t nat -A PREROUTING -i <public interface> -p tcp \
        --sport 1024:65535 -d $MAIL_SERVER --dport 25 \
        -j DNAT --to-destination $DMZ_MAIL_SERVER
```

Destination NAT is applied before the packet reaches the **FORWARD** chain. The rules on the **FORWARD** chain must refer to the internal servers' private IP addresses:

```
iptables -A FORWARD -i <public interface> -o <DMZ interface> -p tcp \
        --sport 1024:65535 -d $DMZ_PUBLIC_WEB_SERVER --dport 80 \
        -m state --state NEW -j ACCEPT
iptables -A FORWARD -i <public interface> -o <DMZ interface> -p tcp \
        --sport 1024:65535 -d $DMZ_CUSTOMER_WEB_SERVER --dport 443 \
        -m state --state NEW -j ACCEPT
iptables -A FORWARD -i <public interface> -o <DMZ interface> -p tcp \
        --sport 1024:65535 -d $DMZ_FTP_SERVER --dport 21 \
        -m state --state NEW -j ACCEPT
iptables -A FORWARD -i <public interface> -o <DMZ interface> -p tcp \
        --sport 1024:65535 -d $DMZ_MAIL_SERVER --dport 25 \
        -m state --state NEW -j ACCEPT
```

As a reminder, the single generic **FORWARD** rule pair for ongoing connections is repeated here:

```
iptables -A FORWARD -i <DMZ interface> -o <public interface> \
        -m state --state ESTABLISHED,RELATED -j ACCEPT
```

```
iptables -A FORWARD -i <public interface> -o <DMZ interface> \
        -m state --state ESTABLISHED,RELATED -j ACCEPT
```

Local Port Redirection—Transparent Proxying

Local port redirection, the REDIRECT target in iptables, is a special case of destination NAT. The packet is redirected to the local host, regardless of the packet's destination address. Incoming packets to be forwarded are redirected from the **nat** table's **PREROUTING** chain to the **filter** table's **INPUT** chain. The incoming interface is the interface that the packet arrived on. Outgoing packets from the local host are redirected from the **nat** table's **OUTPUT** chain to the **filter** table's **INPUT** chain. The incoming interface is the internal loopback interface.

This feature is useful for some of the application-level proxies that you might run. The **squid** web cache server, which is bound to TCP port **3128** by default, is a good example. It can be configured to run transparently. As a local service, the following rules would be used on internal machines rather than on the gateway firewall. The REDIRECT would be applied to outgoing local traffic rather than to incoming remote traffic.

When the **squid** proxy server is configured to run transparently, the browsers use standard HTTP rather than the special proxy protocol. The browsers aren't configured to use a proxy. Their outgoing client requests are simply intercepted and redirected to the local server transparently.

Again, the following example is a bit contrived. **squid** is hosted more securely when it is configured to expect proxy traffic rather than regular HTTP traffic.

In this example, outgoing LAN web client traffic is redirected to the **squid** server running on a local host. That host could be running in the private LAN or in the DMZ:

```
iptables -t nat -A PREROUTING -i <lan interface> -p tcp \
        -s <lan hosts> --sport 1024:65535 --dport 80 \
        -j REDIRECT --to-port 3128
```

The redirected packet will be delivered to the input queue associated with the network interface connected to the LAN on this host. As such, an **INPUT** rule is needed to accept the packet:

```
iptables -A INPUT -i <lan interface> -p tcp \
        -s <lan hosts> --sport 1024:65535 -d <lan address> --dport 3128 \
        -m state --state NEW,ESTABLISHED,RELATED -j ACCEPT
```

squid is a proxy as well as a web cache server, so web traffic isn't forwarded. Instead, the **squid** server establishes connections with the remote web servers, acting as a client itself:

```
iptables -A OUTPUT -o <public interface> -p tcp \
        -s <public address> --sport 1024:65535 --dport 80 \
-m state --state NEW,ESTABLISHED,RELATED -j ACCEPT

iptables -A INPUT -i <public interface> -p tcp \
        --sport 80 -d <public address> --dport 1024:65535  \
        -m state --state ESTABLISHED,RELATED -j ACCEPT
```

squid responds as a server to the LAN client:

```
iptables -A OUTPUT -o <lan interface> -p tcp \
        -s <lan address> --sport 80 --dport 1024:65535 \
        -m state --state ESTABLISHED,RELATED -j ACCEPT
```

Notice that the OUTPUT rule requires the source address to be the host's local LAN interface address. REDIRECT is a form of destination NAT. The returning response appears to be returning from the remote server that the client originally addressed, but the reverse NAT occurs after the packet leaves the filter table's OUTPUT chain.

Summary

This chapter covered Network Address Translation. Initially, three basic types of NAT were described. NAT's original purpose, what it is used for today, and its advantages and disadvantages were discussed as well.

In iptables, NAT features are accessed through the nat table and that table's chains rather than through the filter table and the FORWARD chain. The implications of packet flow through the operating system, and the differences between what address rules match against on the FORWARD chain versus on the nat chains, were discussed.

iptables implements both source NAT and destination NAT. Source NAT is divided into two subcategories, SNAT and MASQUERADE. SNAT is regular source address translation. MASQUERADE is a specialized implementation of source NAT. It removes any NAT table state as soon as a connection is dropped.

Destination NAT is also divided into two subcategories, DNAT and REDIRECT. DNAT is regular destination address translation. REDIRECT is special case of destination address translation. It is an alias for redirecting packets to the local host, regardless of the packet's original destination.

Finally, a series of real-world, practical examples of both source and destination NAT were presented. At least rudimentary FORWARD rules were included in the examples to clarify the distinction between NAT and forwarding, and as a reminder for readers who are used to ipchains and ipfwadm packet flow, forwarding, and NAT.

## CHAPTER 8

Debugging the Firewall Rules

So now the firewall is set up, installed, and activated. But nothing works! You're locked out. Who knows what's going on? Now what? Where do you even begin?

Firewall rules are notoriously difficult to get right. If you're developing by hand, bugs will invariably crop up. Even if you produce a firewall script with an automatic firewall-generation tool, your script undoubtedly will require customized tweaking eventually.

This chapter introduces additional reporting features of the iptables tool and other system tools. The information is invaluable when debugging your firewall rules. This chapter explains what the information can tell you about your firewall. The tools are crude. The process is tedious. Be forewarned.

For additional information on iptables reporting features, see the iptables man page and the "Linux 2.4 Packet Filtering HOWTO," by Rusty Russel.

General Firewall-Development Tips

Tracking down a problem in the firewall is detailed and painstaking. There are no shortcuts to debugging the rules when something goes wrong. In general, the following tips can make the process a bit easier:

- Always execute the rules from a complete test script, like the one I've shown how to build throughout this book. Be sure that the script flushes all existing rules, removes any existing user-defined chains, and resets the default policies first. Otherwise, you can't be sure which rules are in effect or in which order.

- Don't execute new rules from the command line. Especially don't execute the default policy rules from the command line. You'll be cut off immediately if you're logged in using X Windows or remotely from another system, including a system on the LAN.

- Execute the test script from the console if you can. Working in X Windows at the console might be more convenient, but the danger remains of losing access to X Windows locally. Be prepared for the possibility of needing to switch over to a virtual console to regain control. If you must use a remote machine to test the firewall script, use cron to automatically stop the firewall in case you get locked out. Be sure to remove the cron job before going live with the firewall, though.

- Remember that flushing the rule chains does not affect the default policy currently in effect.

- With a deny-by-default policy, always enable the loopback interface immediately.

- When feasible, work on one service at a time. Add rules one at a time, or as input and output rule pairs if you aren't using the state module. Test as you go. This makes it much easier to isolate problem areas in the rules right away. Liberal use of the `echo` command within the firewall script can help to narrow down the location or rules that are being problematic within the script.

- The first matching rule wins. Order is important. Use the `iptables` list commands as you go to get a feel for how the rules are ordered. Trace an imaginary packet through the list.

- Remember that there are at least two independent chains: `INPUT` and `OUTPUT`. If the input rules look right, the problem might be in the `OUTPUT` chain, or vice versa.

- If the script appears to hang, chances are good that a rule is referencing a symbolic hostname rather than an IP address before the DNS rules have been enabled. Any rule using a hostname instead of an address must come after the DNS rules, unless the host has an entry in the `/etc/hosts` file.

- Double-check the `iptables` syntax. It's easy to mistype the rule's direction, to reverse the source and destination addresses or ports, to switch upper- and lowercase-sensitive options, to use `-i` rather than `-o` when referring to an outgoing interface, or to precede an option with the wrong number of hyphens.

- The three tables, `filter`, `nat`, and `mangle`, have different built-in chains. `filter` has `INPUT`, `OUTPUT`, and `FORWARD`. `nat` has `POSTROUTING` for SNAT, and `PREROUTING` and `OUTPUT` for DNAT. `mangle` has `PREROUTING`, `INPUT`, `FORWARD`, `POSTROUTING`, and `OUTPUT`.

- The various built-in chains have differing input and output interface specifications. That is, an `INPUT` rule takes only an incoming interface. An `OUTPUT` rule takes only an outgoing interface. A `FORWARD` rule can take either, both, or no interface specifications. Source

SNAT and MASQUERADE take only an outgoing interface. Destination DNAT and REDIRECT take only an incoming interface on the **PREROUTING** chains and only an outgoing interface on the **OUTPUT** chain.

- The `filter` table is implied by default. The `-t` option and table name must be specified to access the **nat** or **mangle** tables, as in `iptables -t nat`.

- Most match modules require you to reference the module by name with the `-m` option before specifying the module's feature syntax, as in `-m state --state NEW`.

- The `filter` table's **INPUT** and **OUTPUT** chains refer only to the packets addressed to the local machine or originating from the local machine. Forwarded packets do not traverse the `filter` table's **INPUT** or **OUTPUT** chains.

- iptables error messages can be cryptic. If you're having difficulty identifying the problem rule, execute the script with the `-x` or `-v` shell option to list the rules as the script is executed—for example, `sh -v ./rc.firewall`. The `-v` option prints the line in the script as it is read by the shell command interpreter. The `-x` option prints the line in the script as it is executed by the shell. `script` is often useful to capture the output in a `typescript` file.

- When a service doesn't work, log all dropped packets going in both directions, as well as all relevant accepted packets. Do the log entries in `/var/log/messages` or `/var/log/kern.log` show anything being dropped when you try the service? If they do, you can adjust your firewall rules to allow the packets. If not, the problem must be elsewhere.

- When packets aren't crossing an interface, remember that the **FORWARD** chain refers to packets traversing the router. The **INPUT** and **OUTPUT** chains refer to local packets. **NAT** rules are separate from **FORWARD** rules. A **NAT**ed packet requires both **FORWARD** and **NAT** rules.

- Source **NAT** is applied during **POSTROUTING**, after the packet has left the **FORWARD** or **OUTPUT** chain. This means that rules on the **FORWARD** and **OUTPUT** chains must refer to the packet's original source address rather than the **NAT**ed address.

- Destination **NAT** is applied during **PREROUTING**, before the packet arrives on the **FORWARD** or **INPUT** chain. This means that rules on the **PREROUTING** chain must refer to the original destination address, whereas rules on the **FORWARD** and **INPUT** chains must refer to the altered destination address.

- If you have Internet access from the firewall machine but not from the LAN, double-check that IP forwarding is enabled by running `cat /proc/sys/net/ ipv4/ip_forward`. The value `1` should be reported. IP forwarding can be permanently configured by hand in `/etc/sysctl.conf` or in the firewall script itself. The first configuration method takes effect when the network is restarted. If IP forwarding wasn't enabled, you can enable it immediately by typing the following line as **root** or by including it in the firewall script and reexecuting the script:

```
echo "1" > /proc/sys/net/ipv4/ip_forward
```

- If a service works on the LAN but not externally, turn on logging for accepted packets on the internal interface. Use the service *very* briefly to see which ports, addresses, flags, and so forth are in use in both directions. You won't want to log accepted packets for any length of time, or you'll have hundreds or thousands of log entries in /var/log/messages.

- If a service doesn't work at all, temporarily insert input and output rules at the beginning of the firewall script to accept everything in both directions and log all traffic. Is the service available now? If so, check the log entries in /var/log/messages to see which ports are in use.

Listing the Firewall Rules

It's a good idea to list the rules you've defined, to double-check that they are installed and are in the order you expect. The -L command lists the actual rules for a given chain as they exist in the internal kernel table. Rules are listed in the order in which they are matched against a packet.

The basic format of the **iptables** list command is as follows:

```
iptables [-v -n] -L [chain]
```

or

```
iptables [-t <table>] [-v -n] -L [chain]
```

The first format refers to the default **filter** table. If a specific chain isn't specified, the command lists all rules on the three built-in **filter** table chains, plus any user-defined chains.

The second format is needed to list the rules on the **nat** or **mangle** tables.

Adding the -v option is useful to see the interface to which the rule applies. Adding the -n option is useful if the firewall rules refer to remote or illegal addresses, to avoid the lengthy name-resolution time for those addresses. Remember that if a chain is specified, it must follow the -L command. Also note that -L is a command and -v and -n are options. They cannot be combined as in -Lvn.

Unlike using `iptables` to define actual rules, using `iptables` to list existing rules can be done from the command line. The output goes to your terminal or can be redirected into a file.

filter **Table Listing Formats**

The basic format of the `filter` table list command to list all rules on all `filter` table chains is this:

```
iptables -vn -L INPUT
iptables -vn -L OUTPUT
iptables -vn -L FORWARD
```

or

```
iptables -vn -L
```

Notice that the preceding list commands show only the rules in the `filter` table chains.

The next three sections use seven sample rules on the **INPUT** chain to illustrate the differences among the various listing format options available to you with the `filter` table and to explain what the output fields mean. Using the different listing format options, the same seven sample rules are listed with varying degrees of detail and readability. The listing format options and fields are the same for the **INPUT**, **OUTPUT**, and **FORWARD** chains.

iptables -L INPUT

Here is an abbreviated list of seven rules from an **INPUT** chain using the default listing options:

```
> iptables -L INPUT

1    INPUT (policy DROP)
2    target      prot opt source              destination
3    ACCEPT      all  --  anywhere            anywhere
4    LOG         icmp -f  anywhere            anywhere            \
     LOG level warning prefix `Fragmented ICMP: '
5    DROP        tcp  --  anywhere            anywhere            \
     tcp flags:FIN,SYN,RST,PSH,ACK,URG/NONE
6    ACCEPT      all  --  anywhere            anywhere            \
     state RELATED,ESTABLISHED
7    ACCEPT      udp  --  192.168.1.0/25      my.host.domain      \
     udp spts:1024:65535 dpt:domain state NEW
8    REJECT      tcp  --  anywhere            my.host.domain2     \
     tcp dpt:auth reject-with icmp-port-unreachable
9    ACCEPT      tcp  --  192.168.1.0/25      my.host.domain      \
     multiport dports http,https tcp spts:1024:65535 \
     flags:SYN,RST,ACK/SYN state NEW
```

LINE NUMBERS IN LISTINGS

The line numbers in the listings throughout this chapter are not part of the output; they are simply reference markers. Numbers can be generated by adding the --line-numbers option to the command. The "line numbers" generated are the rules' positions within the chain.

Line 1 identifies the listing as being for the **INPUT** chain. The **INPUT** chain's default policy is **DROP**.

Line 2 contains these column headings:

- **target** refers to the target disposition of a packet matching the rule **ACCEPT**, **DROP**, **LOG**, or **REJECT**.

- **prot** is an abbreviation for *protocol*, which can be **all**, **tcp**, **udp**, or **icmp**, as well as a value from **/etc/protocols**.

- **opt** stands for *fragmentation options*, which would have been set with either the **-f** or the **! -f** option. A **!** in the first space indicates the **! -f** option, which means to match either unfragmented packets or the first fragment in a series. An **f** in the second space indicates the **-f** option, which means to match the second and subsequent fragments.

- **source** is the source address in the IP packet header.

- **destination** is the destination address in the IP packet header.

Line 3 illustrates how the simple **-L** list command, without qualifying arguments, lacks some important detail. The rule appears to accept all incoming packets—**tcp**, **udp**, and **icmp**—from anywhere. The missing detail, in this case, is the interface, **lo**. This is the rule accepting all input on the loopback interface.

Line 4 is a rule to log any (second and subsequent) fragmented ICMP packets. The default logging level for **syslog** is **warn**. The **LOG** rule has an associated **--log-prefix** string defined for it.

Line 5 is a rule that drops TCP packets without any state flags set.

Line 6 is a rule that accepts any incoming packet that is part of an **ESTABLISHED** connection, or a packet **RELATED** to such a connection (that is, an associated ICMP error or FTP data connection).

Line 7 is a rule that accepts incoming UDP DNS requests from hosts in the local network, **192.168.1.0/25**. Notice that the network is divided into two subnets, so the hosts could range from **192.168.1.1** to **192.168.1.126**.

Line 8 is a rule that rejects incoming TCP **auth** requests or queries to the local **identd** server. The ICMP Type 3 error message returned contains the default **port-unreachable** code. It isn't evident in the listing that the machine has two network interfaces. Requests are rejected from the "external" network, **domain2**.

Line 9 accepts **incoming** TCP connection requests from the local LAN for standard HTTP web connections and HTTPS web connections. A destination port list was defined with the **multiport** match option.

iptables -n -L INPUT

The **-n** option reports all fields as numeric values rather than symbolic names. This option can save time if your rules use a lot of specific IP addresses that otherwise would require DNS lookups before being listed. Additionally, a port range is more informative if it is listed as **23:79** rather than as **telnet:finger**.

Using the same seven sample rules from the **INPUT** chain, the following shows what the listing output looks like using the **-n** numeric option:

```
> iptables -n -L INPUT

1    INPUT (policy DROP)
2    target      prot opt source             destination
3    ACCEPT      all  --  0.0.0.0/0          0.0.0.0/0
4    LOG         icmp -f  0.0.0.0/0          0.0.0.0/0          \
     LOG flags 0 level 4 prefix `Fragmented ICMP: '
5    DROP        tcp  --  0.0.0.0/0          0.0.0.0/0          \
     tcp flags:0x023F/0x020
6    ACCEPT      all  --  0.0.0.0/0          0.0.0.0/0          \
     state RELATED,ESTABLISHED
7    ACCEPT      udp  --  192.168.1.0/25     192.168.1.2        \
     udp spts:1024:65535 dpt:53 state NEW
8    REJECT      tcp  --  0.0.0.0/0          192.168.1.254      \
     tcp dpt:113 reject-with icmp-port-unreachable
9    ACCEPT      tcp  --  192.168.1.0/25     192.168.1.2        \
     multiport dports 80,443 tcp spts:1024:65535 flags:0x0216/0x022 state NEW
```

Line 1 identifies the listing as being for the **INPUT** chain. The **INPUT** chain's default policy is DROP.

Line 2 contains these column headings:

- **target** refers to the target disposition of a packet matching the rule ACCEPT, DROP, LOG, or REJECT.

- **prot** is an abbreviation for *protocol*, which can be **all**, **tcp**, **udp**, or **icmp**, as well as a value from **/etc/protocols**.

- **opt** stands for *fragmentation options*, which would have been set with either the -f or the ! -f option. A ! in the first space indicates the ! -f option, which means to match either unfragmented packets or the first fragment in a series. An f in the second space indicates the -f option, which means to match the second and subsequent fragments.

- **source** is the source address in the IP packet header.

- **destination** is the destination address in the IP packet header.

Line 3 illustrates how the simple -L list command, without qualifying arguments, lacks some important detail. The rule appears to accept all incoming packets—tcp, udp, and icmp—from anywhere. The missing detail, in this case, is the interface, lo. This is the rule accepting all input on the loopback interface.

Line 4 is a rule to log any (second and subsequent) fragmented ICMP packets. The default logging level for syslog is warn. The LOG rule has an associated --log-prefix string defined for it. The flags value—0, in this case—is an internal value representing which of the logging options was specified, --log-ip-options, --log-tcp-options, or --log-tcp-sequence.

Line 5 is a rule that drops TCP packets without any state flags set. The leading 2 in the mask and comparison fields appears to be a bug in the printing code. It appears that the intent was to define the field as two hexadecimal digits long, with a leading 0, but the length indication (2) was misplaced. So the actual mask value is 0x03F, and the actual comparison value is 0x000.

Line 6 is a rule that accepts any incoming packet that is part of an ESTABLISHED connection, or a packet RELATED to such a connection (that is, an associated ICMP error or FTP data connection).

Line 7 is a rule that accepts incoming UDP DNS requests from hosts in the local network, 192.168.1.0/25. Notice that the network is divided into two subnets, so the hosts could range from 192.168.1.1 to 192.168.1.126.

Line 8 is a rule that rejects incoming TCP auth requests or queries to the local identd server. The ICMP Type 3 error message returned contains the default port-unreachable code. It isn't evident in the listing that the machine has two network interfaces. Requests are rejected from the "external" subnet. Those hosts' IP addresses can range from 129 to 254.

Line 9 accepts incoming TCP connection requests from the local LAN for standard HTTP web connections and HTTPS web connections. A destination port list was defined with the multiport match option. SYN's bit value in the state field is 0x02. (Remember that the leading 2 in both flag fields is a typo in the code.) The 0x016 represents the FIN, SYN, RST, and ACK fields that are being inspected; out of these, only the SYN flag must be set.

iptables -v -L INPUT

The -v option produces more verbose output, including the interface name. Reporting the interface name is especially helpful when the machine has more than one network interface.

Using the same seven sample rules from the INPUT chain, the following shows what the listing output looks like using the -v verbose option:

```
> iptables -v -L INPUT
```

```
1    INPUT (policy DROP 0 packets, 0 bytes)
2    pkts bytes target        prot opt in      out       source              \
       destination
3     32  3416 ACCEPT        all  --  lo      any       anywhere            \
       anywhere
4      0     0 LOG           icmp -f  any     any       anywhere            \
       anywhere           LOG level warning prefix `Fragmented ICMP: '
5      0     0 DROP          tcp  --  any     any       anywhere            \
       anywhere           tcp flags:FIN,SYN,RST,PSH,ACK,URG/NONE
6     94  6586 ACCEPT        all  --  any     any       anywhere            \
       anywhere           state RELATED,ESTABLISHED
7      1    65 ACCEPT        udp  --  eth0    any       192.168.1.0/25      \
       my.host.domain     udp spts:1024:65535 dpt:domain state NEW
8      0     0 REJECT        tcp  --  eth1    any       anywhere            \
       my.host.domain2    tcp dpt:auth reject-with icmp-port-unreachable
9      1    48 ACCEPT        tcp  --  eth0    any       192.168.1.0/25      \
       my.host.domain     multiport dports http,https tcp spts:1024:65535 \
       flags:SYN,RST,ACK/SYN state NEW
```

Line 1 identifies the listing as being for the INPUT chain. The INPUT chain's default policy is DROP. 0 packets have been dropped by the default policy, accounting for 0 bytes of network traffic.

Line 2 contains the following column headings:

- pkts is the number of packets that have matched the rule.

- bytes is the number of bytes contained in the packets matching the rule.

- target refers to the target disposition of a packet matching the rule ACCEPT, DROP, LOG, or REJECT.

- prot is an abbreviation for *protocol*, which can be all, tcp, udp, or icmp, as well as a value from /etc/protocols.

- opt stands for *fragmentation options*, which would have been set with either the -f or the ! -f option. An ! in the first space indicates the ! -f option, which means to match either unfragmented packets or the first fragment in a series. An f in the second space indicates the -f option, which means to match the second and subsequent fragments.

- **in** is the incoming network interface name—such as **eth0**, **eth1**, **lo**, or **ppp0**—to which this rule applies. Only packets arriving on this specific network interface will match the rule. This field becomes important if you have a LAN with separate firewall rules for the different interfaces or if you are forwarding traffic between interfaces.

  Because this is the **INPUT** chain, the **in** field is relevant. The field is also meaningful for the **FORWARD** chain. The field is meaningless with the **OUTPUT** chain.

- **out** is the outgoing network interface name—such as **eth0**, **eth1**, **lo**, or **ppp0**—to which this rule applies. Only packets departing from this specific network interface will match the rule. This field becomes important if you have a LAN with separate firewall rules for the different interfaces or if you are forwarding traffic between interfaces.

  Because this is the **INPUT** chain, the **out** field is meaningless. The field is meaningful with the **OUTPUT** chain. The field is also meaningful for the **FORWARD** chain.

- **source** is the source address in the IP packet header.

- **destination** is the destination address in the IP packet header.

Line 3 is more useful with the **-v** list option. The loopback interface is clearly being referred to. This is the rule accepting all input on the loopback interface.

Line 4 is a rule to log any (second and subsequent) fragmented ICMP packets arriving on any network interface. The default logging level for **syslog** is **warning**. The **LOG** rule has an associated **--log-prefix** string defined for it.

Line 5 is a rule that drops TCP packets arriving on any network interface that doesn't have any state flags set.

Line 6 is a rule that accepts any incoming packet arriving on any network interface that is part of an **ESTABLISHED** connection or a packet **RELATED** to such a connection (such as an associated ICMP error or FTP data connection).

Line 7 is a rule that accepts incoming UDP DNS requests from hosts in the local network, **192.168.1.0/25**. Notice that the network is divided into two subnets, so the hosts could range from **192.168.1.1** to **192.168.1.126**.

Line 8 is a rule that rejects incoming TCP **auth** requests, or queries to the local **identd** server. The ICMP Type 3 error message returned contains the default **port-unreachable** code. It isn't evident in the listing that the machine has two network interfaces. Requests are rejected from the "external" network, **domain2**.

Line 9 accepts **incoming** TCP connection requests from the local LAN for standard HTTP web connections and HTTPS web connections. A destination port list was defined with the **multiport** match option.

nat **Table Listing Formats**

The basic format of the **nat** table list command to list all rules on all **nat** table chains is shown here:

```
iptables -t nat -vn -L PREROUTING
iptables -t nat -vn -L POSTROUTING
iptables -t nat -vn -L OUTPUT
```

or

```
iptables -t nat -vn -L
```

Notice that the preceding list commands show only the rules in the **nat** table chains.

What follows are four sample NAT rules, two on the **PREROUTING** chain and two on the **POSTROUTING** chain. In the interest of brevity, only the -v output is presented:

```
> iptables -t nat -v -L
1   PREROUTING (policy DROP 0 packets, 0 bytes)
2   pkts bytes target      prot opt in    out    source          \
       destination
3   0      0 DNAT          tcp  -- eth1   any    192.168.1.129    \
       this.host          tcp spts:1020:65535 dpt:ssh to:hostA.lan
4   0      0 REDIRECT      tcp  -- eth0   any    anywhere         \
       anywhere           tcp spts:1024:65535 dpt:http

5   POSTROUTING (policy DROP 0 packets, 0 bytes)
6   pkts bytes target      prot opt in    out    source          \
       destination
7   0      0 SNAT          tcp  -- any    eth1   hostA.lan        \
       192.168.1.129      tcp spts:1024:65535 dpt:21 to:this.host
8   0      0 MASQUERADE all -- any    ppp0   lan_network      \
       anywhere
```

Line 1 identifies the listing as being for the **PREROUTING** chain, the point where destination NAT is applied. The **PREROUTING** chain's default policy is **DROP**.

Line 2 contains these column headings:

- **pkts** is the number of packets that have matched the rule.

- **bytes** is the number of bytes contained in the packets matching the rule.

- **target** refers to the target disposition of a packet matching the rule DNAT or REDIRECT.

- **prot** is an abbreviation for *protocol*, which can be **all**, **tcp**, **udp**, or **icmp**, as well as a value from **/etc/protocols**.

- **opt** stands for *fragmentation options*, which would have been set with either the **-f** or the **! -f** option. An **!** in the first space indicates the **! -f** option, which means to match either unfragmented packets or the first fragment in a series. An **f** in the second space indicates the **-f** option, which means to match the second and subsequent fragments.

- **in** is the incoming network interface name—such as **eth0**, **eth1**, **lo**, or **ppp0**—to which this rule applies. Only packets arriving on this specific network interface will match the rule. This field becomes important if you have a LAN with separate firewall rules for the different interfaces or if you are forwarding traffic between interfaces.

  On the **PREROUTING** chain, only the **in** field is relevant. The **out** field is meaningless with the **PREROUTING** chain.

- **out** is the outgoing network interface name—such as **eth0**, **eth1**, **lo**, or **ppp0**—to which this rule applies. Only packets departing from this specific network interface will match the rule. This field becomes important if you have a LAN with separate firewall rules for the different interfaces or if you are forwarding traffic between interfaces.

  On the **POSTROUTING** chain, only the **out** field is relevant. The **in** field is meaningless with the **POSTROUTING** chain.

- **source** is the source address in the IP packet header.

- **destination** is the destination address in the IP packet header.

Line 3 is a DNAT rule to alter the destination address in incoming SSH packets. SSH client connections from external host **192.168.1.129** addressed to the local host are redirected to host A on the LAN.

Line 4 is an example of the specialized form of DNAT, REDIRECT, which redirects packets to the local host. In this case, any HTTP packets arriving on the **eth0** interface, presumably to be forwarded to a remote web server, are redirected to a local proxy server listening on this host's TCP port **80**.

Line 5 identifies the next listing as being for the **POSTROUTING** chain, the point where source NAT is applied. The **POSTROUTING** chain's default policy is **DROP**.

Line 6 contains the column headings and is identical to Line 2.

Line 7 is an SNAT rule to alter the source address in outgoing FTP client packets. FTP client connections from Host A on the LAN addressed to host **192.168.1.129** on the external LAN are modified to appear to be originating from this host.

Line 8 is an example of the specialized form of SNAT, MASQUERADE, which is intended for temporary connections with changeable IP addresses. In this case, all outgoing packets on the

ppp0 interface are masqueraded as coming from this host. Remember that forward rules are also necessary in these cases.

mangle **Table Listing Formats**

The basic format of the **mangle** table list command to list all rules on the **mangle** table chains is as follows:

```
iptables -t mangle -vn -L PREROUTING
iptables -t mangle -vn -L OUTPUT
```

or

```
iptables -t mangle -vn -L
```

Notice that the preceding list commands show only the rules in the **mangle** table chains.

What follows are two sample **mangle** table rules, a MARK rule on the **PREROUTING** chain and a TOS rule on the **OUTPUT** chain. In the interest of brevity, only the -v output is presented:

```
> iptables -t mangle -v -L

1  PREROUTING (policy DROP 0 packets, 0 bytes)
2     pkts bytes target     prot opt in     out     source             \
         destination
3       0    0 MARK       tcp  -- eth0   any     laptop.private.lan \
       anywhere            tcp spts:1024:65535 dpt:ssh MARK set 0x10070

4  OUTPUT (policy DROP 0 packets, 0 bytes)
5     pkts bytes target     prot opt in     out     source             \
         destination
6       0    0 TOS        tcp  -- any    eth1    bastion.firewall.lan \
       anywhere            tcp spts:1024:65535 dpt:ssh TOS set Minimize-Delay
```

Line 1 identifies the listing as being for the **PREROUTING** chain, the point where MANGLE is applied. The **PREROUTING** chain's default policy is DROP.

Line 2 contains these column headings:

- **pkts** is the number of packets that have matched the rule.
- **bytes** is the number of bytes contained in the packets matching the rule.
- **target** refers to the target disposition of a packet matching the rule MARK or TOS.
- **prot** is an abbreviation for *protocol*, which can be **all**, **tcp**, **udp**, or **icmp**, as well as a value from **/etc/protocols**.

- **opt** stands for *fragmentation options*, which would have been set with either the **-f** or the ! **-f** option. An ! in the first space indicates the ! **-f** option, which means to match either unfragmented packets or the first fragment in a series. An **f** in the second space indicates the **-f** option, which means to match the second and subsequent fragments.

- **in** is the incoming network interface name—such as **eth0**, **eth1**, **lo**, or **ppp0**—to which this rule applies. Only packets arriving on this specific network interface will match the rule. This field becomes important if you have a LAN with separate firewall rules for the different interfaces or if you are forwarding traffic between interfaces.

  On the **PREROUTING** chain, only the **in** field is relevant. The **out** field is meaningless on the **PREROUTING** chain.

- **out** is the outgoing network interface name—such as **eth0**, **eth1**, **lo**, or **ppp0**—to which this rule applies. Only packets departing from this specific network interface will match the rule. This field becomes important if you have a LAN with separate firewall rules for the different interfaces or if you are forwarding traffic between interfaces.

  On the **OUTPUT** chain, only the **out** field is relevant. The **in** field is meaningless on the **OUTPUT** chain.

- **source** is the source address in the IP packet header.

- **destination** is the destination address in the IP packet header.

Line 3 is a **MARK** rule to alter the mark value that iptables associates with SSH packets arriving on the incoming interface. SSH client connections from the local laptop addressed to anywhere are assigned the mark value **0x10070**.

Line 4 identifies the listing as being for the **OUTPUT** chain, the chain where **mangle** table operations are applied to locally generated packets. The **OUTPUT** chain's default policy is **DROP**.

Line 5 contains the same column headings as Line 2.

Line 6 is a **TOS** rule to alter the **tos** value in the IP packet header of outgoing SSH client packets. SSH client connections from the local host addressed to the local bastion firewall are assigned the **tos** value **minimize-delay**.

Checking the Input, Output, and Forwarding Rules

Now that you've seen what a firewall chain listing looks like and what formatting options are available, we'll go through brief lists of **INPUT**, **OUT**, and **FORWARD** rules. The sample rules are representative of some of the rules you'll most likely use yourself.

Checking the Input Rules

Your input rules are mostly **ACCEPT** rules when the default policy is **DROP**. Everything is denied, by default, and you explicitly define what will be accepted. Remember that packets arriving on the **INPUT** chain are targeted to the local host. The following example contains a representative sample of input acceptance rules:

```
> iptables -v -L INPUT
```

```
Chain INPUT (policy DROP 0 packets, 0 bytes)
   pkts bytes target       prot opt in      out    source              \
        destination
1    4    390 ACCEPT       all  --  lo      any    anywhere            \
     anywhere
2    59  2599 ACCEPT       all  --  any     any    anywhere            \
     anywhere             state RELATED,ESTABLISHED
3    0     0 DROP          all  --  !lo     any    choke.dmz.lan       \
     anywhere
4    0     0 DROP          all  --  !lo     any    router.private.lan  \
     anywhere
5    0     0 DROP          all  --  eth0    any    ! .private.lan      \
     anywhere
6    0     0 ACCEPT        udp  --  eth0    any    .private.lan        \
     router.private.lan udp spt:1024:65535 dpt:domain state NEW
7    0     0 REJECT        tcp  --  eth1    any    anywhere            \
     choke.dmz.lan tcp spts:1024:65535 dpt:auth state NEW
8    0     0 ACCEPT        udp  --  eth0    any    jet.private.lan     \
     255.255.255.255    udp spt:ntp dpt:ntp state NEW
9    0     0 ACCEPT        tcp  --  any     any    anywhere            \
     anywhere             tcp flags:FIN,ACK/FIN,ACK
10   0     0 LOG           all  --  any     any    anywhere            \
     anywhere             LOG level warning
```

The default policy for incoming packets is **DROP**. Denied packets are simply dropped without any notification being returned to the source address. There are 10 rules on the chain:

- Line 1—All packets arriving on the loopback interface are accepted.

- Line 2—All incoming packets identified as part of a previously accepted connection or exchange, or a packet related to one, are accepted.

- Line 3—Any packet arriving on any interface except the loopback interface that claims to be from this machine's external DMZ network interface is dropped.

- Line 4—Any packet arriving on any interface except the loopback interface that claims to be from this machine's internal private LAN network interface is dropped.

- Line 5—Any packet arriving on the internal private LAN interface that claims to be from a source address other than an address within the internal private LAN network is dropped.

- Line 6—UDP DNS client requests from hosts in the private LAN are accepted.

- Line 7—All incoming TCP packets destined for the local identd server at AUTH service port 113 are rejected. An ICMP error notification Type 3, Service Unavailable, will be returned to the source address.

- Line 8—Limited broadcasts from the local printer to the UDP ntp time server port 123 are accepted.

- Line 9—FIN/ACK packets from anywhere are accepted.

- Line 10—All other incoming packets are logged before being dropped by the default policy.

Checking the Output Rules

Your output rules are mostly ACCEPT rules when the default policy is DROP. Everything is blocked, by default. You explicitly define what will be accepted. The following example contains a representative sample of output acceptance rules:

```
> iptables -L OUTPUT

  Chain OUTPUT (policy DROP 0 packets, 0 bytes)
   pkts bytes target      prot opt in     out      source           \
        destination
 1   34  3558 ACCEPT      all  --  any    lo       anywhere         \
      anywhere
 2   92 12721 ACCEPT      all  --  any    any      anywhere         \
      anywhere             state RELATED,ESTABLISHED
 3    1    82 ACCEPT      udp  --  any    eth1     choke.dmz.lan    \
      nameserver.dmz.lan udp spt:domain dpt:domain state NEW
 4    0     0 ACCEPT      udp  --  any    eth1     choke.dmz.lan    \
      nameserver.dmz.lan udp spts:1024:65535 dpt:domain state NEW
 5    0     0 ACCEPT      tcp  --  any    eth1     choke.dmz.lan    \
      nameserver.dmz.lan tcp spts:1024:65535 dpt:domain state NEW
 6    2   120 ACCEPT      tcp  --  any    eth0     router.private.lan  \
      .private.lan        multiport dports ssh,http,https,auth,ftp   \
      tcp spts:1024:65535 flags:SYN,RST,ACK/SYN state NEW
 7    0     0 ACCEPT      tcp  --  any    eth1     choke.dmz.lan    \
      .dmz.lan            tcp spts:1024:65535 dpt:ssh state NEW
 8    0     0 ACCEPT      tcp  --  any    eth1     choke.dmz.lan    \
      anywhere            multiport dports http,https,auth,ftp,nicname \
      tcp spts:1024:65535 flags:SYN,RST,ACK/SYN state NEW
```

```
9    0    0 ACCEPT       tcp  --  any    eth1    choke.dmz.lan        \
     mail.dmz.lan        tcp spts:1024:65535 dpt:smtp state NEW
10   0    0 ACCEPT       udp  --  any    eth1    choke.dmz.lan        \
     timeserver.edu      udp spts:1024:65535 dpt:ntp state NEW
11   0    0 ACCEPT       icmp --  any    eth1    choke.dmz.lan        \
     anywhere            icmp fragmentation-needed
12   0    0 ACCEPT       icmp --  any    eth0    router.private.lan   \
     .private.lan        icmp echo-request
13   0    0 ACCEPT       icmp --  any    eth0    router.private.lan   \
     .private.lan        icmp echo-reply
14   0    0 ACCEPT       icmp --  any    eth1    choke.dmz.lan        \
     .dmz.lan            icmp echo-request
15   0    0 ACCEPT       icmp --  any    eth1    choke.dmz.lan        \
     firewall.dmz.lan    icmp echo-reply
16   0    0 ACCEPT       tcp  --  any    eth0    router.private.lan   \
     jet.private.lan     tcp dpt:printer state NEW
17   0    0 ACCEPT       tcp  --  any    any     anywhere             \
     anywhere            tcp flags:RST/RST
18   0    0 LOG          all  --  any    any     anywhere             \
     anywhere            LOG level warning
```

The default policy for the **OUTPUT** chain is **DROP**. Denied packets are simply dropped without any notification being returned to the local program. There are 18 rules on the chain:

- Line 1—Any packet going out the loopback interface is allowed.

- Line 2—Any packet that is recognized as being part of a previously **ESTABLISHED** connection or exchange, or a packet that is **RELATED** to one, is allowed.

- Line 3—Local DNS requests that are forwarded to the local name server in the DMZ, server to server, are allowed.

- Line 4—Local DNS client requests over UDP to the local name server in the DMZ are allowed.

- Line 5—Local DNS client requests over TCP to the local name server in the DMZ are allowed.

- Line 6—The local host, the LAN router, is allowed for established connections to local SSH, HTTP, HTTPS, **auth**, and FTP servers in the private LAN.

- Line 7—The local host, the choke firewall, is allowed for established connections to local SSH servers in the DMZ.

- Line 8—The local host, the choke firewall, is allowed for established connections to SSH, HTTP, HTTPS, **auth**, and FTP servers anywhere.

- Line 9—The local host, the choke firewall, is allowed to send mail to the mail gateway in the DMZ.

- Line 10—The local host, the choke firewall, is allowed to send client **ntp** time requests to a specific remote server.

- Line 11—The local host, the choke firewall, is allowed to send ICMP Type 3 **fragmentation-needed** messages anywhere as part of MTU size discovery.

- Line 12—The local host, the LAN router, is allowed to send ICMP **ping** requests to hosts in the private LAN.

- Line 13—The local host, the LAN router, is allowed to send ICMP **ping** responses to hosts in the private LAN.

- Line 14—The local host, the choke firewall, is allowed to send ICMP **ping** requests to hosts in the DMZ.

- Line 15—The local host, the choke firewall, is allowed to send ICMP **ping** responses to the public firewall between the DMZ and the Internet.

- Line 16—The local host, the LAN router, is allowed to access the networked printer in the private LAN.

- Line 17—The local host is allowed to send TCP **RST** messages anywhere.

- Line 18—All other outgoing packets are logged before being dropped by the default policy.

Checking the Forwarding Rules

The forwarding rules apply to packets passing or being routed through the machine. Forwarded packets are inspected only by the rules defined for the **FORWARD** chain. These packets are not inspected against rules on the **INPUT** or **OUTPUT** chains. If the packet's destination address is something other than the address of the interface on which the packet arrived, the packet is inspected by the **FORWARD** chain. If the packet matches a **FORWARD** acceptance rule, the packet is sent out the appropriate interface, after being inspected by any rules defined for the **POSTROUTING** chains.

For the purposes of illustration, the firewall rule pair shown next forwards all TCP connections from the internal network. UDP traffic is not routed. Related ICMP traffic is routed:

```
iptables -A FORWARD -p tcp -m state --state ESTABLISHED,RELATED -j ACCEPT
iptables -A FORWARD -i $LAN_INTERFACE -o $EXTERNAL_INTERFACE -p tcp \
        -s $INTERNAL_LAN_ADDRESSES -m state --state NEW -j ACCEPT
```

This section is based on a representative sample of forwarding rules. The **INPUT** and **OUTPUT** rules are mostly **ACCEPT** rules when the default policy is **DROP**. Everything is denied, by default, and you explicitly define what will be accepted:

```
> iptables -v -L FORWARD

  Chain FORWARD (policy DROP 0 packets, 0 bytes)
    pkts bytes target     prot opt in      out     source              \
        destination
 1  67  6050 ACCEPT       all  --  any     any     anywhere            \
        anywhere             state RELATED,ESTABLISHED
 2   0     0 ACCEPT       tcp  --  eth1    eth0    selected.remote.host \
        host1.private.lan  tcp spts:1024:65535 dpt:ssh                 \
        flags:SYN,RST,ACK/SYN state NEW
 3   0     0 ACCEPT       tcp  --  eth0    eth1    .private.lan         \
        mailserver.dmz.lan multiport dports smtp,pop3 tcp spts:1024:65535 \
        flags:SYN,RST,ACK/SYN state NEW
 4   1    60 ACCEPT       tcp  --  eth0    eth1    .private.lan         \
        web-proxy.dmz.lan  multiport dports http,https tcp spts:1024:65535 \
        flags:SYN,RST,ACK/SYN state NEW
 5   1    60 ACCEPT       tcp  --  eth0    eth1    .private.lan         \
        anywhere             tcp spts:1024:65535 dpts:ssh              \
        flags:SYN,RST,ACK/SYN state NEW
 6   0     0 ACCEPT       tcp  --  eth0    eth1    .private.lan         \
        news-server.net    tcp spts:1024:65535 dpt:nntp                \
        flags:SYN,RST,ACK/SYN state NEW
 7   0     0 REJECT       tcp  --  eth1    any     anywhere            \
        .private.lan         tcp spts:1024:65535 dpt:auth              \
        reject-with icmp-port-unreachable
 8   0     0 ACCEPT       icmp --  any     any     anywhere            \
        anywhere             icmp fragmentation-needed
 9   2   168 ACCEPT       icmp --  eth0    eth1    .private.lan         \
        anywhere             icmp echo-request
10   0     0 ACCEPT       tcp  --  any     any     anywhere            \
        anywhere             tcp flags:FIN,ACK/FIN,ACK
11   0     0 ACCEPT       tcp  --  any     any     anywhere            \
        anywhere             tcp flags:RST/RST
12   0     0 LOG          all  --  any     any     anywhere            \
        anywhere             LOG level warning
```

The default policy for the **FORWARD** chain is **DROP**. Denied packets are simply dropped without any notification being returned to either the local or the remote program. There are 12 rules on the chain:

- Line 1—Any packet recognized as being part of a previously **ESTABLISHED** connection or exchange, or a packet that is **RELATED** to one, is allowed in either direction.

- Line 2—Incoming SSH connections from a particular remote host to **host1** in the private LAN are allowed.

- Line 3—Outgoing client connections to the mail gateway and pop server in the DMZ are allowed.

- Line 4—Outgoing client connections, both HTTP and HTTPS, are allowed to the web proxy in the DMZ.

- Line 5—Outgoing client connections to remote SSH servers anywhere are allowed.

- Line 6—Outgoing client connections to a specific remote news server are allowed.

- Line 7—Incoming `auth` requests to local `identd` servers are rejected.

- Line 8—ICMP Type 3 `fragmentation-needed` messages are allowed in both directions as part of MTU size discovery.

- Line 9—Outgoing `ping` ICMP `echo-requests` are allowed to anywhere.

- Line 10—**FIN/ACK** packets are accepted in either direction.

- Line 11—TCP `RST` packets are accepted in either direction.

- Line 12—All other packets in either direction are logged before being dropped by the default policy.

In this case, the `-v` option is generally helpful to see the incoming and outgoing network interface names. `eth0` is the internal interface to the `.private.lan` network. `eth1` is the external interface to the `.dmz.lan` and the Internet beyond. Remember that **FORWARD** rules are necessary with or without NAT. Also remember that any NAT rules are defined in the `nat` table. These rules are defined in the default `filter` table.

TESTING AN INDIVIDUAL PACKET AGAINST THE FIREWALL RULES

The rule-checking command, the −C command in ipchains, is not yet implemented in iptables.

Interpreting the System Logs

`syslogd` is the service daemon that logs system events. `syslogd`'s main system log file is `/var/log/messages`. Many programs use `syslogd`'s standard logging services. Other programs, such as the Apache web server, maintain their own separate log files.

`syslog` Configuration

Not all log messages are equally important—or even interesting. This is where `/etc/syslog.conf` comes in. The configuration file `/etc/syslog.conf` enables you to tailor the log output to meet your own needs.

Messages are categorized by the subsystem that produces them. In the man pages, these categories are called *facilities* (see Table 8.1).

TABLE 8.1
syslog Log Facility Categories

FACILITY	MESSAGE CATEGORY
auth or security	Security/authorization
authpriv	Private security/authorization
cron	cron daemon messages
daemon	System daemon-generated messages
ftp	FTP server messages
kern	Kernel messages
lpr	Printer subsystem
mail	Mail subsystem
news	Network news subsystem
syslog	syslogd-generated messages
user	User program-generated messages
uucp	UUCP subsystem

Within any given facility category, log messages are divided into *priority* types. The priorities, in increasing order of importance, are listed in Table 8.2.

TABLE 8.2
syslog Log Message Priorities

PRIORITY	MESSAGE TYPE
debug	Debug messages
info	Informational status messages
notice	Normal but important conditions
warning or warn	Warning messages
err or error	Error message
crit	Critical conditions
alert	Immediate attention required
emerg or panic	System is unusable

An entry in `syslog.conf` specifies a logging facility, its priority, and where to write the messages. Not obvious is that the priority is inclusive. It's taken to mean all messages at that priority and higher. If you specify messages at the **error** priority, for example, all messages at priority **error** and higher are included—**crit**, **alert**, and **emerg**.

Logs can be written to devices, such as the console, as well as to files and remote machines.

TIPS ABOUT LOG FILES IN `/var/log`

`syslogd` doesn't create files. It only writes to existing files. If a log file doesn't exist, you can create it with the touch command and then make sure that it is owned by root. For security purposes, log files are often not readable by general users. The security log file, `/var/log/secure`, in particular, is readable by root alone.

These two entries write all kernel messages to both the console and `/var/log/_messages`. Messages can be duplicated to multiple destinations:

```
kern.*                              /dev/console
kern.*                              /var/log/messages
```

This entry writes panic messages to all default locations, including `/var/log/messages`, the console, and all user terminal sessions:

```
*.emerg                             *
```

The next two entries write authentication information related to **root** privilege and connections to `/var/log/secure`, and user authorization information to `/var/log/auth`. With the priority defined at the **info** level, **debug** messages won't be written:

```
authpriv.info                       /var/log/secure
auth.info                           /var/log/auth
```

The next two entries write general daemon information to `/var/log/daemon`, and mail traffic information to `/var/log/maillog`:

```
daemon.notice                       /var/log/daemon
mail.info                           /var/log/maillog
```

Daemon messages at the **debug** and **info** priorities and mail messages at the **debug** priority are not logged (author's preference). **named**, **crond**, and systematic mail checking produce uninteresting informational messages on a regular basis.

The final entry logs all message categories of priority **info** or higher to `/var/log/messages`, with the exception of **auth**, **authpriv**, **daemon**, and **mail**. In this case, the latter four message facilities are set to **none** because their messages are directed to their own dedicated log files:

```
*.info;auth,authpriv,daemon,mail.none          /var/log/messages
```

`syslogd` can be configured to write the system logs to a remote machine. A site that uses a networked server configuration similar to the example in Chapter 6, "Packet Forwarding," with services offered from internal machines in the DMZ, might want to keep a remote copy of the system logs. Maintaining a remote copy offers two advantages: First, log files are consolidated on a single machine, making it easier for a system administrator to monitor the logs. Second, the information is protected if one of the server machines is ever compromised.

Chapter 9, "Intrusion Detection and Response," discusses the importance that system logs play during recovery if a system is ever compromised. One of the first things an attacker does after successfully gaining **root** access to a compromised machine is to either erase the system logs or install trojan programs that won't log his activities. The system log files are either gone or untrustworthy at exactly the time you need them most. Maintaining a remote copy of the logs helps protect this information, at least until the hacker replaces the daemons writing the log file information.

To log system information remotely, both the local logging configuration and the remote logging configuration require slight modifications.

On the remote machine collecting the system logs, add the `-r` option to the `syslogd` invocation. The `-r` option tells `syslogd` to listen on the UDP `syslog` UDP port 514 for incoming log information from remote systems.

On the local machine producing the system logs, edit `syslogd`'s configuration file, `/etc/syslog.conf`, and add lines specifying what log facilities and priorities you want written to a remote host. For example, the following copies all log information to *hostname*:

```
*.*                    @hostname
```

`syslogd` output is sent over UDP. Both the source and the destination ports are 514. The client firewall rule would be as follows:

```
iptables -A OUTPUT -o <out-interface> -p udp \
       -s <this host> --sport 514 \
       -d <log host> --dport 514 -j ACCEPT
```

Firewall Log Messages: What Do They Mean?

To generate firewall logs, the kernel must be compiled with firewall logging enabled. By default, individually matched packets are logged as **kern.warn** (priority 4) messages. The log priority can be changed with the **--log-level** option to **-j LOG**. Most of the IP packet header fields are reported when a packet matches a rule with the **LOG** target. Firewall log messages are written to **/var/log/messages** by default.

You could duplicate the firewall log messages to a different file by creating a new log file and adding a line to **/etc/syslog.conf**:

```
kern.warn                                    /var/log/fwlog
```

As a TCP example, this rule denying access to the **portmap/sunrpc** TCP port **111** would produce the following message in **/var/log/messages**:

```
iptables -A INPUT -i $EXTERNAL_INTERFACE -p tcp \
        --dport 111 -j LOG --log-prefix "DROP portmap: "

iptables -A INPUT -i $EXTERNAL_INTERFACE -p tcp \
        --dport 111 -j DROP
```

```
  (1)      (2)      (3)      (4)         (5)              (6)      (7)
Jun 19 15:24:16 firewall kernel: DROP portmap: IN=eth0 OUT=

                              (8)
              MAC=00:a0:cc:40:9b:a8:00:a0:cc:d4:a7:81:08:00

                  (9)                  (10)           (11)
              SRC=192.168.1.4 DST=192.168.1.2 LEN=60

              (12)        (13)       (14)     (15)     (16)
              TOS=0x00 PREC=0x00 TTL=64 ID=57743   DF

              (17)        (18)         (19)       (20)
              PROTO=TCP SPT=33926 DPT=111 WINDOW=5840

              (21)    (22)  (23)
              RES=0x00 SYN URGP=0
```

The log message fields are numbered for the purposes of discussion:

- Field 1 is the date, **Jun 19**.

- Field 2 is the time the log was written, **15:24:16**.

- Field 3 is the computer's hostname, **firewall**.

- Field 4 is the log facility generating the message, `kernel`.
- Field 5 is the `log-prefix` string defined in the `LOG` rule.
- Field 6 is the incoming network interface that the input rule is attached to, `eth0`.
- Field 7 is the outgoing interface, which has no value in a rule on the `INPUT` chain.
- Field 8 is the MAC address of the interface that the packet is arriving on, followed by eight pairs of garbage hexadecimal digits.
- Field 9 is the packet's source address, `192.168.1.4`.
- Field 10 is the packet's destination address, `192.168.1.2`.
- Field 11 is the IP packet's total length in bytes, `LEN=60`, including both the packet header and its data.
- Field 12 is the type of service (TOS) field's 3 service bits, plus a reserved trailing bit, `TOS=0x00`.
- Field 13 is the TOS field's top 3 precedence bits, `PREC=0x00`.
- Field 14 is the packet's time to live (TTL) field, `TTL=64`. Time to live is the maximum number of hops (that is, routers visited) remaining before the packet expires.
- Field 15 is the packet's datagram ID, `ID=57743`. The datagram ID is either the packet ID or the segment to which this TCP fragment belongs.
- Field 16 is the fragment flags field, indicating that the Don't Fragment (DF) bit is set.
- Field 17 is the message protocol type contained in the packet, `PROTO=TCP`. Field values include 6 (TCP), `17` (UDP), 1 (`ICMP/<code>`), and `PROTO=<number>` for other protocol types.
- Field 18 is the packet's source port, `33926`.
- Field 19 is the packet's destination port, `111`.
- Field 20 is the sender's window size, `WINDOW=5840`, which indicates the amount of data that it is willing to accept and buffer from this host at this time.
- Field 21 reports the reserved field in the TCP header. All 4 bits must be 0.
- Field 22 is the TCP state field. In this case, the `SYN` flag is set.
- Field 23 is the urgent pointer, which indicates the amount of data considered to be urgent. The field is 0 because the `URG` flag isn't set.

When interpreting the log message, the most interesting fields are these:

```
Jun 19 15:24:16 DROP portmap: IN=eth0 SRC=192.168.1.4 DST=192.168.1.2
PROTO=TCP SPT=33926 DPT=111 SYN
```

This says that the dropped packet is a TCP packet coming in on the **eth0** interface from an unprivileged port at **192.168.1.4**. It was a TCP connection request targeted to this machine's (**192.168.1.2**) port **111**, the **sunrpc/portmap** port. (This can be a common message because **portmap** historically is one of the most commonly targeted services.)

As a UDP example, this rule denying access to the **portmap/sunrpc** UDP port **111** would produce the following message in **/var/log/messages**:

```
iptables -A INPUT -i $EXTERNAL_INTERFACE -p udp \
        --dport 111 -j LOG --log-prefix "DROP portmap: "

iptables -A INPUT -i $EXTERNAL_INTERFACE -p udp \
        --dport 111 -j DROP
```

```
   (1)       (2)      (3)       (4)           (5)             (6)     (7)
Jun 19 15:24:16 firewall kernel: DROP portmap: IN=eth0 OUT=

                              (8)
           MAC=00:a0:cc:40:9b:a8:00:a0:cc:d4:a7:81:08:00

                  (9)               (10)          (11)
           SRC=192.168.1.4 DST=192.168.1.2 LEN=28

            (12)        (13)       (14)      (15)
           TOS=0x00 PREC=0x00 TTL=40 ID=50655

             (16)        (17)        (18)      (19)
           PROTO=UDP SPT=33926 DPT=111 LEN=8
```

The log message fields are numbered for the purposes of discussion:

- Field 1 is the date, **Jun 19**.
- Field 2 is the time the log was written, **15:24:16**.
- Field 3 is the computer's hostname, **firewall**.
- Field 4 is the log facility generating the message, **kernel**.
- Field 5 is the **log-prefix** string defined in the **LOG** rule.
- Field 6 is the incoming network interface to which the input rule is attached, **eth0**.
- Field 7 is the outgoing interface, which has no value in a rule on the **INPUT** chain.
- Field 8 is the MAC address of the interface that the packet is arriving on, followed by eight pairs of garbage hexadecimal digits.
- Field 9 is the packet's source address, **192.168.1.4**.

- Field 10 is the packet's destination address, `192.168.1.2`.
- Field 11 is the IP packet's total length in bytes, `LEN=28`, including both the packet header and its data.
- Field 12 is the TOS field's 3 service bits, plus a reserved trailing bit, `TOS=0x00`.
- Field 13 is the TOS field's top 3 precedence bits, `PREC=0x00`.
- Field 14 is the packet's TTL field, `TTL=40`. Time to live is the maximum number of hops (that is, routers visited) remaining before the packet expires.
- Field 15 is the packet's datagram ID, `ID=50655`.
- Field 16 is the message protocol type contained in the packet, `PROTO=UDP`. Field values include 6 (TCP), 17 (UDP), 1 (`ICMP/<code>`), and `PROTO=<number>` for other protocol types.
- Field 17 is the packet's source port, `33926`.
- Field 18 is the packet's destination port, `111`.
- Field 19 is length of the UDP packet, including both the header and data, `LEN=8`.

When interpreting the log message, the most interesting fields are these:

```
Jun 19 15:24:16 DROP portmap: IN=eth0 SRC=192.168.1.4 DST=192.168.1.2
PROTO=UDP SPT=33926 DPT=111
```

This says that the dropped packet is a UDP packet coming in on the `eth0` interface from an unprivileged port at `192.168.1.4`. It was a UDP exchange targeted to this machine's (`192.168.1.2`) port `111`, the `sunrpc/portmap` port. (This can be a common message because `portmap` historically is one of the most commonly targeted services.)

Checking for Open Ports

Listing your firewall rules with `iptables -L` is the main tool available for checking for open ports. Open ports are defined to be open by your `ACCEPT` rules. Beyond the `iptables -L` command, other tools such as `netstat` are helpful for finding out what ports are listening on the firewall.

`netstat` has several uses. In the next section, we'll use it to check for active ports so that we can double-check that the TCP and UDP ports in use are the ports that the firewall rules are accounting for.

Just because `netstat` reports the port as listening or open doesn't mean that it's accessible through the firewall rules. Following this, two third-party port-scanning tools—`strobe` and nmap—are introduced. These tools should be used from an external location to test exactly which ports are listening on the firewall. `netstat` is a good indicator of services that are running on the machine. Remember, if the service isn't absolutely necessary, you should disable it and consider removing it entirely, especially from a firewall. Let firewalls be firewalls—they shouldn't run extra services.

netstat -a [-n -p -A inet]

`netstat` reports various network status information. Quite a few command-line options are documented to select what information `netstat` reports. The following options are useful for identifying open ports, reporting whether they are in active use and by whom, and reporting which programs and which specific processes are listening on the ports:

- `-a` lists all ports that either are in active use or are being listened to by local servers.

- `-n` displays the hostnames and port identifiers in numeric format. Without the `-n` option, the hostnames and port identifiers are displayed as symbolic names, as much as will fit in 80 columns. Using `-n` avoids a potentially long wait while remote hostnames are looked up. Not using `-n` produces a more readable listing.

- `-p` lists the name of the program listening on the socket. You must be logged in as root to use the `-p` option.

- `-A inet` specifies the address family reported. The listing includes the ports in use as they are associated with your network interface cards. Local address family socket connections aren't reported, including local network-based connections in use by programs (such as any X Windows program you might have running).

TYPES OF SOCKETS—TCP/IP AND LINUX

Sockets were introduced in BSD 4.3 UNIX in 1986 and the concepts have largely been adopted by Linux. Two main socket types were the Internet domain, AF_INET, and the UNIX domain, AF_UNIX, sockets. AF_INET is the TCP/IP socket used across a network. AF_UNIX is a socket type local to the kernel. The UNIX domain socket type is used for interprocess communication on the same computer; it is more efficient than using TCP/IP for local sockets. Nothing goes out on the network.

The following `netstat` output is limited to the INET domain sockets. The listing reports all ports being listened to by network services, including the program name and the specific process ID of the listening program:

```
> netstat -a -p -A inet
```

```
1. Active Internet connections (servers and established)
2. Proto Recv-Q Send-Q Local Address    Foreign Address State    PID/
   Program name

3. tcp    0   143 internal:ssh    netserver:62360 ESTABLISHED
   15392/sshd
4. tcp    0    0 *:smtp           *:*                LISTEN
   3674/sendmail: acce
5. tcp    0    0 my.host.domain:www *:*             LISTEN   638/httpd
6. tcp    0    0 internal:domain   *:*             LISTEN   588/named
7. tcp    0    0 localhost:domain  *:*             LISTEN   588/named
8. tcp    0    0 *:pop-3           *:*             LISTEN   574/xinetd
9. udp    0    0 *:domain          *:*                      588/named
10. udp   0    0 internal:domain   *:*                      588/named
11. udp   0    0 localhost:domain  *:*                      588/named
```

Line 1 identifies the listing as including local servers and active Internet connections. This selection was indicated with the -A inet option to netstat.

Line 2 contains these column headings:

- **Proto** refers to the transport protocol the service runs over, TCP or UDP.

- **Recv-Q** is the number of bytes received from the remote host but not yet delivered to the local program.

- **Send-Q** is the number of bytes sent from the local program that haven't been acknowledged by the remote host yet.

- **Local Address** is the local socket, network interface, and service port pair.

- **Foreign Address** is the remote socket, remote network interface, and service port pair.

- **State** is the local socket's connection state for sockets using the TCP protocol, either **ESTABLISHED** connection or **LISTEN**ing for a connection request, as well as a number of intermediate connection establishment and shutdown states.

- **PID/Program name** is the process ID (PID) and program name that owns the local socket.

Line 3 shows that an SSH connection is established over the internal LAN network interface from a machine known as **netserver**. The **netstat** command was typed from this connection.

Line 4 is a `sendmail` listening for incoming mail on the SMTP port associated with all network interfaces, including the external interface connected to the Internet, the internal LAN interface, and the loopback, localhost interface.

Line 5 shows that a local web server is listening for connections on the external interface to the Internet.

Line 6 shows that the name server is listening on the internal LAN interface for DNS lookup connection requests from local machines over TCP.

Line 7 shows that the name server is listening on the loopback interface for DNS lookup connection requests from clients on this machine over TCP.

Line 8 shows that `xinetd` is listening for connections on the POP port associated with all interfaces on behalf of `popd`. (`xinetd` is listening on all interfaces for incoming POP connections. If a connection request arrives, `xinetd` starts a `popd` server to service the request.) The firewall and higher-level security mechanisms at the `tcp_wrappers` level and the `popd` configuration level limit incoming connections to the LAN machines.

Line 9 shows that the name server is listening on all interfaces for DNS server-to-server communications and is accepting local lookup requests over UDP.

Line 10 shows that the name server is listening on the internal LAN network interface for DNS server-to-server communications and lookup requests over UDP.

Line 11 shows that the name server is listening on the loopback interface for DNS lookup requests from local clients on this machine over UDP.

`netstat` OUTPUT REPORTING CONVENTIONS

In `netstat` output, the local and foreign (that is, remote) addresses are listed as `<address:port>`. Under the `Local Address` column, the address is the name or IP address of one of your network interface cards. When the address is listed as *, it means that the server is listening on all network interfaces rather than on just a single interface. The port is either the symbolic or the numeric service port identifier that the server is using. Under the `Foreign Address` column, the address is the name or IP address of the remote client currently participating in a connection. The *.* is printed when the port is idle or for the default daemon. The port is the remote client's port on its end.

Idle servers listening over the TCP protocol are reported as listening for a connection request. Idle servers listening over the UDP protocol are reported as blank. UDP has no state—the `netstat` output is simply making a distinction between stateful TCP and stateless UDP.

Checking a Process Bound to a Particular Port with `fuser`

The `fuser` command identifies which processes are using a particular file, filesystem, or network port. `netstat -a -A inet` will report a port number rather than a service name if the port doesn't have an entry in `/etc/services`. `fuser` can be useful to determine which program is bound to that port.

The general `fuser` command format to identify which program is bound to a given port is as follows:

```
fuser -n tcp|udp -v <port number>[,<remote address>[,<remote port>]
```

For example,

```
> fuser -n tcp -v 515
```

produces the following output:

```
                    USER        PID ACCESS COMMAND
515/tcp             root        718 f....  lpd
```

The `-v` option produces the USER, ACCESS, and COMMAND fields. Without the `-v` option, the port/protocol and PID would be reported. You would need to use `ps` to identify the program assigned that process id.

The access field codes refer to the type of access that the file or filesystem is being accessed by the process as. The `f` indicates that the object is open.

The next two sections describe two third-party tools available from the Internet: `strobe` and `nmap`.

strobe

`strobe` is a simple TCP port scanner. Use it to report which TCP ports are open on your network interfaces. `strobe` is available at http://metalab.unc.edu/pub/Linux/ system/ network/admin.

The following sample `strobe` output reports the TCP ports where `strobe` has found servers listening. `strobe`'s default output includes the scanned hostname and the entry from `/etc/services` describing the port. With a firewall installed, additional servers could be running on the machine, as well, hidden behind publicly blocked ports:

```
> strobe firewall

strobe 1.04 (c) 1995-1997 Julian Assange (proff@suburbia.net).
firewall     ssh        22/tcp # SSH Remote Login Protocol
firewall     smtp       25/tcp mail
```

```
firewall    domain      53/tcp nameserver    # name-domain server
firewall    http        80/tcp www www-http  # WorldWideWeb HTTP
firewall    auth        113/tcp authentication tap ident
```

nmap

nmap is a much more powerful network security auditing tool that includes many of the newer stealth scanning techniques in use today. You should check your system security with **nmap**; it's a given that other people will. **nmap** is available at http://www.insecure.org/nmap/. You should use **nmap** from a host outside of your firewall to check that the firewall isn't listening on unexpected ports.

The following sample **nmap** output reports the state of all TCP and UDP ports. Because the **verbose** option isn't used, **nmap** reports only the ports that are open and that have servers listening on them. **nmap** output includes the scanned hostname, IP address, port, open or closed state, transport protocol in use on that port, and symbolic service port name from **/etc/ services**. Because **choke** is an internal host, additional **ssh** and **ftp** ports are open for internal LAN access:

```
> nmap -sT router

Starting nmap V. 2.54BETA7 ( www.insecure.org/nmap/ )
Interesting ports on choke.private.lan (192.168.1.2):
(The 3100 ports scanned but not shown below are in state: filtered)
Port     State       Service
21/tcp   open        ftp
22/tcp   open        ssh
53/tcp   open        domain
80/tcp   open        http
443/tcp  open        https

Nmap run completed -- 1 IP address (1 host up) scanned in 236 seconds
```

Summary

This chapter introduced the iptables rule-listing mechanism, Linux port and network daemon information available via **netstat**, and a few of the third-party tools available for verifying that the firewall rules are installed and working as you expect.

This chapter emphasized the firewall rules and the ports they protect. Chapter 9 shifts the focus away from firewalls and into the broader topic of network and system security.

PART III

Beyond iptables

9 Intrusion Detection and Response

10 Intrusion Detection Tools

11 Network Monitoring and Attack Detection

12 Filesystem Integrity

13 Kernel Enhancements

Intrusion Detection and Response

Y ou've now built a firewall with Linux using iptables. The layered security approach includes both network and host-based security. Where the firewall provides security for both the network and the hosts, there are also steps that must be undertaken on the firewall machine itself, as well as on the hosts within the network. Whether it takes the form of filesystem integrity checking, virus scanning, or monitoring the network for suspicious activity, these processes help ensure that your data remains safe.

This chapter is about host and network security and intrusion detection. The goal of the chapter is to provide a high-level overview of some of the concepts so that you can do further research into the specific areas of interest. The chapter widens the scope beyond that of the firewall machine to include the security of the network, as well as giving suggestions for individual computers within the network. Chapter 13, "Kernel Enhancements," will provide information on securing the firewall computer itself using kernel enhancements.

Detecting Intrusions

How do you know when you've been attacked successfully? That question has been posed by administrators and intrusion analysts for a long time. The methods used for detecting successful attacks used to be more art than science. Luckily, various tools are now available to make intrusion detection much more science than art.

With that said, the primary tool for intrusion detection still remains a human who can gather data from a number of sources and make an intelligent, educated decision about the meaning of the data. The current tools are sophisticated and can perform some of this correlation themselves, but the true worth of an intrusion analyst is proven in their ability to assess the situation and present likely causes and effects.

With or without tools, determining whether there has been a successful attack is left to the intrusion analyst. At some level, detection of intrusions is only assisted by the tools rather than driven by them. It's still up to a person to correlate the data.

Many times, detection of an attack occurs when a service outage is reported. In this way, it's important to actively monitor your services using a package such as Nagios. By actively monitoring as many services as possible, you can quickly spot an anomaly that warrants further investigation.

If you run a web server, rather than monitoring merely whether the server is listening (usually on TCP port **80**) you should monitor specific text on one or more web pages. If you monitor only the state of the server and whether it's listening, you won't catch a defacement of the website. In essence, you should monitor the behavior of the specific services to ensure that they are running as expected rather than making sure that they are merely running.

It's also important to monitor resources such disk space, memory usage, and load average. Monitoring these resources can indicate if a process has run away and is consuming too many resources (as might be the case with a poorly written exploit). Additionally, monitoring disk space is another useful item. If you normally consume 25% of the disk and suddenly the disk usage jumps to 85%, you'll want to investigate to see whether an attacker is using the server as a drop point for files.

Basic service monitoring, performed as much as you can, as often as you can, will help provide an early warning of anomalies. Monitoring services will also help improve the reliability of the services, all security considerations aside. Monitoring should not, however, replace intrusion detection tools such as Snort, nor should it replace a good security policy implemented through an in-depth strategy.

After an anomaly has been noted, whether through normal service monitoring or through another means, it's up to you to investigate the anomaly. Your investigation should conform to the security policy you have in place. One of the first responses would likely be to determine whether an intrusion has actually taken place. There could be many reasons why the load average just spiked or why the disk usage has increased, so you shouldn't assume that an attack has happened merely because of an outage alert.

Determining the root cause of a service outage is a difficult task that usually ends in a service being restarted or some similar routine procedure being performed to clear up the outage.

However, it's important to look for underlying causes of such outages to ensure that an attack isn't underway or that an attack hasn't already occurred. It is in this area, event correlation, where a human is most necessary. For example, did the disk partition just run out of space because an attacker is using the space or because the log files filled up the partition?

Symptoms Suggesting That the System Might Be Compromised

Often, a successful attacker will try to hide their tracks with greater success, and therefore simple service monitoring won't be of assistance. The attacker might be far more skillful at hiding his tracks than you are at tracking down anomalous system states.

Linux systems are too diverse, customizable, and complicated to define an iron-clad, fully comprehensive list of definitive symptoms proving that the system is compromised. As with any kind of detective or diagnostic work, you must look for clues where you can—as systematically as you can. RFC 2196, "Site Security Handbook," provides a list of signs to check for. The "Steps for Recovering from a UNIX or NT System Compromise," available from CERT at http://www.cert.org/tech_tips/root_compromise.html, provides another list of anomalies to check for.

The following sections incorporate both lists, including all or most of their points in one form or another. The anomalies have been roughly categorized into the following: indications related to the system logs; changes to the system configuration; changes related to the filesystem, file contents, file access permissions, and file size; changes to user accounts, passwords, and user access; problems indicated in the security audit reports; and unexpected performance degradation. The anomalous indications often cross category boundaries.

System Log Indications

System log indications include unusual error and status messages in the logs, truncated log files, deleted log files, and emailed status reports:

- *System log files*—Unexplained entries in the system log files, shrinking log files, and missing log files all suggest that something is wrong. For example, `/var/log/messages` contains the majority of the system log information on most Linux systems. If that log file is zero-sized or is missing large portions, additional investigation is warranted.

- *System daemon status reports*—Instead of (or in addition to) writing to the log files, some daemons such as `crond` send status reports in email. Having unusual or missing reports suggests that something is not right.

- *Anomalous console and terminal messages*—Unexplained messages, possibly meant to announce the hacker's presence, during a login session are obviously suspicious.

- *Repeated access attempts*—Ongoing login attempts or illegal file access attempts through FTP or a web server, particularly attempts to subvert CGI scripts, are suspicious when the attempts are persistent, even if the attempts appear to end in repeated failure.

Chapter 10, "Intrusion Detection Tools," details some automatic log-monitoring programs that can be helpful when putting up an alert or taking some other action in real time.

System Configuration Indications

System configuration indications include modified configuration files and system scripts, unintended processes running inexplicably, unexpected service port usage and assignments, and changes in network device operational status:

- `cron` *jobs*—Check the `cron` configuration scripts and executables for modification.

- *Altered system configuration files*—A filesystem integrity check, manual or using a tool as described in Chapter 12, "Filesystem Integrity," would indicate changed configuration files in `/etc`. These files are critical to proper system functioning. Any change to a file (such as in `/etc/`, like `/etc/passwd`, `/etc/group`, `/etc/hosts.equiv`, and similar files) is important to check.

- *Unexplained services and processes, as shown by* `ps`—Unexpectedly running programs are a bad sign. Be aware that as part of the attack, the `ps` command itself may have been replaced. More on this later.

- *Unexpected connection and unexpected port usage, as shown by* `netstat` *or* `tcpdump`—Unexpected network traffic is a very bad sign.

- *System crashes and missing processes*—System crashes, as well as unexpected server crashes, might be suspect. A system crash can also suggest an attacker-initiated system reboot, which could be necessary to restart certain critical system processes after replacement with a trojan version.

- *Changes in device configuration*—Reconfiguring a network interface to be in promiscuous or debug mode is a sign that a packet sniffer is installed.

Filesystem Indications

Filesystem indications include new files and directories, missing files and directories, altered file contents, MD5sum mismatches, new `setuid` programs, and rapidly growing or overflowing filesystems:

- *New files and directories*—Besides files with suddenly bad digital signatures, you might discover new files and directories. Especially suspicious are filenames starting with one or more dots and legitimate-sounding filenames appearing in unlikely places.

- `setuid` *and* `setgid` *programs*—New `setuid` files, and newly set `setuid` files, are a good place to start looking under the hood for problems.

- *Missing files*—Missing files, particularly log files, indicate a problem of some kind.

- *Rapidly changing filesystem sizes, as shown by* `df`—If the machine is compromised, rapidly growing filesystems might be a sign of a hacker's monitoring program producing large log files.

- *Modified public file archives*—Check the contents of your web and FTP areas for new or modified files.

- *New files or directories in* `/dev`—CERT warns especially to check for the presence of new ASCII files or directories in `/dev`; these are typically Trojan programs' configuration files.

User Account Indications

User account indications include new user accounts, changes to the `passwd` file, unusual activity in the user process accounting reports or missing process accounting reports, changes to user files—especially environmental files—and loss of account access:

- *New and modified user accounts*—New accounts in `/etc/passwd` and processes running under new or unexpected user IDs as shown by `ps` are indications of new accounts. Accounts with suddenly missing passwords indicate an open account.

- *User accounting records*—Unusual user accounting reports, inexplicable logins, missing or edited log files (such as `/var/log/lastlog`, `/var/log/pacct`, or `/var/log/usracct`), and irregular user activity are signs of trouble.

- *Changes to root or user accounts*—A serious sign is if a user's login environment is modified or damaged to the point that the account is inaccessible. Of particular concern are changes to users' `.rhost` and `.forward` files, and changes to their `PATH` environment variable.

- *Loss of account access*—Similar to changes to a user's login environment is intentional access denial, whether by changing the account password, by removing the account, or, for regular users, by changing the runlevel to single-user mode.

Security Audit Tool Indications

Security audit tool indications include filesystem integrity mismatches, file-size changes, changes to file-permission mode bits, new `setuid` and `setgid` programs, alerts from Intrusion detection tools such as Snort, and service monitoring data.

Files with mismatched hash signatures can be files that are new, files whose lengths or creation or modification dates have changed, and files whose access modes are altered. Of particular concern are newly installed trojan horse programs. Frequent targets for replacement are programs managed by `inetd` or `xinetd`, `inetd` or `xinetd` itself, `ls`, `ps`, `netstat`, `ifconfig`, `telnet`, `login`, `su`, `ftp`, `syslogd`, `du`, `df`, `sync`, and the `libc` library.

System Performance Indications

System performance indications include unusually high load averages and heavy disk access.

Unexplained, poor system performance could be caused by unusual process activity, unusually high load averages, excessive network traffic, or heavy filesystem access.

If your system shows signs of a successful compromise, don't panic. Don't reboot the system—important information could be lost. Simply physically disconnect the system from the Internet.

What to Do If Your System Is Compromised

The paper "Steps for Recovering from a UNIX Root Compromise," available from CERT at http://www.cert.org/tech_tips/; RFC 2196, "Site Security Handbook"; and the SANS publication "Computer Security Incident Handling: Step by Step" discuss procedures to follow in the event of a successful security breach. These documents present more formal procedures that a business, government office, or university might follow. The procedures assume some amount of spare storage space for taking snapshots of the system, assume available staff to analyze and diagnose the security problem, and discuss situations in which the victim site might want to initiate formal legal action.

Regardless of how an anomaly is investigated, the intrusion analyst must take care when performing the investigation. If the attacker notices that there's an investigator currently looking around on the same system, it's much more likely that the attacker will slash and burn their way out of the system. If the attacker thinks he or she is being followed or monitored, the attacker might begin deleting anything and everything in the way, causing real damage to the systems in question. An attack that might have resulted in only a defacement of a website might suddenly turn into deletion of entire partitions if the attacker notices the investigation.

After it has been determined that there has been a successful attack or that an attack is currently underway, a number of responses frequently occur. These will, of course, be dependent on your security policy.

If storage space is available, take a snapshot of the entire system in its current state for later analysis. If that isn't an option for you, at least snapshot the system logs under /var/log and the system configuration files under the /etc directory.

Keep a log. Write down everything. Documenting what you do and what you find not only is good for reporting the incident to a response team, your ISP, or a lawyer, but also helps to keep a record of what you've examined and what remains to be done.

If an attack has occurred or is currently underway, one of the first priorities is usually to stop the attack and prevent further damage from occurring. Keeping in mind that an attacker who notices an investigator on the same system is more likely to cause collateral damage, unplugging the system from the network is a common recommendation. With the network cable unplugged, the attacker simply can't cause additional damage. There is, of course, the possibility that the attacker will be using a tool to monitor the network interface and automatically cover his tracks should that interface's status change. However, those types of attacks are as yet unseen in the wild.

Looking for subtle changes to the system is part of this phase. An attacker may have set up a cron job to restart his daemons if they are stopped. In addition, it's quite typical for an attacker to replace common Linux utilities such as ls and ps with his own versions in order to hide their processes and files. In this regard, a program such as Chkrootkit can be helpful for host-based intrusions. Chkrootkit is discussed in Chapter 10.

The tools you use to mitigate damage will be determined by the type of attack. For example, a denial-of-service attack against a router will necessarily use different steps to mitigate the attack. The steps you might take to determine whether the system is compromised are the same steps to take in analyzing the compromised system:

1. Check the system logs and use netstat and lsof to see which processes are running and which ports are bound. Check the contents of the system configuration files. Verify the contents and access modes of all your files and directories by checking their digital signatures. Check for new setuid programs. Compare configuration and user files against clean backup copies.

   It's very likely that the attacker installed trojan horse programs in place of the very system tools you're using to analyze the system.

2. Take stock of any volatile information, such as which processes are running and which ports are in use.

3. Boot off a boot floppy or a backup copy of the system. Examine the system using the clean tools from the unaffected system. As an alternative, install the disk drives as secondary drives in a noncompromised system, and examine the disks as data.

4. Determine how the attacker succeeded in gaining entry, and determine what was done to your system.

5. If possible, completely reinstall the system from the original Linux distribution media.

6. Correct the security vulnerability, whether by making a more careful selection of services to run, by reconfiguring servers more securely, by defining access lists at the `xinetd` or `tcp_wrappers` level and at the individual server level, by installing a packet-filtering firewall, or by installing application proxy servers.

7. Install and configure any system-integrity packages.

8. Enable all logging.

9. Restore user and special configuration files known to be untainted.

10. Create MD5 checksums for the system binaries and static configuration files.

11. Reconnect the system to the network and install any new security upgrades from your Linux vendor.

12. Create MD5 checksums for the newly installed binaries, and store the checksum database on a floppy or some other system.

13. Monitor the system for recurring illegal access attempts.

Incident Reporting

An *incident* can be a number of things; you need to define it for yourself. For example, an incident might be defined as an anomalous attempt to gain or escalate privilege or compromise the confidentiality, integrity, or availability of one or more systems.

It is good practice to monitor your system log files, system-integrity reports, and system-accounting reports as a matter of habit. Even with minimal logging enabled, sooner or later you'll see something that your security policy dictates is important enough to report. With full logging enabled, you'll have plenty of log entries to ponder 24 hours a day.

Some access attempts are more serious than others. Some will annoy you personally more than others. The following sections start by discussing reasons why you might want to report an incident and cover considerations concerning which types of incidents you might report. These are individual decisions. If you choose to report something, the remaining sections focus on the various reporting groups available and the kinds of information you need to supply them.

Why Report an Incident?

You might want to report an incident even if the attack attempt was unsuccessful. These are some of the reasons:

- *To end the probes*—Your firewall ensures that most probes remain harmless. But even harmless probes are annoying if they occur repeatedly. Persistent, repeated, ongoing scans fill your log files. Depending on how you've defined the notification triggers in any log-monitoring software that you run, repeated probes can pester you with continual email notifications. However, in today's age of seemingly endless probes from bots owned by unaware broadband users, especially those in the United States, it would simply be too time-consuming for most people to report every probe.

- *To help protect other sites*—Automated probes and scans are generally building a database of all vulnerable hosts in a large IP address block. When identified as potentially vulnerable to specific exploits, these hosts are targeted for selective attacks. Today's sophisticated analysis and cracking tools can compromise a vulnerable system and hide their tracks in seconds. Reporting an incident might put a stop to the scans before someone somewhere else gets hurt.

- *To inform the system or network administrator*—Attacking sites quite often are compromised systems, host a compromised user account, have misconfigured software, are being spoofed, or have an individual troublemaker. System administrators are usually responsive to an incident report. ISPs tend to stop their troublemaking customers before other customers start complaining that remote sites have blocked access from their address block and that they can't exchange email with a friend or family at a remote site.

- *To receive confirmation of the attack*—Sometimes you might simply want confirmation that what you're seeing in the logs is a problem. Sometimes you might want confirmation that a remote site was indeed leaking packets unintentionally because of a faulty configuration. The remote site also is often glad for the heads-up that its network isn't behaving as it had intended.

- *To increase awareness and monitoring by all involved parties*—If you report the incident to the attacking site, the site hopefully will monitor its configurations and user activities more carefully. If you report the incident to an abuse center, the abuse staff can contact the remote site with more clout than an individual carries, keep an eye out for continued activity, and better help customers who have been compromised. If you report the incident to a security newsgroup, other people can get a better idea of what to watch out for.

What Kinds of Incidents Might You Report?

Which incidents you report depends completely on your tolerance, how serious you consider different probes to be, and how much time you care to devote against what is a global, exponentially growing infestation. It comes down to how you define the term *incident*. In different people's minds, incidents can range anywhere from simple port scans to attempts to access your private files or system resources, to denial-of-service attacks, to crashing your servers or your entire system, to gaining root login access to your system:

- *Denial-of-service attacks*—Any kind of denial-of-service attack is blatantly hostile. It's difficult not to take such an attack personally. These attacks are the electronic form of vandalism, obstruction, harassment, and theft of service. Because some forms of denial-of-service attacks are possible because of the inherent nature of networked devices, you can do little or nothing about some forms of attack other than to report the incidents and block the attacker's entire address block.

- *Attempts to reconfigure your system*—An attacker can't reconfigure your servers without a root login account on your machine, but he could conceivably modify your system's in-memory, network-related tables—or try, at least. Exploits to consider include these:

    - Unauthorized DNS zone transfers to or from your machine over TCP. For more information on zone transfers, see the book *DNS & BIND*, by Albitz and Liu (O'Reilly).

    - Changes to your in-memory routing tables via ICMP Redirect or probes to UDP port **520** for **routed** or **gated**. (Remember, a firewall machine should not support dynamic routing.) For more information on routing table exploits, see the book *Firewalls and Internet Security: Repelling the Wily Hacker*, by Cheswick and Bellovin (Addison-Wesley).

    - Attempts to reconfigure your network interfaces or routing tables via probes to UDP port **161** for **snmpd**.

- *Attempts to gain local configuration and network topology information*—Network information requests are mostly directed to UDP port **161** for **snmpd**. DNS queries over TCP port **53** provide network topology information, as do routing queries to UDP port **520** for **routed** or **gated**.

- *Attempts to gain login account access*—Probes to **telnet** TCP port **23** and **ssh** TCP port **22** are obvious. Less obvious are probes to ports associated with servers known to be exploitable, either historically or currently. Buffer overflow exploits are generally intended ultimately to execute commands and gain shell access. The **mountd** exploit is an example of this.

- *Attempts to access nonpublic files*—Attempts to access private files, such as the /etc/passwd file, configuration files, or proprietary files, show up in your FTP log (/var/log/xferlog or /var/log/messages) and in your web server access log (/var/log/httpd/error_log).

- *Attempts to use private services*—By definition, any service you haven't made available to the Internet is private. These are the private services potentially available through your public servers, such as attempts to relay mail through your mail server. Chances are, people are up to no good if they're trying to use your machine instead of their own or their ISP's. Relay attempts show up in your mail log file (/var/log/maillog).

- *Attempts to store files on your disk*—If you host an improperly configured anonymous FTP site, it's possible for someone to set up a repository of stolen software (WAREZ) on your machine. Attempts to upload files are recorded in your FTP log (/var/log/xferlog) if ftpd is configured to log file uploads.

- *Attempts to crash your system or individual servers*—Buffer overflow attempts against CGI scripts available through your website are possibly the easiest to identify by error messages written in the CGI script's log files. Other reports of erroneous data will appear in your general syslog file (/var/log/_messages), your general daemon log (/var/log/daemon), your mail log (/var/log/maillog), your FTP log (/var/log/xferlog), or your secure access log (/var/log/secure).

- *Attempts to exploit specific, known, currently exploitable vulnerabilities*—Attackers find new vulnerabilities with each new software release (and old ones too). Keep up-to-date with the newest advisories from http://www.cert.org and your Linux software vendor.

To Whom Do You Report an Incident?

You have a number of options in terms of whom you report an incident to:

- **root**, **postmaster**, *or* **abuse** *at the offending site*—The obvious place to lodge a complaint is with the administrator of the offending site. Informing the system administrator is often all that's required to take care of a problem. This isn't always possible, though, because many probes originate from spoofed, nonexistent IP addresses.

- *Network coordinator*—If the IP address doesn't have a DNS entry, contacting the coordinator for the network address block is often helpful. The coordinator can contact the administrator at the offending site or put you in direct contact. If the IP address doesn't resolve through the **host** or **dig** commands, you can almost always find the network coordinator by supplying the address to the **whois** databases. The **whois** command is hard-wired into the ARIN database. Three major databases are available through the web:

- *ARIN*—The American Registry for Internet Numbers maintains the IP address database for the Western hemisphere, the Americas. ARIN is located at http://whois.arin.net/whois/arinwhois.html.

- *APNIC*—The Asia Pacific Network Information Centre maintains the IP address database for Asia. APNIC is located at http://www.apnic.net/apnic-bin/whois.pl.

- *RIPE*—The Réseaux IP Européens maintains the IP address database for Europe. RIPE is located at http://www.ripe.net/db/whois.html.

- *Your ISP abuse center*—If scans are originating from within your ISP's address space, your abuse center is the place to contact. Your ISP can be helpful with scans originating elsewhere, too, by contacting the offending site on your behalf. Chances are good that your machine isn't the only machine being probed on the ISP's network.

- *CERT*—The CERT Coordination Center is unlikely to have the resources to respond to general, run-of-the-mill incidents. CERT's priorities are more likely aimed at global issues, large institutions, and Internet security emergencies. Nevertheless, CERT welcomes incident report information for its tracking and statistical reporting efforts. CERT can be contacted at http://www.cert.org/_contact_cert/contactinfo.html or by email at cert@cert.org.

- *Your Linux vendor*—If your system is compromised because of a software vulnerability in its distribution, your vendor will want to know so that a security upgrade can be developed and released.

What Information Do You Supply?

An incident report must contain enough information to help the incident response team track down the problem. When contacting the site the attack originated from, remember that your contact person might be the individual who intentionally launched the attack. What you include out of the following list depends on whom you are contacting and how comfortable you are including the information, as well as whatever privacy and other policies may be in effect:

- Your email address

- Your phone number, if appropriate

- Your IP address, hostname, and domain name

- The IP addresses and hostnames, if available, involved in the attack

- The date and time of the incident (including your time zone relative to GMT)

- A description of the attack

- How you detected the attack

- Representative log file entries showing the incident

- A description of the log file format

- References to advisories and security notices describing the nature and significance of the attack

- What you want the person to do (fix it, confirm it, explain it, monitor it, or be informed of it)

Where Do You Find More Information?

As network security comes increasingly to the public's mind, the number of security-related websites is growing quickly. CERT and COAST remain excellent sources for security information. The SANS Institute at http://www.sans.org/ and Security Focus at http://www.securityfocus.com/ both provide timely and in-depth information on security as well. The mailing lists on the Security Focus website are particularly good, and I encourage you to not only read the archives but subscribe and participate in the lists. Appendix A, "Security Resources," also contains suggestions with some other sites and locations for security information as well.

Summary

This chapter focused on monitoring system integrity and intrusion detection. If you suspect that a system might be compromised, you can refer to this chapter's list of potential problem indications. If you see some of these indications and conclude that the system is compromised, you can make use of the list of recovery steps discussed. Finally, incident-reporting considerations were discussed, and pointers were given on whom you might report an incident to.

Chapter 10 looks at the implementation of some of the things you learned in this chapter by looking at the specific tools involved in intrusion detection and system testing.

Intrusion Detection Tools

In the preceding chapter you learned the concepts of intrusion detection and intrusion response. Rarely are two attacks exactly the same, though the techniques used frequently rely on a common set of methods and result in many of the same symptoms, as described in the preceding chapter. It is through these common methods and symptoms that intrusion detection tools are able to assist the intrusion analyst with his job.

The intrusion analyst has much to choose from when looking for software tools to assist in problem correlation, diagnosis, and resolution. This chapter focuses on the software tools used in intrusion detection and tools that can help in any administrator's toolkit. The chapter begins with a look at network sniffers and continues through tools to check for rootkits and into filesystem checkers and log file monitoring.

Intrusion Detection Toolkit: Network Tools

Some of the primary tools of security and network administrators alike are network analysis tools. These include network sniffers, intrusion detection software, and network analyzers.

A network sniffer is software that passively listens to traffic received and sent by a network interface. The workhorse sniffer of choice is TCPDump. TCPDump is simple enough that beginners can learn it quickly yet powerful enough to provide the necessary functionality for multiple protocols in multiple situations. Using TCPDump, it's possible to view traffic in numerous formats including ASCII and use expressions to fine-tune the exact traffic to be viewed through the tool.

TCPDump is manual and primitive intrusion detection software. If you know what you're looking for, TCPDump can help you spot the anomalous traffic as it passes through the network. TCPDump in and of itself won't know that an attack just passed under its nose; that's the job of the intrusion analyst (as well as other software). However, TCPDump almost always becomes an integral tool for investigating active attacks because it allows the analyst to watch the attack in real-time.

TCPDump is covered in-depth in Chapter 11, "Network Monitoring and Attack Detection." There you'll find coverage of normal protocol activity, as well as a look at some exploits through the eyes, or nose as it were, of TCPDump.

When it comes to tools that listen to the network and perform some level of analysis on the traffic, none is better than Snort. Snort is provider- and enterprise-class intrusion detection software that's both widely deployed and mature. Snort works using the concept of intrusion signatures. The theory is that many attacks follow the same pattern or look the same or very similar at the network level.

Consider this example: Assume that a packet is received on a certain port with its header flags set a certain way. When this occurs, it is always a precursor to an attack or an attempt to exploit a certain vulnerability. It can be said that this particular attack has, therefore, a signature that identifies it as malicious traffic. This signature, unique to the exploit of this vulnerability, can then be used by software such as Snort to detect that there was an attempt to exploit the vulnerability. Snort can then perform an action based on this detection (or can take no action).

Snort is quite powerful and, when combined with reporting software called ACID, can produce complex reports in addition to the main function of intrusion detection.

Ntop is network analysis software, as opposed to the sniffer that produces reports of usage based on protocol, flow, host, and other parameters. Using ntop is recommended at strategic points in the network to establish a baseline of the normal traffic flows on the network. A sample page with one of ntop's reports is shown in Figure 10.1.

Ntop is just one such analyzer. I chose to feature ntop here because it's simple to get working quickly. However, I also recommend other analysis software for network traffic. Among other analysis software, MRTG and Cricket are two excellent choices for traffic analysis.

Creating baseline traffic reports and keeping them up-to-date helps not only to spot anomalies including both unexpected increases and decreases in the traffic but also to track when new bandwidth might be necessary. It is this dual use—security anomalies and bandwidth usage monitoring—that makes traffic analysis invaluable.

To establish traffic baselines and effectively monitor the network for intrusions using Snort and TCPDump on large networks, it's important to place the tools at strategic locations within the network. Most large networks (even medium and small) use switches to pass traffic.

Understanding the difference between switches and hubs is important when considering where to place network tools.

FIGURE 10.1
An example of one of ntop's reports.

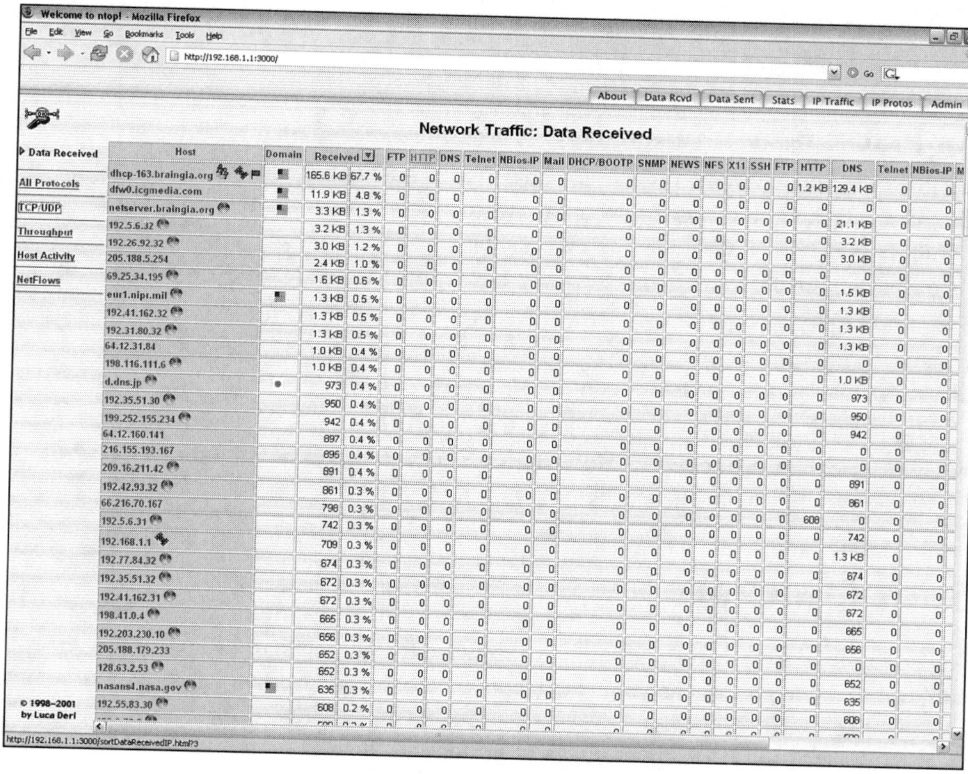

Network Traffic: Data Received

Host	Received	%
dhcp-163.braingia.org	165.6 KB	67.7%
dfw0.icgmedia.com	11.9 KB	4.8%
netserver.braingia.org	3.3 KB	1.3%
192.5.6.32	3.2 KB	1.3%
192.26.92.32	3.0 KB	1.2%
205.188.5.254	2.4 KB	1.0%
69.25.34.195	1.6 KB	0.6%
eur1.nipr.mil	1.3 KB	0.5%
192.41.162.32	1.3 KB	0.5%
192.31.80.32	1.3 KB	0.5%
64.12.31.84	1.0 KB	0.4%
198.116.111.6	1.0 KB	0.4%
d.dns.jp	973	0.4%
192.35.51.30	950	0.4%
199.252.155.234	942	0.4%
64.12.160.141	897	0.4%
216.155.193.167	895	0.4%
209.16.211.42	891	0.4%
192.42.93.32	861	0.3%
66.216.70.167	798	0.3%
192.5.6.31	742	0.3%
192.168.1.1	709	0.3%
192.77.84.32	674	0.3%
192.35.51.32	672	0.3%
192.41.162.31	672	0.3%
198.41.0.4	665	0.3%
192.203.230.10	656	0.3%
205.188.179.233	652	0.3%
128.63.2.53	652	0.3%
nasansl.nasa.gov	635	0.3%
192.55.83.30	608	0.2%

© 1998–2001 by Luca Deri

Switches and Hubs and Why You Care

On a switched network, any given network interface would receive only traffic destined for it as well as broadcast traffic. In a hub network environment the network interface receives all traffic, whether that traffic is destined for it or for another device. This is why switched networks are faster than hubbed networks—the unnecessary traffic isn't sent to all ports of the switch.

There are situations in which a network interface might receive all traffic or a greater subset than merely its own in a switched network, such as those when a switch is configured to mirror the traffic to a specific port. In practice this can be done, but it may result in performance problems for the switch because it now has to copy all traffic to two ports instead of one.

Refer to your switch's documentation for more information. For example, Cisco Catalyst switches call this feature "Switched Port Analyzer," or SPAN. More information on SPAN can be found at http://www.cisco.com/warp/public/473/41.html.

Regardless of where the traffic originates, if it comes into the interface where the sniffer is running, the traffic can be captured. The key, at a network level, is to place sniffers and the related intrusion detection software in the right locations. For host-based traffic sniffing, the placement of the sniffer is obvious, on the host itself.

Sniffer Placement

The placement of network sniffers and traffic-analysis software is key to successfully analyzing the traffic. In a switched network, the switch needs to be configured to mirror all traffic out the sniffer's switch port. Chapter 11 discusses the placement of sniffers. In essence, I recommend placing them in as many points as you can, notably near termination points such as firewalls.

ARPWatch

Another item to be discussed in Chapter 11 is ARPWatch. ARPWatch is software to watch for new network devices on the network. ARPWatch can be helpful for auditing the devices on the network, especially wireless networks.

Rootkit Checkers

A rootkit is a piece of software or a grouping of software that attempts to exploit one or more vulnerabilities with the goal of enabling an attacker to gain elevated privileges or perform any other type of attack against the target. Frequently, rootkits are used by less skilled attackers who use the software built by another attacker but don't really understand the underlying exploit; they're just interested in the results.

Many rootkits not only run the initial exploit to give the attacker root privileges but also attempt to mask or hide the fact that an attack has been launched. They do this by deleting log files or certain entries from log files, planting trojan-horse versions of programs, and employing other means. There is also nothing stopping an attacker from chaining rootkits together for multiple levels of deception and possible exploit.

Like network-centric attacks, rootkits frequently have signatures or leave other traces that identify them. These traces and signatures might be the aforementioned removal of log files, the presence of one or more processes, or other changes to the system that are specific to the rootkit software or the exploit.

Also as with network-centric attacks, there is software to search for the signatures and traces of rootkits as well. One such application is Chkrootkit.

Running Chkrootkit

Before you can run Chkrootkit, you need to get it. Chkrootkit can be downloaded from http://www.chkrootkit.org/. After it's downloaded, Chkrootkit needs to be unarchived and compiled:

```
tar -zxvf chkrootkit.tar.gz
cd chkrootkit-<NNNN>
make sense
```

Yes, that does say `make sense` in the code example. Although Chkrootkit is a shell script, there is some additional functionality gained by compiling the code. Compiling is not required, but because it's quick and adds some additional levels of checking, I'd recommend doing so. Specifically, compiling Chkrootkit will enable these additional checks:

- `ifpromisc`
- `chklastlog`
- `chkwtmp`
- `check_wtmpx`
- `chkproc`
- `chkdirs`
- `strings`

Of all the tools used in this book, Chkrootkit is probably the easiest to use. To run Chkrootkit, from within the `chkrootkit` source directory you simply type this:

```
./chkrootkit | less
```

You aren't required to pipe the output to `less` but there is a copious amount of output. So if you actually want to read the output, you'll probably need to pipe it somewhere—unless, of course, you have a huge scrollback buffer.

Because running Chkrootkit produces a lot of output, it is wise to pipe the output to `more` or `less`, depending on your preference. Alternatively, you could redirect the output to a file:

```
./chkrootkit > output.txt
```

Chkrootkit will output a number of lines informing you what it is currently checking for along with the ultimate status of the check. The output will look similar to this:

```
Checking `amd'... not found
Checking `basename'... not infected
Checking `biff'... not infected
Checking `chfn'... not infected
Checking `chsh'... not infected
Searching for ShitC Worm... nothing found
Searching for Omega Worm... nothing found
Searching for Sadmind/IIS Worm... nothing found
Searching for MonKit... nothing found
Searching for Showtee... nothing found
```

As you can see from the output sample, it doesn't appear that any trojaned files or rootkits were detected. An infected file or detection of a rootkit will look similar to the following:

```
Checking `bindshell'... INFECTED (PORTS:  1524 31337)
```

Even though the output from Chkrootkit seems to indicate that the computer is infected with bindshell, Chkrootkit does sometimes produce false positives. However, if you see the INFECTED output from Chkrootkit, it's in your best interest to assume that Chkrootkit reported correctly and take steps to mitigate the damage.

A false positive occurs when a tool detects and reports a problem when in fact there is no problem. The underlying cause for false positives varies depending on the nature of the software reporting the occurrence. False positives are not as bad as false negatives. A false negative occurs when there really is a problem but the problem is not reported by tools that should find the problem.

False positives and negatives are not limited to computing. Imagine the case in which a person goes to a doctor and gets an ultrasound scan. Based on the scan results, the doctor reports that the person has cancer. However, on further examination it appears that the initial report was incorrect. This is an example of a false positive. Although additional tests were unnecessarily performed based on the false positive, it is still much better than having a false negative, with the cancer going unnoticed and untreated.

Because Chkrootkit reports using tools on the computer, it may report a false negative. There are ways around this problem as described later in this section.

What If Chkrootkit Says the Computer Is Infected?

If Chkrootkit says your computer is infected, the first thing you should do is tell yourself to remain calm. Although you should not assume so, there is a chance that Chkrootkit is reporting a false positive. If Chkrootkit reports an infection, you should immediately take steps to mitigate any further damage.

The preceding chapter of the book looked at incident response. Therefore, it would be redundant to cover that same material in this chapter. However, as with all tools of this nature, false positives come with the territory. It's in your best interest to take the notice seriously, but it might also be wise to try to determine whether Chkrootkit has reported a false positive.

Chkrootkit uses various means to find rootkits. Many times Chkrootkit looks for a certain signature in a file based on a known trojaned version of the file. Other times Chkrootkit looks for ports that are open that have been known to be the result of a rootkit or other attack. This was the case for the report of infection highlighted earlier in this section. Chkrootkit reported that it believed that the computer was infected with the bindshell rootkit. It based this finding on two ports that it found open, 1524 and 31337. In reality, these ports were open because of another security tool, Portsentry, that listens on those ports in hopes of catching other infected hosts. I used the program lsof with the -i option to determine the exact program that was listening on those ports.

With more than 50 rootkits reported by Chkrootkit, you probably won't know the exact ramifications of being infected by a given rootkit. Further, there's a good chance that if one rootkit has been run, multiple rootkits have been run, making cleanup all that much more difficult. To begin the process of damage control, you can search the web for each individual rootkit to determine what actions it takes when it's run. However, realize that, by definition, after a rootkit has been run successfully, the attacker has root privileges on the computer and therefore may have done much greater damage to the system or may be in the process of doing so now!

Whenever Chkrootkit reports an infection, you should take it seriously and always assume the worst. Prudence suggests that you should immediately unplug the computer from the network and take steps to clean up from the rootkit. In reality, it's rarely that easy or cut-and-dried.

Limitations of Chkrootkit and Similar Tools

Chkrootkit is a powerful and incredibly helpful tool but it is not without limitations. These limitations aren't really specific to Chkrootkit but rather are a limitation of any tool that attempts to perform complex checks such as this. One such limitation, false positives, has already been discussed. Another limitation of Chkrootkit and other tools like it is that they rely, by default, on programs included with the Linux computer itself, programs that may have been compromised or altered to avoid detection by prying eyes such as those of Chkrootkit and related utilities.

Here's a list of programs that Chkrootkit uses; keep in mind that these programs may themselves in turn rely on libraries or other things on the Linux computer that also may be compromised:

- awk
- cut
- echo
- egrep
- find
- head
- id
- ls
- netstat
- ps
- sed
- strings
- uname

Another limitation of tools such as Chkrootkit and shared by similar tools is that it can detect only rootkits that have been reported and for which it has been configured. Some unlucky soul has to be the first to have the rootkit run on her computer. If you happen to be that person, Chkrootkit won't help. Realize, though, that there is a fair chance that multiple rootkits will be run on the computer, which will make detection easier. I realize that this is small consolation.

Using Chkrootkit Securely

It's a good idea to use known-good sets of system binaries when using a tool such as Chkrootkit. Many rootkits replace vital system binaries such as /bin/ps with versions of their own. Therefore, if you try to use ps to find unknown processes, you may not be able to see them because the trojaned version of ps hides them.

Chkrootkit gives two methods for working around this problem. The first method involves using a known-good set of binaries, probably mounted from a CD-ROM. The second method involves physically mounting the possibly compromised hard drive into a different computer and then running the check from there. This second method is more appropriate for forensics after a successful attack rather than for investigating a possible attack.

Mounting a CD-ROM with known-good versions of binaries is a safe and easy method for performing a thorough examination using Chkrootkit. This method assumes that you have a CD-ROM with the correct binaries already on the disc. To run Chkrootkit with a CD-ROM copy of the binaries, first mount the CD. This is usually accomplished using the `mount` command, although sometimes it's mounted automatically. A common method for mounting the CD-ROM drive in most modern Linux distributions is shown here:

```
mount -t iso9660 /dev/cdrom /mnt/cdrom
```

Chkrootkit uses the `-p` option to define the location of the binaries it should use. Therefore, if the CD-ROM is mounted at `/mnt/cdrom`, you'd run Chkrootkit like so:

```
./chkrootkit -p /mnt/cdrom
```

The other method for running Chkrootkit is to physically mount the possibly compromised hard drive into another computer and run Chkrootkit against the contents of that drive. This is accomplished by specifying an alternate "root" directory for Chkrootkit. Assume that the second drive is mounted at `/mnt/drive2`:

```
./chkrootkit -r /mnt/drive2
```

When Should Chkrootkit Be Run?

Chkrootkit should be run whenever you'd like. There is no recommended schedule for Chkrootkit. I personally run it at irregular intervals for fun, but then again I'm just that type of guy. You should most definitely run Chkrootkit anytime you observe any suspicious activity on the computer or on other computers that may interact with or reside on the same network block as the computer in question. Whenever you run Chkrootkit, you should always hop out to the website, http://www.chkrootkit.org/, to check for a new version of the tool. A new signature for a rootkit or additional functionality might have been added since the version you're using.

You can also run Chkrootkit nightly from cron. However, I wouldn't rely on such a report being entirely accurate, but it could provide an early warning of an anomaly that needs your attention. Running Chkrootkit from cron might look like this:

```
0 4 * * * /path/to/chkrootkit
```

The cron entry shown will run Chkrootkit every morning at 4:00 a.m. Root (the recipient of cron job output) will receive a report every morning detailing the run of Chkrootkit.

Filesystem Integrity

Hand in hand with a rootkit checker such as Chkrootkit goes filesystem integrity software. Filesystem integrity software monitors important files on the computer and generates reports based on changes to those files. The administrator can then watch for unexpected changes to the files in question. For example, if files such as /etc/resolv.conf or even /etc/shadow change with no apparent reason, the administrator can take action.

Two popular filesystem integrity tools are Tripwire and AIDE. Tripwire had been the choice among administrators for a long time. However, Tripwire's license changed, thus making commercial uses of the software questionable and even making the open-source nature of the software questionable. AIDE was developed as an alternative. In the meantime, the Tripwire license changed back, so as of this writing Tripwire is again a traditional open-source package. However, I'm not going to cover Tripwire in this book due to the license changes. I don't want to have the license change yet again between the time I write this and the time you read it.

AIDE is covered in detail, and a more complete description of how filesystem integrity works is given, in Chapter 12, "Filesystem Integrity."

Log Monitoring

Monitoring log files is used to watch for anomalies that might indicate an attack. Although this method is used successfully, it can result in huge amounts of data and become cumbersome on large networks.

When combined with other tools, log monitoring can be made to work. For example, using log monitoring on a few key systems can reduce the amount of data being received. However, this and other such measures are really stop-gap measures because they do little to ensure the security of the systems that aren't monitored.

Numerous packages are available to monitor log files. Three such packages include Logsnorter, Swatch, and Logcheck. More information on each can be found at their respective websites or from within your system's documentation if the distribution includes them as available packages. I'll briefly cover Swatch here just to give you a taste of some of the capabilities of these types of tools.

Swatch

Swatch is available with many Linux distributions as an add-on package or can be downloaded from http://swatch.sourceforge.net/. Swatch is highly configurable and can perform a number of actions based on a match.

Swatch works in several modes, including a mode called single-pass, which has the program parse a log file once, searching for matches and taking action based on those matches. Another mode sees Swatch perform a running tail (tail -f) of a log file looking for matches. By default, Swatch monitors /var/log/messages but it can be configured to monitor any file or even a socket.

Because Swatch is so powerful, I don't feel as though I can do it justice in a book on Linux firewalls. I invite you to read more about Swatch. For now, I'll give a recipe for monitoring a log file with Swatch. Another such recipe shows up in Chapter 11, in the section on Snort titled "Automated Intrusion Monitoring with Snort."

USING SWATCH TO MONITOR SSH LOGIN FAILURES

In 2004 and 2005, a number of brute-force login attempts were noted against servers running SSH. These usually didn't result in much of anything except annoyance. However, it's general-ly useful to monitor log files for these and other attempts to brute-force attack a server. Swatch can be configured to send an email (or do any number of other actions) when such an attempt is logged. This section shows how to send an email alert when an authentication fail-ure is logged.

The system logs a line similar to the following when a login is attempted and fails:

```
Jun  7 17:09:10 ord sshd[3434]: error: \
     PAM: Authentication failure for root from 192.168.1.10
```

There are a number of unique items on this line, but I'll choose to look for the words "Authentication failure" because that is the type of thing I want to be alerted on. The Swatch syntax is painfully easy yet can be incredibly powerful. This is because Swatch uses regular expression syntax for matching. The match in this case is rather trivial. Simply telling Swatch what to watch for with the aptly titled `watchfor` configuration directive and then giving it one or more actions to perform when a match is noted is all that's required for Swatch configura-tion. For example, to look for the words "Authentication failure" and have an email sent, the Swatch configuration consists of the following:

```
watchfor /Authentication failure/
    mail
```

These two lines are saved in `~/.swatchrc`. In this case, I'm doing so as root because Swatch will need read access to the log file in question.

Next, start Swatch and tell it what file to monitor. Again, the default is `/var/log/messages`. However, I'm creating this example on a Debian system and therefore the authentication fail-ures are logged to `/var/log/auth.log` by default. Therefore, I point Swatch at the correct configuration file and start it:

```
swatch –tail-file=/var/log/auth.log
```

Swatch will now monitor the log file for the words "Authentication failure" and will send an email to root if and when the words are found.

As previously stated, there are several options for alerts, including executing other programs. These programs could be shell scripts or really anything, so the possibilities are virtually limitless.

How to Not Become Compromised

Virtually nothing can be done to stop an attacker with unlimited resources and unlimited time. From DoS attacks to rootkits to physical attacks, if someone wants at your data bad enough, chances are that he can get to it, given no other constraints. That said, there are many things you can do to limit your exposure to most risks.

Neither this chapter nor this book deals with physical attacks on any level. If an attacker is onsite and can simply walk off with the computer or hard drive containing the data, there's no amount of firewalling that will help. If the attacker has physical access to the computer or device holding the data, the attacker can steal the data itself or possibly plant his own malicious trojan software.

This section gives some general suggestions that are field-tested to keep systems secure. The suggestions given here are by no means all-encompassing; rather they are merely things I suggest to help ensure system integrity.

Secure Often

Securing the computing environment is a continual process rather than an endpoint. As you work to secure systems and networks, new vulnerabilities are being discovered and new software is being developed. There is simply no magic bullet that enables you to be done and complete when it comes to securing a computer environment. This book has been devoted to securing a network and its systems through the use of a firewall built on Linux. This chapter has introduced some of the other aspects of a security-in-depth process.

Using the tools available to you, such as those already introduced in this chapter, you can secure a computer and the network on which it resides. There are, of course, additional steps you can take to further enhance the security of the environment.

KERNEL ENHANCEMENTS

There are certain things you can do with the Linux kernel to enhance its security. Naturally, anything you do at this, the lowest, level of the operating system will only serve to help the security of those things above it.

Two such kernel enhancements, SELinux and GrSecurity, are discussed in Chapter 13, "Kernel Enhancements."

BASTILLE LINUX

Bastille Linux is a program that helps automate the process of system security as well as report on the security of the system. Bastille Linux implements many of the security best practices that you could find by reading volumes of material and countless websites. All of those best practices are implemented through a wizard-like interface (command-line or GUI) that contains a lot of information on not only what you're being asked but why it's important.

Bastille Linux goes so far as to give recommendations for certain features. Unlike many tools that try to give recommendations, Bastille gets it right by explaining the reasoning behind the proposed change, as well as the implications that it might have if you choose to use the step.

Finally, Bastille also includes an undo process so that you can quickly undo any changes that might be causing problems. Bastille is welcomed by experienced Linux administrators and those new to Linux alike. Some Linux distributions include Bastille as a package. More information on Bastille Linux can be found at http://www.bastille-linux.org/.

Update Often

Although by far the most effortless of any task in this book, keeping a computer system up-to-date is an often-overlooked aspect of system security. The best way to ensure that a computer will be broken into is to leave it running without updating it.

One of the greatest strengths of Linux and open-source software is security. Some attempt to argue that this security is achieved because open-source software is less popular. Of course, this completely ignores market-share statistics such as Netcraft's web server survey showing that Apache holds nearly 70% of the web server market.

Part of this security strength comes from the open-source community's ability to provide fixes within hours of the security disclosure. It's quite common for fixes to be available the same day as the disclosure, even for security issues that weren't previously disclosed. In events in which a fix might take a little time, the community has historically been excellent at providing workarounds to mitigate and sometimes eliminate the vulnerabilities entirely.

Both of these characteristics, quick fixes and quick workarounds, work to your advantage in maintaining system security. However, for either one to be of use, you need to keep track of their availability by monitoring mailing lists and security websites. Most major Linux vendors offer announce-only security mailing lists in which subscribers receive an email whenever a vulnerability is disclosed. In addition, there are other industry mailing lists that can keep you up-to-date on security issues. Appendix A, "Security Resources," lists some of the more popular sites and lists.

Keeping software up-to-date is an important aspect of system security. I recommend updating as often as possible while obviously paying attention to the software that's being updated to ensure that none of the updates breaks live systems.

Test Often

It's not enough to secure often and update often, though those two items certainly go a long way toward ensuring a secure environment. Another basic point of security in-depth is to test often. Testing ensures that the security policies are being enforced and the implementation of those security policies is successful.

Penetration testing is another important aspect of system security. Penetration testing, or pen-testing, is a process by which the security of a system is tested by trying a number of attack vectors to get the system to behave in an unexpected way. The definition of penetration testing is purposely vague so that it is not limited to attacks of only a certain class or type.

Penetration testing can be both informal and formal. The informal pen-tests are typically run by security administrators or even developers using anything from manual attempts to break into an application to automated attacks using a number of tools. A formal pen-test would be done by a third party who would likely use a combination of both manual and automated attacks to test the system. The type and frequency of pen-testing is a matter for your security policy.

Of course, when you do test, it's important to test both types as if you were a normal attacker and as if you were an insider. Testing as a normal attacker means testing the application or system without any knowledge other than that which can be gleaned from outside of the system. In other words, if you're testing a web application, view the source of the web page to see what form of parameters are being used. Many times, testing as a normal attacker also means that you'll have to test from a location external to the local network. This is especially important when testing a firewall ruleset.

This section examines some of the tools you can use to test a network and computer system. As with other lists presented in this chapter, it is not meant to be all-encompassing or comprehensive. Rather, the tools examined here provide a good starting point on which you can build your knowledge of security and penetration-testing concepts and facilities.

NMAP

Nmap, the Network Mapper, is a program used to identify open ports and available devices on a network. Nmap is frequently used by the intrusion analyst to determine what ports are open and listening on a given host. In the context of a firewall, Nmap can be used from an external location to test the firewall rules to ensure that no unexpected ports are open and available.

Nmap is available as a package on many popular Linux distributions. If Nmap isn't available on your distribution, it can be downloaded from http://www.insecure.org/nmap/.

Nmap includes many options for probing hosts and entire networks. These options are too numerous to cover in-depth here. In practice, I've found the following syntax to be most useful for performing the aforementioned port scan, this one looking for TCP ports:

```
nmap -sS -v <host>
```

For example, to scan the host **192.168.1.10** for open TCP ports, the following syntax would be used:

```
nmap -sS -v 192.168.1.10
```

Note that the use of the **-v** option enables extra verbosity. Although this option is not required, it is recommended, and you can even add additional instances of **-v** to increase the verbosity.

Various types of TCP scans are available with Nmap. I chose a **SYN** scan because I've found it to generally be the most reliable for this type of test.

When Nmap begins a scan, it sends an initial ping or ICMP Echo Request to the target host. Sometimes the target doesn't respond to the ICMP Echo Request. In these cases, you can disable the initial ICMP Echo Request sent by Nmap by using the **-P0** option.

As previously stated, several options are available with Nmap. Typing simply **nmap** at the command line will print a relatively verbose set of usage instructions containing many of these options.

HPING2

Hping2 is another network utility that can be used to test for open ports and also to test the behavior of network applications and devices. Hping2 enables the user to set numerous attributes of a network packet, or craft the packet as it's sometimes called. When packets are crafted, the behavior of the network application or device can be observed.

Hping2 is used in Chapter 11 to show how some attacks might look when viewed with TCPDump.

NIKTO

Nikto is a program to test a web server for known vulnerabilities and also to provide information on that web server. Unlike Nmap, Nikto is not included with many Linux distributions with the notable exception that it is available with Debian. Nikto can be downloaded from http://www.cirt.net/code/nikto.shtml.

Because Nikto is web server specific, its coverage will be limited here. However, if you are running a web server, I highly recommend Nikto to test the server for a number of vulnerabilities.

NESSUS

Nessus is a program used to test a huge number of known vulnerabilities by attempting to exploit them. Nessus works through the concept of plug-ins, and with hundreds of plug-ins available Nessus is one of the best security scanners on the market.

Using Nessus, the intrusion analyst can scan for vulnerable software on both local and remote hosts so that those holes can be patched. Nessus is included with some Linux distributions and can be downloaded from http://www.nessus.org/.

Summary

This chapter provided a look at intrusion detection tools and some basic security principles. From things like TCPDump, to sniffer placement, to filesystem integrity, the chapter showed you around the world of intrusion detection.

These intrusion detection tools are best when coupled with security practices such as regular updating, enhanced security measures, and penetration testing to ensure that the security of the system is as you expect.

The next chapter of the book looks more in-depth at network security by examining TCPDump, a key tool in any administrator's toolbox.

Network Monitoring and Attack Detection

This chapter uses the knowledge you've gained throughout the book and in the preceding couple of chapters specifically to show how you might use some of the tools for every day monitoring and also for investigation.

The chapter begins with an overview of network monitoring, or sniffing. The information in the beginning of this chapter builds on what you've already seen in the first two chapters of the book. This chapter then continues with a look at TCPDump, a key tool in the network security analyst's toolkit. Finally, the chapter also looks at two helpful security software packages: Snort and ARPWatch.

Listening to the Ether

Armed with the basic knowledge of some of the core protocols from the first two chapters, you're ready to begin listening to the network. Exactly what you may see when you begin monitoring your network will depend on several factors, not the least of which is the network topology itself.

A modern Ethernet network is a collection of endpoint devices such as computers with network cards, interconnected using a hub or switch. The difference between a hub and a switch is important to both network performance and security. In a hub environment, every Ethernet frame is copied to every port on the hub, and therefore every device connected to the hub. Contrast a hub environment with a switched environment. In a switched environment, the switch sends frames to the specific port to which a given device is connected. In other words, with a switch, traffic goes only to the devices that should receive it. If an intruder can monitor the network in a hub environment, the intruder will see all frames destined for all devices connected to that hub. In a switch environment, the intruder will see only traffic destined for that host or broadcast traffic that is copied to all ports.

Most managed switches enable the administrator to configure a certain port to receive all traffic. Cisco calls this a "span" port, whereas others call it a "mirror" port. In effect, by copying all traffic to the one port on the switch, the administrator can monitor all the traffic for that switch to look for possible intrusions or other anomalies. Of course, this can also be dangerous. If an attacker gains control over the device at the end of that port, the attacker too can listen to everything! Also, in heavy traffic environments performance degradation will likely occur if you attempt to monitor all ports. Therefore, choosing where to monitor your network is important.

If you don't have a managed switch or a switch that enables you to copy all traffic to one port, you'll need to find another means to listen to the traffic. I don't recommend removing the switch in favor of a hub. However, one method would be to connect a hub to the firewall and then connect your intrusion detection or monitoring computer to that hub as well, and finally connect the hub into the main switch. In this way you can monitor internal firewall traffic without (much) performance degradation and without compromising much of the safety that a switch provides.

As I wrote the sentence about the safety of a switch, I was reminded of some types of attacks that enable an attacker to listen to other traffic on a switch, even if it wasn't destined for the port where the attacker resides. These attacks, primarily ARP spoofing, involve interfering with the normal operation of ARP. A good primer on ARP spoofing can be found in the paper "An Introduction to Arp Spoofing," available online at http://packetstormsecurity.org/papers/protocols/intro_to_arp_spoofing.pdf.

Choosing monitoring points within a network is more art than science and is inevitably debatable. There are those who say that only the interior of the network is important to monitor because the firewall will prevent the outside traffic from being important anyway. There are others who maintain that external points should be monitored so that you can see what is being attempted on the network. And there are those, like myself, who believe that both internal and external points should be monitored. Monitoring the internal network is important for hopefully obvious reasons. You can look for anomalous traffic and also monitor for unexpected conditions and performance. However, I believe that monitoring the external network is important as well. I cut my computer security teeth at an Internet provider where everything important was on the external network by nature. Therefore, I was able to see just how valuable it was to know what's happening on the outside as a means to prevent attacks from being successful.

You have to make decisions that work in your environment. It may not make sense to deploy a computer outside of your firewall just for intrusion detection. All security is a trade-off between the assets you are trying to protect and the limited resources available to protect them.

Three Valuable Tools

An ever-growing number of tools and software exist to monitor network traffic. Some of these tools are free (as in price and speech) and some cost quite a bit of money. I've used both the expensive tools and the free ones, and I'm confident in saying that the free ones are better. The expensive tools are weak on functionality but strong on the pretty. The interfaces for many of the products provide a nice "look and feel" (though many of them seem to be somewhat unstable). In general, the open-source tools are a bit more involved to set up and use, but they provide better functionality and with a little work can produce some of the nicest looking graphs and other pictures that the expensive tools provide. For my money, I'd rather have intrusion detection tools that I could use quickly and easily when investigating a potential attack. Dealing with cumbersome, non-intuitive GUIs only gets in the way of the business of intrusion detection.

This section looks at a few monitoring tools with special emphasis on the tools that are covered later in the book.

TCPDUMP

The primary tool in an intrusion detection analyst's toolkit should be TCPDump. TCPDump places a network interface into promiscuous mode so that it captures every packet that arrives. Of course, this means that TCPDump needs to be run from the computer experiencing the possible intrusion or needs to be run from a computer that is the recipient of a "spanned" port in a switch environment. TCPDump is examined in greater detail in the next section.

SNORT

Snort is one of the best intrusion detection systems available, free or otherwise. Snort captures network traffic in much the same way that TCPDump does. However, Snort uses a database of well-known attack signatures to provide a level of detection as well. Whereas TCPDump is more of a manual monitor, Snort is more automated insofar as the analyst doesn't need to manually examine each packet. You can get more information on Snort at http://www.snort.org/.

ARPWATCH

ARPWatch is a tool used to monitor ARP traffic on a network. The goal would be for an administrator to spot possible ARP spoofing attempts as well as unknown devices that have entered the network. ARPWatch can be downloaded from http://www-nrg.ee.lbl.gov/. Like other tools, ARPWatch needs to be compiled before use. ARPWatch is examined later in this chapter, in the section "Monitoring with ARPWatch."

TCPDump: A Simple Overview

Recall what you've read in earlier chapters. You learned about IP addressing, subnetting, and the headers of some of those core protocols. In this chapter the TCPDump tool will be examined and you will see some of those protocols up close and personal. Armed with an understanding of how to monitor your network at this level, you can be confident that you'll be able to troubleshoot a wide range of problems, not just those related to computer security.

An important tool in the intrusion analyst's toolkit is TCPDump. At a basic level, TCPDump is real-time packet capture and analysis software. This means that TCPDump can be used to eavesdrop on network communication as it travels through the network. As has already been mentioned, however, the amount of traffic that one can eavesdrop on is dictated by the network topology. If the computer from which TCPDump is running is connected to a switched network, TCPDump will see only traffic destined for that host or broadcast/multicast traffic. Because TCPDump (and libpcap) are so lightweight, there's really no reason they couldn't be installed onto as many computers as necessary. However, a better approach in a switched network would be to use a "span" port to which will be copied all network traffic by the switch itself. Of course, none of this is of concern in a hub-based network because all traffic is copied to all ports on the hub.

TCPDump places the network interface into promiscuous mode. Before you get too excited, consider that on busy interfaces this means that a huge amount of traffic will be flying past the screen, which has the potential to slow down the traffic ever so slightly. In any event, a large amount of traffic will be too much for a human to comprehend, so you'll want to capture the output to a file, pipe the output to a pager, or filter the traffic to look for something specific. Filtering through a TCPDump expression is by far the best option, but the choices are by no means mutually exclusive. I'll usually use a filter and a pager such as `less`, just in case something interesting flies past my screen too quickly.

TCPDump can filter traffic by virtually any criteria you can imagine. Most commonly for the intrusion analyst, you'll look at traffic by protocol, host, port number, or a combination thereof. Before I go further, I would be remiss if I didn't recommend reading or at least referring to the TCPDump(1) manual page (type `man tcpdump` to read it). The man page is a comprehensive document providing not only syntax but samples of use, as well as some protocol diagrams. If you get stuck trying to use TCPDump and you don't have a copy of this book handy, maybe you should buy two copies of the book. Alternatively, use the TCPDump man page for reference too.

Obtaining and Installing TCPDump

TCPDump can be downloaded from http://www.tcpdump.org/. TCPDump requires the PCap library libpcap, so while you're downloading TCPDump, you should download libpcap as well. Most popular Linux distributions such as SUSE also include TCPDump as an available package. For example, if you're using Debian you can simply type this:

```
apt-get install tcpdump
```

The package maintenance system will install TCPDump and any prerequisites too. For everyone else, you can probably search your distribution's repository for a package or just download the source and compile it, which I would recommend. TCPDump requires the PCap library, which is not usually installed on most systems. Whichever method you choose for installing TCPDump, you'll also need to grab the PCap library, sometimes referred to as libpcap. Both TCPDump and the PCap library can be downloaded from http://www.tcpdump.org/.

Should you attempt to compile TCPDump without having libpcap installed, you'll see an error similar to the following while running the configure script for TCPDump:

```
checking for main in -lpcap... no
configure: error: see the INSTALL doc for more info
```

Installation of both libpcap and TCPDump is fairly straightforward as far as compiling software goes. Unarchive each piece of source code, run the configure script, compile, and install.

In essence:

```
tar -zxvf libpcap-<version>.tar.gz
cd libpcap-<version>
./configure
make
make install
```

Do the same for TCPDump:

```
tar -zxvf tcpdump-<version>.tar.gz
cd tcpdump-<version>
./configure
make
make install
```

Should you encounter problems while compiling the software, refer to previous chapters where the compile process is detailed further or, as an even better solution, practice your analyst skills by troubleshooting the error on the Internet. Chances are that someone else has encountered and solved the problem that you're working through.

TCPDump Options

TCPDump accepts a wide range of command-line options that alter its behavior, the amount of data captured, and the way in which the data is captured. Such a wide range of options means that you have the power to significantly change how the program operates. For TCPDump, you'll find that you frequently use a common set of options for most data capture activities, and you may not use others at all.

Some of the more commonly used options include those listed in Table 11.1.

TABLE 11.1
Some Common Options for TCPDump

OPTION	DESCRIPTION
-i <interface>	Specifies the interface to use.
-v	Produces output in verbose mode.
-vv	Produces output in really verbose mode.
-x	Causes TCPDump to print the packet itself in hexadecimal format.
-X	Causes TCPDump to also print the output in ASCII.
-n	Tells TCPDump not to perform DNS lookups for the IP addresses seen during the capture.
-F <file>	Reads the expression from <file>.
-D	Prints available interfaces.
-s <length>	Sets the length for each packet of the capture to <length>.

Examining each of these options in turn reveals the steps necessary for performing basic packet capture and analysis. Not all of these options are necessarily required to capture traffic with TCPDump (in fact, none of them is required). It's perfectly valid to simply type the **tcpdump** command on the command line to start capturing traffic. However, in practice many of these options are necessary to gain the level of detail needed in order to properly analyze the traffic.

The -i <interface> option changes the default interface on which TCPDump will listen for packets to capture. By default, TCPDump will listen on the first interface, **eth0**. However, for multihomed machines it may be necessary to use this option so that the correct traffic is captured. For example, on a firewall the **eth0** interface might be connected to the internal network while the **eth1** interface is connected to the Internet. You may be interested in seeing the traffic that's hitting your external interface (**eth1**); thus, you would use the -i <interface> option in TCPDump.

The verbose mode options, -v, -vv, and -vvv (not included in Table 11.1), cause TCPDump to print more (and more, and more) information about each packet received. With -v this information includes such important things as the TTL, packet ID, length, and options. Experimentation is usually necessary during a packet capture to determine which of these options will suit your needs. Different protocols may not have much (or any) additional information to print, so adding verbosity with these switches won't do any good.

The -x option causes TCPDump to also print hex dumps of each packet. For my eyes, this option isn't particularly helpful because I don't read hex so well. However, using the lowercase -x is required to take advantage of the ASCI dump of the packets that can be had by using the uppercase -X. Therefore, I'll rarely if ever use just -x and instead use both -x and -X. Although some parts of the packet may be printed by using just -X, using both can be helpful.

A sometimes-helpful option out of the most common options is the -s <length> option. Using this option is helpful to print the contents of packets themselves rather than the default 68 bytes only. If you're only interested in the headers of packets, this option won't be much, if any, use. However, if you'd like to peek inside the packet itself, this option will help to ensure that the packet capture isn't truncated.

An option that becomes more useful the more you use TCPDump is the -F <file> option. This option tells TCPDump to read the contents of <file> for the filter expression rather than reading the command line. This option is very handy for longer expressions or expressions that are used frequently (or even infrequently). After using TCPDump for a while, you may get tired of typing the same old filter expression to capture the same packets week after week. Storing that expression in a file and then reading the expression from the file when using TCPDump is a great way to save time.

When just starting out with TCPDump, an option that you may find useful is the -D option. The -D option informs TCPDump to print a list of interfaces on which you can perform the packet capture. Because packet captures are interface dependent, knowing which interface to use is the most important thing you will have to choose. In Linux, it's somewhat easier to choose the right interface because interface names are usually simple, like eth0 for the first Ethernet card. However, in Windows, -D is much more important because interface names can be quite difficult to remember.

A final option worth noting is the -n option. Using -n tells TCPDump not to perform reverse DNS lookups on the hosts as it sees them during the capture. Doing reverse lookups frequently slows down packet capture and naturally also increases the amount of traffic. Therefore, adding -n is helpful for speeding up the capture as well as reducing the signal-to-noise ratio. When I forget to set the -n option, I sometimes find myself asking, "Why is this machine performing DNS lookups?" only to realize that the lookups are the result of my packet capture activity.

TCPDump Expressions

Now the fun begins. By default, TCPDump will capture and output every packet that hits the interface. Sometimes this is useful for quickly listening to some traffic on a quiet interface. However, most captures will make use of expressions in TCPDump. A TCPDump expression is a collection of criteria for network traffic that you'd like to view with TCPDump. Expressions consist of one or more qualifiers and possibly a primitive, both of which are discussed in the following subsections. An expression might be used to capture only traffic that originates from a certain host or that is destined for a certain host. The possibilities with expressions and combinations of expressions give you the ability to hone in on exactly the packets you need to see to assess a given network situation.

One of the more powerful features of expressions is the capability to negate. For instance, if you want to listen to all traffic except network traffic on port **80** (usually http traffic), you could have TCPDump capture all traffic except that which is transmitted or received on port **80**. TCPDump can also use other logical terms as well, such as **AND**, **OR**, and the already mentioned negation keyword **NOT**.

TCPDump expressions are enclosed within single quotes (') and can be grouped together by enclosing the various parts of a given expression within parentheses. This means that you can combine multiple expressions to capture only that traffic that is of interest. The key to grouping expressions together is the use of the logical terms **AND**, **OR**, and **NOT**. TCPDump has three qualifiers, each of which is introduced in turn in the discussion that follows. The first kind of qualifier is the type qualifier.

TCPDUMP'S TYPE QUALIFIER

Just as TCPDump has three kinds of qualifiers, the type qualifier itself contains three variations: host, port, and net. The host qualifier is used to specify the host or destination of interesting traffic. The port type qualifier is not surprisingly used to specify the port on which to capture packets. The net type is used to specify the subnet for interesting traffic. You could use the net qualifier in an expression to listen for traffic on an entire range of addresses. Of course, there are times when you don't want to listen to an entire range of addresses. TCPDump also accepts the modifier **mask** with the net qualifier to specify the subnet mask. You can also use CIDR notation to specify the mask bits.

Before I go further, here's an example of a TCPDump expression to capture traffic on port **80**:

```
tcpdump 'port 80'
```

Because this expression uses only a single criterion (port **80**) there's no need to enclose it within parentheses. If, however, the goal was to capture traffic on port **80** with a source or destination of one or more specific hosts, say **192.168.1.10** and **192.168.1.11**, then parentheses would be required, as in this example:

```
tcpdump 'port 80 and (host 192.168.1.10 or host 192.168.1.11)'
```

Parentheses are required only for logical grouping. In practice, you'll suffer no penalty for using them, and truthfully I normally use them just out of habit. When writing the preceding simple port **80** example, I included the parentheses at first only to go back and remove them after I thought about what I was doing. Old habits die hard. Speaking of unnecessary terms, the term **host** in the example isn't required either—more on that later.

Here are some examples using the net type qualifier to listen for traffic:

```
tcpdump 'net 192.168.1'
```

Here's that same example using CIDR notation:

```
tcpdump 'net 192.168.1.0/24'
```

And finally, here's that same example using the mask modifier:

```
tcpdump 'net 192.168.1.0 mask 255.255.255.0'
```

If you fail to specify a type qualifier (host, net, port) within a TCPDump expression, the host type is assumed. Therefore, don't be surprised when you receive a "parse error" when attempting something like this:

```
tcpdump '80'
```

Really, you probably wanted to have TCPDump listen for traffic on port **80**:

```
tcpdump 'port 80'
```

TCPDUMP'S DIRECTION QUALIFIER

Another kind of qualifier within a TCPDump expression is the direction qualifier. The previous examples will look for traffic flowing in either direction, coming or going, on port **80** for instance. For example, this might mean that traffic destined for a web server running at **192.168.1.10** will be captured but so will traffic leaving the computer at **192.168.1.10** and destined for another server on port **80**. You can also specify the direction with which to capture traffic by using a direction qualifier. The terms **src** for the source and **dst** for the destination are the two direction qualifiers used by TCPDump. Adding the destination term to one of the previous examples yields an expression that will look for port **80** traffic going to **192.168.1.10** or **192.168.1.11**:

```
tcpdump 'port 80 and (src 192.168.1.10 or src 192.168.1.11)'
```

The direction qualifier isn't limited to looking for traffic on certain addresses. It's perfectly valid to look for traffic with a source or destination of a specific port, as in this example that looks for traffic with a destination of port **25** (usually SMTP):

```
tcpdump 'dst port 25'
```

Some protocols use the terms **inbound** and **outbound** to specify the direction. See the TCPDump man page for more details.

TCPDUMP'S PROTOCOL QUALIFIER

A final kind of qualifier for use in a TCPDump expression is the protocol qualifier. Not surprisingly, protocol qualifiers enable you to choose which protocols should be captured with TCPDump. The protocols that can be captured with TCPDump include, among others, Ethernet (abbreviated **ether** for TCPDump syntax), TCP, UDP, ICMP, IP, IPv6 (abbreviated **ip6** for TCPDump syntax), ARP, reverse ARP (abbreviated to **rarp**), and more.

PRIMITIVES

Aside from the main three qualifiers (type, direction, and protocol), there are also what are known as primitives for use in TCPDump expressions. Primitives are keywords that help to specify additional parameters for the packet capture. The primitives for use with TCPDump include these:

- Arithmetic operators
- broadcast
- gateway
- greater
- less

The arithmetic operators include +, -, *, /, >, <, >=, <=, =, !=, and a few others. TCPDump can use quite complex arithmetic operators and packet offsets to look into packets. I'd prefer to leave it as an exercise for the reader to dive into these areas should you find it necessary to do so.

The **broadcast** primitive, when prepended with either **ip** or **ether**, will look for packets that are IP or Ethernet broadcasts respectively, though **ether** is the default type to look for. For example, a TCPDump expression looking for **ip broadcast** will search for broadcasts on an IP network. However, if the interface card on which TCPDump is listening has no subnet mask or if the **any** interface is being used, this **broadcast** primitive will not work.

The primitives **greater** and **less** are used to search for packets with a length greater than or equal to or less than or equal to the given length. These primitives are functionally equivalent to using the arithmetic operators for the same. So for example, the syntax

```
len >= 1500
```

is equivalent to this:

`greater 1500`

Beyond the Basics with TCPDump

You should now have a feel for the basic syntax of TCPDump, including some of the options, the syntax, and TCPDump expressions. The amount of troubleshooting and diagnosis that can be accomplished with even a basic grasp of TCPDump syntax makes it an essential tool for anyone managing networked computers. However, even a basic knowledge of TCPDump is sometimes insufficient to examine some problems successfully. To examine more difficult problems, you may find that you need to go beyond the basics of TCPDump.

Going beyond the basics of TCPDump requires deeper understanding of the protocols themselves. Knowing the flags of TCP or the types of ICMP can help to narrow the focus to only the packets of interest. Although this information and knowing how to use it with TCPDump is not mandatory, having the ability to call on the information at any time is valuable to say the least. Take time to familiarize yourself with TCPDump's more involved syntax. It costs nothing but time to test a packet-filtering expression to see how it works under various network conditions.

Using TCPDump to Capture Specific Protocols

In this section, I'll give some examples that show you how to capture various forms of network traffic for monitoring purposes. Included among the examples, you'll see what a DNS query looks like through TCPDump, some ICMP (ping) examples, and various TCP- and UDP-based protocols. After you see how normal traffic looks, I'll then show you some of the fun stuff. Specifically, I'll show what some types of attacks look like through TCPDump so that you might be able to quickly detect these when coming into (or out of) your network.

Throughout this section, I'll be using a few different programs to generate traffic for TCPDump to capture. My primary tool for TCP-related captures will be telnet. I'll use telnet to generate traffic and mirror what the real protocol (or close to it) does in the real world. Generation of DNS queries will be accomplished using both the `dig` command and the `host` command. The `ping` and `traceroute` commands will be used. Finally, the `hping2` command will be used to generate ICMP traffic as well as other interesting packets, especially in the attack section. With the exception of hping2, all of these programs are installed on most major Linux distributions.

Using TCPDump in the Real World

So far in this chapter, you've seen a number of examples for using TCPDump to capture various types of traffic. These examples were given to show the usage of TCPDump in relation to expressions and other options. Now it's time to give you real-life examples of using TCPDump to capture specific types of traffic. The situations in which you might use these examples will vary, but I'll try to give some clue as to why you might use a given example, where I can. It might be helpful to see how a filter expression is built when trying to capture in the real world. I briefly touched on this topic earlier. However, before giving recipe-type solutions, I'll show you how to build a filter with the specific goal of capturing an HTTP conversation.

BUILDING A FILTER TO CAPTURE AN HTTP CONVERSATION

HTTP is the language of the Web. Usually HTTP rides over TCP, which in turn rides on IP. I'm choosing HTTP as the first real-world capture only because people are generally familiar with browsing a web page, even though they may not be familiar with the underlying protocol.

Recall that IP is a connectionless protocol whereas TCP is a connection-oriented protocol. TCP uses a three-way handshake to begin a conversation. HTTP takes advantage of the connection-oriented nature of TCP and in fact knows nothing of lower-layered (remember the OSI model) protocols. As far as HTTP is concerned, it hands its data down to the next lower layer and is done. To that end, when an HTTP conversation is initiated, the first thing you should see through TCPDump is the three-way handshake of TCP followed by protocol-specific data.

For the most part, HTTP traffic flows to a destination of port **80**.

NOTE

The ports on which various services normally operate can be found by examining the file /etc/services. With that in mind, the true source for port-number assignments is IANA. You can view the most current and complete list of official port-number assignments at the URL http://www.iana.org/assignments/port-numbers. However, remember that there's nothing preventing someone from running a service on a port other than the official port numbers!

Because HTTP is usually found on port **80**, it would be a good idea to start with a basic TCPDump expression that looked only for port 80 traffic, such as this one:

```
tcpdump 'port 80'
```

Running that command and then generating some traffic by surfing to a web page yields these results:

```
tcpdump: verbose output suppressed, use -v or -vv for full protocol decode
listening on eth0, link-type EN10MB (Ethernet), capture size 96 bytes

17:15:38.934337 IP client.braingia.org.4485 > test.example.com.www: \
        S 523004834:523004834(0) win 5840 \
            <mss 1460,sackOK,timestamp 249916003 0,nop,wscale 0>

17:15:38.984650 IP test.example.com.www > client.braingia.org.4485: S \
        2810959978:2810959978(0) ack 523004835 win 5792 \
            <mss 1460,sackOK,timestamp 1320060704 249916003,nop,wscale 0>

17:15:38.984684 IP client.braingia.org.4485 > test.example.com.www: \
        . ack 1 win 5840 <nop,nop,timestamp 249916008 1320060704>

17:15:38.985326 IP client.braingia.org.4485 > test.example.com.www: \
        P 1:462(461) ack 1 win 5840 <nop,nop,timestamp 249916008 1320060704>

17:15:39.038067 IP test.example.com.www > client.braingia.org.4485: . \
        ack 462 win 6432 <nop,nop,timestamp 1320060710 249916008>

17:15:39.065141 IP test.example.com.www > client.braingia.org.4485: . \
        1:1449(1448) ack 462 win 6432 <nop,nop,timestamp 1320060712 249916008>

17:15:39.065183 IP client.braingia.org.4485 > test.example.com.www: . \
        ack 1449 win 8688 <nop,nop,timestamp 249916016 1320060712>
```

NOTE

I've separated the results for greater readability, and I'll continue to do so throughout the rest of this chapter.

Notice the first two lines from the TCPDump output. In this case, the first line tells me that I really should have more verbose output enabled in order to see anything interesting within the packet, and the second line gives a status of the interface on which TCPDump is listening, as well as the size of the capture.

The next line is the first line of the capture and is also coincidentally the first packet (SYN) sent in the TCP three-way handshake. The first thing you'll notice on the line is a timestamp, followed by the protocol (IP). Next is the hostname of the computer that initiated the packet (client.braingia.org) together with the source port for the traffic (4485). This combination, source computer and source port, are known as the Source. The greater-than sign (>) shows the direction of the flow in relation to the Destination for this traffic, which, as you can see from that line, is test.example.com.www. The www signifies the destination port that the traffic is headed for on the destination computer.

The next item of interest on the TCPDump output line is the Flags section, in this case indicated by an uppercase **S**. Recall from Chapter 1, "Preliminary Concepts Underlying Packet-Filtering Firewalls," that the TCP header can contain various flags to indicate certain conditions for the packet. If you guessed that **S** indicates a packet with the **SYN** flag set, you may have just won a valuable prize. Following the Flags section is the Sequence Number space for the packet, indicating the sequence numbers that will be covered within this packet. In the case of the example, the Sequence Number space (**523004834:523004834(0)**) is zero length. The next item on this line is the Window size, as indicated by the **win 5840** in the output. Finally, enclosed within brackets are options contained in the packet. Although these options can be of interest at certain times, you'll rarely need to care much about them in the real world.

You've now seen one single packet of a TCP three-way handshake through TCPDump. Don't worry, it does get more exciting than this, really it does. The next line contained in the capture contains the response packet coming back from **test.example.com**. Notice that the time-stamp has increased and the protocol is still IP. However, now the source computer is **test.example.com** on port 80 and the destination is **client.braingia.org.4485**. Notice also that the **SYN** flag is set as evidenced by the **S** following the source > destination area. The sequence number space is different now though, **2810959978:2810959978(0)**. This is because **test.example.com** chose its own sequence number as part of the process. The first difference of real interest because we haven't seen it before is the **ack 523004835**. This is the second part of the TCP three-way handshake, namely, what's commonly referred to as the **SYN-ACK** packet. In this packet, the original destination computer is answering or acknowledging the call to initiate a TCP connection on the specified port. Notice that the number following the **ack** is equal to the original sequence number (**523004834**) plus one. This is the protocol itself in action.

The third packet in the capture, depicted again here for reference, is the final packet in the connection setup for TCP:

```
17:15:38.984684 IP client.braingia.org.4485 > test.example.com.www:  . \
        ack 1 win 5840 <nop,nop,timestamp 249916008 1320060704>
```

In this packet, the original source acknowledges the connection setup. Notice that there is a single dot (.) where the flags would normally show up. This usually means that there are no flags set; however, some flags like **ACK** show up in a different place on the output line. The source side sets the **ACK** flag and also sets an initial sequence number for this connection. At this point, the TCP connection is said to be established. That sure seems like a lot of work, but didn't I promise that this section was about HTTP? Sure enough. The next packets with capture output indicate that an HTTP connection is progressing:

```
17:15:38.985326 IP client.braingia.org.4485 > test.example.com.www: \
        P 1:462(461) ack 1 win 5840 <nop,nop,timestamp 249916008 1320060704>

17:15:39.038067 IP test.example.com.www > client.braingia.org.4485: . ack \
        462 win 6432 <nop,nop,timestamp 1320060710 249916008>

17:15:39.065141 IP test.example.com.www > client.braingia.org.4485: . \
        1:1449(1448) ack 462 win 6432 <nop,nop,timestamp 1320060712 249916008>

17:15:39.065183 IP client.braingia.org.4485 > test.example.com.www: . \
        ack 1449 win 8688 <nop,nop,timestamp 249916016 1320060712>
```

The source sends the beginning of the data for this communication. Notice that the PUSH flag was set in the initial packet and that the sequence numbers increment. The two sides acknowledge sequence numbers and data is transferred. But with the TCPDump command that I ran (`tcpdump 'port 80'`), there isn't much else to see. Therefore, I'll improve that command to include the options I normally include to peek inside the packets. I'll leave it up to the reader to see what each of the options actually does, as explained earlier in the chapter. Here's the improved command for TCPDump:

```
tcpdump -vv -x -X -s 1500 'port 80'
```

With this command running, I can then generate additional web traffic. Here are two-and-a-half packets from the result, picking up from just after the three-way handshake:

```
18:18:51.986230 IP (tos 0x0, ttl 64, id 10907, offset 0, flags [DF], \
        length: 513) client.braingia.org.4564 > test.example.com.www: \
                P [tcp sum ok] 1:462(461) ack 1 win 5840 <nop,nop,timestamp
                        250295308 1320440053>
0x0000:  0090 2741 78f0 00e0 1833 2ee8 0800 4500   ..'Ax....3....E.
0x0010:  0201 2a9b 4000 4006 044b c0a8 010a 455d   ..*.@.@..K....E]
0x0020:  0302 11d4 0050 0c9b 1ea0 9627 33f8 8018   .....P.....'3...
0x0030:  16d0 4915 0000 0101 080a 0eeb 340c 4eb4   ..I.........4.N.
0x0040:  50f5 4745 5420 2f20 4854 5450 2f31 2e30   P.GET./.HTTP/1.0
0x0050:  0d0a 486f 7374 3a20 7777 772e 6272 6169   ..Host:.text.exam
0x0060:  6e67 6961 2e6f 7267 0d0a 4163 6365 7074   ple.com..Accept
0x0070:  3a20 7465 7874 2f68 746d 6c2c 2074 6578   :.text/html,.tex
0x0080:  742f 706c 6169 6e2c 2061 7070 6c69 6361   t/plain,.applica
0x0090:  7469 6f6e 2f6d 7377 6f72 642c 2061 7070   tion/msword,.app
0x00a0:  6c69 6361 7469 6f6e 2f70 6466 2c20 6170   lication/pdf,.ap
0x00b0:  706c 6963 6174 696f 6e2f 6f63 7465 742d   plication/octet-
0x00c0:  7374 7265 616d 2c20 6170 706c 6963 6174   stream,.applicat
0x00d0:  696f 6e2f 782d 7472 6f66 662d 6d61 6e2c   ion/x-troff-man,
0x00e0:  2061 7070 6c69 6361 7469 6f6e 2f78 2d74   .application/x-t
0x00f0:  6172 2c20 6170 706c 6963 6174 696f 6e2f   ar,.application/
0x0100:  782d 6774 6172 2c20 6170 706c 6963 6174   x-gtar,.applicat
0x0110:  696f 6e2f 7274 662c 2061 7070 6c69 6361   ion/rtf,.applica
```

```
0x0120: 7469 6f6e 2f70 6f73 7473 6372 6970 742c   tion/postscript,
0x0130: 2061 7070 6c69 6361 7469 6f6e 2f67 686f    .application/gho
0x0140: 7374 7669 6577 2c20 7465 7874 2f2a 0d0a   stview,.text/*..
0x0150: 4163 6365 7074 3a20 6170 706c 6963 6174   Accept:.applicat
0x0160: 696f 6e2f 782d 6465 6269 616e 2d70 6163   ion/x-debian-pac
0x0170: 6b61 6765 2c20 6175 6469 6f2f 6261 7369   kage,.audio/basi
0x0180: 632c 202a 2f2a 3b71 3d30 2e30 310d 0a41   c,.*/*;q=0.01..A
0x0190: 6363 6570 742d 456e 636f 6469 6e67 3a20   ccept-Encoding:.
0x01a0: 677a 6970 2c20 636f 6d70 7265 7373 0d0a   gzip,.compress..
0x01b0: 4163 6365 7074 2d4c 616e 6775 6167 653a   Accept-Language:
0x01c0: 2065 6e0d 0a55 7365 722d 4167 656e 743a   .en..User-Agent:
0x01d0: 204c 796e 782f 322e 382e 3472 656c 2e31   .Lynx/2.8.4rel.1
0x01e0: 206c 6962 7777 772d 464d 2f32 2e31 3420   .libwww-FM/2.14.
0x01f0: 5353 4c2d 4d4d 2f31 2e34 2e31 204f 7065   SSL-MM/1.4.1.Ope
0x0200: 6e53 534c 2f30 2e39 2e36 630d 0a0d 0a     nSSL/0.9.6c....
18:18:52.039595 IP (tos 0x0, ttl 48, id 25346, offset 0, flags [DF], \
        length: 52) test.example.com.www > client.braingia.org.4564: .
                 [tcp sum ok] 1:1(0) ack 462 win 6432 <nop,nop,timestamp
                        1320440059 250295308>
0x0000: 00e0 1833 2ee8 0090 2741 78f0 0800 4500   ...3....'Ax...E.
0x0010: 0034 6302 4000 3006 ddb0 455d 0302 c0a8   .4c.@.0...E]....
0x0020: 010a 0050 11d4 9627 33f8 0c9b 206d 8010   ...P...'3....m..
0x0030: 1920 6799 0000 0101 080a 4eb4 50fb 0eeb   ..g.......N.P...
0x0040: 340c                                      4.
18:18:52.047021 IP (tos 0x0, ttl 48, id 25347, offset 0, flags [DF], \
        length: 1500) test.example.com.www > client.braingia.org.4564:\
                 . 1:1449(1448) ack 462 win 6432 <nop,nop,timestamp \
                        1320440059 250295308>
0x0000: 00e0 1833 2ee8 0090 2741 78f0 0800 4500   ...3....'Ax...E.
0x0010: 05dc 6303 4000 3006 d807 455d 0302 c0a8   ..c.@.0...E]....
0x0020: 010a 0050 11d4 9627 33f8 0c9b 206d 8010   ...P...'3....m..
0x0030: 1920 b9f7 0000 0101 080a 4eb4 50fb 0eeb   .........N.P...
0x0040: 340c 4854 5450 2f31 2e31 2032 3030 204f   4.HTTP/1.1.200.O
0x0050: 4b0d 0a44 6174 653a 2054 7565 2c20 3237   K..Date:.Tue,.27
0x0060: 204a 756c 2032 3030 3420 3233 3a31 393a   .Jul.2004.23:19:
0x0070: 3030 2047 4d54 0d0a 5365 7276 6572 3a20   00.GMT..Server:.
0x0080: 4170 6163 6865 2f31 2e33 2e32 3620 2855   Apache/1.3.26.(U
0x0090: 6e69 7829 2044 6562 6961 6e20 474e 552f   nix).Debian.GNU/
0x00a0: 4c69 6e75 7820 6d6f 645f 6d6f 6e6f 2f30   Linux.mod_mono/0
0x00b0: 2e31 3120 6d6f 645f 7065 726c 2f31 2e32   .11.mod_perl/1.2
0x00c0: 360d 0a43 6f6e 6e65 6374 696f 6e3a 2063   6..Connection:.c
0x00d0: 6c6f 7365 0d0a 436f 6e74 656e 742d 5479   lose..Content-Ty
0x00e0: 7065 3a20 7465 7874 2f68 746d 6c3b 2063   pe:.text/html;.c
0x00f0: 6861 7273 6574 3d69 736f 2d38 3835 392d   harset=iso-8859-
```

Notice that this output contains an actual request (see the first packet, near GET./.HTTP/1.0) and also contains a portion of the response from the web server. All of this traffic is in plain text because HTTP is not encrypted. This output contains both hex and ASCII. To obtain output with just ASCII, remove the -x and -X from the command and replace them with a single -A. I personally find the dual hex and ASCII output to be helpful at times.

That's all there is to capturing HTTP traffic with TCPDump. Obvious improvements for the command would be to expand the expression to look for a specific source or destination. It's important to understand that only traffic on port **80** will be found with the command as given. If you're running HTTP traffic on another port, substitute that port instead of (or in addition to) the port found in the sample command.

CAPTURING AN SMTP CONVERSATION

Capturing an SMTP conversation is not unlike capturing an HTTP session. Begin with the basic TCPDump options that you'd like to use and then build an expression to grab the appropriate type of data, including protocol, port, and source or destination hosts. For example, here's a simple capture of port **25** traffic along with my normal TCPDump choice of options:

```
tcpdump -vv -x -X -s 1500 'port 25'
```

The TCP three-way handshake is again present, as you might expect:

```
20:40:08.638690 murphy.debian.org.45772 > test.example.com.smtp: \
        S [tcp sum ok] 1485971964:1485971964(0) win 5840 <mss 1460,
            sackOK,timestamp 795074473 0,nop,ws cale 0> (DF) \
                    (ttl 57, id 65109, len 60)
0x0000   4500 003c fe55 4000 3906 deae 9252 8a06     E..<.U@.9....R..
0x0010   455d 0302 b2cc 0019 5892 21fc 0000 0000     E]......X.!.....
0x0020   a002 16d0 8ffe 0000 0204 05b4 0402 080a     ...............
0x0030   2f63 dfa9 0000 0000 0103 0300              /c.........
20:40:08.638769 test.example.com.smtp > murphy.debian.org.45772: S \
        [tcp sum ok] 2853594323:2853594323(0) ack 1485971965 win 5792 \
            <mss 1460,sackOK,timestamp 132 1286843 795074473,nop,wscale 0> \
                    (DF) (ttl 64, id 0, len 60)
0x0000   4500 003c 0000 4000 4006 d604 455d 0302     E..<..@.@...E]..
0x0010   9252 8a06 0019 b2cc aa16 64d3 5892 21fd     .R........d.X.!.
0x0020   a012 16a0 f5b6 0000 0204 05b4 0402 080a     ...............
0x0030   4ec1 3cbb 2f63 dfa9 0103 0300              N.<./c......
20:40:08.640600 murphy.debian.org.45772 > test.example.com.smtp: . \
        [tcp sum ok] 1:1(0) ack 1 win 5840 <nop,nop,timestamp \
            795074473 1321286843> (DF) (ttl 57, id 65110, len 52)
0x0000   4500 0034 fe56 4000 3906 deb5 9252 8a06     E..4.V@.9....R..
0x0010   455d 0302 b2cc 0019 5892 21fd aa16 64d4     E]......X.!...d.
0x0020   8010 16d0 244c 0000 0101 080a 2f63 dfa9     ....$L......./c..
0x0030   4ec1 3cbb                                   N.<.
```

There's nothing really new of interest during the three-way handshake process. Notice that the ASCII output isn't of much use during the three-way handshake though.

As with HTTP, after the initial TCP handshake is done, the SMTP conversation gets underway:

```
20:40:08.683352 test.example.com.smtp > murphy.debian.org.45772: P \
        [tcp sum ok] 1:51(50) ack 1 win 5792 <nop,nop,timestamp \
             1321286848 795074473> (DF) (ttl 64,id 22639, len 102)
0x0000   4500 0066 586f 4000 4006 7d6b 455d 0302    E..fXo@.@.}kE]..
0x0010   9252 8a06 0019 b2cc aa16 64d4 5892 21fd    .R........d.X.!.
0x0020   8018 16a0 bd07 0000 0101 080a 4ec1 3cc0    ............N.<.
0x0030   2f63 dfa9 3232 3020 6466 7730 2e69 6367    /c..220.test.exa
0x0040   6d65 6469 612e 636f 6d20 4553 4d54 5020    mple.com.ESMTP.
0x0050   506f 7374 6669 7820 2844 6562 6961 6e2f    Postfix.(Debian/
0x0060   474e 5529 0d0a                             GNU)..
20:40:08.684581 murphy.debian.org.45772 > test.example.com.smtp: . [tcp sum ok]
 1:1(0) ack 51 win 5840 <nop,nop,timestamp 795074478 1321286848> (DF) (ttl 57, i
d 65111, len 52)
0x0000   4500 0034 fe57 4000 3906 deb4 9252 8a06    E..4.W@.9....R..
0x0010   455d 0302 b2cc 0019 5892 21fd aa16 6506    E]......X.!...e.
0x0020   8010 16d0 2410 0000 0101 080a 2f63 dfae    ....$......./c..
0x0030   4ec1 3cc0                                   N.<.
20:40:08.685428 murphy.debian.org.45772 > test.example.com.smtp: P [tcp sum ok]
 1:25(24) ack 51 win 5840 <nop,nop,timestamp 795074478 1321286848> (DF) (ttl 57,
 id 65112, len 76)
0x0000   4500 004c fe58 4000 3906 de9b 9252 8a06    E..L.X@.9....R..
0x0010   455d 0302 b2cc 0019 5892 21fd aa16 6506    E]......X.!...e.
0x0020   8018 16d0 3cc4 0000 0101 080a 2f63 dfae    ....<......./c..
0x0030   4ec1 3cc0 4548 4c4f 206d 7572 7068 792e    N.<.EHLO.murphy.
0x0040   6465 6269 616e 2e6f 7267 0d0a              debian.org..
```

CAPTURING AN SSH CONVERSATION

Although it's not possible to actually capture an SSH conversation, you can look at some of the connection setup portions of the protocol. Because SSH is encrypted, though, none of the credentials or other data during the actual session is available for you to view. It should be noted, however, that if you can gain access to the private key of the server, you could theoretically decrypt the contents of the SSH connection. Doing this is well beyond the scope of this text.

I'll leave it as an exercise for the reader to capture an SSH connection, including setup, should you want to view what a normal connection looks like for SSH.

CAPTURING OTHER TCP-BASED PROTOCOLS

Capturing other TCP-based protocols follows much the same process as that in the examples shown. For example, capturing POP3 connections can be accomplished and the entire stream can be captured because POP3, like SMTP, is not encrypted during transit. One protocol is of particular interest because it has confounded network administrators for a long time. That protocol is FTP.

FTP utilizes two TCP ports, 20 and 21. Port 21 is normally used for commands and is sometimes referred to as the control channel. Port 20 in FTP is used for data and is sometimes aptly titled the data channel. Therefore, if you want to capture FTP traffic with TCPDump, you need to grab both ports 20 and 21 to see everything.

A trend over the past few years has been protocols that use nonstandard ports to circumvent firewalls and packet capturing and filtering. Such programs, including much of the peer-to-peer software, can be somewhat difficult to find during packet captures because most of the data during the conversation is binary and is thus not human-readable.

CAPTURING A DNS QUERY

TCPDump handles DNS queries a little differently than a packet that's simply TCP. More information can be gleaned from just the initial packet result line as opposed to making it necessary to increase the **snaplen** with the -s option. For example, consider the following trace of a simple DNS query that was looking for the IP address of a host named www.braingia.org:

```
21:18:39.289121 192.168.1.10.1514 > 192.168.1.1.53: 60792+ A?
➡ www.braingia.org. (34) (DF)

21:18:39.289568 192.168.1.1.53 > 192.168.1.10.1514: 60792*- 1/2/
➡2 A 192.168.1.50 (118) (DF)
```

In the packet trace we see host **192.168.1.10** on an ephemeral port communicating with a destination of **192.168.1.1** on port **53**. A query ID number is given; in this case it's **60792**. You see the query ID number is followed by a **+**. This symbol indicates that the querier asked for recursion on this query. The **A?** on the trace line indicates that this was an address query. The query was for **www.braingia.org**, as is shown, and the size of the query is 34 bytes, which does not include IP or UDP overhead.

The answer comes quickly, as we see in the next line of the trace, which shows that the source is now **192.168.1.1** talking to the destination of **192.168.1.10**. As you can see, the answer was contained in the same query ID, **60792**; however, this time there are two extra characters, the ***** and the **-**. The ***** in a response indicates that this is an authoritative answer, and the **-** indicates that recursion is available and not set. The next portion of the response, **1/2/2**, indicates the number of answer records (1), the number of name server records (2), and the number of additional records (2). The first answer given in this case is of type A and is **192.168.1.50**. Finally, the size of the response is given to be 118 bytes.

CAPTURING PINGS

Although it may seem innocent enough, ICMP (the protocol behind ping) has been used fairly often as a means by which to attack hosts and otherwise wreak havoc. Therefore, as a security analyst, an administrator, or a curious bystander, you should know that it's in your best interest to see some of the normal activity for ICMP through TCPDump so that you might be able to spot an anomaly later.

I'll go out onto a limb and say that ICMP is most frequently used for the simple Echo Request and Echo Reply provided by ping. However, ICMP can be and is used for much more than that including informing a fast sender when to slow down (Source Quench), redirecting to other hosts (Redirect), and many other areas. Refer to Chapter 1 for more information on ICMP, or, as always, refer to the original RFC on ICMP for the authoritative information on the protocol.

Attacks Through the Eyes of TCPDump

You've seen what normal TCP and UDP packet traces look like through TCPDump, but how will you know whether someone or something is acting abnormally? Unfortunately, finding nefarious activity is not that easy. Buried in normal packet traces may be signs that someone is attempting an attack on your server. An attacker will obviously attempt to disguise his activity, making detection even more difficult. Not only do you have to wade through all the normal traffic within a packet trace, but you then have to search for the proverbial needle in a haystack to find what may be an attack attempt or even one in progress.

Recall from Chapter 10, "Intrusion Detection Tools," that not everything that falls outside of normal activity can be termed an attack. Some of it is the result of malfunctioning or misconfigured equipment. More often than not, abnormal activity spotted in a packet trace is due to reconnaissance of one form or another. And the large majority of reconnaissance work is done through automation. Rather than spending many fruitless hours searching for a vulnerable host, attackers will automate the process and have the program alert them when it finds an interesting host.

There are naturally exceptions to the rule of automation. Attacks may be the result of directed activity against your server or network. Before the attack there is usually some manual reconnaissance that takes place. This may include the would-be attacker manually crafting or creating packets to attempt to exploit possible holes in your server or network. More often than not, however, the attacker will have had some automated recon data that directed his or her efforts in your direction. If an automated scan alerted the attacker that one of your servers may be vulnerable to a particular type of attack, you may find the hosts or your entire subnet within the sights of the attacker.

Leaving a host vulnerable or making a host appear vulnerable and then observing the attacks is the premise behind a honeypot. A honeypot is a host or device that shows up as vulnerable to an attacker and thus looks like a target for attack. The idea is that by watching the methods that attackers use to exploit a hole or watching what they do when they compromise the host, the observer can learn from it and defend against such activity.

As if all the possible reasons already given for seeing abnormal activity aren't enough, here's one more: You'll also encounter accidental connections that may appear to be attacks. In other words, at times someone simply mistypes an IP address when attempting to connect to his or her server. Anyone who has ever answered the telephone only to find out that the caller dialed incorrectly can relate to this situation.

In summary, there are some basic categories within which abnormal activity might fall:

- Automated or semiautomated recon scan
- Directed attack
- Misconfigured equipment
- Wrong number
- Malfunctioning equipment

With those categories in mind, this section examines some abnormal packet traces or traces that you shouldn't see under normal conditions. By no means does this section include all the possible crafted and abnormal packets. The hope is to give you an understanding of some of the types of things to look for when performing an investigation.

NORMAL SCAN (NMAP)

Sometimes an attacker will scan your subnet or individual IP address for open ports. This scan can be anything from an innocent attempt to look for a service to reconnaissance for an attack. Many times, these scans are completely automated, with an attacker setting up one or more robots (bots) to automatically scan for vulnerable versions of software to exploit.

This simulation was created with the nmap program with the following command line:
```
nmap -sT 192.168.1.2
```

The TCPDump capture of the port scan is shown in the following text; note that I've truncated the output because nmap scanned for more than 1,650 ports. I've divided the capture to make explaining it easier as well.

Nmap scans begin with an ICMP Echo Request to the target host, as shown here. Note, however, that this ICMP exchange can be disabled by the person running the nmap scan, so it might not always show up:

```
12:31:21.834284 IP 192.168.1.10 > 192.168.1.2: icmp 8: echo request seq 27074
12:31:21.834508 IP 192.168.1.2 > 192.168.1.10: icmp 8: echo reply seq 27074
```

Next nmap looks for port **80**, the default HTTP port. Notice that the scan comes from an ephemeral port on the scanner's side aimed for port **80** on the recipient. In this case, the recipient host **192.168.1.2** is listening on port **80** and a TCP response is sent back to the scanning host with the TCP **RST** flag set and the sequence number set:

```
12:31:21.834318 IP 192.168.1.10.60034 > 192.168.1.2.80: . ack 2624625246 win 4096
12:31:21.834363 IP 192.168.1.2.80 > 192.168.1.10.60034: R \
        2624625246:2624625246(0) win 0
```

Next, nmap looks for the telnet port (**tcp/23**). Notice the difference between this and the preceding scan. Aside from the ports being different, the response packet is also different. In this case, the recipient host is not listening on TCP port **23**, so it responds with a packet with the TCP **RST** flag set but with the TCP sequence number set to **0**:

```
12:31:21.935005 IP 192.168.1.10.3171 > 192.168.1.2.23: S 752173650:752173650(0) \
        win 5840 <mss 1460,sackOK,timestamp 1421906912 0,nop,wscale 0>
12:31:21.935046 IP 192.168.1.2.23 > 192.168.1.10.3171: R 0:0(0) ack 752173651 win 0
```

The following packets are essentially the same as the preceding telnet port scan insofar as the recipient host is not listening on the ports being scanned:

```
12:31:21.935129 IP 192.168.1.10.3172 > 192.168.1.2.554: S 758180552:758180552(0) \
        win 5840 <mss 1460,sackOK,timestamp 1421906912 0,nop,wscale 0>
12:31:21.935186 IP 192.168.1.2.554 > 192.168.1.10.3172: R 0:0(0) ack 758180553 win 0
12:31:21.935149 IP 192.168.1.10.3174 > 192.168.1.2.21: S 751983738:751983738(0) \
        win 5840 <mss 1460,sackOK,timestamp 1421906912 0,nop,wscale 0>
12:31:21.935289 IP 192.168.1.2.21 > 192.168.1.10.3174: R 0:0(0) ack 751983739 win 0
12:31:21.935255 IP 192.168.1.10.3175 > 192.168.1.2.1723: S 757954867:757954867(0) \
        win 5840 <mss 1460,sackOK,timestamp 1421906912 0,nop,wscale 0>
12:31:21.935320 IP 192.168.1.2.1723 > 192.168.1.10.3175: R 0:0(0) \
        ack 757954868 win 0
```

Finally, another open port is found. This time the open port is **tcp/25**, the well-known SMTP port:

```
12:31:21.935381 IP 192.168.1.10.3176 > 192.168.1.2.25: S 762467904:762467904(0) \
        win 5840 <mss 1460,sackOK,timestamp 1421906912 0,nop,wscale 0>
12:31:21.935448 IP 192.168.1.2.25 > 192.168.1.10.3176: S 2645882457:2645882457(0) \
        ack 762467905 win 5792 <mss 1460,sackOK,timestamp \
                921140115 1421906912,nop,wscale 7>
```

As stated previously, the nmap scan continues for another 1,650 or so ports. I chose to save a tree by not showing the remainder of the port scans here. Rest assured that they look largely the same as the ones already shown.

The response you take when port scanned depends on your security policy. If I notice a wide port scan, one in which a large number of ports are scanned, I'll usually take steps to block the host. However, because I'm not at the computer 24 hours a day (close, but not quite), I use a tool called PortSentry to monitor for this type of activity. PortSentry has apparently fallen out of active development since being purchased by Cisco. You can still download the last version of PortSentry at http://sourceforge.net/projects/sentrytools/. However, I won't cover the tool in this chapter because it's quite unclear whether it will exist by the time you're reading this book. Other anti–port scan software exists, including a plug-in for Snort.

SMURF ATTACK

A Smurf attack is a DoS attack whereby the attacker sends ICMP Echo Requests with a forged source address to one or more broadcast addresses. The forged source address is the recipient of the attack, and it will be inundated with echo replies from the broadcast addresses of other networks. Imagine echo replies coming from 254 hosts directed at a machine with a small or slow Internet connection. Now imagine those replies coming from 100 networks of 254 hosts each. It doesn't take long for an entire network to become bogged down receiving ICMP replies.

The following trace was created with the `hping2` command:

```
hping2 -1 -a 192.168.1.2 192.168.1.255
```

On the network under attack, only one host responded to the broadcasted ping; however, there's no way to guarantee that other networks wouldn't have a large number of hosts that respond:

```
12:57:06.871156 IP 192.168.1.2 > 192.168.1.255: icmp 8: echo request seq 0
12:57:06.871637 IP 192.168.1.8 > 192.168.1.2: icmp 8: echo reply seq 0
12:57:07.870259 IP 192.168.1.2 > 192.168.1.255: icmp 8: echo request seq 256
12:57:07.871008 IP 192.168.1.8 > 192.168.1.2: icmp 8: echo reply seq 256
12:57:08.870132 IP 192.168.1.2 > 192.168.1.255: icmp 8: echo request seq 512
12:57:08.870880 IP 192.168.1.8 > 192.168.1.2: icmp 8: echo reply seq 512
```

There is no good host-based defense for a Smurf attack. Even if ICMP replies are disabled on the individual host, the bandwidth is still being consumed by all the replies coming into the network.

To effectively counter a Smurf attack, ICMP Echo Requests directed to broadcast addresses mustn't cross router boundaries. This means that you're relying on others to be good netizens. In addition, ICMP echo replies must be filtered as far upstream from your location as possible. However, I'm not an advocate of filtering ICMP echo replies. A better solution is to rate-limit the echo replies as far upstream as possible while still allowing the replies for all the good that they do in problem diagnosis.

XMAS TREE AND TCP HEADER FLAGS

The Xmas Tree attack is so named because all the bit flags are set on within the TCP header. The idea is to cause the recipient host to respond, thus causing a DoS. Recall the TCP flag bits SYN, RST, ACK, URG, and others from Chapter 1. These bits should never all appear at the same time, and when they do it's an indication of a crafted packet.

Xmas Tree attacks are quite uncommon. However, it's important to consider the TCP flags when examining packets. Setting these flags with invalid combinations is almost always an indication of a crafted packet (though it also could in a few instances indicate broken or mis-configured software). The goal of the crafted packet might be anything from reconnaissance to an active attack such as one to get through a firewall.

The following capture sets the TCP flags SYN, FIN, RST, and PUSH, which should never show up in a real packet. It was created with the hping2 command:

```
hping2 -SFRP 192.168.1.2
```

There are three packets in this capture. Notice the source port increments and that the destination port is 0. The TCP flags are also shown, SFRP in this case. Seeing this in the wild should cause the intrusion analyst to immediately begin investigating the packets according to the security policy.

```
13:20:03.989780 IP (tos 0x0, ttl 64, id 2270, offset 0, flags [none], length: \
        40) 192.168.1.10.2687 > 192.168.1.2.0: SFRP [tcp sum ok] \
            925164686:925164686(0) win 512
13:20:04.989734 IP (tos 0x0, ttl 64, id 9285, offset 0, flags [none], \
        length: 40) 192.168.1.10.2688 > 192.168.1.2.0: SFRP [tcp sum ok] \
            1113258177:1113258177(0) win 512
13:20:05.989731 IP (tos 0x0, ttl 64, id 26951, offset 0, flags [none], \
        length: 40) 192.168.1.10.2689 > 192.168.1.2.0: SFRP [tcp sum ok] \
            2097818687:2097818687(0) win 512
```

LAND ATTACK

The LAND attack is a DoS attack against computers running Microsoft Windows. The attack was originally reported to affect Windows 95 and Windows NT back in 1997. Microsoft eventually patched the vulnerability for the operating systems. However, the vulnerability resurfaced in Microsoft's newer operating systems, including Windows XP Service Pack 2 and even Windows Server 2003. Obviously, a problem of this type resurfacing was quite embarrassing for Microsoft, especially because it has undertaken countless initiatives to secure its operating systems and software.

The LAND attack is quite trivial and occurs when the source and destination addresses and ports are set to the recipient host and the SYN flag is set.

`hping2` again provides an easy way to re-create this for testing:

```
hping2 -k -S -s 25 -p 25 -a 192.168.1.2 192.168.1.2
```

The capture through TCPDump is shown next. Notice that the source and destination addresses and ports are the same and that the source port is not incrementing and that it's also below the ephemeral ports:

```
13:42:28.079339 IP 192.168.1.2.25 > 192.168.1.2.25: S 764505725:764505725(0) win 512
13:42:29.079462 IP 192.168.1.2.25 > 192.168.1.2.25: S 2081780101:2081780101(0) \
        win 512
13:42:30.079461 IP 192.168.1.2.25 > 192.168.1.2.25: S 390202112:390202112(0) win 512
```

Recording Traffic with TCPDump

While consulting for a small Internet provider, I noticed that there was a routine and significant spike in network traffic at about 3 a.m. every morning and lasting anywhere from 15 minutes to an hour. My goal was to determine the cause of this traffic spike. Because the traffic was routine and at an odd hour, my initial thought was that the traffic was the result of an automatic update process for the servers on the network.

Most of the servers in the network were running Debian Linux and using apt-proxy. This meant that only one local server would contact the off-site Debian update servers and obtain any updates necessary. All the other servers in the local network would then contact that local master server. This setup cut the Internet utilization immensely.

Although the master server could certainly be a contributing factor, I didn't feel that there would be enough update traffic on a nightly basis to warrant such a significant spike in traffic. My assumption was confirmed when I looked at the update schedule on the master server and found that it was actually looking for updates at a different time anyway, and thus it wasn't contributing to the 3 a.m. spike at all.

With that cause eliminated, I needed to look at the traffic itself at 3 a.m. However, I wasn't really looking forward to staying awake until that hour, and if I was awake, I might not be in shape to read a packet trace. Enter cron. By using cron to fire TCPDump, I could capture the packet trace to a file for later analysis. No great surprise here and I wasn't breaking any new ground, but it seemed like a fair solution to the problem. I configured the switch to copy packets to the port on which the monitoring machine was connected and got to work on the TCPDump portion.

TCPDump offers a couple features that come in handy for this type of trace. The first feature is the capability to write the output to a file (record, if you will) and then read that file in later (playback). The second helpful feature is the capability to exit after capturing a certain number of packets. Granted, I could've used another means to stop the packet trace, such as another cron job to kill the TCPDump capture, but I thought that using TCPDump's native capability was the quickest and easiest solution.

All the TCPDump commands I've shown so far in this chapter have used expressions such as `port 80` or `host <n>.<n>.<n>.<n>`. Expressions are helpful when you're looking for specific and known traffic. However, expressions aren't of much help when you're unsure of what exactly you're searching for, as was the case here. The best option was to capture everything and then work on a filter during playback.

The two TCPDump options of interest that haven't been covered yet in the chapter are `-w` and `-c`. The `-w` option causes TCPDump to place the raw output into the specified file so that it can later be fed back through TCPDump. The resulting file is in TCPDump's native format and is thus not readable by a plain-text pager such as `cat`, `less`, or `more`. The `-c` option informs TCPDump that it should exit after it captures `<N>` packets. Getting `<N>` correct seemed to be the most difficult part of the capture.

The capture results needed to show me only basic information about the packet, including source and destination, as well as a few bits of the packet. To that end, the TCPDump command was rather easy to craft:

```
/usr/sbin/tcpdump -c 25000 -w dumpfile -n
```

In this command I have TCPDump exiting after capturing 25,000 packets, writing the capture to a file called `dumpfile`, and not performing DNS queries for the source and destination. Getting to this command did require some level of testing to see just how long it took to capture 25,000 packets and what information was included in the capture. After it was tested, I entered the command into cron with this schedule:

```
5 3 * * * /usr/sbin/tcpdump -c 25000 -w dumpfile -n
```

That is, every morning at 3:05 a.m. the capture would take place. Then at a saner hour, like 11 a.m. when I get out of bed, I'd look to see whether indeed there was traffic the prior evening that required me to look at the `dumpfile`. If there was traffic, I'd log in to the server and run a command to read the `dumpfile`:

```
tcpdump -r dumpfile -X -vv
```

Running this command gave me an idea of what traffic was out there. Intermingled with the normal traffic was an FTP conversation between one of the ISP's larger customers and another host on the Internet. The FTP traffic was easily the most frequent packet I was seeing within the trace. Another night's packet trace confirmed it. I had the ISP contact its customer to find out whether this was known activity and, if so, to let the customer know that it might be going over its bandwidth allocation for the month.

This example is somewhat typical of a security analyst's job. Spot an anomaly, investigate the anomaly while ruling out possibilities, and take action based on the investigation. Although the ultimate cause of this particular anomaly turned out not to be any type of unauthorized attack, the result of the investigation was a happier customer because that customer could take corrective action before exceeding its bandwidth for the month.

Automated Intrusion Monitoring with Snort

Snort is an excellent intrusion detection software package combining best-in-class technology with open-source configurability. Snort actually has a few different modes of operation, including a sniffer mode, a packet logger mode, an intrusion detection mode, and what is called inline mode. It is the intrusion detection mode that is of interest in this section. However, inline mode is also notable because it provides a way to configure Snort and iptables to work together to dynamically accept or drop packets based on Snort rules. For the purposes of this chapter, when referring to Snort I'm referring specifically to the intrusion detection mode.

When in intrusion detection mode, Snort works by using a number of rules that define anomalous traffic. Many of these rules come predefined for you by Sourcefire, the makers of Snort. Many other rules are available from the community, and of course you can also write your own rules as necessary. CERT has a good paper on writing rules, aptly titled "Writing Rules and Understanding Alerts for Snort," available at http://www.cert.org/security-improvement/implementations/i042.14.html.

In addition to rules, Snort has a number of preprocessors that enable modules to view and alter packets before they are handled by the intrusion detection engine of the software. Preprocessors can be developed to suit your needs, though the preprocessors already available are helpful. The preexisting preprocessors include two types of port scan detectors to help detect and take action when a port scan is detected. There are also preprocessors to reassemble TCP streams to provide stateful analysis and preprocessors to decode RPC traffic and inspect HTTP traffic. Other preprocessors are described in detail in the Snort documentation available with Snort or online at http://www.snort.org/docs/.

Snort works by detecting and reporting on events. The actual process of reporting on events can be configured through event handling within Snort. Event handling calls for configuration based on thresholds. This highly configurable aspect of Snort helps to prevent being inundated with log entries and alerts.

Normally you'd want to be notified in some way when certain Snort rules are triggered. Snort uses output modules that can be configured to send the output to various locations. The primary or most commonly used output module is the alert_syslog module, which sends alerts to the local syslog facility. Other output modules exist, including alert_fast and alert_full. The former puts a fast entry into the file specified, and the latter sends the entire packet header along with the event message. Other output modules exist and more information on them can be found within the Snort documentation.

One interesting output module is the database output module. The database module enables Snort alerts to be sent to an SQL database. Using this output module enables you to leverage software called ACID, which can generate reports on the alerts and events in Snort.

Snort has numerous additional features and nuances that help make it one of the best, if not the best, intrusion detection software available.

Obtaining and Installing Snort

Snort is available with many Linux distributions as an additional package, and most distributions also include the Snort rules, either included with the Snort package or as an add-on package. You can also download Snort from http://www.snort.org/.

Installation of Snort and the default rules should nearly always be done by installing the package available with your distribution. If this isn't possible or if the available package doesn't include the options you'd like, you'll need to compile from source.

The Snort package comes in a gzip archive and therefore needs to be unzipped and unarchived prior to being compiled:

```
tar -zxvf snort-<version>.tar.gz
```

After it's unzipped and unarchived, you can **cd** into the Snort source directory and run the configure script:

```
cd snort-<version>
./configure
```

It is at the point of running the configure script where many compile-time options can be set. To obtain a list of some of these options, notably options to enable support for certain databases or enable certain other features, type the following:

```
./configure --help
```

In addition, the INSTALL document and other documentation within the **<snort-source>/doc** directory explain these and other options available when compiling Snort from source.

Running the configure script, along with any options, will result in Snort looking for various prerequisites. For example, when compiling Snort from source, you might receive an error indicating that one or more prerequisites can't be found, such as this error:

```
checking for pcre.h... no

  ERROR! Libpcre header not found, go get it from
  http://www.pcre.org
```

With that error in mind, I was able to install the **pcre** development files, rerun the configure script, and continue.

After the configure script has run successfully, compile the software by typing this:

```
make
```

The software will now compile. Should you get any errors during this phase, consult the Snort documentation and mailing list archives to see whether you've received a known error for your architecture.

Finally, after the software is compiled, install it by typing the following:

```
make install
```

The software will now be installed and should be ready to use. By default, the software is installed into **/usr/local/bin**. You can test the basic Snort command by typing this:

```
/usr/local/bin/snort -?
```

You should see output with help options, similar to this:

```
  ,,_    -*> Snort! <*-
o" )~  Version 2.3.3 (Build 14)
  ''''   By Martin Roesch & The Snort Team: http://www.snort.org/team.html
       (C) Copyright 1998-2004 Sourcefire Inc., et al.

USAGE: ./snort [-options] <filter options>
Options:
   -A      Set alert mode: fast, full, console, or none (alert file alerts only)
           "unsock" enables UNIX socket logging (experimental).
...
<output truncated>
```

Configuring Snort

The source code for Snort includes a sample configuration file. If you've installed from your distribution's package, that too should include a sample Snort configuration file. Usually this file is called **snort.conf**. On most popular distributions, including SUSE and Debian, this file (along with a number of Snort rules) is placed in **/etc/snort/**.

If you're working with a source installation, the sample **snort.conf** configuration file is located in **<snort-source>/etc/** and sample rules are located in **<snort-source>/rules/**. For those working with a source-code version, I recommend creating a directory in either **/etc/** or **/usr/local/etc/** called **snort** and placing the **snort.conf** configuration file and the Snort rules in that directory. In addition, the default Snort configuration file calls various map and extra configuration files as well. These files can also be found in the **<snort-source>/etc/** directory. Creating the directory and copying all the files into it would look like this (again, this is applicable only to those who have compiled Snort from source):

```
mkdir /etc/snort
cp <snort-source>/etc/snort.conf /etc/snort/
cp <snort-source>/etc/*.map /etc/snort/
cp <snort-source>/etc/*.config /etc/snort/
cp <snort-source>/rules/*.rules /etc/snort/
```

One additional and important change is done to the **snort.conf** configuration file. After you've copied it to the **/etc/snort** directory, edit the file and change the RULE_PATH variable from its default of **../rules** to **/etc/snort**. The line should look like this when you're done:

```
var RULE_PATH /etc/snort
```

Finally, create the Snort log directory with the following command:

```
mkdir /var/log/snort
```

With all the groundwork done, it's time to officially start Snort for the first time. If you've installed from your distribution's package, it's likely that you can start Snort through the normal run control mechanism, such as **/etc/init.d/snort start**. If you've compiled from source, you'll need to start Snort manually and point to the location of its configuration file:

```
/usr/local/bin/snort -c /etc/snort/snort.conf
```

If you receive any errors, chances are that there are missing files. Check the Snort source directory structure for the missing files and copy them to the appropriate location, based on the configuration file.

If all goes well, you should see a message such as this, near the end of the output:

```
--== Initialization Complete ==--
```

As you can see, the shell prompt didn't return. This is because Snort was not told to fork into daemon mode. Press Ctrl+C to kill Snort and add a **-D** to the command line. It should now look like this:

```
/usr/local/bin/snort -c /etc/snort/snort.conf -D
```

Snort will start again and this time fork off into the background, returning you to the shell prompt.

There is, of course, much more to Snort configuration than merely getting it running with the default options and rulesets. For more information on specific Snort configurations, refer to the Snort documentation.

Testing Snort

With Snort now running in the background, you could assume that it's running perfectly fine and that log entries will be placed into /var/log/snort for you. However, I'm not one to assume things, especially about computer security. Therefore, to test the Snort installation I'll use the handy hping2 tool to craft a packet or two and fire them toward the host running Snort.

In this case, I'm just looking for verification that Snort is running and monitoring something. The default rules look for bad packets, so crafting one of those should be trivial with hping2. From another host on the network (192.168.1.10), I ran the following hping2 command toward the host running Snort (192.168.1.2):

```
hping2 -X 192.168.1.2
```

The -X option causes an Xmas scan to be run. Looking in /var/log/snort on the host running Snort reveals that the alert file has received some information and there is also a new directory called 192.168.1.10, which was the source of the test packets. Inside that directory are files corresponding to the packets I sent, the contents of which are shown here:

```
[**] BAD-TRAFFIC tcp port 0 traffic [**]
06/07-16:19:00.712543 192.168.1.10:1984 -> 192.168.1.2:0
TCP TTL:64 TOS:0x0 ID:48557 IpLen:20 DgmLen:40
*2****** Seq: 0xED1609B Ack: 0x13E893C5 Win: 0x200 TcpLen: 20
=+=+=+=+=+=+=+=+=+=+=+=+=+=+=+=+=+=+=+=+=+=+=+=+=+=+=+=+=+=+=+=+

[**] BAD-TRAFFIC tcp port 0 traffic [**]
06/07-16:19:00.712610 192.168.1.2:0 -> 192.168.1.10:1984
TCP TTL:64 TOS:0x0 ID:10034 IpLen:20 DgmLen:40 DF
***A*R** Seq: 0x0 Ack: 0xED1609B Win: 0x0 TcpLen: 20
=+=+=+=+=+=+=+=+=+=+=+=+=+=+=+=+=+=+=+=+=+=+=+=+=+=+=+=+=+=+=+=+
```

As you can see from the output, Snort has captured what it believes to be (correctly so) bad TCP packets. The alert log file /var/log/snort/alert also contains information that is especially useful for sorting the alerts. Here are the log entries from the alert log file that correspond to the previously shown entries from the specific host file:

```
[**] [1:524:8] BAD-TRAFFIC tcp port 0 traffic [**]
[Classification: Misc activity] [Priority: 3]
06/07-16:19:00.712543 192.168.1.10:1984 -> 192.168.1.2:0
TCP TTL:64 TOS:0x0 ID:48557 IpLen:20 DgmLen:40
*2****** Seq: 0xED1609B Ack: 0x13E893C5 Win: 0x200 TcpLen: 20


[**] [1:524:8] BAD-TRAFFIC tcp port 0 traffic [**]
[Classification: Misc activity] [Priority: 3]
06/07-16:19:00.712610 192.168.1.2:0 -> 192.168.1.10:1984
TCP TTL:64 TOS:0x0 ID:10034 IpLen:20 DgmLen:40 DF
***A*R** Seq: 0x0 Ack: 0xED1609B Win: 0x0 TcpLen: 20
```

As you can see from these entries, there are some additional items such as `Classification`
and `Priority` that can help to, well, classify and prioritize the alert. Both the classification
and the priority can be configured within the alert log file.

Receiving Alerts

I recommend working with Snort to gain experience with rules and configuration options
before configuring it to send alerts in email or via another means. You might easily find yourself overwhelmed by alerts with the default Snort rules, depending on your network layout.

Recall from Chapter 10 that log file monitoring software was introduced and a recipe was
given for using Swatch to monitor log files for certain events, at which time it would send an
email based on the alert. If you see where I'm going with this, then congratulations!

USING SWATCH TO MONITOR FOR SNORT ALERTS

With its default configuration, Snort logs to `/var/log/snort/alert`. Therefore, creating a
Swatch configuration to monitor this file is quite easy. Again, it would be easy to overwhelm
yourself or the system with alerts and emails from Swatch, so you should use caution when configuring any actions based on Snort alerts until you've had a chance to configure Snort further.

Recall that Snort logs some prioritization data within `/var/log/snort/alert`. Therefore, you
could set up a Swatch rule to watch for anything with a certain priority, say 3, for example,
and send an email when that's seen. This would be placed within your Swatch configuration
file which, by default, is `~/.swatchrc`. Here's the configuration entry:

```
watchfor /Priority: 3/
  mail
```

Starting Swatch and pointing it toward the Snort alert file, `/var/log/snort/alert`, looks like
this:

```
swatch --tail-file=/var/log/snort/alert
```

Now when an alert with `Priority: 3` is logged, an email will be sent by Swatch.

Final Thoughts on Snort

Snort comes highly recommended as a means to automate the task of intrusion detection. I've only been able to touch on the very basics of Snort here in hopes of giving you a starting point for working with it. From here, you can combine Snort with MySQL and ACID to create an enterprise-class intrusion detection system. Snort can be configured just as you need and extended to fit any size of organization.

Monitoring with ARPWatch

ARPWatch is a daemon that watches for new Ethernet interfaces on a network. If a new ARP entry is seen, it could be indicative of a rogue computer somewhere within the network.

ARPWatch uses the PCap library, which may not (yet) be on your system. If it's not, you'll find out during the configuration process for ARPWatch. The PCap library, commonly known as libpcap, can be downloaded from http://www.tcpdump.org/. The PCap library is used for other network and security-related programs such as TCPDump. Because TCPDump was already covered, I'll forego repeating the instructions for installing libpcap in this chapter and instead I'll refer you to the section "TCPDump: A Simple Overview" for those instructions.

Installation of ARPWatch involves untarring the ARPWatch archive that you download, usually something like `tar -zxvf arpwatch.tar.Z`. From there, change directory into the ARPWatch directory and run the configure script:

```
./configure
```

You'll see a (hopefully somewhat) familiar series of output statements, something like this:

```
creating cache ./config.cache
checking host system type... i686-pc-linux-gnu
checking target system type... i686-pc-linux-gnu
checking build system type... i686-pc-linux-gnu
checking for gcc... gcc
checking whether the C compiler (gcc ) works... yes
... (output truncated) ...
```

If you see an error to the effect of the following, you'll need to install libpcap:

```
checking for main in -lpcap... no
configure: error: see the INSTALL doc for more info
```

Refer to the section on TCPDump earlier in this chapter for information on installing the PCap library.

For the rest of you, and if you're joining us again after installing PCap, the next step to compile ARPWatch is to **make** it. From the command line within the ARPWatch source code directory, type this:

```
make
```

ARPWatch will now compile and you'll see messages indicating the progress, as well as possibly a warning or two:

```
report.o(.text+0x409): the use of `mktemp' is dangerous, better use `mkstemp'
gcc -O2 -DDEBUG -DHAVE_FCNTL_H=1 -DHAVE_MEMORY_H=1 -DTIME_WITH_SYS_TIME=1 \
        -DHAVE_BCOPY=1 -DHAVE_STRERROR=1 -DRETSIGTYPE=void -DRETSIGVAL= \
            -DHAVE_SIGSET=1 -DDECLWAITSTATUS=int -DSTDC_HEADERS=1 \
                -DARPDIR=\"/usr/local/arpwatch\" -DPATH \
                    _SENDMAIL=\"/usr/sbin/sendmail\" -I.\
                        -Ilinux-include -c ./arpsnmp.c
gcc -O2 -DDEBUG -DHAVE_FCNTL_H=1 -DHAVE_MEMORY_H=1 -DTIME_WITH_SYS_TIME=1 \
        -DHAVE_BCOPY=1 -DHAVE_STRERROR=1 -DRETSIGTYPE=void -DRETSIGVAL= \
            -DHAVE_SIGSET=1 -DDECLWAITSTATUS=int -DSTDC_HEADERS=1 \
                -DARPDIR=\"/usr/local/arpwatch\" \
                    -DPATH_SENDMAIL=\"/usr/sbin/sendmail\" \
                        -I. -Ilinux-include -o arpsnmp \
                            arpsnmp.o db.o dns.o \
                                ec.o file.o intoa.o \
        machdep.o util.o report.o setsignal.o version.o
report.o: In function `report':
report.o(.text+0x409): the use of `mktemp' is dangerous, better use `mkstemp'
```

After it's compiled, install ARPWatch with the following command:

```
make install
```

ARPWatch will be installed (by default) into **/usr/local/sbin**. This directory is usually in **root**'s path, but if you type **arpwatch** and receive a **command not found** error, you probably need to preface the command with its directory, like this:

```
/usr/local/bin/arpwatch
```

As ARPWatch runs, it will report to the SYSLOG daemon about new MAC addresses found on the network. This means that ARPWatch will usually output to **/var/log/messages**, so you can run a **grep** command to find out about the new hosts as ARPWatch finds them:

```
grep arpwatch /var/log/messages
```

Additionally, ARPWatch will also send email to the root account on a system detailing the new hosts as well. The email contains details such as the date, the IP address, and the MAC address:

```
    hostname: client.example.com
  ip address: 192.168.1.10
ethernet address: 0:e1:18:34:2f:e8
ethernet vendor: <unknown>
    timestamp: Saturday, May 22, 2004 11:25:59 -0500
```

In both of these ways, it's possible to know virtually instantly when a new host appears on the network. Such information would be helpful to the security administrator in monitoring for possible unauthorized use of a network.

ARPWatch will run in the background as a daemon, silently (or hopefully silently) going about its business and reporting back to you as needed. If, for some reason, ARPWatch shuts off, maybe due to the machine rebooting, the existing entries will be written to a file called `arp.dat` (the location of this file varies greatly; if you need to find it run `find / -name "arp.dat"`). If you need to reset ARPWatch's monitoring database so that it will "pick up" all the hosts on the network again, run these commands from within the directory in which you locate ARPWatch:

```
rm arp.dat
touch arp.dat
```

A tip about using ARPWatch: Make sure that the ARPWatch data file, `arp.dat`, is monitored for unauthorized changes. If an attacker can alter this file and add his own entry manually, ARPWatch won't alert you to the presence of the new host. Make sure that the `arp.dat` file is monitored by AIDE (covered in Chapter 12, "Filesystem Integrity") or through other similar means.

Summary

This chapter showed you some of the tools used in intrusion detection. The goal was to provide you with some hands-on experience based on the concepts introduced in previous chapters. You learned about network sniffers in this chapter and focused specifically on TCPDump. Some packets and attack types were viewed through the eyes of TCPDump as well.

Other tools were introduced and discussed in this chapter as well. These included Snort, which provides an excellent intrusion detection system. Finally, using ARPWatch to monitor for new and unexpected ARP entries on the network was also discussed.

The next chapter looks at filesystem integrity through the eyes of AIDE, a filesystem integrity checker.

Filesystem Integrity

Integrity is one of three commonly used principles of computer security; confidentiality and availability are the other two. In the purest sense of the three principles, integrity simply refers to the means by which you ensure that data is authentic and has not been altered or tampered with in any way. One aspect of ensuring data integrity is ensuring the integrity of the system on which the data is housed.

This chapter looks at some very specific means you have at your disposal when running Linux to ensure data integrity. These include examining the files on a Linux system to make sure that they haven't been altered without your knowledge, and they include looking for anomalies that may indicate the presence of an intruder on the system.

Filesystem Integrity Defined

Maintaining system integrity is yet another layer of security meant to give you, the security administrator, a warm, fuzzy feeling. For the purposes of this chapter, the term *filesystem integrity* refers to the verifiable knowledge that the computer system and the objects contained therein are in a known-good state. Although that's a wide definition, filesystem integrity in this chapter will simply entail verification that the files located on the computer have not been tampered with or altered. As such, this chapter concentrates on tools to assist you in checking the files.

Practical Filesystem Integrity

Various tools are available to check the integrity of files on the system. Tripwire is a commercial offering in the area that's now been open sourced. Well, it was open source and then closed and now open, or something entirely too confusing. See Chapter 10, "Intrusion Detection Tools," for a description of Tripwire's licensing issues. In this chapter, I'll show AIDE, the Advanced Intrusion Detection Environment. AIDE is an open-source filesystem integrity-checking tool.

A basic integrity check of a file usually involves obtaining checksum values of the files on the computer and comparing that checksum against a known-good value. Checksums are sometimes also referred to as hash values or signatures. More complex checking is done by tools such as AIDE, as you'll see later in the chapter.

Checksums are frequently used to verify the integrity of a downloaded file. For example, many Linux FTP repositories contain a file called md5sums. Inside of that md5sums file are the checksums of the files as they reside on the FTP server. When you download the file, you can then run a checksum against the downloaded file. If your checksum value matches the checksum on the server, you know you have a good file. If the values don't match, something went wrong with the download and you can save some time rather than trying to work with a corrupt file or wasting a CDR.

A hands-on example would be helpful. Jump into a console and type the following:

```
md5sum /etc/passwd
```

You'll see a value such as this:

```
fc8053d1be0dcc33e8ef8264e8b8e502 /etc/passwd
```

Note that your value will be substantially different from mine, unless you're running the command against my password file, in which case I have other problems that need attention.

If you add a user, delete a user, or make any change that affects the password file, that md5sum value will change. For example, if you make a change to someone's name within the passwd file, the md5sum of the passwd file will change because the file's contents are now different. Continuing with the preceding example, you can change the name of the root user by running this (as root):

```
chfn root
```

You'll be presented with various options for changing the account information for the user, beginning with the Full Name. Change the Full Name value to whatever you'd like, and continue with changes to other values if you'd like. Now running an md5sum against /etc/passwd will show a different checksum for the file:

```
md5sum /etc/passwd
5a916699b172ab44c75bbfd2582849bf /etc/passwd
```

Installing AIDE

AIDE is a filesystem integrity-checking tool offering many of the features you'd expect from such a program. More information on AIDE, including links to download, are available at http://www.cs.tut.fi/~rammer/aide.html and http://sourceforge.net/projects/aide.

After it's downloaded, AIDE needs to be compiled. However, you will probably also need some prerequisites before attempting to compile AIDE. If this is the case, the configure script for AIDE will inform you of these prerequisites, which you will then need to download and compile before continuing with AIDE's compilation. One such prerequisite commonly needed is the mhash library. The mhash library can be downloaded from http://sourceforge.net/projects/mhash/.

The mhash library should be compiled statically for use with AIDE. Follow the normal steps for unarchiving and compiling a software package:

```
tar -zxvf mhash-<NNNN>.tar.gz
cd mhash-<NNNN>
```

I recommend these compile options for the configure script:

```
./configure --prefix=/usr --enable-static=yes
```

After mhash has been configured, compile and install it with these commands:

```
make
make install
```

Compiling AIDE follows the same pattern as other software compilation, such as this in Linux:

```
tar -zxvf aide-<NNNN>.tar.gz
cd aide-<NNNN>
./configure
make
make install
```

Configuring AIDE

AIDE, like many other Linux applications, operates using a configuration file. The configuration file is text-based and contains information that the program uses to determine the characteristics it will use when it runs. The first time you run AIDE you'll create and initialize the database that will be used for future checks of the filesystem's integrity. That database is then manually checked over for sanity, and you'll run an update process that will be used from then on to look for changes that occur on the filesystem.

Creating an AIDE Configuration File

After AIDE has been installed, the first thing you'll want to do is create a configuration file. Unlike most other software in Linux, AIDE doesn't include a default configuration file from which you can build a customized version. There is a sample configuration file in the `<AIDE-source>/doc/` directory, but it explicitly states that you shouldn't use it as a system-wide configuration file. Therefore, you'll have to build one of your own. Don't worry, I'm here to help.

The AIDE configuration file is normally called `aide.conf` and is located in `/etc/`. Comments within the AIDE configuration file begin with a pound sign (#). There are three categories of lines within the AIDE configuration file: configuration lines, macro lines, and selection lines. The heart of the AIDE configuration file is the selection lines that you use to determine what objects on the filesystem will be monitored. Configuration lines are also important in determining how AIDE will operate, and macro lines are important for creating advanced configurations. AIDE uses a series of *parameter=value* directives to indicate the type of checking to perform on a given object. Table 12.1 lists those directives.

TABLE 12.1
AIDE Configuration Directives

DIRECTIVE	DESCRIPTION
p	permissions
i	inode
n	number of links
u	user
g	group
s	size
b	block count
m	Mtime
a	Atime
c	Ctime
S	check for growing size
md5	md5 checksum
sha1	sha1 checksum
rmd160	rmd160 checksum
tiger	tiger checksum
R	p+i+n+u+g+s+m+c+md5

TABLE 12.1

AIDE Configuration Directives (continued)

DIRECTIVE	DESCRIPTION
L	p+i+n+u+g
E	Empty group
>	Growing logfile p+u+g+i+n+S
haval	haval checksum
gost	gost checksum
crc32	crc32 checksum

AIDE also enables the administrator to create custom groups containing the default groups. Doing so can save you time and improve the readability of the configuration file. You might use a custom group to combine other groups of commonly used checks. For example, to create a group called MyGroup with commonly used types of checks, it's as simple as this:

MyGroup p+i+n+m+md5

These groupings, whether default or custom, are used to determine the type of check that will be performed on a given selection. You also configure the files and directories to be checked using a selection line in the configuration file. Selection lines consist of the object to be checked together with the type of check to be performed. The object can be a file, a directory, a regular expression, or more commonly a combination of a file along with some regular expression syntax. I'll take a glance at regular expressions in a later section, but for now I'll show simple examples of the selection process.

The following selection line would examine everything in the /etc directory, specifically looking at the number of links, the user who owns a given file, the group who owns a given file, and the size of the file:

/etc n+u+g+s

A change to one of those attributes that occurs unexpectedly might indicate tampering. The next example uses a custom group called MyGroup as the check for the files within the /bin directory:

/bin MyGroup

Objects can be ignored or skipped by using an exclamation point (!), as in the following example, which causes AIDE to ignore everything in /var/log:

!/var/log/.*

Ignoring objects that change frequently can drastically reduce the number of irrelevant lines that appear in the AIDE report. However, you should be careful so as not to ignore too much; otherwise, you might miss important filesystem changes.

Rule lines in the configuration file use regular expressions to enable powerful matching capabilities. Don't worry if you're not familiar with the black magic involved in regular expressions; I'll go easy on you here.

A primary concern with matching files in AIDE is that you don't leave room for an attacker to circumvent the file integrity checker. This could occur if you specified a filename without fully qualifying the file. For example, if you wanted to skip checking a file in the /var/log/ directory because it changes, you might use this (seemingly correct) syntax:

```
!/var/log/maillog
```

However, due to the regular expression matching that occurs, an attacker could create a file called this:

```
/var/log/maillog.crack
```

Because you've excluded /var/log/maillog already, AIDE will not check anything that begins with /var/log/maillog. To solve this problem you add a dollar sign ($) to the end of the file. In regular expression syntax, a $ indicates the end-of-line. Therefore, by changing the syntax for the file you want to exclude and adding a $, you use the most specific match for that filesystem check:

```
!/var/log/maillog$
```

By default, AIDE will create a file-based database in /usr/local/etc/ called aide.db.new. This file is then moved (manually) to /usr/local/etc/aide.db for future checks. Therefore, there's not really a need to alter this behavior within the context of the configuration file; however, you certainly can change the path and name of this file using the configuration options:

```
database=file:<filename>
database_out=file:<filename>
```

AIDE can also use an SQL database server such as PostgreSQL to store database contents, although that configuration is beyond the scope of this book.

A Sample AIDE Configuration File

At the very least you need to tell AIDE what parts of the filesystem to check and what rules to use for those checks. You can also add numerous other bits to the configuration to alter how AIDE performs. For the purposes of this section, I'll show a very basic configuration file with the caveat that you should add to it as you see necessary for your Linux installation.

Open the file `/usr/local/etc/aide.conf`. If the file doesn't exist, create it. Place the following lines within the file:

```
/bin R
/sbin R
/etc R+a
/lib R
/usr/lib R
```

Initializing the AIDE DB

With a quick and basic configuration file in hand, it's time to initialize the AIDE database. This process can take a varying length of time depending on how many files you're checking and the amount of resources the computer has available. Initializing the AIDE database is as simple as running the following:

```
/usr/local/bin/aide --init
```

AIDE will now initialize the database based on the criteria you chose in the configuration file. When it's complete, you'll see a message similar to this:

```
AIDE, version 0.10

### AIDE database initialized.
```

The next step is to rename (move) the newly created database to `aide.db` so that it becomes the default or master database:

```
mv /usr/local/etc/aide.db.new /usr/local/etc/aide.db
```

Now you should be able to run a check of the database to verify that everything is working okay:

```
/usr/local/bin/aide --check
```

If everything goes well, you'll see output similar to the following:

```
AIDE, version 0.10

### All files match AIDE database. Looks okay!
```

With the AIDE database initialized, you should immediately copy the database to a disk, preferably a read-only media such as a CD-R, or you should securely copy it to another computer. If you leave the AIDE database on the computer, an attacker may be able to simply alter the AIDE database to cover her tracks after replacing system files with her own! Each time you update the AIDE database from this point forward, you should always copy the resulting database file to secure media.

Scheduling AIDE to Run Automatically

AIDE is best run using a cron job (scheduled task). Therefore, you should schedule AIDE to run automatically without your intervention. AIDE is commonly run once per day, but you should schedule it to run according to your security policy. The easiest and quickest method to have AIDE run daily is to create a crontab entry.

Creating a crontab entry is a matter of running this (as root):

```
crontab -e
```

To run AIDE nightly at 2:00 a.m., enter the following line into crontab:

```
0 2 * * * /usr/local/bin/aide --check
```

For more information on the format of crontab entries, see your distribution's documentation.

Monitoring AIDE for Bad Things

Okay, so you have this shiny new filesystem integrity-checking tool all set up and running. But now what? Now you sit and wait for something to happen. Usually nothing does, and even when it appears that something bad might have happened, many times it hasn't.

AIDE will continue to monitor the filesystem according to the rules you configured. Thanks to the cron job, you'll receive reports nightly containing the files and the attributes for those files that have changed since the database was initialized or last updated. Many times these changes will be completely benign. Recall the example from the beginning of the chapter. If you add a user, files such as /etc/passwd and /etc/shadow will change. AIDE will notice and report accordingly, assuming that you're checking /etc. However, if you didn't add a user or make other changes to /etc/passwd or /etc/shadow, it might bear closer examination to make sure that an attacker hasn't altered either one of those important files.

Of course, there are other files that AIDE will be reporting on. You should closely monitor the AIDE report for files that were altered unexpectedly. For example, the files /bin/su or /usr/bin/passwd should rarely be altered and then only by certain known software updates. Therefore, if a file such as /bin/su shows up in an AIDE report, you need to look into it immediately to see when and why that file changed. Taking this example one step further, assume for a moment that AIDE ran overnight through its normal process. In the morning you awake to find an email containing some of the following lines:

```
AIDE found differences between database and filesystem!!
Start timestamp: 2004-03-09 20:24:33
Summary:
Total number of files=1488,added files=0,removed files=0,changed files=1
```

```
Changed files:
changed:/bin/su
Detailed information about changes:

File: /bin/su
  Size   : 23176                 , 0
  Permissions: -rwsr-xr-x             , -rwxr-xr-x
  Mtime  : 2002-04-07 10:59:14       , 2004-03-09 20:24:31
  Ctime  : 2002-04-08 20:45:36       , 2004-03-09 20:24:31
  Inode  : 98564             , 100922
  MD5    : XTJKOhKy/492djesGoBx7A==       , 1B2M2Y8AsgTpgAmY7PhCfg==
```

The AIDE check that you scheduled found something. You can quickly tell from the summary line what has been found:

```
Summary:
Total number of files=1488,added files=0,removed files=0,changed files=1
```

Next you'll see a slightly more detailed summary of the files that have been added, changed, or removed since the database was initialized or last updated. In this case, there's only one file that's been changed, /bin/su:

```
Changed files:
changed:/bin/su
```

Finally, you see the gory details of exactly what AIDE found for the files in the report. The items you see in the detail section of the report correspond to the type of check that you configured in aide.conf; you do remember that, right? In this case, six items changed, the file size, permissions, Mtime (modified time), Ctime (creation time), inode, and MD5 hash:

```
File: /bin/su
  Size   : 23176                 , 23948
  Permissions: -rwsr-xr-x             , -rwsr-xr-x
  Mtime  : 2002-04-07 10:59:14       , 2004-03-09 20:24:31
  Ctime  : 2002-04-08 20:45:36       , 2004-03-09 20:24:31
  Inode  : 98564             , 100922
  MD5    : XTJKOhKy/492djesGoBx7A==       , 1B2M2Y8AsgTpgAmY7PhCfg==
```

Based on this report, it's easy to see that something changed with /bin/su and probably not for the better. Knowing that I didn't perform any updates to the server in the past few days, I can reasonably assume that a break-in has occurred and someone has replaced the normal su program with one of his own. An attacker might do this so that he can steal the root password or, more likely, he would do it so that he always has a way to get root access into the server. The attacker's trojaned su program might always allow users to go to root if they type a certain password (not the real root password) or if they log in as a certain user. In this manner, no matter what I change the root password to, the attacker can always get root access.

Without a utility such as AIDE I might not see that /bin/su has changed. It's still roughly the same size and the permissions are the same. A more skilled attacker would've also changed the Ctime to match an earlier time, to make it appear that the file is older than it really is. In that way, an ls -la on the file wouldn't have given many clues as to the real status of this important program.

The /bin/su example is just one of many in a long line of similar examples. Attackers can and will replace your programs with their own versions to hide their activity or give them elevated privileges. For example, a common attack practice is to place a trojaned ps program on a server to hide the attacker's processes. Performing a ps awux to look at what processes are running wouldn't reveal the attacker's processes if the trojaned version is in place. Another attacker might replace the cron scheduling program with one of his own that automatically runs his attack again after you've cleaned up from it the first time!

Cleaning Up the AIDE Database

Over time, you'll notice that AIDE check reports become longer and longer. This is usually the result of normal activity on the server, such as adding and deleting users, updating software, and changing settings in configuration files. You should regularly update the AIDE database not only to shorten reports but also to better track when unexpected changes occur. If you don't regularly update the AIDE database, you might miss a change that resulted from an attack.

You may be asking, "How often should I update the AIDE database?" The answer depends largely on your needs and your security policy. When you first start to use AIDE, I expect that you should be updating the database at least for the first few runs (again, depending on your security policy) and, more important, refining the configuration file. You'll find that certain files change so often that you need to either exclude them entirely or change the types of checks that occur on those files.

It is much better to change the types of checks than to simply skip the files altogether. Some file attributes that AIDE can check will not change often or at all for the same file. Attributes such as inode and Ctime shouldn't change. Therefore, if you notice certain files that keep showing up in the AIDE report and you've ruled out nefarious activity, you should change the type of check that occurs on that file within the AIDE configuration file.

A file that regularly changes on some systems is the Samba password file, /etc/samba/smbpasswd. On such systems, the file regularly shows up in the report where everything in the /etc/ directory is examined using the R check (refer to Table 12.1 for a refresher). A more appropriate check type for this file might include things that don't change often such as inode and Ctime. Such a check would appear like this in the AIDE configuration file:

```
/etc/samba/smbpasswd$ c+i
```

Note the use of the $ at the end of the filename in the example to indicate the end of line.

As the AIDE report runs, you'll be able to use more granularity to refine the files that are checked and the checks themselves. After you update the AIDE configuration file, you'll need to update the database so that the changes take effect. This process is accomplished by running this command:

```
/usr/local/bin/aide --update
```

After the update is complete, you'll have a new database file, `/usr/local/etc/aide.db.new` by default. This file should be moved to overwrite the existing database:

```
mv /usr/local/etc/aide.db.new /usr/local/etc/aide.db
```

Now running `aide --check` will give a clean result:

```
AIDE, version 0.10

### All files match AIDE database. Looks okay!
```

After you update the database, you should copy the file to secure media or to another computer to ensure the integrity of the database.

With the AIDE configuration file and database updated and AIDE scheduled to run nightly, you now have an infrastructure in place to verify the integrity of your filesystem. From here you can read on to find out about more advanced configurations for AIDE, or you can jump ahead to the next part of the chapter to find out about the rootkit checking tool called Chkrootkit.

Changing the Output of the AIDE Report

You might want a little more flexibility in the location of the AIDE report. For example, you may not want to receive emails if everything is okay with the AIDE report, or you may want to have AIDE report into a file instead of providing standard output. AIDE has four basic options for configuring output that can be configured through the AIDE configuration file.

LINUX OUTPUT STREAMS

Linux has three generic streams of output that are created when a program runs. These streams are referred to as STDIN, STDOUT, and STDERR, which are abbreviations for Standard Input, Standard Output, and Standard Error, respectively. When you see a referral to STDOUT, it refers to the normal method of output to the screen, and STDERR indicates output as a result of an error condition. As you might expect, STDIN refers to the method of input when read from the input file descriptor.

The general AIDE configuration option called **report_url** configures how output is displayed. By default, output is displayed to **STDOUT**. Output can be displayed to any or all of the following:

- **STDOUT** (default)
- **STDERR**
- Text file
- File descriptor

Of these four possibilities, **STDOUT**, **STDERR**, and text file are of interest. Future versions of AIDE may include output configurations for automated email and automated output to the SYSLOG facility.

Of particular interest is the text file type of output for AIDE. This output type is specified using this configuration line:

```
report_url=file:/<path>/<filename>
```

For example, to configure AIDE reports to go to a file called **aidereport.txt** in the **/var/log/aide** directory that you create, you would use this configuration option in the AIDE configuration file:

```
report_url=file:/var/log/aide/aidereport.txt
```

However, the **report_url** configuration option is only one means for getting output into a file. Because you're running the AIDE report from cron, you could also simply redirect the output to a file. For example, recall the crontab entry shown earlier in the chapter:

```
0 2 * * * /usr/local/bin/aide --check
```

You could alter that cron entry to redirect the output to a file. Doing so would cause all output to go to that file and would also enable additional features such as date-based naming. This can be done with a little shell trick using runquotes (sometimes called a backtick, usually found with the tilde [~] on the keyboard). Here's the new cron entry:

```
0 2 * * * /usr/local/bin/aide --check >/var/log/aide/aidereport-`date +%m%d%Y`.txt
```

Now the AIDE report will run and redirect **STDOUT** to a file called

```
/var/log/aide/aidereport-<date>.txt
```

For example, for a report run on March 12, 2004, the file would be called

```
/var/log/aide/aidereport-03122004.txt
```

With a redirected configuration such as the one shown, you will no longer receive emails when AIDE runs through its normal cron job. Rather, you will receive emails only when an error occurs with the AIDE cron job. Because you'll no longer be receiving the emails, you may be tempted to ignore your monitoring duties and just let all the AIDE reports pile up. However, you should still monitor the AIDE reports by looking at the reports for anomalies and cleaning them up as appropriate.

Obtaining More Verbose Output

AIDE reports can be configured with additional verbosity. Adding verbosity to AIDE is valuable when you're troubleshooting rule matching. For example, when you set the verbose configuration option, you'll be able to see how AIDE builds the list of files to check. If you're seeing unexpected results or if files are being included or excluded for mysterious reasons, adding this option to the configuration or adding it as a command-line option will help.

The configuration option to add verbosity is as follows:

```
verbose=<N>
```

In this case, <N> is a positive integer with a maximum value of 255. In practice, only numbers above 200 give additional debugging output for most of the checks. Therefore, to add the maximum verbosity level, you would use this configuration setting:

```
verbose=255
```

With this configuration set, you'll see much additional output during an AIDE run:

```
Mhash library initialization
inserting 4096
update_md called
close_md called
md2line
Line has 4096
copying 4096
/bin/ash attr=7100
/bin/ash attr=7101
Adding child /bin/ash
encode base64, data length: 10
encode base64, data length: 10
encode base64, data length: 16
r->childs 135736080, r->parent 135383536, r->checked 512
dropping back to parent
r->childs 135388080, r->parent 0, r->checked 1024
```

The output is much more verbose (like you would expect) and includes the functions being called within the AIDE program itself, as well as details on the files that AIDE is checking as it is checking them. Using this output can be invaluable when you're trying to troubleshoot a problem with your AIDE configuration.

Defining Macros in AIDE

Macros are used in AIDE to define commonly used objects and objects to be used as variables throughout an AIDE configuration file. You might use an AIDE macro to define the top-level directory to be used within the configuration. You would then use this macro within selection lines, and it would be substituted like a variable in that selection line. You also might use a macro to set a variable based on certain criteria. Macros can then be used within the AIDE configuration within control structures (decisional blocks of code) to alter the configuration of AIDE based on the outcome of the control structure.

Macros are defined using the following syntax:

```
@@define <macro> <definition>
```

Macros can also be undefined with this syntax:

```
@@undef <macro>
```

Macros are used within the configuration with the following syntax:

```
@@{<macro>}
```

An example of using a macro in a simple way is to create a macro for a complex directory hierarchy so that you don't have to type it into the configuration file multiple times. Assume that you have a certain structure of directories on the computer that you want to define using a macro:

```
@@define BASEDIR /usr/src/linux
```

This macro could then be used later within the configuration of selections for AIDE:

```
@@{BASEDIR}/.config R
!@@{BASEDIR}/doc
```

A more powerful use of macros involves changing the configuration based on some criteria. For example, macros can be used within two types of control structures, one based on whether the macro has been defined and the other based on the host from which the AIDE program is being run.

These control structures are basically if/then/else statements, and they have associated negations as well. The syntax for determining whether a macro has been defined is this:

```
@@ifdef <macro>
```

The negation for the @@ifdef evaluation is as shown here:

```
@@ifndef <macro>
```

For determining the current host, this is the syntax:

```
@@ifhost <hostname>
```

The negation for the @@ifhost evaluation is, as you might guess, the following:

```
@@ifnhost <hostname>
```

Regardless of which control structure is used, it must be closed using the statement:

```
@@endif
```

Multiple control structures can be grouped using an **else** type of structure that you would expect for an associated **if** statement. The syntax is simply as follows:

```
@@else
```

Here's an example of how each of these might be used. The first example checks to see whether the macro called **SOURCE** has been defined, and if not, defines it:

```
@@ifndef SOURCE
@@define SOURCE /usr/src
@@endif
```

The second example looks at the hostname of the computer from which AIDE is being run and sets a macro based on the results of that check. This might be helpful if you have differing directory structures between various hosts and you'd like to use only one common AIDE configuration file among them. Here's the second example:

```
@@ifhost netserver
@@define LOCALBINDIR /usr/local/sbin
@@endif
```

Finally, here is an example using an **else** statement:

```
@@ifhost netserver
@@define LOCALBINDIR /usr/local/sbin
@@ELSE
@@define LOCALBINDIR /usr/local/bin
@@endif
```

For all the examples, recall that you'd use these macros later within the configuration using the following syntax:

```
@@{<macro>}
```

The Types of AIDE Checks

You may be wondering about the different types of checks AIDE can perform. The checks are described again in Table 12.2.

TABLE 12.2
AIDE Check Types

DIRECTIVE	DESCRIPTION
p	permissions
i	inode
n	number of links
u	user
g	group
s	size
b	block count
m	Mtime
a	Atime
c	Ctime
S	check for growing size
md5	md5 checksum
sha1	sha1 checksum
rmd160	rmd160 checksum
tiger	tiger checksum
R	p+i+n+u+g+s+m+c+md5
L	p+i+n+u+g
E	Empty group
>	Growing logfile p+u+g+i+n+S
haval	haval checksum
gost	gost checksum
crc32	crc32 checksum

It's probably helpful to break down the types of AIDE checks into categories. There are three basic categories of AIDE checks: what I will term standard checks, grouped checks, and checksums. The standard type of AIDE check looks for information that can be gathered from the file or the file's descriptor. These checks are listed in Table 12.3.

TABLE 12.3
Standard Checks in AIDE

DIRECTIVE	DESCRIPTION
p	permissions
i	inode
n	number of links
u	user
g	group
s	size
b	block count
m	Mtime
a	Atime
c	Ctime
S	check for growing size

These standard checks all utilize filesystem functions that are built-in or native in Linux and can be found from the inode entry for the file. As such, running a given standard check is less resource intensive than a checksum check. Some of these checks lend themselves to certain files, whereas others will cause the file to show up in a report nearly every time the check is run. For example, the Ctime of a given file should not change unless the file is deleted or replaced with another.

It may not be readily apparent what some of the standard checks actually do. Table 12.4 describes what may be the more obscure checks within this group.

TABLE 12.4
Explanation of Some Standard Checks

CHECK NAME	EXPLANATION
inode	The inode is a data structure that holds information about a given file in Linux. The inode contains information such as the location of the file, the permissions, the owner and group information, and many other useful bits.
Number of links	Links are akin to shortcuts in the Windows world. This type of check looks to see how many links exist to the given file.
Mtime	The Mtime of a file is the time when the file was last modified.
Atime	The Atime of a file is the time when the file was last accessed.
Ctime	The Ctime of a file is the time when the file was created.

On the other hand, grouped checks combine some of the more commonly used standard checks, as described in Table 12.5.

TABLE 12.5
Grouped Checks in AIDE

DIRECTIVE	DEFINITION
R	p+i+n+u+g+s+m+c+md5
L	p+i+n+u+g
E	Empty group
>	Growing logfile p+u+g+i+n+S

Finally, checksums utilize cryptographic checksums of the files, as explained earlier in the chapter and defined in Table 12.6.

TABLE 12.6
Checksum Checks in AIDE

DIRECTIVE	DEFINITION
md5	md5 checksum
sha1	sha1 checksum
rmd160	rmd160 checksum
tiger	tiger checksum
haval	haval checksum
gost	gost checksum
crc32	crc32 checksum

The differences in the various checksum check types can be explained simply as the differences in the cryptographic algorithms used to create the checksums. I'll leave it up to you to do further research on the types of cryptographic algorithms used by AIDE. I recommend *Applied Cryptography*, by Bruce Schneier, as a great reference for this purpose.

Summary

This chapter looked at filesystem integrity and how it can help your system security by ensuring that files haven't been unexpectedly altered. The chapter began with a look at how checksums are used to check files. The chapter continued with an in-depth look at one filesystem integrity software package, AIDE. You saw how to install, configure, and use AIDE on your system.

The next chapter looks at system security from its lowest level for an operating system: the kernel.

Kernel Enhancements

Up until this point, you've seen how to create, install, and troubleshoot a Linux firewall using iptables. A firewall is an integral piece, a layer if you will, of the defense-in-depth strategy that has become popular. However, a firewall doesn't protect against attacks on your data that originate from the inside of the firewall. A firewall is also only as good as the security of the device or computer on which it runs. If you don't keep the firewall's software up-to-date or if you run unnecessary services on the firewall computer, that could compromise the security.

Various kernel enhancements can be applied to make the computer that much more secure at this important level. Specifically, this chapter looks at two kernel enhancements: Security Enhanced Linux, known as SELinux, and Greater Security, known as GrSecurity. This chapter also walks through how to build your own kernel and apply the GrSecurity patch.

Security Enhanced Linux

SELinux was developed by the National Security Agency in the United States. SELinux is software to protect against some kinds of security attacks, to limit the success of others, and to log much additional information. SELinux is included in the stock 2.6 Linux kernel; therefore, it's no longer necessary to add the SELinux patch to the kernel to take advantage of its enhancements.

SELinux works by placing processes inside of a sandbox known as a domain. By limiting processes to their own sandbox or domain, it limits the damage that can be done by an attacker who uses that process to gain or escalate privilege.

This section gives an elementary overview of SELinux. If you'd like to explore SELinux further, I recommend visiting the NSA website at http://www.nsa.gov/selinux/.

SELinux Architecture

SELinux is more than kernel code. SELinux consists of the kernel code plus related library, files, and administration tools. The system or security administrator creates a security policy for SELinux to use. This policy is then implemented on the system and administered through SELinux tools such as newrole, setfiles, checkpolicy, and a whole host of others.

In addition to the SELinux-specific tools, some standard Linux tools are also modified to work with SELinux, including commands such as `ps`, `ls`, `cron`, and others.

SUBJECTS, OBJECTS, AND ACTIONS, OH MY!

Three elements compose SELinux's security model: Subjects, Objects, and Actions. Subjects are the protagonists within the context of SELinux; they are the things that work on or perform actions on objects. Objects are, therefore, the items on which subjects act. Examples of objects include files; processes; special devices like block devices, character devices, and sockets; directories; and filesystems. Objects are actually divided into classes of objects and include those listed above plus many more. And, yes, processes can be both subjects and objects. In other words, a process can perform the action or it can have the action performed on it.

OBJECT PERSISTENCE

Objects are either persistent or transient. Persistent objects are those that are long-lived, such as files. Transient objects are short-lived, such as a process while running.

Each domain has a limited number of files and operations it can access. Each domain's definition classifies the operations it can perform on files within a certain class. Processes can also transition into other domains under certain conditions.

When an action is requested, for example, a program attempting to read `/etc/shadow`, an Access Decision must be made. This Access Decision is made based on three security attributes:

- User identity
- Role
- Type

The user identity is exactly what you'd think, the userid of the subject or object. This information is stored in an SELinux file as opposed to being stored in /etc/passwd. The role is a given set of permissions for the user identity. Users can be in only one role at a time, and roles are managed through the SELinux newrole command. Finally, types are groupings of subjects and objects and are the primary attribute used to make decisions with SELinux.

Combined, the three security attributes make up the Security Identifier (SID). The SID is an integer value used by SELinux to optimize the myriad access and transition decisions that must take place on a Linux system.

SELinux gives a level of security not previously possible with Linux. As you can imagine, SELinux is much more complex than this overview could hope to convey. I invite the reader to visit the SELinux website at http://www.nsa.gov/selinux/ for more information on SELinux.

Greater Security with GrSecurity

GrSecurity, formally known as Greater Security, is a kernel patch and userspace program for enhancing the security of a Linux system. GrSecurity, also referred to as Grsec, closes some avenues for attack and makes others much more difficult. Grsec implements a sophisticated Access Control List (ACL) for objects in Linux. The ACL can be used to provide much more granular control over files and other resources. For example, using a Grsec ACL, you can control what files will be shown as the result of a find command or which processes are included in process accounting logs.

Grsec also enables a system called PaX to restrict the capability of processes to alter memory space. This aspect alone renders many types of attacks involving overflows completely ineffective. Grsec also provides other protections such as stack randomization to make attacking the computer a more difficult task.

Throughout this chapter, I'll be taking a recipe-style approach to get the quickest results with a Grsec kernel. At the end of the chapter, I'll take more time to explain some of the features of Grsec. In other words, I'll show you how before telling you why, for the most part.

A Quick Look Around the Kernel

I'd like to introduce the kernel. If this is the first time you've met, say hello and treat it nicely. The kernel is the piece of software responsible for talking to the hardware and creating the background environment within which programs are run. You usually don't encounter the kernel until you have to load hardware or need to recompile it for additional features or security updates. Most Linux vendors now include modular kernels along with their regular updates, thus greatly reducing the number of people who compile their own kernel, or roll their own kernel as it is sometimes called.

What'd You Call That?

Before I go too far, I should get some terms out of the way in relation to the kernel. First is differentiation between the various kernels now available. Because Linux is open source and free (as in free speech), numerous forks and customizations have taken place on the kernel. Some of these are discussed a bit later, but for now take my word that multiple versions of the kernel exist. When you hear someone refer to a "stock" or "vanilla" kernel, they are (or should be) referring to the official kernel source code available from http://www.kernel.org/. These kernels are named as such because they come from the official Linus Torvalds–based Linux kernel implementation.

Stock or vanilla kernels are in contrast to customized or distribution-specific kernels released by some Linux vendors. You'll hear the vendors refer to the kernels as "enhanced" or some other marketing-type term. These vendors usually add functionality to the kernel, thus making it custom to that distribution. One example of this is the Advanced Server released by Red Hat, which includes some Red Hat–specific additions to the kernel. Although these additions provide some functionality for specific needs, they also create a problem for those of us who want to add security or otherwise customize the kernel. Further, the updates to those distribution-specific kernels frequently lag behind the vanilla kernel, which leaves users of those distribution-specific kernels vulnerable to attack for longer than they should be.

What's Your Number?

Version numbering of kernels can be confusing to those new to the kernel. This fact is multiplied by the use of distribution-specific kernels and their own naming and numbering conventions. This section briefly examines the version numbering involved in Linux kernels.

Kernel numbering consists of three numbers separated by a dot, as in 2.6.4. In this numbering scheme the initial 2.6 indicates the major version number, and the final .4 indicates the minor version number. Major changes to the kernel are usually encompassed within the major version number, 2.0, 2.2, 2.4, 2.6, and so on. As you can see, the second digit within the kernel version number consists only of even-numbered integers. Kernel versions declared "stable" are given even-numbered second digits. For example, the development version of the kernel known as 2.3.N was eventually released as 2.4.0, and the development version known as 2.5.N was eventually released as 2.6.0. Work continues on the 2.7.N branch, which will eventually be released as 2.8.0. It's important to note that only the second number connotes the type of release, development (odd) or stable (even).

The final number is the minor release, beginning with 0 and continuing on as minor bug fixes and driver additions are released for the stock kernel. This last number can be either even or odd, and neither indicates any special type of kernel.

Kernels are also sometimes given an RC status to indicate that they are a Release Candidate. The number will resemble something like 2.6.5-rc2 or 2.6.8-rc3. As with the development releases of the kernel, these release candidates aren't meant for general use but rather are for testing purposes.

The Kernel: From 20,000 Feet

The kernel is really a bunch of source-code files written in C (mostly). You choose the stuff you want to include within the kernel, such as drivers and other functionality, and then you compile it. The kernel is modular, which means that pieces of its functionality can be loaded on demand. This is helpful for desktop-type systems in which you might need the USB driver only when a USB device is plugged in. A modular kernel is less useful (and can be harmful) from a security standpoint.

The act of compiling the kernel consists of a few steps, the first of which is obtaining the source code itself. Beyond that, you unarchive the source and run a command to help you select which drivers and functionality to include in the kernel. From there you build the kernel and then install it.

The de facto location for kernel source code is in **/usr/src/linux**. The kernel, as source code, includes a few main variations for selecting the options to include within the kernel. These options are all accessed with the **make** command; two of them are appropriate from the command line, whereas one is used for X Windows kernel compiles. For this discussion I'll be concentrating on the methods available from the command line. Don't worry about following along in this section; there will be plenty of time for that later. For now I'll give a high-level overview of the kernel.

The primary (and easiest) method for selecting kernel compile options from the command line is with this command:

```
make menuconfig
```

Running that command from the kernel source directory results in the kernel configuration interface running, as shown in Figure 13.1.

As you can see from Figure 13.1, there are quite a few options within the kernel. The configuration is such that the options are organized hierarchically, so there could be multiple levels within each of the options shown in Figure 13.1.

FIGURE 13.1
The kernel configuration interface is used to configure options to include with the kernel in Linux.

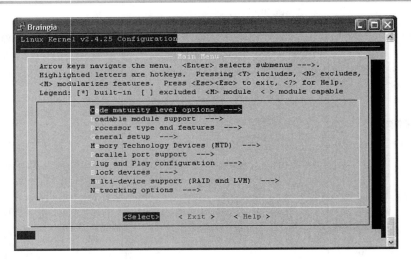

Probably the biggest hurdle when compiling a kernel for the first time on a new computer, whether you're experienced or not, is knowing exactly what to include within the compile. Much of the process involves finding the hardware that the computer uses and determining which driver to include for that hardware. At the end of the day, some of the process of compiling a kernel comes down to guesswork, some educated guesses, some not. Good troubleshooting techniques and trial and error both play a part in a kernel compile. These are fine when you're at the console but much less fun when you're 1,000 miles away from the computer.

To Patch or Not to Patch

When you patch software source code, whether the kernel or not, you change the code to add or remove lines of code based on a patch file created for that software. The patch may be something as simple as a software update or as complex as changing the functionality of the software itself. When a new version of the kernel is released, the kernel maintainers release a full version of the kernel along with a patch file for those wanting to simply update to the next version of the kernel by patching.

When you run a patch to change software functionality, you are, in effect, altering that software from its base state. This involves a trade-off. The trade-off is that from that point forward, to take advantage of the additional functionality added by the patch, you must also patch any updates to the base software. In the context of Grsec, it means that you're moving away from the concept of the vanilla or stock kernel in favor of the added security.

Enhanced Security Without Grsec

Beginning with the 2.6 stream of kernels, some functionality that was previously available only as a kernel patch was introduced into the main kernel. This functionality comes in the form of the SELinux area of the kernel covered earlier.

The advantage to using SELinux is that it's included with the stock kernel and thus doesn't require a patch for every kernel update. However, the additional functionality included with Grsec makes the patch trade-off well worth it for enhancing security.

Other software such as Exec-Shield offers some of the same protections as Grsec. However, information gathered on Grsec and Exec-Shield seems to indicate that Grsec is the more robust implementation and provides some functionality not offered by Exec-Shield. Exec-Shield does have the advantage of being included with some major vendors' Linux implementations.

Using a GrSecurity Kernel

A logical order exists for implementing a kernel with Grsec. If you've compiled your own kernel before, some of these steps aren't necessary. Truthfully, some of the steps within this section aren't fully required either, but I'll go through them to lessen the chance of something going wrong during the process of getting up to speed with Grsec.

Downloading Grsec and a Fresh Kernel

Both GrSecurity and a fresh kernel need to be downloaded from their respective Internet sites. The kernel source can be downloaded in a few different archive formats with bzip2 being the smallest in download size. Download the kernel source from http://www.kernel.org/. The kernel.org site will contain a few versions of the kernel right on the main home page. I'd recommend using the kernel labeled with a phrase such as "the latest stable kernel." Figure 13.2 contains a look at the kernel.org home page so that you can see the area to which I'm referring. The kernel can be downloaded by clicking on the link labeled "F" (which is an abbreviation for "Full").

The kernel source will take a few minutes to a few hours to download, depending on the speed of your Internet connection. It will be downloaded in a bzip2-formatted tar archive.

Grsec is downloaded from the GrSecurity website at http://www.grsecurity.net/. Grab the latest stable Grsec patch. This file will download very quickly because it's just a patch containing the differences between it and the main kernel that you just downloaded.

FIGURE 13.2

The kernel.org site. You should look for the latest stable kernel.

Compiling Your First Kernel

Before you apply the Grsec patch, it will be helpful for you to get a working customized version of the kernel going on the computer. After the new kernel is up and running, I'll show how to apply the patch. This section examines how to compile a kernel from the vanilla source.

A good place to start when considering how to approach your first kernel compile is the Kernel-HOWTO or the Kernel Rebuild Guide. The Kernel-HOWTO is located at http://www.tldp.org/HOWTO/Kernel-HOWTO/index.html; the Kernel Rebuild Guide is currently located at http://www.digitalhermit.com/~kwan/kernel.html. These documents provide valuable insight and tips for first-time kernel compilers.

The first thing to do is to unpack the kernel sources into the right place. Normally Linux kernel source files are stored in **/usr/src** within a directory called **linux**. When you unpack the kernel source, it'll be named something like **linux-N.N.NN**. I'll show you how to create a symbolic link (it's like a shortcut in Windows) to link that directory to **/usr/src/linux**.

Copy the source files that you downloaded into **/usr/src**. For example, for kernel 2.6.4 the command is this:

```
cp linux-2.6.4.tar.bz2 /usr/src
```

Unpack the Linux kernel source using a combination of bzip2 and tar, like this (don't forget to change into the /usr/src directory):

```
bunzip2 -c linux-2.6.4.tar.bz2 | tar -x
```

You'll now have a directory containing the uncompressed Linux kernel source code. Traditionally the source code is stored in /usr/src/linux but the kernel source was unpacked to /usr/src/linux-2.6.4. To solve this problem, make a symbolic link, sometimes called a symlink:

```
ln -s linux-2.6.4 linux
```

Now there will be a symlink in the traditional spot that you can cd into:

```
cd /usr/src/linux
```

Or just use this:

```
cd linux
```

When you attempt to run the ln command, you may receive an error saying that the file linux already exists. If this is the case, it appears that you already have kernel source lying around in the directory. For example, in SUSE if you install the kernel source during initial installation, it will be unpacked to a directory within /usr/src, and then a symlink is created to /usr/src/linux. The symlink can safely be removed so that you can re-create it for linking to your kernel source. If you received the error about linux already existing when you attempted to create the symlink, delete the old one with the command (from within /usr/src):

```
rm linux
```

There are three primary methods for configuring the options to include with the customized kernel, and all three are based on the options presented in the Linux kernel Makefile. When configured, the options you choose (and don't choose) are stored in a file called .config within the Linux kernel source-code directory:

```
make config
make menuconfig
make xconfig
```

Additionally, there's a method called oldconfig to update the configuration to a new version by using an old version of the config file. This function is quite helpful for upgrading between minor versions of the kernel without having to start from a vanilla configuration and possibly forgetting to compile in some vital bits here or there. The oldconfig method assumes that you have the old configuration already located in the kernel source directory (/usr/src/linux in the examples here) and that the configuration file is called .config within that directory. You can update to the new kernel with the **oldconfig** method by typing this:

```
make oldconfig
```

The method you choose to configure the kernel is at least somewhat a matter of personal preference, but the result of the computer's configuration as well. You can't use **xconfig** if you don't have X Windows installed. Likewise, **menuconfig** requires some **ncurses** libraries that are usually, but not always, installed. The standard **config** option for compiling a kernel will always work, but it's also the most cumbersome, especially for newcomers.

All things considered, I recommend **menuconfig** as the option to use for configuration of the kernel. **Menuconfig** can be used regardless of whether the computer has X Windows, and it can be used through a remote SSH connection as well. However, if you have an existing version of a configuration file, I recommend using **oldconfig** first and then using **menuconfig** to further tune the configuration options.

You should spend some time determining the hardware in the computer as well as the kernel driver responsible for that hardware's operation. The program **/sbin/lspci** will show the current PCI hardware configuration, which you can then use to find out which drivers are necessary to run that hardware. Also, examine **/proc/cpuinfo** using a pager such as less or more or another program such as cat:

```
cat /proc/cpuinfo
```

This will tell you the type of processor you have so that you can choose the appropriate architecture in that area of the kernel **config**. Keep track of this information and use a tool such as Google to determine the appropriate Linux drivers that correspond to the hardware in the computer.

You can frequently find a copy of the kernel configuration for the current kernel within the **/boot** directory. For example, in SUSE the file will be located in **/boot** and named **vmlinuz.config**. To incorporate this configuration as a starting point for your new kernel, copy this file into the **/usr/src/linux** directory:

```
cp -i /boot/vmlinuz.config /usr/src/linux/.config
```

If the command runs correctly, you won't receive any feedback; silence indicates success. However, if you receive a question asking whether to overwrite an existing **.config**, cancel out of the copy operation and find out why there is an existing configuration file in **/usr/src/linux**. This might be caused if you didn't delete the symlink to a previous kernel in **/usr/src/linux** or if you've already run one of the make options for a kernel. When you run make for a kernel, it will save a new copy of the **.config** file, so if you've already run a kernel compile process, chances are you don't want to overwrite that configuration file with a default one.

After you've copied the default configuration file over, it's wise to run the `oldconfig` process on the config file to update it to the new version of the kernel. From within the `/usr/src/linux` directory, run the following:

```
make oldconfig
```

You'll be asked several questions, based on the differences between the existing (default) configuration file that you just copied over and the new configuration options available with this version of the kernel. The `oldconfig` process is accomplished through a text-based interface, so you'll see things like this:

```
Kernel support for ELF binaries (CONFIG_BINFMT_ELF) [Y/m/n/?]
Kernel support for MISC binaries (CONFIG_BINFMT_MISC) [M/n/y/?]
Select task to kill on out of memory condition (CONFIG_OOM_KILLER) [N/y/?] (NEW)
```

As each new feature is encountered within the new kernel, you'll be asked whether you'd like to include the feature in the new kernel. It's almost always safe to assume the defaults by just pressing Enter for these options, unless you're looking for some specific functionality with the new kernel.

After you get through all the `oldconfig` process, you'll be placed back at the command prompt within `/usr/src/linux`. You've now reached another fork in the road. If you'd like, you can jump into the `menuconfig` interface (`make menuconfig`) to further customize the drivers and features included in your kernel. If you'd like to try compiling the kernel without that additional customization, you can do so right now as well. I strongly recommend that you do go into the `menuconfig` process to ensure that the correct drivers are included for your hardware. If you choose to skip the `menuconfig` process, the chances of a failed boot increase.

If you choose to enter into the `menuconfig` process, you'll have a chance to further customize the kernel through a friendlier interface than the `oldconfig` process. The `menuconfig` interface makes it easier to access help for the various kernel options as well.

Within the `menuconfig` interface, walk through each of the options by pressing Enter; using the keyboard arrows; using Tab to move among Select, Exit, and Help; using the spacebar to select or deselect; and pressing Esc to back up. Be careful not to press Esc too many times because that's also how you exit. While you're configuring through the `menuconfig` interface, look specifically for drivers that relate to your hardware and make sure that they are included in the kernel, as indicated by an asterisk (*). For example, I have a network card that's based off of the AMD PCNet32 driver, so I need to include this in the kernel. I navigate to Network Device Support; then Ethernet (10 or 100Mbit); and then EISA, VLB, PCI and On Board Controllers; and then make sure that AMD PCnet32 PCI Support is checked by pressing the spacebar.

When you're ready to begin the actual build process, there are three primary commands used to build the kernel. Actually, for now, most likely four commands will be used because I'm going to assume that modules are included in the default kernel that you're building. Eventually, when you disable modules for added security, you won't have to run the final **make** command that I'll show because it's just used to build the modules.

The first build step generates the dependencies. From within the **/usr/src/linux** directory, type the following:

```
make dep
```

This command should run relatively quickly. Continue the build process by typing this:

```
make clean
```

The **make clean** step is also somewhat fast, obviously depending on the available resources. Finally, create the kernel itself by typing this:

```
make bzImage
```

The **bzImage** option compresses the kernel using bzip2. Another alternative used on systems without bzip2 is **make zImage**, which uses gzip instead of bzip2. Because you have bzip2 on this system (you had to in order to uncompress the kernel source), you can use **bzImage**.

The kernel will now compile. This process will take a varying amount of time depending on a couple factors. First and foremost, the speed of and load on the processor(s) and available RAM will be the biggest factors that will determine the amount of time that the kernel will take to compile. On a hardly used dual-Intel Xeon processor machine with 1GB RAM, the kernel takes less than five minutes to compile. On the other hand, an Intel Pentium 60 with 24MB RAM will take many hours to compile the kernel. The second factor in determining the amount of time a kernel takes to compile is the number of options you included with the kernel. Adding SMP code and many (possibly unnecessary) drivers will cause the compile time to increase.

Sit back and relax or go do something else while the kernel is compiling. Now is a good time to read the kernel HOWTO that I recommended earlier, that is, if you haven't already read it. Hopefully the kernel compile won't fail with an error, though this does sometimes happen. Usually it's due to a troublesome driver or a conflict between two drivers. You'll know that the compile failed if the kernel stops compiling and you're left with something like this on the screen:

```
Error 1
***[make]***
Error 2
```

If this happens, examine the last few lines above the errors to see whether you can discern in which portion of the kernel compile the error occurred. Many times the name of the file that was compiling is shown within the text on the screen. Also, examine the end of the file config.log within /usr/src/linux to see whether there is any information in there. If necessary, copy the contents of any error messages into a search engine like Google to see whether someone else has encountered the problem. One of the biggest strengths of open-source software is the availability of help online within forums and Google for just this sort of thing.

If the kernel compile fails with an error, you'll need to trace down the troublesome driver(s) or area of the kernel and deselect the drivers or exclude them. When you believe you've found the cause of the error, the first task is to clean up the environment and start over. Countless compiles of software fail because the administrator didn't clean up the source tree after a failed compile. Before undertaking this process, you should copy the existing .config configuration file to a safe location. The clean up process will delete the .config file, so if you've made customizations they'll be lost.

To clean up the kernel source tree, type the following:

```
make mrproper
```

The environment will now be clean just as if you had unarchived fresh kernel source. Start the process over from the beginning by copying the existing configuration file (usually in /boot) into the kernel source tree and follow the steps as before. This time, however, go into the menuconfig interface and deselect the troublesome drivers or other parts of the kernel that you believe caused the failure.

Whew. Hopefully nothing goes wrong! If the kernel stops compiling and you didn't receive any errors, you'll see something close to this on the screen (your text will vary):

```
tools/build -b bbootsect bsetup compressed/bvmlinux.out CURRENT >bzImage
Root device is (8, 2)
Boot sector 512 bytes.
Setup is 4769 bytes.
System is 1086 kB
warning: kernel is too big for standalone boot from floppy
make[1]: Leaving directory `/usr/src/linux-2.4.25/arch/i386/boot'
```

Congratulations, the kernel compiled. Because this is your first kernel and you've used the default configuration file, the kernel that's compiling most likely requires modules in order to run. As you become more comfortable with compiling kernels, I recommend that you compile a monolithic kernel rather than including modules for server environments.

There's less of a chance of an attacker injecting his own code into the kernel if the capability to use modules isn't even included in the kernel. However, the reality of the situation is that modular kernels are the de facto standard for installed kernels today. Therefore, you'll need to compile and install the modules as part of the kernel build process.

After you compile the necessary drivers into the kernel rather than including them as modules, the module-related steps will no longer be necessary as part of the kernel build process. After the kernel itself compiles successfully, the next step is to compile the modules. This is accomplished with the following command:

```
make modules
```

The module compile process will take a varying amount of time depending on the factors discussed earlier for kernel compile time. The same caveat and troubleshooting steps also apply in relation to the module compile as well. If the module compile fails with an error, track down the troublesome module code and deselect it, or, if it's necessary for your system to run, try including it within the kernel itself rather than including it as a module.

The module compile process will complete without much fanfare, probably something like this:

```
make[1]: Entering directory `/usr/src/linux-2.4.25/arch/i386/lib'
make[1]: Nothing to be done for `modules'.
make[1]: Leaving directory `/usr/src/linux-2.4.25/arch/i386/lib'
```

If you see anything resembling the word **Error**, the module compile didn't complete successfully.

Assuming that the modules compiled, install the modules by typing this:

```
make modules_install
```

Now it's time to install the new kernel. The kernel is installed within an architecture-independent directory structure. Allow me to assume that the architecture you're using is an Intel x86-based type of computer. If that's the case, your kernel is located in /usr/src/linux/arch/i386/boot. Because you should already be in the /usr/src/linux directory, you can copy the new kernel to its home in **/boot** with the command as follows, substituting the kernel version for **<version>**:

```
cp -i arch/i386/boot/bzImage /boot/vmlinuz-<version>
```

For example, to copy a compiled kernel version 2.4.25, you'd type this:

```
cp -i arch/i386/boot/bzImage /boot/vmlinuz-2425
```

When using a modularized kernel, the computer frequently requires an initial ramdisk, known as **initrd**, to successfully preload modules required for the computer to boot. This is often the case when disk or disk controller drivers are included as modules rather than compiled directly into the kernel. If you're using a modular kernel, you'll also need to create the initial ramdisk before attempting to boot. The initial ramdisk is created with the mkinitrd program. The use of the mkinitrd program is slightly different with various flavors of Linux.

Assume that you've compiled a modularized kernel version 2.4.25, compiled the modules, and installed them. Now it's time to create an **initrd** for that kernel. The new kernel has been copied to **/boot/vmlinuz-2425**. There's also an existing kernel named **/boot/vmlinuz**. In SUSE, you'd accomplish this task with the following command:

```
mkinitrd -k "vmlinuz vmlinuz-2425" -i "initrd initrd-2425"
```

The **initrd** files will be created in **/boot** and named **initrd** and **initrd-2425** for the existing and new kernels respectively.

The next step depends entirely on whether your version of Linux uses the Lilo or Grub boot loader. I'll include instructions for both Lilo and Grub, but you only have to follow the one that applies to your computer.

Here's how to tell which loader you're using. Find out whether you're running Lilo by typing this command:

```
ls /etc/lilo.conf
```

If you receive an error similar to the following, you're probably running Grub:

```
ls: /etc/lilo.conf: No such file or directory
```

NOTE

It's possible to have both Lilo and Grub installed, so finding lilo.conf does not 100% guarantee that you are using Lilo. If you're in doubt, most boot loaders such as Lilo and Grub will identify themselves when you boot the system.

First I'll handle adding the new kernel to the Grub menu for boot. Edit the Grub menu file, usually **/boot/grub/menu.lst**, in your favorite text editor. Within the **menu.lst** file, you'll see sections relating to the current kernel. Simply copy and paste one of those existing sections. Be careful so as not to alter any of the existing lines in the file. For example, you might add the following lines:

```
title customlinux
    kernel (hd0,1)/boot/vmlinuz-2425 root=/dev/sda2
    initrd (hd0,1)/boot/initrd-2425
```

Note that your **hd** and **root** devices will probably be different. Look at what's there already and simply copy it. For Grub, that's all you need to do. You can reboot the computer by typing **reboot** or **shutdown -r now**.

The process is similar for Lilo. Edit the file **/etc/lilo.conf**, find an existing section related to the current kernel, copy the section, and paste it back in, being careful not to alter any existing lines of the Lilo configuration file. An example in the Lilo configuration file might be something like this:

```
image=/boot/vmlinuz
        label=Linux
        read-only
```

One additional step is necessary after you're done editing the Lilo configuration file, and that's to run the Lilo program. This step is overlooked by many an administrator. At the command prompt, simply type this:

```
lilo
```

You'll see output similar to the following:

```
Added Linux *
Added LinuxOLD
```

The asterisk (*) indicates the kernel that will load by default. Now you can reboot the computer by typing reboot.

WHAT HAPPENS IF THERE'S A PROBLEM?

When you've compiled a kernel, there is always a chance that the computer won't boot when you attempt to reboot using the new kernel. This will be evidenced by a few different error conditions, the end result of which will be that the computer won't get booted fully into Linux. You may receive an error on the console such as this:

```
Kernel panic:  Unable to mount root fs
```

If this happens, don't spend too much time worrying. Write down the error message along with key words from lines preceding the error. Power down the computer and start it again, this time selecting the old kernel when presented with the Lilo or Grub prompt. The computer will boot as it did before.

Another problem that's not as noticeable is when the computer boots but some functionality is missing. This occurs frequently when the incorrect network drivers are compiled into the kernel and the networking won't work, but many other driver-related issues might show up as well.

Unfortunately, if you do get a kernel panic or choose an incorrect driver, it means that you'll end up having to start the kernel compile process over. Use your troubleshooting skills to try to determine the problem or, in other words, what wasn't included in the kernel that should've been.

There's no magic bullet to fix the new kernel. It will take your solid troubleshooting skills along with patience. Again, people who are experienced in working with the kernel can still have problems with the first kernel on a new computer. So don't feel bad if it happens to you!

Improving the Kernel Build

If everything has gone according to plan, the new kernel will be booted and devices such as networking will work correctly. You can confirm the kernel that the computer is using with the following command:

```
uname -a
```

If the version reported doesn't match the version that you compiled in the previous steps, verify that you placed the kernel in the correct place in the Grub configuration or that you chose the right kernel to boot from either the Lilo or the Grub prompt. Also, if you're running Lilo, did you remember to run the `lilo` command after editing the Lilo configuration file? It's a frequent oversight.

From here, it's up to you whether you want to improve the kernel compile to add further customization for the computer. From both server administration and security standpoints, improving the kernel compile is a good idea.

As starting points, I recommend removing support for modules and compiling the necessary drivers directly into the kernel. You'll probably find that many of the drivers compiled in as modules are actually unnecessary. Again, a monolithic kernel reduces the attack paths available by making it impossible for an attacker to inject a trojaned module.

I also recommend using a minimum set of drivers that match the computer's hardware and role. For example, is printer support really necessary on a Linux server that acts solely as a web server? Probably not. Therefore, these drivers can be removed from the kernel. Not only will the kernel be smaller and use less resources, but the attack path through those drivers will also be removed.

GrSecurity

Now that the new kernel is running, it's time to recompile it! This time you'll be adding the GrSecurity patch and compiling in options to greatly enhance the security of the computer system. This section examines the steps involved in this undertaking.

Applying the Grsec Patch

Because you've already downloaded the patch in a previous step, now it's time to patch the kernel source. The problem is that you have an already-compiled version of the kernel in /usr/src/linux. That version has a known-good configuration file, but there are other files that will interfere with the patching process. Therefore, you'll need to clean up that area before patching the kernel with Grsec.

Usually the configuration file is copied to the /boot directory. However, at this point there's no reason to assume anything. Therefore, as a first step, copy the existing kernel configuration file to another location so as to preserve its contents:

```
cp /usr/src/linux/.config /root/.config-kernel-<NNNN>
```

Replace <NNNN> with the kernel version.

Now change directory into /usr/src/linux and clean up the source tree:

```
cd /usr/src/linux
make mrproper
```

Copy the configuration file back into the kernel source tree:

```
cp /root/.config-kernel-<NNNN> /usr/src/linux/.config
```

Now it's (finally) time to apply the Grsec patch. Change directory into /usr/src; if the Grsec patch isn't there already, copy it there from the location you saved it to when you downloaded the patch earlier in the chapter.

```
cd /usr/src
```

Optionally, if the patch isn't already there, use this:

```
cp <download-location>/grsec-<NNNN>.patch /usr/src
```

Apply the patch, replacing <NNNN> with the Grsec version corresponding to your kernel:

```
patch -p0 < grsec-<NNNN>.patch
```

You'll now see output similar to the following, which was generated from a patch application on version 2.4.25 of the kernel:

```
patching file linux-2.4.25/Documentation/Configure.help
patching file linux-2.4.25/Makefile
... (continued)
patching file linux-2.4.25/net/socket.c
patching file linux-2.4.25/net/sunrpc/xprt.c
patching file linux-2.4.25/net/unix/af_unix.c
```

Choosing Grsec Features

Grsec includes more than a few features, not all of which are relevant to every situation. Some of the features available with Grsec are specialized to certain situations, and some are very advanced, requiring extensive additional configuration to work properly. Enabling some of the Grsec options is simply a matter of turning them on within the kernel configuration. This section examines the Grsec options.

SECURITY LEVEL

Grsec enables you to select one of four security levels, three of which are predefined. The predefined security levels include Low, Medium, and High, with the fourth level called Customized. One method for evaluating Grsec and its features is to apply the Low Security Level, compile, and run with the kernel as such. If you notice no ill effects of running with the Grsec-Enhanced Low Security Level, apply the Medium Security Level, compile, and run with that. Increase the security level to the highest level possible.

Recommendation:

Choose one of the default provided security levels and increase as much as possible, or choose a customized level and work through the other options contained in this section.

PAX CONTROL

PaX Control provides a means to defend against certain types of exploits that attack a program's address space. For instance, PaX Control can give protection against both stack and heap-based buffer overflows, among other things. Also included is integration between PaX and Mandatory Access Control (MAC) functions.

Recommendation:

Use your discretion. Some of the PaX options can be more involved to configure properly.

ADDRESS SPACE PROTECTION

Address Space Protection provides many useful options that can enhance security, including prevention of methods to inject code into a running monolithic kernel. Some of the options included within Address Space Protection can break applications, most notably X Windows. Therefore, if you use X Windows, extra caution should be taken when choosing Address Space Protection options.

Recommendation:

Enable these options unless you're running X Windows. If you're running X Windows, be wary of these options. These protections are great enough that it is worth a potential recompile in case one of the options breaks an application.

ACL OPTIONS

ACL Options provide some additional features that can be used when the Access Control List system is enabled through Grsec. Some options are set based on your policy, such as password lockout for the ACL system.

Recommendation:

If you're going to be using the Grsec ACL system, set these options as appropriate for your environment.

FILESYSTEM PROTECTIONS

The Filesystem Protections provided by Grsec enable the additional **chroot** restrictions that should be used if you're running applications in a **chroot**. Other protections are also provided within this option area, including restrictions on symlinks, the proc filesystem, and FIFO restrictions.

Recommendation:

You can greatly enhance security by enabling these options, especially including the **chroot** options if you're using **chroot**ed applications.

KERNEL AUDITING

A group of options that provides useful logging and tracking options can be found within the Kernel Auditing area. Included within this area are such things as logging for time changes, filesystem mounting and unmounting, and even logging every call to the **execve()** system. Some of these options can create huge log files but are invaluable when performing forensics on a successful attack.

Recommendation:

Enable as many of these options as possible. However, be careful not to fill up your log directory filesystems because of the number of entries created with things like **Exec logging**.

EXECUTABLE PROTECTIONS

Four important options appear within Executable Protections. These include options to prevent local users from possibly gaining extra privilege or gathering information about the system. Even if you aren't intending to allow "shell" (think: command-line) access to users on the system, an attacker's goal in life is to gain that shell access. These options can help prevent the attacker from gaining additional privileges if the attacker happens to gain shell access.

Recommendation:

Enable these options if possible in your environment.

NETWORK PROTECTIONS

Providing a broad range of helpful additional security are the Network Protections within Grsec. Randomization is a key component of these protections and can make it more difficult for an automated scan or probe to identify your operating system.

Recommendation:

Enable as many of these options as possible in your environment.

SYSCTL SUPPORT

Using Sysctl, you can enable many of the features of Grsec individually to help in troubleshooting. This is particularly helpful when you're first using Grsec in case an application won't start and you believe it to be because of a Grsec option. Using Sysctl, you issue an **echo** command to enable some of the various features that were compiled into the Grsec kernel. When you have a stable system, you then issue another **echo** command to effectively "lock" the environment, preventing the Grsec features from being disabled without a reboot. If you fail to lock the environment and you don't recompile to disable Sysctl support, an attacker can remove the Grsec protections, thus making them useless!

Recommendation:

Enable Sysctl support when first getting acquainted with Grsec. When you have a system that is stable with the various Grsec options that you've chosen, recompile the kernel to remove Sysctl support. Failure to do so can completely negate any Grsec enhancements.

LOGGING OPTIONS

The Logging Options area controls the performance of Grsec logging. Within this area you'll find options to configure the number of messages that can be sent within a certain (configurable) time period. This can help prevent possible denial-of-service attacks resulting from an attacker causing log file filesystems to fill up or creating noisy logs.

Recommendation:

Set these options as appropriate for your environment.

Building the Grsec Kernel

Building the kernel with Grsec is, in effect, no different from building another kernel. You've already applied the patch and, hopefully, chosen the options you would like to try. From here, back up to earlier in the chapter and follow the instructions for compiling the kernel from source.

After you've compiled the kernel and restarted, you can begin testing the new environment. The first thing to do is to make sure that the Grsec kernel is actually running. This task is accomplished by typing this:

```
uname -a
```

You should see output containing a portion similar to the following:

```
2.4.25-grsec
```

Obviously, the kernel revision number will probably be different, but the key is to ensure that grsec appears in that name. If it does, you're running with a Grsec kernel. If it doesn't, you should examine why the kernel booted to a different version other than the one you compiled. This could be because you forgot to run Lilo or forgot to install the kernel as the final step of the compile. Refer to the section "Compiling Your First Kernel" for possible causes.

If you've chosen to enable Sysctl support so that you can enable and disable certain Grsec features on the fly, you'll find a number of files located in the **/proc/sys/kernel/grsecurity** directory. You can enable these options within Grsec by typing this:

```
echo "1" >/proc/sys/kernel/grsecurity/<filename>
```

Here, **<filename>** is the name of the option as found by doing an **ls** within **/proc/sys/ kernel/grsecurity**. For example, if you want to enable the randomized process IDs (PIDs), the file is called **rand_pids**. You'd enable it with this line:

```
echo "1" >/proc/sys/kernel/grsecurity/rand_pids
```

After this particular option is enabled, you can run the **ps** command and watch new processes as they are created. They will have pseudo-random ID numbers rather than the traditional incrementing PIDs. I'd probably use the command **ps auwx** as root to see all the processes.

To disable a Grsec feature, simply echo a **0** to the file. For example, to disable the PID randomization that you just enabled, run the following command:

```
echo "0" >/proc/sys/kernel/grsecurity/rand_pids
```

It's important to remember that until you "lock" the Grsec features, an attacker can undo those features. The drawback is that after you lock the features, you can't undo them yourself without rebooting the computer. By locking, you prevent other features from being enabled or disabled until the server is rebooted, and this applies only if you're using the Sysctl option within Grsec. Lock the features with this command:

```
echo "1" >/proc/sys/kernel/grsecurity/grsec_lock
```

Beyond the Basics with GrSecurity

I've only scratched the surface of the benefits of GrSecurity. One of the greatest benefits of Grsec is its capability to enhance the available permissions on a file, known as Role Based Access Control (RBAC). Windows administrators who are familiar with and use the Advanced permissions that can be given to a file in Windows will want to explore these features in Grsec as well. This chapter has examined only the kernel patch portion of Grsec. There is also administration software for RBAC called gradm that enables a large set of specialized file and object permissions.

More information on the GrSecurity ACL system can be found on the GrSecurity website at http://www.grsecurity.net/gracldoc.htm.

Conclusion: Custom Kernels

This chapter covered an important topic and one that is vital for a good Linux administrator to know, namely, compiling a custom kernel. Custom kernels enhance security by enabling the administrator to choose only those options necessary for the specific computer on which the kernel will reside. By disabling unnecessary drivers and module support, you can reduce the number of attack paths available for an exploit.

Using a security-enhanced kernel such as a kernel with SELinux or a GrSecurity kernel significantly decreases the risk posed by some of the more advanced exploit techniques available. As with other security options, GrSecurity provides only one facet of a host's security. Without things like `chroot`, and even simply keeping the server patched, Grsec won't be as helpful. However, for all the benefits that Grsec can provide, it should be used whenever possible. It's worth the time and effort and is certainly a much better option than cleaning up after an attack that could've been prevented.

PART IV

Appendices

A   Security Resources

B   Firewall Examples and Support Scripts

C   VPNs

D   Glossary

Security Resources

This appendix lists some common sources of security-related notices, information, tools, updates, and patches currently on the Internet. Many more sites exist, and new sites pop up every day—consider this list a starting point, not a complete list. The appendix also serves as a general reference section for this book.

Security Information Sources

Security information of all kinds, notices and alerts, whitepapers, tutorials, and so on can be found in the following sources:

BugTraq:
http://www.securityfocus.com/archive/1

CERT Coordination Center:
http://www.cert.org/

CIAC (Computer Incident Advisory Capability):
http://www.ciac.org/ciac/

Freshmeat:
http://www.freshmeat.net/

Geektools:
http://www.geektools.com/

Internet Engineering Task Force (IETF):
http://www.ietf.org/

Packet Storm:
http://packetstormsecurity.org/

RFC Editor:
http://www.rfc-editor.org/

SANS Institute:
http://www.sans.org/

Security Focus:
http://www.securityfocus.com/

Reference Papers and FAQs

Some useful reference papers, some of which were cited within the book, can be found on these sites:

"Help Defeat Denial of Service Attacks: Step-by-Step":
http://www.sans.org/dosstep/index.php

"Internet Firewalls Frequently Asked Questions":
http://www.interhack.net/pubs/fwfaq/

"TCP SYN Flooding and IP Spoofing Attacks" (CERT Advisory CA-96.21):
http://www.cert.org/advisories/CA-1996-21.html

"TCP/UDP Service Port Numbers" (IANA):
http://www.iana.org/assignments/port-numbers

"UDP Port Denial of Service Attack" (CERT Advisory CA-1996.01):
http://www.cert.org/advisories/CA-1996-01.html

Books

Building Internet Firewalls, Second Edition, by Elizabeth D. Zwicky, Simon Cooper, and D. Brent Chapman. O'Reilly & Associates, Inc.

Intrusion Signatures and Analysis, by Stephen Northcutt, Mark Cooper, Matt Fearnow, and Karen Frederick. New Riders Publishing.

Network Intrusion Detection, An Analyst's Handbook, Third Edition, by Stephen Northcutt and Judy Novak. New Riders Publishing.

Practical Unix & Internet Security, by Simson Garfinkel, et al. O'Reilly & Associates, Inc.

TCP/IP Illustrated, Volume 1: The Protocols, by W. Richard Stevens. Addison-Wesley Professional.

Firewall Examples and Support Scripts

A firewall for a standalone system is described in Chapter 4, "Building and Installing a Standalone Firewall." The standalone example is optimized in Chapter 5, "Firewall Optimization." The same example is extended in Chapter 6, "Packet Forwarding," to function as either a gateway or a choke firewall, with a full set of firewall rules applied to both the external public interface and the internal local network interface. The gateway serves as the link between the Internet and a DMZ network containing public servers. The choke serves as the link between a private LAN and the DMZ.

The sample firewalls are presented piecemeal in Chapters 4, 5, and 6. This appendix presents the same firewall examples as they would appear in a firewall script.

iptables Firewall for a Standalone System from Chapter 4

Chapter 4 covers the application protocols and firewall rules for the types of services most likely to be used on an individual, standalone Linux box. Additionally, both client and server rules are presented for services that not everyone will use. The complete iptables firewall script, as it would appear in /etc/rc.d/rc.firewall or /etc/init.d/firewall, follows:

```
#!/bin/sh

/sbin/modprobe ip_conntrack_ftp
```

```
CONNECTION_TRACKING="1"
ACCEPT_AUTH="0"
SSH_SERVER="0"
FTP_SERVER="0"
WEB_SERVER="0"
SSL_SERVER="0"
DHCP_CLIENT="1"

IPT="/sbin/iptables"                      # Location of iptables on your system
INTERNET="eth0"                           # Internet-connected interface
LOOPBACK_INTERFACE="lo"                   # however your system names it
IPADDR="my.ip.address"                    # your IP address
SUBNET_BASE="my.subnet.base"            # ISP network segment base address
SUBNET_BROADCAST="my.subnet.bcast" # network segment broadcast address
MY_ISP="my.isp.address.range"             # ISP server & NOC address range

NAMESERVER="isp.name.server.1"            # address of a remote name server
POP_SERVER="isp.pop.server"               # address of a remote pop server
MAIL_SERVER="isp.mail.server"             # address of a remote mail gateway
NEWS_SERVER="isp.news.server"             # address of a remote news server
TIME_SERVER="some.time.server"         # address of a remote time server
DHCP_SERVER="isp.dhcp.server"             # address of your ISP dhcp server

LOOPBACK="127.0.0.0/8"                     # reserved loopback address range
CLASS_A="10.0.0.0/8"                       # Class A private networks
CLASS_B="172.16.0.0/12"                    # Class B private networks
CLASS_C="192.168.0.0/16"                   # Class C private networks
CLASS_D_MULTICAST="224.0.0.0/4"           # Class D multicast addresses
CLASS_E_RESERVED_NET="240.0.0.0/5"        # Class E reserved addresses
BROADCAST_SRC="0.0.0.0"                    # broadcast source address
BROADCAST_DEST="255.255.255.255"          # broadcast destination address

PRIVPORTS="0:1023"                         # well-known, privileged port range
UNPRIVPORTS="1024:65535"                   # unprivileged port range

SSH_PORTS="1024:65535"

NFS_PORT="2049"
LOCKD_PORT="4045"
SOCKS_PORT="1080"
OPENWINDOWS_PORT="2000"
XWINDOW_PORTS="6000:6063"
SQUID_PORT="3128"
```

```
###############################################################

# Enable broadcast echo Protection
echo 1 > /proc/sys/net/ipv4/icmp_echo_ignore_broadcasts

# Disable Source Routed Packets
for f in /proc/sys/net/ipv4/conf/*/accept_source_route; do
    echo 0 > $f
done

# Enable TCP SYN Cookie Protection
echo 1 > /proc/sys/net/ipv4/tcp_syncookies

# Disable ICMP Redirect Acceptance
for f in /proc/sys/net/ipv4/conf/*/accept_redirects; do
    echo 0 > $f
done

# Don't send Redirect Messages
for f in /proc/sys/net/ipv4/conf/*/send_redirects; do
    echo 0 > $f
done

# Drop Spoofed Packets coming in on an interface, which, if replied to,
# would result in the reply going out a different interface.
for f in /proc/sys/net/ipv4/conf/*/rp_filter; do
    echo 1 > $f
done

# Log packets with impossible addresses.
for f in /proc/sys/net/ipv4/conf/*/log_martians; do
    echo 1 > $f
done

###############################################################

# Remove any existing rules from all chains
$IPT --flush
$IPT -t nat --flush
$IPT -t mangle --flush
$IPT -X
$IPT -t nat -X
$IPT -t mangle -X
$IPT --policy INPUT    ACCEPT
$IPT --policy OUTPUT   ACCEPT
$IPT --policy FORWARD ACCEPT
```

```
$IPT -t nat --policy PREROUTING  ACCEPT
$IPT -t nat --policy OUTPUT ACCEPT
$IPT -t nat --policy POSTROUTING ACCEPT
$IPT -t mangle --policy PREROUTING ACCEPT
$IPT -t mangle --policy OUTPUT ACCEPT
if [ "$1" = "stop" ]
then
echo "Firewall completely stopped!  WARNING: THIS HOST HAS NO FIREWALL RUNNING."
exit 0
fi
# Unlimited traffic on the loopback interface
$IPT -A INPUT  -i lo -j ACCEPT
$IPT -A OUTPUT -o lo -j ACCEPT

# Set the default policy to drop
$IPT --policy INPUT   DROP
$IPT --policy OUTPUT  DROP
$IPT --policy FORWARD DROP

$IPT -t nat --policy PREROUTING  DROP
$IPT -t nat --policy OUTPUT DROP
$IPT -t nat --policy POSTROUTING DROP

$IPT -t mangle --policy PREROUTING DROP
$IPT -t mangle --policy OUTPUT DROP

###############################################################
# Stealth Scans and TCP State Flags

# Unclean
$IPT -A INPUT -m unclean -j DROP
# All of the bits are cleared
$IPT -A INPUT -p tcp --tcp-flags ALL NONE -j DROP
# SYN and FIN are both set
$IPT -A INPUT -p tcp --tcp-flags SYN,FIN SYN,FIN -j DROP
# SYN and RST are both set
$IPT -A INPUT -p tcp --tcp-flags SYN,RST SYN,RST -j DROP
# FIN and RST are both set
$IPT -A INPUT -p tcp --tcp-flags FIN,RST FIN,RST -j DROP
# FIN is the only bit set, without the expected accompanying ACK
$IPT -A INPUT -p tcp --tcp-flags ACK,FIN FIN -j DROP
# PSH is the only bit set, without the expected accompanying ACK
$IPT -A INPUT -p tcp --tcp-flags ACK,PSH PSH -j DROP
# URG is the only bit set, without the expected accompanying ACK
$IPT -A INPUT -p tcp --tcp-flags ACK,URG URG -j DROP
```

```
##############################################################
# Using Connection State to By-pass Rule Checking

if [ "$CONNECTION_TRACKING" = "1" ]; then
    $IPT -A INPUT  -m state --state ESTABLISHED,RELATED -j ACCEPT
    $IPT -A OUTPUT -m state --state ESTABLISHED,RELATED -j ACCEPT

    # Using the state module alone, INVALID will break protocols that use
    # bi-directional connections or multiple connections or exchanges,
    # unless an ALG is provided for the protocol. At this time, FTP and
    # IRC are the only protocols with ALG support.

    $IPT -A INPUT -m state --state INVALID -j LOG \
            --log-prefix "INVALID input: "
    $IPT -A INPUT -m state --state INVALID -j DROP

    $IPT -A OUTPUT -m state --state INVALID -j LOG \
            --log-prefix "INVALID output: "
    $IPT -A OUTPUT -m state --state INVALID -j DROP
fi

##############################################################
# Source Address Spoofing and Other Bad Addresses

# Refuse spoofed packets pretending to be from
# the external interface's IP address
$IPT -A INPUT  -i $INTERNET -s $IPADDR -j DROP

# Refuse packets claiming to be from a Class A private network
$IPT -A INPUT  -i $INTERNET -s $CLASS_A -j DROP

# Refuse packets claiming to be from a Class B private network
$IPT -A INPUT  -i $INTERNET -s $CLASS_B -j DROP

# Refuse packets claiming to be from a Class C private network
$IPT -A INPUT  -i $INTERNET -s $CLASS_C -j DROP
# Refuse packets claiming to be from the loopback interface
$IPT -A INPUT  -i $INTERNET -s $LOOPBACK -j DROP

# Refuse malformed broadcast packets
$IPT -A INPUT  -i $INTERNET -s $BROADCAST_DEST -j LOG
$IPT -A INPUT  -i $INTERNET -s $BROADCAST_DEST -j DROP

$IPT -A INPUT  -i $INTERNET -d $BROADCAST_SRC  -j LOG
$IPT -A INPUT  -i $INTERNET -d $BROADCAST_SRC  -j DROP
```

```
if [ "$DHCP_CLIENT" = "0" ]; then
    # Refuse directed broadcasts
    # Used to map networks and in Denial of Service attacks
    $IPT -A INPUT -i $INTERNET -d $SUBNET_BASE -j DROP
    $IPT -A INPUT -i $INTERNET -d $SUBNET_BROADCAST -j DROP

    # Refuse limited broadcasts
    $IPT -A INPUT -i $INTERNET -d $BROADCAST_DEST -j DROP
fi

# Refuse Class D multicast addresses
# illegal as a source address
$IPT -A INPUT -i $INTERNET -s $CLASS_D_MULTICAST -j DROP

$IPT -A INPUT -i $INTERNET -p ! udp -d $CLASS_D_MULTICAST -j DROP

$IPT -A INPUT  -i $INTERNET -p udp -d $CLASS_D_MULTICAST -j ACCEPT

# Refuse Class E reserved IP addresses
$IPT -A INPUT  -i $INTERNET -s $CLASS_E_RESERVED_NET -j DROP

if [ "$DHCP_CLIENT" = "1" ]; then
    $IPT -A INPUT  -i $INTERNET -p udp \
            -s $BROADCAST_SRC --sport 67 \
            -d $BROADCAST_DEST --dport 68 -j ACCEPT
fi

# refuse addresses defined as reserved by the IANA
# 0.*.*.*            - Can't be blocked unilaterally with DHCP
# 169.254.0.0/16   - Link Local Networks
# 192.0.2.0/24     - TEST-NET

$IPT -A INPUT -i $INTERNET -s 0.0.0.0/8 -j DROP
$IPT -A INPUT -i $INTERNET -s 169.254.0.0/16 -j DROP
$IPT -A INPUT -i $INTERNET -s 192.0.2.0/24 -j DROP

###############################################################
# Disallowing Connections to Common TCP Unprivileged Server Ports

# X Window connection establishment
$IPT -A OUTPUT -o $INTERNET -p tcp --syn \
        --destination-port $XWINDOW_PORTS -j REJECT

# X Window: incoming connection attempt
$IPT -A INPUT -i $INTERNET -p tcp --syn \
        --destination-port $XWINDOW_PORTS -j DROP
```

```
# Establishing a connection over TCP to NFS, OpenWindows, SOCKS, or squid
$IPT -A OUTPUT -o $INTERNET -p tcp \
        -m multiport --destination-port \
        $NFS_PORT,$OPENWINDOWS_PORT,$SOCKS_PORT,$SQUID_PORT \
        --syn -j REJECT

$IPT -A INPUT -i $INTERNET -p tcp \
        -m multiport --destination-port \
        $NFS_PORT,$OPENWINDOWS_PORT,$SOCKS_PORT,$SQUID_PORT \
        --syn -j DROP
##############################################################
# Disallowing Connections to Common UDP Unprivileged Server Ports

# NFS and lockd
if [ "$CONNECTION_TRACKING" = "1" ]; then
    $IPT -A OUTPUT -o $INTERNET -p udp \
            -m multiport --destination-port $NFS_PORT,$LOCKD_PORT \
            -m state --state NEW -j REJECT

    $IPT -A INPUT -i $INTERNET -p udp \
            -m multiport --destination-port $NFS_PORT,$LOCKD_PORT \
            -m state --state NEW -j DROP
else
    $IPT -A OUTPUT -o $INTERNET -p udp \
            -m multiport --destination-port $NFS_PORT,$LOCKD_PORT \
            -j REJECT

    $IPT -A input -i $INTERNET -p udp \
            -m multiport --destination-port $NFS_PORT,$LOCKD_PORT \
            -j DROP
fi


##############################################################
# DNS Name Server

# DNS Forwarding Name Server or client requests

if [ "$CONNECTION_TRACKING" = "1" ]; then
    $IPT -A OUTPUT -o $INTERNET -p udp \
            -s $IPADDR --sport $UNPRIVPORTS \
            -d $NAMESERVER --dport 53 \
            -m state --state NEW -j ACCEPT
fi

$IPT -A OUTPUT -o $INTERNET -p udp \
        -s $IPADDR --sport $UNPRIVPORTS \
```

```
                    -d $NAMESERVER --dport 53 -j ACCEPT

$IPT -A INPUT  -i $INTERNET -p udp \
         -s $NAMESERVER --sport 53 \
         -d $IPADDR --dport $UNPRIVPORTS -j ACCEPT


#...............................................................
# TCP is used for large responses

if [ "$CONNECTION_TRACKING" = "1" ]; then
    $IPT -A OUTPUT -o $INTERNET -p tcp \
            -s $IPADDR --sport $UNPRIVPORTS \
            -d $NAMESERVER --dport 53 \
            -m state --state NEW -j ACCEPT
fi

$IPT -A OUTPUT -o $INTERNET -p tcp \
         -s $IPADDR --sport $UNPRIVPORTS \
         -d $NAMESERVER --dport 53 -j ACCEPT

$IPT -A INPUT -i $INTERNET -p tcp ! --syn \
         -s $NAMESERVER --sport 53 \
         -d $IPADDR --dport $UNPRIVPORTS -j ACCEPT


#...............................................................
# DNS Caching Name Server (local server to primary server)

if [ "$CONNECTION_TRACKING" = "1" ]; then
    $IPT -A OUTPUT -o $INTERNET -p udp \
            -s $IPADDR --sport 53 \
            -d $NAMESERVER --dport 53 \
            -m state --state NEW -j ACCEPT
fi

$IPT -A OUTPUT -o $INTERNET -p udp \
         -s $IPADDR --sport 53 \
         -d $NAMESERVER --dport 53 -j ACCEPT

$IPT -A INPUT  -i $INTERNET -p udp \
         -s $NAMESERVER --sport 53 \
         -d $IPADDR --dport 53 -j ACCEPT
```

```
##############################################################
# Filtering the AUTH User Identification Service (TCP Port 113)

# Outgoing Local Client Requests to Remote Servers

    $IPT -A OUTPUT -o $INTERNET -p tcp \
            -s $IPADDR --sport $UNPRIVPORTS \
            --dport 113 -m state --state NEW -j ACCEPT
fi
$IPT -A OUTPUT -o $INTERNET -p tcp \
        -s $IPADDR --sport $UNPRIVPORTS \
        --dport 113 -j ACCEPT

$IPT -A INPUT -i $INTERNET -p tcp ! --syn \
        --sport 113 \
        -d $IPADDR --dport $UNPRIVPORTS -j ACCEPT

#..........................................................
# Incoming Remote Client Requests to Local Servers


if [ "$ACCEPT_AUTH" = "1" ]; then
    if [ "$CONNECTION_TRACKING" = "1" ]; then
    $IPT -A INPUT  -i $INTERNET -p tcp \
            --sport $UNPRIVPORTS \
            -d $IPADDR --dport 113 \
            -m state --state NEW -j ACCEPT
    fi

$IPT -A INPUT  -i $INTERNET -p tcp \
        --sport $UNPRIVPORTS \
        -d $IPADDR --dport 113 -j ACCEPT

$IPT -A OUTPUT -o $INTERNET -p tcp ! --syn \
        -s $IPADDR --sport 113 \
        --dport $UNPRIVPORTS -j ACCEPT
else
$IPT -A INPUT -i $INTERNET -p tcp \
        --sport $UNPRIVPORTS \
        -d $IPADDR --dport 113 -j REJECT --reject-with tcp-reset
fi

##############################################################
# Sending Mail to Any External Mail Server
# Use "-d $MAIL_SERVER" if an ISP mail gateway is used instead
```

```
if [ "$CONNECTION_TRACKING" = "1" ]; then
    $IPT -A OUTPUT -o $INTERNET -p tcp \
            -s $IPADDR --sport $UNPRIVPORTS \
            --dport 25 -m state --state NEW -j ACCEPT
fi

$IPT -A OUTPUT -o $INTERNET -p tcp \
        -s $IPADDR --sport $UNPRIVPORTS \
        --dport 25 -j ACCEPT

$IPT -A INPUT -i $INTERNET -p tcp ! --syn \
        --sport 25 \
        -d $IPADDR --dport $UNPRIVPORTS -j ACCEPT

##############################################################
# Retrieving Mail as a POP Client (TCP Port 110)

if [ "$CONNECTION_TRACKING" = "1" ]; then
    $IPT -A OUTPUT -o $INTERNET -p tcp \
            -s $IPADDR --sport $UNPRIVPORTS \
            -d $POP_SERVER --dport 110 -m state --state NEW -j ACCEPT
fi

$IPT -A OUTPUT -o $INTERNET -p tcp \
        -s $IPADDR --sport $UNPRIVPORTS \
        -d $POP_SERVER --dport 110 -j ACCEPT

$IPT -A INPUT -i $INTERNET -p tcp ! --syn \
        -s $POP_SERVER --sport 110 \
        -d $IPADDR --dport $UNPRIVPORTS -j ACCEPT

##############################################################
# Accessing Usenet News Services (TCP NNTP Port 119)

if [ "$CONNECTION_TRACKING" = "1" ]; then
    $IPT -A OUTPUT -o $INTERNET -p tcp \
            -s $IPADDR --sport $UNPRIVPORTS \
            -d $NEWS_SERVER --dport 119 -m state --state NEW -j ACCEPT
fi

$IPT -A OUTPUT -o $INTERNET -p tcp \
        -s $IPADDR --sport $UNPRIVPORTS \
        -d $NEWS_SERVER --dport 119 -j ACCEPT

$IPT -A INPUT -i $INTERNET -p tcp ! --syn \
        -s $NEWS_SERVER --sport 119 \
        -d $IPADDR --dport $UNPRIVPORTS -j ACCEPT
```

```
###############################################################
# ssh (TCP Port 22)

# Outgoing Local Client Requests to Remote Servers

if [ "$CONNECTION_TRACKING" = "1" ]; then
    $IPT -A OUTPUT -o $INTERNET -p tcp \
            -s $IPADDR --sport $SSH_PORTS \
            --dport 22 -m state --state NEW -j ACCEPT
fi

$IPT -A OUTPUT -o $INTERNET -p tcp \
        -s $IPADDR --sport $SSH_PORTS \
        --dport 22 -j ACCEPT

$IPT -A INPUT -i $INTERNET -p tcp ! --syn \
        --sport 22 \
        -d $IPADDR --dport $SSH_PORTS -j ACCEPT

#..............................................................
# Incoming Remote Client Requests to Local Servers

if [ "$SSH_SERVER" = "1" ]; then
    if [ "$CONNECTION_TRACKING" = "1" ]; then
    $IPT -A INPUT   -i $INTERNET -p tcp \
            --sport $SSH_PORTS \
            -d $IPADDR --dport 22 \
            -m state --state NEW -j ACCEPT
    fi

$IPT -A INPUT   -i $INTERNET -p tcp \
        --sport $SSH_PORTS \
        -d $IPADDR --dport 22 -j ACCEPT

$IPT -A OUTPUT -o $INTERNET -p tcp ! --syn \
        -s $IPADDR --sport 22 \
        --dport $SSH_PORTS -j ACCEPT
fi

###############################################################
# ftp (TCP Ports 21, 20)

# Outgoing Local Client Requests to Remote Servers

# Outgoing Control Connection to Port 21
if [ "$CONNECTION_TRACKING" = "1" ]; then
```

```
        $IPT -A OUTPUT -o $INTERNET -p tcp \
                -s $IPADDR --sport $UNPRIVPORTS \
                --dport 21 -m state --state NEW -j ACCEPT
fi


$IPT -A OUTPUT -o $INTERNET -p tcp \
        -s $IPADDR --sport $UNPRIVPORTS \
        --dport 21 -j ACCEPT

$IPT -A INPUT -i $INTERNET -p tcp ! --syn \
        --sport 21 \
        -d $IPADDR --dport $UNPRIVPORTS -j ACCEPT


# Incoming Port Mode Data Channel Connection from Port 20
if [ "$CONNECTION_TRACKING" = "1" ]; then
    # This rule is not necessary if the ip_conntrack_ftp
    # module is used.
    $IPT -A INPUT  -i $INTERNET -p tcp \
            --sport 20 \
            -d $IPADDR --dport $UNPRIVPORTS \
            -m state --state NEW -j ACCEPT
fi


$IPT -A INPUT  -i $INTERNET -p tcp \
        --sport 20 \
        -d $IPADDR --dport $UNPRIVPORTS -j ACCEPT

$IPT -A OUTPUT -o $INTERNET -p tcp ! --syn \
        -s $IPADDR --sport $UNPRIVPORTS \
        --dport 20 -j ACCEPT


# Outgoing Passive Mode Data Channel Connection Between Unprivileged Ports
if [ "$CONNECTION_TRACKING" = "1" ]; then
    # This rule is not necessary if the ip_conntrack_ftp
    # module is used.
    $IPT -A OUTPUT -o $INTERNET -p tcp \
            -s $IPADDR --sport $UNPRIVPORTS \
            --dport $UNPRIVPORTS -m state --state NEW -j ACCEPT
fi

    $IPT -A OUTPUT -o $INTERNET -p tcp \
            -s $IPADDR --sport $UNPRIVPORTS \
            --dport $UNPRIVPORTS -j ACCEPT

    $IPT -A INPUT -i $INTERNET -p tcp ! --syn \
            --sport $UNPRIVPORTS \
```

```
                 -d $IPADDR --dport $UNPRIVPORTS -j ACCEPT

#........................................................
# Incoming Remote Client Requests to Local Servers

if [ "$FTP_SERVER" = "1" ]; then

    # Incoming Control Connection to Port 21
    if [ "$CONNECTION_TRACKING" = "1" ]; then
    $IPT -A INPUT  -i $INTERNET -p tcp \
            --sport $UNPRIVPORTS \
            -d $IPADDR --dport 21 \
            -m state --state NEW -j ACCEPT
    fi

$IPT -A INPUT  -i $INTERNET -p tcp \
        --sport $UNPRIVPORTS \
        -d $IPADDR --dport 21 -j ACCEPT

$IPT -A OUTPUT -o $INTERNET -p tcp ! --syn \
        -s $IPADDR --sport 21 \
        --dport $UNPRIVPORTS -j ACCEPT

    # Outgoing Port Mode Data Channel Connection to Port 20
    if [ "$CONNECTION_TRACKING" = "1" ]; then
    $IPT -A OUTPUT -o $INTERNET -p tcp \
            -s $IPADDR --sport 20\
            --dport $UNPRIVPORTS -m state --state NEW -j ACCEPT
    fi

$IPT -A OUTPUT -o $INTERNET -p tcp \
        -s $IPADDR --sport 20 \
        --dport $UNPRIVPORTS -j ACCEPT

$IPT -A INPUT -i $INTERNET -p tcp ! --syn \
        --sport $UNPRIVPORTS \
        -d $IPADDR --dport 20 -j ACCEPT

    # Incoming Passive Mode Data Channel Connection Between Unprivileged Ports
if [ "$CONNECTION_TRACKING" = "1" ]; then
    $IPT -A INPUT  -i $INTERNET -p tcp \
            --sport $UNPRIVPORTS \
            -d $IPADDR --dport $UNPRIVPORTS \
            -m state --state NEW -j ACCEPT
    fi
```

```
$IPT -A INPUT  -i $INTERNET -p tcp \
        --sport $UNPRIVPORTS \
        -d $IPADDR --dport $UNPRIVPORTS -j ACCEPT

$IPT -A OUTPUT -o $INTERNET -p tcp ! --syn \
        -s $IPADDR --sport $UNPRIVPORTS \
        --dport $UNPRIVPORTS -j ACCEPT
fi
################################################################
# HTTP Web Traffic (TCP Port 80)

# Outgoing Local Client Requests to Remote Servers

if [ "$CONNECTION_TRACKING" = "1" ]; then
    $IPT -A OUTPUT -o $INTERNET -p tcp \
            -s $IPADDR --sport $UNPRIVPORTS \
            --dport 80 -m state --state NEW -j ACCEPT
fi

$IPT -A OUTPUT -o $INTERNET -p tcp \
        -s $IPADDR --sport $UNPRIVPORTS \
        --dport 80 -j ACCEPT

$IPT -A INPUT -i $INTERNET -p tcp ! --syn \
        --sport 80 \
        -d $IPADDR --dport $UNPRIVPORTS -j ACCEPT

#.............................................................
# Incoming Remote Client Requests to Local Servers

if [ "$WEB_SERVER" = "1" ]; then
    if [ "$CONNECTION_TRACKING" = "1" ]; then
    $IPT -A INPUT  -i $INTERNET -p tcp \
            --sport $UNPRIVPORTS \
            -d $IPADDR --dport 80 \
            -m state --state NEW -j ACCEPT
fi

$IPT -A INPUT  -i $INTERNET -p tcp \
        --sport $UNPRIVPORTS \
        -d $IPADDR --dport 80 -j ACCEPT

$IPT -A OUTPUT -o $INTERNET -p tcp ! --syn \
        -s $IPADDR --sport 80 \
        --dport $UNPRIVPORTS -j ACCEPT
fi
```

```
############################################################
# SSL Web Traffic (TCP Port 443)

# Outgoing Local Client Requests to Remote Servers

if [ "$CONNECTION_TRACKING" = "1" ]; then
    $IPT -A OUTPUT -o $INTERNET -p tcp \
            -s $IPADDR --sport $UNPRIVPORTS \
            --dport 443 -m state --state NEW -j ACCEPT
fi

$IPT -A OUTPUT -o $INTERNET -p tcp \
        -s $IPADDR --sport $UNPRIVPORTS \
        --dport 443 -j ACCEPT

$IPT -A INPUT -i $INTERNET -p tcp ! --syn \
        --sport 443 \
        -d $IPADDR --dport $UNPRIVPORTS -j ACCEPT

#...........................................................
# Incoming Remote Client Requests to Local Servers

if [ "$SSL_SERVER" = "1" ]; then
    if [ "$CONNECTION_TRACKING" = "1" ]; then
    $IPT -A INPUT  -i $INTERNET -p tcp \
            --sport $UNPRIVPORTS \
            -d $IPADDR --dport 443 \
            -m state --state NEW -j ACCEPT
fi

$IPT -A INPUT  -i $INTERNET -p tcp \
        --sport $UNPRIVPORTS \
        -d $IPADDR --dport 443 -j ACCEPT

$IPT -A OUTPUT -o $INTERNET -p tcp ! --syn \
        -s $IPADDR --sport 443 \
        --dport $UNPRIVPORTS -j ACCEPT
fi

############################################################
# whois (TCP Port 43)

# Outgoing Local Client Requests to Remote Servers

if [ "$CONNECTION_TRACKING" = "1" ]; then
    $IPT -A OUTPUT -o $INTERNET -p tcp \
```

```
                -s $IPADDR --sport $UNPRIVPORTS \
                --dport 43 -m state --state NEW -j ACCEPT
fi

$IPT -A OUTPUT -o $INTERNET -p tcp \
        -s $IPADDR --sport $UNPRIVPORTS \
        --dport 43 -j ACCEPT

$IPT -A INPUT -i $INTERNET -p tcp ! --syn \
        --sport 43 \
        -d $IPADDR --dport $UNPRIVPORTS -j ACCEPT


##############################################################
# Accessing Remote Network Time Servers (UDP 123)
# Note: Some client and servers use source port 123
# when querying a remote server on destination port 123.

if [ "$CONNECTION_TRACKING" = "1" ]; then
    $IPT -A OUTPUT -o $INTERNET -p udp \
            -s $IPADDR --sport $UNPRIVPORTS \
            -d $TIME_SERVER --dport 123 \
            -m state --state NEW -j ACCEPT
fi

$IPT -A OUTPUT -o $INTERNET -p udp \
        -s $IPADDR --sport $UNPRIVPORTS \
        -d $TIME_SERVER --dport 123 -j ACCEPT

$IPT -A INPUT  -i $INTERNET -p udp \
        -s $TIME_SERVER --sport 123 \
        -d $IPADDR --dport $UNPRIVPORTS -j ACCEPT

##############################################################
# Accessing Your ISP's DHCP Server (UDP Ports 67, 68)

# Some broadcast packets are explicitly ignored by the firewall.
# Others are dropped by the default policy.
# DHCP tests must precede broadcast-related rules, as DHCP relies
# on broadcast traffic initially.

if [ "$DHCP_CLIENT" = "1" ]; then
    # Initialization or rebinding: No lease or Lease time expired.
```

```
$IPT -A OUTPUT -o $INTERNET -p udp \
        -s $BROADCAST_SRC --sport 68 \
        -d $BROADCAST_DEST --dport 67 -j ACCEPT

    # Incoming DHCPOFFER from available DHCP servers

$IPT -A INPUT  -i $INTERNET -p udp \
        -s $BROADCAST_SRC --sport 67 \
        -d $BROADCAST_DEST --dport 68 -j ACCEPT

    # Fall back to initialization
    # The client knows its server, but has either lost its lease,
    # or else needs to reconfirm the IP address after rebooting.

$IPT -A OUTPUT -o $INTERNET -p udp \
        -s $BROADCAST_SRC --sport 68 \
        -d $DHCP_SERVER --dport 67 -j ACCEPT

$IPT -A INPUT  -i $INTERNET -p udp \
        -s $DHCP_SERVER --sport 67 \
        -d $BROADCAST_DEST --dport 68 -j ACCEPT


    # As a result of the above, we're supposed to change our IP
    # address with this message, which is addressed to our new
    # address before the dhcp client has received the update.
    # Depending on the server implementation, the destination address
    # can be the new IP address, the subnet address, or the limited
    # broadcast address.

    # If the network subnet address is used as the destination,
    # the next rule must allow incoming packets destined to the
    # subnet address, and the rule must precede any general rules
    # that block such incoming broadcast packets.

$IPT -A INPUT  -i $INTERNET -p udp \
        -s $DHCP_SERVER --sport 67 \
        --dport 68 -j ACCEPT

    # Lease renewal

$IPT -A OUTPUT -o $INTERNET -p udp \
        -s $IPADDR --sport 68 \
        -d $DHCP_SERVER --dport 67 -j ACCEPT
```

```
$IPT -A INPUT  -i $INTERNET -p udp \
        -s $DHCP_SERVER --sport 67 \
        -d $IPADDR --dport 68 -j ACCEPT

    # Refuse directed broadcasts
    # Used to map networks and in Denial of Service attacks
    iptables -A INPUT -i $INTERNET -d $SUBNET_BASE -j DROP
    iptables -A INPUT -i $INTERNET -d $SUBNET_BROADCAST -j DROP

    # Refuse limited broadcasts
    iptables -A INPUT -i $INTERNET -d $BROADCAST_DEST -j DROP

fi
###############################################################
# ICMP Control and Status Messages

# Log and drop initial ICMP fragments
$IPT -A INPUT  -i $INTERNET --fragment -p icmp -j LOG \
        --log-prefix "Fragmented ICMP: "

$IPT -A INPUT  -i $INTERNET --fragment -p icmp -j DROP

$IPT -A INPUT  -i $INTERNET -p icmp \
        --icmp-type source-quench -d $IPADDR -j ACCEPT

$IPT -A OUTPUT -o $INTERNET -p icmp \
        -s $IPADDR --icmp-type source-quench -j ACCEPT

$IPT -A INPUT  -i $INTERNET -p icmp \
        --icmp-type parameter-problem -d $IPADDR -j ACCEPT

$IPT -A OUTPUT -o $INTERNET -p icmp \
        -s $IPADDR --icmp-type parameter-problem -j ACCEPT

$IPT -A INPUT  -i $INTERNET -p icmp \
        --icmp-type destination-unreachable -d $IPADDR -j ACCEPT

$IPT -A OUTPUT -o $INTERNET -p icmp \
        -s $IPADDR --icmp-type fragmentation-needed -j ACCEPT

# Don't log dropped outgoing ICMP error messages
$IPT -A OUTPUT -o $INTERNET -p icmp \
        -s $IPADDR --icmp-type destination-unreachable -j DROP
```

```
# Intermediate traceroute responses
$IPT -A INPUT  -i $INTERNET -p icmp \
        --icmp-type time-exceeded -d $IPADDR -j ACCEPT

# allow outgoing pings to anywhere
if [ "$CONNECTION_TRACKING" = "1" ]; then
    $IPT -A OUTPUT -o $INTERNET -p icmp \
            -s $IPADDR --icmp-type echo-request \
            -m state --state NEW -j ACCEPT
fi

$IPT -A OUTPUT -o $INTERNET -p icmp \
        -s $IPADDR --icmp-type echo-request -j ACCEPT

$IPT -A INPUT  -i $INTERNET -p icmp \
        --icmp-type echo-reply -d $IPADDR -j ACCEPT

# allow incoming pings from trusted hosts
if [ "$CONNECTION_TRACKING" = "1" ]; then
    $IPT -A INPUT  -i $INTERNET -p icmp \
            -s $MY_ISP --icmp-type echo-request -d $IPADDR \
            -m state --state NEW -j ACCEPT
fi

$IPT -A INPUT  -i $INTERNET -p icmp \
        -s $MY_ISP --icmp-type echo-request -d $IPADDR -j ACCEPT

$IPT -A OUTPUT -o $INTERNET -p icmp \
        -s $IPADDR --icmp-type echo-reply -d $MY_ISP -j ACCEPT


###############################################################
# Logging Dropped Packets

# Don't log dropped incoming echo-requests
$IPT -A INPUT -i $INTERNET -p icmp \
        --icmp-type ! 8 -d $IPADDR -j LOG

$IPT -A INPUT -i $INTERNET -p tcp \
        -d $IPADDR -j LOG

$IPT -A OUTPUT -o $INTERNET -j LOG

exit 0
```

Optimized iptables Firewall from Chapter 5

For most systems on DSL, cable modem, and lower-speed leased line connections, the chances are good that the Linux network code can handle packets faster than the network connection can. Particularly because firewall rules are order-dependent and difficult to construct, organizing the rules for readability is probably a bigger win than organizing for speed.

In addition to general rule ordering, iptables supports user-defined rule lists, or chains, that you can use to optimize your firewall rules. Passing a packet from one chain to another based on values in the packet header provides a means to selectively test the packet against a subset of the INPUT, OUTPUT, or FORWARD rules rather than testing the packet against every rule in the list until a match is found.

Based on these particular scripts, an input packet from an NTP time server must be tested against numerous input rules in the unoptimized firewall script before the packet matches its ACCEPT rule. Using user-defined chains to optimize the firewall, the same input packet is tested against far fewer rules before matching its ACCEPT rule. With the addition of connection state tracking, the same input packet is tested against only a handful rules before matching its ACCEPT rule.

With user-defined chains, rules are used to pass packets between chains, as well as to define under what conditions the packet is accepted or dropped. If a packet doesn't match any rule in the user-defined chain, control returns to the calling chain. If the packet doesn't match a top-level chain-selection rule, the packet isn't passed to that chain for testing against the chain's rules. The packet is simply tested against the next chain selection rule.

Following is the Chapter 5 firewall script, optimized with user-defined chains:

```sh
#!/bin/sh

/sbin/modprobe ip_conntrack_ftp

CONNECTION_TRACKING="1"
ACCEPT_AUTH="0"
DHCP_CLIENT="0"
IPT="/sbin/iptables"                      # Location of iptables on your system
INTERNET="eth0"                           # Internet-connected interface
LOOPBACK_INTERFACE="lo"                   # however your system names it
IPADDR="my.ip.address"                    # your IP address
SUBNET_BASE="network.address"             # ISP network segment base address
SUBNET_BROADCAST="directed.broadcast"     # network segment broadcast address
MY_ISP="my.isp.address.range"             # ISP server & NOC address range
```

```
NAMESERVER_1="isp.name.server.1"      # address of a remote name server
NAMESERVER_2="isp.name.server.2"      # address of a remote name server
NAMESERVER_3="isp.name.server.3"      # address of a remote name server
POP_SERVER="isp.pop.server"           # address of a remote pop server
MAIL_SERVER="isp.mail.server"         # address of a remote mail gateway
NEWS_SERVER="isp.news.server"         # address of a remote news server
TIME_SERVER="some.timne.server"       # address of a remote time server
DHCP_SERVER="isp.dhcp.server"         # address of your ISP dhcp server
SSH_CLIENT="some.ssh.client"

LOOPBACK="127.0.0.0/8"                # reserved loopback address range
CLASS_A="10.0.0.0/8"                  # Class A private networks
CLASS_B="172.16.0.0/12"              # Class B private networks
CLASS_C="192.168.0.0/16"            # Class C private networks
CLASS_D_MULTICAST="224.0.0.0/4"     # Class D multicast addresses
CLASS_E_RESERVED_NET="240.0.0.0/5"  # Class E reserved addresses
BROADCAST_SRC="0.0.0.0"              # broadcast source address
BROADCAST_DEST="255.255.255.255"    # broadcast destination address

PRIVPORTS="0:1023"                   # well-known, privileged port range
UNPRIVPORTS="1024:65535"             # unprivileged port range

NFS_PORT="2049"
LOCKD_PORT="4045"
SOCKS_PORT="1080"
OPENWINDOWS_PORT="2000"
XWINDOW_PORTS="6000:6063"
SQUID_PORT="3128"


# traceroute usually uses -S 32769:65535 -D 33434:33523
TRACEROUTE_SRC_PORTS="32769:65535"
TRACEROUTE_DEST_PORTS="33434:33523"


USER_CHAINS="EXT-input                EXT-output \
            tcp-state-flags          connection-tracking  \
            source-address-check     destination-address-check  \
            local-dns-server-query   remote-dns-server-response  \
            local-tcp-client-request remote-tcp-server-response \
            remote-tcp-client-request local-tcp-server-response \
            local-udp-client-request remote-udp-server-response \
            local-dhcp-client-query  remote-dhcp-server-response \
            EXT-icmp-out             EXT-icmp-in \
            EXT-log-in               EXT-log-out \
            log-tcp-state"
```

```
############################################################

# Enable broadcast echo Protection
echo 1 > /proc/sys/net/ipv4/icmp_echo_ignore_broadcasts

# Disable Source Routed Packets
for f in /proc/sys/net/ipv4/conf/*/accept_source_route; do
    echo 0 > $f
done

# Enable TCP SYN Cookie Protection
echo 1 > /proc/sys/net/ipv4/tcp_syncookies

# Disable ICMP Redirect Acceptance
for f in /proc/sys/net/ipv4/conf/*/accept_redirects; do
    echo 0 > $f
done

# Don't send Redirect Messages
for f in /proc/sys/net/ipv4/conf/*/send_redirects; do
    echo 0 > $f
done

# Drop Spoofed Packets coming in on an interface, which, if replied to,
# would result in the reply going out a different interface.
for f in /proc/sys/net/ipv4/conf/*/rp_filter; do
    echo 1 > $f
done

# Log packets with impossible addresses.
for f in /proc/sys/net/ipv4/conf/*/log_martians; do
    echo 1 > $f
done

############################################################

# Remove any existing rules from all chains
$IPT --flush
$IPT -t nat --flush
$IPT -t mangle --flush
$IPT -X
$IPT -t nat -X
$IPT -t mangle -X

$IPT --policy INPUT    ACCEPT
$IPT --policy OUTPUT   ACCEPT
```

```
$IPT --policy FORWARD ACCEPT
$IPT -t nat --policy PREROUTING  ACCEPT
$IPT -t nat --policy OUTPUT ACCEPT
$IPT -t nat --policy POSTROUTING ACCEPT
$IPT -t mangle --policy PREROUTING ACCEPT
$IPT -t mangle --policy OUTPUT ACCEPT
if [ "$1" = "stop" ]
then
echo "Firewall completely stopped!  WARNING: THIS HOST HAS NO FIREWALL RUNNING."
exit 0
fi

# Unlimited traffic on the loopback interface
$IPT -A INPUT   -i lo -j ACCEPT
$IPT -A OUTPUT -o lo -j ACCEPT

# Set the default policy to drop
$IPT --policy INPUT DROP
$IPT --policy OUTPUT DROP
$IPT --policy FORWARD DROP
$IPT -t nat --policy PREROUTING DROP
$IPT -t nat --policy OUTPUT DROP
$IPT -t nat --policy POSTROUTING DROP
$IPT -t mangle --policy PREROUTING DROPT
$IPT -t mangle --policy OUTPUT DROP

# Create the user-defined chains
for i in $USER_CHAINS; do
    $IPT -N $i
done

###############################################################
# DNS Caching Name Server (query to remote, primary server)

$IPT -A EXT-output -p udp --sport 53 --dport 53 \
        -j local-dns-server-query

$IPT -A EXT-input -p udp --sport 53 --dport 53 \
        -j remote-dns-server-response

# DNS Caching Name Server (query to remote server over TCP)

$IPT -A EXT-output -p tcp \
        --sport $UNPRIVPORTS --dport 53 \
        -j local-dns-server-query
```

```
$IPT -A EXT-input -p tcp ! --syn \
        --sport 53 --dport $UNPRIVPORTS \
        -j remote-dns-server-response

##############################################################
# DNS Forwarding Name Server or client requests

if [ "$CONNECTION_TRACKING" = "1" ]; then
    $IPT -A local-dns-server-query \
            -d $NAMESERVER_1 \
            -m state --state NEW -j ACCEPT

    $IPT -A local-dns-server-query \
            -d $NAMESERVER_2 \
            -m state --state NEW -j ACCEPT

    $IPT -A local-dns-server-query \
            -d $NAMESERVER_3 \
            -m state --state NEW -j ACCEPT
fi

$IPT -A local-dns-server-query \
        -d $NAMESERVER_1 -j ACCEPT

$IPT -A local-dns-server-query \
        -d $NAMESERVER_2 -j ACCEPT

$IPT -A local-dns-server-query \
        -d $NAMESERVER_3 -j ACCEPT

# DNS server responses to local requests

$IPT -A remote-dns-server-response \
        -s $NAMESERVER_1 -j ACCEPT

$IPT -A remote-dns-server-response \
        -s $NAMESERVER_2 -j ACCEPT

$IPT -A remote-dns-server-response \
        -s $NAMESERVER_3 -j ACCEPT

##############################################################
# Local TCP client, remote server

$IPT -A EXT-output -p tcp \
        --sport $UNPRIVPORTS \
        -j local-tcp-client-request
```

```
$IPT -A EXT-input -p tcp ! --syn \
        --dport $UNPRIVPORTS \
        -j remote-tcp-server-response

##############################################################
# Local TCP client output and remote server input chains

# SSH client

if [ "$CONNECTION_TRACKING" = "1" ]; then
    $IPT -A local-tcp-client-request -p tcp \
            -d <selected host> --dport 22 \
            -m state --state NEW \
            -j ACCEPT
fi

$IPT -A local-tcp-client-request -p tcp \
        -d <selected host> --dport 22 \
        -j ACCEPT

$IPT -A remote-tcp-server-response -p tcp ! --syn \
        -s <selected host> --sport 22  \
        -j ACCEPT

#...........................................................
# Client rules for HTTP, HTTPS, AUTH, and FTP control requests

if [ "$CONNECTION_TRACKING" = "1" ]; then
    $IPT -A local-tcp-client-request -p tcp \
            -m multiport --destination-port 80,443,21 \
            --syn -m state --state NEW \
            -j ACCEPT
fi

$IPT -A local-tcp-client-request -p tcp \
        -m multiport --destination-port 80,443,21 \
        -j ACCEPT

$IPT -A remote-tcp-server-response -p tcp \
        -m multiport --source-port 80,443,21  ! --syn \
        -j ACCEPT

#...........................................................
# POP client
```

```
if [ "$CONNECTION_TRACKING" = "1" ]; then
    $IPT -A local-tcp-client-request -p tcp \
            -d $POP_SERVER --dport 110 \
            -m state --state NEW \
            -j ACCEPT
fi

$IPT -A local-tcp-client-request -p tcp \
        -d $POP_SERVER --dport 110 \
        -j ACCEPT

$IPT -A remote-tcp-server-response -p tcp ! --syn \
        -s $POP_SERVER --sport 110  \
        -j ACCEPT
#................................................................
# SMTP mail client

if [ "$CONNECTION_TRACKING" = "1" ]; then
    $IPT -A local-tcp-client-request -p tcp \
            -d $MAIL_SERVER --dport 25 \
            -m state --state NEW \
            -j ACCEPT
fi

$IPT -A local-tcp-client-request -p tcp \
        -d $MAIL_SERVER --dport 25 \
        -j ACCEPT

$IPT -A remote-tcp-server-response -p tcp ! --syn \
        -s $MAIL_SERVER --sport 25  \
        -j ACCEPT


#................................................................
# Usenet news client

if [ "$CONNECTION_TRACKING" = "1" ]; then
    $IPT -A local-tcp-client-request -p tcp \
            -d $NEWS_SERVER --dport 119 \
            -m state --state NEW \
            -j ACCEPT
fi
$IPT -A local-tcp-client-request -p tcp \
        -d $NEWS_SERVER --dport 119 \
        -j ACCEPT
```

```
$IPT -A remote-tcp-server-response -p tcp ! --syn \
        -s $NEWS_SERVER --sport 119 \
        -j ACCEPT


#...........................................................
# FTP client - passive mode data channel connection

if [ "$CONNECTION_TRACKING" = "1" ]; then
    $IPT -A local-tcp-client-request -p tcp \
            --dport $UNPRIVPORTS \
            -m state --state NEW \
            -j ACCEPT
fi

$IPT -A local-tcp-client-request -p tcp \
        --dport $UNPRIVPORTS -j ACCEPT

$IPT -A remote-tcp-server-response -p tcp  ! --syn \
        --sport $UNPRIVPORTS -j ACCEPT
############################################################
# Local TCP server, remote client

$IPT -A EXT-input -p tcp \
        --sport $UNPRIVPORTS \
        -j remote-tcp-client-request

$IPT -A EXT-output -p tcp ! --syn \
        --dport $UNPRIVPORTS \
        -j local-tcp-server-response

# Kludge for incoming FTP data channel connections
# from remote servers using port mode.
# The state modules treat this connection as RELATED
# if the ip_conntrack_ftp module is loaded.

$IPT -A EXT-input -p tcp \
        --sport 20 --dport $UNPRIVPORTS \
        -j ACCEPT

$IPT -A EXT-output -p tcp ! --syn \
        --sport $UNPRIVPORTS --dport 20 \
        -j ACCEPT
```

```
###############################################################
# Remote TCP client input and local server output chains

# SSH server

if [ "$CONNECTION_TRACKING" = "1" ]; then
    $IPT -A remote-tcp-client-request -p tcp \
            -s <selected host> --destination-port 22 \
            -m state --state NEW \
            -j ACCEPT
fi

$IPT -A remote-tcp-client-request -p tcp \
        -s <selected host> --destination-port 22 \
        -j ACCEPT

$IPT -A local-tcp-server-response -p tcp  ! --syn \
        --source-port 22 -d <selected host> \
        -j ACCEPT

#................................................................
# AUTH identd server

if [ "$ACCEPT_AUTH" = "0" ]; then
    $IPT -A remote-tcp-client-request -p tcp \
        --destination-port 113 \
        -j REJECT --reject-with tcp-reset
else
    $IPT -A remote-tcp-client-request -p tcp \
            --destination-port 113 \
            -j ACCEPT

    $IPT -A local-tcp-server-response -p tcp  ! --syn \
            --source-port 113 \
            -j ACCEPT
fi

###############################################################
# Local UDP client, remote server

$IPT -A EXT-output -p udp \
        --sport $UNPRIVPORTS \
        -j local-udp-client-request

$IPT -A EXT-input -p udp \
        --dport $UNPRIVPORTS \
        -j remote-udp-server-response
```

```
##############################################################
# NTP time client

if [ "$CONNECTION_TRACKING" = "1" ]; then
    $IPT -A local-udp-client-request -p udp \
            -d $TIME_SERVER --dport 123 \
            -m state --state NEW \
            -j ACCEPT
fi
$IPT -A local-udp-client-request -p udp \
        -d $TIME_SERVER --dport 123 \
        -j ACCEPT

$IPT -A remote-udp-server-response -p udp \
        -s $TIME_SERVER --sport 123 \
        -j ACCEPT


##############################################################
# ICMP

$IPT -A EXT-input -p icmp -j EXT-icmp-in

$IPT -A EXT-output -p icmp -j EXT-icmp-out

##############################################################
# ICMP traffic

# Log and drop initial ICMP fragments
$IPT -A EXT-icmp-in --fragment -j LOG \
        --log-prefix "Fragmented incoming ICMP: "

$IPT -A EXT-icmp-in --fragment -j DROP

$IPT -A EXT-icmp-out --fragment -j LOG \
        --log-prefix "Fragmented outgoing ICMP: "

$IPT -A EXT-icmp-out --fragment -j DROP

# Outgoing ping

if [ "$CONNECTION_TRACKING" = "1" ]; then
    $IPT -A EXT-icmp-out -p icmp \
            --icmp-type echo-request \
            -m state --state NEW \
            -j ACCEPT
fi
```

```
$IPT -A EXT-icmp-out -p icmp \
        --icmp-type echo-request -j ACCEPT

$IPT -A EXT-icmp-in -p icmp \
        --icmp-type echo-reply -j ACCEPT

# Incoming ping

if [ "$CONNECTION_TRACKING" = "1" ]; then
    $IPT -A EXT-icmp-in -p icmp \
            -s $MY_ISP \
            --icmp-type echo-request \
            -m state --state NEW \
            -j ACCEPT
fi

$IPT -A EXT-icmp-in -p icmp \
        --icmp-type echo-request \
        -s $MY_ISP -j ACCEPT

$IPT -A EXT-icmp-out -p icmp \
        --icmp-type echo-reply \
        -d $MY_ISP -j ACCEPT

# Destination Unreachable Type 3
$IPT -A EXT-icmp-out -p icmp \
        --icmp-type fragmentation-needed -j ACCEPT

$IPT -A EXT-icmp-in -p icmp \
        --icmp-type destination-unreachable -j ACCEPT

# Parameter Problem
$IPT -A EXT-icmp-out -p icmp \
        --icmp-type parameter-problem -j ACCEPT

$IPT -A EXT-icmp-in -p icmp \
        --icmp-type parameter-problem -j ACCEPT

# Time Exceeded
$IPT -A EXT-icmp-in -p icmp \
        --icmp-type time-exceeded -j ACCEPT

# Source Quench
$IPT -A EXT-icmp-out -p icmp \
        --icmp-type source-quench -j ACCEPT
```

```
##############################################################
# TCP State Flags

# All of the bits are cleared
$IPT -A tcp-state-flags -p tcp --tcp-flags ALL NONE -j log-tcp-state

# SYN and FIN are both set
$IPT -A tcp-state-flags -p tcp --tcp-flags SYN,FIN SYN,FIN -j log-tcp-state

# SYN and RST are both set
$IPT -A tcp-state-flags -p tcp --tcp-flags SYN,RST SYN,RST -j log-tcp-state

# FIN and RST are both set
$IPT -A tcp-state-flags -p tcp --tcp-flags FIN,RST FIN,RST -j log-tcp-state

# FIN is the only bit set, without the expected accompanying ACK
$IPT -A tcp-state-flags -p tcp --tcp-flags ACK,FIN FIN -j log-tcp-state

# PSH is the only bit set, without the expected accompanying ACK
$IPT -A tcp-state-flags -p tcp --tcp-flags ACK,PSH PSH -j log-tcp-state

# URG is the only bit set, without the expected accompanying ACK
$IPT -A tcp-state-flags -p tcp --tcp-flags ACK,URG URG -j log-tcp-state

##############################################################
# Log and drop TCP packets with bad state combinations

$IPT -A log-tcp-state -p tcp -j LOG \
        --log-prefix "Illegal TCP state: " \
        --log-ip-options --log-tcp-options

$IPT -A log-tcp-state -j DROP

##############################################################
# By-pass rule checking for ESTABLISHED exchanges

if [ "$CONNECTION_TRACKING" = "1" ]; then
    # By-pass the firewall filters for established exchanges
    $IPT -A connection-tracking -m state \
            --state ESTABLISHED,RELATED \
            -j ACCEPT

    $IPT -A connection-tracking -m state --state INVALID \
            -j LOG --log-prefix "INVALID packet: "
    $IPT -A connection-tracking -m state --state INVALID -j DROP
fi
```

```
################################################################
# DHCP traffic

# Some broadcast packets are explicitly ignored by the firewall.
# Others are dropped by the default policy.
# DHCP tests must precede broadcast-related rules, as DHCP relies
# on broadcast traffic initially.

if [ "$DHCP_CLIENT" = "1" ]; then

    # Initialization or rebinding: No lease or Lease time expired.

    $IPT -A local-dhcp-client-query \
            -s $BROADCAST_SRC \
            -d $BROADCAST_DEST -j ACCEPT

    # Incoming DHCPOFFER from available DHCP servers

    $IPT -A remote-dhcp-server-response \
            -s $BROADCAST_SRC \
            -d $BROADCAST_DEST -j ACCEPT

    # Fall back to initialization
    # The client knows its server, but has either lost its lease,
    # or else needs to reconfirm the IP address after rebooting.

    $IPT -A local-dhcp-client-query \
            -s $BROADCAST_SRC \
            -d $DHCP_SERVER -j ACCEPT

    $IPT -A remote-dhcp-server-response \
            -s $DHCP_SERVER \
            -d $BROADCAST_DEST -j ACCEPT

    # As a result of the above, we're supposed to change our IP
    # address with this message, which is addressed to our new
    # address before the dhcp client has received the update.
    # Depending on the server implementation, the destination address
    # can be the new IP address, the subnet address, or the limited
    # broadcast address.

    # If the network subnet address is used as the destination,
    # the next rule must allow incoming packets destined to the
    # subnet address, and the rule must precede any general rules
    # that block such incoming broadcast packets.
```

```
      $IPT -A remote-dhcp-server-response \
            -s $DHCP_SERVER -j ACCEPT

      # Lease renewal

      $IPT -A local-dhcp-client-query \
            -s $IPADDR \
            -d $DHCP_SERVER -j ACCEPT
fi
###############################################################
# Source Address Spoof Checks

# Drop packets pretending to be originating from the receiving interface
$IPT -A source-address-check -s $IPADDR -j DROP

# Refuse packets claiming to be from private networks

$IPT -A source-address-check -s $CLASS_A -j DROP
$IPT -A source-address-check -s $CLASS_B -j DROP
$IPT -A source-address-check -s $CLASS_C -j DROP
$IPT -A source-address-check -s $CLASS_D_MULTICAST -j DROP
$IPT -A source-address-check -s $CLASS_E_RESERVED_NET -j DROP
$IPT -A source-address-check -s $LOOPBACK   -j DROP

$IPT -A source-address-check -s 0.0.0.0/8 -j DROP
$IPT -A source-address-check -s 169.254.0.0/16 -j DROP
$IPT -A source-address-check -s 192.0.2.0/24 -j DROP


###############################################################
# Bad Destination Address and Port Checks

# Block directed broadcasts from the Internet

$IPT -A destination-address-check -d $BROADCAST_DEST -j DROP
$IPT -A destination-address-check -d $SUBNET_BASE -j DROP
$IPT -A destination-address-check -d $SUBNET_BROADCAST -j DROP
$IPT -A destination-address-check -p ! udp \
        -d $CLASS_D_MULTICAST -j DROP

# Avoid ports subject to protocol and system administration problems

# TCP unprivileged ports
# Deny connection requests to NFS, SOCKS, and X Window ports
$IPT -A destination-address-check -p tcp -m multiport \
        --destination-port $NFS_PORT,$OPENWINDOWS_PORT,$SOCKS_PORT,$SQUID_PORT \
        --syn -j DROP
```

```
$IPT -A destination-address-check -p tcp --syn \
        --destination-port $XWINDOW_PORTS -j DROP

# UDP unprivileged ports
# Deny connection requests to NFS and lockd ports
$IPT -A destination-address-check -p udp -m multiport \
        --destination-port $NFS_PORT,$LOCKD_PORT -j DROP

#############################################################
# Logging Rules Prior to Dropping by the Default Policy

# ICMP rules

$IPT -A EXT-log-in -p icmp \
        --icmp-type ! echo-request -m limit -j LOG

# TCP rules

$IPT -A EXT-log-in -p tcp \
        --dport 0:19 -j LOG

# skip ftp, telnet, ssh
$IPT -A EXT-log-in -p tcp \
        --dport 24 -j LOG

# skip smtp
$IPT -A EXT-log-in -p tcp \
        --dport 26:78 -j LOG

# skip finger, www
$IPT -A EXT-log-in -p tcp \
        --dport 81:109 -j LOG

# skip pop-3, sunrpc
$IPT -A EXT-log-in -p tcp \
        --dport 112:136 -j LOG

# skip NetBIOS
$IPT -A EXT-log-in -p tcp \
        --dport 140:142 -j LOG

# skip imap
$IPT -A EXT-log-in -p tcp \
        --dport 144:442 -j LOG
```

```
# skip secure_web/SSL
$IPT -A EXT-log-in -p tcp \
        --dport 444:65535 -j LOG

#UDP rules

$IPT -A EXT-log-in -p udp \
        --dport 0:110 -j LOG

# skip sunrpc
$IPT -A EXT-log-in -p udp \
        --dport 112:160 -j LOG

# skip snmp
$IPT -A EXT-log-in -p udp \
        --dport 163:634 -j LOG

# skip NFS mountd
$IPT -A EXT-log-in -p udp \
        --dport 636:5631 -j LOG

# skip pcAnywhere
$IPT -A EXT-log-in -p udp \
        --dport 5633:31336 -j LOG

# skip traceroute's default ports
$IPT -A EXT-log-in -p udp \
        --sport $TRACEROUTE_SRC_PORTS \
        --dport $TRACEROUTE_DEST_PORTS -j LOG

# skip the rest
$IPT -A EXT-log-in -p udp \
        --dport 33434:65535 -j LOG

# Outgoing Packets

# Don't log rejected outgoing ICMP destination-unreachable packets
$IPT -A EXT-log-out -p icmp \
        --icmp-type destination-unreachable -j DROP

$IPT -A EXT-log-out -j LOG

###############################################################
# Install the User-defined Chains on the built-in
# INPUT and OUTPUT chains
```

```
# If TCP: Check for common stealth scan TCP state patterns
$IPT -A INPUT  -p tcp -j tcp-state-flags
$IPT -A OUTPUT -p tcp -j tcp-state-flags

if [ "$CONNECTION_TRACKING" = "1" ]; then
    # By-pass the firewall filters for established exchanges
    $IPT -A INPUT  -j connection-tracking
    $IPT -A OUTPUT -j connection-tracking
fi

if [ "$DHCP_CLIENT" = "1" ]; then
    $IPT -A INPUT  -i $INTERNET -p udp \
            --sport 67 --dport 68 -j remote-dhcp-server-response
    $IPT -A OUTPUT -o $INTERNET -p udp \
            --sport 68 --dport 67 -j local-dhcp-client-query
fi

# Test for illegal source and destination addresses in incoming packets
$IPT -A INPUT  -p ! tcp -j source-address-check
$IPT -A INPUT  -p tcp --syn -j source-address-check
$IPT -A INPUT  -j destination-address-check

# Test for illegal destination addresses in outgoing packets
$IPT -A OUTPUT -j destination-address-check

# Begin standard firewall tests for packets addressed to this host
$IPT -A INPUT -i $INTERNET -d $IPADDR -j EXT-input

# Multicast traffic
$IPT -A INPUT  -i $INTERNET -p udp -d $CLASS_D_MULTICAST -j [ DROP | ACCEPT ]
$IPT -A OUTPUT -o $INTERNET -p udp -s $IPADDR -d $CLASS_D_MULTICAST \_
-j [ DROP | ACCEPT ]

# Begin standard firewall tests for packets sent from this host
# Source address spoofing by this host is not allowed due to the
# test on source address in this rule.
$IPT -A OUTPUT -o $INTERNET -s $IPADDR -j EXT-output

# Log anything of interest that fell through,
# before the default policy drops the packet.
$IPT -A INPUT  -j EXT-log-in
$IPT -A OUTPUT -j EXT-log-out

exit 0
```

iptables Firewall for a Choke Firewall from Chapter 6

Chapter 6 built on the standalone firewall example to develop either a gateway or a choke firewall. The gateway separated the Internet from the DMZ. The choke separated the DMZ from the LAN. The two firewalls were largely identical in terms of what they forwarded. They differed in that the gateway host didn't host any services, whereas the choke firewall did for the LAN.

NAT wasn't used in the Chapter 6 sample scripts. A private Class C network block was divided between the DMZ and LAN as a demonstration, and the assumption was made that both networks' address spaces were not within the private address space. The forward rules perform the actual firewall filtering. The **nat** table is used to perform NAT. To adapt the script to perform NAT, a single rule must be added:

```
$IPT -t nat -A POSTROUTING -o $DMZ_INTERFACE \
        -j SNAT --to-source $DMZ_IPADDR
```

Following is the Chapter 6 choke firewall script. The fallback rules for the case where the connection state is lost are not included.

```
#!/bin/sh

/sbin/modprobe ip_conntrack_ftp

CONNECTION_TRACKING="1"
ACCEPT_AUTH="0"
DHCP_SERVER="1"
IPT="/sbin/iptables"                  # Location of iptables on your system

DMZ_INTERFACE="eth0"                  # network interface to the DMZ
LAN_INTERFACE="eth1"                  # network interface to the LAN
LOOPBACK_INTERFACE="lo"               # however your system names it

DMZ_IPADDR="192.168.1.126"            # DMZ IP address
GATEWAY_IPADDR="192.168.1.65"         # gateway firewall - the router
DMZ_ADDRESSES="192.168.1.64/26"       # DMZ IP address range
DMZ_NETWORK="192.168.1.64"           # DMZ subnet base address
DMZ_BROADCAST="192.168.1.127"         # DMZ broadcast address
LAN_IPADDR="192.168.1.129"            # LAN IP address
LAN_ADDRESSES="192.168.1.128/26"      # LAN IP address range
LAN_NETWORK="192.168.1.128"           # DMZ subnet base address
LAN_BROADCAST="192.168.1.191"         # DMZ broadcast address
LAN_NETMASK="255.255.255.192"
```

```
NAMESERVER="isp.name.server.1"        # address of a remote name server
POP_SERVER="isp.pop.server"           # address of a remote pop server
MAIL_SERVER="isp.mail.server"         # address of a remote mail gateway
NEWS_SERVER="isp.news.server"         # address of a remote news server
TIME_SERVER="some.timne.server"       # address of a remote time server
DHCP_SERVER="isp.dhcp.server"         # address of your ISP dhcp server
SSH_CLIENT="some.ssh.client"
PRINTER_ADDRESS="local networked printer"

LOOPBACK="127.0.0.0/8"                # reserved loopback address range
CLASS_A="10.0.0.0/8"                  # Class A private networks
CLASS_B="172.16.0.0/12"              # Class B private networks
CLASS_C="192.168.0.0/16"            # Class C private networks
CLASS_D_MULTICAST="224.0.0.0/4"     # Class D multicast addresses
CLASS_E_RESERVED_NET="240.0.0.0/5"  # Class E reserved addresses
BROADCAST_SRC="0.0.0.0"             # broadcast source address
BROADCAST_DEST="255.255.255.255"    # broadcast destination address

PRIVPORTS="0:1023"                   # well-known, privileged port range
UNPRIVPORTS="1024:65535"            # unprivileged port range


###############################################################

# Enable broadcast echo Protection
echo 1 > /proc/sys/net/ipv4/icmp_echo_ignore_broadcasts

# Disable Source Routed Packets
for f in /proc/sys/net/ipv4/conf/*/accept_source_route; do
    echo 0 > $f
done

# Enable TCP SYN Cookie Protection
echo 1 > /proc/sys/net/ipv4/tcp_syncookies

# Disable ICMP Redirect Acceptance
for f in /proc/sys/net/ipv4/conf/*/accept_redirects; do
    echo 0 > $f
done

# Don't send Redirect Messages
for f in /proc/sys/net/ipv4/conf/*/send_redirects; do
    echo 0 > $f
done

# Drop Spoofed Packets coming in on an interface, which, if replied to,
# would result in the reply going out a different interface.
```

```
for f in /proc/sys/net/ipv4/conf/*/rp_filter; do
    echo 1 > $f
done

# Log packets with impossible addresses.
for f in /proc/sys/net/ipv4/conf/*/log_martians; do
    echo 1 > $f
done

##############################################################

# Remove any existing rules from all chains
$IPT --flush
$IPT -t nat --flush
$IPT -t mangle --flush
$IPT -X
$IPT -t nat -X
$IPT -t mangle -X
$IPT --policy INPUT   ACCEPT
$IPT --policy OUTPUT  ACCEPT
$IPT --policy FORWARD ACCEPT
$IPT -t nat --policy PREROUTING  ACCEPT
$IPT -t nat --policy OUTPUT ACCEPT
$IPT -t nat --policy POSTROUTING ACCEPT
$IPT -t mangle --policy PREROUTING ACCEPT
$IPT -t mangle --policy OUTPUT ACCEPT
if [ "$1" = "stop" ]
then
echo "Firewall completely stopped!  WARNING: THIS HOST HAS NO FIREWALL RUNNING."
exit 0
fi

# Unlimited traffic on the loopback interface
$IPT -A INPUT  -i $LOOPBACK_INTERFACE -j ACCEPT
$IPT -A OUTPUT -o $LOOPBACK_INTERFACE -j ACCEPT

# Set the default policy to drop
$IPT --policy INPUT REJECT
$IPT --policy OUTPUT REJECT
$IPT --policy FORWARD REJECT

##############################################################
# Stealth Scans and TCP State Flags

# All of the bits are cleared
$IPT -A INPUT   -p tcp --tcp-flags ALL NONE -j DROP
$IPT -A FORWARD -p tcp --tcp-flags ALL NONE -j DROP
```

```
# SYN and FIN are both set
$IPT -A INPUT   -p tcp --tcp-flags SYN,FIN SYN,FIN -j DROP
$IPT -A FORWARD -p tcp --tcp-flags SYN,FIN SYN,FIN -j DROP

# SYN and RST are both set
$IPT -A INPUT   -p tcp --tcp-flags SYN,RST SYN,RST -j DROP
$IPT -A FORWARD -p tcp --tcp-flags SYN,RST SYN,RST -j DROP

# FIN and RST are both set
$IPT -A INPUT   -p tcp --tcp-flags FIN,RST FIN,RST -j DROP
$IPT -A FORWARD -p tcp --tcp-flags FIN,RST FIN,RST -j DROP

# FIN is the only bit set, without the expected accompanying ACK
$IPT -A INPUT   -p tcp --tcp-flags ACK,FIN FIN -j DROP
$IPT -A FORWARD -p tcp --tcp-flags ACK,FIN FIN -j DROP

# PSH is the only bit set, without the expected accompanying ACK
$IPT -A INPUT   -p tcp --tcp-flags ACK,PSH PSH -j DROP
$IPT -A FORWARD -p tcp --tcp-flags ACK,PSH PSH -j DROP

# URG is the only bit set, without the expected accompanying ACK
$IPT -A INPUT   -p tcp --tcp-flags ACK,URG URG -j DROP
$IPT -A FORWARD -p tcp --tcp-flags ACK,URG URG -j DROP

##############################################################
# Using Connection State to By-pass Rule Checking

# Using the state module alone, INVALID will break protocols that use
# bidirectional connections or multiple connections or exchanges,
# unless an ALG is provided for the protocol. At this time, FTP is the
# only protocol with ALG support.

    $IPT -A INPUT  -m state --state ESTABLISHED,RELATED -j ACCEPT
    $IPT -A OUTPUT -m state --state ESTABLISHED,RELATED -j ACCEPT
    $IPT -A FORWARD -m state --state ESTABLISHED,RELATED -j ACCEPT

    $IPT -A INPUT -m state --state INVALID -j LOG \
            --log-prefix "INVALID input: "
    $IPT -A INPUT -m state --state INVALID -j DROP

    $IPT -A OUTPUT -m state --state INVALID -j LOG \
            --log-prefix "INVALID output: "
    $IPT -A OUTPUT -m state --state INVALID -j DROP

    $IPT -A FORWARD -m state --state INVALID -j LOG \
            --log-prefix "INVALID forward: "
    $IPT -A FORWARD -m state --state INVALID -j DROP
```

```
#############################################################
# Source Address Spoofing and Other Bad Addresses

# Refuse spoofed packets pretending to be from you
$IPT -A INPUT -s $DMZ_IPADDR -j DROP
$IPT -A INPUT -s $LAN_IPADDR -j DROP

$IPT -A FORWARD -s $DMZ_IPADDR -j DROP
$IPT -A FORWARD -s $LAN_IPADDR -j DROP

$IPT -A INPUT -i $DMZ_INTERFACE \
        -s $LAN_ADDRESSES -j DROP
$IPT -A FORWARD -i $DMZ_INTERFACE \
        -s $LAN_ADDRESSES -j DROP

$IPT -A FORWARD  -i $LAN_INTERFACE \
        -s ! $LAN_ADDRESSES -j DROP

$IPT -A OUTPUT -o $DMZ_INTERFACE -s ! $DMZ_IPADDR -j DROP
$IPT -A OUTPUT -o $LAN_INTERFACE -s ! $LAN_IPADDR -j DROP

if [ "$DHCP_SERVER" = "1" ]; then
    $IPT -A OUTPUT -o $LAN_INTERFACE -p udp \
            -s $BROADCAST_SRC --sport 67 \
            -d $BROADCAST_DEST --dport 68 -j ACCEPT
fi

$IPT -A OUTPUT -o $LAN_INTERFACE -s ! $LAN_IPADDR -j DROP

# Refuse malformed broadcast packets
$IPT -A FORWARD -i $LAN_INTERFACE -o $DMZ_INTERFACE \
        -d $BROADCAST_SRC  -j DROP

$IPT -A FORWARD -i $LAN_INTERFACE -o $DMZ_INTERFACE \
        -d $BROADCAST_SRC  -j DROP

# Don't forward directed broadcasts
$IPT -A FORWARD -i $LAN_INTERFACE -o $DMZ_INTERFACE \
        -d $DMZ_NETWORK -j DROP
$IPT -A FORWARD -i $LAN_INTERFACE -o $DMZ_INTERFACE \
        -d $DMZ_BROADCAST -j DROP

# Don't forward limited broadcasts in either direction
$IPT -A FORWARD -d $BROADCAST_DEST -j DROP

$IPT -A INPUT   -p ! udp -d $CLASS_D_MULTICAST -j DROP
$IPT -A FORWARD -p ! udp -d $CLASS_D_MULTICAST -j DROP
```

```
################################################################
# ICMP Control and Status Messages

# Log and drop initial ICMP fragments
$IPT -A INPUT --fragment -p icmp -j LOG \
        --log-prefix "Fragmented incoming ICMP: "
$IPT -A INPUT --fragment -p icmp -j DROP

$IPT -A OUTPUT --fragment -p icmp -j LOG \
        --log-prefix "Fragmented outgoing ICMP: "
$IPT -A OUTPUT --fragment -p icmp -j DROP

$IPT -A FORWARD --fragment -p icmp -j LOG \
        --log-prefix "Fragmented forwarded ICMP: "
$IPT -A FORWARD --fragment -p icmp -j DROP

$IPT -A INPUT -p icmp \
        --icmp-type source-quench -d $DMZ_IPADDR -j ACCEPT

$IPT -A OUTPUT -p icmp \
        --icmp-type source-quench -j ACCEPT
$IPT -A FORWARD -p icmp \
        --icmp-type source-quench -j ACCEPT

$IPT -A INPUT -p icmp \
        --icmp-type parameter-problem -j ACCEPT

$IPT -A OUTPUT -p icmp \
        --icmp-type parameter-problem -j ACCEPT

$IPT -A FORWARD -p icmp \
        --icmp-type parameter-problem -j ACCEPT

$IPT -A INPUT -p icmp \
        --icmp-type destination-unreachable -j ACCEPT

$IPT -A OUTPUT -o $LAN_INTERFACE -p icmp \
        --icmp-type destination-unreachable -d $LAN_ADDRESSES -j ACCEPT

$IPT -A FORWARD -o $LAN_INTERFACE -p icmp \
        --icmp-type destination-unreachable -d $LAN_ADDRESSES -j ACCEPT

$IPT -A OUTPUT -p icmp \
        --icmp-type fragmentation-needed -j ACCEPT
```

```
$IPT -A FORWARD -p icmp \
        --icmp-type fragmentation-needed -j ACCEPT

# Don't log dropped outgoing ICMP error messages
$IPT -A OUTPUT  -p icmp \
        --icmp-type destination-unreachable -j DROP

$IPT -A FORWARD -o $DMZ_INTERFACE -p icmp \
        --icmp-type destination-unreachable -j DROP

# Intermediate traceroute responses
$IPT -A INPUT -p icmp \
        --icmp-type time-exceeded -j ACCEPT

$IPT -A FORWARD -o $LAN_INTERFACE -p icmp \
        --icmp-type time-exceeded -d $LAN_ADDRESSES -j ACCEPT

# allow outgoing pings to anywhere
if [ "$CONNECTION_TRACKING" = "1" ]; then
    $IPT -A OUTPUT -p icmp \
            --icmp-type echo-request \
            -m state --state NEW -j ACCEPT

    $IPT -A FORWARD -o $DMZ_INTERFACE -p icmp \
            --icmp-type echo-request -s $LAN_ADDRESSES \
            -m state --state NEW -j ACCEPT
fi

# allow incoming pings from trusted hosts
if [ "$CONNECTION_TRACKING" = "1" ]; then
    $IPT -A INPUT  -i $DMZ_INTERFACE -p icmp \
            -s $GATEWAY_IPADDR --icmp-type echo-request -d $DMZ_IPADDR \
            -m state --state NEW -j ACCEPT

    $IPT -A INPUT  -i $LAN_INTERFACE -p icmp \
            -s $LAN_ADDRESSES --icmp-type echo-request -d $LAN_IPADDR \
            -m state --state NEW -j ACCEPT
fi

##############################################################
# DNS Name Server

# DNS LAN clients to private server (53)

$IPT -A INPUT  -i $LAN_INTERFACE -p udp \
        -s $LAN_ADDRESSES --sport $UNPRIVPORTS \
```

```
                   -d $LAN_IPADDR --dport 53 \
                   -m state --state NEW -j ACCEPT

$IPT -A INPUT  -i $LAN_INTERFACE -p tcp \
                   -s $LAN_ADDRESSES --sport $UNPRIVPORTS \
                   -d $LAN_IPADDR --dport 53 \
                   -m state --state NEW -j ACCEPT

$IPT -A INPUT  -i $DMZ_INTERFACE -p udp \
                   -s $DMZ_ADDRESSES --sport $UNPRIVPORTS \
                   -d $DMZ_IPADDR --dport 53 \
                   -m state --state NEW -j ACCEPT

# DNS caching & forwarding name server (53)

$IPT -A OUTPUT -o $DMZ_INTERFACE -p udp \
                   -s $DMZ_IPADDR --sport 53 \
                   -d $NAMESERVER --dport 53 \
                   -m state --state NEW -j ACCEPT

$IPT -A OUTPUT -o $DMZ_INTERFACE -p udp \
                   -s $DMZ_IPADDR --sport $UNPRIVPORTS \
                   -d $NAMESERVER --dport 53 \
                   -m state --state NEW -j ACCEPT

$IPT -A OUTPUT -o $DMZ_INTERFACE -p tcp \
                   -s $DMZ_IPADDR --sport $UNPRIVPORTS \
                   -d $NAMESERVER --dport 53 \
                   -m state --state NEW -j ACCEPT

###############################################################
# Filtering the AUTH User Identification Service (TCP Port 113)

$IPT -A FORWARD -i $LAN_INTERFACE -o $DMZ_INTERFACE -p tcp \
                   -s $LAN_ADDRESSES --sport $UNPRIVPORTS --dport 113 \
                   -m state --state NEW -j ACCEPT

$IPT -A FORWARD -i $DMZ_INTERFACE -o $LAN_INTERFACE -p tcp \
                   --sport $UNPRIVPORTS -d $LAN_ADDRESSES --dport 113 \
                   -m state --state NEW -j ACCEPT

$IPT -A INPUT -i $LAN_INTERFACE -p tcp \
                   -s $LAN_ADDRESSES --sport $UNPRIVPORTS -d $LAN_IPADDR --dport 113 \
                   -m state --state NEW -j ACCEPT
```

```
$IPT -A INPUT -i $DMZ_INTERFACE -p tcp \
        -s $DMZ_ADDRESSES --sport $UNPRIVPORTS -d $DMZ_IPADDR --dport 113 \
        -m state --state NEW -j ACCEPT

##############################################################
# Sending Mail to the Mail Gateway Server (TCP Port 25)

$IPT -A FORWARD -i $LAN_INTERFACE -o $DMZ_INTERFACE -p tcp \
        -s $LAN_ADDRESSES --sport $UNPRIVPORTS \
        -d $MAIL_SERVER --dport 25 \
        -m state --state NEW -j ACCEPT

$IPT -A OUTPUT -o $DMZ_INTERFACE -p tcp \
        -s $DMZ_IPADDR --sport $UNPRIVPORTS \
        -d $MAIL_SERVER --dport 25 \
        -m state --state NEW -j ACCEPT

##############################################################
# Retrieving Mail as a POP Client (TCP Port 110)

$IPT -A FORWARD -i $LAN_INTERFACE -o $DMZ_INTERFACE -p tcp \
        -s $LAN_ADDRESSES --sport $UNPRIVPORTS \
        -d $POP_SERVER --dport 110 \
        -m state --state NEW -j ACCEPT

$IPT -A OUTPUT -o $DMZ_INTERFACE -p tcp \
        -s $DMZ_IPADDR --sport $UNPRIVPORTS \
        -d $POP_SERVER --dport 110 \
        -m state --state NEW -j ACCEPT

##############################################################
# Accessing Usenet News Services (TCP NNTP Port 119)

$IPT -A FORWARD -i $LAN_INTERFACE -o $DMZ_INTERFACE -p tcp \
        -s $LAN_ADDRESSES --sport $UNPRIVPORTS \
        -d $NEWS_SERVER --dport 119 \
        -m state --state NEW -j ACCEPT

##############################################################
# ssh (TCP Port 22)

$IPT -A OUTPUT  -o $DMZ_INTERFACE -p tcp \
        -s $DMZ_IPADDR --sport $UNPRIVPORTS \
        -d $DMZ_ADDRESSES --dport  22 \
        -m state --state NEW -j ACCEPT
```

```
$IPT -A FORWARD  -i $LAN_INTERFACE -o $DMZ_INTERFACE -p tcp \
        -s $LAN_ADDRESSES --sport $UNPRIVPORTS --dport 22 \
        -m state --state NEW -j ACCEPT

$IPT -A FORWARD  -i $DMZ_INTERFACE -o $LAN_INTERFACE -p tcp \
        -s $SSH_CLIENT --sport $UNPRIVPORTS \
        -d $SSH_CLIENT --dport 22 \
        -m state --state NEW -j ACCEPT

############################################################
# ftp (TCP Ports 21, 20)
# Outgoing Local Client Requests to Remote Servers

$IPT -A FORWARD -i $LAN_INTERFACE -o $DMZ_INTERFACE -p tcp \
        -s $LAN_ADDRESSES --sport $UNPRIVPORTS --dport 21 \
        -m state --state NEW -j ACCEPT

$IPT -A OUTPUT -o $DMZ_INTERFACE -p tcp  \
        -s $DMZ_IPADDR --sport $UNPRIVPORTS --dport 21 \
        -m state --state NEW -j ACCEPT

############################################################
# HTTP Web Traffic (TCP Port 80)

$IPT -A FORWARD  -i $LAN_INTERFACE -o $DMZ_INTERFACE -p tcp \
        -s $LAN_ADDRESSES --sport  $UNPRIVPORTS --dport 80 \
        -m state --state NEW -j ACCEPT

$IPT -A OUTPUT  -o $DMZ_INTERFACE -p tcp \
        -s $DMZ_IPADDR --sport  $UNPRIVPORTS --dport 80 \
        -m state --state NEW -j ACCEPT

############################################################
# SSL Web Traffic (TCP Port 443)

$IPT -A FORWARD  -i $LAN_INTERFACE -o $DMZ_INTERFACE -p tcp \
        -s $LAN_ADDRESSES --sport  $UNPRIVPORTS --dport 443 \
        -m state --state NEW -j ACCEPT

$IPT -A OUTPUT  -o $DMZ_INTERFACE -p tcp \
        -s $DMZ_IPADDR --sport  $UNPRIVPORTS --dport 443 \
        -m state --state NEW -j ACCEPT

############################################################
# whois (TCP Port 43)
```

```
$IPT -A FORWARD  -i $LAN_INTERFACE -o $DMZ_INTERFACE -p tcp \
        -s $LAN_ADDRESSES --sport $UNPRIVPORTS --dport 43 \
        -m state --state NEW -j ACCEPT

$IPT -A OUTPUT -o $DMZ_INTERFACE -p tcp  \
        -s $DMZ_IPADDR --sport $UNPRIVPORTS --dport 43 \
        -m state --state NEW -j ACCEPT

##############################################################
# Networked Printer (TCP Port 515)

$IPT -A OUTPUT -o $LAN_INTERFACE -p tcp  \
        -s $LAN_IPADDR --sport $PRIVPORTS \
        -d $PRINTER_ADDRESS --dport 515 \
        -m state --state NEW -j ACCEPT

$IPT -A FORWARD -i $DMZ_INTERFACE -o $LAN_INTERFACE -p tcp \
        -s $DMZ_ADDRESSES --sport $UNPRIVPORTS \
        -d $PRINTER_ADDRESS --dport 515 \
        -m state --state NEW -j ACCEPT

##############################################################
# Accessing Network Time Server (UDP 123)
# Note: Some client and servers use source port 123
# when querying a remote server on destination port 123.

$IPT -A OUTPUT  -o $DMZ_INTERFACE -p udp \
        -s $DMZ_IPADDR --sport $UNPRIVPORTS \
        -d $GATEWAY_IPADDR --dport 123 \
        -m state --state NEW -j ACCEPT

$IPT -A INPUT  -i $LAN_INTERFACE -p udp \
        -s $LAN_ADDRESSES --sport $UNPRIVPORTS \
        -d $LAN_IPADDR --dport 123 \
        -m state --state NEW -j ACCEPT

$IPT -A INPUT  -i $LAN_INTERFACE -p udp \
        -s $LAN_ADDRESSES --sport 123 \
        -d $LAN_IPADDR --dport 123 \
        -m state --state NEW -j ACCEPT

##############################################################
# Accessing a Local DHCP Server (UDP Ports 67, 68)

$IPT -A INPUT  -i $LAN_INTERFACE -p udp \
        -s $BROADCAST_SRC --sport 68 \
        -d $BROADCAST_DEST --dport 67 -j ACCEPT
```

```
$IPT -A OUTPUT -o $LAN_INTERFACE -p udp \
        -s $BROADCAST_SRC --sport 67 \
        -d $BROADCAST_DEST --dport 68 -j ACCEPT

$IPT -A OUTPUT -o $LAN_INTERFACE -p udp \
        -s $LAN_IPADDR --sport 67 \
        -d $BROADCAST_DEST --dport 68 -j ACCEPT

$IPT -A INPUT  -i $LAN_INTERFACE -p udp \
        -s $BROADCAST_SRC --sport 68 \
        -d $LAN_IPADDR --dport 67 -j ACCEPT

$IPT -A OUTPUT -o $LAN_INTERFACE -p udp \
        -s $LAN_IPADDR --sport 67 \
        -d $LAN_ADDRESSES --dport 68 -j ACCEPT

$IPT -A OUTPUT -o $LAN_INTERFACE -p udp \
        -s $LAN_IPADDR --sport 67 \
        -d $LAN_ADDRESSES --dport 68 -j ACCEPT

$IPT -A INPUT  -i $LAN_INTERFACE -p udp \
        -s $LAN_ADDRESSES --sport 68 \
        -d $LAN_IPADDR --dport 67 -j ACCEPT
$IPT -A OUTPUT -o $LAN_INTERFACE  -j LOG

##############################################################
# Logging Dropped Packets

$IPT -A INPUT   -i $LAN_INTERFACE -j LOG
$IPT -A OUTPUT  -o $LAN_INTERFACE -j LOG
$IPT -A FORWARD  -i $LAN_INTERFACE -o $DMZ_INTERFACE -j LOG
$IPT -A FORWARD  -i $DMZ_INTERFACE -o $LAN_INTERFACE -j LOG

exit 0
```

VPNs

contributed by Carl B. Constantine

The use of virtual private networks, or VPNs, is fast becoming the preferred method for accessing remote and private networks by home users and business users alike. This appendix discusses VPNs, providing both some background on VPNs themselves and insight on how you might implement a VPN using Linux.

Overview of Virtual Private Networks

VPN systems are designed to connect two or more devices or networks securely over a public network such as the Internet. A VPN is so named because it is virtual, using an already existing infrastructure; it is private, having the data encapsulated through a secure protocol; and it is a network, because it connects two or more devices or networks together. VPNs are popular today because they provide a better value proposition than setting up individual leased connections between locations, especially for road warriors or other short-lived connections. VPNs can also provide seamless operation. After initial configuration is done, the networks connected with a VPN can operate as if they were one network.

VPN Protocols

Most VPN systems use one of two main protocols: Point-to-Point Tunneling Protocol (PPTP) or IP Security (IPSec). IPSec is the more widely used protocol for VPNs. Other VPN systems use varying degrees of both protocols. Additionally, Microsoft and Cisco jointly developed another VPN protocol called Layer Two Tunneling Protocol (L2TP).

PPTP

Point-to-Point Tunneling Protocol was originally designed and developed by a consortium of companies to encapsulate non-TCP/IP protocols such as IPX over the Internet using Generic Routing Encapsulation (GRE). Security in the protocol was added later.

> **GENERIC ROUTING ENCAPSULATION**
>
> Many protocols are currently available that are designed to encapsulate or hide one protocol in another, normally IP. GRE is designed to be more generic (hence the name) than these other protocols. As such, however, it may not fit the need of specifically encapsulating protocol X over protocol Y; instead, it is designed to be a simple, general-purpose encapsulation protocol that reduces the overhead of providing encapsulation. RFC 2784 describes GRE in detail. GRE is supported by the Linux kernel, however.

PPTP is very popular in many corporate environments, particularly those that are Windows-centric. For the most part, PPTP relies on a Windows NT host and includes clients for all flavors of Windows from Windows 95 on up, as well as the Mac OS. However, PPTP is considered to be less secure than IPSec, which is one of the reasons many people have switched to IPSec.

PPTP has many security concerns, including these:

- *Poor encryption*—Nonrandom keys are generated, session keys are a hash of user passwords, and key lengths are too short.
- *Bad password management*—Static passwords are easily compromised.
- *Vulnerability to attacks*—Server spoofing attacks make this system vulnerable partly because packet authentication is not implemented. PPTP also is vulnerable to denial-of-service (DoS) attacks.

PPTP is still a widely used VPN protocol despite the noted security flaws and weaknesses. Because of its wide use, two main PPTP efforts are ongoing for Linux at this time; one is a server and the other is a client. More on this later.

IPSec

IPSec was designed with security in mind and is considered the de facto standard for secure private communication across public networks such as the Internet. As mentioned previously, IPSec has been included in the upcoming IPv6 implementation, but it also can be used in the current IPv4 standard.

IPSec provides data integrity, authentication, and confidentiality. All IPSec services are at the IP layer and provide protection for IP and upper-layer protocols. These services are provided by two traffic security protocols, the Authentication Header (AH) and the Encapsulating Security Payload (ESP). IPSec uses a cryptographic key-management system through the Internet Key Exchange (IKE) protocol and a managed Security Association (SA) connection system.

IPSec offers many advantages compared to other secure network access methods. One of the biggest advantages is that IPSec can work in the background without the user even knowing what's happening.

AUTHENTICATION HEADER

Normal IP packets consist of a header and a payload. The header contains both source and destination IP addresses that are required for routing. The payload consists of information that may be confidential. Headers can be spoofed or altered using a "man in the middle" type of attack. The AH actually signs the outbound packet digitally, verifying the identity of source and destination addresses and the integrity of the payload data.

AH provides only authentication, not encryption, and can be configured in one of two ways: in transport mode or in tunnel mode. Transport mode really applies only to the host implementation and provides protection for the upper-level protocols as well as selected IP header fields. Using transport mode, the AH is inserted after the IP header and before the upper-layer protocol (TCP, UDP, ICMP, and so forth), or before other IPSec headers that may already have been inserted.

The AH in tunnel mode protects the entire IP packet, including the entire inner IP header. As in transport mode, the AH is inserted after the outer IP header of the packet.

The AH is inserted after the IP header. In IPv4 implementations, the IP header contains the protocol number 51 (AH). The AH is shown in Figure C.1.

FIGURE C.1
The AH header format.

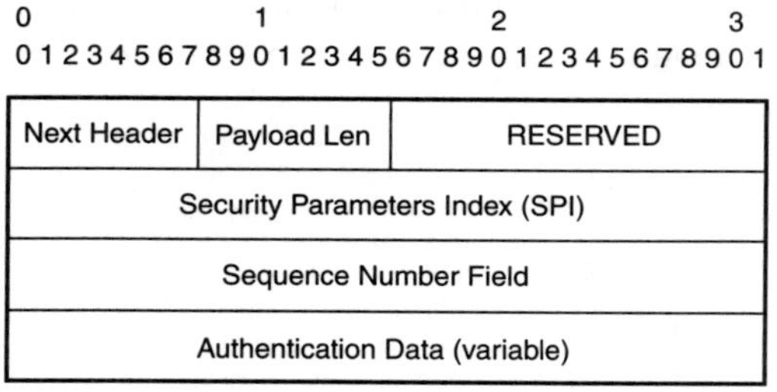

```
       0               1               2               3
       0 1 2 3 4 5 6 7 8 9 0 1 2 3 4 5 6 7 8 9 0 1 2 3 4 5 6 7 8 9 0 1
      +---------------+---------------+-------------------------------+
      |  Next Header  |  Payload Len  |           RESERVED            |
      +---------------+---------------+-------------------------------+
      |               Security Parameters Index (SPI)                |
      +---------------------------------------------------------------+
      |                    Sequence Number Field                     |
      +---------------------------------------------------------------+
      |                 Authentication Data (variable)               |
      +---------------------------------------------------------------+
```

All fields in AH format must always be present and are included in the Integrity Check Value (ICV) computation.

ENCAPSULATING SECURITY PAYLOAD

Using ESP guarantees the integrity and confidentiality of the data in the original message by means of a secure encryption of either the original payload by itself or the combination of the headers and payload of the original packet.

ESP can be used in transport mode or tunnel mode, like AH, to provide encryption and authentication. Transport mode is applicable only to host implementations. It provides protection for the upper-layer protocols, but not for the IP header. For tunnel mode, the ESP is inserted after the IP header and before any upper-layer protocol such as TCP and UDP, or before any other IPSec headers that may already be inserted. In the current IPv4 implementation of TCP/IP, the ESP is placed after the IP header but before the upper-layer protocol. This makes ESP compatible with non–IPSec-aware hardware.

ESP's tunnel mode may be used in either hosts or security gateways. You must use ESP in tunnel mode if you deploy a security gateway. In tunnel mode, the inner IP header carries the proper source and destination addresses, whereas the outer IP header may contain distinct IP addresses such as addresses of security gateways. ESP protects the entire packet in tunnel mode, including the inner IP header. The position of the ESP packet is similar to that of transport mode.

ESP can use a wide variety of encryption algorithms, including 3DES, DES, CAST128, and Blowfish, to provide security services.

TRANSPORT AND TUNNEL MODES

In transport mode, the IPSec gateway is the destination of the protected packets—a machine acts as its own gateway. In tunnel mode, an IPSec gateway provides protection for packets to and from other systems.

The ESP is inserted after the IP header. In IPv4 implementations, the IP header contains the protocol number 50 (ESP). Figure C.2 shows an example of an ESP.

FIGURE C.2
The ESP format.

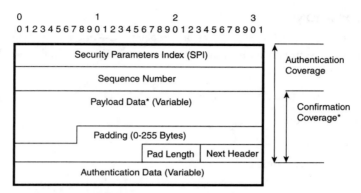

* If included in the Payload field, cryptographic synchronization
data, e.g., an Initialization Vector, usually is not encrypted,
although it often is referred to as being part of the ciphertext.

INTERNET KEY EXCHANGE

The Internet Key Exchange, or IKE, is an important part of an IPSec VPN. IKE itself is a hybrid protocol and allows for negotiation and authentication of keyed material for security associations in a protected manner. IKE consists of the following components:

- *ISAKMP*—A framework for authentication and key exchange. ISAKMP is designed to be independent of the key exchange so that it can support many different key exchanges.

- *Oakley*—A series of key exchanges, known as modes, and details of the services provided by each, such as perfect forward secrecy for keys, identity protection, and authentication.

- *SKEME*—A key exchange technique that provides anonymity, reputability, and quick key refreshment.

IKE uses parts of these protocols to obtain authenticated keying material for ISAKMP and other security associations, such as AH and ESP. ISAKMP/Oakley is used by many VPN vendors to perform key exchange between IPSec devices.

ISAKMP/Oakley works in two phases when hosts need to set up connections between them. In the first phase, the hosts establish a secure channel between themselves by creating a bidirectional ISAKMP security association. This channel can then be used for the next phase to negotiate the required IPSec SAs. After this is done, IPSec can provide its security services with the established SAs. When the security associations expire, ISAKMP/Oakley is again used to negotiate new SAs.

SECURITY ASSOCIATIONS

To have secure traffic, there must be two security associations—one for each direction. The security association is essentially a one-way channel negotiated by the higher-level IPSec system and used by the lower level.

A security association is defined by three things:

- The destination IP address
- The protocol (AH or ESP)
- The security parameter index (SPI)

You cannot use both AH and ESP unless you create two or more SAs at each end of the VPN network. An SA can be used in transport mode or tunnel mode. A transport-mode SA is a security association between two hosts. A tunnel-mode SA is a security association applied to an IP tunnel. If either end of an SA is a security gateway, the SA is a tunnel-mode security association. Security association between two security gateways is always the tunnel-mode SA, just like an SA between a host and a security gateway.

Linux and VPN Products

Now that you know most everything you need to in order to understand VPNs, it's time to take a look at different Linux VPN products and what issues need to be addressed when using VPNs in concert with firewalls. It should be noted that IPSec support is now available with the Linux 2.6 kernel series as well.

Let's start by looking at some VPN systems available for Linux and discussing their merits. This is by no means an exhaustive list, but it does provide a good place to start.

Openswan

Openswan is an open-source implementation of VPN software that works very well with Linux. Openswan is included with many Linux distributions, including SUSE, Debian, and Red Hat. Openswan currently has two main development branches: the 1.X branch for 2.X kernels prior to 2.6, and the 2.X development branch of Openswan for the 2.6 kernel series.

Openswan is one of the easier Linux implementations of VPN software to set up. More information can be found at http://www.openswan.org/.

FreeS/WAN

Linux FreeS/WAN is another good IPSec VPN implementation for Linux. FreeS/WAN is maintained and supported at http://www.freeswan.org.

Linux FreeS/WAN gets its name as a variation of SWAN, which means secure wide area network. Because it's free, it's called FreeS/WAN to differentiate it from the various RSA implementations of SWAN.

FreeS/WAN can be used by itself or as part of a firewall solution. In fact, the product is used in various other IPSec VPN firewalls and router products, and it is also part of some Linux distributions. There is a development version that works with the newer kernels, but the release version is guaranteed to work only on current stable series kernels. The documentation available is extensive, and the mailing list is extremely helpful.

Virtual Private Network Daemon

Virtual Private Network Daemon (VPND) is a network daemon that can connect two networks using either a leased line or standard TCP/IP over Ethernet. All traffic going between the two sites is encrypted using the Blowfish algorithm.

VPND has a lot of merit. It's simple to set up and use, and it is probably a good solution for people who just want to share resources and data securely without going through a lot of hassle.

However, VPND is not without problems. First, it has not been updated to work with the latest kernels and really hasn't been actively developed or improved on for a couple of years. You can find more information on VPND at http://sunsite.dk/vpnd/.

PPTP Linux Solutions

As mentioned before, a couple of PPTP solutions are in active development. Why use a PPTP solution if there are security problems? To fit into an existing PPTP VPN solution while still using Linux as your operating system.

For example, if you work for a company that uses a PPTP VPN system and you occasionally work at home, you can use a PPTP Linux client to connect to the office network. Similarly, if you're in the office and want to connect to your Linux system at home, you can use a PPTP VPN client to access your home network.

POPTOP

PoPToP is a PPTP VPN server solution for Linux developed by Lineo. This package requires a new version of PPP, with some patches applied to it, to work correctly. PoPToP is an excellent

PPTP "server" solution that can be used with the Linux PPTP "client" as well as standard PPTP clients. You can find more information, including install instructions, mail list archives, and more, at http://www.poptop.org/.

Virtual Tunnel

One other product deserves mention here: the Virtual Tunnel (VTUN) project. VTUN is an open-source project that creates an encrypted tunnel between two computers or networks. It can run over TCP or UDP, and it uses good cryptographic algorithms such as Blowfish and 3DES to encrypt the data.

VTUN is under active development and works with newer kernels. Someone with simple requirements would do well to look into this project. More information on VTUN is available at http://vtun.sourceforge.net.

VPN Configurations

From this point on, I'm going to talk only about IPSec-based VPN systems because I believe them to be the best VPN solution and because IPSec is now considered the de facto standard in the industry. A great deal of time could be spent discussing different VPN configurations and how things actually work. I describe the most common configurations here.

Roaming User

Let's first look at a typical VPN setup, in which there is a roaming "client" machine and a VPN gateway server located on the home network.

Let's say that you are at a conference and you occasionally want to get your email and transfer files from your home network. Typically, you would bring a laptop with you to the conference. It could be a Win32-, Mac OSX-, or Linux-based laptop. You connect to the Internet through some local means. You then start the IPSec software on the laptop and direct it to your VPN gateway at home. The client and the VPN gateway negotiate and exchange authentication keys, and you then have access to your network as though you were sitting right next to your server. A roaming user like this is often referred to as a "road warrior," a user who does not have a fixed IP address.

In this configuration, your VPN gateway must have IP forwarding enabled in **/proc/sys/net/ipv4/ip_forward** to permit routing to your LAN. All computers on your internal network must use the IPSec gateway as their default gateway because the packets need to come from your LAN to your laptop, as well as go to your LAN from your laptop.

For an added twist, you may have your VPN server set up to accept dial-in connections so that you do not have to go through the Internet at all.

The point to make with this example is that you, the user, must do something such as start a program on the laptop to initiate a VPN connection. If it's a Linux-based laptop, you may need to start IPSec services using a script after you are connected to the Internet.

Connecting Networks

Let's contrast the preceding case with the case in which you want to connect two networks. These networks could be in separate physical locations, or they could just be two separate subnets of the same network.

In this configuration, the VPN gateways have startup scripts to start IPSec services at boot time. The servers establish a secure connection with each other. Both gateways have a static route to the other gateway. From a user perspective, they don't need to do anything to communicate and share information between networks. All communication is taken care of by the VPN gateways. From the perspective of the user, it looks as though Network 2 is on the same network as Network 1. This may be a slight oversimplification, of course, but that is essentially what happens.

AUTHENTICATION

It's important to note that, in both of these configurations, the user is not being authenticated. Instead, the computer that the VPN software is running on is authenticated. This is particularly noticeable in the dual-network configuration. Only the gateways know about each other and authenticate traffic coming from the other. This process differs greatly from the traditional client/server thinking and technology we have today.

You can set up a lot more complex configurations than those shown here. However, they all have similarities. All VPN gateways know about and have routes to the other VPN gateways in any configuration. Authentication occurs at the gateway level, not the user level.

VPN and Firewalls

A VPN can be placed in front of a firewall, be placed behind a firewall, or be part of a firewall implementation. Placing the VPN in front of a firewall is not very common. It is more common to use a firewall/VPN combo or to put the VPN behind the firewall itself.

Combining a VPN system and a firewall is one of the more flexible solutions. It also requires less hardware and thus unfortunately also gives a single point of failure. However, it should be stressed that the best solution is to have a VPN behind the firewall or as part of a DMZ configuration. A separate firewall and VPN is set up because it is more secure. If a potential attacker managed to break your firewall/VPN, your network and also your remote networks could potentially be compromised. You want to avoid this problem and make it as hard for the attacker as possible.

If your firewall also performs NAT, you may run into some troubles with some VPN configurations. In particular, your firewall must be set up to route packets based on the protocol (GRE, AH, ESP) instead of on the port alone.

A NAT/firewall is incompatible with the AH protocol regardless of the mode (transport or tunnel). IPSec VPNs using AH digitally sign the outbound packet, both data payload and headers, with a hash value appended to the packet. AH doesn't encrypt the packet contents (data payload). If a NAT/firewall is between the IPSec endpoints, it rewrites either the source address or the destination address with one of its own (depending on the NAT setup). The VPN at the receiving end tries to verify the integrity of the inbound packet by computing its own hash value and complains that the hash value appended to the packet doesn't match. The VPN, unaware of the NAT/firewall in the middle, thinks that the packet has been altered.

You can use IPSec with ESP in tunnel mode with authentication. ESP in tunnel mode encapsulates the entire original packet (including headers) in a new IP packet. The new packet's source address is the outbound address of the sending VPN gateway, and its destination address is the inbound address of the VPN at the receiving end. When using ESP in tunnel mode with authentication, the packet contents are encrypted. The encrypted contents (the original packet), not the new headers, are signed with a hash value appended to the packet.

Integrity checks are performed over the combination of the original header plus the original payload. If you're using ESP in tunnel mode with authentication, these are not changed by the NAT/firewall.

A NAT/firewall may interfere with IPSec (both AH and ESP) if it prevents the two VPN gateways from successfully negotiating security associations using ISAKMP/IKE with X.509 certificates. If the two VPN gateways exchange signed certificates that bind each gateway's identity to its IP address, NAT address rewriting will cause the IKE negotiation to fail.

It is for this reason that combination VPN and firewall configurations are becoming so popular. Rules to manage this situation can be set up and maintained easily.

Summary

Virtual private networks are popular because they leverage existing infrastructure to provide a seamless network experience to end users. Numerous implementations of VPNs are available, taking advantage of the different protocols available for creating VPNs. As you would expect, Linux has several options available, including Openswan and PoPToP, among others.

Some problems exist when connecting VPNs through NAT-enabled firewalls. This is because IPSec creates a digital signature based on the IP header, which is altered during the NAT process.

Glossary

This glossary defines terms and acronyms used in the book. Multiword terms are alphabetized on the major noun in the term, followed by a comma and the rest of the term.

ACCEPT   A firewall-filtering rule decision to pass a packet through to its next destination.

accept-everything-by-default policy   A policy that accepts all packets that don't match a firewall rule in the chain. Therefore, most firewall rules are **DENY** rules defining the exceptions to the default accept policy.

ACK   The TCP flag that acknowledges receipt of a previously received TCP segment.

application-level gateway   *See also* proxy, application-level. Often referred to as ALG, an application-level (or layer) gateway is an overloaded term. In firewall terms, ALG often refers to application-specific support modules that inspect application payload for embedded addresses and ports, and that recognize secondary streams associated with the session.

AUTH   TCP service port **113**, associated with the `identd` user authentication server.

authentication   The process of determining that an entity is who or what it claims to be.

authorization   The process of determining what services and resources an entity can use.

bastion   *See* firewall, bastion.

BIND   Berkeley Internet Name Domain, the Berkeley implementation of the DNS protocol.

BOOTP Bootstrap Protocol, which is used by diskless workstations to discover their IP address and the location of the boot server, and to initiate the system download over TFTP before booting. BOOTP was developed to replace RARP.

BOOTPC UDP service port **68**, associated with the BOOTP and DHCP clients.

bootpd The BOOTP server program.

BOOTPS UDP service port **67**, associated with the BOOTP and DHCP servers.

border router A device to route packets that resides on the edge or boundary of a network.

broadcast An IP packet that is addressed and sent to all interfaces connected to the same network or subnet.

CERT Computer Emergency Response Team, an information coordination center and Internet security emergency prevention center formed at the Software Engineering Institute of Carnegie Mellon University after the Internet Worm incident in 1988.

CGI Common Gateway Interface. CGI programs are local programs executed by the web server on behalf of the remote client. CGI programs are often Perl scripts, so these programs are often called CGI scripts.

chain The list of rules defining which packets can come in and which can go out through a network interface.

checksum A number produced by performing some arithmetic computation on the numeric value of each byte in a file or packet. If the file is changed, or the packet corrupted, a second checksum produced for the same object will not match the original checksum.

choke *See* firewall, choke.

chroot Both a program and a system call that defines a directory to be the root of the filesystem, and that then executes a program to run confined to that virtual filesystem.

circuit gateway *See* proxy, circuit-level.

class, network address Historically, one of five classes of network addresses. An IPv4 address is a 32-bit value. The address space is divided into Class A through Class E addresses, depending on the value of the first 4 most significant bits in the 32-bit value. The Class A network address space maps 128 separate networks, each addressing more than 16 million hosts. The Class B network address space maps 16,384 networks, each addressing up to 64,534 hosts. The Class C network address space maps about 2 million networks, each addressing up to 254 hosts. Class D is used for multicast addresses. Class E is reserved for unspecified or experimental purposes. The network classes have largely become an artifact with the introduction of CIDR. People refer to them out of familiarity and because their byte-boundary characteristics make them convenient to use in examples.

Classless Inter-Domain Routing   CIDR replaces the concept of network address classes for space allocation with the concept of variable-length network fields. A conceptual extension of the idea of variable-length subnet masks, CIDR is intended to improve router table scalability and to solve the allocation problems caused by the exhaustion of the classful address space for midsize organizations.

client/server model   The model for distributed network services, in which a centralized program, a server, provides a service to remote client programs requesting that service, whether the service is receiving a copy of a web page, downloading a file from a central repository, performing a database lookup, sending or receiving electronic mail, performing some kind of computation on client-supplied data, or establishing human communication connections between two or more people.

daemon   A basic system services server running in the background.

DARPA   Defense Advanced Research Projects Agency.

Datalink layer   In the OSI reference model, the second layer, which represents point-to-point data signal delivery between two adjacent network devices, such as the delivery of an Ethernet frame from your computer to your external router. (In the TCP/IP reference model, this functionality is included as part of the first layer, the subnet layer.)

default policy   A policy for a firewall ruleset—whether for an INPUT chain, an OUTPUT chain, or a FORWARD chain in the filter table—that defines a packet's disposition when the packet doesn't match any rule in the set. *See also* accept-everything-by-default policy and deny-everything-by-default policy.

denial-of-service attack   An attack based on the idea of sending unexpected data or flooding your system with packets to disrupt or seriously degrade service, tie up local servers to the extent that legitimate requests can't be honored, or, in the worst case, crash a system or systems altogether.

deny-everything-by-default policy   A policy that silently drops all packets that don't match a firewall rule in the chain. Most firewall rules are ACCEPT rules defining the exceptions to the default deny policy.

DHCP   Dynamic Host Configuration Protocol, which is used to dynamically assign IP addresses and provide server and router information to clients without registered IP addresses. DHCP was developed to replace BOOTP.

DMZ   The demilitarized zone, a perimeter network containing machines hosting public services, separated from a local, private network. The less-secure public servers are isolated from the private LAN.

DNS   Domain name service, a global Internet database service primarily providing host-to-IP and IP-to-host mapping.

DROP   A firewall-filtering rule decision to silently drop a packet without returning any notification to the sender. DROP is identical to DENY in earlier Linux firewall technologies.

dual-homed   A computer that has two network interfaces. *See also* multihomed.

dynamically assigned address   IP addresses temporarily assigned to a client network interface by a central server, such as a DHCP server.

Ethernet frame   Over an Ethernet network, IP datagrams are encapsulated in Ethernet frames.

filter, firewall   A firewall packet-filtering rule defining the characteristics of the packet's IP and transport headers, which, if matched, determines whether the packet is to be allowed through the network interface or is to be dropped. Filters are defined in terms of such fields as a packet's source and destination addresses, source and destination ports, protocol type, TCP connection state, and ICMP message type.

finger   A user information lookup program.

firewall   A device or group of devices that enforces an access control policy between networks.

firewall, bastion   Frequently, a firewall that has two or more network interfaces and is the gateway or connection point between those networks, most typically between a local site and the Internet. Because a bastion firewall is the single point of connection between networks, the bastion is secured to the greatest extent possible. More generally, a bastion is a firewall that remote sites have direct access to, whether that host connects networks or protects a server that provides public services.

firewall, choke   A LAN firewall that has two or more network interfaces and is the gateway or connection point between those networks. One side connects to a DMZ perimeter network between the choke firewall and a bastion gateway firewall. The other network interface connects to an internal, private LAN.

firewall, dual-homed   A single-host, gateway firewall that either requires local users to specifically connect to the firewall machine to access the Internet from the firewall machine, or proxies all remote services accessible to the site. In a dual-homed gateway firewall system, no traffic is allowed to pass between the LAN and the Internet.

firewall, screened-host   Almost identical to a dual-homed firewall, the single-host firewall does not sit directly between the Internet and the local network. The screened-host firewall is separated from the public network by an intermediate router and a packet filter. Local users must either specifically connect to the firewall machine to access the Internet or go through proxies on the firewall machine. The screening router ensures that all traffic between networks, or at least specific kinds of traffic, goes through the screened host. The difference between the screened-host firewall and the dual-host firewall is primarily in the location of the firewall within the local network.

firewall, screened-subnet   A firewall system incorporating a gateway firewall, a DMZ network housing public servers, and an internal choke firewall that screens the LAN from both the DMZ and direct Internet access. Public services are not hosted from the choke firewall.

flooding, packet   A denial-of-service attack in which the victim host or network is sent more packets of a given type than the victim can accommodate.

forward   To route packets from one network to another in the process of delivering a packet from one computer to another.

fragment   An IP packet containing a piece of a TCP segment.

FTP   File Transfer Protocol. The protocol and programs used to copy files between networked computers.

FTP, anonymous   FTP service accessible to any client that requests the service.

FTP, authenticated   FTP service accessible to predefined accounts, which must be authenticated before using the service.

gateway   A computer or program serving as either the conduit or the termination point and relay between two networks.

hosts.allow, **hosts.deny**   TCP wrappers' configuration files are `/etc/hosts.allow` and `/etc/hosts.deny`.

HOWTO   In addition to the standard man pages, Linux includes user-supplied online documentation on numerous topics, in many languages and in multiple formats. The HOWTO documents are coordinated and maintained by the Linux Documentation Project.

HTTP   Hypertext Transfer Protocol, used by web servers and browsers.

hub   A hardware signal repeater used to physically connect multiple network segments, extend the distance of a physical network, or connect network segments of different physical types.

IANA   Internet Assigned Numbers Authority.

ICMP   Internet Control Message Protocol. A Network layer IP status and control message.

identd   The user authentication (AUTH) server.

IMAP   Internet Message Access Protocol, used to retrieve mail from mail hosts running an IMAP server.

inetd   A network superserver that listens for incoming connections to service ports used by servers that it manages. When a connection request arrives, inetd starts a copy of the request server to handle the connection. By default, inetd has been replaced by an extended version called xinetd.

IP datagram   An IP Network layer packet.

ipchains   With the introduction of the newer implementation of the IPFW firewall mechanism in Linux, the firewall administration program that replaced ipfwadm. iptables is supplied with an ipchains compatibility module for sites that want to continue using their existing firewall scripts.

IPFW   IP firewall mechanism, now replaced by Netfilter.

ipfwadm   Before the introduction of ipchains, the Linux IPFW firewall administration program. iptables is supplied with an ipfwadm compatibility module for sites that want to continue using their existing firewall scripts.

iptables   The firewall administration program for the current Netfilter firewall mechanism in Linux.

klogd   The kernel logging daemon that collects operating-system error and status messages from the kernel message buffers and, in conjunction with syslogd, writes the messages to a system log file.

LAN   Local area network.

localhost   The symbolic name often given to a machine's loopback interface in /etc/hosts.

loopback interface   A special software network interface used by the system to deliver locally generated network messages destined to the local machine, bypassing the hardware network interface and associated network driver.

man page   The standard Linux online documentation format. Manual pages are written for almost all user and system administration programs, as well as system calls, library calls, device types, and system file formats.

masquerading   The process of replacing an outgoing packet's local source address with that of the firewall or gateway machine so that the LAN's IP addresses remain hidden. In the IPFW firewall mechanism, masquerading referred to the source NAT functionality implemented in

Linux. In Netfilter, masquerading refers to a specialized form of source NAT for use with connections that are dynamically assigned temporary IP addresses that tend to change with each connection.

MD5   A cryptographic checksum algorithm used to ensure data integrity by creating digital signatures, called message digests, of objects.

MTU   Maximum Transmission Unit, the maximum packet size based on the underlying network.

multicast   An IP packet specially addressed to a Class D multicast IP address. Multicast clients are registered with the intermediate routers to receive packets addressed to a particular multicast address.

multihomed   A computer that has two or more network interfaces. *See also* dual-homed.

name server, primary   An authoritative server for a domain or a zone of the domain space. The server maintains a complete database of hostnames and IP addresses for this zone.

name server, secondary   A backup or peer to a primary name server.

NAT   Network address translation, the process of replacing a packet's source or destination address with that of some other network interface. NAT is primarily intended to allow traffic between incompatible network address spaces, such as between the Internet and a LAN that is assigned private addresses internally.

Netfilter   The firewall mechanism included with the Linux 2.4 and 2.6 kernels.

netstat   A program that reports various kinds of network status based on the various network-related kernel tables.

Network layer   In the OSI reference model, the third layer, which represents end-to-end communication between two computers, such as routing and delivery of an IP datagram from your source computer to some external destination computer. In the TCP/IP reference model, this is referred to as the second layer, the Internet layer.

NFS   Network File System, used to share filesystems between networked computers.

NIS   Network Information Service, used to centrally manage and provide user account and host information.

nmap   A network security auditing (that is, port-scanning) tool that includes many of the newer scanning techniques in use today.

NNTP   Network News Transfer Protocol, used by Usenet.

NTP   Network Time Protocol, used by `ntpd` and `ntpdate`.

OSI (Open System Interconnection) reference model   A seven-layer model developed by the International Organization for Standardization (ISO) to provide a framework or guide for network interconnection standards.

OSPF   The Open Shortest Path First routing protocol for TCP/IP, which is the most commonly used routing protocol today.

packet   An IP network datagram.

packet filtering   *See* firewall.

PATH   The shell environmental variable defining which directories the shell should search for unqualified executable commands and in which order the shell should search those directories.

peer-to-peer   A communication mode used for communication between two server programs. A peer-to-peer communication protocol is often, but not always, different from the protocol used to communicate between the server and a client.

Physical layer   In the OSI reference model, the first layer, which represents the physical medium used to carry the signals between two adjacent network devices, such as copper wire, optical fiber, packet radio, or infrared. In the TCP/IP reference model, this is included as part of the first layer, the subnet layer.

PID   Process ID, which is a process's unique numeric identifier on the system, usually associated with the process's slot in the system process table.

ping   A simple network-analysis tool used to determine whether a remote host is reachable and responding. Ping sends an ICMP Echo Request message. The recipient host returns an ICMP Echo Reply message in response.

POP   Post Office Protocol, used to retrieve mail from mail hosts running a POP server.

port   In TCP or UDP, the numeric designator of a particular network communication channel. Port assignments are managed by IANA. Some ports are assigned to particular application communication protocols as part of the protocol standard. Some ports are registered as being associated with a particular service by convention. Some ports are unassigned and free to be dynamically assigned for use by clients and user programs:

- *privileged*   A port in the range from 0 to 1023. Many of these ports are assigned to application protocols by international standard. On a Linux system, access to the privileged ports requires system-level privilege.
- *unprivileged*   A port in the range from 1024 to 65535. Some of these ports are registered for use by certain programs by convention. Any port in this range can be used by a client program to establish a connection with a networked server.

port scan   A probe of all or a set of a host computer's service ports, typically service ports that are often associated with security vulnerabilities.

portmap   An RPC manager daemon, used to map between a particular RPC service number that a client is requesting to access and the service port to which the associated server is bound.

probe   To send some kind of packet to a service port on a host computer. The purpose of a probe is to determine whether a response is generated from the target host.

proxy   A program that creates and maintains a network connection on behalf of another program, providing an application-level conduit between a client and a server. The actual client and server have no direct communication. The proxy appears to be the server to the client program and appears to be the client to the server program. Application proxies generally are categorized into application gateways and circuit gateways.

proxy, application-level   A proxy server for a particular service. Application-level gateway proxies understand the particular application protocol that they proxy for. The proxy is capable of inspecting the application payload and making decisions based on information at the application level, instead of making decisions merely at the IP and transport levels.

proxy, circuit-level   A proxy server that can be implemented either as separate applications for each service being proxied or as a single generalized connection relay. A circuit-level proxy doesn't have any specific knowledge about the application protocols. The proxy makes decisions based on the same IP and transport information that a packet-filtering firewall does, with the possible addition of some amount of user authentication functionality.

QoS   Quality of Service.

RARP   Reverse Address Resolution Protocol, developed to enable diskless machines to ask servers for their IP address based on their MAC hardware address.

REJECT rule   A firewall-filtering rule decision to drop a packet and return an error message to the sender.

resolver   The client side of DNS. The resolver is implemented as library code that is linked to programs requiring network access. The DNS client configuration file is `/etc/resolv.conf`.

RFC   Request for Comments, a note or memo published through the Internet Society or the Internet Engineering Task Force. Some RFCs become standards. RFCs typically concern a topic related to the Internet or the TCP/IP protocol suite.

RIP   Routing Information Protocol, an older routing protocol still in use today, especially within a large LAN. The `routed` daemon uses RIP.

RPC   Remote procedure call.

rule   *See* firewall and filter, firewall.

runlevel   A booting and system state concept taken from System V UNIX. A system normally operates at one of runlevels 2, 3, or 5. Runlevel 3 is the default, normal, multiuser system state. Runlevel 2 is similar to runlevel 3, without `xinetd`, `portmap`, or Network File System (NFS) services running. Runlevel 5 is the same as runlevel 3, with the addition of the X Window Display Manager, which presents an X-based login and host-selection screen.

screened host   *See* firewall, screened-host.

screened subnet   *See* firewall, screened-subnet.

script   An ASCII file that can contain either shell or Linux program commands. These scripts are interpreted by shell programs such as sh, csh, bash, zsh, or ksh, or by programs such as perl, awk, or sed.

segment, TCP   A TCP message.

setgid   A program that, when executed, assumes the group ID of the program's owner rather than the group ID of the process running the program.

setuid   A program that, when executed, assumes the user ID of the program's owner rather than the user ID of the process running the program.

shell   A command interpreter, such as sh, csh, bash, zsh, and ksh.

SMTP   Simple Mail Transfer Protocol, used to exchange mail between mail servers and between mail programs and mail servers.

SNMP   Simple Network Management Protocol, used to manage network device configuration from a remote workstation.

socket   The unique network connection point defined by the pairing of an IP address with a particular TCP or UDP service port.

SOCKS   A circuit gateway proxy package available from NEC.

spoofing, source address   Forging the source address in an IP packet header so that it appears to be that of some other address.

SSH   Secure shell protocol, used for authenticated, encrypted network connections.

SSL   Secure Socket Layer protocol, used for encrypted communication. SSL is most commonly used by web servers and browsers for exchanging personal information for e-commerce.

statically assigned address   Permanently assigned, hard-coded IP addresses, whether publicly registered addresses or private class addresses.

subnet layer   In the TCP/IP reference model, the first layer, which represents both the physical media used to carry the signals between two adjacent network devices and point-to-point data signal delivery between two adjacent network devices, such as the delivery of an Ethernet frame from your computer to your external router.

SYN   The TCP connection synchronization request flag. A SYN message is the first message sent from a program seeking to open a connection with another networked program.

syslog.conf   The system-logging daemon's configuration file.

syslogd   The system-logging daemon, which collects error and status messages generated by system programs that post messages using the syslog() system call.

TCP   Transmission Control Protocol, used for reliable, ongoing network connections between two programs.

TCP/IP reference model   An informal network communication model developed when TCP/IP became the de facto standard for Internet communication among UNIX machines during the late 1970s and early 1980s. Rather than being a formal, academic ideal, the TCP/IP reference model is based on what manufacturers and developers finally came to agree on for communication across the Internet.

tcp_wrapper   An authorization scheme used to control which local services are available to which remote hosts on the network.

TFTP   Trivial File Transfer Protocol, the protocol used to download a boot image to a diskless workstation or router. The protocol is a UDP-based, simplified version of FTP.

three-way handshake   The TCP connection establishment protocol. When a client program sends its first message to a server, the connection request message, the SYN flag is set and accompanied by a synchronization sequence number that the client will use as the starting point to number all the rest of the messages that the client will send. The server responds with an acknowledgment (ACK) to the SYN message, along with its own synchronization request (SYN). The server includes the client's sequence number incremented by the number of contiguous data bytes received, plus 1. The purpose of the acknowledgment is to acknowledge the message to which the client referred by its sequence number. As with the client's first message, the SYN flag is accompanied by a synchronization sequence number. The server is passing along its own starting sequence number for its half of the connection. The client responds with an ACK of the server's SYN-ACK, incrementing the server's sequence number by the number of contiguous data bytes received, plus 1 to indicate receipt of the message. The connection is established.

TOS   Type of Service, the field in the IP packet header that was intended to provide a hint of the preferred routing policy or packet-routing preference.

traceroute   A network analysis tool used to determine the path from one computer to another across the network.

Transport layer   In the OSI reference model, the fourth layer, which represents end-to-end communication between two programs, such as the delivery of a packet from a client program to a server program. In the TCP/IP reference model, this is referred to as the third layer, also the Transport layer. However, the TCP/IP Layer 3 transport-level abstraction includes the concept of the OSI Layer 5 Session layer, which includes the concepts of an orderly and synchronized exchange of messages.

TTL   Time to live, an IP packet header field that is a maximum count of the number of routers the packet can pass through before reaching its destination.

UDP   User Datagram Protocol, used to send individual network messages between programs, without any guarantee of delivery or delivery order.

unicast   An IP packet sent point to point, from one computer's network interface to another's.

UUCP   UNIX-to-UNIX Copy Protocol.

world-readable   Filesystem objects—files, directories, and entire filesystems—that are readable by any account or program on the system.

world-writable   Filesystem objects—files, directories, and entire filesystems—that are writable by any account or program on the system.

X Windows   The Linux graphical user interface window display system.

Index

Symbols

[] (brackets), 75

: (colon), 75

| (pipe symbol), 75

0.0.0.0 IP addresses, 116

A

abuse, reporting, 325

accept-everything-by-default policy, 37

access

    DHCP servers, 162-165

    incoming access to FTP servers

        incoming FTP requests, 152

        passive-mode FTP data channel responses, 153

        port-mode FTP data channel responses, 152

    incoming access to local servers, 146

    outgoing client access to remote FTP servers, 150-152

    remote access, 145

        as clients, 154

        network time servers, 165-166

        SSH servers, 147-148

Access Decisions (SELinux), 400

ACK flag, 22, 29, 43, 182

ACL options (GrSec), 418

actions (SELinux), 400

Address Resolution Protocol (ARP), 24

address space protection (GrSec), 417

addresses

    destination addresses

        branching, 186

        iptables, 104-105

    Ethernet addresses, 24-25

    illegal addresses, 39-41

    IP addresses, 12-16

        addresses to avoid, 39-41

        assignments, 118

        broadcast addresses, 13-17

        classes, 13, 39-40

        expressed as symbolic names, 105

        headers, 14

        installing firewalls, 176

        limited broadcast addresses, 13

        loopback addresses, 13

        multicast, 15

        network address 0, 13, 116

        network-directed broadcast addresses, 13

        subnetting to create multiple networks, 223

        unicast, 15

    link local network addresses, 40

    loopback interface addresses, 40

    malformed broadcast addresses, 40

    multicast destination addresses, 117

    ranges, 225

    source addresses

        iptables, 104-105

        source address checking, bypassing, 201

        spoofing, 39-41, 114-119, 238-239

        TEST-NENT addresses, 40

addrtype filter table match extensions, 93-94

Advanced Intrusion Detection Environment. See AIDE

AIDE (Advanced Intrusion Detection Environment)

    check types, 396-398

    configuration files

        creating, 384-386

        example, 386-387

    database updates, 390-391

    initialization, 387

    installation, 383

    macros, 394-395

    monitoring filesystems with, 388-390

    reports, customizing, 391-393

    scheduling to run automatically, 388

    verbose output, 393

alerts (Snort), 376

ALGs (application-level gateways), 32

allocation of IP addresses, 118

allowing DNS, 124-127

    DNS lookups as clients, 127-128

    DNS lookups as forwarding servers, 128-130

    zone transfers, 125

American Registry for Internet Numbers (ARIN), 326

APNIC (Asia Pacific Network Information Centre), 326

application-level gateways (ALGs), 32

Applied Cryptography, 398

ARIN (American Registry for Internet Numbers), 326

ARP (Address Resolution Protocol), 24

ARPWatch, 332, 347, 377-379

Asia Pacific Network Information Centre (APNIC), 326

assigning
addresses, 118
port numbers, 119

attacks
detecting. *See* intrusion detection
preventing
Bastille Linux, 341
kernel enhancements, 340
penetration testing, 342-344
testing, 342-344
updates, 341-342

auditing (GrSecurity), 418

AUTH clients, 131

AUTH requests, filtering, 131-132, 246

authentication
IPSec authentication headers, 477-478
VPNs, 483

B

BALANCE nat table target extensions, 97

Bastille Linux, 341

bastion firewalls, 7

bidirectional NAT, 71, 263

BIND, 128-130

blocking
attempts to unprivileged ports, 119
directed broadcasts, 116
problem sites, 41

boot process, starting firewalls at
Debian, 175-176
Red Hat and SUSE, 175

border routers, 31

brackets ([]), 75

branching user-defined chains, 186

broadcast addresses, 13-17

broadcasting (IP), 17-18

BSD remote access commands, 59

buffer overflows, 54

bypassing
rule checking, 113-114, 238
source address checking, 201

C

capturing
FTP conversations, 363
HTTP conversations, 356-361
ICMP pings, 364
SMTP conversations, 361-362
SSH conversations, 362

CERT, reporting incidents to, 326

chains, 33. *See also* user-defined chains
chain commands on rules, 77
installing, 192-195

POSTROUTING, 267

PREROUTING, 267

channels

passive-mode FTP data channels, 151-153

port-mode FTP data channels, 151-152

chargen services, 52

check types (AIDE), 396-398

checking

forwarding rules, 298-300

input rules, 295-296

open ports, 307-308

fuser, 311

netstat, 308-310

nmap, 312

strobe, 311-312

output rules, 296-298

processes bound to particular ports, 311

checksums, 382

Chkrootkit, 332-333

downloading, 333

limitations, 335-336

responding to infections, 334-335

running, 333-334

security, 336-337

system binaries, 336-337

when to use, 337

choke firewalls, 232

conduits/clients to remote FTP servers, 253

constants, 234

default policies, 236

DMZ configurations as private name servers, 244-245

email

IMAP clients, 248

POP clients, 247

enabling loopback interfaces, 237

forwarders and web clients, 254

local DHCP servers, 256-257

NNTP client DMZ configurations, 249

preexisting rules, removing, 235

public web servers, 255

sample iptables choke firewall (code listing), 463-474

setting stage for, 234-235

SMTP client configurations, 247

SSH configuration, 251

CIDR (Classless Inter Domain Routing), 15

Class A addresses, 39-40

Class B addresses, 39

Class C addresses, 39

Class D addresses, 40

Class E addresses, 40

Classless Inter Domain Routing (CIDR), 15

classless subnetting, 15

clients

AUTH clients, 131

DNS lookups, 127-128

outgoing client access to remote FTP servers

outgoing FTP requests over control channels, 150

passive-mode FTP data channels, 151-152

port-mode FTP data channels, 151

remote clients

email, 141-142

hosting Usenet news servers for, 143-144

remote site access, 145

SSH server access, 147-148

colon (:), 75

commands. *See specific command names*

compiling kernel, 403-411

compromised systems. *See* intrusion detection

config option (make command), 407

configuration

AIDE (Advanced Intrusion Detection Environment), 384-387

choke NNTP client DMZ, 249

choke SMTP clients, 247

choke SSH, 251

gateway NNTP conduit, 248

gateway SSH, 250

GrSecurity (Greater Security), 417

ACL options, 418

address space protection, 417

executable protections, 418

filesystem protections, 418

kernel auditing, 418

logging options, 419

network protections, 419

PaX Control, 417

security levels, 417

Sysctl support, 419

internal LANs, 226-227

intrusion detection, 318

large or less trusted LANs, 222-223

selective internal access, 225

subnetting to create multiple networks, 223-225

multiple LANs, 227-231

Serer DMZ, 248

Snort, 373, 375

syslog, 300-303

trusted home LANs, 218-219

LAN access to gateway firewalls, 220

LAN access to other LANs, 221-222

VPNs

network connections, 483

roaming users, 482-483

connection-oriented protocols, 11-12

connection state, 113-114

connection-tracking chain, 188, 205-206

connectionless protocols, 11-12

constants, 232-233

private choke firewalls, 234

symbolic constants used in firewall examples, 107

control channels, 150

control messages (ICMP), 166-168

conversations, capturing with TCPDump

DNS queries, 363

FTP, 363

HTTP, 356-361

pings, 364

SMTP, 361-362

SSH, 362

converting gateway firewalls from local services to forwarding, 258

Cricket, 330

custom kernels, 104

customizing AIDE (Advanced Intrusion Detection Environment) reports, 391-393

D

daemons, 25

  ntpd, 165-166

  status reports, 317

  syslogd, 300

  VPND, 481

DARPA model, 11

databases, AIDE (Advanced Intrusion Detection Environment), 390-391

Datalink layer (OSI model), 10

Debian firewalls, starting on boot, 175-176

debugging, 174-175

  firewall rules, checking

    forwarding rules, 298-300

    input rules, 295-296

    output rules, 296-298

  firewall rules, listing, 284-285

    filter table listing formats, 285-292

    mangle table listing formats, 293-294

    nat table listing formats, 291

  system logs, 300

    firewall log messages, 304-307

    syslog configuration, 300-303

  tips, 281-284

default policies

  defining, 111, 236

  packet-filtering firewalls, 35-37

  rules, 112

demilitarized zone. See DMZ

denial-of-service attacks, 324

  areas of consideration, 55

  "Denial of Service" (paper), 48

  incoming packets

    buffer overflows, 54

    fragmentation bombs, 53-54

    ICMP redirect bombs, 54-55

    ping flooding, 50

    Ping of Death, 50-51

    TCP SYN flooding, 48-50

    UDP flooding, 52

  Smurf attacks, 169, 367

deny-everything-by-default policy, 36, 120

denying

  access to problem sites, 172-173

  packets, 38

destination addresses

  branching, 186

  iptables, 104-105

destination NAT. See DNAT

Destination Unreachable messages, 168

destination-address-check chain, 188, 208

detecting intrusions, 315-317, 329, 345-347

  AIDE (Advanced Intrusion Detection Environment)

    check types, 396-398

    configuration files, 384-387

    database updates, 390-391

    initialization, 387

    installation, 383

    macros, 394-395

    monitoring filesystems with, 388-390

    reports, customizing, 391-393

    scheduling to run automatically, 388

    verbose output, 393

  ARPWatch, 347, 377-379

Chkrootkit, 332-333
  downloading, 333
  limitations, 335-336
  responding to infections, 334-335
  running, 333-334
  security, 336-337
  system binaries, 336-337
  when to use, 337
filesystems, 318-319, 337-338
incident reporting, 322-323
  advantages of, 323
  denial-of-service attacks, 324
  incident types, 324-325
  information to include, 326-327
  online resources, 327
  where to report incidents, 325-326
log monitoring, 338-340
network analysis tools, 329-332
  ARPWatch, 332
  Cricket, 330
  MRTG, 330
  ntop, 330
  sniffer placement, 332
  Snort, 330
  switches/hubs, 331-332
  TCPDump, 329-330
penetration testing
  Hping2, 343
  Nessus, 344
  Nikto, 343-344
  Nmap, 342-343
preventing attacks
  Bastille Linux, 341
  kernel enhancements, 340

  penetration testing, 344
  updates, 341-342
responding to, 320-322
security audit tools, 320
Snort, 347, 371-372
  alerts, 376
  configuring, 373-375
  downloading, 372
  installing, 372-373
  Swatch, 376
  testing, 375-376
system configuration, 318
system logs, 317-318
system performance, 320
TCPDump, 347-348
  abnormal packet activity, 364-365
  command-line options, 350-351
  DNS queries, capturing, 363
  downloading, 349
  expressions, 352-354
  FTP conversations, capturing, 363
  HTTP conversations, capturing, 356-361
  ICMP pings, capturing, 364
  installing, 349
  LAND attacks, 368-369
  normal scan (nmap) attacks, 365-367
  recording traffic with, 369-371
  SMTP conversations, capturing, 361-362
  Smurf attacks, 367
  SSH conversations, capturing, 362
  Xmas Tree attacks, 368
user accounts, 319

developing firewalls, 281-284

DHCP (Dynamic Host Configuration Protocol)

choke firewalls as local DHCP servers, 256-257

messages, 162-163

protocols, 163

servers, accessing, 162-165

DHCPACK messages, 162

DHCPDECLINE messages, 163

DHCPDISCOVER messages, 162

DHCPINFORM messages, 163

DHCPNAK messages, 162

DHCPOFFER messages, 162

DHCPRELEASE messages, 163

DHCPREQUEST messages, 162

Differentiated Services (DS) field, 92

Differentiated Services Control Protocol (DSCP), 92

directed broadcasts, blocking, 116

direction qualifiers (TCPDump), 353-354

directives (AIDE), 384-385

DMZ (demilitarized zone), 215

choke DMZ configurations as private name servers, 244-245

gateway configurations for name servers, 243-244

implementing, 231-232

public web servers, 255

web proxies, 255-256

DNAT (Destination NAT), 69, 270

host forwarding, 274-275

port redirection, 275-276

to server farms, 276

to servers in privately addressed DMZ, 277-278

local port redirection, 279-280

nat table target extensions, 96-97

port redirection, 275-276

REDIRECT DNAT, 271

standard DNAT, 270

DNS (Domain Name Service), 24

BIND port usage, 129

enabling, 124-127, 241-243

choke DMZ configuration, 244-245

DMZ name server gateway configuration, 243-244

DNS lookups as clients, 127-128

DNS lookups as forwarding servers, 128-130

zone transfers, 125

queries, capturing with TCPDump, 363

traffic, 195-197

Domain Name Service. See DNS

DoS attacks. See denial-of-service attacks

downloading

Chkrootkit, 333

GrSecurity (Greater Security), 405

Snort, 372

TCPDump, 349

dropped packets, logging, 258

incoming packets, 170-172

optimized example, 208-210

outgoing packets, 172

dropping spoofed multicast network packets, 117

DS (Differentiated Services) field, 92

DSCP (Differentiated Services Control Protocol), 92

dstlimit filter table match extensions, 85-86

duplicating firewall log messages, 304

Dynamic Host Configuration Protocol. *See* DHCP

dynamic IP addresses, 176

E

echo services, 52

echo-reply messages, 169-170, 240

echo-request messages, 108, 169-170, 240

email, 133

    client/server email combinations, 137

    DMZ, 246-248

    IMAP, 133-137, 248

    POP, 133-136, 247

    remote clients, 141-142

    SMTP, 133-134

        SMTP clients, 137-140

        SMTP servers, 134-136, 140-141

"Email Bombing and Spamming," 55

enabling

    DNS, 124-127, 241-243

        choke DMZ configuration, 244-245

        DMZ name server gateway configuration, 243-244

        DNS lookups as clients, 127-128

        DNS lookups as forwarding servers, 128-130

        zone transfers, 125

    Internet services, 124, 130-132

    kernel-monitoring support, 108-109

    loopback interfaces, 111, 237

    outgoing traceroute requests, 161

encapsulating security payload (ESP), 478

end-to-end transparencies, 8

ESP (encapsulating security payload), 478

ESTABLISHED matches, 88, 182

Ethernet addresses, 24-25

executable protections (GrSec), 418

expressions (TCPDump)

    direction qualifiers, 353-354

    primitives, 354

    protocol qualifiers, 354

    type qualifiers, 352-353

EXT, 189

EXT-icmp-in, 189, 203-204

EXT-icmp-out, 189, 203-204

EXT-input, 188, 195

    DNS traffic, 195-197

    ICMP traffic, 203-204

    local client traffic over TCP, 197-200

    local client traffic over UDP, 201-202

    local server traffic over TCP, 200-201

EXT-log-in chain, 189

EXT-log-out chain, 189

EXT-output, 189, 195

    DNS traffic, 195-196

    ICMP traffic, 203-204

    local client traffic over TCP, 197-200

    local client traffic over UDP, 201-202

    local server traffic over TCP, 200-201

F

File Transfer Protocol. *See* FTP

file (log). *See* logging

filesystem integrity, 337-338, 381

AIDE (Advanced Intrusion Detection Environment)

check types, 396-398

configuration files, 384-387

database updates, 390-391

initialization, 387

installation, 383

macros, 394-395

monitoring filesystems with, 388-390

reports, customizing, 391-393

scheduling to run automatically, 388

verbose output, 393

checksums, 382

definition of, 381

GrSec, 418

intrusion detection, 318-319

Tripwire, 381

filter table, 68-69, 74-75

addrtype filter table match extensions, 93-94

dstlimit filter table match extensions, 85-86

filter table target extensions, 80-81

icmp filter table match operator, 79-80

iprange filter table match, 94

iptables, 68, 71

length filter table match, 94

limit filter table match extensions, 84-85

listing formats

iptables –L INPUT, 285-287

iptables -n –L INPUT, 287-288

iptables -v –L INPUT, 289-290

mac filter table match extensions, 90

mark filter table match extensions, 91

match operations, 77-78

multiport filter table match extensions, 82-84

operations on entire chains, 76

operations on rules, 77

owner filter table match extensions, 90-91

state filter table match extensions, 86-90

target extensions, 81

tcp filter table match operations, 79

tos filter table match extensions, 91-92

udp filter table match operations, 79

ULOG table target extensions, 81-82

unclean filter table match extensions, 92-93

filtering. *See also* **denial-of-service attacks**

AUTH requests, 131-132, 246

FTP, 150

ICMP control messages, 240

incoming packets, 33-38

chains, 33

default policies, 35-37

general port scans, 44

incoming TCP connection-state filtering, 43

iptables, 102-103

local destination address filtering, 42

local destination port filtering, 43

port scans, 47-48

remote source address filtering, 38-41

remote source port filtering, 43

source-routed packets, 56

stealth scans, 46

targeted port scans, 44-46

outgoing packets, 56

local source address filtering, 57

local source port filtering, 58

outgoing TCP connection-state filtering, 59

remote destination address filtering, 57-58

remote destination port filtering, 58

rp filter, 109

FIN flag, 22

firewall log messages

duplicating, 304

TCP example, 304-305

UDP example, 306-307

firewall rules. *See* **rules**

first matching rule wins, 112

flags

ACK, 43

TCP state flags, 112-113, 237

flooding

ping flooding, 50

TCP SYN flooding, 48-50

UDP flooding, 52

FORWARD chain, 74

FORWARD policy, 111

FORWARD rules, 272

forwarding, 266

converting gateway firewalls from local services, 258

local traffic among multiple LANs, 221-222

mail through gateways, 246-247

rule checking, 298-300

fragmentation, 16-17

fragmentation bombs on incoming packets, 53-54

fragmented ICMP messages, 167

FreeS/WAN, 481

FTP (File Transfer Protocol), 148-149, 251

choke firewalls as conduits/clients to remote FTP servers, 253

conversations, capturing with TCPDump, 363

gateway firewalls

remote FTP servers, 251-252

FTP DMZ servers, 253

incoming access to FTP servers

incoming FTP requests, 152

passive-mode FTP data channel responses, 153

port mode FTP data channel responses, 152

outgoing access to FTP servers

outgoing FTP requests over control channels, 150

passive-mode FTP data channels, 151-152

port-mode FTP data channels, 151

packet-filtering, 150

port mode, 150

protocols, 150

TFTP, 153

fuser, 311

G

gateway firewalls, 215-217, 231

ALGs (application-level gateways), 32

conduits to FTP DMZ servers, 253

conduits for local web clients, 254

conduits to remote FTP servers, 251-252

converting from local services to forwarding, 258

forwarding mail through, 246-247

NNTP conduit and server DMZ configurations, 248

public DMZ name servers, 243-244

setting stage for, 234-235

SSH configurations, 250

general port scans, 44

GrSec (Greater Security), 401, 405

ACL options, 418

address space protections, 417

building, 419-420

downloading, 405

executable protections, 418

filesystem protections, 418

GrSec patch, applying, 416

kernel auditing, 418

logging options, 419

network protections, 419

PaX Control, 417

RBAC (Role Based Access Control), 421

security levels, 417

Sysctl support, 419

website, 421

H

-h help command, 76

headers

IP, 14

IPSec authentication headers, 477-478

TCP (Transmission Control Protocol), 20-22

history of NAT, 261-262

host forwarding (DNAT), 274-275

port redirection, 275-276

to server farms, 276

to servers in privately addressed DMZ, 277-278

host type qualifiers (TCPDump), 352

hosting

IMAP servers, 142

POP servers, 141

Usenet news servers, 143-144

hostnames, 24

"How to Remove Meta-Characters from User-Supplied Data in CGI," 54

Hping2, 343

HTTP (Hypertext Transport Protocol)

remote websites, accessing, 154-155

conversations, capturing with TCPDump, 356-361

hubs, 331-332

I

IANA (Internet Assigned Numbers Authority), 25

IP address registration and allocation, 118

port number assignment, 119

ICMP (Internet Control Message Protocol), 18-19

control and status messages, 166-167

Destination Unreachable, 168

echo-reply, 240

echo-request, 108, 240

fragmented messages, 167

Parameter Problem, 168

Source Quench, 167

Time Exceeded, 168, 240

icmp filter table match operator, 79-80

ping messages

capturing with TCPDump, 364

incoming pings, 169-170

outgoing pings, 169

redirect messages, 54-55, 108

rule organization, 183

traffic, 203-204

ICV (Integrity Check Value), 478

identd protocol, 130-131

IKE (Internet Key Exchange), 477-479

illegal addresses, 39-41

IMAP (Internet Message Access Protocol), 133-134

hosting IMAP servers for remote clients, 142

email, receiving, 136-139, 248

incidents, reporting

advantages of, 323

denial-of-service attacks, 324

incident types, 324-325

information to include, 326-327

online resources, 327

where to report incidents, 325-326

incoming Destination Unreachable messages, 167

incoming packets

denial-of-service attacks, 324

areas of consideration, 55

buffer overflows, 54

fragmentation bombs, 53-54

ICMP redirect bombs, 54-55

ping flooding, 50

Ping of Death, 50-51

Smurf attacks, 169, 367

TCP SYN flooding, 48-50

UDP flooding, 52

filtering

incoming TCP connection-state filtering, 43

local destination address filtering, 42

local destination port filtering, 43

remote source address filtering, 38-41

remote source port filtering, 43

source-routed packets, 56

iptables, 70

limiting to selected remote sites, 41

probes, 43

scans, 43

general port scans, 44

responding to port scans, 47-48

stealth scans, 46

targeted port scans, 44-46

incoming TCP connection-state filtering, 43

initialization

AIDE (Advanced Intrusion Detection Environment), 387

firewalls, 106-107

defining default policies, 111

kernel-monitoring support, 108-109

loopback interfaces, 111

optimized example, 190-192

preexisting rules, removing, 109-110

rule checking, bypassing, 113-114

source address spoofing, 114-119

stealth scans, 112-113

symbolic constants, 107

TCP state flags, 112-113

input rules, checking, 295-296

installation

AIDE (Advanced Intrusion Detection Environment), 383

chains, 192-195

firewalls, 173-176

kernels, 412-414

Snort, 372-373

TCPDump, 349

Integrity Check Value (ICV), 478

integrity of filesystems, 337-338, 381

AIDE (Advanced Intrusion Detection Environment)

check types, 396-398

configuration files, 384-387

database updates, 390-391

initialization, 387

installation, 383

macros, 394-395

monitoring filesystems with, 388-390

reports, customizing, 391-393

scheduling to run automatically, 388

verbose output, 393

checksums, 382

definition of, 381

Tripwire, 381

internal choke firewalls. *See* **choke firewalls**

Internet Assigned Numbers Authority. *See* **IANA**

Internet Control Message Protocol. *See* **ICMP**

Internet Key Exchange (IKE), 477-479

Internet Message Access Protocol. *See* **IMAP**

Internet Protocol. *See* **IP**

Internet services, enabling, 124, 130-132. *See also* **DNS (Domain Name System)**

intrusion detection, 315-317, 329, 345-347

AIDE (Advanced Intrusion Detection Environment)

check types, 396-398

configuration files, 384-387

database updates, 390-391

initialization, 387

installation, 383

macros, 394-395

monitoring filesystems with, 388-390

reports, customizing, 391-393

scheduling to run automatically, 388

verbose output, 393

ARPWatch, 347, 377-379

Chkrootkit, 332-333

downloading, 333

limitations, 335-336

responding to infections, 334-335

running, 333-334

security, 336-337

system binaries, 336-337

when to use, 337

filesystems, 318-319, 337-338

incident reporting, 322-323

advantages of, 323

denial-of-service attacks, 324

incident types, 324-325

information to include, 326-327

online resources, 327

where to report incidents, 325-326

log monitoring, 338-340

network analysis tools, 329-332

ARPWatch, 332

Cricket, 330

MRTG, 330

ntop, 330

sniffer placement, 332

Snort, 330

switches/hubs, 331-332

TCPDump, 329-330

penetration testing

Hping2, 343

Nessus, 344

Nikto, 343-344

Nmap, 342-343

preventing attacks

Bastille Linux, 341

kernel enhancements, 340

penetration testing, 344

updates, 341-342

responding to, 320-322

security audit tools, 320

Snort, 347, 371-372

alerts, 376

configuring, 373-375

downloading, 372

installing, 372-373

Swatch, 376

testing, 375-376

system configuration, 318

system logs, 317-318

system performance, 320

TCPDump, 347-348

abnormal packet activity, 364-365

command-line options, 350-351

DNS queries, capturing, 363

downloading, 349

expressions, 352-354

FTP conversations, capturing, 363

HTTP conversations, capturing, 356-361

ICMP pings, capturing, 364

installing, 349

LAND attacks, 368-369

normal scan (nmap) attacks, 365-367

recording traffic with, 369-371

SMTP conversations, capturing, 361-362

Smurf attacks, 367

SSH conversations, capturing, 362

Xmas Tree attacks, 368

user accounts, 319

IP (Internet Protocol). *See also* IPSec

addresses, 12-16

assignments, 118

broadcast addresses, 13-17

classes, 13, 39-40

expressed as symbolic names, 105

headers, 14

installing firewalls, 176

limited broadcast addresses, 13

loopback addresses, 13

multicast, 15

network address 0, 13, 116

network-directed broadcast addresses, 13

subnetting to create multiple networks, 223

unicast, 15

broadcasting, 17-18

Ethernet addresses, 24-25

fragmentation, 16-17

headers, 14

hostnames, 24

multicasting, 17-18

subnet masks, 15

subnets, 12-16, 223

IP Security Protocol. *See* **IPSec**

ipchains, 102

compared to iptables, 64

packet traversal, 65

IPFW packet traversal, 65

ipfwadm, 102

iprange filter table match, 94

IPSec (IP Security Protocol), 476-477, 482

authentication headers, 477-478

configuring, 482-483

ESP (encapsulating security payload), 478

IKE (Internet Key Exchange), 479

security associations, 480

iptables, 63, 102-103. *See also* **user-defined chains**

command syntax, 67-68, 75

-L, 284-285

-L INPUT, 285-287

-n -L INPUT, 287-288

-v -L INPUT, 289-290

compared to ipchains, 64

destination addresses, 104-105

filter table, 68-71, 74-75, 82

addrtype filter table match extensions, 93-94

dstlimit filter table match extensions, 85-86

filter table target extensions, 80-81

icmp filter table match operator, 79-80

iprange filter table match, 94

length filter table match, 94

limit filter table match extensions, 84-85

mac filter table match extensions, 90

mark filter table match extensions, 91

match operations, 77-78

multiport filter table match extensions, 82-84

operations on entire chains, 76

operations on rules, 77

owner filter table match extensions, 90-91

state filter table match extensions, 86-90

target extensions, 81

tcp filter table match operations, 79

tos filter table match extensions, 91-92

udp filter table match operations, 79

ULOG table target extensions, 81-82

unclean filter table match extensions, 92-93

incoming packets, 70

ipchains compatibility, 102

mangle table, 69, 73-74, 98

masquerading, 72

NAT, 266-268

nat table, 69-74

BALANCE nat table target extensions, 97

DNAT nat table target extensions, 96-97

MASQUERADE nat table target extensions, 96

REDIRECT nat table target extensions, 97

SNAT nat table target extensions, 95-96

target extensions, 95

packet matches, 70

packet traversal, 66-67

packet-filtering rules, 102-103

QUEUE target, 71

REJECT target, 70

RETURN target, 71

sample firewall scripts

    firewall for standalone system, 427-445

    iptables choke firewall, 463-474

    optimized iptables firewall, 446-462

source addresses, 104-105

TCP state flags, 70

TOS (Type of Service), 70

upcoming features of, 69

iptables choke firewall (code listing), 463-474

IPv6, 261

ISAKMP, 479

ISP abuse centers, reporting incidents to, 326

Sysctl support, 419

    website, 421

improving kernel build, 415

installing, 412-414

location, 403

Kernel-HOWTO, 406

kernel-monitoring support, enabling, 108-109

Kernel Rebuild Guide, 406

modular nature of, 403

patching, 404-405

SELinux, 399-401

stock/vanilla kernel, 402

troubleshooting, 414-415

version numbering, 402-403

J-K

kernels, 340, 401-402

compiling, 403-411

confirming version of, 415

custom kernels, 104

GrSecurity (Greater Security), 401

    ACL options, 418

    address space protection, 417

    applying GrSec patch, 416

    building, 419-420

    downloading, 405

    executable protections, 418

    filesystem protections, 418

    kernel auditing, 418

    logging options, 419

    network protections, 419

    PaX Control, 417

    RBAC (Role Based Access Control), 421

    security levels, 417

L

-L INPUT option (iptables), 285-287

-L option (iptables), 284-285

LAND attacks, 368-369

LANs, 217-218

DNS setup, 241-243

    choke DMZ configuration, 244-245

    DMZ name server gateway configuration, 243-244

internal LANs, 226-227

multiple LANs, 227-231

large or less trusted LANs, 222-223

    selective internal access, 225

    subnetting to create multiple networks, 223-225

trusted home LANs, 218-219

    LAN access to gateway firewalls, 220

    LAN access to other LANs, 221-222

public web servers, 255

traffic

    forwarding, 221-222

    masquerading, 271-273

    standard NAT, 273-274

web proxies, 255-256

length filter table match, 94

limit filter table match extensions, 84-85

limited broadcast addresses, 13

limiting incoming packets, 41

link local network addresses, 40

Linux Firewall Administration Program. *See* iptables

Linux kernels. *See* kernels

Linux vendors, reporting incidents to, 326

Linux VPN products

    FreeS/WAN, 481

    Openswan, 480

    PoPToP, 481

    VPND (Virtual Private Network Daemon), 481

    VTUN (Virtual Tunnel), 482

listing firewall rules, 284-285

listing formats

    filter table

        iptables –L INPUT, 285-287

        iptables -n –L INPUT, 287-288

        iptables -v –L INPUT, 289-290

    mangle table, 293-294

    nat table, 291-292

local client traffic

    over TCP, 197-200

    over UDP, 201-202

local destination address filtering, 42

local destination port filtering, 43

local port redirection, 279-280

local server traffic, 200-201

local services, protecting, 60

local source address filtering, 57

local source port filtering, 58

local_dhcp_client_request chain, 189, 206-207

local_dns_client_request chain, 189, 197

local_dns_server_query chain, 189, 196-197

local_tcp_server_response chain, 189, 200-201

local_udp_client_request chain, 189

LOG target extensions, 80

log-tcp-state chain, 189, 205

logging

    dropped packets, 258

        incoming packets, 170-172

        optimized example, 208-210

        outgoing packets, 172

    firewall log messages, 114, 304-307

        duplicating, 304

        TCP example, 304-305

        UDP example, 306-307

    GrSec options, 419

    intrusion detection, 317-318

    log monitoring, 338-340

    matching packets, 115

    syslog configuration, 300-303

    tips for, 302

login failures, monitoring, 339-340

lookups

> DNS lookups as clients, 127-128
>
> DNS lookups as forwarding servers, 128, 130

loopback addresses, 13, 40, 115

loopback interfaces, enabling, 111, 237

M

mac filter table match extensions, 90

macros, 394-395

make clean command, 410

make command, 407

make config command, 407

make dep command, 410

make menuconfig command, 408

make modules command, 412

make oldconfig command, 407

make xconfig command, 407

malformed broadcast addresses, 40

mangle table, 69, 73-74

> commands, 98
>
> listing formats, 293-294
>
> mark mangle table target extensions, 98

mark filter table match extensions, 91

mark mangle table target extensions, 98

MASQUERADE, 69

> MASQUERADE nat table target extensions, 96
>
> MASQUERADE SNAT, 269-273

masquerading. *See* NAT (Network Address Translation)

match extensions, 68

> addrtype filter table, 93-94
>
> dstlimit filter table, 85-86
>
> filter table, 82
>
> iprange filter table, 94
>
> length filter table, 94
>
> limit filter table, 84-85
>
> mac filter table, 90
>
> mark filter table, 91
>
> multiport filter table, 82-84
>
> owner filter table, 90-91
>
> state filter table, 86-90
>
> tos filter table, 91-92
>
> unclean filter table, 92-93

menuconfig option (make command), 408

messages

> firewall log messages, 304-307
>
> > duplicating, 304
> >
> > TCP example, 304-305
> >
> > UDP example, 306-307
>
> ICMP control and status messages, 166-167
>
> > Destination Unreachable, 168
> >
> > echo-reply, 240
> >
> > echo-request, 108, 240
> >
> > fragmented messages, 167
> >
> > Parameter Problem, 168
> >
> > Source Quench, 167
> >
> > Time Exceeded, 168, 240
>
> redirect messages, 108

mobile users, VPN configuration, 482-483

modules, compiling/installing, 412

monitoring

> filesystems, 388-390
>
> login failures, 339-340

logs, 338-340

networks. *See* network analysis tools

MRTG (Multi Router Traffic Grapher), 330

multicast addresses (IP), 15

multicast destination addresses, 117

multicast packets, 117

multicast registration, 117

multicasting (IP), 17-18

multihomed firewalls, 101

multiport filter table match extensions, 82-84

multiport module, 184

N

-n -L INPUT option (iptables), 287-288

-n option (iptables), 284

names, hostnames, 24

NAPT (Network Address Port Translation), 71, 263

NAT (Network Address Translation), 8, 32, 64, 71, 261, 266. *See also* nat table

advantages of, 264

bidirectional NAT, 71, 263

destination NAT, 267

disadvantages of, 264-265

DNAT

REDIRECT DNAT, 271

standard DNAT, 270

firewalls, 262

history of, 261-262

iptables, 266-268

packet traversal, 73

SNAT, 69, 72-73, 268

applying to LAN traffic, 273-274

MASQUERADE SNAT, 269

masquerading LAN traffic, 271-273

nat table target extensions, 95-96

rules, 273

standard SNAT, 268-269

syntax, 268

traditional NAT, 263

transparent translation, 262

Twice NAT, 72, 264

nat table, 69-74

listing formats, 291-292

target extensions

BALANCE nat table target extensions, 97

DNAT nat table target extensions, 96-97

MASQUERADE nat table target extensions, 96

REDIRECT nat table target extensions, 97

SNAT nat table target extensions, 95-96

net type qualifiers (TCPDump), 352

Netfilter, 63. *See also* iptables

compared to ipchains, 64

packet traversal, 66-67

netstat

open ports, checking for, 308-310

output reporting conventions, 310

network address 0, 13, 116

Network Address Port Translation (NAPT), 71, 263

Network Address Translation. *See* NAT

network analysis tools, 329-332, 345-347

ARPWatch, 332, 347, 377-379

Cricket, 330

MRTG, 330

ntop, 330

sniffer placement, 332

Snort, 330, 347, 371-372

    alerts, 376

    configuring, 373-375

    downloading, 372

    installing, 372-373

    Swatch, 376

    testing, 375-376

switches/hubs, 331-332

TCPDump, 329-330, 347-348

    abnormal packet activity, 364-365

    command-line options, 350-351

    DNS queries, capturing, 363

    downloading, 349

    expressions, 352-354

    FTP conversations, capturing, 363

    HTTP conversations, capturing, 356-361

    ICMP pings, capturing, 364

    installing, 349

    LAND attacks, 368-369

    normal scan (nmap) attacks, 365-367

    recording traffic with, 369-371

    SMTP conversations, capturing, 361-362

    Smurf attacks, 367

    SSH conversations, capturing, 362

    Xmas Tree attacks, 368

network coordinators, reporting incidents to, 325

network-directed broadcasts, 13

Network File System (NFS), 122

Network layer (OSI model), 11

Network Mapper (Nmap), 342-343

Network News Transport Protocol (NNTP), 142-143

network protections (GrSec), 419

network services. *See* services

Network Time Protocol (NTP), 165

networks. *See also* network analysis tools

    connecting with VPNs, 483

    hubs, 331-332

    OSI (Open System Interconnection) model, 9-12

        connectionless versus connection-oriented protocols, 11-12

        Datalink layer, 10

        Network layer, 11

        Physical layer, 10

        Presentation layer, 11

        Session layer, 11

        Transport layer, 11

    subnetting to create multiple networks, 223-225

    switches, 331-332

    VPNs (virtual private networks)

        configuring, 482-483

        firewalls and, 483-484

        FreeS/WAN, 481

        Openswan, 480

        PoPToP, 481

        protocols, 475-482

        VPND (Virtual Private Network Daemon), 481

news feeds, 144

NFS (Network File System), 122

nmap 342-343

    normal scan attacks, 365-367

    open ports, checking for, 312

NNTP (Network News Transport Protocol), 142-143

normal scan (nmap) attacks, 365-367

ntop, 330

NTP (Network Time Protocol), 165

ntpd daemon, 165-166

numbering kernel versions, 402-403

O

Oakley, 479

object persistence, 400

oldconfig option (make command), 407

open ports, checking for, 307-308

    fuser, 311

    netstat, 308-310

    nmap, 312

    strobe, 311-312

Open System Interconnection model. *See* OSI model

Openswan, 480

optimization

    goal of, 210-211

    optimized iptables firewall (code listing), 446-462

    rule organization, 181-182

        heavily used services, 184

        multiport module, 184

        state module for ESTABLISHED and RELATED matches, 182

        traffic flow to determine rule placement, 184-185

        transport protocols, 182-183

        where to begin, 182

    user-defined chains, 185-189

        branching, 186

        characteristics of, 187-188

        connection-tracking, 188, 205-206

        destination-address-check, 188, 208

        EXT-icmp-in, 189

        EXT-icmp-out, 189

        EXT-input, 188, 195-202

        EXT-log-in, 189

        EXT-log-out, 189

        EXT-output, 189, 195-202

        firewall initialization, 190-192

        installing, 192-195

        local_dhcp_client_query, 189

        local_dhcp_client_request, 206-207

        local_dns_client_request, 189

        local_dns_server_query, 189

        local_tcp_server_response, 189

        local_udp_client_request, 189

        log-tcp-state, 189

        logging dropped packets, 208-210

        remote_dhcp_server_response, 189, 206-207

        remote_dns_server_response, 189

        remote_tcp_client_request, 189

        remote_udp_server_response, 189

        source-address-check, 188, 207-208

        tcp-state-flags, 188, 204-205

organizing rules, 181-182

    heavily used services, 184

    multiport module, 184

state module for ESTABLISHED and RELAT-
ED matches, 182

traffic flow to determine rule placement,
184-185

transport protocols, 182-183

where to begin, 182

OSI (Open System Interconnection) model, 9-12

connectionless versus connection-oriented
protocols, 11-12

Datalink layer, 10

Network layer, 11

Physical layer, 10

Presentation layer, 11

Session layer, 11

Transport layer, 11

outgoing Destination Unreachable messages,
167

outgoing packets, filtering, 56

local source address filtering, 57

local source port filtering, 58

outgoing TCP connection-state filtering, 59

remote destination address filtering, 57-58

remote destination port filtering, 58

OUTPUT chain

mangle table, 74

nat table, 72

output reporting conventions (netstat), 310

output rules, checking, 296-298

owner filter table match extensions, 90-91

P

packet filtering. See filtering

packet routing, 25

packet traversal

IPFW, 65

NAT, 73

Netfilter, 66-67

packets. See also filtering

dropped packets, logging, 170-172, 208-210,
258

incoming packets

iptables, 70

limiting to selected remote sites, 41

probes, 43

scans, 43-48

IPFW packet traversal, 65

matching packets, 70, 115

multicast network packets, dropping, 117

multicast packets, 117

NAT packet traversal, 73

rejecting versus denying, 38

Parameter Problem messages, 167-168

passive-mode FTP data channels, 151-153

patching kernel, 404-405

PaX Control (GrSec), 417

penetration testing

Hping2, 343

Nessus, 344

Nikto, 343-344

Nmap, 342-343

persistence (objects), 400

Physical layer (OSI model), 10

ping

capturing with TCPDump, 364

Echo Request and Echo Reply messages,
169-170

ping flooding on incoming packets, 50

ping messages, limiting, 85

Ping of Death, 50-51

pipe symbol (|), 75

Point-to-Point Tunneling Protocol. *See* PPTP

policies

default policies

defining, 111, 236

packet-filtering firewalls, 35-37

rules, 11

deny-everything-by-default policies, 120

FORWARD policy, 111

POP (Post Office Protocol), 133-134, 225

email

retrieving, 136, 247

sending, 137-138

POP servers for remote clients, 141

PoPToP, 481

port mode (FTP), 150

port type qualifiers (TCPDump), 352

port-mode FTP data channels, 151-152

ports

numbers, 119

open ports, checking for, 307

fuser, 311

netstat, 308-310

nmap, 312

strobe, 311-312

processes bound to particular ports, checking, 311

redirection, 275-276

scans

problems with, 120

responding to, 47-48

selective internal access, 225

service ports, 25-27

unprivileged ports, 26

posting news (Usenet), 143

postmaster, reporting incidents to, 325

POSTROUTING chain, 267

mangle table, 74

nat table, 72

Post Office Protocol. *See* POP

POSTROUTING rules, 272

PPTP (Point-to-Point Tunneling Protocol), 476

PoPToP, 481

security, 476

preexisting rules

removing, 109-110

removing from choke firewalls, 235

PREROUTING chain, 267

mangle table, 73

nat table, 72

Presentation layer (OSI model), 11

primitives (TCPDump), 354

private network services, 59-60

probes, 43

problem sites, blocking, 41, 172-173

protocol qualifiers (TCPDump), 354

proxying, transparent, 279-280

PSH flag, 22

public gateway firewalls, 233-234

public network services, 59-60

Q-R

qualifiers (TCPDump)
  direction qualifiers, 353-354
  primitives, 354
  protocol qualifiers, 354
  type qualifiers, 352-353

query lookup requests, 125

QUEUE target, 71

QuickTime, 158-160

RBAC (Role Based Access Control), 421

reading Usenet news, 143

RealAudio, 158-160

RealVideo, 158-160

receiving email
  IMAP clients, 136-139
  POP clients, 137-138
  SMTP servers, 135-136, 139-141

REDIRECT, 69

REDIRECT DNAT, 271

redirect messages, 85, 108

REDIRECT nat table target extensions, 97

reference papers, 426

registration
  IP addresses, 118
  multicast registration, 117

REJECT target, 70, 81

rejecting
  AUTH requests, 246
  packets, 38

RELATED matches, 182

relaying mail through external gateway SMTP servers, 134-135

remote clients
  AUTH clients, 131
  DNS lookups, 127-128
  outgoing client access to remote FTP servers
    outgoing FTP requests over control channels, 150
    passive-mode FTP data channels, 151-152
    port-mode FTP data channels, 151
  remote clients
    email, 141-142
    hosting Usenet news servers for, 143-144
    remote site access, 145
    SSH server access, 147-148

remote destination address filtering, 57-58

remote destination port filtering, 58

remote hosts, 255

remote network time servers, 165-166

remote sites, accessing, 27-30, 145, 154-155

remote source address filtering, 38
  illegal addresses, 39-41
  incoming packets, limiting, 41
  problem sites, blocking, 41
  source address spoofing, 39-41

remote source port filtering, 43

remote_dhcp_server_response chain, 189, 206-207

remote_dns_server_response chain, 189, 197

remote_tcp_client_request chain, 189, 200-201

remote_udp_server_response chain, 189

removing preexisting rules, 109-110, 235

reporting incidents

    advantages of, 323

    AIDE (Advanced Intrusion Detection Environment) reports, customizing, 391-393

    denial-of-service attacks, 324

    incident types, 324-325

    information to include, 326-327

    online resources, 327

    where to report incidents, 325-326

Reseaux IP Europe (RIPE), 326

resources

    books, 426

    reference papers, 426

    websites, 425-426

responding

    to intrusion detection, 320-322

    to port scans, 47-48

RETURN target, 71

RIPE (Reseaux IP Europe), 326

roaming users, VPN configuration, 482-483

Role Based Access Control (RBAC), 421

root, 325

rootkit checkers. See Chkrootkit

routers

    border routers, 31

    compared to firewalls, 9

    source address spoofing, 115

routing encapsulation, 476

routing packets, 25

rp filter, 109

RST flag, 22

RTSP (Real-Time Streaming Protocol), 158

rules, 284-285

    blocking directed broadcasts, 116

    chain commands on, 77

    debugging tips, 281-284

    default policies, 112

    filter table listing formats

        iptables –L INPUT, 285-287

        iptables -n –L INPUT, 287-288

        iptables -v –L INPUT, 289-290

    FORWARD, 272

    forwarding rules, 298-300

    input rules, 295-296

    mangle table listing formats, 293-294

    nat table listing formats, 291-292

    organization, 181-182

        heavily used services, 184

        multiport module, 184

        state module for ESTABLISHED and RELATED matches, 182

        traffic flow to determine rule placement, 184-185

        transport protocols, 182-183

        where to begin, 182

    output rules, 296-298

    packet-filtering rules, 102-103

    packets

        disallowing, 115

        dropping, 117-118

        logging, 115

POSTROUTING, 272

preexisting rules

    removing, 109-110

    removing from choke firewalls, 235

rule checking, bypassing, 113-114, 238

telnet connections, 89

SNAT, 273

user-defined chains, 186

S

SAs (security associations), 477, 480

scans

    incoming packets, 43

        general port scans, 44

        responding to port scans, 47-48

        stealth scans, 46

        targeted port scans, 44-46

    service port targets, 45-46

    TCP stealth scans, 237

scheduling AIDE (Advanced Intrusion Detection Environment), 388

Schneier, Bruce, 398

screened-subnet firewalls, 231-232

    AUTH user identification service, filtering, 246

    choke firewalls as local DHCP servers, 256-257

    DNS, 241-243

        choke DMZ configuration, 244-245

        DMZ name server gateway configuration, 243-244

    email

        forwarding through gateways, 246-247

        retrieving as IMAP client, 248

        retrieving as POP client, 247

    FTP

        choke firewalls as conduits/clients to remote FTP servers, 253

        gateway firewalls as conduits to FTP DMZ servers, 253

        gateway firewalls as conduits to remote FTP servers, 251-252

    ICMP control and status messages, filtering, 240

    rule checking, bypassing, 238

    source-address spoofing, 238-239

    SSH

        choke SSH configuration, 251

        gateway SSH configurations, 250

    TCP stealth scans and TCP state flags, 237

    Telnet, 249-250

    Usenet news services

        choke NNTP client DMZ configurations, 249

        gateway NNTP conduit and server DMZ configurations, 248

    web services, 253

        choke firewalls as forwarders and web clients, 254

        gateway firewalls as conduits for local web clients, 254

        public web servers in DMZ, 255

        web proxies in DMZ, 255-256

scripts

    iptables choke firewall, 463-474

    iptables firewall for standalone system, 427-445

    optimized iptables firewall, 446-462

Secure Message Transport Protocol. *See* SMTP

Secure Network Address Translation. *See* SNAT

Secure Shell. *See* SSH

Secure Socket Layer (SSL), 155-156

security associations (SAs), 477, 480

Security Enhanced Linux (SELinux), 399-401

Security Identifiers (SIDs), 401

selective internal access

by host, address range, or ports, 225

configuration options for internal LANS, 226-227

configuration options for multiple LANS, 227-231

SELinux, 399-401

sending email, 134

as SMTP clients and receiving as IMAP clients, 138-139

as SMTP clients and receiving as POP clients, 137-138

as SMTP clients and receiving as SMTP servers, 139-140

as SMTP servers and receiving as SMTP servers, 140-141

service daemons, syslogd, 300

service port targets, 45-46

service ports, 25-27

services, 25-27. *See also* TCP (Transmission Control Protocol)

AUTH user identification service, 130-132

choosing which services to run, 60

network-based services, 25-27

nonsecure local services, protecting, 60

protecting on assigned unprivileged ports, 119-120

local TCP services, 120-122

local UDP services, 122-123

public versus private, 59-60

Usenet news services

news servers, hosting, 143-144

NNTP, 142-143, 248-249

peer news feeds, 144

reading and posting news, 143

Session layer (OSI model), 11

SIDs (Security Identifiers), 401

SKEME, 479

SMTP (Secure Message Transport Protocol), 133-134

choke configurations, 247

conversations, capturing with TCPDump, 361-362

email, 134

receiving as local SMTP servers, 135-136

relaying mail through external gateway SMTP servers, 134-135

sending as SMTP clients and receiving as IMAP clients, 138-139

sending as SMTP clients and receiving as POP clients, 137-138

sending as SMTP clients and receiving as SMTP servers, 139-140

sending as SMTP servers and receiving as SMTP servers, 140-141

sending to any external mail servers, 135

smurf attacks, 169, 367

SNAT (Source Network Address Translation), 69, 72-73, 268

applying to LAN traffic, 273-274

MASQUERADE SNAT, 269

masquerading LAN traffic, 271-273

nat table target extensions, 95-96

rules, 273

standard SNAT, 268-269

sniffers, 329, 345-347

ARPWatch, 347, 377-379

Cricket, 330

MRTG, 330

ntop, 330

placement of, 332

Snort, 330, 347, 371-372

alerts, 376

configuring, 373-375

downloading, 372

installing, 372-373

Swatch, 376

testing, 375-376

switches/hubs, 331-332

TCPDump, 329-330, 347-348

abnormal packet activity, 364-365

command-line options, 350-351

DNS queries, capturing, 363

downloading, 349

expressions, 352-354

FTP conversations, capturing, 363

HTTP conversations, capturing, 356-361

ICMP pings, capturing, 364

installing, 349

LAND attacks, 368-369

normal scan (nmap) attacks, 365-367

recording traffic with, 369-371

SMTP conversations, capturing, 361-362

Smurf attacks, 367

SSH conversations, capturing, 362

Xmas Tree attacks, 368

Snort, 330, 347, 371-372

alerts, 376

configuring, 373-375

downloading, 372

installing, 372-373

Swatch, 376

testing, 375-376

sockets, 308

source addresses

iptables, 104-105

source address checking, bypassing, 201

spoofing, 39-41, 114-119

loopback addresses, 115

routers, 115

screened-subnet firewalls, 238-239

Source Network Address Translation. *See* SNAT

Source Quench messages, 167

source-address-check chain, 188, 207-208

source-routed packets, 56

spoofing source addresses, 39-41, 114-119

loopback addresses, 115

routers, 115

screened-subnet firewalls, 238-239

squid, 279

SSH (Secure Shell), 146-147

choke SSH configuration, 251

client access to remote SSH servers, 147-148

conversations, capturing with TCPDump, 362

gateway SSH configurations, 250

login failures, monitoring, 339-340

SSL (Secure Socket Layer), 155-156

standalone systems

    iptables choke firewall, 463-474

    limitations of, 213-215

    optimized iptables firewall, 446-462

    sample iptables firewall script, 427-445

standard DNAT, 270

standard SNAT, 268-269

starting firewalls on boot

    Debian, 175-176

    Red Hat and SUSE, 175

state filter table match extensions, 86-90

state flags (TCP), 237

stateful firewalls, 31

stateless firewalls, 31

status messages (ICMP), 166-167

    Destination Unreachable, 168

    echo-reply, 240

    echo-request, 108, 240

    fragmented messages, 167

    Parameter Problem, 168

    Source Quench, 167

    Time Exceeded, 168, 240

STDERR, 391

STDIN, 391

STDOUT, 391-392

stealth scans, 112-113

    incoming packets, filtering, 46

    TCP, 237

"Steps for Recovering from a UNIX or NT System Compromise" (paper), 317

Stevens, Richard, 12

stock kernel, 402

strobe, 311-312

subjects (SELinux), 400

subnet masks, 15

subnets, 12-16, 223-225

SUSE Linux, 175

Swatch, 338-340, 376

switches, 331-332

symbolic constants, 107, 232-233

    private choke firewalls, 234

    public gateway firewalls, 233-234

SYN ACK, 49

SYN flag, 22, 27-29, 49, 59, 182

Sysctl support (GrSec), 419

syslog, 300-303

syslogd, 300-303

system logs

    firewall log messages, 304-307

        duplicating, 304

        TCP example, 304-305

        UDP example, 306-307

    intrusion detection, 317-318

    syslog configuration, 300-303

T

tables

    filter table, 68-69, 74-75

        addrtype filter table match extensions, 93-94

        dstlimit filter table match extensions, 85-86

filter table target extensions, 80-81

icmp filter table match operator, 79-80

iprange filter table match, 94

iptables, 68, 71

length filter table match, 94

limit filter table match extensions, 84-85

listing formats, 285-290

mac filter table match extensions, 90

mark filter table match extensions, 91

match operations, 77-78

multiport filter table match extensions, 82-84

operations on entire chains, 76

operations on rules, 77

owner filter table match extensions, 90-91

state filter table match extensions, 86-90

target extensions, 81

tcp filter table match operations, 79

tos filter table match extensions, 91-92

udp filter table match operations, 79

ULOG table target extensions, 81-82

unclean filter table match extensions, 92-93

mangle, 69, 73-74

  commands, 98

  listing formats, 293-294

  mark mangle table target extensions, 98

nat, 69-74

  BALANCE nat table target extensions, 97

  DNAT nat table target extensions, 96-97

  listing formats, 291-292

  MASQUERADE nat table target extensions, 96

  REDIRECT nat table target extensions, 97

  SNAT nat table target extensions, 95-96

  service protocol tables, 123-124

target extensions, 68

  filter table, 80-81

  mangle table, 98

  nat table

    BALANCE nat table target extensions, 97

    DNAT nat table target extensions, 96-97

    MASQUERADE nat table target extensions, 96

    REDIRECT nat table target extensions, 97

    SNAT nat table target extensions, 95-96

  ULOG table, 81-82

targeted port scans, 44-46

targets, service port, 45-46

TCP (Transmission Control Protocol), 20-23, 132. *See also* **email; TCPDump; Usenet news services**

  connection sequence, 22-23

  firewall log messages, 304-305

  FTP, 148-149

    incoming access to FTP servers, 152-153

    outgoing client access to remote FTP servers, 150-152

    packet-filtering, 150

    port mode, 150

    TFTP, 153

  headers, 20-22

  iptables, 70

  LAND attacks, 368-369

  local client traffic over TCP, 197-200

  local server over traffic, 200-201

  rule organization, 182-183

  service protocol tables, 123-124

SSH, 146-148

state flags, 112-113, 237

stealth scans, 112-113, 237

SYN flooding, 48-50

telnet, 144-146

unprivileged ports, 120-122

Xmas Tree attacks, 368

web services, 153

    HTTP, 154-155

    QuickTime, 158-160

    RealAudio, 158-160

    RealVideo, 158-160

    SSL, 155-156

    TLS, 155-156

    Web Proxy access, 156-157

    whois, 157-158

websites, connecting to, 27-30

tcp filter table match operations, 79

tcp-state-flags chain, 188, 204-205

TCP/IP (Transmission Control Protocol/Internet Protocol)

sockets, 308

TCP/IP Illustrated, Volume 1, 12

TCPDump, 329-330, 347-348

abnormal packet activity, 364-365

command-line options, 350-351

DNS queries, capturing, 363

downloading, 349

expressions

    direction qualifiers, 353-354

    protocol qualifiers, 354

    type qualifiers, 352-353

FTP conversations, capturing, 363

HTTP conversations, capturing, 356-361

ICMP pings, capturing, 364

installing, 349

LAND attacks, 368-369

normal scan (nmap) attacks, 365-367

recording traffic with, 369-371

SMTP conversations, capturing, 361-362

Smurf attacks, 367

SSH conversations, capturing, 362

Xmas Tree attacks, 368

telnet, 144-145, 249-250

incoming access to local servers, 146

outgoing client access to remote sites, 145

rules, 89

TEST-NET addresses, 40

testing

penetration testing

    Hping2, 343

    Nessus, 344

    Nikto, 343-344

    Nmap, 342-343

    Snort, 375-376

TFTP (Trivial File Transfer Protocol), 153

Time Exceeded messages, 168

time exceeded status messages, 240

TLS (Transport Layer Security), 155-156

TOS (Type of Service)

iptables, 70

TOS bits, 92

TOS field, 74, 92

tos filter table match extensions, 91-92

traceroute, 160-162

traditional NAT, 263

traffic

forwarding traffic among multiple LANs, 221-222

ICMP, 203-204

placement of rules for multiple network interfaces, 184-185

recording with TCPDump, 369-371

Transmission Control Protocol. *See* TCP

transparent proxying (DNAT), 279-280

transparent translation (NAT), 262

Transport layer (OSI model), 11. *See also* UDP (User Datagram Protocol); TCP (Transport Control Protocol)

Transport Layer Security (TLS), 155-156

transport mode (IPSec), 478

transport protocol

ICMP services, 183

TCP services, 182-183

TCP versus UDP services, 183

UDP services, 183

Tripwire, 381

Trivial File Transfer Protocol (TFTP), 153

troubleshooting kernels, 414-415

trusted home LANs, 218-219

LAN access to gateway firewalls, 220

LAN access to other LANs, 221-222

tunnel mode (IPSec), 478

twice NAT, 72, 264

type qualifiers (TCPDump), 352-353

U

UDP (User Datagram Protocol), 20, 160

denial-of-service attacks, 53

DHCP servers

accessing, 162-165

message types, 162-163

firewall log messages, 306-307

flooding on incoming packets, 52

local client traffic over, 201-202

protecting on unprivileged ports, 122-123

query lookup requests, 125

remote network time servers, accessing, 165-166

rule organization, 183

service protocol tables, 123-124

traceroute, 160-162

udp filter table match operations, 79

ULOG target extensions, 81-82

unclean filter table match extensions, 92-93

unicast addresses (IP), 15

UNIX sockets, 308

unprivileged ports, 26, 119-120

local TCP services, 120-122

local UDP services, 122-123

updates, 341-342, 390-391

URG flag, 22

Usenet news services

news servers, hosting, 143-144

NNTP, 142-143

choke NNTP client DMZ configurations, 249

gateway NNTP conduit and server DMZ configurations, 248

peer news feeds, 144

reading and posting news, 143

user accounts, intrusion detection, 319

User Datagram Protocol. *See* UDP

user-defined chains, 185-186

branching, 186

characteristics of, 187-188

example, 188-189

connection-tracking, 188, 205-206

destination-address-check, 188, 208

EXT-icmp-in, 189

EXT-icmp-out, 189

EXT-input, 188, 195-202

EXT-log-in, 189

EXT-log-out, 189

EXT-output, 189, 195-202

firewall initialization, 190-192

installing chains, 192-195

local_dhcp_client_query, 189

local_dhcp_client_request, 206-207

local_dns_client_request, 189

local_dns_server_query, 189

local_tcp_server_response, 189

local_udp_client_request, 189

log-tcp-state, 189

logging dropped packets, 208-210

remote_dhcp_server_response, 189, 206-207

remote_dns_server_response, 189

remote_tcp_client_request, 189

remote_udp_server_response, 189

source-address-check, 188, 207-208

tcp-state-flags, 188, 204-205

V

-v -L INPUT option (iptables), 289-290

-v option (iptables), 284

"vanilla" kernel, 402

verbose output (AIDE), 393

version numbering (kernels), 402-403

Virtual Private Network Daemon (VPND), 481

virtual private networks. *See* VPNs

Virtual Tunnel (VTUN), 482

VPND (Virtual Private Network Daemon), 481

VPNs (virtual private networks)

configuring

network connections, 483

roaming users, 482-483

firewalls and, 483-484

FreeS/WAN, 481

Openswan, 480

PoPToP, 481

protocols, 475

ESP (encapsulating security payload), 478

IKE (Internet Key Exchange), 479-480

IPSec (IP Security Protocol), 476-480

PPTP (Point-to-Point Tunneling Protocol), 476

VTUN (Virtual Tunnel), 482

VPND (Virtual Private Network Daemon), 481

VTUN (Virtual Tunnel), 482

W

web proxies, 156-157, 255-256

web servers, allowing remote access to, 154-155

web services, 153, 253

    choke firewalls as forwarders and web clients, 254

    gateway firewalls as conduits for local web clients, 254

    HTTP, 154-155

    public web servers in DMZ, 255

    QuickTime, 158-160

    RealAudio, 158-160

    RealVideo, 158-160

    SSL, 155-156

    TLS, 155-156

    web proxies, 156-157, 255-256

    whois, 157-158

websites

    denying access to, 172-173

    reference papers, 426

    security information sources, 425-426

    visiting with TCP connections, 27-30

whois, 157-158

X-Y-Z

xconfig option (make command), 407

Xmas Tree attacks, 368

zone transfers, 125

Ignoring Nature No More